S0-ABC-772

★ **Cathedral of St. John the Divine** ⑫
See pages 224–5

Morningside Heights and Harlem ⑫

Upper West Side ⑨

Central Park

Upper East Side

⑪ ⑩

★ **Solomon R. Guggenheim Museum** ⑪
See pages 186–7

④
⑤
⑥
⑧

Upper Midtown

Lower Midtown

★ **Metropolitan Museum** ⑩
See pages 188–95

EAST RIVER

N

★ **United Nations** ⑧
See pages 158–61

★ **St. Patrick's Cathedral** ⑤
See pages 176–7

0 kilometers	2
0 miles	1

★ **Grand Central Terminal** ⑥
See pages 154–5

STAR SIGHTS FARTHER AFIELD

★ **The Cloisters** *See pages 234–7*

★ **Botanical Garden** *See pages 240–41*

★ **Bronx Zoo** *See pages 242–3*

★ **Brooklyn Museum** *See pages 248–51*

EYEWITNESS TRAVEL GUIDES

NEW YORK

EMPIRE STATE

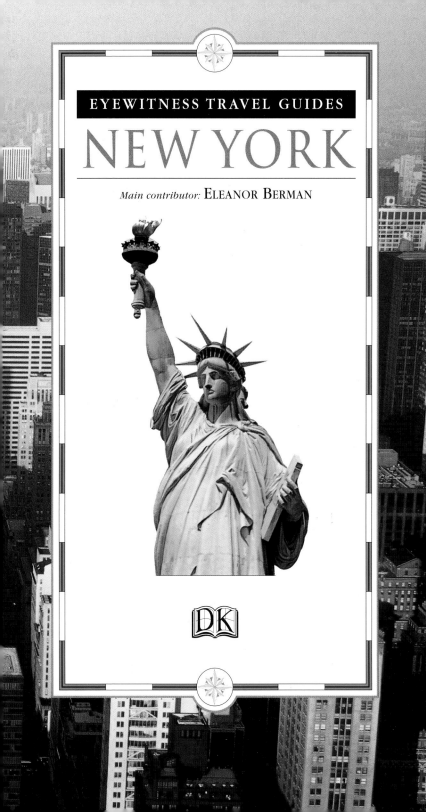

EYEWITNESS TRAVEL GUIDES

NEW YORK

Main contributor: ELEANOR BERMAN

DK

LONDON, NEW YORK,
MELBOURNE, MUNICH AND DELHI
www.dk.com

PROJECT EDITOR Fay Franklin
ART EDITOR Tony Foo
EDITORS Donna Dailey, Ellen Dupont, Esther Labi
DESIGNERS Steve Bere, Louise Parsons, Mark Stevens
EDITORIAL ASSISTANT Fiona Morgan

CONTRIBUTORS
Lester Brooks, Patricia Brooks, Susan Farewell

PHOTOGRAPHERS
Max Alexander, Dave King, Michael Moran

ILLUSTRATORS
Richard Draper, Robbie Polley, Hamish Simpson

This book was produced with the assistance of
Websters International Publishers.

Reproduced by Colourscan (Singapore)
Printed and bound by South China Printing Co. Ltd, China.

First published in Great Britain in 1993
by Dorling Kindersley Limited
80 Strand, London WC2R 0RL

**Reprinted with revisions 1994, 1995 (twice),
1997, 1999, 2000, 2001, 2002, 2003, 2004, 2005**

Copyright 1993, 2005 © Dorling Kindersley Limited, London
A Penguin Company

ALL RIGHTS RESERVED. NO PART OF THIS PUBLICATION MAY BE
REPRODUCED, STORED IN A RETRIEVAL SYSTEM, OR TRANSMITTED
IN ANY FORM OR BY ANY MEANS, ELECTRONIC, MECHANICAL,
PHOTOCOPYING, RECORDING OR OTHERWISE, WITHOUT THE
PRIOR WRITTEN PERMISSION OF THE COPYRIGHT OWNER.

A CIP CATALOGUE RECORD IS AVAILABLE FROM THE BRITISH LIBRARY.

ISBN 1 4053 0771 4

THROUGHOUT THIS BOOK, FLOORS ARE REFERRED TO IN ACCORDANCE
WITH AMERICAN USAGE, IE THE "FIRST FLOOR" IS AT GROUND LEVEL.

**The information in this
DK Eyewitness Guide is checked annually**.
Every effort has been made to ensure that this book is as up-to-date as
possible at the time of going to press. Some details, however, such as
telephone numbers, opening hours, prices, gallery hanging
arrangements and travel information are liable to change. The
publishers cannot accept responsibility for any consequences arising
from the use of this book, nor for any material on third party websites,
and cannot guarantee that any website address in this book will be a
suitable source of travel information. We value the views and
suggestions of our readers very highly. Please write to:
Publisher, DK Eyewitness Travel Guides, Dorling Kindersley,
80 Strand, London WC2R 0RL, Great Britain.

CONTENTS

Baseball star,
Babe Ruth
(1895–1948)

South Manhattan skyline

Vesuvio Bakery, SoHo

Trump Tower, Upper Midtown

The New York City Ballet

Tug boat at the North Wind Undersea Institute Museum

TRAVELLERS' NEEDS

Bagel from a New York deli

SURVIVAL GUIDE

Solomon R Guggenheim Museum, Upper East Side

HOW TO USE THIS GUIDE

THIS EYEWITNESS TRAVEL GUIDE helps you get the most from your stay in New York with the minimum of practical difficulty. The opening section, *Introducing New York*, locates the city geographically, sets modern New York in its historical context and describes the highlights of the year. *New York at a Glance* is an overview of the city's attractions. Section two, *New York Area by Area*, guides you through the city's sightseeing areas. It describes all the main sights with maps, photographs and detailed illustrations. In addition, five planned walks take you step-by-step through special areas.

Well-researched tips on where to stay, eat, shop, and on sports and entertainment are in section three, *Travelers' Needs. Children's New York* lists highlights for young visitors, and section four, *Survival Guide*, shows you how to do everything from mailing a letter to using the subway.

NEW YORK AREA BY AREA

Manhattan has been divided into 15 sightseeing areas, each described separately. Each area opens with a portrait, summing up the area's character and history and listing all the sights to be covered. Sights are numbered and clearly located on an *Area Map*. After this comes a large-scale *Street-by-Street Map* focusing on the most interesting part of the area. Finding your way around each area is made simple by the numbering system. This refers to the order in which sights are described on the pages that follow.

Sights at a Glance lists the sights in the area by category, including: Historic Streets and Buildings, Modern Architecture, Museums and Galleries, Churches, Monuments, and Parks and Squares.

The area covered in greater detail on the *Street-by-Street Map* is shaded red.

Numbered circles pinpoint all the listed sights on the area map. Trump Tower, for example, is ❷

Travel tips help you reach the area quickly by public transportation.

1 The Area Map

For easy reference, the sights in each area are numbered and located on an Area Map. *To help the visitor, the map also shows subway stations, heliports and ferry embarkation points.*

Photographs of facades and distinctive details of buildings help you locate the sights.

Color-coding on each page makes the area easy to find in the book.

2 The Street-by-Street Map

This gives a bird's-eye view of the heart of each sightseeing area. The most important buildings are illustrated, to help you spot them easily as you walk around.

A locator map shows you where you are in relation to surrounding areas. The area of the *Street-by-Street Map* is shown in red.

Trump Tower ❷ is also shown on this map.

A suggested route for a walk takes you past some of the area's most interesting sights.

Red stars indicate the sights that no visitor should miss.

NEW YORK AT A GLANCE
Each map in this section
concentrates on a specific
theme: *Museums, Architecture,
Multicultural New York*, and
Celebrated New Yorkers. The
top sights are shown on the
map; other sights are
described on the two pages
following and cross-referenced
to their full entries in the
Area by Area section.

Each sightseeing area
is color-coded.

The theme is explored in greater
detail on the pages following the map.

3 Detailed information on each sight
*All important sights in each area are
described in depth here. They are
listed in order, following the numbering
on the opening* Area Map. *Practical
information is also provided.*

PRACTICAL INFORMATION
Each entry provides all the information
needed to plan a visit to the sight. The
key to the symbols is inside the back
cover.

Map reference to Street
Finder at back of book

Address

Sight Number

Trump Tower ②

725 5th Ave. **Map** 12 F3.

C 832-2000. **M** 5th Ave–53rd St.

Garden level, shops open 10am–6pm
Mon–Sat. Building open 8am–10pm
daily. Adm free. See Shopping p311.

Concerts.

Opening hours

**Services and
facilities available**

**Telephone
number**

Nearest subway station

4 New York's major sights
*These are given two or more full pages in
the sightseeing area in which they are
found. Important buildings are dissected
to reveal their interiors; museums have
color-coded floor plans to help you find
particular exhibits.*

The Visitors' Checklist
provides the practical
information you will need
to plan your visit.

The facade of each major
sight is shown to help you
spot it quickly.

Red stars indicate the
most important
exhibits or works of
art on display inside,
or the most interesting
architectural details of
the building.

A color key helps
you find your way
easily around the
collection.

Floors are referred to in
accordance with American
usage, i.e., the "first floor"
is at ground level.

INTRODUCING
NEW YORK

Putting New York on the Map

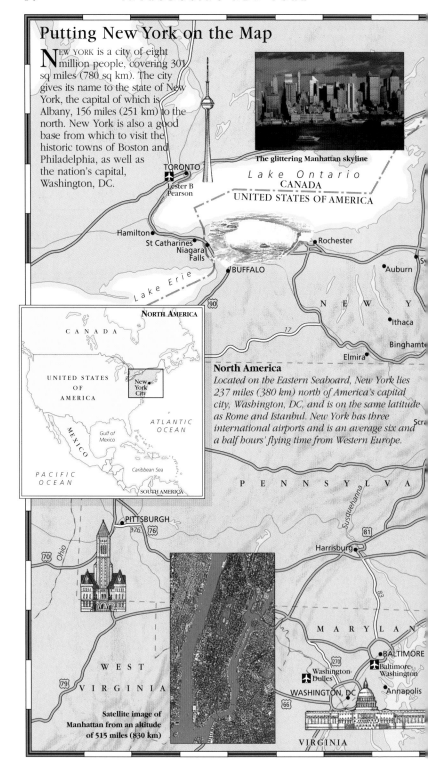

Nᴇᴡ Yᴏʀᴋ is a city of eight million people, covering 301 sq miles (780 sq km). The city gives its name to the state of New York, the capital of which is Albany, 156 miles (251 km) to the north. New York is also a good base from which to visit the historic towns of Boston and Philadelphia, as well as the nation's capital, Washington, DC.

The glittering Manhattan skyline

Lake Ontario

CANADA
UNITED STATES OF AMERICA

TORONTO

Lester B Pearson

Hamilton

St Catharines

Niagara Falls

BUFFALO

Rochester

Auburn

Lake Erie

90

N E W   Y

Ithaca

17

Binghamte

Elmira

NORTH AMERICA

CANADA

UNITED STATES OF AMERICA

New York City

ATLANTIC OCEAN

MEXICO

Gulf of Mexico

Caribbean Sea

PACIFIC OCEAN

SOUTH AMERICA

North America

Located on the Eastern Seaboard, New York lies 237 miles (380 km) north of America's capital city, Washington, DC, and is on the same latitude as Rome and Istanbul. New York has three international airports and is an average six and a half hours' flying time from Western Europe.

Scra

P E N N S Y L V A

Susquehanna

81

PITTSBURGH

376   76

70

Ohio

Harrisburg

83

M A R Y L A N

BALTIMORE

270

Washington-Dulles

Baltimore-Washington

WEST

79

V I R G I N I A

Satellite image of Manhattan from an altitude of 515 miles (830 km)

WASHINGTON, DC

66

Annapolis

VIRGINIA

GREATER NEW YORK

Greater New York

New York City is made
[u]p of five distinct boroughs:
Manhattan (where the
[v]ast majority of sights are
[lo]cated), the Bronx, Queens,
[Br]ooklyn, and Staten Island.
Details of important sights
[ou]tside central New York but
[w]ithin the city's boundaries
can be found on pages
231–53. Day trips in New
York State and beyond are
suggested on page 377.

Yonkers
New Rochelle
Mount Vernon
Englewood
Passaic
Bronx
Port Washington
Bloomfield
see next page
LaGuardia ✈
Flushing
East Orange
Union City
Manhattan
Newark
Jersey City
Queens
LONG ISLAND
Valley Stream
Newark ✈
Upper New York Bay
John F. Kennedy (JFK) ✈
Elizabeth
Brooklyn
Staten Island
Lower New York Bay

A T L A N T I C
O C E A N

0 kilometers   10
0 miles   5

Troy
Albany
MASSACHUSETTS
BOSTON
Worcester
Catskill Mountains
Hudson
Springfield
RHODE ISLAND
Hartford
Providence
CONNECTICUT
Poughkeepsie
91
95
New Haven
Bridgeport
Long Island Sound
Long Island
N
NEW YORK CITY
Newark ✈ LaGuardia ✈ John F. Kennedy (JFK) ✈
llentown
Delaware
NEW
JERSEY
A T L A N T I C
O C E A N
Liverpool
Southampton
Gibraltar ➝
PHILADELPHIA
elphia ✈ Camden
Wilmington
KEY
Dover
Atlantic City
Delaware Bay
DELAWARE
San Juan
Panama
Recife
Rio de Janeiro
Cape Town

☐ Greater New York
✈ Airport
66 Interstate highway
═ State highway
— Major railroad line
- - International border
- ● - Shipping route
- - State line

0 kilometers   100
0 miles   50

Manhattan

MOST OF THE SIGHTS described in this book lie within 15 areas of Manhattan. Each of these has its own section in the book. If you are short of time, you could restrict your sightseeing to one or two areas. Many of New York's oldest and newest buildings rub shoulders in Lower Manhattan. It is from here, too, that you can take the Staten Island ferry for breathtaking views of the famous skyline and the Statue of Liberty. Midtown includes the Theater District and Fifth Avenue's glittering shops as well as museums, entertainment and such landmark skyscrapers as the glorious Chrysler Building. Museum Mile on the Upper East Side is a cultural paradise and, since it runs alongside Central Park, you can rest en route and watch New Yorkers at play.

PAGES 138–47
Street Finder maps
8, 11-12

PAGES 128–37
Street Finder maps
7–8

PAGES 106–13
Street Finder maps
3–4

PAGES 100–105
Street Finder map
4

Chelsea and the Garment District

Grame and Flatir Distri

Greenwich Village

SoHo and TriBeCa

East Villag

Lower East Side

Lower Manhattan

Seaport and the Civic Center

PAGES 64–79
Street Finder maps
1–2

PAGES 80–91
Street Finder maps
1–2

PAGES 92–9
Street Finder maps
4, 5

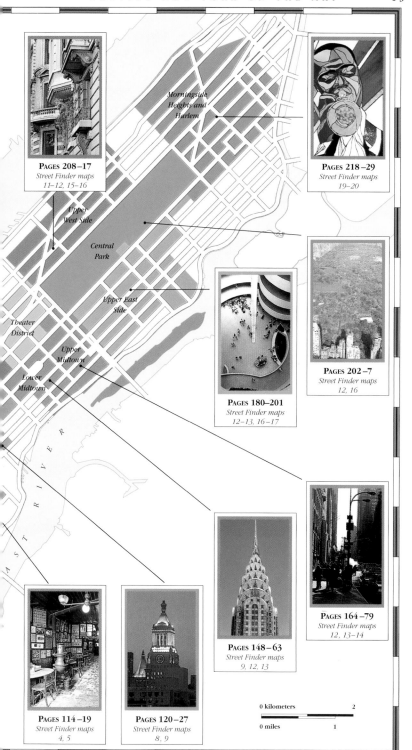

Morningside
Heights and
Harlem

PAGES 208–17
*Street Finder maps
11–12, 15–16*

PAGES 218–29
*Street Finder maps
19–20*

Upper
West Side

Central
Park

Upper East
Side

PAGES 202–7
*Street Finder maps
12, 16*

Theater
District

Upper
Midtown

Lower
Midtown

PAGES 180–201
*Street Finder maps
12–13, 16–17*

PAGES 164–79
*Street Finder maps
12, 13–14*

PAGES 148–63
*Street Finder maps
9, 12, 13*

PAGES 114–19
*Street Finder maps
4, 5*

PAGES 120–27
*Street Finder maps
8, 9*

E A S T   R I V E R

0 kilometers   2

0 miles   1

THE HISTORY OF NEW YORK

ROM ITS FIRST sighting almost 500 years ago by Giovanni da Verrazano, New York's harbor was the prize that all of Europe wanted to capture. The Dutch first sent fur traders to the area in 1621, but they lost the colony they called New Amsterdam to the English in 1664. The settlement was re-christened New York and the name stayed, even after the English lost the colony in 1783, at the end of the Revolutionary War.

A shell-work cloak worn by an Indian chief

THE GROWING CITY

In the 19th century, New York grew rapidly and became a major port. Ease of shipping spawned manufacturing, commerce was king and great fortunes were made. In 1898, Manhattan was joined with the four outer boroughs to form the world's second-largest city. From 1800 to 1900, the population grew from 79,000 to 3 million people. New York City became the country's cultural and entertainment mecca as well as its business center.

THE MELTING POT

The city continued to grow as thousands of immigrants came seeking a better life. Overpopulation meant that many at first lived in slums. Today, the mix of cultures has enriched the city and become its defining quality. Its eight million inhabitants speak some 100 languages.

Manhattan's skyline took shape as the city grew skyward to make space for its ever-increasing population. Throughout its history, the city has experienced alternating periods of economic decline and growth, but in both good times and bad, it remains one of the world's most vital cities.

The following pages illustrate significant periods in New York's history.

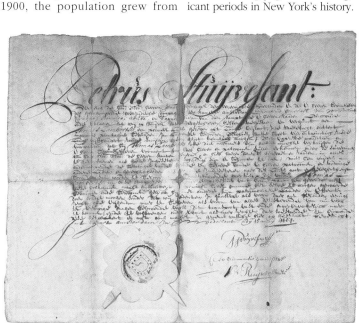
A deed signed by New Amsterdam's last Dutch governor, Peter Stuyvesant, in 1664

◁ The southern half of Manhattan and part of Brooklyn in 1767

Early New York

Indian husk mask

Mᴀɴʜᴀᴛᴛᴀɴ ᴡᴀs a forested land populated by Algonquian-speaking Natives when the Dutch West India Company established a fur trading post called New Amsterdam in 1625. The first settlers built houses helter-skelter, so even today the streets of Lower Manhattan still twist. Broadway, then called by the Dutch name *Breede Wegh*, began as an Indian trail known as the Week-quaesgeek Trail. Harlem has also kept its Dutch name. The town was unruly until Peter Stuyvesant arrived to bring order. But the colony did not produce the expected revenues, and in 1664 the Dutch let it fall to the English, who renamed it New York.

GROWTH OF THE METROPOLIS
☐ *1664*   ☐ *Today*

Seal of New Netherland
The beaver pelt and wampum (Indian shell beads) on the seal were the currency of the colony of New Netherland.

FIRST VIEW OF MANHATTAN (1626)
The southern tip of Manhattan resembled a Dutch town, down to the windmill. Although shown here, the fort had not yet been built.

Dutch ships

The First New Yorkers
Algonquian-speaking Natives were the first inhabitants of Manhattan.

Iroquois Pot
Iroquois Indians were frequent visitors to early Manhattan.

Indian Village
Some Algonquians lived in longhouses on Manhattan before the Dutch arrived.

Native canoe

TIMELINE

1524 Giovanni da Verrazano sails into New York harbor	**1626** Peter Minuit buys Manhattan from the Natives	**1653** Wall is built for protection from attack; adjacent street is called Wall Street
	1625 Dutch establish first permanent trading post	
1600	**1620**	**1640**
1609 Henry Hudson sails up the Hudson River in search of the Northwest Passage	**1643–45** Indian skirmishes end with temporary peace treaty	**1654** First Jewish settlers arrive
	1625 First black slaves brought from Africa	**1647** Peter Stuyvesant becomes colonial governor

Dutch Delftware
Colonists brought this popular tin-glazed earthenware pottery from Holland.

Tiger timbers

Manhattan Skyline
The Strand, now Whitehall Street, was the site of the city's first brick house.

WHERE TO SEE DUTCH NEW YORK

Dug up by workmen in 1916, these remnants of a Dutch ship, the *Tiger*, which burned in 1613, are the earliest artifacts of the period and are now in the Museum of the City of New York *(see p197)*. Rooms in this museum, as well as in the Morris-Jumel Mansion *(see p233)* and the Van Cortlandt House Museum *(see p238)*, display Dutch pottery, tiles and furniture.

Purchase of Manhattan
Peter Minuit bought the island from the Natives in 1626 for $24 worth of trinkets.

Dutch windmill

Fort Amsterdam

Peter Stuyvesant
The last Dutch governor was a tyrant who imposed strict laws – such as an edict closing all the city's taverns at 9 o'clock.

1660 First city hospital established

1664 British forces oust Dutch without a fight and change name to New York

1676 Great Dock built on East River

1698 Trinity Church dedicated

1660

1680

1700

The surrender of New Amsterdam to the British

1680s Bolting Laws give New York exclusive right to process and ship grain

1683 First New York city charter established

1689 Merchant Jacob Leisler leads revolt against taxes and takes over the city for two years

1691 Leisler sentenced to death for treason

1693 Ninety-two cannons installed for protection; area becomes known as the Battery

Colonial New York

Colonial
gentleman

U NDER BRITISH RULE, New York prospered and the population grew rapidly. The bolting of flour (grinding grain) was the main commercial enterprise. Shipbuilding also flourished. As the city prospered, an elite emerged that could afford a more refined way of life, and fine furniture and household silver were made for use in their homes during the Colonial period. During more than a century of governing New York, Britain proved more interested in profit than in the welfare of the colony. The Crown imposed hated taxes, and the spirit of rebellion grew, although especially in New York, loyalties were divided. On the the eve of Revolution, New York was the second-largest city in the 13 colonies, with 20,000 citizens.

Colonial currency

GROWTH OF THE METROPOLIS

■ *1760* □ *Today*

Bedroom

Colonial Street
Pigs and dogs roamed free on the streets of Colonial New York.

Dining
room

Kas
This Dutch-style pine wardrobe was made in New York's Hudson River valley around 1720.

Shipping
Trade with the West Indies and Britain helped New York prosper. In some years, 200 or more vessels visited the port.

TIMELINE

1702 Lord Cornbury appointed Colonial governor; he often wore women's clothes

1711 Slave market set up at the foot of Wall Street

1720 First shipyard opens

| 1700 | 1710 | 1720 | 1730 |

1710 Iroquois chief Hendrick visits England

1720 First shipyard opens

1732 First city theater opens

1725 *New York Gazette*, city's first newspaper, is established

Captain Kidd
The English pirate William Kidd was a respected citizen, lending a block and tackle to help build Trinity Church (see p68).

VAN CORTLANDT HOUSE
Frederick Van Cortlandt built this Georgian-style house in 1748 on a wheat plantation in what is now the Bronx. Today a museum (see p238), it shows how a well-to-do Dutch-English family once lived.

West parlor

WHERE TO SEE COLONIAL NEW YORK
Colonial buildings are open to the public at Historic Richmond Town on Staten Island *(see p252).* Fine examples of Colonial silver and furniture are on display at the Museum of the City of New York *(see p197).*

Richmond Town General Store

Colonial Kitchen
Plain white cheese, called "white meat," was often served in place of meat. Waffles, introduced by the Dutch, were popular. Fresh fruit was rare, but preserved fruits were eaten.

Pewter baby bottle   **Cheese mold**   **Waffle iron**

Decorative Carvings
A face carved in stone peers over each of the front windows.

Sucket fork, for eating preserved fruits

1734 John Peter Zenger's libel trial upholds freedom of the press

1741 Slave uprising creates hysteria; 31 slaves are executed, 150 imprisoned

1754 French and Indian War begins; King's College (now Columbia University) founded

British soldier

1759 First jail built

1740 **1750** **1760**

1733 Bowling Green becomes first city park; first ferries to Brooklyn

King's College

1762 First paid police force

1763 War ends; British gain control of North America

Revolutionary New York

DUG UP INTO TRENCHES for defense, heavily shelled by British troops and scarred by recurring fires, New York suffered during the American Revolution. But despite the hardships, many continued to enjoy cricket games, horse races, balls and boxing matches. After the British took the city in 1776, it became their headquarters. The Continental army did not return to Manhattan until November 25, 1783, two years after the fighting ended.

George Washington, Revolutionary general

GROWTH OF THE METROPOLIS

☐ *1776*   ☐ *Today*

Battle Dress
The Continental (Patriot) army wore blue uniforms, while the British wore red.

British soldier

Soldier's Haversack
American soldiers in the War of Independence carried their supplies in haversacks.

TOPPLING THE KING
New Yorkers tore down the statue of King George III in Bowling Green and melted it down to make ammunition.

Battle of Harlem Heights
Washington won this battle on September 16, 1776. But he did not have enough troops to hold New York so retreated, leaving it to the British.

American soldier

Patriot

Death of a Patriot
While working behind British lines in 1776, Nathan Hale was captured and hanged by the British without trial for spying.

TIMELINE

1765 British pass Stamp Act; New Yorkers protest; Sons of Liberty formed

1767 New duties imposed with Townshend Act; after protests, the act is repealed

1770 Sons of Liberty fight British in the "Battle of Golden Hill"

1774 Rebels dump tea in New York harbor to protest taxes

1760

1770

1780

St. Paul's Chapel

1766 St. Paul's Chapel completed; Stamp Act repealed; Statue of George III erected on Bowling Green

General William Howe, commander in chief of the British troops

1776 War begins; 500 ships under General Howe assemble in New York harbor

Fire Fighters
Fires had long threatened the city, but during the war a series of fires nearly destroyed it. In the wake of the patriot retreat, on September 21, 1776, a devastating fire razed Trinity Church and 1,000 houses.

Leather fire bucket

Statue of George III

General Washington Returns
Washington received a hero's welcome when he reentered New York on November 25, 1783, after the British withdrawal.

Cheering patriots

Flags of the Revolution
Washington's army flew the Continental colors, with a stripe for each of the 13 colonies and a Union Jack in the corner. The Stars and Stripes became the official flag in 1777.

First Stars and Stripes

Continental colors

WHERE TO SEE THE REVOLUTIONARY CITY
In 1776, George Washington used the Morris-Jumel Mansion in upper Manhattan as a headquarters *(see p233)*. He also slept at the Van Cortlandt House *(see p19 and p238)*. After the war he bade farewell to his officers at Fraunces Tavern *(see p76)*.

Morris-Jumel mansion

1783 Treaty of Paris signed, US wins independence; British evacuate New York

1784 Bank of New York chartered

1785 New York named US capital

1789 George Washington inaugurated as first president at Federal Hall

Washington's inauguration

1790 US capital is moved to Philadelphia

1791 New York Hospital, city's oldest, opens

1792 Tontine Coffee House built – first home of the Stock Exchange

1794 Bellevue Hospital opens on the East River

1790

1800

1801 *New York Post* founded by Alexander Hamilton

1804 Vice President Aaron Burr kills political rival Alexander Hamilton in a duel

New York in the 19th Century

FIRMLY ESTABLISHED as the nation's largest city and preeminent seaport, New York grew increasingly wealthy. Manufacturing increased due to the ease of shipping; tycoons like John Jacob Astor made millions. The rich moved uptown; public transportation followed. With rapid growth came fires, epidemics and financial panics.

Governor De Witt Clinton

Immigrants from Ireland, Germany, and other nations arrived. Some found prosperity; others crowded into slums in Lower Manhattan.

GROWTH OF THE METROPOLIS
☐ *1840*   ☐ *Today*

Sheet Music
The Stephen Foster ballad Jeanie With the Light Brown Hair *was popular at this time.*

Croton Distributing Reservoir was built in 1842. Until then, New Yorkers had no fresh drinking water – they relied on deliveries of bottled water.

Omnibus
The horse-drawn omnibus was introduced for public transportation in 1832 and remained on New York streets until World War I.

Keeping Fit
Gymnasiums such as Dr. Rich's Institute for Physical Education were established in New York in the 1830s and 1840s.

TIMELINE

1805 First free state schools established in New York

1811 Randel Plan divides Manhattan into grid pattern above 14th Street

1812–14 War of 1812; British blockade New York harbor

The Constitution, *most famous ship in War of 1812*

1835 Much of old New York razed in city's worst fire

| 1810 | 1820 | 1830 |

1807 Robert Fulton launches first steamboat, on the Hudson River

1822 Yellow fever epidemic; people evacuate to Greenwich Village

1823 New York surpasses Boston and Philadelphia to become nation's largest city

1827 New York abolishes slavery

1837 New Yorker Samuel Morse sends first telegraph message

The Brownstone
Many brownstone row houses were built in the first half of the century. The raised stoop allowed separate entry to the parlor and ground-floor servants' quarters.

Crystal Palace was an iron and glass exhibition hall erected for the 1853 World's Fair.

NEW YORK IN 1855
Looking south from 42nd Street, Crystal Palace and the Croton Distributing Reservoir stood where the main public library and Bryant Park are today.

THE PORT OF NEW YORK
New York's importance as a port city grew by leaps and bounds in the early 19th century. Robert Fulton launched his first steamboat, the *Clermont*, in 1807. Steamboats made travel much quicker – it now took 72 hours to reach Albany, which was both the state capital and the gateway to the West. Trade with the West by steamboat and canal boat, and with the rest of the world by clipper ship, made the fortunes of many New Yorkers.

The steamboat *Clermont*

Crystal Palace in Flames
On October 5, 1858, New York's Crystal Palace exhibition hall burned to the ground, just as its predecessor in London did.

Grand Canal Celebration
Ships in New York harbor lined up to celebrate the 1825 Erie Canal opening. In connecting the Great Lakes with Albany, the state capital, on the Hudson River, the canal opened a water link between the Midwest and the Port of New York. New York realized huge profits.

1849 Astor Place riots; ships set sail for California Gold Rush

1851 *New York Times* first published

1853 New York hosts first World's Fair

1861 Civil War begins

1857 Financial panic and depression

1863 Draft riots last four days, many die

1865 Abraham Lincoln lies in state in City Hall

1840

1850

1860

Early baseball player

1845 New York Knickerbockers, first organized baseball team chartered

Clipper ship card

1858 Vaux and Olmsted design Central Park; Macy's founded

1842 Croton Reservoir built

FOR SAN FRANCISCO
FREE TRADE

Crowds in Central Park

The Age of Extravagance

Industrialist Andrew Carnegie

As NEW YORK's merchant princes grew ever wealthier, the city entered into a gilded era during which many of its most opulent buildings went up. Millions were lavished on the arts with the founding of the Metropolitan Museum, Public Library and Carnegie Hall. Luxury hotels like the Plaza and the original Waldorf-Astoria were built, and elegant department stores arose to serve the wealthy. Such flamboyant figures as William "Boss" Tweed, political strongman and king of corruption, and circus man Phineas T. Barnum were also larger than life.

GROWTH OF THE METROPOLIS

☐ *1890*   ☐ *Today*

Overlooking the Park
The Dakota (1880) was the first grand luxury apartment house on the Upper West Side (see p216).

Palatial Living
Mansions lined Fifth Avenue. When it was built in 1882, W.K. Vanderbilt's Italianate palace at 660 Fifth Avenue, was one of the farthest north.

Fashion City
Lord & Taylor built a new store on Broadway's Ladies' Mile; 6th Avenue between 14th and 23rd streets was known as Fashion Row.

BATHING SUITS.

A GREAT SPECIALTY AT
LORD & TAYLOR'S, Broadway and 20th Street, N.Y.
CHEAPEST AND BEST QUALITY OF BATHING SUITS IN THE CITY.

THE ELEVATED RAILROAD
By the mid 1870s, elevated railroads or "Els" ran along 2nd, 3rd, 6th and 9th avenues. They made travel faster, but left noise, grime and pollution in their wake.

TIMELINE

		1870 J.D. Rockefeller founds Standard Oil	
1867 Brooklyn's Prospect Park completed	**1868** First elevated railroad built on Greenwich Street	**1871** The first Grand Central Depot opens on 42nd St.; "Boss" Tweed is arrested and imprisoned	**1877** A.G. Bell demonstrates the telephone in New York

1865 ———— **1870** ———— **1875**

1869 First apartment house built on 18th Street; Black Friday financial crisis hits Wall Street

The interior of the Stock Exchange

1873 Banks fail: Stock Exchange panics

1872 Bloomingdale's opens

1879 St. Patrick's Cathedral completed; first city telephone exchange opened on Nassau Street

Mark Twain's Birthday
Mark Twain, whose 1873 novel The Gilded Age *portrayed the decadent lifestyle of New Yorkers, celebrated his birthday at Delmonico's.*

WHERE TO SEE THE AGE OF EXTRAVAGANCE

The Gold Room in the Henry Villard Houses *(see p174)* is a good place to experience the city's past. Formerly the Music Room, it is now a venue for afternoon tea. The Museum of the City of New York also has two period rooms *(p197)*.

Elevated train

Streetcar

Bowery

Rural Fifth Avenue
This painting by Ralph Blakelock shows a shantytown at 86th Street. Today it is one of New York's most expensive addresses.

The Tweed Ring
William "Boss" Tweed led Tammany Hall, which dominated city government. He stole millions in city funds.

Nast's cartoon of "Boss" Tweed

Tammany Tiger
The Museum of the City of New York has "Boss" Tweed's cane, which sports a gold Tammany Tiger mascot on its handle.

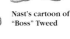

1880 Canned fruits and meats first appear in stores; Metropolitan Museum of Art opens; streets lit by electricity

1883 Metropolitan Opera opens on Broadway; Brooklyn Bridge completed

1886 Statue of Liberty unveiled

1891 Carnegie Hall opens

1880	1885	1890

1888 Great Blizzard dumps 22 in (56 cm) of snow

1890 First moving picture shows appear in New York

Grand display of fireworks over Brooklyn Bridge, 1883

1892 Cathedral of St. John the Divine begun; Ellis Island opens

New York at the Turn of the Century

Horse-drawn carriage

B Y 1900, NEW YORK was a hub of American industry: 70% of the country's corporations were based there, and the port handled two-thirds of all imported goods. The rich got richer, but in the crowded slums, disease spread. Even so, immigrants kept their rich traditions alive, and political and social reform emerged. In 1900, the International Ladies' Garment Workers' Union was founded to battle for the rights of the women and children who toiled in dangerous factories for low wages. The Triangle Shirtwaist Factory fire in 1911 also sped reform.

GROWTH OF THE METROPOLIS

☐ *1914*   ☐ *Today*

Crowded Conditions
Tenements were unhealthy and overcrowded. They often lacked windows, air shafts or proper sanitary facilities.

Gateway to America
Almost five times as crowded as the rest of New York, the Lower East Side was the most densely populated place in the world.

WHERE TO SEE TURN-OF-THE-CENTURY NEW YORK
The Lower East Side Tenement Museum *(see p97)* has exhibits on tenement life.

Tailor's scissors

Hip bath

Inside a Sweatshop
Workers toiled long hours for low wages in the overcrowded sweatshops of the garment district. This view of Moe Levy's shop was taken in 1912.

Streetcars on Broadway

TIMELINE

1895 Olympia Theater is first to open in the Broadway area

1898 Five boroughs merge to form world's second-largest city

1901 Macy's opens Broadway department store

1895   **1900**

1896 First bagel served in a Clinton Street bakery

1897 Waldorf-Astoria Hotel opens: the largest hotel in the world

1900 Mayor Robert Van Wyck breaks ground for city's first subway with silver shovel

1903 Lyceum Theater opens – oldest Broadway house still in use

FLATIRON BUILDING

Overlooking Madison Square where Broadway, Fifth Avenue and 23rd Street meet, the 21-story tower was one of the city's first skyscrapers (1902). Triangle-shaped, it was dubbed the Flatiron Building (see p125).

Underlying
steel structure

Elaborate
limestone facade

Only 6 ft (185 cm) wide
at apex of
triangle

Supper in the Saddle
Decadent parties were all the rage. C.K.G. Billings's horseback dinner at Sherry's restaurant in 1903 was the talk of all New York.

Plaza Promenade
The section of Fifth Avenue in front of the Plaza Hotel was considered the most elegant in the city.

Ventilated hairpiece

High Fashion
In 1900 styles were stiff, with wire hoops and bustles worn beneath ornate dresses. Later, clothes became softer and more practical.

Long bustle

Wire hoops

1906 Architect Stanford White shot at Madison Square Garden, which he had built in 1890

1909 Wilbur Wright flies first plane over New York

1910 Pennsylvania Station opens

1913 Woolworth Building is world's tallest; new Grand Central Terminal opens; Harlem's Apollo Theater opens

1905

1910

1905 First crossing of the Staten Island Ferry

1907 First metered taxicabs; first Ziegfeld Follies

1911 Triangle Shirtwaist Factory fire kills 146 sweatshop workers; New York Public Library completed

Woolworth Building

New York Between the Wars

Entrance card to the Cotton Club

THE 1920s WERE a time of high living for many New Yorkers. Mayor Jimmy Walker set the pace, whether squiring chorus girls, drinking in speakeasies or watching the Yankees. But the good times ended with the 1929 stock market crash. By 1932, Walker had resigned, charged with corruption, and one-quarter of New Yorkers were unemployed. With Mayor Fiorello La Guardia's 1933 election, New York began to recover and thrive.

GROWTH OF THE METROPOLIS
☐ *1933*   ☐ *Today*

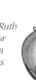

Exotic Costumes
Chorus girls were a major Cotton Club attraction.

THE COTTON CLUB
This Harlem nightclub was host to the best jazz in town, as first Duke Ellington and then Cab Calloway led the band. People flocked from all over the city to hear them.

Defying Prohibition
Although alcohol was outlawed, speakeasies – semi-secret illegal drinking dens – still sold it.

Home-Run Hitter
In 1927, baseball star Babe Ruth hit a record 60 home runs for the Yankees. Yankee Stadium (see p239) became known as "the house that Ruth built."

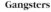

Sawed-off shotgun concealed in violin case

Gangsters
Dutch Schultz was the kingpin of an illegal booze racket.

TIMELINE

Opening of the Holland Tunnel

1918 End of World War I

1919 18th Amendment bans alcohol, launches Prohibition Era

1920 US women get the vote

1926 Jimmy Walker becomes mayor

1931 Empire State Building becomes world's tallest

1920	1925	1930

1924 Novelist James Baldwin is born in Harlem

1925 *The New Yorker* magazine is launched

1927 Lindbergh flies across the Atlantic; first talking movie, *The Jazz Singer*, opens; Holland Tunnel opens

1929 Stock market crash; Great Depression begins

1930 Chrysler Building completed

Big Band Leaders
Banned from many downtown clubs, black artists like Cab Calloway starred at the Cotton Club.

Broadway Melodies
The 1920s were the heyday of the Broadway musical, with a record number of plays opening.

THE GREAT DEPRESSION

The Roaring Twenties ended with the stock market crash of October 29, 1929, which set off the Depression. New York was hard hit: squatters' shacks sprang up in Central Park and thousands were out of work. But art flourished as artists went to work for the Works Projects Administration (WPA), creating outstanding murals and artworks throughout the city.

Waiting to receive benefits in 1931

Breakfast menu

Lindbergh's plane,
Spirit of St. Louis

Lindbergh's Flight
New Yorkers celebrated Lindbergh's nonstop solo flight across the Atlantic in 1927 in a variety of ways, including a breakfast in his honor.

Rockefeller Center
Millionaire John D. Rockefeller drives the final rivet to celebrate the opening of Rockefeller Center on May 1, 1939.

Mass Event
Forty-five million people visited the 1939 World's Fair in New York.

NEW YORK WORLD'S FAIR
1939

1933 Prohibition ends; Fiorello LaGuardia begins three terms as mayor

1940 Queens-Midtown Tunnel opens

1942 Times Square blacked out during World War II; Idlewild International Airport (now JFK) opens

1935

1940

1945

1936 Parks Department headed by Robert Moses; new parks created

1939 Rockefeller Center is completed

1941 US enters World War II

1944 Black leader Adam Clayton Powell elected to Congress

Postwar New York

Since World War II, New York has seen both the best of times and the worst. Although established as the financial capital of the world, the city itself almost went bankrupt in the 1970s. Wall Street hit its peak in the 1980s, then experienced its worst crash since 1929. Since the early 1990s, New York has seen a dramatic drop in the crime rate and an increase in the restoration and renewal of such landmarks as Grand Central Terminal and the "new" Times Square. This constant rebuilding is emblematic of the city's position at the cultural and financial hub of the United States.

1967 Hippie musical *Hair* opens on Off-Broadway, then transfers to the Biltmore Theater

1971 Pop artist Andy Warhol has a retrospective show of his work at the Whitney Museum

1966 Newspaper and transit strikes

1975 Federal loan saves New York from bankruptcy

1953 Merce Cunningham founds dance company

1963 Pennsylvania Station razed

1959 Guggenheim Museum opens

1945 End of World War II

1946 UN headquarters established in New York

1954 Ellis Island closes

1945	1950	1955	1960	1965	1970	1975
MAYORS:	IMPELLITERI	WAGNER			LINDSAY	BEAME
1945	1950	1955	1960	1965	1970	1975

1947 Jackie Robinson, first black baseball player in the major leagues, signs with Brooklyn Dodgers

1964 New York World's Fair; race riots in Harlem and Bedford-Stuyvesant; Verrazano Narrows Bridge links Brooklyn and Staten Island; Beatles play at Shea Stadium

1973 World Trade Center completed

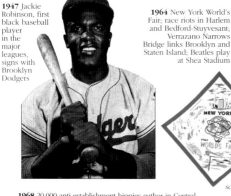

Souvenir scarf

1968 20,000 anti-establishment hippies gather in Central Park; student sit-ins at Columbia University

Andy Warhol with actresses Candy Darling and Ultra Violet

1983 Economic boom: property prices skyrocket; Trump Tower completed by real estate tycoon Donald Trump, who symbolizes the "yuppie" wealth of the 1980s

31 New York regains solvency

1988 Twenty-five percent of New Yorkers live below the poverty line

1990 David Dinkins, New York's first black mayor, takes office; Ellis Island reopens as an immigration museum

2001 Terrorist attack on the World Trade Center; Mayor Giuliani is a great support to the people of New York. President George W Bush declares war on terrorism

1987 Stock market crash

1994 Rudolph Giuliani takes office as mayor

1980	1985	1990	1995	2000	2005
CH		**DINKINS**	**GIULIANI**		**BLOOMBERG**
1980	1985	1990	1995	2000	2005

1986 Shock of corruption scandals rock Mayor Koch's administration; Centennial of Statue of Liberty

2000 Population reaches just over 8 million

2003 A major power outage on August 14 leaves 50 million people in the North East (including New York City), mid-West, and ports of Canada, blacked out for up to 24 hours

1995 The neglected Chelsea Piers are renovated and open as a mammoth sports and entertainment complex *(see p136)*

2002 The lights go on in a regenerated 42nd Street, which crosses Broadway at Times Square. Along with neighboring Chelsea and its cutting-edge galleries, the area out-shines SoHo as the city's chic spot

NEW YORK AT A GLANCE

THERE ARE ALMOST 300 places of interest described in the *Area by Area* section of this book. They range from the bustling New York Stock Exchange *(see pp70–71)* to Central Park's peaceful Strawberry Fields *(see p206)* and from synagogues to skyscrapers. The following 16 pages are a time-saving guide to New York's most interesting sights. Museums and architecture each have a section, and there are guides to the people and cultures that have given the city its unique character. Each sight is cross-referenced to its own full entry. Below are the top ten tourist attractions to start you off.

NEW YORK'S TOP TEN TOURIST ATTRACTIONS

Ellis Island
See pp78–9.

Empire State Building
See pp134–5.

South Street Seaport
See p84.

Museum of Modern Art
See pp170–73.

Rockefeller Center
See p142.

Central Park
See pp202–7.

Statue of Liberty
See pp74–5.

Metropolitan Museum of Art
See pp188–95.

Brooklyn Bridge
See pp86–9.

Chinatown
See p96.

◁ **Park Avenue's relentless flow of traffic**

New York's Best: Museums

NEW YORK'S MUSEUMS range from the vast scope of the Metropolitan Museum to the personal treasures of financier J. Pierpont Morgan's own collection. Several museums celebrate New York's heritage, giving visitors an insight into the people and events that made the city what it is today. This map features some highlights, with a detailed overview on pages 36 and 37.

Museum of Modern Art
Picasso's Goat (1950) is among the impressive collection in the newly-renovated and expanded Museum of Modern Art.

***Intrepid* Sea-Air-Space Museum**
Situated on a large aircraft carrier on the Hudson River, this naval museum also traces the progress of flight and undersea exploration.

Morgan Library
One of the world's finest collections of manuscripts, prints and books includes this rare French Bible from 1230.

Merchant's House Museum
This perfectly preserved 1832 house belonged to a wealthy trader.

Ellis Island
This museum vividly re-creates the experiences of many millions of immigrant families.

Upper West Side

Theater District

Chelsea and the Garment District

Lower Midtown

Gramercy and the Flatiron District

Greenwich Village

SoHo and TriBeCa

East Village

Lower East Side

Lower Manhattan

Seaport and the Civic Center

Ellis Island

0 kilometers   2

0 miles   1

American Museum of Natural History
Dinosaurs, meteorites and much more have fascinated generations of visitors here.

Morningside Heights and Harlem

N

Museum of the City of New York
Costumes, works of art and household objects (such as this 1725 silver dish) create an intricate and detailed picture of New York's past.

Cooper-Hewitt Museum
A wealth of decorative arts is displayed in industrialist Andrew Carnegie's former Upper East Side mansion.

Central Park

Upper East Side

Solomon R. Guggenheim Museum
Ellsworth Kelly's Blue, Green, Yellow, Orange, Red *(1966) is part of the collection housed in Frank Lloyd Wright's only New York building.*

oper town

Metropolitan Museum of Art
Of the millions of works in its collection, this 12th-dynasty Egyptian faïence hippo is the museum's own mascot.

Whitney Museum of American Art
This exceptional collection includes many views of New York. One of the best is Brooklyn Bridge: Variation on an Old Theme *(1939), by Joseph Stella.*

Frick Collection
The collection of 19th-century rail-road magnate Henry Clay Frick is displayed in his former home. Master-pieces include St. Francis in the Desert *(about 1480) by Giovanni Bellini.*

Exploring New York's Museums

YOU COULD DEVOTE an entire month to visiting New York's museums and still not do them justice. There are more than 60 museums in Manhattan alone, half that number again in the other boroughs. The wealth of art and the huge variety of offerings – from old masters to old fire engines, dinosaurs to dolls, Tibetan tapestries to African masks – is equal to that of any city in the world. Note that some museums close on Monday as well as on another day. Many stay open late one or two evenings a week, and some have one evening when admission is free. Not every museum charges for admission, but donations are always welcome.

Richmond Town tobacco tin

PAINTING AND SCULPTURE

NEW YORK is best known for its art museums. The **Metropolitan Museum of Art** houses an extensive collection of American art as well as world-famous master-pieces. **The Cloisters**, a branch of the "Met" in Upper Manhattan, is a treasury of medieval art and architecture. The **Frick Collection** has a superb display of Old Masters. In contrast, the newly-renovated **Museum of Modern Art (MoMA)** houses Impressionist and modern paintings. **The Whitney Museum of American Art** and the **Solomon R. Guggenheim Museum** also specialize in modern art, the Whitney's biennial show being the foremost display of work by living artists. Today's cutting edge is at the **New Museum of Contemporary Art**, and the work of untrained artists can be seen at the

American Folk Art Museum. The **National Academy of Design** displays a collection of 19th- and 20th- century art, donated by its members. In Harlem, the **Studio Museum** shows the work of black artists.

CRAFTS AND DESIGN

IF YOU ARE interested in textiles, porcelain and glass, embroideries and laces, wallpaper and prints, visit the **Cooper-Hewitt Museum**, the decorative arts out-post of Washington's Smithsonian Institu-tion. The design collections at **MoMA** trace the history of design from clocks to couches. The **American Craft Museum** offers the finest work of today's skilled artisans in mediums from furniture to art glass, and the **American Folk Art Museum** presents folk forms, from quilts to canes. Silver collections are notable at the **Museum of the City of New York**. The fine displays of native art at the **National Museum of the American Indian** include jewelry, rugs and pottery.

Corn husk doll, American Museum of Natural History

PRINTS AND PHOTOGRAPHY

THE **International Center of Photography** is the only museum in New York that is totally devoted to this medium. Collections can also be seen at the **Metropolitan Museum of Art** and there are many examples of early photography at the **Museum of the City of New York** and **Ellis Island**.

Prints and drawings by such great book illustrators as Kate Greenaway and John Tenniel are featured at the **Morgan Library**. The **Cooper-Hewitt Museum** has examples of the use of prints in the decorative arts.

FURNITURE AND COSTUMES

THE ANNUAL exhibition of the Costume Institute at the **Metropolitan Museum of Art** is always worth a visit. Also impressive is the American Wing, with its 24 rooms of original furnishings tracing life from 1640 to the 20th century. Period rooms depicting New York in various settings, beginning with the 17th century Dutch, are on display at the **Museum of the City of New York**. There are also some house museums that give a realistic picture of furnishings and life in old New York. The **Merchant's House Museum**, a preserved residence from 1832, was occupied by the same family for 98 years. **Gracie Mansion** was the residence of mayor Archibald Gracie who bought it in 1798 from a shipping merchant and is open periodically for public tours. The **Theodore Roosevelt Birthplace** is the brownstone where the 26th president of the United States grew up, and the **Mount Vernon Hotel Museum** was an early 19th-century resort.

The Peaceable Kingdom (c.1840–1845) by Edward Hicks, at the Brooklyn Museum

HISTORY

Palm pistol at the New York City Police Museum

AMERICAN HISTORY unfolds at **Federal Hall**, the first US capital: George Washington took his oath as America's first president on the balcony in April 1789. Visit the **Fraunces Tavern Museum** for a glimpse of colonial New York. **Ellis Island** and **Lower East Side Tenement Museum** re-create the hardships faced by immigrants. The new **Museum of Jewish Heritage** in Battery City is a living memorial to the Holocaust. The **NYC Fire Museum** and the **New York City Police Museum** chronicle heroism and tragedy, while the **South Street Seaport Museum** re-creates early maritime history.

TECHNOLOGY AND NATURAL HISTORY

Forest-dwelling bonga, American Museum of Natural History

SCIENCE MUSEUMS hold exhibitions from nature to space-age technology. The **American Museum of Natural History** has vast collections covering flora, fauna and cultures from around the world. Its Rose Center/Hayden Planetarium offers a unique view of space. The *Intrepid* **Sea-Air-Space Museum** is a repository of technology that chronicles military progress. It is based on the decks of an aircraft carrier.

If you missed a classic Lucille Ball sitcom or footage of the first man on the moon, the place to visit is the **Museum of Television and Radio**, which holds these and many other classics of TV and radio.

ART FROM OTHER CULTURES

ARTWORK of other nations is the focus of several special collections. Oriental art is the specialty of the **Asia Society** and the **Japan Society**. The **Jewish Museum** features major collections of Judaica and has changing exhibitions of Jewish life. **El Museo del Barrio** is dedicated to the arts of Puerto Rico, including many pre-Columbian artifacts. For an impressive review of African-American art and history, visit the **Schomburg Center for Research in Black Culture**. Finally, the **Metropolitan Museum of Art** excels in its multicultural displays of art, ranging from ancient Egypt to contemporary Africa.

Egyptian mummy, Brooklyn Museum

LIBRARIES

NEW YORK's notable libraries, such as the **Morgan Library**, offer some superb art collections as well as a chance to view pages from rare books. The **New York Public Library** shows a collection that includes manuscripts of many famous works.

BEYOND MANHATTAN

OTHER MUSEUMS worth a visit include the **Brooklyn Museum**, with more than one million paintings. The

American Museum of the Moving Image in Queens has a unique collection of motion-picture history. The **Jacques Marchais Museum of Tibetan Art** is a rare find on Staten Island as is **Historic Richmond Town**, a well-restored village dating from the 1600s.

New York's Best: Architecture

E VEN WHEN FOLLOWING world trends, New York has given its own twist to the turns of architectural fashion, the style of its buildings influenced by both geography and economy. An island city, with space at a premium, must look upward to grow. This trend was reflected early on with tall, narrow town houses and later with the city's apartment buildings and sky-scrapers. Building materials such as cast-iron and brownstone were chosen for their local availability and practical appeal. The result is a city that has developed by finding flamboyant answers to practical needs. A more detailed overview of New York's architecture is on pages 40 to 41.

Apartment Buildings
The Majestic is one of five Art Deco twin-towered apartment buildings on Central Park West.

Cast-Iron Architecture
Mass-produced cast-iron was often used for building facades. SoHo has many of the best examples, such as this building at 28–30 Greene Street.

Post-Modernism
The quirky, yet elegant, shapes of buildings like the World Financial Center, built in 1985 (see p69), mark a bold departure from the sleek steel-and-glass boxes of the 1950s and 1960s.

Brownstones
Built from local sand-stone, brownstones were favored by the 19th-century middle classes. India House, built in a Florentine palazzo style on Wall Street, is typical of many brownstone commercial buildings.

Théâtre District

Chelsea and the Garment District

Greenwich Village

Gramercy and the Flatiron District

SoHo and TriBeCa

East Village

Lower East Side

Lower Manhattan

HUDSON RIVER

Central Park

Morningside Heights and Harlem

Upper West Side

Upper East Side

Upper Midtown

Lower Midtown

EAST RIVER

19th-Century Mansions
The Jewish Museum (see p184), formerly the home of Felix M. Warburg, is a fine example of the French Renaissance style that typified these mansions.

Beaux Arts
Opulent style, created for the richest of owners, is exemplified by the Beaux Arts grandeur of the Frick mansion.

Modernism
The Seagram Building's sleek bronze-and-glass walls, scant decoration and monumental scale typify postwar architecture. (See p175.)

The Skyscraper
The glory of New York architecture, these buildings expressed a perfect blend of practical engineering skill together with fabulous decoration, such as this gargoyle on the Chrysler Building.

0 kilometers 2
0 miles 1

Tenements
Constructed as an economic form of housing, for many these buildings were a stark introduction to new lives. Mainly built on the Lower East Side, the apartments were hopelessly overcrowded. In addition, the buildings' design, with inadequate air shafts, resulted in apartments with little or no ventilation.

Federal Architecture
Federal style was popular in civic architecture of the 19th century; City Hall combines it with French Renaissance influences.

Exploring New York's Architecture

A Federal-style front door

IN ITS FIRST 200 YEARS, New York, like all of America, looked to Europe for architectural inspiration. None of the buildings from the Dutch colonial period survive in Manhattan today; most were lost in the great fire of 1776 or torn down to make way for new developments in the early 1800s. Throughout the 18th and 19th centuries, the city's major architectural trends followed those of Europe. With the advent of cast-iron architecture in the 1850s, the Art Deco period and the ever-higher rise of the skyscraper, New York's architecture came into its own.

FEDERAL ARCHITECTURE

THIS AMERICAN adaptation of the Neoclassical Adam style flowered in the early decades of the new nation, featuring square buildings two or three stories tall, with low hipped roofs, balustrades and decorative elements – all carefully balanced. **City Hall** (1811, John McComb, Jr. and Joseph François Mangin) is a blend of Federal and French Renaissance influences. The restored warehouses of **Schermerhorn Row** (c1812) in the Seaport district are also in Federal style.

BROWNSTONES

PLENTIFUL AND CHEAP, the brown sandstone found in the nearby Connecticut River Valley and along the banks of the Hackensack River in New

A typical brownstone with stoop leading up to the main entrance

Jersey was the most common building material in the 1800s. It is found all over the city's residential neighborhoods, used for small homes or small apartments – some of the best examples of brownstone can be found in **Chelsea**. Because street space was limited, these buildings were very narrow in width, but also very deep. A typical brownstone has a flight of steps, called a stoop, leading up to the living floors. Separate stairs lead down to the basement, which was originally the servants' quarters.

TENEMENTS

TENEMENTS WERE built to house the huge influx of immigrants who arrived from the 1840s up to World War I. The six-story blocks, 100 ft (30 m) long and 25 ft (8 m) wide, offered very little light and air except from tiny side-wall air shafts and windows at each end, leaving the middle rooms in darkness. The tiny apartments were called railroad flats after their similarity to railroad cars. Later designs had air shafts between buildings, but these helped the spread of fire. The **Lower East Side Tenement Museum** has scale models of the old tenements.

CAST-IRON ARCHITECTURE

AN AMERICAN architectural innovation of the 19th century, cast iron was cheaper than stone or brick and allowed ornate features to be prefabricated in foundries from molds and used as building facades. Today, New York has the world's largest concentration of full and partial cast-iron facades. The best, built in the 1870s, are in the **SoHo Cast-Iron Historic District**.

The original cast-iron facade of 72–76 Greene Street, SoHo

BEAUX ARTS

THIS FRENCH school of architecture dominated public buildings and wealthy residential properties during New York's gilded age. This era (from 1880 to about 1920) produced many of the city's most prominent architects, including Richard Morris Hunt (**Carnegie Hall**, 1891; **Metropolitan Museum**, 1895), who in 1845 was the first American architect to study in Paris; Cass Gilbert (**Custom House**, 1907; **New York Life Insurance**

ARCHITECTURAL DISGUISES

Some of the most fanciful forms on the New York skyline were devised by clever architects to disguise the city's essential but utilitarian – and rather unattractive – rooftop water tanks. Look skyward to discover the ornate cupolas, spires and domes that transform the most mundane of features into veritable castles in the air. Examples that are easy to spot are atop two neighboring Fifth Avenue hotels: the Sherry Netherland at 60th Street and the Pierre at 61st Street.

Standard water tower

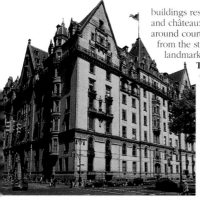

The Dakota Apartments, built in 1884, on the Upper West Side across from Central Park

Building, 1928; the **US Courthouse**, 1936); the teams of Warren & Wetmore (**Grand Central Terminal**, 1913; **Helmsley Building**, 1929); Carrère & Hastings (**New York Public Library**, 1911; **Frick mansion**, 1914); and McKim, Mead & White, the city's most famous firm of architects (**Villard Houses**, 1884; **United States General Post Office**, 1913; **Municipal Building**, 1914).

APARTMENT BUILDINGS

A S THE CITY'S population grew and space became ever more precious, family homes in Manhattan became much too expensive for most New Yorkers, and even the wealthy joined the trend toward communal living. In 1884 Henry Hardenbergh's Dakota *(see p216)*, one of the first luxury apartment buildings, started a spate of turn-of-the-century construction on the Upper West Side. Many of the

buildings resembled castles and châteaux, and were built around courtyards not visible from the street. Favorite landmarks are the five **Twin Towers** on Central Park West, the San Remo, Eldorado, Century, the Beresford, and the Majestic. Built during the peak of Art Deco (1929 to 1931), they create the distinctive skyline seen from the park.

SKYSCRAPERS

A LTHOUGH CHICAGO gave birth to the skyscraper, New York has seen some of the greatest innovations. In 1902 Daniel Burnham, a Chicago architect, built the **Flatiron Building**, so tall at 300 ft (91 m) that skeptics said it would collapse. By 1913, the **Woolworth Building** had risen to 792 ft (241 m). Soon, zoning laws were passed requiring "setbacks" – upper stories were stepped back to allow light to reach street level. This suited the Art Deco style. The **Chrysler Building** (1930) was the world's tallest until the

Art Deco arched pattern on the spire of the Chrysler Building

Empire State Building (1931) was completed. Both are Art Deco classics, but it was Raymond Hood's **Group Health Insurance Building**, formerly the McGraw-Hill Building, that represented New York in 1932 in the *International Style* architectural survey.

The World Trade Center *(see p72)* was New York's tallest building until September 2001 *(see p54)*. It represented the "glass box" Modernist style, now superseded by the Post-Modern style, such as the **Citigroup Center** (1977).

WHERE TO FIND THE BUILDINGS

**245 Fifth Avenue
(Apartment Building)**

**60 Gramercy Park
North (Brownstone)**

**Hotel Pierre
(Beaux Arts)**

**Sherry Netherland
Hotel (Beaux Arts)**

Multicultural New York

WHEREVER YOU GO in New York, even in pockets of the hectic high-rise city center, you will find evidence of the richly ethnic flavor of the city. A bus ride can take you from Madras to Moscow, Hong Kong to Haiti. Immigrants are still coming to New York, though numbers are fewer than in the peak years from 1880 to 1910, when 17 million people arrived. In the 1980s, a million newcomers, largely from Caribbean countries and Asia, arrived and found their own special corner of the city. Throughout the year you will encounter crowds celebrating one of many festivals. To find out more about national celebrations and parades, see pages 50 to 53.

Hell's Kitchen
For a while called "Clinton" to reflect a new neighborhood mix, this was the first home of early Irish immigrants.

Little Ukraine
Services are held at T. Shevchenko Place as part of the May 17 festivities to mark the Ukrainians' conversion to Christianity.

Little Korea
Not far from Herald Square, a small enclave of Koreans has made a niche.

Thea Distr

Chelsea and the Garment District

Gramercy and the Flatiron District

Greenwich Village

Little Italy
For ten days in September, the Italian community gathers around the Mulberry Street area, and the streets are taken over by the celebrations of the Festa di San Gennaro.

SoHo and TriBeCa

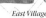

East Village

Chinatown
Every year, in January or February, Mott Street is packed as residents celebrate the Chinese New Year.

Seaport and the Civic Center

Lower Manhattan

Lower East Side

0 kilometers   2

0 miles   1

The Lower East Side
The synagogues around Rivington Street reflect the religious traditions of this old Jewish area.

Morningside
Heights and
Harlem

Upper West
Side

Central
Park

Upper East
Side

Upper
Midtown

Lower
Midtown

Harlem
The Sunday morning gospel service at the Abyssinian Baptist Church is one of Harlem's finest.

El Barrio
The vibrant Hispanic community of Harlem's El Barrio district is centered around the street market, La Marquetta.

Yorkville
Only a few cafés and bierkellers remain to keep the flavor of this former uptown German district. The Steuben Day Parade is still held here each September.

Upper East Side
The magnificent St. Nicholas Russian Orthodox Cathedral on East 97th Street is a reminder of the dispersed White Russian community. Mass is held in Russian each Sunday.

Little India
The restaurants of East 6th Street offer Eastern atmosphere at affordable prices.

Exploring New York's Many Cultures

Stained glass at the Cotton Club

EVEN "NATIVE" NEW YORKERS have ancestral roots in other countries. Throughout the 17th century, the Dutch and English settled here, establishing trade colonies in the New World. Soon America became a symbol of hope for the downtrodden elsewhere in Europe. Many flocked across the ocean, some penniless and with little knowledge of the language. The potato famine of the 1840s led to the first wave of Irish immigrants, followed by German and other European workers displaced by political unrest and the Industrial Revolution. Immigrants continue to enrich New York in countless ways, and today an estimated 100 languages are spoken.

Turkish immigrants arriving at former Idlewild Airport in 1963

THE JEWS

THERE HAS BEEN a Jewish community in New York since 1654. The first synagogue, Shearith Israel, was established by refugees from a Dutch colony in Brazil and is still active today. These first settlers, Sephardic Jews of Spanish descent, included such prominent families as the Baruchs. They were followed by the German Jews, who set up successful retailing enterprises, like the Straus brothers at Macy's. Russian persecution led to the mass immigration that began in the late 1800s. By the start of World War I, there were 600,000 Jews living on the Lower East Side. Today, this area is more Hispanic and Asian than Jewish, but it holds reminders of its role as a place of refuge and new beginnings.

THE GERMANS

THE GERMANS began to settle in New York in the 18th century. From John Peter Zenger onward *(see p19)*, the city's German community has championed the freedom to express ideas and opinions. It has also produced giants of industry, such as John Jacob Astor, the city's first millionaire.

THE ITALIANS

ITALIANS FIRST came to New York in the 1830s and 1840s. Many came from northern Italy to escape the failing revolution at home. In the 1870s, poverty in southern Italy drove many more Italians across the ocean. In time, they became a potent political force in the city, exemplified by Fiorello La Guardia, one of New York's finest mayors.

THE CHINESE

THE CHINESE were late arrivals to New York. In 1880, the population of the Mott Street district was a mere

Eastern States Buddhist Temple, in central Chinatown *(see pp96–7)*

700. By the 1940s, they were the city's fastest-growing and most upwardly mobile ethnic group, extending the old boundaries of Chinatown and establishing new neighborhoods in parts of Brooklyn and Queens. Once a closed community, Chinatown now bustles with tourists exploring the streets and markets, and sampling the restaurant food.

THE HISPANIC AMERICANS

Hispanic religious carving at El Museo del Barrio *(see p229)*

PUERTO RICANS were in New York as early as 1838, but it was not until after World War II that they arrived in large numbers in search of work. Most live in El Barrio, formerly known as Spanish Harlem. Professionals who fled Fidel Castro's Cuba have moved out of the city itself but are still influential in Hispanic commerce and culture. Parts of Washington Heights have large Dominican and Columbian communities.

THE IRISH

THE IRISH, who first arrived in New York in the 1840s, had to overcome harsh odds. Starving and with barely a penny to their names, they labored hard to escape the slums of Five Points and Hell's Kitchen, helping to build the modern city in the process. Many joined the police and fire-fighting forces, rising to high rank through dedication to duty. Others set up successful businesses, such as the Irish bars that act as a focus for the now-scattered New York Irish community.

THE AFRICAN AMERICANS

PERHAPS the best-known black inner-city community in the Western world, Harlem is noted for the Harlem Renaissance of writing *(see pp28-9)* as much as it is for great entertainment, gospel music and soul food. The move of black African Americans from the South to the North began with emancipation in the 1860s and increased markedly in the 1920s, when Harlem's black population rose from 83,000 to 204,000. Today Harlem is undergoing revitalization in many areas. The African American population has also dispersed throughout the city.

THE MELTING POT

OTHER NEW YORK cultures are not distinctly defined but are still easily found. Ukrainians gather in the East Village, around St. George's Ukrainian Catholic Church on East 7th Street. Little India can be spotted by the restaurants along East 6th Street. Koreans own many of the small grocery stores in Manhattan, but most tend to live in the Flushing area of Queens. The religious diversity of New York can be seen in the Islamic Center on Riverside Drive, the

A woman celebrating at the Greek Independence Day parade

Russian Orthodox Cathedral on East 97th Street *(see p197)*; and the new Islamic Cultural Center on 96th Street – Manhattan's first major mosque.

THE OUTER BOROUGHS

BROOKLYN IS by far the most international borough. Caribbean newcomers from Jamaica and Haiti are one of

the fastest-growing immigrant groups. West Indians tend to cluster along Eastern Parkway between Grand Army Plaza and Utica Avenue, the route of the lavish, exotically-costumed West Indian Day Parade in September. Recently arrived Russian Jewish immigrants have turned Brighton Beach into "Little Odessa by the Sea," and the Scandinavians and Lebanese have settled in Bay Ridge and the Finns in Sunset Park. Borough Park and Williamsburg are home to Orthodox Jews, and Midwood has an Israeli – Middle East accent. Italians live in the Bensonhurst area. Greenpoint is little Poland, and Atlantic Avenue is home to the largest Arab community in America.

The Irish were among the earliest groups to cross the Harlem River into the Bronx. Japanese executives favor the more exclusive Riverdale area. One of the most distinctive ethnic areas is Astoria, Queens, which has the largest Greek population outside the motherland. Jackson Heights is home to a large Latin American quarter, including 300,000 Colombians. Indians also favor this area and neighboring Flushing. But it is the Asians who have transformed Flushing, so much so that the local train is known as "The Orient Express."

The New York police, a haven for Irish Americans

NEWCOMERS WHO MADE THEIR MARK See also pp46–9.

The dates mark the year these immigrants entered the US via New York.

- **1893** Irving Berlin (Russia), musician
- **1894** Al Jolson (Lithuania), singer
- **1896** Samuel Goldwyn (Poland), movie mogul
- **1902** Joe Hill (Sweden), labor activist
- **1903** Frank Capra (Italy), film director
- **1904** Hyman Rickover (Russia), developer of nuclear submarine
- **1906** "Lucky" Luciano (Italy), gangster (deported 1946)
- **1908** Bob Hope (England), comedian
- **1909** Lee Strasberg (Austria), theater director
- **1912** Claudette Colbert (France), film star
- **1913** Rudolph Valentino (Italy), film star
- **1921** Bela Lugosi (Hungary), star of *Dracula*
- **1923** Isaac Asimov (Russia), scientist and writer
- **1932** George Balanchine (Russia), ballet choreographer
- **1933** Albert Einstein (Germany), scientist
- **1938** von Trapp family (Austria), singers

1890	1895	1900	1905	1910	1915	1920	1925	1930	1935	1940

Celebrated Visitors and Residents

NEARLY ALL New Yorkers have immigrant roots if you go back far enough. Indeed, many of the city's most prominent residents have migrated here, coming to New York to find creative freedom and sometimes fleeing from constraints or repression in their native countries. As a result, some of the most brilliant contributions to New York's colorful history and culture have been made by first-generation immigrants and visitors.

George Balanchine *(1904–83)*
The ballet choreographer migrated from Russia in 1933 and formed the New York City Ballet.

Dylan Thomas
(1914–53)
The Welsh poet drank himself to a tragically early death; he frequented the White Horse Tavern in Greenwich Village.

Marcel Duchamp
(1887–1968)
In 1917 the French Dadaist climbed Washington Square arch to protest against US partici-pation in World War I.

Theater District

Chelsea and the Garment District

Gramercy and the Flatiron District

Lower Midt

Giuseppe Garibaldi *(1807–82)*
A statue in Greenwich Village honors the Italian freedom fighter who spent four years in exile on Staten Island before returning to unify Italy.

East Village

Greenwich Village

SoHo & TriBeCa

Lower East Side

Seaport and the Civic Center

Irving Berlin *(1888–1989)*
Born Israel Baline in Siberia, he grew up on the Lower East Side and composed the hit tune "White Christmas."

Lower Manhattan

Isaac Bashevis Singer
*(1904–91)
The Polish
Jewish novelist
lived on West 86th
Street for
many
years.*

N

*Morningside
Heights and Harlem*

John Audubon
*(1785–1851)
America's most
famous ornithol-
ogist grew up in
France. His New
York estate was
in Washington
Heights.*

**Marcus
Garvey**
*(1887–1940) During
the 1920s Jamaican-
born Garvey lived
in Harlem, where
he was an
influential black
leader.*

*Upper
West Side*

*Central
Park*

John Lennon
*(1940–80)
The Liverpool-
born musician
and his wife,
Yoko Ono,
made their
home on the
Upper West Side.*

*Upper East
Side*

**Harry
Houdini**
*(1874–1926)
The escape
artist from
Budapest had
a vision of his
death at age 52
and left his West 113th Street
house weeping.*

*Upper
Midtown*

Andrew Carnegie *(1835–1919)
The Scottish-born industrialist and
philanthropist's home is now the
Cooper-Hewitt Museum (see p184).*

Sarah Bernhardt *(1844–1923)
The French actress attended
services at the Little Church
Around the Corner (see p127)
during her time in New York.*

0 kilometers   2

0 miles   1

Jacob Riis *(1849–1914)
A Danish immigrant,
he slept in Bowery
doorways before writing
How the Other Half Lives,
which helped alleviate
New York's squalor.*

Remarkable New Yorkers

NEW YORK HAS NOURISHED some of the best creative talents of this century. Pop art began here, and Manhattan is still the world center for modern art. The alternative writers of the 1950s and '60s – known as the Beat Generation – took inspiration from the city's jazz clubs. And since it is the financial capital, many leading world financiers have made New York their home.

Pop artist Andy Warhol

WRITERS

Novelist James Baldwin

MUCH GREAT AMERICAN literature was created in New York. *Charlotte Temple, A Tale of Truth*, first published in 1791 by Susanna Rowson (c1762–1824), was a tale of seduction in the city and a best-seller for 50 years.

America's first professional author was Charles Brockden Brown (1771–1810), who came to New York in 1791. The novels of Edgar Allan Poe (1809–49), the pioneer of the modern detective story, expanded the thriller genre. Henry James (1843–1916) published *The Bostonians* (1886) and became the master of the psychological novel, and his friend Edith Wharton (1861–1937) became known for her satirical novels about American society.

American literature finally received international recognition with Washington Irving's (1783–1859) satire, *A History of New York* (1809). It earned him $2,000. Irving coined the names "Gotham" for New York and "Knickerbockers" for New Yorkers. He and James Fenimore Cooper (1789–1851), whose books gave birth to the "Western" novel, formed the Knicker-

bocker group of US writers. Greenwich Village has always attracted writers, including Herman Melville (1819–91) whose masterpiece, *Moby Dick* (1851), was very poorly received at first. Jack Kerouac (1922–69), Allen Ginsberg and William Burroughs all went to Columbia University and drank at the San Remo Café in Greenwich Village. Dylan Thomas (1914–53) lived at the Chelsea Hotel *(see p137)*. Novelist Nathanael West (1902–40) worked in the Gramercy Park Hotel, and Dashiell Hammett (1894–1961) wrote *The Maltese Falcon* while living there. James Baldwin (1924–87), born in Harlem, wrote *Another Country* (1963) on his return to New York from Europe.

ARTISTS

THE NEW YORK School of Abstract Expressionists founded the first influential American art movement. It was launched by Hans Hofmann (1880–1966) with Franz Kline and Willem de Kooning, whose first job in America was as a house-painter. Adolph Gottlieb, Mark Rothko (1903–70) and Jackson Pollock (1912–56) went on to popularize this style. Pollock, Kline and de Kooning all had their studios on the Lower East Side.

Pop art began in New York in the 1960s with Roy Lichtenstein and

Andy Warhol (1926–87), who made some of his cult films at 33 Union Square. Keith Haring (1958–90) was a very prolific graffiti artist whose work as a pop artist is now receiving recognition.

Robert Mapplethorpe (1946–89) acquired notoriety for his homoerotic photos of men. Jeff Koons has now superseded him as the *bête noire* of the art establishment.

The illusionistic murals by Richard Haas enliven many walls throughout the city.

ACTORS

IN 1849 the British actor Charles Macready started a riot by saying Americans were vulgar. A mob stormed the Astor Place Opera House, where Macready was playing Macbeth, police opened fire, and 22 rioters were killed. In 1927 Mae West (1893–1980) spent 10 days in a workhouse on Roosevelt Island and was fined $500 for giving a lewd performance in her Broadway show *Sex*. Marc Blitzstein's radical pro-labor opera *The Cradle Will Rock* produced by Orson Welles (1915–85) and John Houseman (1902–88), was immediately banned and the show had to move to

Vaudeville actress Mae West

another theater. The actors managed to get around the ban by buying tickets and singing their roles from the audience.

The musical has been New York's special contribution to the theater. Florenz Ziegfeld's (1869–1932) *Follies* ran from 1907 to 1931. The opening of *Oklahoma!* on Broadway in 1943 began the age of musicals by Richard Rodgers (1902–79) and Oscar Hammerstein, Jr. (1895–1960).

Off Broadway, the Provincetown Players at 33 MacDougal Street were the first to produce Eugene O'Neill's (1888–1953) *Beyond the Horizon* (1920). His successor as the major innovative force in US theater was Edward Albee, author of *Who's Afraid of Virginia Woolf?* (1962).

Josephine Baker

as Charlie Parker (1920–55) and Josephine Baker (1906–75).

Between 1940 and 1965, New York became a world dance capital with George Balanchine's (1904–83) New York City Ballet and the American Ballet Theater. In 1958, choreographer Alvin Ailey (1931–89) started the American Dance Theate, while Bob Fosse (1927–87) changed the course of musicals.

In business, New York's "robber barons" did what they liked with apparent impunity. Financiers Jay Gould (1836–92) and James Fisk (1834–72) beat Vanderbilt in the war for the Erie Railroad by manipulating stock. In September 1869 they caused Wall Street's first "Black Friday" when they tried to corner the gold market, but fled when their fraud was discovered. Gould died a happy billionaire, and Fisk was killed in a fight over a woman.

Modern entrepreneurs include Donald Trump *(see p31)*, owner of Trump Tower, and Leona and the late Harry Helmsley. Despite Leona's imprisonment for tax evasion, their property empire remains intact and includes such New York sites as the Helmsley Building *(see p156)*.

MUSICIANS AND DANCERS

LEONARD BERNSTEIN (1918–90) followed a long line of great conductors at the New York Philharmonic, including Bruno Walter (1876–1962), Arturo Toscanini (1867–1957) and Leopold Stokowski (1882–1977). Maria Callas (1923–77) was born in New York but moved to Europe.

Carnegie Hall *(see p146)* has featured Enrico Caruso (1873–1921), Bob Dylan and the Beatles. A record concert attendance was set in 1991 when Paul Simon drew a million people for his free concert in Central Park.

The legendary swinging jazz clubs of the 1930s and 1940s are now gone from 52nd Street. Plaques on "Jazz Walk" outside the CBS building honor such famous performers

INDUSTRIALISTS AND ENTREPRENEURS

Tycoon Cornelius Vanderbilt

THE RAGS-TO-RICHES story is an American dream. Andrew Carnegie (1835–1919), "the steel baron with a heart of gold," started with nothing and died having given away $350 million. His beneficiaries included public libraries and universities throughout America. Many other foundations are legacies of wealthy philanthropists. Some, like Cornelius Vanderbilt (1794–1877) tried to shake off their rough beginnings by patronizing the arts.

ARCHITECTS

CASS GILBERT (1858–1934), who built such Neo-Gothic skyscrapers as the Woolworth Building of 1913 *(see p91)* was one of the men who literally shaped the city. His caricature can be seen in the lobby, clutching a model of his masterpiece. Stanford White (1853–1906) was as well known for his scandalous private life as for his fine Beaux Arts buildings, such as the Players Club *(p126)*. For most of his life, Frank Lloyd Wright (1867–1959) spurned city architecture. When he was persuaded to leave his mark on the city, it was in the form of the Guggenheim Museum *(pp186–7)*. German-born Ludwig Mies van der Rohe (1886–1969), who built the Seagram Building, did not believe in "inventing a new architecture every Monday morning," although some might argue that this is just what New York has always done best.

Musical producer Florenz Ziegfeld

NEW YORK THROUGH THE YEAR

SPRINGTIME IN NEW YORK sees Park Avenue filled with blooms, while Fifth Avenue goes green for St. Patrick's Day, the first of the year's many big parades. Summer in the city is hot and humid, but it is worth forsaking an air-conditioned interior to step outside, where parks and squares are the setting for free open-air music and theater. The first Monday in September marks Labor Day and the advent of comfortable temperatures and the orange-red colors of autumn. Then, as Christmas nears, the shops and streets begin to sparkle with dazzling window displays.

Dates of the events on the following pages may vary. For details consult the listings magazines *(see p353)*. The New York Convention and Visitors Bureau *(see p352)* also issues a useful quarterly free calendar of events.

SPRING

EVERY SEASON in New York brings its own tempo and temptations. In spring, the city shakes off the winter with tulips and cherry blossoms in the parks and spring fashions in the stores. Everyone window shops and gallery hops. The hugely popular St. Patrick's Day Parade draws the crowds, and thousands don their finery for the Easter Parade down Fifth Avenue.

Inventive Easter bonnets in New York's Easter Parade

MARCH

St. Patrick's Day Parade *(Mar 17)*, Fifth Ave, from 44th to 86th St. Green clothes, beer and flowers, plus bagpipes.
Greek Independence Day Parade *(Mar 25)*, Fifth Ave, from 49th to 59th St. Greek dancing and food.
New York City Opera Spring Season *(Mar–Apr)*, Lincoln Center *(p338)*.
Ringling Bros and Barnum & Bailey Circus *(Mar–Apr)*, Madison Square Garden *(p133)*.

Yellow tulips and cabs shine on Park Avenue

EASTER

Easter Flower Show *(week before Easter)*, Macy's department store *(pp132–3)*.
Easter Parade *(Easter Sun)*, Fifth Ave, from 44th to 59th St. Paraders in costumes and outrageous millinery gather around St. Patrick's Cathedral.

APRIL

Cherry Blossom Festival *(late Mar–Apr)*, Brooklyn Botanic Garden. Famous for Japanese cherry trees and beautifully laid out ornamental gardens.
Annual Earth Day Festival Activities *(varies)*.
Baseball *(Apr–May)*, Major league season starts for Yankees and Mets *(p344)*.
New York City Ballet Spring Season *(Apr–Jun)*, New York State Theater and Metropolitan Opera House in Lincoln Center *(p212)*.

MAY

Martin Luther King Jr. Parade *(third Sun)*, Fifth Ave, from 57th to 79th St. A parade to honor the memory of the black civil rights leader who was assassinated in Memphis in 1968.

Parading in national costume on Greek Independence Day

Ninth Avenue Street Festival *(mid-May)*, from W 37th to W 57th St. A feast of ethnic foods, music and dance.
Washington Square Outdoor Art Exhibit *(last weekend May, first weekend Jun)*.
Memorial Day Activities *(last weekend)* A parade down Fifth Ave, festivities at South Street Seaport.

AVERAGE DAYS OF SUNSHINE PER MONTH

Jan Feb Mar Apr May Jun Jul Aug Sep Oct Nov Dec

Days of Sunshine

New York enjoys long hours of summer sun from June to August, with July the month of greatest sunshine. The winter days are much shorter, but many are clear and bright. Autumn has more sunshine than spring, although both are sunny.

SUMMER

NEW YORKERS escape the hot city streets when possible, for picnics, boat rides and the beaches. Macy's fireworks light up the Fourth of July skies, and more sparks fly when the New York Yankees and Mets baseball teams are in town. Summer also brings street fairs, outdoor concerts, and free Shakespeare and opera in Central Park.

Policeman dancing in the Puerto Rican Day Parade

JUNE

Puerto Rican Day Parade *(early Jun)*, Fifth Ave, from 44th to 86th St. Floats and marching bands.
Museum Mile Festival *(second Tue)*, Fifth Ave, from 82nd to 105th St. Free entry to museums.
Central Park Summerstage *(Jun–Aug)*, Central Park. Music and dance of every variety, almost daily, rain or shine.
Metropolitan Opera Parks Concerts. Free evening concerts in parks throughout the city *(pp338–9)*.
Goldman Memorial Band Concerts *(Jun–Aug)*, Lincoln Center *(p212)*. Traditional band concerts.

Shakespeare in the Park *(Jun–Sep)*. Star actors take on the bard at Delacorte Theater, Central Park *(p335)*.
Lesbian and Gay Pride Day Parade *(Jun)*, from Columbus Circle along Fifth Ave to Washington Sq *(p113)*.
JVC Jazz Festival *(late Jun–early Jul)*. Top jazz musicians perform in various halls in the city *(p341)*.

JULY

Macy's Firework Display *(Jul 4)*, East River. High point of the city's Independence Day celebrations, featuring the best fireworks in town.
American Crafts Festival *(mid Jun–early Jul)*, Lincoln Center *(p212)*. High-quality crafts.
Mostly Mozart Festival, *(end Jul–end Aug)*, Avery Fisher Hall, Lincoln Center *(pp338-9)*.
NY Philharmonic Parks Concerts *(late Jul–early Aug)*. Free concerts in parks

Festivities at a summer street fair in Greenwich Village

throughout the city *(p339)*.
Lincoln Center Festival *(Jul)*, Dance. opera, other performing arts from around the world.

AUGUST

Harlem Week *(mid-Aug)*. Films, art, music, dance, fashion, sports and tours.
Out-of-Doors Festival *(Aug)*, Lincoln Center. Free dance and theater performances *(p334)*.
US Open Tennis Championships *(late Aug–early Sep)*, Flushing Meadows *(p345)*.

Crowds of spectators flock to the US Open Tennis Championships

AVERAGE MONTHLY TEMPERATURE

Temperature
The chart shows the average minimum and maximum temperatures for each month in New York. With top temperatures averaging 84° F (29° C), the city can become hot and humid. In contrast, the months of winter, although rarely below freezing, can seem bitterly cold.

AUTUMN

LABOR DAY marks the end of the summer. The Giants and the Jets kick off the football season, the Broadway season begins and the Festa di San Gennaro in Little Italy is the high point in a succession of colorful neighborhood fairs. Macy's Thanksgiving Day Parade is the nation's symbol that the holiday season has arrived.

SEPTEMBER

Richmond County Fair
(Labor Day weekend), in the grounds of Historic Richmond Town *(p252)*. New York's only authentic county fair.
West Indian Carnival
(Labor Day weekend), Brooklyn. Parade, floats, music, dancing and food.
Brazilian Festival *(early Sep)*, E 46th St, between Times Sq and Madison Ave.

Exotic Caribbean carnival costume in the streets of Brooklyn

Brazilian music, food, and crafts.
New York is Book Country *(mid-Sep)*, Fifth Ave, from 48th to 59th Sts. Book fair.
Festa di San Gennaro *(third week)*, Little Italy *(p96)*. Ten days of festivities and processions.
New York Film Festival *(mid-Sep – early Oct)*, Lincoln Center *(p212)*. American films and international art films.
Von Steuben Day Parade *(third week)*, Upper Fifth Ave. German-American celebrations.
American Football *(season begins)*, Giants Stadium, home to the Giants and the Jets *(p344)*.

OCTOBER

Columbus Day Parade *(2nd Mon)*, Fifth Ave, from 44th to 86th Sts. Parades and music to celebrate Columbus's first sighting of America.
Pulaski Day Parade *(Sun closest to Oct 5)*, Fifth Ave, from 26th to 52nd Sts. Celebrations for Polish-American hero Casimir Pulaski.
Halloween Parade *(Oct 31)*, Greenwich Village. Brilliant event with fantastic costumes.
Big Apple Circus *(Oct–Jan)*, Damrosch Park, Lincoln Center. Special themes are presented each year *(p349)*.
Basketball *(season begins)*, Madison Square Garden. Local team is the Knicks *(p344)*.
New York City Marathon *(early Nov)*. From Staten Island through all the city boroughs.

Huge Superman balloon floating above Macy's Thanksgiving Day Parade

NOVEMBER

Macy's Thanksgiving Day Parade *(fourth Thu)*, from Central Park West and W 79th St to Broadway and W 34th St. A joy for children, with floats, huge balloons and Santa.
Rockefeller Center Ice Skating Rink *(Oct–Mar)*, Open to the public. You can skate beneath the famous Christmas Tree.
Christmas Spectacular *(Nov–Dec)*, Radio City Music Hall. Variety show, with the Rockettes.

Revelers in Greenwich Village's Halloween Parade

AVERAGE MONTHLY RAINFALL

Rainfall
*March and August
are the months of
heaviest rainfall in
New York. Rainfall
in spring is unpre-
dictable, so be
prepared. Sudden
heavy snowfalls in
winter can cause
chaos in the city.*

☐ Rainfall

☐ Snowfall

WINTER

NEW YORK is magical at
Christmas – even the
stone lions at the Public
Library don wreaths for the
occasion, and shops become
works of art. From Times
Square to Chinatown, New
Year celebrations punctuate
the season, and Central Park
becomes a winter sports arena.

**Statue of Alice in Wonderland
in Central Park**

DECEMBER

Tree-Lighting Ceremony
(early Dec), Rockefeller
Center *(p142).* Lighting of the
giant Christmas tree in front
of the RCA Building.
Messiah Sing-In *(mid-Dec),*
Lincoln Center *(p212).* The
audience rehearses and
performs under the guidance
of various conductors.
Hanukkah Menorah
(mid–late Dec), Grand Army
Plaza, Brooklyn. Lighting of
the huge menorah (candel-
abra) every night during the
eight-day Festival of Lights.
New Year's Eve. Fireworks
display in Central Park
(pp204–5); festivities in Times
Square *(p145);* 5-mile (8-km)
run in Central Park; poetry
reading in St. Mark's Church.

JANUARY

National Boat Show
(Jan), Jacob K. Javits
Convention Center
(p136).
Chinese New Year
(late Jan/Feb), China-
town *(pp96–7).*
Dragons, fireworks
and food.
**Winter Antiques
Show** *(Jan),* Seventh
Regiment Armory
(p185). NYC's most
prestigious antiques fair.

FEBRUARY

Black History Month.
African-American events take
place throughout the city.
**Empire State Building Run-
Up** *(early Feb).* Runners race
to the 102nd floor *(pp134–5).*
**Lincoln and Washington
Birthday Sales** *(Feb 12–22)*
Big department stores sales
throughout the city.
**Westminster Kennel Club
Dog Show** *(mid-Feb),*
Madison Square Garden
(p133). Major dog show.

Chinese New Year celebrations in Chinatown

PUBLIC HOLIDAYS

New Year's Day (Jan 1)
Martin Luther King Day
(3rd Mon, Jan)
President's Day (mid-Feb)
Memorial Day (end May)
Independence Day (Jul 4)
Labor Day (1st Mon, Sep)
Columbus Day
(2nd Mon, Oct)
Election Day
(1st Tue, Nov)
Veterans Day (Nov 11)
Thanksgiving Day
(4th Thu, Nov)
Christmas Day (Dec 25)

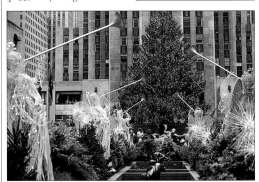

The giant Christmas tree and decorations at Rockefeller Center

The Southern Tip of Manhattan

THIS VIEW OF Lower Manhattan, seen from the Hudson River, encompasses some of the most striking modern additions to the New York skyline, including the distinctively topped quartet of the World Financial Center. You will also catch glimpses of an earlier Manhattan: Castle Clinton set against the green space of Battery Park and, behind it, the noble Custom House building. From 1973 until September 2001 the area also boasted the World Trade Center, in its day the city's tallest building. Its landmark towers were destroyed in a terrorist attack on the city.

LOCATOR MAP

◻ *The Southern Tip*

DESTRUCTION OF THE WORLD TRADE CENTER

On September 11, 2001, two planes bound for Los Angeles were hijacked and targeted at the World Trade Center. Hundreds of people died in the impact, but thousands more were killed when the twin towers collapsed. Two other planes were also hijacked that morning; the first struck the Pentagon, while the second came to ground near Pittsburgh. The death toll exceeded the number of troops killed in the Revolutionary War *(see pp20–21)*, and comparisons were made with the bombing of Pearl Harbor. Images of the destruction were seen across the world, drawing wide support for a "war against terrorism."

World Financial Center
At the heart of this complex is the Winter Garden – a place to shop, dine, be entertained or just enjoy the Hudson River views (see p69).

World Trade Center
Twin 110-story towers dominated the sky-line (see p72).

The Upper Room
This walk-around sculpture by Ned Smyth is one of many works of art in Battery Park City (see p72).

An Earlier View
This 1898 photograph shows a skyline now changed beyond recognition.

Detail from the *Upper Room*

Downtown Athletic Club

The Heisman Trophy for football is kept in this fine Art Deco building.

US Custom House

This magnificent 1907 Beaux Arts building now houses the Museum of the American Indian (see p73).

East Coast War Memorial

In Battery Park, a huge bronze eagle by Albino Manca honors the dead of World War II.

26 Broadway

The tower of the former Standard Oil Building resembles an oil lamp. The interior is still decorated with company symbols.

Bank of New York

17 State Street

26 Broadway

1 Liberty Plaza

Liberty View

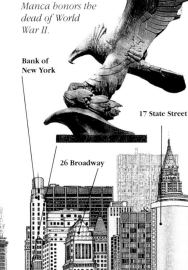

Castle Clinton   US Custom House

American Merchant Mariners' Memorial (1991)

This sculpture by Marisol is on Pier A, the last of Manhattan's old piers. The pier also has a clock tower that chimes the hours on ships' bells.

Shrine of Mother Seton

The first US-born saint lived here (see p76).

Lower Manhattan from the East River

A<small>T FIRST SIGHT</small>, this stretch of East River shoreline, running up from the tip of Manhattan Island, is a seamless array of 20th-century office buildings. But from sea level, streets and slips are still visible, offering glimpses of old New York and the Financial District to the west. On the skyline itself, a few of the district's early skyscrapers still proudly display their ornate crowns above their more anonymous modern counterparts.

LOCATOR MAP

☐ East River View

India House
The handsome brownstone at One Hanover Square is one of the finest of its kind.

Vietnam Veterans Plaza
An engraved green-glass memorial dominates the former Coenties Slip, a wharf filled in to make a park in the late 19th century (see p76).

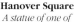

Hanover Square
A statue of one of the Dutch mayors, Abraham De Peyster, sits near the house where he was born in 1657.

One New York Plaza

55 Water Street

Barclay's Bank Building

Downtown Heliport
Air-Sea Rescue and sightseeing flights operate from here.

Battery Maritime Building
This historic ferry terminal serves only Governors Island (see p77).

Delmonico's
High society dined here a century ago.

New York Stock Exchange
Although hidden from view by more modern edifices, this is still the hub of the hectic Financial District (see pp70–71).

40 Wall Street
In the 1940s, the pyramid-topped tower of the former Bank of Manhattan was hit by a light aircraft.

70 Pine Street
Replicas of this elegant Gothic-style tower can be seen near the Pine and Cedar Street entrances.

Bank of New York
This serene 1928 interior is part of the bank set up in 1784 by Alexander Hamilton (see p21).

Morgan Bank
Columns from lobby to rooftop are the theme of this striking modern building.

1 Financial Square

New York Stock Exchange

Chase Manhattan Bank Tower

120 Wall Street

Citibank Building

100 Old Slip
Now in the shadow of One Financial Square, the small palazzo-style First Precinct Police Department was the city's most modern police station when it was built in 1911.

Carved medallion, 100 Old Slip

***Queen Elizabeth* Monument**
The ocean liner that sank in 1972 is remembered here.

South Street Seaport

As the financial district ends, the skyline, as seen from the East River or Brooklyn, changes dramatically. The corporate headquarters are replaced by the piers, low-rise streets and warehouses of the old seaport area, now restored as the South Street Seaport *(see pp82–3)*. The Civic Center lies not far inland, and a few of its monumental buildings can be seen. The Brooklyn Bridge marks the end of this stretch of skyline. Between here and midtown, apartment blocks make up the majority of riverside features.

LOCATOR MAP

☐ *South Street Area*

Stonework on
the Woolworth
Building

Woolworth Building
The handsomely decorated spire marks the headquarters of F.W. Woolworth's empire. It is still the finest "cathedral of commerce" ever built (see p91).

Pier 17
A focal point of the Seaport, this traditional-style leisure pier is packed with exciting shops, vendors and restaurants.

Fleet
Bank
Building

Seaport
Plaza

Transportation
Building

Bogardus
Building

Maritime Crafts Center
At Pier 15, craftspeople demonstrate traditional seafaring skills such as woodcarving and modelmaking.

Titanic Memorial
The lighthouse on Fulton Street commemorates the sinking of the Titanic, the largest steam ship ever built.

Police Plaza

Five in One (1971–4), in Police Plaza, is a sculpture by Bernard Rosenthal. It represents the five boroughs of New York.

United States Courthouse

The Civic Center is marked on the skyline by the golden pyramid of architect Cass Gilbert's courthouse (see p85).

Municipal Building

Among the offices of this vast building is the Marriage Chapel, where weddings "at City Hall" actually take place. The copper statue on the skyline is Civic Fame *by Adolph Weinman (see p85).*

Surrogate's Court and Hall of Records

Archives dating back to 1664 are stored and displayed here (see p85).

Verizon Telephone Company

Pace University

Southbridge Towers

Police Plaza

Con Edison Mural

In 1975, artist Richard Haas re-created the Brooklyn Bridge on the side wall of a former electrical substation.

Brooklyn Bridge

Views of, and from, the bridge have made it one of New York's best-loved landmarks (see pp86–9).

Midtown Manhattan

Tʜᴇ ꜱᴋʏʟɪɴᴇ ᴏꜰ midtown Manhattan is graced with some of the city's most spectacular towers and spires – from the familiar beauty of the Empire State Building's Art Deco pinnacle to the dramatic wedge shape of Citicorp's modern headquarters. As the shoreline progresses uptown, so the architecture becomes more varied; the United Nations complex dominates a long stretch, and then Beekman Place begins a strand of exclusive residential enclaves that offer the rich and famous some seclusion in this busy part of the city.

Chrysler Building
Glinting in the sun by day or lit up by night, this stainless-steel spire is, for many, the ultimate New York skyscraper (see p153).

Grand Central Terminal
Now dwarfed by its neighbors, this landmark building is full of period details, such as this fine clock (see pp154–5).

Empire State Building
At 1250 ft (381 m), this was the tallest building in the world for many years (see p134–5).

The Highpoint

MetLife Building

Tudor City
Built in the 1920s, this complex is mock Tudor on a grand scale, with over 3,000 apartments (see p156).

United Nations
Works of art from member countries include this Barbara Hepworth sculpture, a gift from Britain (see pp158–61).

1 and 2 UN Plaza
Angular glass towers house offices and the UN Millennium Plaza Hotel (see p156).

General Electric Building
Built of brick in 1931, this Art Deco building has a tall spiked crown that resembles radio waves. (see p174).

Citigroup Center
St. Peter's Church nestles in one corner of the Citigroup Center, with its raked tower (see p175).

Waldorf–Astoria
The splendid interior of one of the city's finest hotels lies beneath twin copper-capped towers (see p175).

Rockefeller Center
The outdoor skating rink and walkways of this complex of office buildings are a great place to people watch (see p142).

The Nail, by Arnoldo Pomodoro, St. Peter's Church, Citicorp Center

General Electric Building

100 UN Plaza

866 UN Plaza

Trump World Tower

Japan Society
Japanese culture, from avant-garde plays to ancient art, can be seen here (see p156–7).

Beekman Tower
Now an all-suite hotel, this Art Deco tower was built in 1928 as a hotel for women who were members of US college sororities.

St. Mary's Garden
The garden at Holy Family Church is a peaceful haven.

NEW YORK
AREA BY AREA

LOWER MANHATTAN

THE OLD AND THE NEW converge at Lower Manhattan, where Colonial churches and early American monuments stand in the shadow of skyscrapers. New York was born here, and this was the site of the nation's first capitol. Commerce has flourished since 1626, when Dutchman Peter Minuit purchased the island of Man-a-hatt-ta from the Algonquian Indians for goods valued at $24 *(see p17)*. At the time of revising this guide a number of landmark buildings in the area were being repaired following the destruction of the World Trade Center *(see p54)*. Visitors are advised to call all sights to check opening and transportation information.

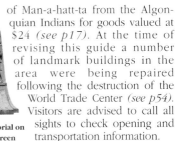

Minuit memorial on Bowling Green

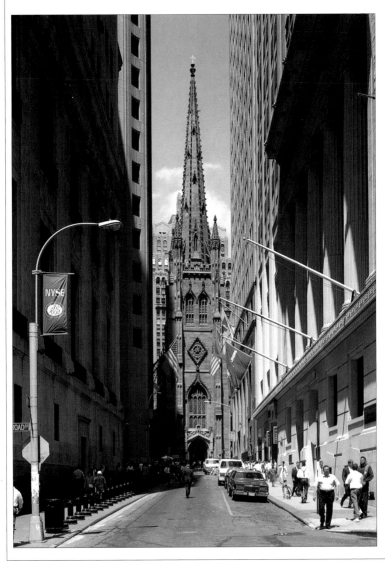

Trinity Church at the foot of Wall Street

SIGHTS AT A GLANCE

Historic Buildings and Important Sites
Federal Reserve Bank ❶
Federal Hall ❷
New York Stock Exchange pp70–71 ❸
World Trade Center Site ❻
Downtown Athletic Club ❽
Cunard Building ❾
Fraunces Tavern Museum ❸
Battery Maritime Building ⑯

Museums and Galleries
US Custom House ⑪
Ellis Island pp78–9 ⑱

Castle Clinton National Monument ⑳
Museum of Jewish Heritage ㉑

Monuments and Statues
Statue of Liberty pp74–5 ⑰

Parks and Squares
Bowling Green ⑩
Vietnam Veterans' Plaza ⑭
Battery Park ⑲

Boat Trips
Staten Island Ferry ⑮

Churches
Trinity Church ❹
Shrine of Saint Elizabeth Ann Seton ⑫

Modern Architecture
World Financial Center ❺
Battery Park City ❼

Bronze statue of a bull, symbol of Wall Street, near the Custom House

GETTING THERE
The best subway routes to the tip of Manhattan are the Lexington Ave 4 or 5 trains to Bowling Green; N or R to Whitehall St; or the 7th Ave 1 or 9 trains to South Ferry. For Wall St, take subways 2, 3, 4 or 5 to Wall St, or N or R to Rector St. The M1, M6 and M15 buses and the M22 crosstown route all serve the area.

0 meters 500

0 yards 500

KEY

Street-by-Street map

M Subway station

Ferry boarding point

Heliport

Street by Street: Wall Street

No INTERSECTION has been of greater importance to the city, past or present, than the corners of Wall and Broad streets. Three important sites are located here. Federal Hall National Monument marks the place where, in 1789, George Washington was sworn in as president. Trinity Church is one of the nation's oldest Anglican parishes. The New York Stock Exchange, founded in 1817, is to this day a financial nerve center whose ups and downs cause tremors around the globe. The surrounding buildings are the very heart of New York's famous financial district.

The Marine Midland Bank rises straight up 55 stories. This dark, glass tower occupies only 40% of its site. The other 60% is a plaza in which a large red sculpture by Isamu Noguchi, *Cube*, balances on one of its points.

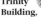

Trinity Building, an early 20th-century Gothic skyscraper, was designed to complement nearby Trinity Church.

The Equitable Building (1915) deprived its neighbors of light, prompting a change in the law: skyscrapers had to be set back from the street.

Wall Street subway (lines 4, 5)

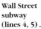

★ **Trinity Church**
Built in 1846 in a Gothic style, this is the third church on this site. Once the tallest structure in the city, the bell tower is now dwarfed by the skyscrapers that surround it. Many famous early New Yorkers are buried in the churchyard ❹

The Irving Trust Company, built in 1932, has an outer wall patterned to look like fabric. In the lobby is an Art Deco mosaic in shades of flame and gold.

26 Broadway was built as the home of the Standard Oil Trust. An oil lamp rests on top of it.

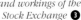

New York Stock Exchange ★
The hub of the world's financial markets is housed in a 17-story building constructed in 1903. Its visitors' center explains the history and workings of the Stock Exchange ❸

The Liberty Tower is clad in white terra-cotta and is in the Gothic style. It was later turned into apartments.

The Chamber of Commerce is a fine Beaux-Arts building of 1901.

STAR SIGHTS

★ **Federal Hall National Monument**

★ **Federal Reserve Bank**

★ **New York Stock Exchange**

★ **Trinity Church**

LOCATOR MAP
See Manhattan Map pp12–13

KEY

– – – Suggested route

| 0 meters | 100 |
| 0 yards | 100 |

Chase Manhattan Bank and Plaza has the famous Jean Dubuffet sculpture, *Four Trees*, located in the plaza.

★ **Federal Reserve Bank**
In the style of a Renaissance palace, this is a bank for banks. US currency is issued here ❶

Louise Nevelson Plaza is a park containing Nevelson's sculpture *Shadows and Flags*.

Wall Street is named for the wall that kept enemies and warring Indians out of Manhattan – the street is now the heart of the city's business center.

Wall Street in the 1920s

★ **Federal Hall National Monument**
Originally the US Custom House, this classical building now houses an exhibit about the Constitution ❷

Federal Reserve Bank ❶

33 Liberty St. **Map** 1 C2. 🏛 *(212) 720-6130*. Ⓜ *Fulton St – Broadway Nassau*. 🕐 *8:30am–5pm Mon–Fri*; ● *public hols*. 🚫 ♿ 🎥 *free 9:30, 10:30, 11:30am, 1:30, 2:30pm Mon–Fri*.

Entrance to Federal Reserve Bank

This is a government bank *for* banks – it is one of the 12 Federal Reserve banks, and therefore issues US currency. You can identify bank notes originating from this branch by the letter B in the Federal Reserve seal on each note.

Five stories below ground is the largest storehouse for international gold. Each nation's hoard is stored in its own compartment within the subterranean vault, guarded by 90-ton doors. Payments between nations used to be made by physical transfers of gold. An exhibition of "The History of Money", with 800 items, runs from 10am to 4pm.

Designed by York & Sawyer and inspired by the Italian Renaissance, the 1924 building occupies a full block and is adorned with fine wrought-iron grillwork.

Federal Hall ❷

26 Wall St. **Map** 1 C3. 🏛 *(212) 825-6888*. Ⓜ *Wall St*. 🕐 *9am–5pm Mon–Fri; Sat, Sun in Jul & Aug*. ● *public holidays*. 📷 ♿ 🎥 🛗 ⓦ www.nps.gov/feha

A bronze statue of George Washington on the steps of Federal Hall marks the site where the nation's first president took his oath of office in 1789. Thousands of New Yorkers jammed Wall and Broad Streets for the occasion. They roared their approval when the Chancellor of the State of New York shouted, "Long live George Washington, President of the United States."

The present imposing structure, built between 1834 and 1842 as the US Customs House, is one of the finest Classical designs in the city. Display rooms off the Rotunda include the Bill of Rights Room and an interactive computer exhibit about the Constitution.

New York Stock Exchange ❸

See pp70–71.

Trinity Churchyard

Trinity Church ❹

Broadway at Wall St. **Map** 1 C3. 🏛 *(212) 602-0872*. Ⓜ *Wall St, Rector St*. 🕐 *7am–6pm daily (church), 7am–4pm daily (churchyard)*. 🛗 *noon Mon–Fri, 9, 11:15am Sun*. 📷 *except during services*. 🎥 *2pm daily and Sun after 11.15 service*. **Concerts** Thu. 🖥 🛗 ⓦ www.trinitywallstreet.org

This square-towered Episcopal church at the head of Wall Street is the third one on this site in one of America's oldest Anglican parishes, founded in 1697. Designed in 1846 by Richard Upjohn, it was among the grandest churches of its day, marking the beginning of the best period of Gothic Revival architecture in America. Richard Morris Hunt's design for the sculpted brass doors was inspired by Ghiberti's *Doors of Paradise* in Florence.

Restoration has uncovered the original rosy sandstone, long buried beneath layers of city grime. The 280-ft (86-m) steeple, the tallest structure in New York until the 1860s, still commands respect despite its towering neighbors.

Many prominent early New Yorkers are buried in the graveyard: statesman Alexander Hamilton; steamboat inventor Robert Fulton; and William Bradford, founder of New York's first newspaper in 1725.

Marble-columned rotunda within Federal Hall

New York Stock Exchange

IN 1790, TRADING in stocks and shares took place haphazardly on or around Wall Street, but in 1792, 24 brokers who traded under a button-wood tree at 68 Wall Street signed an agreement to deal only with one another, and the basis of the New York Stock Exchange was formed. Membership is strictly limited. In 1817, a "seat" cost $25; today the cost is more than two million dollars, and a rigorous test of suitability is required. Visitors can watch the bustle of the trading posts from a gallery overlooking the trading floor. The NYSE has weathered slumps ("bear markets") and booms ("bull markets"), and has seen advances in technology, from tickertape to microchip, turn a local marketplace into a global one.

QUOTATIONS FURNISHED BY THE
WESTERN UNION TELEGRAPH CO
APPLY TO LOCAL MANAGER

Ticker-tape Machine
Introduced in the 1870s, these machines printed out up-to-the-minute details of purchase prices on ribbons of paper tape.

Public entrance, Broad Street

Computerized stock tickers
flash a steady stream of prices as fast as the human eye is able to read them.

WHAT A TRADING POST DOES

The 17 trading posts each consist of 22 groups or "sections" of traders and technology, each trading the stock of up to 10 listed companies. Commission brokers work for brokerage firms, and rush between booth and trading post, buying and selling securities (stocks and bonds) for the public. A specialist trades in just one stock at a time, quoting bids to other brokers, and independent floor brokers handle orders for busy brokerage firms. Clerks process the orders that come into the trading post via SuperDOT computer into the Exchange's Market Data System. The supervisor's job is to monitor the smooth and legal running of the post. The pages help on the busy exchange floor,

Trading post

bringing orders from the booths to the brokers and specialists. Post display units show stock prices, and flat screens show prices and trades for the specialist.

The 48-Hour Day
During the 1929 Crash, stock exchange clerks worked nonstop for 48 hours. Their mood stayed cheerful despite the panic outside.

VISITORS' CHECKLIST

20 Broad St. **Map** 1 C3.
[C] (212) 656-5168. [M] 2, 3, 4, 5 to Wall St, N, R to Rector St.
[bus] M1, M6, M15. **Visitors' gallery** ● currently closed for security reasons. [∅] [&]
[📷] [▯] **Video displays.**
[W] www.nyse.com

Public viewing gallery

Trading post

Members' entrance, Wall Street

Trading Floor
On the busiest days, some 2 billion shares are traded for more than 2,000 listed companies. The advanced electronics that support the Designated Order Turnaround (SuperDOT) computer are carried above the chaos of the trading floor in a web of gold piping.

Great Crash of 1929
On Tuesday, October 29, over 16 million shares changed hands as the stock market crashed. Investors thronged Wall Street in bewilderment but, contrary to popular myth, traders did not leap from windows in panic.

TIMELINE

1792 Buttonwood Agreement signed on May 17

1844 Invention of the telegraph allows trading nationwide

1867 Ticker-tape machines introduced

1903 Present Stock Exchange building opens

1976 DOT system replaces ticker-tape

1987 "Black Monday" crash, October 19. Dow Jones Index drops 508 points

1750	1800	1850	1900	1950	2000

1817 New York Stock & Exchange Board created

Crowds gather outside during the 1929 Crash

1863 Name changed to New York Stock Exchange

1865 New Exchange Building opens at Wall and Broad Streets

1869 "Black Friday" gold crash, September 24

1929 Wall St. Crash, October 29

1981 Trading posts upgraded with electronic units

2001 After 8 years of bull markets, economy falters after September 11

World Trade Center Site ❻

Map 1 B2. Ⓜ *Chambers St, Rector St.* ⭘ *Viewing wall on Church St.* ⓦ *www.wtcsitememorial.org* ⓦ *www.renewnyc.org*

IMMORTALIZED by film-makers and photographers, the twin towers of the World Trade Center dominated the skyline of Manhattan for 27 years, until September 2001's terrorist attack *(see p54)*. The enormous weight of each building was supported by an inner wire cage, which melted from the heat of the fire caused by the two passenger aircraft that were flown into the towers.

These towers were part of a buildings complex consisting of six office blocks and a hotel, connected by a vast underground concourse lined with shops and restaurants. A bridge linked the complex to the World Financial Center *(see p69)*, which survived the attack. The World Trade Center was home to some 450 companies with 50,000 employees. Large numbers of visitors used to come to see the unparalleled views from the observation deck or the rooftop promenade at Two World Trade Center. The elevator took 58 seconds to reach the 107th floor. At One World Trade Center, this speedy ascent could be taken to the Windows on the World restaurant on the 107th floor. One of the Center's most memorable days was on August 7, 1974, when Philippe Petit stepped onto a

The tightrope act in progress

tightrope between the two towers and entertained crowds of office workers for almost an hour with a high-rise balancing act.

The "Ground Zero" perimeter continues to shrink as buildings around the site are reoccupied. Plans to erect a new skyscraper, designed by architect Daniel Liebskind, are underway and the site will also be home to a memorial dedicated to the thousands who died here.

Philippe Petit about to step out between the two towers in 1974

Battery Park City ❼

Map 1 A3. Ⓜ *1, 9 to Rector St.* 📷 ♿ 🍽 🏛 ⓦ *www.batteryparkcity.org* ⓦ *www.skyscraper.org*

Battery Park City esplanade

GOVERNOR MARIO CUOMO set the tone for this project in 1983 when he urged the developers, "Give it a social purpose – give it a soul." The ambitious new neighborhood is on 92 reclaimed acres (37 ha) along the Hudson River.

The restaurants, apartments, sculptures and gardens emphasize quality and are built on a human scale.

Battery Park City is designed to house more than 25,000 people. The most visible part of it is the World Financial Center *(see p69)* and total costs are estimated at $4 billion. Among new attractions is The Skyscraper Museum, which is located on the first floor of the Ritz-Carlton hotel.

The 1.2 mile walk along the river offers unobstructed views of the Statue of Liberty.

Downtown Athletic Club ❽

19 West St. **Map** 1 B4. 📞 *(212) 425-7000.* Ⓜ *4, 5 to Bowling Green. Lobby open to visitors.* ⓦ *www.dacnyc.org*

ONE OF DOWNTOWN's most striking buildings, this 1926 Art Deco creation features a front arcade of arches with a Moorish flavor and a facade of patterned salt-glazed tiles in a range of colors from burnt orange to brown. Open only to members and their guests, the club is home of the Heisman Trophy, given every year to the most outstanding college football player and named after the club's first Athletic Director, John Heisman.

Downtown Athletic Club façade

Ornate ceiling of the Cunard Building's Great Hall

Cunard Building ❾

25 Broadway. **Map** 1 C3.
🅲 Postal Service: 800 275 8777.
Ⓜ Bowling Green. ◯ post office hours (see p361).

Go PAST the ornate facade, the brass doors, and wrought-iron gates of the US Post Office to see the elaborate, domed Great Hall of this 1921 building. The first transatlantic Cunard ship arrived in New York in 1867, and by 1915, when victims and survivors of the torpedoed *Lusitania* were brought here, the company had its own wharf.

In the 1920s Cunard merged with the White Star Line to become the largest passenger shipping line in the world and tickets were booked here for classic liners such as the *Queen Mary* and the original *Queen Elizabeth*. The hall has magnificent murals and frescoes, and an ornately decorated ceiling. Paintings by Ezra Winter on the vaulting show the ships of early explorers.

Bowling Green ❿

Map 1 C4. Ⓜ Bowling Green.

THIS TRIANGULAR plot north of Battery Park was the city's earliest park, used first as a cattle market and later as a bowling ground. A statue of King George III stood here until the signing of the Declaration of Independence, when, as a symbol of British rule, the statue was hacked to pieces and smelted for ammunition *(see pp20–21)*. The wife of the governor of Connecticut is said to have melted down enough pieces to mold 42,000 bullets.

The fence, erected in 1771, is still standing, but minus the royal crowns that once adorned it. They met the same fate as the statue. The Green was once surrounded by elegant homes. Beyond it is the start of Broadway, which runs the length of Manhattan and, under its formal name of Route 9, all the way north to the State capital in Albany.

Top of a column at the US Custom House

Fountain at Bowling Green

US Custom House ⓫

1 Bowling Green St. **Map** 1 C4.
Ⓜ Bowling Green. **National Museum of the American Indian**
🅲 (212) 514-3700. ◯ 10am–5pm daily, 10am–8pm Thu. Free. ● Dec 25.
📷 ♿ Ⓦ www.nmai.si.edu

ONE OF NEW YORK'S finest Beaux Arts designs, this 1907 granite palace by Cass Gilbert is a fitting monument to the city's role as a great seaport, decorated by the best sculptors and artists of the time. Forty-four Ionic columns stand guard, with an ornate frieze. Heroic sculptures by Daniel Chester French depict four continents as seated women: Asia (contemplative), America (facing optimistically forward), Europe (surrounded by symbols of past glories) and Africa (still sleeping).

Inside, murals by Reginald Marsh decorate the fine marble rotunda, showing the progress of ships into the harbor. Opposite the entrance is a portrait of movie star Greta Garbo giving a press conference on board ship. In 1973 the US Customs Service moved out, leaving the building empty but for a small bankruptcy court.

The Custom House took on a new function in 1994, when the George Gustav Heye Center of the **National Museum of the American Indian** was unveiled on three floors of the building. The museum's outstanding collection of about a million artifacts along with an archive of many thousands of photographs, spans the breadth of the native cultures of North, Central and South America.

Exhibitions include works by contemporary Native American artists as well as changing displays drawn from the permanent collection.

Statue of Liberty ⓱

A GIFT FROM THE FRENCH to the American people, the statue was the brainchild of sculptor Frédéric-Auguste Bartholdi and has become a symbol of freedom throughout the world. In Emma Lazarus's poem, which is engraved on the base, Lady Liberty says: "Give me your tired, your poor,/ Your huddled masses yearning to breathe free." Unveiled by President Grover Cleveland on October 28, 1886, the statue was restored in time for its 100th anniversary in 1986. Visitors were able to go right up to the crown, but this was closed after the September 11 terrorist attack. However, the base is still open.

★ Golden Torch
In 1986, a new torch replaced the corroded original. The replica's flame is coated in 24-carat gold leaf.

The crown cannot currently be visited.

The frame was designed by Gustave Eiffel, who later built the Eiffel Tower. The copper shell hangs on iron bars from a central iron pylon.

A central pylon anchors the 225-ton statue to its base.

354 steps lead from the entrance to the crown.

Observation deck and museum

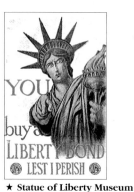

From Her Toes to Her Torch
Three hundred molded copper sheets riveted together make up Lady Liberty.

THE STATUE
With a height of 305 ft (93 m) from ground to torch, the Statue of Liberty dominates New York harbor.

The pedestal is set within the walls of an army fort. It was the largest concrete mass ever poured.

★ Statue of Liberty Museum
Posters featuring the statue are among the items on display.

The original torch now stands in the main lobby.

★ **Ferries to Liberty Island**
Ferries cross New York Harbor to Liberty Island, where the Statue offers some of the city's finest views

VISITORS' CHECKLIST

Liberty Island. **Map** 1 A5.
(212) 363-3200. **M** 1, 9, N, R to South Ferry, 4, 5 to Bowling Green. **M6, M15** to South Ferry, then Circle Line–Statue of Liberty Ferry from the Battery every 30–45 mins, 9:15am–3:30pm summer (winter hours vary). *(212) 269-5755.* Jul–Aug: 9am–6pm daily; Sep–Jun: 9:30am–5pm daily. ● Dec 25. Ferry fare includes entry to Ellis and Liberty Is. elevator to observation deck only. W www.nps.gov/stli/

Portrait of Liberty
Bartholdi's mother was the model for Liberty. The seven rays of her crown represent the seven seas and seven continents.

Making the Hand
To mold the copper shell, the hand was made first in plaster, then wood.

A Model Figure
A series of graduated scale models enabled Bartholdi to build the largest metal statue ever constructed.

FRÉDÉRIC-AUGUSTE BARTHOLDI

The French sculptor who designed the Statue of Liberty intended it as a monument to the freedom he found lacking in his own country. He said "I will try to glorify the Republic and Liberty over there, in the hope that someday I will find it again here." Bartholdi devoted 21 years of his life to making the statue a reality, even traveling to America in 1871 to talk President Ulysses S. Grant and others into funding it and installing it in New York's harbor.

STAR FEATURES

★**Golden Torch**

★**Statue of Liberty Museum**

★**Ferries to Liberty Island**

Restoration Celebration
On July 3, 1986, after a $100 million restoration, the statue was unveiled. The $2 million fireworks display was the largest ever seen in America.

St. Elizabeth Ann Seton Shrine

7 State St. **Map** 1 C4. ☎ (212) 269-6865. Ⓜ Whitehall, South Ferry. ◷ 6:30am– 5pm Mon–Fri; services. ✝ frequent. ◙ �W www.setonshrine.org

Elizabeth Ann Seton

Eₗᵢzₐᵦₑₜₕ ₐₙₙ Seton (1774–1821), the first native-born American to be canonized by the Catholic Church, lived here from 1801 to 1803. Mother Seton founded the American Sisters of Charity, the first order of nuns in the United States.

After the Civil War, the Mission of Our Lady of the Rosary turned the building into a shelter for homeless Irish immigrant women – 170,000 passed through on their way to a new life in America. The adjoining church was built in 1883. The Mission established and maintains the shrine to Mother Seton.

Fraunces Tavern Museum ⓲

54 Pearl St. **Map** 1 C4. ☎ (212) 425-1778. Ⓜ Wall St, Broad St, Bowling Green. ◷ 10am–5pm Tue, Wed, Fri, 10am–7pm Thu, 11am–5pm Sat ● public hols, day after Thanksgiving. ⓖ ⓖ groups only. **Lectures, films.** ⛔ ⚑ �W www.fraunces tavern museum.org **NYC Police Museum** 100 Old Slip, South Street. **Map** 1 D3. ☎ (212) 480 3100. ◷ 10am–5pm Tue–Sat. Donation suggested. �W www.nycpolicemuseum.org

Nₑw york's only remaining block of 18th-century commercial buildings contains an exact replica of the 1719 Fraunces Tavern where George Washington said farewell to his officers in 1783. The tavern had been an early casualty of the Revolution: the British ship *Asia* shot a cannon-ball through its roof in August 1775. The building was bought in 1904 by the Sons of the Revolution. Its restoration in 1907 was one of the first efforts to preserve the nation's heritage.

The ground floor restaurant has wood-burning fires and great charm. An upstairs museum has changing exhibits interpreting the history and cul-ture of early America.

The **Police Museum** is down by South Street. Exhibits include NYPD artifacts, interactive displays, seminars, and special events. Visit the Hall of Heroes and try your hand at the firearms training simulator.

Vietnam Veterans' Plaza ⓮

Between Water St and South St. **Map** 2 D4. Ⓜ Whitehall, South Ferry.

Tₕᵢₛ newly renovated multilevel brick plaza has an upscale shopping mall below. However, in its center is a huge wall of translucent green glass, engraved with excerpts from speeches, news stories and moving letters to families from servicemen and women who died in the war.

Staten Island Ferry – one of the city's best bargains

Staten Island Ferry ⓯

Whitehall St. **Map** 2 D5. ☎ (718) 815-BOAT. Ⓜ South Ferry. ◷ 24 hrs. **Free.** ◙ ♿ See **Practical Information** p353.

Tₕₑ first business venture of a promising Staten Island boy named Cornelius Vanderbilt, who later became the railroad magnate, the ferry has operated since 1810, carrying island commuters to

The 18th-century Fraunces Tavern Museum and restaurant

and from the city and offering visitors an unforgettable close-up of the harbor, the Statue of Liberty, Ellis Island and Lower Manhattan's incredible skyline. The fare is still the city's best bargain: it's free.

Battery Maritime Building ⓰

11 South St. **Map** 2 D4. Ⓜ *South Ferry.* ⬤ *to the public.*

F ROM 1909 TO 1938, the municipal terminal for ferries to Brooklyn operated here on the site of a small wharf known as Schreijers Hoek, from which Dutch Colonial ships once set sail for the mother country. At the height of the ferry era, 17 lines made regular runs from these bustling piers, which are used now only by the Coast Guard service for Governors Island.

The building was designed in 1907. Arriving boats face 300-ft (91-m) arched openings guarded by tall, ornately scrolled columns and adorned with latticework, molding and rosettes typical of the Beaux Arts period. This is actually a false front of sheet metal and steel, painted green to resemble copper.

Ironwork railing on the Battery Maritime Building

Statue of Liberty ⓱

See pp74–5.

Ellis Island ⓲

See pp78–9.

Castle Clinton National Monument in Battery Park

Battery Park ⓳

Map 1 B4. Ⓜ *South Ferry, Bowling Green.*

N AMED FOR the cannons that once protected the harbor, the park is wedged between the water and the crush of buildings, and is one of the best places in the city for gazing out to sea. Over the years, landfill has extended the greenery far beyond its original State Street boundary.

The park is rimmed with

Beaux Arts subway entrance at the corner of Battery Park

statues and monuments, such as the Netherlands Memorial Monument and memorials to New York's first Jewish immigrants and the Coast Guard. Others honored are Giovanni da Verrazano, the first explorer to see these shores, and also the poet Emma Lazarus.

Castle Clinton National Monument ⓴

Battery Park. **Map** 1 B4. 🕿 *(212) 344-7220.* Ⓜ *Bowling Green, South Ferry.* 🕐 *8:30am–5pm daily.* ⬤ *Dec 25.* 📷 ♿ 🎫 *Concerts.* 🔲 �𝕎 *www.nps.gov/cacl*

C ASTLE CLINTON WAS built in 1811 as an artillery defense post 300 ft (91 m)

offshore, connected to Battery Park by a causeway; but landfill gradually linked it to the mainland. None of its 28 guns was ever used in battle.

The fort was enclosed in 1824 to become a fashionable theater, where Phineas T. Barnum introduced "Swedish nightingale" Jenny Lind in 1850. In 1855 it preceded Ellis Island as the city's immigration point processing over 8 million newcomers. In 1896, it became the New York Aquarium, which moved to Coney Island in 1941 *(see p247).*

Now it is a monument and visitors' center for Manhattan's National Park Service sites, with historical panoramas of the city. The complex is the departure point for the Statue of Liberty–Ellis Island ferry *(see p353).*

Museum of Jewish Heritage ㉑

18 First Place between West Street and Battery Place. **Map** 1 B4. 🕿 *(646) 437-4200.* Ⓜ *Bowling Green, South Ferry.* 🕐 *10am–5:45pm Sun – Tue, Thu, 10am–8pm Wed, 10am–3pm Fri and eve of Jewish holidays.* ⬤ *Sat, Jewish holidays, Thanksgiving.* 🈺 ♿ 🎧 🔲 *Lectures.* ⟨w⟩ *www.mjhnyc.org*

C URRENT EXPANSION will more than triple the exhibition and meeting space at the Museum of Jewish Heritage: A Living Memorial to the Holocaust. The four-story, 70,000 sq ft (6,500sq m) east wing will contain a state-of-the-art theater for films, lectures and performances; a memorial garden; classrooms; a resource center and library; a family history center; expanded gallery space for temporary exhibitions; offices; a cafe and event hall.

Ellis Island ⑱

Half of America's population can trace its roots to Ellis Island, which served as the country's immigration depot from 1892 until 1954. Nearly 12 million people passed through its gates and dispersed across the country in the greatest wave of migration the world has ever known. Centered on the Great Hall or Registry Room, the site today houses the three-story *Ellis Island Immigration Museum* with permanent exhibits. Much of this story is told with photos and the voices of actual immigrants, and an electronic database traces ancestors. Outside, the *American Immigrant Wall of Honor* is the largest wall of names in the world. No other place explains so well the "melting pot" that formed the character of the nation.

Main building

The railroad office sold tickets onward to the final destination.

Rail Ticket
A special fare for emigrants led many on to California.

★ **Dormitory**
There were separate sleeping quarters for male and female detainees.

THE RESTORATION

In 1990 a $156 million project by the Statue of Liberty-Ellis Island Foundation, Inc., renewed several ruined buildings, replacing the copper domes and restoring the interior with original fixtures.

The ferry office sold tickets to New Jersey.

★ **Baggage Room** *The immigrants' meager possessions were checked here on arrival.*

Great Hall ★
Immigrant families were made to wait for "processing" in the Registry Room. The old metal railings were replaced with wooden benches in 1911.

The metal and glass awning is a re-creation of the original.

VISITORS' CHECKLIST

Map 1 A5. 🛈 (212) 363-3200.
Ⓜ 4, 5 to Bowling Green; 1, 9,
N, R to Whitehall/South Ferry,
then Circle Line/Statue of Liberty
Ferry from the Battery.
Departures every 30 mins
9am–3:30pm summer (winter
hours vary). 🕿 269-5755.
◯ Jul–Aug: 9am–6pm daily;
Sep–Jun: 9:30am–5pm daily.
● Dec 25. 🎫 entry inc Ellis and
Liberty Is. 🚻 ◎ ✂ 🎁 🍴 🖵
W www.nps.gov/stli W www.
statueoflibertyferry.com

Arrival *Steerage passengers crowd the deck as the ship approaches Ellis Island.*

Main entrance

Immigrant Family
An Italian mother and her children arrive in 1905.

STAR FEATURES

★ **Great Hall**

★ **Dormitory**

★ **Baggage Room**

Medical Examining Rooms
Immigrants with contagious diseases could be refused entry and sent back home.

SEAPORT AND
THE CIVIC CENTER

MANHATTAN'S BUSY Civic Center is the hub of the city, state and federal governments' court systems and the city's police department. In the 1880s it was the heart of the newspaper publishing business as well. The area is still a handsome enclave of imposing architecture with fine landmarks from every period in the city's history, from the 20th-century Woolworth Building to 19th-century City Hall and 18th-century St. Paul's

*Ship's figurehead,
South Street Seaport*

Chapel, New York's oldest building in continuous use. Nearby is South Street Seaport. Called the "street of sails" in the 19th century because of the many ships that were moored there, the seaport underwent a decline when sailing ships became unprofitable. The area has now been restored and is home to a museum and many shops and restaurants. The Brooklyn Bridge, once the largest suspension bridge in the world, lies to the north.

SIGHTS AT A GLANCE

Historic Streets and Buildings
South Street Seaport ❶
Schermerhorn Row ❷
Brooklyn Bridge pp86–9 ❸
Criminal Courts Building ❹
New York County Courthouse ❺
United States Courthouse ❻
Municipal Building ❼
Surrogate's Court, Hall of Records ❽
Old New York County Courthouse ❾
City Hall ❿
Woolworth Building ⓬
AT&T Building ⓮

Churches
St. Paul's Chapel ⓭

Parks and Squares
City Hall Park and Park Row ⓫

GETTING THERE
Many subway lines serve the area: the 7th Ave/Broadway 2 and 3 trains to Park Pl or Fulton St; the Lexington Ave 4, 5 and 6 to Brooklyn Bridge; the 8th Ave A, C and E to Chambers St and the W and R to City Hall. By bus take the M1, M6, M9, M10, M15, M101/102 or the M22 crosstown.

SEE ALSO

KEY

▦	Street-by-Street map
Ⓜ	Subway station
⛴	Riverboat boarding point

0 meters   500

0 yards   500

◁ **South Street Seaport**

Street by Street: South Street Seaport

PART COMMERCIAL, part historical, the development of South Street Seaport has turned the former heart of the 19th-century port of New York, which had long been neglected, into a lively part of the city. Shops and cafés abound; tall ships are once again moored here. The South Street Seaport museum tells the story of New York's maritime past through craft demonstrations, ship tours and river cruises. Workers from Wall Street come here to eat and drink.

★ **South Street Seaport**
Once full of sailors and sailing ships, the seaport is now a lively complex of shops, restaurants and museums ❶

Cannon's Walk is a 19th- and 20th-century block of buildings, with an outdoor café, shops and a very lively marketplace.

The Titanic Memorial
is a lighthouse built in 1913 in memory of those who died on the *Titanic*. It now stands on Fulton Street.

To Fulton St. subway (4 blocks)

Schermerhorn Row
Built as warehouses in 1813 and due to house The World Port New York exhibit, the Row contains The North Star Pub (see p308) and Brookstone ❷

The Boat-Building Shop
lets you watch as skilled craftspeople build and restore small wooden vessels.

At the Maritime Crafts Center
woodcarvers and painters can be seen at work on models, ship carvings and figureheads.

Ship in a bottle

The Pilothouse
was originally from a steam tugboat built in 1923 by New York Central. The Seaport's admission and information center is to be found here.

STAR SIGHTS

★ **Brooklyn Bridge**

★ **South Street Seaport**

The Consolidated Edison electrical substation, built in 1975, has an illusionistic mural of the Brooklyn Bridge by Richard Haas on one side to help it blend in with its historic neighbors.

LOCATOR MAP
See Manhattan Map pp12–13

SOHO & TRIBECA

LOWER EAST SIDE

SEAPORT & THE CIVIC CENTER

LOWER MANHATTAN

East River

KEY

- - - Suggested route

0 meters   100

0 yards   100

N

Meyer's Hotel, built in 1873, became a hotel in 1881. Now a bar, it retains a feel of days gone by when marks-woman Annie Oakley stayed here.

★ Brooklyn Bridge
An engineering wonder when it was built in 1883, the bridge is still remarkable. From the pedestrian walkway there are fine views of the city and the bridge itself ❸

Pier 17 offers three floors of shops, restaurants, and food stands in an impressive glass and steel pavilion. From the top floor there are great views of the Brooklyn Bridge and historic ships moored in the harbor.

The schooner *Pioneer* is used for river cruises from the Seaport. The 1908 *Ambrose* lightship, which guided ships into port, is also moored here.

The Ambrose lightship at a South Street Seaport pier on the East River

South Street Seaport ❶

Fulton St. **Map** 2 E2. ☎ (212) SEA-PORT. Ⓜ Fulton St. ◯ 10am–9pm Mon–Sat, 11am–8pm Sun. ◙ ♿ ⚞ **Concerts.** ⅋ ◙ **South Street Seaport Museum** 207 Front St. ⓕ (212) 748-8600. ◯ 10am–5pm daily. ● Jan 1, Thanksgiving, Dec 25. ◙ ◙ ♿ ⚞ **Lectures, exhibits, films.** ⅋ ◙ Ⓦ www.southstreetseaport.com Ⓦ www.southstseaport.org (museum)

Tʜᴇ ʜᴇᴀʀᴛ of New York's 19th-century seaport has been given an imaginative new lease on life. Glitzy stores and restaurants sit harmoniously beside seafaring craft, historic buildings, and museums, with spectacular views of Brooklyn Bridge and the East River from the cobblestone streets. Historic ships berthed here range from the little tugboat *W.O. Decker* to the four-masted *Peking*, the second-largest sailing ship in existence. Mini-trips on the schooner *Pioneer* are a great way to see the river.

The **Museum** covers the 11 blocks of what was once America's leading port. Not only is it home to the largest fleet of privately maintained historic vessels in the US, but there are also more than 20,000 artifacts, artworks, and documents from the 19th- and early 20th-century maritime world.

The New York City Police Museum chronicles the history of law enforcement. Exhibits include an array of weapons, the art of fingerprinting and forensics, and the arrest records of famous criminals.

Fulton Fish Market, which was a popular attraction at Seaport for more than 150 years, moved to a new home in the Bronx in 2005.

Schermerhorn Row ❷

Fulton and South Sts. **Map** 2 D3. Ⓜ Fulton St.

Tʜɪs ɪs ᴛʜᴇ architectural showpiece of the seaport. Built in 1811 by shipowner and chandler Peter Schermerhorn on land reclaimed from the river, the buildings were originally warehouses and counting-houses. The opening of the Brooklyn Ferry terminus in 1814 and of Fulton Market in 1822 made the block desirable property.

The Row has been restored as part of the South Street Seaport development, and it now houses 24 museum galleries, as well as shops, and restaurants.

Restored buildings on Schermerhorn Row

Brooklyn Bridge ❸

See pp86–9.

Criminal Courts Building ❹

100 Centre St. **Map** 4 F5. Ⓜ Canal St. **Open** 9am–5pm Mon–Fri. **Closed** public hols.

Tʜɪs 1939 ʙᴜɪʟᴅɪɴɢ is Art Moderne in style, with towers reminiscent of a Babylonian temple. The three-story-high entrance is set back in a court, behind two huge, square free-standing granite columns – an intimidating sight for the accused. The building also houses the Manhattan Detention Center for Men, which was formerly across the street in a building known as "The Tombs" because of its Egyptian-style architecture. The nickname has stuck, although the original is long gone. An aerial walkway, or "bridge of sighs," links the courts with the correctional facility across Centre Street.

The building also houses the night courts, where cases are heard from 5pm to 1am on weekdays.

Entrance to the Criminal Courts Building

New York County Courthouse ❺

60 Centre St. **Map** 2 D1. Ⓜ Brooklyn Br-City Hall. **Open** 9am–5pm Mon–Fri. **Closed** public hols.

Bᴜɪʟᴛ ᴛᴏ ʀᴇᴘʟᴀᴄᴇ the Tweed Courthouse (see p90), this new county courthouse was completed in 1926.

The fluted Corinthian portico at the top of a wide staircase is the main feature of the hexagonal building. The austere exterior is offset by a circular-columned interior rotunda featuring Tiffany lighting fixtures and a series of rich marble and ceiling murals by Attilio Pusterla on themes of law and justice. Six wings radiate from the rotunda, each housing a single court and its facilities.

The courtroom drama *Twelve Angry Men,* starring Henry Fonda, was filmed here.

New York County Courthouse

United States Courthouse ❻

40 Centre St. **Map** 2 D1. 🅜
Brooklyn Br-City Hall. ⬜ 9am–5pm Mon–Fri. ⬤ public hols.

THIS COURTHOUSE is the last work by noted architect Cass Gilbert, designer of the Woolworth Building. Begun in 1933, the year before his death, it was finished by his son. The 31-story structure is

United States Courthouse

a pyramid-topped tower set on a classical temple base. The bronzework on the doors is handsome, but the interior lacks the colorful decoration Gilbert had outlined in his sketchbooks. Aerial walkways link the building with its Police Plaza Annex.

Municipal Building ❼

1 Centre St. **Map** 1 C1. 🅜
Brooklyn Br-City Hall. ⬛ ♿

THE MUNICIPAL Building, constructed in 1914, dominates the Civic Center and straddles Chambers Street. It was McKim, Mead & White's first skyscraper and houses government offices and a marriage chapel. The exterior, in harmony with City Hall, has no excess detail to detract from the earlier building. The most notable feature is the top, a fantasy of towers capped by Adolph Wienman's statue *Civic Fame.*

A railway passage (no longer in use) through the base, and the plaza joining the building to the IRT subway station entrance were built as concessions to modern transportation needs. The building has had a far-reaching influence on architectural style; the main building at Moscow University is said to have been modeled on its design.

Surrogate's Court, Hall of Records ❽

31 Chambers St. **Map** 1 C1. 🅜 City Hall. ⬜ 9am–5pm Mon–Fri. ⬤ public hols. ⬛ ♿ 🚻

A BEAUX ARTS triumph, the original Hall of Records was begun in 1899 and completed in 1911. The elaborate columned facade is of white Maine granite, with a high mansard roof. The figures by Henry K. Bush-Brown in the roof area represent life's stages from childhood to old age; the statues by Philip Martiny over the colonnade are of notable New Yorkers

Municipal Building

such as Peter Stuyvesant. Martiny also made the representations of New York in its infancy and New York in revolutionary times at the Chambers Street entrance.

The Paris Opéra Garnier was the inspiration for the twin marble stairways and painted ceiling of the dazzling central hall. The ceiling mosaic by William de Leftwich Dodge features the signs of the zodiac and symbols of record keeping.

The Hall of Records holds public records dating back to 1664. A permanent exhibition, *Windows on the Archives,* features historical papers, drawings, letters and photographs illustrating what life was like in New York from 1626 to the present.

Surrogate's Court

Brooklyn Bridge ❸

COMPLETED IN 1883, the Brooklyn Bridge was the largest suspension bridge and the first to be constructed of steel. Engineer John A. Roebling conceived of a bridge spanning the East River while ice-bound on a ferry to Brooklyn. The bridge took 16 years to build, required 600 workers and claimed over 20 lives, including Roebling's. Most died of caisson disease (known as "the bends") after coming up from the underwater excavation chambers. When finished, the bridge linked Manhattan and Brooklyn, then two separate cities.

Souvenir medal cast for the opening of the bridge

BROOKLYN BRIDGE
From making the wire to sinking the supports, the bridge was built using new techniques.

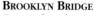

Anchorage
The ends of the bridge's four steel cables are fastened to a series of anchor bars held in place by anchor plates. These are held down by giant granite vaults up to three stories high. Their vast interiors once used for storage are now used for summer art displays.

Granite vault

Cable to tower

Anchor bar

Vault

Anchor plate

Caisson
The towers rose up above caissons, each the size of four tennis courts, which provided a dry area for underwater excavation. As work went on, they sank deeper beneath the river.

Shaft

Anchor Plates
Each of the four cast-iron anchor plates holds one cable. The masonry was built up around them after they were placed in position.

Anchor plates

Central span is 1,595 ft (486 m) long

Vault

Roadway from anchorage to anchorage is 3,579 ft (1,091 m)

First Crossing
Master mechanic E.F. Farrington in 1876 was the first to cross the river on the bridge-in-progress, using a steam-driven traveler rope. His journey took 22 minutes.

VISITORS' CHECKLIST

Map 2 D2. **M** 4, 5, 6 to Brooklyn Bridge-City Hall (Manhattan side); A, C to High St, Brooklyn Bridge (Brooklyn side). M9, M22, M101, M102.

Steel Cable Wire
Each cable contains 3,515 miles (5,657 km) of wire, galvanized with zinc for protection from the wind, rain and snow.

Brooklyn Tower (1875)
Two Gothic double arches, each 271 ft (83 m) high, one in Brooklyn, the other in Manhattan, were meant to be the portals of the cities.

JOHN A. ROEBLING
The German-born Roebling designed the bridge. In 1869, just before construction started, his foot was crushed between an incoming ferry and the ferry slip. He died three weeks later. His son, Washington Roebling, finished the bridge, but in 1872 he was taken from a caisson suffering from the bends and became partly paralyzed. His wife, under his tutelage, then took over.

Inside the Caisson
Immigrant workers broke up rocks in the riverbed.

MAKING THE CABLES

Thickness of steel wire (actual size)

End of wire

How the Cables Were Made
Each of the four main cables has 19 strands, each made of 278 steel wires. The wires were not twisted, but laid parallel.

The 19 strands of a main cable

The strands were laid in order: after the bottom 12 strands were laid, the center strands were bound together.

Iron clamp

Bolt

Cable Wrapping
Wire was wound off the drum and around the cable to form a tight final wrapping.

A massive iron clamp compressed all the strands into an even cylinder once they had been positioned.

1983 Centennial Fireworks over the Brooklyn Bridge
Celebrating the bridge's 100th year, this display was awesome.

Bustling Bridge
This 1883 view from the Manhattan side shows the original two outer lanes for horse-drawn carriages, two middle lanes for cable cars and the elevated center walkway.

Panic of May 30, 1883
After a woman tripped on the bridge, panic broke out. Of the estimated 20,000 people on the bridge, 12 were crushed to death.

Holding the Cables
Saddle plates anchor the cables at the top of each of the two towers.

Cable

Diagonal stays

Suspender wires

Nearing Completion (1883)
Vertical suspender wires lashed to diagonal stays hold the floor beams in place.

Floor Beams
The steel floor beams weigh 4 tons each.

Odlum's Jump
Robert Odlum was the first to jump off the bridge, on a bet, in May 1885. He later died from internal bleeding.

Elevated Walkway
Poet Walt Whitman said that the view from the walkway – 18 ft (5.5 m) above the road – was "the best, most effective medicine my soul has yet partaken."

Old New York County Courthouse 9

52 Chambers St. **Map** 1 C1.
M Chambers St-City Hall.

THIS BUILDING is best known for the scandal it caused. It is nicknamed the "Tweed Courthouse" after the political boss who spent 20 times the budget for the building and pocketed $9 million of the total $14 million cost. "Boss" Tweed even bought a marble quarry and sold materials to the city at huge profit. Public outrage eventually led to his downfall in 1871 – ironically, he was tried in his own courthouse and died in a New York jail *(see p25)*.

After an $85 million restoration, including the 85-ft (26-m) rotunda and the grand staircase, this vibrant 19th-century landmark became the home of the Department of Education.

City Hall's imposing early 19th-century facade

City Hall 10

City Hall Park. **Map** 1 C1. **C** *(212) 88-6865.* **M** *Brooklyn Br-City Hall.* **□** *for prearranged tours only.* **📷** **♿ 📷** *319-9300.*

CITY HALL, has been the seat of the New York city government since 1812, and is one of the finest examples of early 19th-century American architecture. A stately Federal-style building (with a bit of French Renaissance

P.T. Barnum's museum blazes as crowds watch from City Hall Park

influence), it was designed by John McComb, Jr., the first prominent American-born architect, and French emigré Joseph Mangin.

Marble cladding was not used for the building's rear, since it was not expected that the city would ever develop farther to the north. In 1954, a program of restoration remedied this and the interior was refurbished.

Mangin is usually given credit for the exterior, McComb for the beautiful interior with its fine domed rotunda encircled by 10 columns. The space beneath it opens onto an elegant marble stairway, leading to the splendid second-floor City Council chambers and the Governor's Room, which houses a portrait gallery of early New York leaders. This magnificent entrance has welcomed rulers and heroes for nearly 200 years. In 1865 Abraham Lincoln's body lay in state in this hall.

Stand on the steps and look to your right to see a statue of Nathan Hale, a US soldier hanged by the British as a spy in September 1776 during the Revolutionary War. His last words – "My only regret is that I have not more lives than one to offer in the service of my country" – won him a permanent place in the history books and hearts of America.

City Hall Park and Park Row 11

Map 1 C2. **M** *Brooklyn Br-City Hall.*

THIS WAS New York's village green 250 years ago, complete with stocks and whipping post. It was the scene of pre-Revolution protests against English rule, and there is a memorial to the "Liberty Poles" (symbols of revolt) on City Hall's west lawn. The Declaration of Independence was read to George Washington and his troops here on July 9, 1776.

Later, Phineas T. Barnum's American Museum at the park's southern tip drew crowds from 1842 until it burned down in 1865. The Park Row building was the site of the Park Theater. From 1798 to 1848, the best actors of the day, such as Edmund Kean and Fanny Kemble, performed there. Park Row runs along the east side of City Hall Park. Once called "Newspaper Row," it was lined with the lofty offices of the *Sun*, *World*, *Tribune* and other papers. Printing

Statue of Benjamin Franklin in Printing House Square

House Square has a statue of Benjamin Franklin with his *Pennsylvania Gazette*.

In 1999 City Hall Park underwent major renovations; its clean, open space is a fine place to sit and relax.

Woolworth Building ⓬

233 Broadway. **Map** 1 C2. Ⓜ *City Hall.* ☐ *office hours.*

Bas-relief caricature of architect Gilbert in the Woolworth lobby

IN 1879, SALESCLERK Frank W. Woolworth opened a new kind of store, where shoppers could see and touch the goods, and everything cost five cents. The chain of stores that followed made him a fortune and changed the face of retailing forever.

The 1913 Gothic headquarters of his empire was New York's tallest building until 1930. It set the standard for the great skyscrapers.

Architect Cass Gilbert's soaring two-tiered design, adorned with gargoyles of bats and other wildlife, is topped with a pyramid roof, flying buttresses, pinnacles and four small towers. The marble interior is rich with filigree, sculptured reliefs and painted decoration, and has a high glass-tile mosaic ceiling that almost seems to glow. The lobby is one of the city's treasures. Gilbert showed his sense of humor here, in bas-relief caricatures of the founder counting out his fortune in nickels and dimes; of the real estate broker closing a deal; and of Cass Gilbert himself cradling a large model of the building. Paid for with $13.5 million in cash, the building has never had a mortgage. Woolworth's went out of business in 1997. The building is now owned by the Witkoff Group.

St. Paul's Chapel ⓭

209-11 Broadway. **Map** 1 C2. Ⓒ (212) 233-4164. Ⓜ *Fulton St.* ☐ 9am– 3pm Mon–Fri, 7am-3pm Sun. ● *most public hols.* ✝ *8am Sun.* ☐ ☐ *by appt.* **Concerts** *1pm Mon.* Ⓦ *www.saintpaulschapel.org*

MIRACULOUSLY untouched when the World Trade Center towers collapsed,

The Georgian interior of St. Paul's Chapel

St. Paul's is Manhattan's only remaining church built before the Revolutionary War. It is a Georgian gem. The colorful interior, lit by Waterford chandeliers, is the setting for free concerts. The pew where newly inaugurated George Washington prayed has been preserved. In the churchyard, the Actor's Monument commemorates George F. Cooke, who played many great roles at the Park Theater; he drank himself to death at the Shakespeare Tavern on Fulton Street.

AT&T Building ⓮

195 Broadway. **Map** 1 C2. Ⓜ *Broadway-Nassau.* ☐ *office hours.*

COLUMNS, columns everywhere mark this former headquarters designed by Welles Bosworth from 1915 to 1922. The facade is said to have more columns than any other building in the world, and the interior of the building is a forest of marble pillars. The whole edifice looks like a gigantic squaretopped layer cake.

A sea sprite above the door of the AT&T (American Telephone and Telegraph) Building

LOWER EAST SIDE

19th-century tin, Lower East Side Tenement Museum

NOWHERE DOES the strong ethnic flavor of New York come through more clearly than in Lower Manhattan, where many immigrants first settled. Here Italians, Chinese and Jews established distinct neighborhoods, preserving their languages, customs, foods and religions in the midst of a strange land. New immigrants from many nations now occupy some of these neighborhoods of low-rise buildings, but the old flavor remains. The area brims with restaurants, some of the city's greatest bargains and a spirit found nowhere else. The composer Irving Berlin grew up here. Looking back on those days he said: "Everybody ought to have a Lower East Side in their life."

SIGHTS AT A GLANCE

Historic Streets and Buildings
Home Savings of America ❶
Police Headquarters Building ❷
Little Italy ❸
Chinatown ❹
Orchard Street ❽
Delancey Street ❿
East Houston Street ⓫
Puck Building ⓬
Engine Company No. 31 ⓮

Parks and Squares
Columbus Park ❺

Museums and Galleries
Lower East Side Tenement Museum ❼

Churches and Synagogues
Eldridge Street Synagogue ❻
Bialystoker Synagogue ❾
Old St. Patrick's Cathedral ⓭

GETTING THERE

Chinatown and Little Italy can be reached by subway on the N, R and W or the Lexington Ave 4, 5 and 6 trains to Canal St, or by taking the M101/102 bus. The Lower East Side is served by the F and V trains to Grand St, the F train to Delancey St or the M15 bus.

SEE ALSO

- **Street Finder,** maps 4, 5
- **Where to Stay** pp272–3
- **Restaurants** p288
- **Lower East Side Walk** pp258–9

KEY

▢ Street-by-Street map
Ⓜ Subway station

◁ **Dragon puppet in Chinatown at Chinese New Year**

Street by Street: Little Italy and Chinatown

N EW YORK'S LARGEST and most colorful ethnic neighborhood is Chinatown, which is growing so rapidly that it is overrunning nearby Little Italy as well as the Lower East Side. Streets here teem with grocery stores, gift shops and hundreds of Chinese restaurants; even the plainest offer good food. What is left of Little Italy can be found at Mulberry and Grand streets, where old-world flavor abounds.

★ **Little Italy**
The scents of Italy still waft from the restaurants and bakeries of this area, once home to thousands of immigrants. ❸

The Market on Canal Street has a wide range of bargains in new and used clothes and fresh produce.

M Canal Street subway (lines N, R, 4, 5, 6)

★ **Chinatown**
Home to a thriving – and still expanding – community of Chinese immigrants, this area is famous for its restaurants and hectic street life. The area truly comes alive around the Chinese New Year in January or February ❹

The Eastern States Buddhist Temple at 64b Mott Street contains over 100 golden Buddhas.

The Wall of Democracy on Bayard Street is covered with newspapers and posters describing the situation in China.

Columbus Park ❺
This park was once the site of 19th century New York's worst slum.

Confucius Plaza is marked by sculptor Liu Shih's monument to the Oriental philosopher.

Chatham Square has a memorial to Chinese-American war dead.

Police Headquarters Building
The dome of this Baroque civic building towers over the City Hall area. In 1973, the police moved out; ten years later the building was turned into apartments **2**

LOCATOR MAP
See Manhattan Map pp12–13

Umbertos Clam House
serves Italian seafood. It is also known as the place where Mafia boss Joey Gallo was shot in 1972.

KEY

— — — Suggested route

| 0 meters | 100 |
| 0 yards | 100 |

Home Savings of America
Stanford White designed this in 1894 for the old Bowery Savings Bank **1**

★ **Eldridge Street Synagogue**
Built in 1887, this was the first large temple built in the US by European Jews **6**

Bloody Angle, where Doyers Street turns sharply, was the gruesome site of many gangland ambushes during the 1920s.

STAR SIGHTS

★ **Eldridge Street Synagogue**

★ **Chinatown**

★ **Little Italy**

Home Savings of America ❶

130 Bowery. **Map** 4 F4. Ⓜ *Grand St, Bowery.* 🔲 *banking hours.*

IMPOSING INSIDE and out, this Classical Revival building was built for the Bowery Savings Bank in 1894. Architect Stanford White designed the ornamented lime-stone facade to wrap around the rival Butchers' and Drovers' Bank, which refused to sell the corner plot. The interior is decorated with marble pillars and a ceiling scattered with gilded rosettes.

Detail from Home Savings of America

By the middle of the 20th century, the bank was a contrast to the Bowery with its vagrants and flophouses.

Police Headquarters Building ❷

240 Centre St. **Map** 4 F4. Ⓜ *Canal St.* ⚫ *to the public.*

COMPLETED IN 1909, this was a fitting home for the city's new professional police force. Corinthian columns line the main portico and the end pavilions, and the dome dom-inates the skyline. However, lack of space meant the head-quarters had to conform to an awkward, wedge-shaped site in the midst of Little Italy.

For nearly three-quarters of a century, this was where "New York's finest" came to

work. During Prohibition, Grand Street from here to the Bowery was known as "Bootleggers' Row," and alcohol was easily obtained except when a police raid was due. The liquor merchants paid handsomely for a tip-off from inside police headquarters. The police moved to new headquarters in 1973, and in 1985 the building was converted into a luxury cooperative apartment project.

Little Italy ❸

Streets around Mulberry St. **Map** 4 F4. Ⓜ *Canal St.* 🌐 www.littleitalynyc.com

THE SOUTHERN Italians who came to New York in the late 19th century found themselves living in the squalor of "dumbbell" apartments. These were built so close together that sunlight never reached the lower windows or backyards. With over 40,000 people living in 17 small, unsanitary blocks, diseases such as tuberculosis were rife.

Despite the privations of life on the Lower East Side, the community that grew up around Mulberry Street was lively with the colors, flavors and atmosphere of Italy. These have lingered on, though the Italian population has dwindled to 5,000 and

Chinatown has encroached on the traditional "Little Italy."

The most exciting time to visit is during the Feast of San Gennaro around September 19 (*see p52*). For nine days Mulberry Street is renamed Via San Gennaro. On the saint's day, his shrine and relics are paraded through the streets. Throughout the feast there is music, dancing, sideshows and stalls selling Italian food and drink, as well as other ethnic cuisines.

Little Italy's restaurants offer simple, rustic food served in friendly surroundings at reasonable prices.

NoLIta, North of Little Italy, is filled with boutiques. Actresses, models and the fashionable flock here for the coolest small labels.

Italian café in Little Italy

Chinatown ❹

Streets around Mott St. **Map** 4 F5. Ⓜ *Canal St.* **Eastern States Buddhist Temple** 64b Mott St. ☎ *(212) 966-6229.* 🔲 *9am–6pm daily.*

THE CHINATOWN of the early 20th century was primarily a male community, made up of immigrants who had first gone to California. Wages were sent home to their families in China who were prevented from joining them by US immigration laws. The men relaxed by gambling at mahjong. The community remained isolated from the rest of the city, financed and controlled by its own secret organizations, the Tongs. Some of the Tongs were simply family associations who provided loans. Others, such as the On Leong and the Hip Sing, who were at war with one another, were criminal fraternities. Tiny, crooked Doyers Street was called "Bloody Angle"; enemies

Stonework figures adorning the Police Headquarters Building

A Chinese grocer tending his shop on Canal Street

were lured there and set upon by gang members waiting around the bend.

A truce between the Tongs in 1933 brought peace to Chinatown. By 1940 it was home to many middle-class families. Immigrants and businesses from Hong Kong also brought postwar prosperity to the community. Today over 80,000 Chinese-Americans live here.

Many visit the neighborhood simply to feast on Chinese cuisine, but there is more to do here than eat. There are galleries, antiques and curio shops, and Oriental festivals *(see p53)*. To glimpse another side of Chinatown, step into the incense-scented dimness of the Eastern States Buddhist Temple at 64b Mott Street, where offerings are piled up and over 100 golden Buddhas gleam in the candlelight.

Columbus Park **⑤**

Map 4 F5. **M** *Canal St.*

THE TRANQUILLITY of Columbus Park today could not be further removed from the scene near this site in the early 1800s. The area, known as Mulberry Bend, was a red-light district, part of the infamous Five Points slum. Gangs with names like the Dead Rabbits and the Plug Uglies roamed the streets. A murder a day was commonplace; even the police were afraid to pass through. Partly as a result of the writings of reformer Jacob Riis *(see p47)*, the slum was taken down in 1892. The park is now the only open space in Chinatown.

Eldridge Street Synagogue **⑥**

12 Eldridge Street. **Map** 5 A5.
C *(212) 219-0888.* **M** *East Broadway.*
◯ *11am-4pm Sun.* **✡** *Fri sundown, Sat 10am onward* 🎫 🚫 **C** *11:30am & 2:30pm Tue, Thu, and by appt.* **◻**
W *www.eldridgestreet.org*

WHEN THIS HOUSE of worship was built by the Orthodox Ashkenazi from Eastern Europe in 1887, it was the most flamboyant temple in the neighborhood. But many immigrant Jews saw the Lower East Side as just the beginning of a new life, and later moved out of this massive synagogue.

In the 1930s, the huge sanctuary, rich with stained glass, brass chandeliers, marbleized wood paneling and fine carving, was closed. Three decades later a group of citizens raised funds for preservation, and restoration is now complete. A brief audiovisual presentation recounts the history of the synagogue and its renovation.

Even after years of neglect, the facade, with touches of Romanesque, Gothic and Moorish designs, is impressive. Inside, the Italian hand-carved ark and sculpted wooden balcony show why this building was the pride of the area.

Lower East Side Tenement Museum **⑦**

90 Orchard St. **Map** 5 A4. **C** *(212) 431-0233.* **M** *Delancey, Grand St.* **◻** *for* **C** *only (book ahead), 1:20pm– 4:45pm Tue– Fri, 11:15am–4:45pm Sat–Sun.* **◯** *Jan 1, Thanksgiving, Dec 25.* 🎫 🚫 🛗 *Lectures, films, videos.* **W** *www.tenement.org*

Street vendor's pushcart (1890s) from the museum

THE INTERIOR of this building was restored to re-create apartments as they appeared in the late 1870s, in 1916, 1918, and 1935. There were no regulations on tenement living conditions until 1879. Many rooms had no windows, and indoor plumbing was rare. The rooms give a sense of the cramped and deplorable conditions in which so many lived. The museum program includes the newest exhibit "The Sweatshop Apartment" and offers excellent walking tours of the area.

Stained glass from the Synagogue

Orchard Street ❽

Map 5 A3. Ⓜ *Delancey, Grand St.*
See **Shopping** *p312.*
Ⓦ www.lowereastsideny.com

Jewish immigrants founded the New York garment industry on Orchard Street, named after the orchards that once stood here on James De Lancey's colonial estate. For many years the street was filled with pushcarts loaded with goods for sale, many of which were made at home in the teeming tenements of the neighborhood.

The pushcarts are long gone and not all the shop-keepers are Jewish, but the flavor remains and the stores still close on Saturday, the Jewish Sabbath. On Sunday there is an outdoor market, and shoppers fill the street from Houston to Canal, looking for clothing bargains.

Zodiac mural from the synagogue

Bialystoker Synagogue ❾

7–11 Willett St. **Map** 5 C4.
Ⓒ *(212) 475-0165.* Ⓜ *Essex St.*
✡ *frequent services.* ◻

This 1826 Federal-style building was originally the Willett Street Methodist Church. It was bought in 1905 by Jewish immigrants from the Bialystok province in Poland, who converted it into a synagogue. For this reason, it faces west instead of the traditional east. It has a beautiful interior, with lovely stained-glass windows, a

Canal Street Market vegetable stall

three-story carved wooden ark and murals representing the signs of the zodiac and views of the Holy Land.

Delancey Street ❿

Map 5 C4. Ⓜ *Essex St. See*
Shopping *p312.*

Once a majestic boulevard, Delancey Street today is little more than an obligatory entrance to the Williamsburg Bridge. The street was named for James De Lancey, whose farm was situated here during colonial days. De Lancey re-mained loyal to George III during the Revolution and fled to England after the war, before his land was seized.

Most of the stores on this once-grand shopping street are now run-down, but you can still buy an authentic English bowler hat (not to mention an authentic American Stetson cowboy hat, or almost any other kind of hat) at the Buranelli Hat Company at 101 Delancey.

East Houston Street ⓫

East Houston Street. **Map** 4 F3, 5A3.
Ⓜ *Second Avenue.*

The dividing line between Lower East Side and the East Village, East Houston between Forsyth and Ludlow streets clearly demonstrates the changing mix of old and new in the area. Between Forsyth and Eldridge is a new small hotel next door to the

Yonah Schimmel Knish Bakery, a fixture for more than 90 years, still with its original showcases. Further down the block is the Sunshine Theater, constructed as a Dutch Church in the 1840s and later used as a boxing arena and a Yiddish vaudeville theater. Today it shows art films.

While much of the Jewish flavor of the Lower East Side has disappeared, there are two survivors further along East Houston. Russ and Daughters is a culinary landmark, a third-generation family business that began on a pushcart, circa 1900. At this location since 1914, the store has seen its fortunes change with the neighborhood. It is famed for traditional smoked fish and herring, and has an impressive stock of caviar. At the corner of Ludlow street is perhaps the best known survivor, the bustling Katz's Delicatessen, well past its

Bagels in East Houston Street

100th birthday and still packing them in for pastrami and corned beef sandwiches and spicy hot dogs.

Puck Building **12**

295–309 Lafayette St. **Map** 4 F3.
M *Lafayette.* ○ *to the public during business hours.* **C** *(212) 274-8900.*

Puck statue on building's north-east corner

THIS BLOCK-SQUARE architectural curiosity was built in 1885 by Albert and Herman Wagner. It is an adaptation of the German *Rundbogenstil*, a mid-19th-century style characterized by horizontal bands of arched windows and the skillful use of molded red brick.

The building is part of the city's publishing history. Situated on the edge of Manhattan's old printing district, from 1887 to 1916 it housed the satirical *Puck*, a magazine similar to the British *Punch*. At the turn of the century it was the largest building in the world devoted to lithography and publishing.

Today it is used as the site of some of New York's most stylish parties and artiest fashion-photography shoots. The only connection remaining to the mythical Puck is the gold-leaf statue on the third-floor corner of Mulberry and Houston, and the smaller version over the entrance on Lafayette Street.

Walk half a block and you will see a display of *Puck* covers in Bars and Backbars at 49 East Houston.

Old St. Patrick's Cathedral **13**

263 Mulberry St. **Map** 4 F3.
C *(212) 226-8075.* **M**
Prince St. ○ *daily 8am–1pm, 3:30–9pm.*
● *Wed.* ✝ *5:30pm Sat, 9:30am,12:30pm Sun; Spanish: 10:45am Sun.*
W www.oldsaintpatricks.com

THE FIRST St. Patrick's was begun in 1809 – one of the oldest churches in the city. When fire destroyed the original in the 1860s, it was rebuilt much as it is today. When the archdiocese moved the cathedral uptown *(see pp176–7)*, it became the local parish church, and has flourished despite a constantly changing ethnic congregation.

Below the church are vaults containing the remains of, among others, one of New York's most famous families of restaurateurs, the Delmonicos. Pierre Toussaint was also buried here. In 1990 his remains were moved from the old graveyard beside the church to a more prestigious burial place in a crypt in the uptown St. Patrick's. Born as a slave in Haiti in 1766, Toussaint was brought to New York, where he became

Old St. Patrick's Cathedral

a prosperous wig-maker as a free man. He later devoted himself to the poor, tending cholera victims and using his money to build an orphanage. The Vatican is now considering him for sainthood.

Engine Company No. 31 **14**

87 Lafayette St. **Map** 4 F3.
C *(212) 966-4510.* **M** *Canal St.*
● *to the public.*

IN THE 19TH CENTURY, fire stations were considered important enough to merit a building of architectural importance and the Le Brun firm was the acknowledged master of the art. This 1895 station is one of their best. The building resembles a Loire château, with its steep roof, dormers and towers, seeming almost fairy tale-like in this location.

The present-day tenant is the Downtown Community Television Center, which offers courses and workshops to members but which is no longer open to the public.

Facade of Engine Company 31, in the style of a French château

SoHo and TriBeCa

ART AND architecture are the twin lures that have transformed these formerly industrial districts. SoHo (south of Houston) was threatened with demolition in the 1960s until preservationists drew attention to the rare cast-iron architecture. The district was saved, and artists began to move into the loft spaces.

Storefront of a SoHo bakery

Galleries, cafés, shops and designer boutiques followed. Brunch and gallery hopping in SoHo is now a favorite weekend outing. As rents rose, many artists were priced out of SoHo and moved to TriBeCa (triangle below Canal). Now, trendy TriBeCa has galleries, many new restaurants, and the Tribeca Film Festival in May.

Sights at a Glance

Historic Streets and Buildings
Haughwout Building ❶
St. Nicholas Hotel ❷
Greene Street ❸
Singer Building ❹

Harrison Street ❽
White Street ❾

Museums and Galleries
New Museum of Contemporary Art ❺

New York City Fire Museum ❼
New York Earth Room ❻

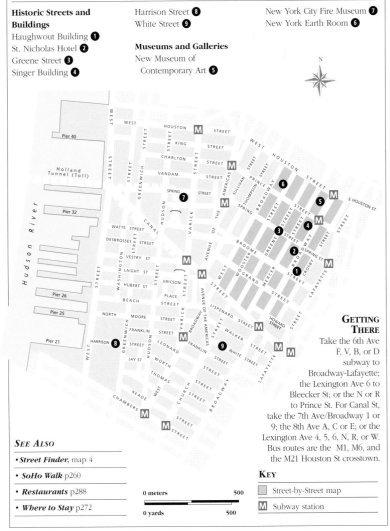

Getting There

Take the 6th Ave F, V, B, or D subway to Broadway-Lafayette; the Lexington Ave 6 to Bleecker St; or the N or R to Prince St. For Canal St, take the 7th Ave/Broadway 1 or 9; the 8th Ave A, C or E; or the Lexington Ave 4, 5, 6, N, R, or W. Bus routes are the M1, M6, and the M21 Houston St crosstown.

See Also

- **Street Finder**, map 4
- **SoHo Walk** p260
- **Restaurants** p288
- **Where to Stay** p272

0 meters 500
0 yards 500

Key

☐ Street-by-street map
Ⓜ Subway station

◁ **Cast-iron facades on Greene Street**

Street by Street: SoHo Cast-Iron Historic District

THE LARGEST concentration of cast-iron architecture in the world *(see p40)* survives in the area between West Houston and Canal streets. The heart of the district is Greene Street, where 50 buildings erected between 1869 and 1895 are found on five cobblestoned blocks. The intricately designed facades were mass-produced in a foundry but are now rare works of industrial art, well suited to the character of the district.

72–76 Greene Street, the "King of Greene Street," is a splendid Corinthian-columned building. It was the creation of Isaac F. Duckworth, one of the masters of cast-iron design.

West Broadway, as it passes through SoHo, combines striking architecture with a string of art galleries, art shops, designer boutiques, and small restaurants.

Creature from the Enchanted Forest

Enchanted Forest casts a magic spell, just as its name suggests, selling children's toys and books in a fairy-tale forest setting. *(See p314.)*

Performing Garage is a tiny experimental theater that pioneers the work of avant-garde artists.

Canal Street–Broadway subway (2 blocks)

★ Greene Street
Of all Greene Street's fine cast-iron architecture, one of the best is 28–30, the "Queen," which was built by Duckworth in 1872, and has a tall mansard roof **❸**

10–14 Greene Street dates from 1869. Note the glass circles in the risers of the iron stoop, which allowed daylight to reach the basement.

15–17 Greene Street is a late addition from 1895, in a simple Corinthian style.

★ **Singer Building**
This terra-cotta beauty was built in 1904 for the famous sewing machine company ❹

Richard Haas, the prolific muralist, has transformed a blank wall into a convincing cast-iron frontage.

LOCATOR MAP
See Manhattan Map pp12–13

KEY

– – – Suggested route

New Museum of Contemporary Art
This museum is dedicated to showing innovative work by living artists ❺

Prince Street subway station (lines N, R, W)

Dean & DeLuca is one of the best gourmet food stores in New York. Its range includes a global choice of coffee beans. *(See p326.)*

101 Spring Street, with its simple, geometric facade and large windows, is a fine example of the style that led to the skyscraper.

St. Nicholas Hotel
During the Civil War, this former luxury hotel was used as a headquarters for the Union Army ❷

| 0 meters | 100 |
| 0 yards | 100 |

STAR SIGHTS

★ **Greene Street**

★ **Singer Building**

Haughwout Building
In 1857 this was an elegant store, featuring the first Otis safety elevator ❶

Haughwout Building ❶

488–492 Broadway. **Map** 4 E4.
Ⓜ *Canal St.*

Haughwout Building facade

THIS CAST-IRON building was erected in 1857 for the E.V. Haughwout china and glassware company, which once supplied the White House. Beneath the grime, the design is superb: rows of windows are framed by arches set on columns flanked by taller columns. Mass-produced sections repeat the pattern over and over. The building was the first to use a steam-driven Otis safety elevator, an innovation that made the skyscraper a possibility.

St. Nicholas Hotel ❷

521–523 Broadway. **Map** 4 E4.
Ⓜ *Prince St.*

ENGLISH PARLIAMENTARIAN W.E. Baxter, visiting New York in 1854, reported of the recently opened St. Nicholas Hotel: "Every carpet is of velvet pile; chair covers and curtains are made of silk or satin damask … and the embroidery on the mosquito nettings itself

St. Nicholas Hotel in its heyday in the mid-19th century

might be exhibited to royalty." It is small wonder, then, that it cost over $1 million to build – and with profits of over $50,000 for that year it must have seemed money well spent. Its glory was short-lived, however. In the Civil War it served as a Union Army head-quarters. Afterward, the better hotels followed the entertainment district uptown, and by the mid-1870s the St. Nicholas had closed. There is little left on the ground floor to attest to its former opulence, but look up to the remains of its once-stunning marble facade.

Greene Street ❸

Map 4 E4. Ⓜ *Canal St.*

Haas mural on Greene Street

THIS IS THE HEART of SoHo's Cast-Iron District. Along five cobblestoned blocks are 50 cast-iron buildings dating from 1869 to 1895. The block between Broome and Spring streets has 13 full cast-iron facades and from 8–34 is the longest row of cast-iron buildings anywhere. Those at 72–76 are known as the "King of Greene Street," but 28–30, the "Queen," is considered to be the finest. The architecture is best appreciated as a streetscape, with row upon row of columned facades. Walk into any of the galleries housed within to see the spacious interior lofts.

At the corner of Greene and Prince streets, the illusionistic muralist Richard Haas has created an eye-catching work, disguising a plain brick side wall as a cast-iron frontage. Look for the detail of the little gray cat, which sits primly in an "open window."

Singer Building ❹

561–563 Broadway. **Map** 4 E3.
Ⓜ *Prince St.*

THE "LITTLE" Singer Building built by Ernest Flagg in 1904 is the second and smaller Flagg structure by this name, and many critics think it superior to the 41-story tower on lower Broadway that was torn down in 1967. The charmingly ornate building is adorned with wrought-iron balconies and graceful arches painted in striking dark green. The 12-story facade of terra-cotta, glass and steel was advanced for its day, a forerunner of the metal and glass walls to come in the 1940s and 1950s. The building was an office and warehouse for the Singer sewing machine company, and the original Singer name can be seen cast in iron above the entrance to the store on Prince Street.

Early electric-powered Singer sewing machine

New Museum of Contemporary Art ❺

583 Broadway. **Map** 4 E3. 📞 *(212) 219-1222.* Ⓜ *Prince St.* 🕐 *noon–6pm Tue–Sat, noon–8pm Thu.* 📷 🚫 ♿ 📷 *Lectures, readings.* 🏠 ⓦ www.newmuseum.org
Temporary address Chelsea Art Museum, 556 W 22nd St at 11th Ave.

Marcia Tucker left her post as the Whitney Museum's Curator of Painting and Sculpture in 1977 to found this museum. Jeff Koons and the late John Cage are among those whose work has been featured in thematic shows. Tucker exhibits the kind of work she feels is missing from more traditional museums. The Zenith Media

Les Enfants de Dijon by Christian Boltanski, at the New Museum

Lounge explores digital art, video and sound works.
The museum is temporarily located on the ground floor of the Chelsea Art Museum until its move to a new state-of-the-art facility on Bowery in 2006.

New York Earth Room ❻

141 Wooster St. **Map** 4 E3. 📞 *(212) 473-8072.* Ⓜ *B, C, D, E, F, N, Q, R, 6.* 🕐 *noon–3pm & 3:30–6pm Wed–Sat.* ♿ ⓦ www.earthroom.org

Of the three Earth Rooms created by conceptual artist Walter De Maria, this is the only one still in existence. Commissioned by the Dia Art Foundation in 1977, the in-terior earth sculpture consists of 280,000 lbs (127,000 kg) of dirt piled 22 in (56 cm) deep in a 3,600 sq ft (335 sq m) room. *The Broken Kilometer*, another sculpture by De Maria, can be seen at 393 W Broad-way. This piece is composed of 500 round, highly-polished brass rods placed in five parallel rows.

1901 La France horse-drawn steam pumper in the City Fire Museum

New York City Fire Museum ❼

278 Spring St. **Map** 4 D4. 📞 *691-1303.* Ⓜ *Spring St.* 🕐 *10am– 5pm Tue–Sat, 10am–4pm Sun.* 📷 📷 ♿ ⓦ nycfiremuseum.org

This splendid museum is housed in a Beaux Arts–style 1904 firehouse. New York city's unsurpassed collection of fire-fighting equipment and memorabilia from the 18th century to 1917 includes scale models, bells and hydrants. Upstairs, fire engines are neatly lined up for an 1890 parade. A new interactive fire simulation exhibit is great for kids.

Harrison Street ❽

Map 4 D5. Ⓜ *Chambers St.*

Surrounded by modern high-rise blocks, this rare row of eight beautifully restored Federal town houses, with their pitched roofs and distinctive dormer windows, almost seems like a stage set. The houses were constructed in the late 1700s and early 1800s. Two of the buildings were designed by John McComb, Jr., New York's first major native-born architect, and were moved from Washington Street, their original site, for preservation purposes. The houses had previously been used as warehouses and were about to be razed to the ground, when, in 1969, the Landmarks Preservation Commission intervened and helped secure the necessary funding to enable them to be completely restored. They are now privately owned.
On the other side of the high-rise complex is Washington Market Park. this area was formerly the site of New York city's wholesale produce center. The market moved from this historic district and relocated to the Bronx at the beginning of the 1970s.

White Street ❾

Map 4 E5. Ⓜ *Franklin St.*

While not as fine and intricate as some of the SoHo blocks, this sampling of TriBeCa cast-iron architecture shows a considerably wide range of styles. The house at No. 2 has carefully balanced Federal features and a rare gambrel roof, in contrast with the mansard roof of No. 17. Numbers 8 to 10 White, designed by Silesian-born Henry Fernbach, in 1869, have impressive Tuscan columns and arches, with Neo-Renaissance shorter upper stories to give an illusion of height. In contrast, 38 White is the home of neon artist Rudi Stern's gallery, Let There Be Neon.

Rudi Stern's Let There Be Neon gallery in White Street

GREENWICH VILLAGE

NEW YORKERS call it "the Village," and it began as a country village, an escape for city dwellers during the yellow fever epidemic of 1822. The crazy-quilt pattern of streets, reflecting early farm boundaries or streams, makes it a natural enclave that has been a bohemian haven and home to many celebrated artists and writers. A popular gay district is here, but the area has become mainstream and expensive. Near Washington Square, it is dominated by New York University students. The cheaper East Village attracts nonconformists, while the West Village and the Meatpacking District, which is still functioning, have become spotted with exclusive boutiques and restaurants.

Jazz club flag on West 3rd Street

SIGHTS AT A GLANCE

Historic Streets and Buildings

St. Luke's Place ❶
75½ Bedford Street ❷
Isaacs-Hendricks House ❸
Grove Court ❹
Jefferson Market Courthouse ❻
Patchin Place ❼
Salmagundi Club ❾
Washington Mews ⓬
New York University ⓭

Museums and Galleries

Forbes Magazine Building ❽

Churches

First Presbyterian Church ❿
Church of the Ascension ⓫
Judson Memorial Church ⓮

Parks and Squares

Sheridan Square ❺
Washington Square ⓯

GETTING THERE

By subway, take lines A, B, C, D, E, F or V to West 4th St-Washington Sq, the 7th Ave 1 and 9 to Christopher St-Sheridan Sq or the R or W to 8th St. By bus take the M1, M5, M6 or the M8 crosstown.

0 meters   500

0 yards   500

KEY

▨ Street-by-Street map

Ⓜ Subway station

◁ **Billboards on the corner of Christopher Street and Seventh Avenue South**

Street by Street: Greenwich Village

A STROLL THROUGH HISTORIC Greenwich Village is a feast of unexpected small pleasures – charming row houses, hidden alleys and leafy courtyards. The often quirky architecture suits the bohemian air of the Village. Many famous people, particularly artists and writers, such as playwright Eugene O'Neill and actor Dustin Hoffman, have made their homes in the houses and apartments that line these old-fashioned narrow streets. By night, the Village really comes alive. Late-night coffeehouses and cafés, experimental theaters and music clubs, including some of the best jazz venues, beckon you at every turn.

The Lucille Lortel Theater is at No. 121 Christopher Street; it opened in 1955 with *The Threepenny Opera*.

Christopher Street, a part of New York's gay community, is lined with all kinds of shops, bookstores and bars.

Twin Peaks at No. 102 Bedford Street began life in 1830 as an ordinary house. It was rebuilt in 1926 by architect Clifford Daily to house artists, writers and actors. Daily believed that the quirky house would help their creativity flourish.

Grove Court
Six houses dating from 1853 to 1854 are set at the back of a quiet leafy courtyard **4**

Chumley's at No. 86 Bedford Street (*see p309*), once a speakeasy, now a restaurant, still seems secret. There is no sign outside, just a small menu.

No. 75½ Bedford Street
Built in 1873 in an alley, this is the city's narrowest house **2**

★ St. Luke's Place
This beautiful row of Italianate houses was built in the 1850s **1**

To Houston Street subway (2 blocks)

The Cherry Lane Theater was founded in 1924. Originally a brewery, it was one of the first of the Off-Broadway theaters.

Patchin Place
Built in 1848 to house waiters from the Brevoort Hotel, it was later home to poet e e cummings and other famous writers of the 1920s and 1930s ❼

To W 14th St subway (3 blocks)

To W 14th St subway (3 blocks)

LOCATOR MAP
See Manhattan Map pp12–13

STAR SIGHTS

★ **St. Luke's Place**

★ **Jefferson Market Courthouse**

GREENWICH AVENUE

PERRY ST

10TH STREET

WAVERLEY PLACE

STREET

GTON PLACE

SIXTH AVENUE

★ **Jefferson Market Courthouse**
The courthouse was built in 1877, and has been voted the fifth most beautiful building in the US. It was converted into a public library in 1967 ❻

KEY

– – – Suggested route

0 meters	100
0 yards	100

West 4th eet subway blocks)

The Northern Dispensary has offered free medical care to the poor since 1827. Edgar Allan Poe was treated here for a cold.

Gay Street attracted many aspiring artists, writers, and musicians during the 1920s. It was the setting for Ruth McKenney's novel, *My Sister Eileen*, and the film *Carlito's Way*.

Row houses on St. Luke's Place

St. Luke's Place ❶

Map 3 C3. **M** *Houston St.*

FIFTEEN ATTRACTIVE row houses, dating from the 1850s, line the north side of this street. The park opposite is named after a previous resident of St. Luke's Place, Mayor Jimmy Walker, the popular dandy who ran the city from 1926 until he was forced to resign after a financial scandal in 1932. In front of No. 6 are the lamps that always identify a mayor's home in New York. In recent years, the most recognizable house on the block has been No. 10, shown on television as the home of the Huxtable family in *The Cosby Show* (although the series sets it in Brooklyn). This is also the block where *Wait Until Dark* was filmed, starring Audrey Hepburn as a blind woman living at No. 4. Theodore Dreiser was one of several writers, including the poet Marianne Moore, who lived here. He wrote *An American Tragedy* while living at No. 16. One block north, the corner of Hudson and Morton Streets marked the edge of the Hudson River three centuries ago.

Mayor's lamp at No. 6

75½ Bedford Street ❷

Map 3 C2. **M** *Houston St.* ● *to the public.* **W** www.cherrylanetheatre.com

NEW YORK'S narrowest home, just 9½ ft (2.9 m) wide, was built in 1893 in a former passageway. The poet Edna St. Vincent Millay lived here briefly, followed by the actor John Barrymore, and later Cary Grant. The three-story building has been recently renovated and is marked by a plaque.

Just around the corner, at 38 Commerce Street, Miss Millay founded the Cherry Lane Theater in 1924 as a site for avant-garde drama. It still premieres new works. Its biggest hit was the 1960s musical *Godspell*.

Cottage on Bedford Street

Isaacs-Hendricks House ❸

77 Bedford St. **Map** 3 C2. **M** *Houston St.* ● *to the public.*

THIS IS THE OLDEST surviving home in the Village, built in 1799. The old clapboard walls are visible on the sides

Isaacs-Hendricks House

and rear; the brickwork and third floor came later. The first owner, John Isaacs, bought the land for $295 in 1794. Next came Harmon Hendricks, a copper dealer and associate of revolutionary Paul Revere. Robert Fulton, who used copper for the boilers in his steamboat, was a customer.

Grove Court ❹

Map 3 C2. **M** *Christopher St/ Sheridan Sq.*

AN ENTERPRISING grocer named Samuel Cocks was responsible for this group of six town houses, fitting snugly into an area formed by the bend in the street. (The bends in this part of the Village originally marked divisions between colonial properties.) Cocks reckoned that having residents in the empty passage between Nos. 10 and 12 Grove Street would help his business at No. 18.

But residential courts, now prized as exclusive private addresses, were not considered respectable in 1854, and the lowbrow residents attracted to the area soon earned it the nickname "Mixed Ale Alley." O. Henry later used this block as the setting for his 1902 work *The Last Leaf.*

The mid-19th-century town houses at Grove Court

Sheridan Square **5**

Map 3 C2. M *Christopher St-Sheridan Sq.*

THIS IS THE HEART of the Village, where seven streets come together in such a maze that early guidebooks called it "the mousetrap." It was named after the Civil War General Philip Sheridan who became commander in chief of the US Army in 1883. His statue stands in nearby Christopher Park.

The Draft Riots of 1863 took place in the square, when mobs revolting against army service tried to lynch freed slaves. More than a century later, another famous disturbance rocked the

Sheridan Square scene

square. The Stonewall Inn on Christopher Street was a gay bar that had stayed in business (it was then illegal for gays to gather in bars) by paying off the police. However, on June 28, 1969, the patrons rebelled, and the pitched close combat that resulted found police officers barricaded inside the bar for hours while crowds taunted them from outside. It was a landmark moral victory for the budding Gay Rights movement. The inn that stands today is not the original. The Village remains a focus for the city's gay community. The spirited gay Halloween Parade *(see p52)* through the Village, noted for its outrageous costumes, brings thousands out.

Pointed tower of "Old Jeff"

Jefferson Market Courthouse **6**

425 6th Ave. **Map** 4 D1. 243-4334. M *W 4th St-Washington Sq.* noon–8pm Mon, Wed, 10am–6pm Tue, Thu, noon–6pm Fri, 10am–5pm Sat. Sun, public hols. w www.nypl.org

THIS TREASURED Village landmark was saved from the wrecking ball and converted into a branch of the New York Public Library through a spirited campaign that began at a Christmas party in the late 1950s.

The site became a market in 1833, named after former president Thomas Jefferson. Its fire lookout tower had a giant bell that alerted the neighborhood's volunteer fire fighters. In 1865, the founding of the municipal fire department made the bell obsolete, and the Third Judicial District, or Jefferson Market, Courthouse was built. With its Venetian Gothic–style spires and turrets, it was named one of the 10 most beautiful buildings in the country when it opened in 1877. The old fire bell was

Statue of General Sheridan in Christopher Park

installed in the tower. Here, in 1906 Harry Thaw was tried for Stanford White's murder *(see p124).*

By 1945, the market had moved, court sessions were discontinued, the four-sided clock had stopped and the building was endangered. In the 1950s, preservationists campaigned first to restore the clock and then the whole building. Architect Giorgio Cavaglieri has preserved many original details, including the stained glass and a spiral staircase that now leads to a dungeonlike reference room.

Facade and an ailanthus tree at Patchin Place

Patchin Place **7**

W 10th St. **Map** 4 D1. M *W 4th St-Washington Sq.*

ONE OF MANY delightful unexpected pockets in the Village is this tiny block of small residences, lined with ailanthus trees planted in order to "absorb the bad air." The houses were built in the mid-19th century to house Basque waiters from the Fifth Avenue Brevoort Hotel.

Later the houses became fashionable addresses, with many writers living here. The poet e e cummings lived at No. 4 from 1923 until his death in 1962. English poet laureate John Masefield also lived on the block. So did playwright Eugene O'Neill and John Reed, whose eyewitness account of the Russian Revolution, *Ten Days That Shook The World* was filmed by Warren Beatty as *Reds.*

Toy battleship from the Forbes Magazine Collection

Forbes Magazine Building **8**

60 5th Ave. **Map** 4 E1. **C** (212) 206-5548. **M** 14th St-Union Sq. **Galleries** ◌ 10am–4pm Tue, Wed, Fri, Sat (times may vary). No strollers ⬦ ▣ Thu.

Some architectural critics have called this 1925 limestone cube by Carrère & Hastings pompous. It was originally the headquarters of the Macmillan Publishing Company. When Macmillan moved uptown, the late Malcolm Forbes moved in with his financial magazine, *Forbes*. The Forbes Magazine Galleries here show Forbes's diverse tastes, with Fabergé eggs made for the last Russian czar; over 500 antique toy boats; 12,000 toy soldiers; and a signed copy of Abraham Lincoln's Gettysburg Address, among other presidential memorabilia. There are also exhibitions of paintings, from French to American Military works.

Salmagundi Club **9**

47 5th Ave. **Map** 4 E1. **C** (212) 255-7740. **M** 14th St-Union Sq. ◌ 1–5pm daily. ⬦ �W www.salmagundi.org

America's oldest artists club resides in the last remaining mansion on lower Fifth Avenue. Built in 1853 for Irad Hawley, it now houses the American Artists' Professional League, the American Watercolor Society and the

Greenwich Village Society for Historic Preservation. Washington Irving's satiric periodical, *The Salmagundi Papers,* gave the club its name.

Founded in 1871, the club moved here in 1917. Periodic art exhibits open the late 19th-century interior to the public.

Exterior of the Salmagundi Club

First Presbyterian Church **10**

5th Ave at 12th St. **Map** 4 D1. **C** (212) 675-6150 **M** 7th Ave-Union Sq. ◌ noon–12:45pm Mon, Wed, Fri, 11am–12:30pm Sun. ✝ 6pm Wed in chapel. �W www.firstpresnyc.org

Designed by Joseph C. Wells in 1846, this Gothic church was modeled on the Church of Saint Saviour in Bath, England. The church is noteworthy for its brownstone tower. The carved wooden plaques on the altar list every pastor since 1716. The south transept by McKim, Mead & White was added in 1893. The fence of iron and wood was built in 1844 and then restored in 1981.

Church of the Ascension **11**

5th Ave at 10th St. **Map** 4 E1. **C** (212) 254-8620. **M** 14th St-Union Sq. ◌ noon–2pm, 5–7pm daily. ✝ 6pm Mon–Fri, 9am, 11am Sun. ◙ (except during services). �W www.ascensionnyc.org

Church of the Ascension

This English Gothic Revival church was designed in 1840–41 by Richard Upjohn, architect of Trinity Church. The interior was redone in 1888 by Stanford White, with an altar relief by Augustus Saint-Gaudens. Above the altar hangs *The Ascension*, a mural by John La Farge, who also designed some of the stained glass. The belfry tower is lit at night to show off the colors.

In 1844 President John Tyler married Julia Gardiner here; she lived in nearby Colonnade Row (*see p118*).

Washington Mews **12**

Washington Sq N at E 8th St. **Map** 4 E2. **M** W 4th St.

Built as stables, this hidden enclave was turned into carriage houses around 1900. The south side was added in 1939. Gertrude Vanderbilt Whitney, founder of the Whitney Museum, lived and worked here.

On the corner of University Place is NYU's French House, remodeled in a French style, where movies, lectures and classes in French are held.

New York University ⑬

Washington Sq. **Map** 4 E2.
☎ (212) 998-1212, (212) 998-4636. Ⓜ W 4th St. ◯ 8:30am–8pm Mon–Fri. ⓦ www.nyu.edu

ORIGINALLY CALLED the University of the City of New York, NYU was founded in 1831 as an alternative to Episcopalian Columbia University. It is now the largest private university in the US and extends for blocks around Washington Square.

Construction of the school's first building on Waverly Place sparked the Stone-cutters' Guild Riot of 1833: contractors protested the use of inmates from a state prison to cut stone. The National Guard restored order. The original building no longer exists, but a memorial with a piece of the original tower is on a pedestal set into the pavement on Washington Square South. Samuel Morse's telegraph, John W. Draper's first-ever photographic

Bust of Sylvette by Picasso, between Bleecker and West Houston streets

portrait and Samuel Colt's six-shooter were invented here.

The Brown Building, on Washington Place near Greene Street, was the site of the Triangle Shirtwaist Company. In 1911, 146 factory workers died in a fire here, leading to new fire safety and labor laws.

A 36-ft (11-m) enlargement of Picasso's *Bust of Sylvette* is in University Village.

Judson Memorial Church ⑭

55 Washington Sq S. **Map** 4 D2.
☎ (212) 477-0351. Ⓜ W 4th St.
◯ 10am–1pm, 2pm–6pm Mon–Fri.
✝ Sun 11am. ⓦ www.judson.org

BUILT IN 1892, this McKim, Mead & White church is an impressive Romanesque building with stained glass by John La Farge. Designed by Stanford White, it is named after the first American missionary sent to foreign soil, Adoniram Judson, who served in Burma in 1811. A copy of his Burmese translation of the Bible was put in the cornerstone when the building was dedicated.

It is the unique spirit of this church, not the architecture, that makes it stand out. Judson Memorial has played an active role in local and world concerns and has been the site of activism on issues ranging from AIDS to the arms race. It is also home to avant-garde art exhibitions and off-Off Broadway plays.

Arch on the north side of Washington Square

Washington Square ⑮

Map 4 D2. Ⓜ W 4th St.

NOW ONE of the city's most vibrant open spaces, Washington Square was once marshland through which the quiet Minetta Brook flowed. By the late 1700s, the area had been turned into a public cemetery – when excavation began for the park, some 10,000 skeletal remains were exhumed. The square was used as a dueling ground for

a time, then as a site for public hangings until 1819. The "hanging elm" in the northwest corner remains. In 1826 the marsh was filled in and the brook diverted underground, where it still flows; a small sign on a fountain at the entrance to Two Fifth Avenue marks its course.

The magnificent marble arch by Stanford White, completed in 1895, replaced an earlier wooden version that had spanned lower Fifth Avenue to mark the centenary of George Washington's inauguration. A stairway is hidden in the right side of the arch. In 1916, a group of artists led by Marcel Duchamp and John Sloan broke in, climbed atop the arch, and declared the "free and independent republic of Washington Square, the state of New Bohemia."

Across the street is "the Row." Now part of NYU, this block was once home to New York's most prominent families. The Delano family, writers Edith Wharton, Henry James and John dos Passos, and artist Edward Hopper all lived here. Number 8 was once the mayor's official home.

Today students, families and free spirits mingle and enjoy the park side by side. A few drug dealers frequent the park, but it is safe by day.

Window on the corner of West 4th Street and Washington Square

EAST VILLAGE

PETER STUYVESANT had a country estate in the East Village, and in the 19th century, the Astors and Vanderbilts lived here. But around 1900, high society moved uptown and immigrants moved in. The Irish, Germans, Jews, Poles, Ukrainians and Puerto Ricans all left their mark in the area's churches, landmarks and the city's most varied

Mosaic, facade of St. George's Ukrainian Catholic Church

and least expensive ethnic restaurants. In the 1950s low rents attracted the "beat generation." Later, Hippies were followed by punks. The area's experimental music clubs and theaters still feature the latest styles. Astor Place buzzes with students. To the east are Avenues A, B, C and D, an area known as "Alphabet City," which is slowly being redeveloped.

SIGHTS AT A GLANCE

Historic Streets and Buildings
Cooper Union ❶
Colonnade Row ❸
Bayard-Condict Building ❽

Museums and Galleries
Merchant's House Museum ❹

Churches
St. Mark's-in-the-Bowery Church ❺
Grace Church ❻

Parks and Squares
Tompkins Square ❼

Famous Theaters
Public Theater ❷

SEE ALSO

• *Street Finder*, map 4, 5
• *Where to Stay* p273
• *Restaurants* p289

GETTING THERE
By subway, the Lexington Ave 6 train stop at Astor Pl is the most convenient; the area is also served by the M15 and M101/102 buses and the M8 crosstown bus.

| 0 meters | 500 |
| 0 yards | 500 |

KEY
▦ Street-by-Street map
Ⓜ Subway station

Gothic bas-relief on the facade of Grace Church

◁ **The interior of McSorley's Old Ale House**

Street by Street: East Village

A T THE SPOT WHERE Tenth and Stuyvesant
streets now intersect, Peter Stuyvesant's
country house once stood. His grandson, also
named Peter, inherited most of the property and
had it divided into streets in 1787. Among the
prize sites of the St. Mark's Historic District are the
St. Mark's-in-the-Bowery Church, the Stuyvesant-
Fish house and the 1795 home of Nicholas
Stuyvesant, both on Stuyvesant Street. Many
other homes in the
district were built
between 1871 and
1890 and still have
their original stoops,
lintels and other
architectural details.

Astor Place saw rioting in
1849. English actor William
Macready, playing *Hamlet*
at the Astor Place Opera
House, criticized American
actor Edwin Forrest.
Forrest's fans revolted and
there were 34 deaths.

Astor Place subway (line 6)

Alamo is the title of the
15-ft (4.5-m) steel cube
in Astor Place designed
by Bernard Rosenthal.
It revolves when
pushed.

Colonnade Row

*Now in shabby disrepair, these buildings were once
expensive town houses. The houses, of which only four
are left, are unified by one facade in the European style.
The marble was quarried by Sing Sing prisoners* ❸

Public Theater
*In 1965 the late Joseph
Papp convinced the city
to buy the Astor Library
(1849) as a home for the
theater. Now restored, it
sees the opening of
many famous plays* ❷

★ **Merchant's House**
*This museum contains the
house's original Federal,
American Empire and
Victorian furniture* ❹

STAR SIGHTS

★ **Cooper Union**

★ **Merchant's House
Museum**

★ **Cooper Union**
Founded by self-made man Peter Cooper in 1859, it still provides a free education to its students ❶

The Stuyvesant-Fish House
(1803–4) was constructed out of brick. It is a classic example of a Federal-style house.

St. Mark's-in-the-Bowery-Church
The church was built in 1799 and the steeple added in 1828 ❺

Renwick Triangle
is a group of 16 houses built in 1861 in the Italianate style.

LOCATOR MAP
See Manhattan Map pp12–13

Stuyvesant Polyclinic
was founded in 1857 as the German Dispensary, and it is still a health clinic. The facade is decorated with the busts of many famous physicians and scientists.

St. Mark's Place was once the main street of hippie life. It is still the hub of the East Village youth scene. Funky shops now occupy many of the basements.

Little India, the row of Indian eateries on the south side of East Sixth Street, offers a taste of India at budget prices.

Little Ukraine is home to 30,000 Ukrainians. The focus of the community is St. George's Ukrainian Catholic Church.

KEY

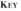 — — — Suggested route

0 meters	100
0 yards	100

McSorley's Old Ale House still brews its own ale and serves it in surroundings seemingly unchanged since it opened in 1854. *(See p309.)*

Great Hall at Cooper Union, where Abraham Lincoln spoke

Cooper Union ❶

30 Cooper Sq. **Map** 4 F2.
📞 (212) 353-4000. Ⓜ Astor Pl.
◑ by appointment only, and for
lectures and concerts in Great Hall.
⬤ Jun–Aug, public hols. ✗ ♿
🅦 www.cooper.edu

PETER COOPER, the wealthy
industrialist who built the
first US steam locomotive,
made the first steel rails and
was a partner in the first trans-
atlantic cable venture, had no
formal schooling. In 1859 He
founded New York's first free,
non-sectarian coeducational
college specializing in design,
engineering, and architecture.
Still free, the school inspires
intense competition for
places. The six-story building,
renovated in 1973–4, was the
first with a steel frame, made
of Cooper's own rails. The
Great Hall was inaugurated in
1859 by Mark Twain, and
Lincoln delivered his "Right
Makes Might" speech there
in 1860. Cooper Union still
sponsors a Public Forum.

Public Theater ❷

425 Lafayette St. **Map** 4 F2. 📞 (212)
239-6200 (tickets). Admin (212) 539-
8500 Ⓜ Astor Pl. See also **Entertainment** p332. 🅦 www.publictheater.org

THE LARGE redbrick and
brownstone building that
is the home of the New York
Shakespeare
Festival

The Public Theater on Lafayette Street

began its life in 1849 as the
Astor Library, the city's first
free library, now part of the
New York Public Library. It is
a prime American example of
German Romanesque Revival
style. When the building was
threatened with demolition in
1965, Joseph Papp, founder of
the Shakespeare
Festival,
persuaded
New York City to buy
it as a home for the
company. Renovation
began in 1967,
and much of the
handsome interior
was preserved
during conversion
into six theaters.
Although much of
the work shown is
experimental, the
Public Theater was
the original home
of hit musicals *Hair*
and *A Chorus Line*.
The latter moved
uptown to become a long-
running Broadway production.

Colonnade Row ❸

428–434 Lafayette St. **Map** 4 F2.
Ⓜ Astor Pl. ◑ to the public.

THE CORINTHIAN columns
across these four buildings
are all that remain of a once-
magnificent row of nine Greek
Revival town houses. They
were completed in 1833 by
developer Seth Geer and
were known as "Geer's Folly"
by skeptics who
thought no one
would live so far
east. They were
proved wrong
when the houses
were taken by
such eminent
citizens as John

Jacob Astor and Cornelius
Vanderbilt. Washington Irving,
author of *Rip Van Winkle* and
other classic American tales,
lived here for a time, as did
two English novelists, William
Makepeace Thackeray and
Charles Dickens. Five of the
houses were lost when the
John Wanamaker Department
Store razed them in the early
20th century to make room
for a garage. The remaining
buildings are falling to ruin.

Merchant's House Museum ❹

29 E 4th St. **Map** 4 F2. 📞 (212) 777-
1089. Ⓜ Astor Pl. ◑ 1–5pm Tue, Fri,
noon–5pm Sat–Mon and by appt. 🆗
✗ (no flashes permitted). 📷 **Lectures**
🅞 🅦 www.merchantshouse.com

**The original 19th-century iron stove in the
kitchen of the Merchant's House Museum**

THIS REMARKABLE Greek
Revival brick town house,
improbably tucked away on
an East Village block, is a
time capsule of a vanished
way of life. It still has both its
original fixtures and its
kitchen, and is filled with the
actual furniture, ornaments
and utensils of the family that
lived here for almost 100
years. Built in 1832, it was
bought in 1835 by Seabury
Tredwell, a wealthy merchant,
and stayed in the family until
Gertrude Tredwell, the last
member, died in 1933. She
had maintained her father's
home just as he would have
liked it, and a relative
opened the house as a
museum in 1936. The first-
floor parlors are very grand,
a sign of how well New
York's merchant class lived
in the 1800s.

St. Mark's-in-the-Bowery Church ❺

131 E 10th St. **Map** 4 F1. ☎ *(212) 674-6377.* Ⓜ *Astor Pl.* ⏰ *8:30am–4pm Mon–Fri.* ✝ *6:30pm Wed, 10:30am Sun.* 🚫 Ⓦ *www.saintmarkschurch.org*

O NE OF New York's oldest churches, this 1799 building replaced a 1660 church on the *bouwerie* (farm) of Governor Peter Stuyvesant. He is buried here with seven generations of descendants and many other prominent early New Yorkers. Poet W.H. Auden was a parishioner and is also commemorated here.

In 1878, a grisly kidnapping took place in the churchyard, when the remains of department store magnate A.T. Stewart were removed and held for $20,000 ransom.

The church rectory at 232 East 11th Street is a little-known work, from 1900, by Ernest Flagg. He achieved renown for his Singer Building *(see p104).*

Grace Church ❻

802 Broadway. **Map** 4 F1. ☎ *(212) 254-2000.* Ⓜ *Astor Pl, Union Sq.* ⏰ *10am–5:30pm Mon–Fri, noon–4pm Sat.* ● *public hols.* ✝ *6pm Wed, 9am, 11am, 6pm Sun.* 🚫 ♿ *Concerts.* Ⓦ *www.gracechurchnyc.org*

J AMES RENWICK, JR., the architect of St. Patrick's Cathedral, was only 23 when he designed this church, yet many consider it his finest achievement. Its delicate early Gothic lines have a grace befitting the church's name. The interior is just as beautiful, with Pre-Raphaelite stained glass and a handsome mosaic floor.

The church's peace and serenity were briefly shattered in 1863, when Phineas T. Barnum

staged the wedding of midget General Tom Thumb here; the crowds turned the event into complete chaos.

The marble spire replaced a wooden steeple in 1888 amid fears that it might prove too heavy for the church – and it has since developed a distinct lean. The church is visible from afar, because it is on a bend on Broadway. Henry Brevoort forced the city to bend Broadway to divert it around his apple orchard.

Grace Church altar and window

Tompkins Square ❼

Map 5 B1. Ⓜ *2nd Ave, 1st Ave.*

T HIS ENGLISH-STYLE park has the makings of a peaceful spot, but its past has more often been dominated by strife. It was the site of America's first organized labor demonstration in 1874, the main gathering place during the neighborhood's hippie era of the 1960s and, in 1991, an arena for violent riots when the police tried to evict homeless people who had taken over the grounds.

The square also contains a poignant monument to the neighborhood's greatest tragedy. A small statue of a boy

Tom Thumb and his bride at Grace Church

and a girl looking at a steamboat commemorates the deaths of over 1,000 local residents in the *General Slocum* steamer disaster. On June 15, 1904, the boat caught fire during a pleasure cruise on the East River. The boat was crowded with women and children from this then-German neighborhood. Many local men lost their entire families and moved away, leaving the area and its memories behind.

Bayard-Condict Building ❽

65 Bleecker St. **Map** 4 F3. Ⓜ *Bleecker St.*

T HE GRACEFUL columns, elegant filigreed terra-cotta facade and magnificent cornice on this 1898 building mark the only New York work by Louis Sullivan, the great Chicago architect who taught Frank Lloyd Wright. He died in poverty and obscurity in Chicago in 1924.

Sullivan is said to have objected vigorously to the sentimental angels supporting the Bayard-Condict Building's cornice, but he eventually gave in to the wishes of Silas Alden Condict, the owner.

Because this building is squeezed into a commercial block, it is better appreciated from a distance. Cross the street and walk a little way down Crosby Street for the best view.

The Bayard-Condict Building

GRAMERCY AND THE FLATIRON DISTRICT

FOUR SQUARES were laid out in this area by real estate developers in the 19th century to emulate the quiet, private residential areas in many European cities. Gramercy Park, still mainly residential, was one of them. The townhouses around the square were designed by some of the country's best architects, such as Calvert Vaux and Stanford White, and occupied by some of New York's most prominent citizens. Today, not far away, boutiques, trendy cafés, and high-rise apartments have taken over the stretch of lower Fifth Avenue just south of the famous Flatiron Building.

Lizard on a statue in Union Square

SIGHTS AT A GLANCE

Historic Streets and Buildings
New York Life Insurance Company **2**
Appellate Division of the Supreme Court of the State of New York **3**
Metropolitan Life Insurance Company **4**
Flatiron Building **5**
Ladies' Mile **6**
National Arts Club **8**
The Library at the Players **9**
Block Beautiful **11**
Gramercy Park Hotel **12**
Con Edison Headquarters **14**

Museums and Galleries
Theodore Roosevelt Birthplace **7**

Churches
The Little Church Around the Corner **16**

Parks and Squares
Madison Square **1**
Gramercy Park **10**
Stuyvesant Square **13**
Union Square **15**

SEE ALSO
- *Street Finder,* maps 8, 9
- *Where to Stay* pp273–4
- *Restaurants* p289

GETTING THERE
The closest subway station is at 23rd St, where the N, R, W, and Lexington Ave No. 6 train stop. Buses to the area include the M101/102 on 3rd Ave, and the M1, M2 or M3 on 5th and Madison Avenues. The crosstown bus is the M26.

0 meters 500
0 yards 500

KEY

Street-by-Street map

M Subway station

◁ **Con Edison Headquarters by night**

Street by Street: Gramercy Park

GRAMERCY PARK AND nearby Madison Square tell a tale of two cities. Madison Square is ringed by offices and traffic and is used mainly by those who work nearby, but the fine surrounding commercial architecture and statues make it well worth visiting. It was once the home of Stanford White's famous pleasure palace, the old Madison Square Garden, a place where revelers always thronged. Gramercy Park, however, retains the air of dignified tranquility it has become known for. Here, the residences and clubs remain, set around New York's last private park, for which only those who live on the square have a key.

Statue of Diana atop the old Madison Square Garden

★ Madison Square
The Knickerbocker Club played baseball here in the 1840s and was the first to codify the game's rules.
Today office workers enjoy the park's many statues of 19th-century figures, among them Admiral David Farragut **1**

23rd Street subway (lines N, R, W)

★ Flatiron Building
The triangle made by Fifth Avenue, Broadway and 23rd Street is the site of one of New York's most famous early skyscrapers. When it was built in 1903, it was the world's tallest building **5**

A sidewalk clock found in front of 200 Fifth Avenue marks the very end of the once-fashionable shopping area, known as Ladies' Mile.

Ladies' Mile
Broadway from Union Square to Madison Square was once New York's finest shopping area. **6**

Theodore Roosevelt Birthplace
The house is a replica of the one in which the 26th American president was born **7**

National Arts Club
This is a private club for the arts, on the south side of the park **8**

KEY
- - - Suggested route

0 meters   100
0 yards   100

Appellate Court
This small marble palace is said to be the world's busiest courthouse ③

LOCATOR MAP
See Manhattan Map pp12–13

New York Life Insurance Company
This spectacular building by Cass Gilbert bears his trademark pyramid-shaped top ②

STAR SIGHTS
★ **Flatiron Building**
★ **Madison Square**

Metropolitan Life Insurance Company
Vast vaulted entrances mark each corner ④

Gramercy Park
Only residents can use the park itself, but all can enjoy the peace and charm of the area around it ⑩

23rd Street subway (line 6)

The Library at the Players
Actor Edwin Booth founded this club in 1888 ⑨

The Brotherhood Synagogue was a Friends' Meeting House from 1859 to 1975, when it became a synagogue.

The Block Beautiful
This is a tree-lined stretch of East 19th Street. No particular house is outstanding, but the street as a whole is lovely ⑪

Pete's Tavern
has been here since 1903. Short story writer O. Henry, a well-known chronicler of the city, wrote "The Gift of the Magi" in the second booth.

Madison Square ❶

Map 8 F4. **Ⓜ** *23rd St.*

Farragut's statue, Madison Square

PLANNED AS the center of a fashionable residential district, this square became a popular entertainment center after the Civil War. It was bordered by the elegant Fifth Avenue Hotel, the Madison Square Theater and Stanford White's Madison Square Garden. The torch-bearing arm of the Statue of Liberty was exhibited here in 1884.

Quiet once again, it is a lunchtime spot for neighborhood office workers, and a place to stroll and admire the sculptures. The 1880 statue of Admiral David Farragut is by Augustus Saint-Gaudens, with a pedestal by Stanford White. Farragut was the hero of a Civil War sea battle; figures representing Courage and Loyalty arising from the waves are carved on the base. The statue of Roscoe Conkling commemorates a US senator who died of exposure during the great blizzard of 1888. The Eternal Light flagpole, by Carrère & Hastings, honors the soldiers who fell in France during World War I.

New York Life Insurance Company ❷

51 Madison Ave. **Map** 9 A3.
Ⓜ *28th St.* ◯ *office hours.*

THIS IMPOSING building was designed in 1928 by Cass Gilbert of Woolworth Building fame. The interior is a masterpiece, adorned with enormous hanging lamps, bronze doors and paneling, and a grand staircase leading, of all places, to the subway station.

Other famous buildings have stood on this site. Barnum's Hippodrome was here in 1874, then the first Madison Square Garden opened in 1879. A wide range of entertainments were put on, including the prizefights of heavyweight boxing hero John L. Sullivan in the 1880s. The next Madison Square Garden – Stanford White's legendary pleasure palace – opened on the same site in 1890. Lavish musical shows and social events were attended by New York's elite, who paid over $500 for a box at the prestigious annual horse show.

The building had street-level arcades and a tower modeled on the Giralda in Seville. A gold statue of the goddess Diana stood atop the tower. Her nudity was shocking, but far more scandalous was the decadent life and death of White himself. In 1906, while watching a revue in the roof garden, he was shot dead by millionaire Harry K. Thaw, the husband of White's former mistress, showgirl Evelyn Nesbit. The headline in the journal *Vanity Fair* summed up popular feeling: "Stanford White, Voluptuary and Pervert, Dies the Death of a Dog." The ensuing trial's revelations about decadent Broadway high society leave modern soap operas far behind.

New York Life Insurance Company's golden pyramid roof

Appellate Division of the Supreme Court of the State of New York ❸

E. 25th St. at Madison Ave. **Map** 9 A4.
Ⓜ *23rd St.* ◯ *9am–5pm Mon–Fri (court in session from 2pm Tue, Wed, Thu, from 10am Fri). public hols.* 🚫

APPEALS RELATING TO civil and criminal cases for New York and the Bronx are heard here, in what is widely considered to be the busiest court of its kind in the world. James Brown Lord designed the small yet noble Palladian Revival building in 1900. It is decorated with more than a

Statues of *Justice* and *Study* above the Appellate Court

dozen handsome sculptures, including Daniel Chester French's *Justice* flanked by *Power* and *Study*. During the week, the public is invited to step inside to admire the fine interior, designed by the Herter brothers, including the courtroom when it is not in session. Among the elegant details worth looking for are the fine stained-glass windows and dome, the murals and the striking cabinetwork.

Displays in the lobby often feature some of the more famous – and infamous – cases that have been heard in this court. Among the celebrity names that have been involved in appeals settled here are Babe Ruth, Charlie Chaplin, Fred Astaire, Harry Houdini, Theodore Dreiser and Edgar Allan Poe.

Clock tower of the Metropolitan Life Insurance Company

Metropolitan Life Insurance Company **4**

1 Madison Ave. **Map** 9 A4. 578-2211. **M** 23rd St. to the public, except lobby.

I N 1909, THE ADDITION of a 700-ft (210-m) tower to this 1893 building ousted the Flatiron as the tallest in the world. The huge four-sided clock has minute hands said to weigh 1000 lb (454 kg) each. The building is lit up at night, and is a familiar part of the evening skyline. It served as the company symbol "the light that never fails."

A series of historical murals by N.C. Wyeth, the famed illustrator of such classics as *Robin Hood*, *Treasure Island* and *Robinson Crusoe* (and the father of painter Andrew Wyeth), once graced the walls of the cafeteria. They are now on display in the lobby.

Flatiron Building **5**

175 5th Ave. **Map** 8 F4. **M** 23rd St. office hours.

O RIGINALLY NAMED the Fuller Building after the construction company that owned it, this building by Chicago architect David Burnham was the tallest in the world when it was completed in 1902. One of the first buildings to use a steel frame, it heralded the era of the skyscrapers.

It soon became known as the Flatiron for its unusual triangular shape, but some called it "Burnham's folly," predicting that the winds created by the building's shape would knock it down. It has withstood the test of time, but the winds along 23rd Street did have one notable effect. In the building's early days, they drew crowds of males hoping to get a peek at women's ankles as their long skirts got blown about. Police officers had to keep people moving along, and their call, "23-skidoo" became slang for "scram."

The stretch of Fifth Avenue to the south of the building was, until recently, rather run down but is fast coming to life with chic shops such as Emporio Armani and Paul Smith, giving the area new cachet and a new name, "the Flatiron District."

Flatiron Building during its construction

Ladies' Mile **6**

Broadway (Union Sq. to Madison Sq.). **Map** 4 E1 to 8 F4. **M** 14th St, 23rd St.

Arnold Constable store

I N THE 19TH CENTURY, the "carriage trade" came here in shiny traps from their town houses nearby, to shop at stores such as Arnold Constable (Nos. 881–887) and Lord & Taylor (No. 901). The ground-floor exteriors have changed beyond recognition; look up to see the remains of once-grand facades.

President Teddy Roosevelt

Theodore Roosevelt Birthplace **7**

28 E. 20th St. **Map** 9 A5. (212) 260-1616 **M** 14th St.-Union Sq. 9am–5pm Tue–Sat (last adm: 4pm). public hols. **Lectures, concerts, films, videos.** W www.nps.gov/thrb

T HE RECONSTRUCTED boyhood home of the colorful 26th president displays everything from the toys with which the young Teddy played to campaign buttons and emblems of the trademark "Rough Rider" hat that Roosevelt wore in the Spanish-American War. One exhibit features his explorations and interests; the other covers his political career.

Bas-relief faces of great writers at the National Arts Club

National Arts Club ⑧

15 Gramercy Pk S. **Map** 9 A5. ☎ (212) 475-3424. Ⓜ 14th St-Union Sq, 6 to 23rd St. ◯ noon–5pm for exhibitions. ⓦ www.nationalartsclub.org

THIS BROWNSTONE was the residence of New York governor Samuel Tilden, who condemned "Boss" Tweed (see p25) and established a free public library. He had the facade redesigned by Calvert Vaux in 1881–84. In 1906 the National Arts Club bought the home and kept the original high ceilings and stained glass by John La Farge. Members have included most leading American artists of the late 19th and early 20th century, who were asked to donate a painting or sculpture in return for life membership; these gifts form the permanent collection. The club is open to the public for exhibitions only.

The Library at the Players ⑨

18 Gramercy Pk S. **Map** 9 A5. ☎ (212) 228-7610. Ⓜ 14th St-Union Sq, 6 to 23rd St. ◯ exc for pre-booked group tours. 📷

THIS TWO-STORY brownstone was the home of actor Edwin Booth, brother of John Wilkes Booth, President Lincoln's assassin. Architect Stanford White remodeled the building as a club in 1888. Although intended primarily for actors, members have included White himself, author Mark Twain, publisher Thomas Nast and Winston Churchill, whose mother, Jennie Jerome, was born nearby. A statue of Booth playing Hamlet is across the street in Gramercy Park.

Decorative grille at The Players club

Gramercy Park ⑩

Map 9 A4. Ⓜ 23rd St, 14th St-Union Sq.

GRAMERCY PARK is one of four squares (with Union, Stuyvesant and Madison) laid out in the 1830s and 1840s to attract society residences. It is the city's only private park, and residents in the surrounding buildings have keys to the park gate as the original owners once did. Look through the railings at the southeast corner to see Greg Wyatt's fountain, with giraffes leaping around a smiling sun.

The buildings around the square were designed by some of the city's most famous architects, including Stanford White, whose house was located on the site of today's Gramercy Park Hotel. Particularly fine are 3 and 4, with graceful cast-iron gates and porches. The lanterns in front of 4 serve as symbols marking the house of a former mayor of the city, James Harper. Number 34 (1883) has been the home of the sculptor Daniel Chester French, the actor James Cagney and circus impresario John Ringling (who had a massive pipe organ installed in his apartment).

Block Beautiful ⑪

E. 19th St. **Map** 9 A5. Ⓜ 14th St-Union Sq, 6 to 23rd St.

House facade on the Block Beautiful on East 19th Street

THIS IS A SERENE, tree-lined block of 1920s residences, beautifully restored. None of them is exceptional on its own, but together they create a wonderfully harmonious whole. Number 132 had two famous theatrical tenants: Theda Bara, silent movie star and Hollywood's first sex symbol, and the fine Shakespearean actress Mrs. Patrick Campbell, who originated the role of Eliza Doolittle in George Bernard Shaw's *Pygmalion* in 1914. The hitching posts outside 141 and the ceramic relief of giraffes outside 147-149 are two of the many details to look for as you walk along the block.

Fountain with sun and giraffes by Greg Wyatt in Gramercy Park

Gramercy Park Hotel ⓬

2 Lexington Ave at 21st St. **Map** 9 B4. 📞 (212) 475-4320. Ⓜ 14th St-Union Sq. 🅦 www.gramercyparkhotel.com

Located on the site of Stanford White's house, this hotel has, for more than sixty years, been a home away from home for many international visitors and New Yorkers alike. The hotel's delightfully old-fashioned bar, with its antique sconces, candles, and wood-slat windows, is one of New York's best-kept secrets and seems made to order for romantic or clandestine trysts. Here, you might well find yourself seated next to a wealthy, very old matron or a wealthy, very young rock star. The hotel is right next to the only private park in Manhattan. If you want to go into the park and pretend you live in this rarified neighborhood, ask at the reception desk for a guest key to the park.

Stuyvesant Square ⓭

Map 9 B5. Ⓜ 14th St-Union Sq.

This oasis, in the form of a pair of parks divided by Second Avenue, was part of Peter Stuyvesant's original farm in the 1600s. It was still in the Stuyvesant family when the park was designed in 1836; Peter G. Stuyvesant sold the land to the city for the nominal sum of $5 (much to the delight of those living nearby, who saw real estate values jump). A statue of Stuyvesant by Gertrude Vanderbilt Whitney stands in the park. The park separated the Stuyvesant area from the poorer Gas House district.

Con Edison Headquarters ⓮

145 E 14th St. **Map** 9 A5. Ⓜ 3rd Ave, 14th St-Union Sq. ⬤ to the public.

The clock tower of this building, which dates from 1911, is a local

The towers of Con Edison (right), Metropolitan Life and the Empire State

land-mark. Originally conceived by Henry Hardenbergh, the architect best known for such buildings as the Dakota (see p216) and the Plaza (see p179). The 26-story tower was built by the same firm who designed Grand Central Terminal. Near the top of the tower, a 38-ft (11.6-m) bronze lantern was built as a memorial to Con Ed's employees who died in World War I. The tower itself is not as tall as nearby Empire State Building, but when it is lit up at night, it makes an attractive showpiece, in addition to a potent symbol of the company that keeps Manhattan and the other four boroughs shining.

Union Square ⓯

Map 9 A5. Ⓜ 14th St-Union Sq. **Farmers' Market 8am–6pm** Mon, Wed, Fri, Sat.

Greenmarket day at Union Square

Opened in 1839, this park joined Bloomingdale Road (now Broadway) with the Bowery Road (Fourth Avenue or Park), and hence its name. Later, the center of

the square was lifted up for a subway to run beneath it. The park became popular with soapbox orators. During the Depression in 1930, more than 35,000 unemployed people rallied here, before marching on to City Hall to demand jobs. The square hosts a popular greenmarket where farmers from all over New York State sell their fresh and organic produce.

The Little Church Around the Corner ⓰

1 E 29th St. **Map** 8 F3. 📞 (212) 684-6770. Ⓜ 28th St. 🕘 9am–5pm daily. ✝ 5:30pm Mon–Sat, 8:30am, 11am Sun. 📷 ♿ ✉ Sun after 11am service. **Lectures, concerts, recitals.** 🔗 www.littlechurch.org

Built from 1849 to 1856, the Episcopal Church of the Transfiguration is a tranquil retreat. It has been known by its nickname since 1870 when Joseph Jefferson tried to arrange the funeral of fellow actor George Holland. The pastor at a nearby church refused to bury a person of so lowly a profession. Instead, he suggested "the little church around the corner." The name stuck and the church has had special ties with the theater ever since. Sarah Bernhardt attended services here.

The south transept window, by John La Farge, shows Edwin Booth playing Hamlet. Jefferson's cry of "God bless the little church around the corner" is commemorated in a window in the south aisle.

CHELSEA AND THE GARMENT DISTRICT

THIS WAS OPEN farmland in 1750, but by the 1830s it was a city suburb, and in the 1870s, with the coming of the elevated railroads *(see pp24–5)*, it had become quite commercial. Music halls and theaters lined 23rd Street. Fashion Row grew in the shadow of the El, with department stores serving middle-class New York. As fashion moved uptown, Chelsea drifted farther downhill. It became a warehouse district, until the Els were removed and New Yorkers rediscovered the 19th-century town houses. When Macy's arrived at Herald Square to the north, the retailing and garment districts grew around it. Today Chelsea's warehouses are the heart of New York's avant-garde art galleries.

Statue of garment worker, at 555 7th Avenue

Inside Chelsea's Empire Diner

SIGHTS AT A GLANCE

Historic Streets and Buildings
*Empire State Building
pp134–5* 2
General Post Office 7
General Theological
  Seminary 11

Chelsea Historic District 12
Hugh O'Neill Dry Goods
Store 14

Churches
Marble Collegiate Reformed
Church 1
St. John the Baptist Church 5

Modern Architecture
Madison Square Garden 6
  Jacob K. Javits Convention
    Center 8

Chelsea Piers Sports and
Entertainment Complex 9

Monuments
Worth Monument 15

Parks and Squares
Herald Square 3

**Landmark Hotels and
Restaurants**
Empire Diner 10
Chelsea Hotel 13

Landmark Stores
Macy's 4

Medallion
celebrating technology
at the Empire State Building

GETTING THERE
To Chelsea, take the 7th Ave/
Broadway 1 or 9 subway trains
to 18th or 23rd St. The 8th Ave
A, C and E trains go to 23rd St.
Buses include the M10 and
M11, M14 or the M23 cross-
town. To reach the area
around Macy's, take the 1 or 9
or the 2 or 3 express trains to
34th St/Penn Station. The 8th
Ave trains also stop at 34th St.

KEY

Street-by-Street map

M Subway station

Heliport

0 meters   500
0 yards   500

Street by Street: Herald Square

HERALD SQUARE is named for the New York *Herald*, which had its office there from 1894 to 1921. Today full of shoppers, the area was once one of the raunchiest parts of New York. During the 1880s and '90s, it was known as the Tenderloin District and was filled with dance halls and bordellos. When Macy's opened in 1901, the focus moved from flesh to fashion. New York's Garment District now fills the streets near Macy's around Seventh Avenue, also known as Fashion Avenue. To the east on Fifth Avenue is the Empire State Building, with the city's best eagle's-eye views from the observation deck.

Manhattan Mall, the site of Gimbel's, Macy's former archrival, holds 90 stores, a huge food court, and a floor for children's wares.

Fashion Avenue is another name for the stretch of Seventh Avenue around 34th Street. This area is the heart of New York's garment industry. The streets are full of men pushing racks of clothes.

34th Street-Penn Station subway (1, 2, 3, 9, A, C, E)

The Ramada Hotel Pennsylvania was a center for the 1930s big bands – Glenn Miller's song "Pennsylvania 6-5000" made its telephone number famous.

St. John the Baptist Church
A beautiful set of carved Stations of the Cross is hung on the walls of the white marble interior of this church **5**

The SJM Building is at 130 West 30th Street. Mesopotamian-style friezes adorn the outside of the building.

The Fur District is at the southern end of the Garment District. Furriers ply their trade between West 27th and 30th streets.

The Flower District, around Sixth Avenue and West 28th Street, hums with activity in the early part of the day as florists pack their vans with their highly scented, brightly colored wares.

28th Street subway (lines 1, 9, N, R, W)

★ **Macy's**
The biggest department store in the world has something for everyone ❹

The Greenwich Savings Bank (now the HSBC) is a Greek temple to banking with huge columns on three sides.

34th Street subway (lines B, D, F, N, Q, R, V, W)

Herald Square
The New York Herald Building's clock now is situated where Broadway meets Sixth Avenue ❸

LOCATOR MAP
See Manhattan Map pp12–13

KEY
– – – Suggested route

0 meters   100
0 yards   100

Greeley Square is more of a traffic island than a square, but it does have a fine statue of Horace Greeley, founder of the New York Tribune.

★ **Empire State Building**
The observation deck of this quintessential skyscraper is a great place to view the city ❷

Little Korea is an area of Korean businesses. In addition to shops, there are restaurants nearby on West 31st and 32nd streets.

The Life Building at 19 West 31st Street housed *Life* magazine when it was a satirical weekly. Carrère & Hastings designed the building in 1894. It is now a hotel.

Marble Collegiate Church
This 1854 church was built in the Gothic Revival style. It became famous when Norman Vincent Peale was pastor here ❶

STAR SIGHTS
★ Macy's
★ Empire State Building

Marble Collegiate's Tiffany stained-glass windows

Marble Collegiate Reformed Church ❶

1 W. 29th St. **Map** 8 F3. 【 *(212) 686-2770.* Ⓜ *28th St.* ◯ *8:30am–8:30pm Mon–Fri, 9am–4pm Sat, 8am–3pm Sun.* ✝ *11:15am Sun.* 🚫 *during services.* ♿ **Sanctuary** *3 W. 29th St.* ◯ *10am–noon, 2–4pm Mon–Fri.* Ⓦ *www.marblechurch.org*

T HIS CHURCH is best known for its former pastor Norman Vincent Peale, who wrote *The Power of Positive Thinking.* Another positive thinker, Richard M. Nixon, attended services here when he was a lawyer in his pre-White House days.

The church was built in 1854 using the marble blocks that give it its name. Fifth Avenue was then no more than a dusty country road, and the cast-iron fence was there to keep livestock out.

The original white and gold interior walls were replaced with a stenciled gold *fleur-de-lis* design on a soft rust background. Two stained-glass Tiffany windows, depicting Old Testament scenes, were placed in the south wall in 1893.

Empire State Building ❷

See pp134–5.

Herald Square ❸

6th Ave. **Map** 8 E2. Ⓜ *34th St-Penn Station. See **Shopping** p313.*

N AMED AFTER the New York *Herald,* which occupied a fine arcaded, Italianate Stanford White building here from 1893 to 1921, the square was the hub of the rowdy Tenderloin district in the 1870s and 1880s. Theaters, such as the Manhattan Opera House, dance halls, hotels and restaurants kept the area humming with life until reformers clamped down on sleaze in the 1890s. The ornamental Bennett clock, named for James Gordon Bennett Jr., publisher of the *Herald,* is now all that is left of the Herald Building.

The Opera House was razed in 1901 to make way for Macy's and, soon after, other department stores followed, making Herald Square a mecca for shoppers. One such store was the now-defunct Gimbel Brothers Department Store, once arch rival to Macy's. (The rivalry was affectionately portrayed in the New York Christmas movie *A Miracle on 34th Street*). In 1988 the store was converted into a vertical mall with a glittery neon front. Although most of the old names have gone, Herald Square is still a key shopping district.

Macy's ❹

151 W. 34th St. **Map** 8 E2. 【 *(212) 695-4400* Ⓜ *34th St-Penn Station.* ◯ *10am–8:30pm Mon–Sat; 11am–7pm Sun. See **Shopping** p311.* 🌐 *public hols.* Ⓦ *www.macys.com*

T HE "WORLD'S LARGEST STORE" covers a square block, and the merchandise inside covers just about any item you could imagine in every price range.

Macy's was founded by a former whaler named Rowland Hussey Macy, who opened a small store on West 14th Street in 1857. The store's red star logo came from Macy's tattoo, a souvenir of his sailing days.

By the time Macy died in 1877, his little store had grown to a row of 11 buildings. It was to expand further under two brothers, Isidor and Nathan Straus, who had operated Macy's china and glassware department. By 1902 Macy's had outgrown its 14th Street premises, and the firm acquired its present site. The eastern facade has a new

Macy's 34th Street facade

The nave of St. John the Baptist Church

entrance but still bears the bay windows and Corinthian pillars of the 1902 design. The 34th Street facade still has its original caryatids guarding the entrance, along with the clock, canopy and lettering. Inside, many of the original wooden escalators are still in good working order.

The sea featured again in Macy's history in 1912 – a plaque by the main entrance commemorates the death of Isidor and his wife in the sinking of the *Titanic*.

Macy's sponsors New York's renowned Thanksgiving Day parade and the Fourth of July fireworks. The store's Spring Flower Show draws thousands of visitors.

St. John the Baptist Church ❺

210 W. 31st St. **Map** 8 E3. (212) 564-9070. 34th St-Penn Station. 6:45am–6pm daily. throughout the day.

FOUNDED IN 1840 to serve a congregation of newly arrived immigrants, today this small Roman Catholic church is almost lost in the heart of the Fur District. The exterior has a single spire. Although the brownstone facade on 30th Street is dark with city soot, many treasures lie within this dull exterior. The entrance is through the modern Friary on 31st Street.

The sanctuary by Napoleon Le Brun is a marvel of Gothic arches in glowing white marble surmounted by gilded capitals. Painted reliefs of religious scenes line the walls; sunlight streams through the stained-glass windows. Also off the Friary is the Prayer Garden, a small, green and peaceful oasis with religious statuary, a fountain and stone benches.

Madison Square Garden ❻

4 Pennsylvania Plaza. **Map** 8 D2. (212) 465-6741. 34th St-Penn Station. Mon–Sun, times vary according to shows. See **Entertainment** p344. www.thegarden.com

THERE'S ONLY ONE good thing to be said for the razing of the extraordinarily lovely McKim, Mead & White Pennsylvania Station building in favor of this undistinguished 1968 complex: it so enraged city preservationists that they formed an alliance to ensure that such a thing would never be allowed to happen again.

Madison Square Garden itself, which sits atop underground Pennsylvania Station, is a cylinder of precast concrete, functional enough as a 20,000-seat, centrally located home for the famous New York Knickerbockers (the Knicks) basketball, Liberty (women's basketball), and New York Rangers hockey teams. It has a packed calendar of other events: rock concerts, championship tennis and boxing, outrageously staged wrestling, the Ringling Bros. and Barnum & Bailey Circus, an antiques show, a dog show and more. There is also a 5,600-seat theater.

Despite renovation work, Madison Square Garden lacks the panache of its earlier location, which combined a stunning Stanford White building with extravagant entertainment *(see p124).*

The massive interior of Madison Square Garden

General Post Office ❼

421 8th Ave. **Map** 8 D2. (212) 967-8585. 34th St-Penn Station. 24 hrs a day, every day, (incl public hols). See **Practical Information** p361.

DESIGNED BY McKim, Mead & White in 1913, in a style to complement their 1910 Pennsylvania Station across the street, the General Post Office is a perfect example of a public building of the Beaux Arts period. The imposing, two-block-long structure has a broad staircase leading to a facade with 20 Corinthian columns and a pavilion at each end. The 280-ft (85-m) inscription across it is based on a description of the Persian Empire's postal service, from around 520 BC: "Neither snow nor rain nor heat nor gloom of night stays these couriers from the swift completion of their appointed rounds."

The Corinthian colonnade of the General Post Office

Empire State Building ❷

102nd-floor observatory

Empire State Building

THE EMPIRE STATE BUILDING is the tallest skyscraper in New York. Construction began in March 1930, not long after the Wall Street Crash, and by the time it opened in 1931, space was so diffi cult to rent that it was nicknamed "the Empty State Building." Only the immediate popularity of the observatories saved the building from bankruptcy – to date, they have attracted more than 110 million visitors – and the building soon became a symbol of the city the world over.

The Empire State was planned to be 86 stories high, but a then 150 ft (46 m) mooring mast for zeppelins was added. The mast, now 204 ft (62 m), transmits TV and radio to the city and four states.

Colored floodlighting of the top 30 floors marks special and seasonal events.

Symbols of the modern age are depicted on these bronze Art Deco medallions placed throughout the lobby.

CONSTRUCTION
The building was designed for ease and speed of construction. Everything possible was prefabricated and slotted into place at a rate of about four stories per week.

High-speed elevators travel at up to 1,200 ft (366 m) a minute.

The framework is made from 60,000 tons of steel and was built in 23 weeks.

Aluminum panels were used instead of stone around the 6,500 windows. The steel trim masks rough edges on the facing.

Ten million bricks were used to line the whole building.

Ten minutes is all it takes for fit runners to race up the 1,575 steps from the lobby to the 86th floor, in the annual Empire State Run-Up.

Sandwich space between the floors houses the wiring, pipes and cables.

Over 200 steel and concrete piles support the 365,000-ton building.

STAR FEATURES

★ **Fifth Avenue Entrance Lobby**

★ **Views from 86th-floor Observatory**

★ Views from the Observatories
The 86th floor has outdoor observation decks for bird's-eye views of Manhattan. From the 102nd floor, 1,250 ft (381 m) high, you can see more than 80 miles (125 km) on a clear day, but this has been closed to the public for several years.

VISITORS' CHECKLIST

350 5th Ave. **Map** 8 F2. 📞 *(212) 736-3100.* Ⓜ *A, B, C, D, E, F, N, Q, R, 1, 2, 3, 9 to 34th St; 6 to 33rd St.* 🚌 *M4, M10, M16, M34, Q32.* **86th-floor Observatory** ⬤ *9: 30am–midnight (last adm: 11: 15pm); 9am–5pm Dec 24; 11am– 7pm Dec 25; 11am–7pm Jan 1.* 📷 ♿ 🍴 Ⓦ *www.esbnyc.com*

Sky Boy
Photographer Lewis Hine documented the workers' bravery during the 1930s construction. Here, a worker climbs up a cable. The wide Hudson River appears small in the background.

**Empire State
1454 ft (443 m)
with mast**

**Eiffel Tower
1045 ft
(319 m)**

**Great Pyramid
350 ft (107 m)**

**Big Ben 220 ft
(67 m)**

Lightning Strikes
The Empire State is a natural lightning conductor, struck up to 100 times a year. The observation deck is closed during unfavorable weather.

Pecking Order
New Yorkers are justly proud of their city's symbol, which towers above the icons of other countries.

★ Fifth Avenue Entrance Lobby
A relief image of the skyscraper is superimposed on a map of New York State in the marble-lined lobby.

ENCOUNTERS IN THE SKY
The Empire State Building has been seen in many films. However, the finale from the 1933 classic *King Kong* is easily its most famous guest appearance, as the giant ape straddles the spire to do battle with army aircraft. In 1945 a real bomber flew too low over Manhattan in fog and struck the building just above the 78th floor. The luckiest escape was that of a young elevator operator whose cabin plunged 79 floors. The emergency brakes saved her life.

Jacob K. Javits Convention Center ⑧

655 W. 34th St. **Map** 7 B2. ⚏ (212) 216-2000. Ⓜ 34th St-Penn Station, 42nd St. ▦ M34, M42. ◯ only on show days – times vary. 🗓 🚫 ♿ � ⓦ www.javitscenter.com

The Convention Center – modern New York architecture at its best

STRIKINGLY MODERNISTIC in appearance, this glass building facing the Hudson, which opened in 1986, was designed by I.M. Pei to give New York the space for large-scale expositions. The 15-story building is constructed of 16,000 panes of glass, the two main halls can accommodate thousands of delegates and the lobby is high enough to hold the Statue of Liberty. In 1989 the final completion of the Galleria River Pavilion added another 40,000 sq ft (3,750 sq m) of open space and two outdoor terraces overlooking the river.

Chelsea Piers Complex ⑨

11th Ave (17th & 23rd Sts) **Map** 7 B5. ⚏ (212) 336-6666. Ⓜ 14th St, 23rd St. ▦ M14, M23. ◯ daily. 🗓 ⓦ www.chelseapiers.com

THIS MAMMOTH complex, which opened in 1995, has converted four neglected piers into a center for a vast range of sports and leisure activities *(see p31)*. The facilities include skating rinks, running tracks, a golf driving range, a marina, and 11 TV and film production sound stages.

Empire Diner ⑩

210 10th Ave. **Map** 7 C4. ⚏ (212) 924-0011. Ⓜ 23rd St. ◯ 24hrs daily . ● 4–8am Tue.

THIS ART DECO beauty is a faithful refurbishing of a classic 1929 American diner, complete with stainless steel bar and black and chrome trim. Bette Davis reputedly declared it her favorite diner. Its cuisine and clientele are up-to-date New York style.

A 15th-century music manuscript from the Seminary's collection

General Theological Seminary ⑪

20th–21st Sts. **Map** 7 C4. ⚏ (212) 243-5150. Ⓜ 23rd St. ◯ noon–3pm Mon–Fri, 11am–3pm Sat. 🚫 ♿ ⓦ www.gts.edu

FOUNDED IN 1817, this block-square campus accepts 150 students at a time to train for the priesthood. Clement Clarke Moore, a professor of Biblical Learning, donated the site, officially known as Chelsea Square. The earliest remaining building dates from 1836; the most modern, St. Mark's Library, was built in 1960 and holds the largest collection of Latin Bibles in the world.

The campus can be entered from Ninth Avenue only. Inside, the garden is laid out in two quadrangles like an English cathedral close: it is especially lovely in spring.

The Empire Diner before hungry club-goers arrive for breakfast

Chelsea Historic District ⑫

From 9th to 10th Aves. and from W. 20th to 21st Sts. **Map** 8 D5. **M** *18th St.*

Aᴌᴛʜᴏᴜɢʜ ʜᴇ is more well-known as the author of the poem "A Visit from St. Nicholas" than as an urban planner, Clement Clarke Moore owned an estate here and divided it into lots in the 1830s creating handsome rows of town houses. Restoration has since rescued many of the original buildings.

Of these, the finest are seven houses known as Cushman Row, running from 406– 418 West 20th Street, which were built from 1839–1840 for Don Alonzo Cushman. He was a merchant who also founded the Greenwich Savings Bank. He joined Moore and James N. Wells in the development of Chelsea. Rich in detail and intricate ironwork, Cushman Row is ranked with Washington Square North as supreme examples of Greek Revival architecture. Look for cast-iron wreaths around attic windows and the pineapples on the newel posts of two of the houses – old symbols of hospitality.

Farther along West 20th Street, from 446–450, there are fine examples of the Italianate style for which Chelsea is also renowned.

A house on Cushman Row

The detailed brickwork arches of windows and fanlights subtly implied the wealth of the owner, being able to afford this expensive effect.

Hugh O'Neill Dry Goods Store

Chelsea Hotel ⑬

222 W. 23rd St. **Map** 8 D4. **C** (212) 243-3700. **M** *23rd St.* **W** www.chelseahotel.com

Fᴇᴡ ʜᴏᴛᴇʟs can match the Chelsea for artistic and literary heritage – and notoriety. Many former guests have been commemorated in the brass plaques on the hotel's facade. They include

A guest's-eye view of the Chelsea Hotel's cast-iron stairwell

Tennessee Williams, Mark Twain, Jack Kerouac and Brendan Behan. Dylan Thomas spent his last years here. In 1966 Andy Warhol's movie *Chelsea Girls* was set here, reviving its cult status, and in 1978 punk band member Sid Vicious killed his girlfriend in the hotel. The Chelsea still draws musicians, artists and writers who hope their names will one day be remembered. Stop by the bar to soak in the decadent decay of this creative atmsphere.

Hugh O'Neill Dry Goods Store ⑭

655–671 6th Avenue. **Map** 8 E4. **M** *23rd St.*

Tʜᴏᴜɢʜ ᴛʜᴇ sᴛᴏʀᴇ is long gone, the 1876 cast-iron columned and pilastered facade clearly shows the scale and grandeur of the

emporiums that once lined Sixth Avenue from 18th to 23rd streets, the area known as Fashion Row. O'Neill, whose sign can still be seen on the facade, was a showman and super-salesman whose trademark was a fleet of shiny delivery wagons. His customers came in droves via the conveniently close Sixth Avenue El. They were not the "carriage trade" enjoyed by Ladies' Mile *(see p125)*, but their numbers allowed the Row to flourish until the turn of the century, when the retailing district continued its move uptown. Now mostly restored, the buildings have turned into superstores and the headquarters of bargain places like Filene's Basement.

Worth Monument ⑮

5th Ave. **Map** 8 F4. **M** *23rd St-Broadway.*

Hɪᴅᴅᴇɴ ᴀᴡᴀʏ ʙᴇʜɪɴᴅ a water meter on a triangle amid city traffic is an obelisk erected in 1857 to mark the grave of the one public figure to be buried under the streets of Manhattan. That honor belongs to General William Worth, a hero of the Mexican wars of the mid-1800s. A cast-iron fence of swords embedded in the ground surrounds the monument.

The Worth Monument

THEATER DISTRICT

I<small>T WAS THE</small> move of the Metropolitan Opera House to Broadway at 40th Street in 1883 that first drew lavish theaters and restaurants to this area. In the 1920s, movie palaces added the glamour of neon to Broadway, the signs getting bigger and brighter until eventually the street became known as the "Great White Way." After World War II,

Lee Lawrie design in Rockefeller Center

the pull of the movies waned and the glitter was replaced by grime. In recent years, however, a redevelopment program has brought the public and the bright lights back. Pockets of calm also exist away from the bustle. Explore the Public Library or relax in Bryant Park. For the best of both worlds, though, visit Rockefeller Center.

The heart of the Theater District, around Times Square

SIGHTS AT A GLANCE

Historic Streets and Buildings
New York Yacht Club ⑤
New York Public Library ⑧
Times Square ⑩
Group Health Insurance Building ⑫
Paramount Building ⑬
Shubert Alley ⑭
Alwyn Court Apartments ⑱

Museums and Galleries
International Center of Photography ⑨
Intrepid Sea-Air-Space Museum ⑲

Modern Architecture
Rockefeller Center ①
MONY Tower ⑮

Parks and Squares
Bryant Park ⑥

Famous Theaters
Lyceum Theater ③
New Amsterdam Theater ⑪
City Center of Music and Dance ⑯
Carnegie Hall ⑰

Landmark Hotels and Restaurants
Algonquin Hotel ④
Bryant Park Hotel ⑦

Landmark Stores
Diamond Row ②

GETTING THERE

Convenient subway routes are the 7th Ave/Broadway 1, 2, 3 and 9 trains to 50th or 42nd St, and N, Q, R or W trains to 57th, 49th or 42nd St. Other nearby lines include the 8th Ave A, C or E trains and 6th Ave, B, D, F or Q trains. Bus routes through the area are the M5, M6, M7, M10, M34, M42, M50, M57 and the M58 Street crosstown.

SEE ALSO

- *Street Finder,* maps 8, 11–12
- *Where to Stay* pp276–79
- *Restaurants* p289

Mermaid and dolphin fountain in the Channel Gardens

KEY

▨ Street-by-Street map
Ⓜ Subway station
🚢 Riverboat boarding point

0 meters   500
0 yards   500

Street by street:Times Square

Named for the 25-story New York Times Tower, which opened in 1906, Times Square has been at the heart of the city's theater district since 1899, when Oscar Hammerstein built the Victoria and Republic theaters. Since the 1920s, the glowing neon of theater billboards has combined with the *Times'* illuminated newswire and other advertising to create a spectacular lightshow. After a period of decline starting in the 1930s, which saw sex shows taking over many of the grand theatres, rejuvenation of the district began in the 1990s. Old-style Broadway glamour again rubs shoulders with modern entertainment in this enticing part of the city.

Paramount Hotel
This hotel (*see p277*), designed by Philippe Starck, is the hip haunt of the theatre crowd, in the Whiskey Bar for a late-night drink.

MTV Studios
Crowds gather outside at 3pm Monday through Friday to watch interviews being filmed in the second-floor studios. Roving cameras often seek reactions on the street.

Sardi's
In Times Square since 1921, Sardi's walls are lined with caricatures of Broadway stars of yesterday and today.

★ E Walk
This vast entertainment and retail complex is home to a state-of-the-art multiplex cinema, restaurants, a hotel and the BB King Blues Club.

★ New Victory Theater
Renovated in 1995, this classic Broadway theater reopened as a dedicated young people's performance space.

W 45TH ST

W 43RD ST

W 41ST ST

SEVENTH AV

BROA

★ Times Square ⑩
Every New Years Eve at midnight, the famed silver ball drops from the top of One Times Square. There are great views from the front of this New York landmark.

0 meters   100

0 yards   100

Electronic Ticker Tape
The figures on the Morgan Stanley LED tickertape are 10 feet (3 m) high. It is only one of the eye-catching lighting displays that illuminate Times Square day and night. City ordinances require office buildings to carry neon advertising.

KEY

— — — Suggested Route

STAR SIGHTS

★ **E Walk**

★ **Times Square**

★ **New Victory Theater**

McGraw-Hill Building

J.P. Stevens Tower

Celanese Building

BROADWAY

AVENUE

SEVENTH

W 47TH ST

W 46TH ST

3RD ST

Times Square Visitors Center

Duffy Square
A statue of actor, composer, and writer George M Cohan, responsible for many of Broadway's hits, stands proud in this small square. Duffy Square is named for World War I hero, "Fighting" Father Duffy, immortalized in a statue. It is also home to the TKTS booth, where cut-price tickets are sold daily.

Lyceum Theater
The oldest Broadway theatre, the Lyceum has a beautifully ornate Baroque façade. ❸

Belasco Theater
Built in 1907 by producer David Belasco, it was the most technically advanced theater of its time. Original Tiffany glass and Everett Shinn murals decorate the interior. It is rumored that Belasco's ghost still treads the boards some nights.

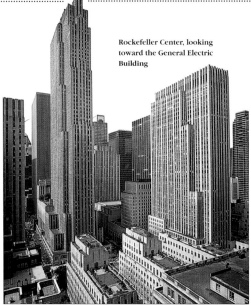

Rockefeller Center, looking toward the General Electric Building

Rockefeller Center ❶

Map 12 F5. **M** *47th-50th Sts.*

W HEN THE New York City Landmarks Preservation Commission unanimously voted to declare Rockefeller Center a landmark in 1985, they rightly called it "the heart of New York . . . a great unifying presence in the chaotic core of midtown Manhattan."

It is the largest privately owned complex of its kind and the inspiration for many cities to emulate its perfect urban mix. The Art Deco design was by a team of top architects headed by Raymond Hood. Works by 30 artists can be found in foyers, on facades, and in the gardens.

The site, once a botanic garden owned by Columbia University, was leased in 1928 by John D. Rockefeller, Jr., as an ideal central home for a new opera house. When the 1929 Depression scuttled the plans,

Rockefeller, stuck with a long lease, went ahead with his own development. The 14 buildings erected between 1931 and 1940 provided jobs for 225,000 during the Depression and by 1973 there were a total of 19 buildings.

In December 1932, Radio City Music Hall opened within the complex. It hosts dazzling events; the annual Christmas and Easter shows feature the famous Rockettes. In 1999, a complete renovation of the Hall brought

***Wisdom* by Lee Lawrie, on the GE Building**

back the glitter and sparkle of the original interior. NBC's studios are here and people line up for a chance on camera on the *Today Show*.

Diamond Row ❷

47th St. **Map** 12 F5. **M** *47th-50th Sts. See* **Shopping** *p320.*

N EARLY EVERY SHOP window on 47th Street glitters with gold and diamonds. The buildings are filled with booths and workshops where jewelers vie for customers while, upstairs, millions of dollars change hands. The diamond district was born in the 1930s, when the Jewish diamond cutters of Antwerp and Amsterdam fled to America to escape Nazism. Hasidic Jews with black hats, beards and long earlocks are still an integral part of the scene. Although mainly a wholesale district, individual customers are welcome. Bring cash, compare prices, haggle, and stay away if you know nothing about the value of diamonds.

Diamond Row's main commodity

In the midst of all this, look for the sign saying "Wise men fish here" – here is the Gotham Book Mart, a tiny, much-loved treasure house of literary gems *(see p322)*.

Lyceum Theater ❸

149 W 45th St. **Map** 12 E5. **C** *Telecharge (212) 239-6200.* **M** *42nd St-5th Ave. See* **Entertainment** *p333.*

T HE OLDEST New York theater still active is a Baroque-style bandbox as frilly as a wedding cake. This 1903 triumph was the first theater by Herts and Tallant, later renowned for their extravagant style. The Lyceum made history with a record run of 1,600 performances of the comedy *Born Yesterday*. It was the first theater to be designated a historic landmark and though the Theater District has shifted westward, there are still many shows here.

The Rose Room in the Algonquin Hotel

Algonquin Hotel ❹

59 W 44th St. **Map** 12 F5. [C] *(212) 840-6800.* [M] *42nd St-5th Ave. See* **Where to Stay** *p277.* [W] *www.thealgonquin.net*

THE EXTERIOR is a bit fussy – iron bay windows in vertical rows, red brick, too much detail – but it is the ambience, not the 1902 architecture, that makes the Algonquin special. In the 1920s, the Rose Room was home to America's best-known luncheon club, the Round Table, with literary lights such as Alexander Woollcott, Franklin P. Adams, Dorothy Parker, Robert Benchley and Harold Ross. All were associated with the *New Yorker* (Ross was the founding editor), whose 25 West 43rd Street headquarters had a back door opening into the hotel.

Renovations have preserved the old-fashioned, civilized feel of the Rose Room, as well as the cozy, paneled lobby where publishing types and theater-goers still like to gather for drinks, settling into comfortable armchairs and ringing a small brass bell in order to summon the waiters.

Statue of poet William Cullen Bryant in Bryant Park

New York Yacht Club ❺

37 W 44th St. **Map** 12 F5. [M] *42nd St-5th Ave.* [●] *to the public (members only).* [W] *www.nyyc.org*

A WHIMSICAL 1899 creation, this private club has the carved sterns of 16th-century Dutch galleons in the three bay windows. The prows of the ships are borne up by sculpted dolphins and waves spilling over the windowsills and splashing down to the pavement. (The building, just over 100 years old, has been spruced up for its next century.)

This is the birthplace of the America's Cup yacht race, which was based in the US from 1857 to 1983. That was the year the much coveted prize was taken from the table where it had stood for more than a century, when the *Australia II* sailed to a historic victory.

The America's Cup, the coveted yachting prize

Bryant Park ❻

Map 8 F1. [M] *42nd St-5th Ave.* [W] *www.bryantpark.org*

IN 1853, WITH the New York Public Library site still occupied by Croton Reservoir, Bryant Park (then Reservoir Park) housed a dazzling Crystal Palace, built for the World's Fair of that year *(see p23)*.

In the 1960s the park was a hangout for drug dealers and other undesirables. In 1989 the city renovated the park, reclaiming it for workers and visitors to relax in. In spring and fall, world-famous fashion shows take place here; in the summer, classic movies are screened. Over seven million books lie in storage stacks beneath the park.

Bryant Park Hotel ❼

40 W 40th St. **Map** 8 F1. [M] *42nd St-Grand Central, Times Sq, 42nd St-5th Ave.* [W] *www.bryantparkhotel.com*

THE AMERICAN Radiator building (now the Bryant Park Hotel) was the first major New York work by Raymond Hood and John Howells, who went on to design the Daily News Building *(see p153)*, the McGraw-Hill building, and Rockefeller Center. The 1924 structure is reminiscent of one of Hood's best-known Gothic buildings, Chicago's Tribune Tower. Here, the design is sleeker, giving the building the illusion of being taller than its actual 23 stories. The black brick facade is set off by gold terra-cotta trim, evoking images of flaming coals: a comparison that would have suited its original owners well, since they made heating equipment.

The building is now a luxury hotel right in the heart of Midtown, across the street from the New York Public Library, Bryant Park and Fifth Avenue.

The Bryant Park Hotel, formerly the American Radiator Building

The New York Public Library **8**

5th Ave and 42nd St. **Map** 8 F1. ☎ (212) 930-0800. Ⓜ 42nd St-Grand Central, 42nd St-5th Ave. ◯ Tue–Sat. ● public hols. ◉ ⓓ ☑ **Lectures, workshops, readings.** ◻ Ⓦ www.nypl.org

The doorway leading to the Main Reading Room

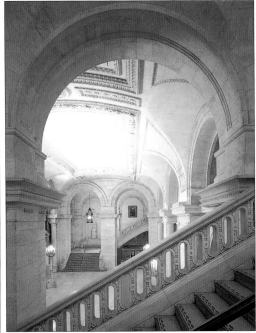

Barrel vaults of carved white marble over the stairs in the Astor Hall

I N 1897 THE COVETED JOB of designing New York's main public library was awarded to architects Carrère & Hastings. The library's first director envisaged a light, quiet, airy place for study, where millions of books could be stored and yet be available to readers as promptly as possible. In the hands of Carrère & Hastings, his vision came true, in what is considered the epitome of New York's Beaux Arts period.

Built on the site of the former Croton Reservoir *(see p22)*, it opened in 1911 to immediate acclaim, despite having cost the city $9 million.

One of the library's two stone lions, named Patience and Fortitude by Mayor LaGuardia

The vast, paneled Main Reading Room stretches two full blocks and is suffused with daylight from the two interior courtyards. Below it are 88 miles (140 km) of shelves, holding over seven million volumes. A staff of over 100 and a computerized dumb-waiter can supply any book within 10 minutes.

The Periodicals Room holds 10,000 current periodicals from 128 countries. On its walls are murals by Richard Haas, honoring New York's great publishing houses. The original library combined the collections of John Jacob Astor and James Lenox. Its collections today range from Thomas Jefferson's handwritten copy of the Declaration of Independence to T.S. Eliot's typed copy of "The Waste Land." More than 1,000 queries

The Main Reading Room, with its original bronze reading lamps

are answered daily, using the vast database of the CATNYP computer catalog.

This library is the hub of a network of 82 branches, with nearly seven million users. Some branches are very well known, such as the New York Public Library for the Performing Arts at the Lincoln Center *(see p210)* and the Schomburg Center in Harlem *(see p227)*.

International Center of Photography 9

1133 Avenue of the Americas (43rd St) **Map** 8 F1. **C** *(212) 857-0000.* **M** *42nd St-Times Sq.* ○ *10am–5pm Tue–Thu, 10am–8pm Fri, 10am–6pm Sat & Sun* **⅃ ⬛ ⬛ w** *www.icp.org*

THIS MUSEUM was founded by Cornell Capa in 1974 to conserve the work of such photojournalists as his brother Robert, who was killed on assignment in 1954. The ICP's collection of 12,500 original prints contains work by many top photographers, including Ansel Adams and Henri Cartier-Bresson. Special exhibitions are organized from the contents of the archive, as well as from outside sources. There are also films, lectures, and classes.

Times Square 10

Map 8 E1. **M** *42nd St-Times Sq.* **i** *Times Square Visitors Center, 1560 Broadway (46th St) 8am–8pm daily.* **⬛** *noon Fri, (212) 869-1890.* **w** *www.timessquarebid.org*

THE 1990s saw a huge transformation in Times Square, reversing a decline that began during the Depression – the square is now a safe and vibrant place for theatergoers and tourists, where Broadway traditions comfortably coexist with modern innovations.

Although the *New York Times* has moved on from its original headquarters at the south end of the square, the silver ball still drops at midnight on New Years Eve, as it has since the building opened with fanfare and fireworks in 1906. New buildings, such as the Bertlesmann and the fashionably minimalist Condé Nast offices, sit comfortably alongside the classic Broadway theaters.

Broadway's fortunes have also revived. Many theaters, such as the New Victory and the New Amsterdam, have been reclaimed and renovated. They are again housing new productions, and theatergoers throng the area's bars and restaurants each evening.

The newest landmark is the 57-story skyscraper designed by Miami architects Arquitectonica, that tops the E-Walk entertainment and retail complex at 42nd Street and Eighth Avenue *(see p140).* Other new attractions include an outpost of Madame Tussaud's Wax Museum at 42nd Street, between Seventh and Eighth Avenue, and Lazer Park, a huge lazer tag arena, at 46th Street and Broadway.

W.C. Fields (far left) and Eddie Cantor (holding top hat, right) in the 1918 *Ziegfeld Follies* at the New Amsterdam Theater

New Amsterdam Theater 11

214 W 42nd St. **Map** 8 E1. **C** *(212) 282-2900.* **M** *42nd St-Times Sq.* **⬛** *10am–5pm Mon, 10am–12pm Tues.*

THIS WAS the most opulent theater in the United States when it opened in 1903, and the first to have an Art Nouveau interior. It was owned for a time by Florenz Ziegfeld, who produced his famous *Follies* revue here between 1914 and 1918 – with Broadway's first $5 ticket price. He remodeled the roof garden into another theater, the Aerial Gardens. This is one of the fine early theaters on 42nd Street that fell on hard times. With the rehabilitation of Times Square its fortunes rose again, and it is once more in Show Business.

The Art Deco top of the Paramount Building

Group Health Insurance Building 12

330 W 42nd St. **Map** 8 D1. **M** *42nd St.* ○ *office hours.*

THIS 1931 design by Raymond Hood was the only New York building selected for the influential International Style survey of 1932 *(see p41).* Its unusual design gives it a stepped profile seen from east and west, but a slab effect viewed from north or south. The exterior's horizontal bands of blue-green terra-cotta have earned it the nickname "jolly green giant." Step inside to see the classic Art Deco lobby of opaque glass and stainless steel.

One block west is Theater Row, a pleasant group of Off-Broadway theaters and cafés.

Paramount Building 13

1501 Broadway. **Map** 8 E1. **M** *34th St.*

THE FABULOUS ground-floor movie theater where bobby-soxers stood in line in the 1940s to hear Frank Sinatra perform is gone, but there's still a theatrical feel to the massive building designed by Rapp & Rapp in 1927. On each side are symmetrical setbacks, 14 in all, rising like building blocks to an Art Deco crown – a tower, clock and globe. In the heyday of the "Great White Way," the tower was lit, with an observation deck at the top.

Shubert Alley ❹

Between W 44th and W 45th St.
Map 12 E5. **M** *42nd St-Times Sq.*

THE PLAYHOUSES on the streets west of Broadway are rich in theater lore – and in notable architecture. Two classic theaters built in 1913 are the Booth (22 West 45th Street), named after actor Edwin Booth, and the Shubert (221 West 44th), after theater baron Sam S. Shubert. They form the west wall of Shubert Alley, where aspiring actors lined up, hoping for a casting in a Shubert play.

A Chorus Line ran at the Shubert until 1990, for a record 6,137 performances; Katharine Hepburn starred earlier in The Philadelphia Story. Across from the 44th Street end of the alley is the St. James, where Rodgers and Hammerstein made their debut with Oklahoma! in 1941, followed by The King and I. Nearby is Sardi's, the restaurant where actors waited for opening night reviews. Irving Berlin staged The Music Box Revue opposite the other end of the alley in 1921. His Music Box Theater has since housed many famous shows.

The tiled Moorish facade of the City Center of Music and Drama

MONY Tower ❺

1740 Broadway. **Map** 12 E4.
M *57th St.* ● *to the public.*

BUILT IN 1950, the head office of the Mutual of New York insurance company (now MONY Financial Services) has a weather vane that tells you everything except the wind direction. The mast turns green for fair, orange for cloudy, flashing orange for rain and white for snow. Lights moving up the mast mean warmer weather; lights going down mean get out your overcoat!

City Center of Music and Dance ❻

131 W 55th St. **Map** 12 E4.
C *(212) 581-1212.* **M** *57th St.* Ø
& *See* **Entertainment** *p334.*
W www.citycenter.org

THIS HIGHLY ornate Moorish structure with its dome of Spanish tiles was designed in 1924 as a Masonic Shriners' Temple. It was saved from the developers by Mayor La Guardia, becoming home to the New York City Opera and Ballet in 1943. When the troupes moved to Lincoln Center, City Center lived on as a major venue for dance. Renovation work has preserved the delightful excesses of the architecture.

Carnegie Hall ❼

154 W 57th Street. **Map** 12 E3.
C *(212) 903-9765.* **M** *57th St,
59th St.* **Museum** ○ *11am–4:30pm
daily & after concerts.* ● *Wed.* Ø
& ♿ ⌂ *See* **Entertainment** *p338.*
W www.carnegiehall.org

FINANCED BY millionaire philanthropist Andrew Carnegie, New York's first great concert hall opened in 1891 in what was then a suburb of the city. The terra-cotta and brick Italian Renaissance–style building has among the best acoustics in the world. On opening night, Tchaikovsky was a guest conductor and New York's finest families attended.

Auditorium of the Shubert Theater, built by Henry Herts in 1913

Carnegie Hall offering some of the best acoustics in the world

For many years Carnegie Hall was home to the New York Philharmonic, under such conductors as Arturo Toscanini, Leopold Stokowski, Bruno Walter and Leonard Bernstein. Playing Carnegie Hall quickly became an international symbol of success for both classical and popular musicians.

A campaign led by violinist Isaac Stern in the 1950s saved the site from re-development, and in 1964 it was made a national landmark. Renovation in 1986 brought the bronze balconies and the ornamental plaster back to their original splendor. In 1991, a museum opened next to the first-tier level, telling the story of the first 100 years of "The House that Music Built." In 2003, the Judy and Arthur Zankel Hall re-established the lower level as a performance venue.

Top orchestras and performers from around the world still fill Carnegie Hall, and the corridors are lined with memorabilia of artists who have performed here.

Millionaire Andrew Carnegie

Alwyn Court Apartments ⑱

180 W 58th St. **Map** 12 E3. **M** *57th St.* ⬤ *to the public.*

YOU CAN'T miss it – not with the fanciful crowns, dragons and other French Renaissance-style terra-cotta carvings covering the exterior of this 1909 Harde and Short apartment building. The ground floor has lost its cornice, but the rest of the building is intact, and it's one of a kind in the city.

The façade follows the style of François I, whose symbol, a crowned salamander, can be seen above the entrance to the building.

The interior courtyard features a dazzling display of the illusionistic skills of artist Richard Haas, in which plain walls are transformed into "carved" stonework.

The Salamander on Alwyn Court, the symbol of François I

The flight deck of the *Intrepid* with fighter and spy planes on display

Intrepid Sea-Air-Space Museum ⑲

Pier 86, W 46th St. **Map** 11 A5. 📋 *(212) 245-0072.* **M** *M42, M16, M50.* ⬚ *Apr–Sep: 10am–5pm Mon–Fri; 10am–7pm Sat–Sun and hols; Oct–Mar: 10am–5pm Tue–Sun and hols.* 🎫 📷 W www.intrepidmuseum.org

ON THE *Intrepid*, a World War II US aircraft carrier, exhibits include fighter planes from the 1940s and the A-12, the world's fastest spy plane. The *Growler*, a guided-missile submarine, and the destroyer *Edson* are also open.

The workings of today's super-carriers are traced in Pioneers Hall, while Techno-logies Hall looks at ocean exploration and the rockets of the future. Mission Control offers live coverage of NASA shuttle missions. The museum's newest addition is Concorde.

LOWER MIDTOWN

ROM BEAUX ARTS to Art Deco, this section of midtown boasts some fine architecture. Quiet, residential Murray Hill was named for a country estate that once occupied the site. By the turn of the century, it was home to many of New York's first families, including the financier J.P. Morgan, whose library,

Brass door, Fred F. French Building

now a museum, reveals the grandeur of the age. The commercial pace quickens at 42nd Street, near Grand Central Terminal, where tall office buildings line the streets. However, few of the newer buildings have equaled the Beaux Arts Terminal itself or such Art Deco beauties as the Chrysler Building.

SIGHTS AT A GLANCE

Historic Streets and Buildings
Grand Central Terminal pp154–5 ❷
Home Savings of America ❸
Chanin Building ❹
Chrysler Building ❺
Daily News Building ❻
Tudor City ❼
Helmsley Building ❽
Fred F. French Building ❿
Sniffen Court ⓯

Museums and Galleries
Morgan Library pp162–3 ⓮
Japan Society ⓫

Modern Architecture
MetLife Building ❶
Nos. 1 and 2 United Nations Plaza ❾
United Nations pp158–61 ❿

Churches
Church of the Incarnation ⓭

GETTING THERE
By subway, take the Lexington Avenue 4, 5 or 6 trains to 42nd Street–Grand Central. Buses M15, M101/102, M1, M2, M3 and M4 run along the area's avenues, while the M34 and M42 are the crosstown buses.

Flower box in Sniffen Court

SEE ALSO

- **Street Finder**, maps 9, 12, 13
- **Where to Stay** pp279–80
- **Restaurants** p289

KEY

▨	Street-by-Street map
Ⓜ	Subway station

0 meters   500
0 yards   500

◁ **The stainless-steel–coated spire of the Chrysler Building**

Street by Street: Lower Midtown

A WALK IN THE neighborhood allows you to see an eclectic mix of New York's architectural styles. Step back to appreciate the contours of the tallest skyscrapers, and step inside to experience the many fine interiors, from modern atriums such as those in the Philip Morris Building and Ford Foundation buildings to the ornate details of the Home Savings Bank and the soaring spaces of Grand Central Terminal.

MetLife Building
This skyscraper, built by Pan Am in 1963, towers above Park Avenue. ❶

★ **Grand Central Terminal**
The vast, vaulted interior is a splendid reminder of the heyday of train travel ❷

Grand Central-42nd St. subway (lines S, 4, 5, 6, 7)

The Philip Morris Building is the headquarters of a tobacco company. It houses a branch of the Whitney Museum, which specializes in modern American art.

Chanin Building
Built for self-made real estate mogul Irwin Chanin in the 1920s, this building has a fine Art Deco lobby ❹

STAR SIGHTS

★ **Grand Central Terminal**

★ **Chrysler Building**

★ **Home Savings of America**

★ **Daily News Building**

The Mobil Building has a self-cleaning stainless steel facade that is embossed in geometric patterns to prevent it from warping. It was built in 1955.

Brass door, Home Savings Bank

★ **Home Savings of America**
Formerly the headquarters of the Bowery Savings Bank, this is one of the finest bank buildings in New York. Architects York & Sawyer designed it to resemble a Romanesque palace ❸

Helmsley Building
Straddling Park Avenue between 45th and 46th, its ornate entrance symbolized the wealth of its first occupants, New York Central Railroad. **8**

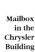

Mailbox in the Chrysler Building

LOCATOR MAP
See Manhattan Map pp12–13

KEY

— — — Suggested route

| 0 meters | 100 |
| 0 yards | 100 |

★ **Chrysler Building**
Ornamented with automotive motifs, this Art Deco delight was built in 1930 for the Chrysler car company **5**

Worker resting during construction of the Chrysler Building

N

The Ford Foundation Building
is the headquarters of Ford's philanthropic arm. It has a lovely interior garden surrounded by a cube-shaped building made of pinkish gray granite, glass and steel.

Ralph J. Bunche Park

E 43RD STREET

42ND STREET

Daily News ★ Building
The Art Deco former home of the news-paper has a revolving globe in the lobby **6**

Tudor City
This 1928 private residential complex has 3,000 apart-ments. Built in the Tudor style, it features fine stone-work details **7**

MetLife Building ●

200 Park Ave. **Map** 13 A5.
Ⓜ *42nd St-Grand Central.*
◯ *office hours.* 🍴 🚻

Lobby of the MetLife Building

Oᴺᴄᴇ, ᴛʜᴇ ꜱᴄᴜʟᴘᴛᴜʀᴇꜱ atop the Grand Central Terminal stood out against the sky. Then this colossus, formerly called the Pan Am Building and designed by Walter Gropius, Emery Roth and Sons and Pietro Belluschi, rose up in 1963 to block the Park Avenue view. It dwarfed the terminal and aroused universal dislike. At the time it was the largest commercial building in the world, and the dismay over its scale helped thwart a later plan to build a tower over the terminal itself.

It is ironic that the New York skies were blocked by Pan Am, a company that had opened up the skies as a means of travel for millions of people. When the company began in 1927, Charles Lindbergh, fresh from his solo trans-atlantic flight, was one of their pilots and an adviser on new routes. By 1936, Pan Am managed to introduce the first trans-Pacific passenger route, and in 1947 they introduced the first round-the-world route.

The building's famous roof-top heliport was abandoned in 1977 after a freak accident showered debris on to the surrounding streets. Now Pan Am itself has gone, too, and in 1981 the entire building was sold to the Metropolitan Life organization.

Grand Central Terminal ●

See pp154–5.

Home Savings of America ●

110 E 42nd St. **Map** 9 A1.
Ⓜ *42nd St-Grand Central.* ◯ *banking hours.*

Mᴀɴʏ ᴄᴏɴꜱɪᴅᴇʀ this 1923 building the best work of the best bank architects of the 1920s. York & Sawyer chose the style of a Romanesque basilica for the uptown offices of the venerable Bowery Savings Bank (now Home Savings of America). An arched entry leads into the vast banking room, with a high beamed ceiling, marble mosaic floors and marble columns that support the stone arches that soar overhead.

Façade of Home Savings of America building

Between the columns are unpolished mosaic panels of marble from France and Italy. The rich detailing includes symbolic animal motifs, such as a squirrel representing thrift and a lion for power.

Chanin Building ●

122 E 42nd St. **Map** 9 A1.
Ⓜ *42nd St-Grand Central.*
◯ *office hours.*

Stonework detail on the Chanin Building

Oɴᴄᴇ ᴛʜᴇ headquarters of Irwin S. Chanin, one of New York's leading real estate developers, the 56-story tower was the first skyscraper in the Grand Central area, a harbinger of things to come. It was designed by Sloan & Robertson in 1929 and is one of the best examples of the Art Deco period. A wide bronze band, patterned with birds and fish, runs the full length of the facade; the terra-cotta base is decorated with a luxuriant tangle of stylized leaves and flowers. Inside, Radio City's sculptor René Chambellan worked on the reliefs and the bronze grills, elevator doors, mailboxes, clocks and pattern of waves in the floor. The vestibule reliefs chart the career of Chanin, who was a self-made man.

Carved detail in the banking hall of Home Savings of America

Chrysler Building ❺

405 Lexington Ave. **Map** 9 A1.
☎ (212) 682-3070. Ⓜ 42nd St-
Grand Central. ◯ office hours,
lobby only. 📷 ♿

**Stainless steel
gargoyle on the
Chrysler Building**

Walter P. Chrysler began
his career in a Union
Pacific Railroad machine
shop, but his passion for the
motor car helped him
rise swiftly to the top
of the new industry,
to found, in 1925, the
corporation bearing
his name. His wish for
a headquarters in New
York that symbolized
his company led to a
building that will
always be linked with
the golden age of
motoring. Following
Chrysler's wishes, the
stainless-steel Art
Deco spire resembles
a car radiator grill; the
building's series of
stepped setbacks are
emblazoned with
winged radiator caps,
wheels and stylized
automobiles; and there
are gargoyles modeled
on hood ornaments
from the 1929
Chrysler Plymouth.

It stands at 1,046ft
(320 m) but it lost the
title of tallest building
in the world to the
Empire State Building
a few months after its
completion in 1930.
William Van Alen's
77-story Chrysler Building and
its shining crown are still
among the city's best-known
and most-loved landmarks.

The crowning spire was
kept a secret until the last
moment, when, having been

built in the fire shaft, it was
raised into position through
the roof, ensuring that the
building would be higher
than the Bank of Manhattan,
then just completed down-
town by Van Alen's great
rival, H. Craig
Severance.

Van Alen was
poorly rewarded
for his labors.
Chrysler accused him
of accepting bribes from
contractors and refused to
pay him. Van Alen's career
never recovered from the slur.

The stunning lobby, once
used as a showroom for
Chrysler cars, was perfectly
restored in 1978. It is lavishly
decorated with patterned
marbles and granite from
around the world and has
chromed steel trim. A vast
painted ceiling by Edward

Elevator door at the Chrysler Building

Trumball shows transportation scenes of the late 1920s.

Although the Chrysler Corporation never occupied the
building as their headquarters,
their name remains, as firm a
fixture as the gargoyles.

Entrance to the News Building

Daily News Building ❻

220 E 42nd St. **Map** 9 B1.
Ⓜ 42nd St-Grand Central.
◯ 8am–6pm Mon–Fri.

The *Daily News* was founded
in 1919, and by 1925 it
was a million-seller. It was
known, rather scathingly, as
"the servant girl's bible," for
its concentration on scandals,
celebrities and murders, its
readable style and heavy use
of illustration. Over the years
it has stuck to what it does
best, and the formula paid off
handsomely. It revealed
stories such as the romance of
Edward VIII and Mrs.
Simpson, and has become
renowned for its punchy
headlines that sum up the
mood of the moment. Its
circulation figures are still
among the highest in the
United States.

Its headquarters, designed by
Raymond Hood in 1930, has
rows of brown and black brick
alternating with windows to
create a vertical striped effect.
Hood's lobby is familiar to
many as that of the *Daily
Planet* in the 1980s *Superman*
movies. It includes the world's
largest interior globe, and
bronze lines on the floor
indicate the direction of world
cities and the position of the
planets. At night, the intricate
detail over the front entrance of
the building is lit from within
by neon. The newspaper's
offices are now on West 33rd
Street, and the future of the
building is in some doubt.

Grand Central Terminal ❷

IN 1871 CORNELIUS VANDERBILT opened a railway station on 42nd Street. Although often revamped, it was never large enough and was finally demolished. The present station opened in 1913. This Beaux Arts gem has been a gateway to and symbol of the city ever since. Its glory is the soaring main concourse and the way it separates pedestrian and train traffic. The building has a steel frame covered with plaster and marble. Reed & Stern were in charge of the logistical planning; Warren & Wetmore for the overall design. The restoration by architects Beyer Blinder Belle is awesome.

42nd Street colonnaded facade

Statuary on the 42nd Street Facade
Jules-Alexis Coutans sculptures of Mercury, Hercules and Minerva crown the main entrance.

Main Concourse Level

Circumferential Road

Subway

Cornelius Vanderbilt
The railroad magnate was known as the "Commodore."

Commuters use the terminal. Half a million people pass through it each day. An escalator leads up into the MetLife Building, where there are specialty shops and restaurants.

Vanderbilt Hall, adjacent to the Main Concourse, is a good example of Beaux Arts architecture. It is decorated with gold chandeliers and pink marble.

STAR SIGHTS

★ **Grand Staircases**

★ **Main Concourse**

★ **Central Information**

Grand Central Oyster Bar
This popular spot (see p301), with its yellow Guastavino tiles, is one of the many eateries in the station. The dining concourse is enormous, with food, snacks, and drinks to suit all tastes.

VISITORS' CHECKLIST

E 42nd St at Park Ave. **Map** 13 A5.
(212) 532-4900. M *4, 5, 6,
7, S to Grand Central.* M1–5,
*M42, M98, M101, M102, M104,
Q32.* 5:30am–1:30am daily.
Wed 12:30pm (free).
935-3960. Fri 12:30pm
(free). *697-1245.*
Baggage check; lost & found.
W www.grandcentralterminal.com

★ Main Concourse

This vast pedestrian area
with its high vaulted ceiling
is dominated by three
great arched
windows, 75 ft
(23 m) high on
each side.

Vaulted Ceiling

A medieval manu-
script provided the
basis for French artist
Paul Helleu's zodiac
design containing
over 2,500 stars.
Lights pinpoint the
major constellations.

The Lower Level
is linked to the other
levels by stairways,
ramps and brand
new escalators.

★ Grand Staircase

There are now two of
these double flights
of marble steps, styled
after the staircase in
Paris' Opera House,
and a vivid reminder
of the glamorous days
of early rail travel.

★ Central Information

This four-faced clock tops the
travel information booth on
the main concourse.

Tudor City ⓱

E. 42nd St. **Map** 9 B1.
Ⓜ 42nd St-Grand Central.
ⓦ www.tudorcity.com

THIS EARLY URBAN renewal
effort, developed between
1925 and 1928 by the Fred
F. French Company, was
designed as a middle-class
city within the city. Rents
were modest, thanks to the
"large-scale production." There
are 12 buildings containing
3,000 apartments, a hotel,
shops, restaurants, a post office
and two small private parks, all
built in the Tudor Gothic style.

In the mid-19th century the
area was the haunt of gangs
and criminals and was known
as Corcoran's Roost, after
Paddy Corcoran, the leader of
the notorious "Rag Gang." The
East River shore was lined
with glue factories, slaughter-
houses, breweries and a
gasworks. Some were still
there when Tudor City was
planned, so its buildings have
only a few outward-facing
windows from which residents
might enjoy what is
now a great view
of the river.

Upper stories of Tudor City

Helmsley Building ⓲

230 Park Ave. **Map** 13 A5.
Ⓜ 42nd St-Grand Central. ◯ office
hours.

ONE OF THE GREAT New
York views looks south
down Park Avenue to the
Helmsley Building straddling
the busy traffic flow beneath.
There is just one flaw – the
monolithic MetLife Building
(which was built by Pan Am
as its corporate headquarters

Performance at the Japan Society

in 1963) that towers behind it,
replacing the building's
former backdrop, the sky.

Built by Warren & Whetmore
in 1929, the Helmsley Building
was originally the headquarters
of the New York Central Railroad Company. Its current
owner is Leona Helmsley,
wife of the late
Harry Helmsley, a
billionaire who
began his career
as a New York
office boy for
$12 per week.
Leona was a
prominent
feature in all the
advertise-
ments for
their hotel
chain – until her imprisonment in 1989 for tax evasion
on a grand scale. Many
observers believe that the
extravagant glitter of the
building's face-lift is due to
Leona's over-blown
taste in decor.

1 & 2 United Nations Plaza ⓳

Map 13 B5. Ⓜ 42nd St-
Grand Central.

THESE TWO
GREAT columns
of lovely blue-
green mirrored
glass are set at an
angle to each other;
the play of light and reflections
on their gleaming sides and
sloping setbacks make them
seem an ever-changing,
giant work of modern art.
The marble and mirrored
interiors are also stunning.
They house streamlined
modern offices and, in
No. 1, the Millennium
United Nations
Plaza Hotel.
Here, the
guest list
frequently includes many UN
delegates from all over the
world as well as a number of
visiting heads of state. Even
the stresses of international
diplomacy must ease when
one is floating lazily in the
glassed-in swimming pool,
enjoying the bird's-eye views
of the city and the United
Nations itself.

United Nations ⓴

See pp158–61.

Japan Society ㉑

333 E 47th St. **Map** 13 B5.
Ⓒ (212) 832-1155. Ⓜ 42nd St-
Grand Central. **Gallery** ◯ 11am–
6pm Tue–Sun. Ⓩ ☒ Ⓩ
ⓦ www.japansociety.org

THE HEADQUARTERS of the
Japan Society, founded in
1907 to foster understanding
and cultural exchange
between Japan and the
US, was under-
written by
John D.
Rockefeller

Roman gods reclining against the Helmsley Building clock

III at a cost of some $4.3 million. The striking black building with its delicate sun grilles was designed by Tokyo architects Junzo Yoshimura and George Shimamoto in 1971. It includes an auditorium, a language center, a research library, a museum gallery and serene, traditional Oriental gardens.

Changing exhibits include a variety of Japanese arts, from swords to kimonos to scrolls. The society offers programs of Japanese performing arts, lectures, language classes and many business workshops for American and Japanese executives and managers.

Fred F. French Building ⑫

521 5th Ave. **Map** 12 F5.
Ⓜ *42nd St-Grand Central.*
◯ *office hours.*

Built in 1927 to house the best-known real estate firm of the day, this is a fabulously opulent creation. It was designed by French's chief architect, H. Douglas Ives, in collaboration with Sloan & Robertson, whose

Lobby of the Fred F. French Building

Tiffany stained-glass window in the Church of the Incarnation

other work included the Chanin Building *(see p152)*. They handsomely blended Near Eastern, ancient Egyptian and Greek styles with early Art Deco forms.

Multicolored faïence ornaments decorate the upper facade, and the water tower is hidden in a false top level of the building. Its disguise is an elaborate one, with reliefs showing a rising sun flanked by griffins and bees and symbols of virtues such as integrity and industry. Winged Assyrian beasts ride on a bronze frieze over the entrance. These exotic themes continue into the vaulted lobby, with its elaborate polychrome ceiling decoration and 25 gilt-bronze doors.

This was the first building project to employ members of the Native Canadian Caughnawaga tribe as construction workers. They did not fear heights and soon became highly sought-after scaffolders for many of the city's most famous skyscrapers.

Church of the Incarnation ⑬

209 Madison Ave. **Map** 9 A2. Ⓒ *(212) 689-6350.* Ⓜ *42nd St-Grand Central, 33rd St.* ◯ *11:30am–2pm Mon–Wed, Fri (also 5–7:30pm Wed), 8am–1pm Sun.* ✝ *8:30am, 11am Sun.* ◉ & *By appointment.* ⬛ Ⓦ *www.churchoftheincarnation.org*

This episcopal church and parish house date from 1864, when Madison Avenue was home to the elite. Its patterned sandstone and brownstone exterior is representative of the period.

The interior has an oak communion rail by Daniel Chester French; a chancel mural, *Adoration of the Magi,* by John La Farge; and stained-glass windows by La Farge, Tiffany, William Morris and Edward Burne-Jones.

Morgan Library ⑭

See pp162–3.

Sniffen Court ⑮

150–158 E 36th St. **Map** 9 A2.
Ⓜ *33rd St.*

Here is a delightful, intimate courtyard of ten brick Romanesque revival carriage houses, built by John Sniffen in the 1850s.

They are perfectly and improbably preserved off a busy block in modern New York. The house at the south end was used as a studio by the American sculptor Malvina Hoffman, whose plaques of Greek horsemen decorate the exterior wall.

Malvina Hoffman's studio

United Nations

F OUNDED IN 1945 near the end of World War II with 51 members, the United Nations now numbers 189 nations. Its aims are to preserve world peace, promote self-determination and to aid economic and social well-being around the globe. New York was chosen as the UN headquarters, and John D. Rockefeller, Jr. donated $8.5 million for the purchase of the East River site. The chief architect was American Wallace Harrison, who worked with an international Board of Design Consultants. The 18-acre (7-ha) site is not on US territory. It is an international zone and has its own stamps and post office. Daily guided tours show visitors the various council chambers and General Assembly hall.

**Flag of the
United Nations**

**United Nations
headquarters**

**Secretariat
building**

The Conference Building houses meeting rooms for the Security Council, the Trusteeship Council and the Economic and Social Council.

**Trusteeship
Council**

★ **Security Council**
*Delegates and their
assistants confer around
the horseshoe-shaped
table while verbatim
reporters and other UN
staff members sit at the
long table in the center.*

**Economic
and Social
Council**

★ **Peace Bell**
*Cast from the coins of
60 nations, this gift
from Japan hangs on a
cypress pagoda shaped
like a Shinto shrine.*

Rose Garden
*Twenty-five varieties of roses
adorn the manicured
gardens on the East River.*

STAR FEATURES

★ **General Assembly**

★ **Security Council**

★ **Peace Bell**

★ **Reclining Figure**

★ **Reclining Figure** *(1982)*
This bronze statue was a gift from the Henry Moore Foundation.

VISITORS' CHECKLIST

1st Ave at 46th St. **Map** 13 C5.
(212) 963-8687. 4, 5, 6, 7 and
S to 42nd St-Grand Central Station.
M15, M27, M42, M104.
Mar–Dec: 9:30am–4:45pm Mon–
Fri, 10am–4:30pm Sat–Sun; Jan–
Feb: Mon–Fri. Jan 1, Thanksgiving, Dec 25 (limited hours during
year-end hols). for tours.
in 17 languages. **Lectures,
films.** www.un.org

Colors of the World
Flags of member nations fly in front of the UN complex.

General ★ Assembly
This is the only UN organ in which all member states are represented. One regular, three-month session is held each year.

Non-Violence *(1988)*
Luxembourg donated this peace sculpture by Karl Fredrik Reutersward.

The statue of peace was a gift from Yugoslavia.

Visitors' entrance

Let Us Beat Swords Into Plowshares
This bronze statue (1958) by Soviet sculptor Evgeny Vuchetich symbolizes the main goal of the United Nations.

The Work of the United Nations

THE GOALS of the United Nations are pursued by three UN councils and a General Assembly comprising all member nations. The Secretariat carries out the administrative work of the organization. Guided tours allow visitors to see the Security Council Chamber and General Assembly Hall.

Secretary General

Translators interpret debates in Arabic, Chinese, French, Russian, Spanish or English.

Reporters

Nation delegates sit in alphabetical order by country, but who sits at the front is decided before every session by drawing lots.

Public gallery

Public entrance

GENERAL ASSEMBLY HALL

GENERAL ASSEMBLY

THE GENERAL ASSEMBLY is the governing body of the UN and has regular sessions each year from mid-September to mid-December. Special sessions are also held when the Security Council or a majority of members request one. All member states are represented with an equal vote, regardless of size. The General Assembly may discuss any international problem raised by the members or by other UN bodies. Although it cannot enact laws, recommendations strongly influence world opinion; these require a two-thirds majority vote.

Lots are drawn before each session to determine the seating in the chamber for the delegations. All 1,898 seats in the chamber are equipped with earphones that offer simultaneous translations in

Foucault's Pendulum (Holland); its slowly rotating swing is proof of the earth's rotation on its axis

several languages. The General Assembly also appoints the Secretary General (on the recommendation of the Security Council), approves the UN budgets and elects the non-permanent members of the Councils. Together with the Security Council, it also appoints the judges of the International Court of Justice, based in the Netherlands.

SECURITY COUNCIL

THE MOST POWERFUL part of the UN is the Security Council. It strives to achieve

Mural symbolizing peace and freedom by Per Krohg (Norway)

international peace and security and intervenes in crises such as the fighting in Kuwait, the former Yugoslavia and Kosovo. It is the only body whose decisions member states are obliged to obey as well as the only one in continuous session.

Five of its members – China, France, the Russian Federation, the United Kingdom and the United States – are permanent. The other nations are elected by the General Assembly to serve two-year terms.

When international conflicts arise, the Council first tries to seek agreement by mediation. If fighting breaks out, it may issue cease-fire orders and impose military or economic sanctions. It could also decide to send UN peace-keeping missions into troubled areas to separate opposing factions until issues can be resolved through diplomatic channels.

Military intervention is the Council's last resort. UN forces may be deployed, and peace-keeping forces are resident in such places as Cyprus and the Middle East.

TRUSTEESHIP COUNCIL

THE SMALLEST OF the councils, this is the only UN body whose workload is decreasing. The council was established in 1945 with the goal of fostering peaceful independence for non–self-governing territories or colonies. Since then, more than 80 colonies have gained self-rule, and the number of people living in dependent territories has been reduced from 750 million to about 3 million. The council currently consists of the five permanent members of the Security Council.

Zanetti mural (Dominican Republic) in the Conference Building depicting the struggle for peace

plays a key role as a spokes-person in the organization's peace-keeping efforts. The Secretary General is appointed by the General Assembly for a five-year term.

IMPORTANT EVENTS IN UN HISTORY

Soviet premier Krushchev speaking to the General Assembly in 1960

W ITH NO PERMANENT police force to deal with disputes, the UN depends on voluntary compliance and

military support from members. As a result, it has had successes and failures in its efforts to keep the peace. In 1948, the UN declared South Korea the legitimate government of Korea; two years later, it played a leading role in defending South Korea against North Korea. In 1949, the UN helped negotiate a cease-fire between Indonesia and the Netherlands and set up a conference that led to the Dutch granting independence to Indonesia, returning in 2002 to supervise elections in East Timor.

In 1964 a UN military force was sent to Cyprus to keep peace between the Greeks and Turks, and still remains. Persistent problems in the Middle East have kept UN forces in the area since 1974, the year that the People's Republic of China – long refused membership in favor of Taiwan – gained UN membership. In the 1990s the UN was heavily involved in the break-up of Yugoslavia.

At any given time there are more than half a dozen UN peacekeeping and observer missions active somewhere in the world. The organisation was awarded the Nobel Peace Prize in 1988 and in 2001.

Trusteeship Council Chamber

ECONOMIC AND SOCIAL COUNCIL

T HE 54 MEMBERS OF this Council work to improve the standard of living and social welfare around the world, goals that consume 80% of the UN's resources. It makes recommendations to the General Assembly, to each member nation and to the UN's specialized agencies. The Council is assisted by com-missions dealing with regional economic problems, human rights abuses, population, narcotics and women's rights. It also works with the Inter-national Labor Organization, the World Health Organization, UNICEF and other global welfare organizations.

SECRETARIAT

A N INTERNATIONAL STAFF of 16,000 works for the Secretariat to carry out the day-to-day work of the United Nations, providing services to all UN councils, commissions and agencies. The Secretariat is headed by the Secretary General, who

WORKS OF ART AT THE UN

The UN Building has acquired numerous works of art and reproductions by major artists; many have been gifts from member nations. Most of them have either a peace or inter-national friendship theme. The legend on Norman Rockwell's *The Golden Rule* reads "Do unto others as you would have them do unto you." Marc Chagall designed a large stained-glass window as a memorial to former Secretary General Dag Hammarskjöld, who was accidentally killed while on a peace mission in 1961. There is a Henry Moore sculpture in the grounds (currently closed) and many other sculptures and paintings by the artists of many nations.

The Golden Rule (1985), a large mosaic by Norman Rockwell

Morgan Library ⑭

T HE MORGAN LIBRARY is closed until 2006 due to an expansion program. The collection, accumulated by banker Pierpont Morgan, is housed in a magnificent palazzo-style 1902 building by architects McKim, Mead & White. Morgan's son, J.P. Morgan, Jr., made it a public institution in 1924. One of the world's finest collections of rare manuscripts, prints, books and bindings is on display in a complex that includes the original library and the home of J.P. Morgan, Jr.

Exterior of the original library building

The Song of Los *(1795)*
Mystic poet William Blake designed and engraved this plate for one of his most innovative works.

Morgan House

Main entrance

Gallery

KEY TO FLOOR PLAN

☐ Exhibition space

☐ Non-exhibition space

Gutenberg Bible *(1455)*
Printed on vellum, this volume is one of only eleven surviving copies.

STAR EXHIBITS

★ **The West Room**

★ **The Rotunda**

★ **East Room**

The Nursery Alice
Lewis Carroll's characters are immortalized in John Tenniel's classic illustrations (c. 1865).

LIBRARY GUIDE

Mr. Morgan's Study and the original library contain some of his favorite paintings, objets d'art and rare acquisitions. Changing exhibitions provide visitors access to some of the world's most significant cultural artifacts.

West Room (Mr. Morgan's study)

Mozart's Horn Concerto in E-flat Major

The six surviving leaves of this score are written in different colored inks.

VISITORS' CHECKLIST

29 E. 36th St. **Map** 9 A2.
685-0008. 6 to 33rd St;
4, 5, 6, 7 to Grand Central; B, D,
F, Q to 42nd St. M2, M3, M4

Concerts, lectures, film/video.
www.morganlibrary.org
Due to an expansion
program, the Morgan Library
is closed until 2006.

★ East Room

The walls are lined from floor to ceiling with triple tiers of bookcases. Murals show historical figures and their muses, and signs of the zodiac.

★ The Rotunda (1504)

The entrance foyer of the Library has marble columns and pilasters; the marble floor is modeled on the floor in Villa Pia in the Vatican gardens.

★ The West Room

Renaissance art and an antique, Florentine wooden ceiling adorn this room.

PIERPONT MORGAN

Pierpont Morgan (1837–1913) was not only a leading financier but also one of the great collectors of his time. Rare books and original manuscripts were his passion, and inclusion in his collection was an honor. In 1909, when Morgan requested the donation of the manuscript of *Pudd'nhead Wilson*, Mark Twain responded, "One of my high ambitions is gratified."

UPPER MIDTOWN

U PSCALE NEW YORK in all its diversity is here, in this area of churches, synagogues, clubs, museums, luxury hotels, famous stores, trend-setting skyscrapers and pockets of luxury living. For almost 30 years from 1833, it was home to society names

1946 Cisitalia in the MoMA

such as Astor and Vanderbilt. In the 1950s, architectural history was made when the Lever and Seagram buildings were erected. These first great modern towers marked mid-town Park Avenue's change from a residential street to a prestigious office address.

SIGHTS AT A GLANCE

Historic Streets and Buildings
Villard Houses **10**
General Electric Building **12**
Sutton Place and Beekman Place **18**
Roosevelt Island **19**
Fuller Building **21**

Modern Architecture
Trump Tower **2**
IBM Building **3**
Lever House **14**
Seagram Building **15**
Citigroup Center **16**

Museums and Galleries
Museum of Modern Art (MoMA) pp170–73 **5**
American Craft Museum **6**
American Folk Art Museum **7**

Museum of Television and Radio **8**

Churches and Synagogues
St. Thomas' Church **4**
St. Patrick's Cathedral pp176–7 **9**
St. Bartholomew's Church **11**
Central Synagogue **17**

Landmark Hotels
Waldorf–Astoria **13**
Plaza Hotel **22**

Landmark Stores
Fifth Avenue **1**
Bloomingdale's **20**

[Map of Upper Midtown showing Central Park, Grand Army Plaza, numbered sights, and Roosevelt Island with the East River]

N

SEE ALSO

- *Street Finder*, maps 12, 13–14
- *Where to Stay* pp280–81
- *Restaurants* pp289–90

0 meters	500
0 yards	500

KEY

▢ Street-by-Street map

Ⓜ Subway station

GETTING THERE
Take the Lexington Ave 6 subway to 51st St, the F to 5th Ave, the E and V to 51st St–5th Ave or the N, R or W to 5th Ave. Bus routes are the M15, M101/102 and M1, M2, M3 and M4. Crosstown buses are the M50, M57 and M58.

◁ **View down Fifth Avenue**

Street by Street: Upper Midtown

THE LUXURY STORES that are synonymous with Fifth Avenue first blossomed as society moved on uptown. In 1917, Cartier's acquired the mansion of banker Morton F. Plant in exchange for a string of pearls, setting the style for other retailers to follow. But this stretch of midtown is not simply for shoppers. There are three distinctive museums and an equally diverse assembly of architectural styles to enjoy, too.

Fifth Avenue
Today's carriage rides offer a taste of past elegance ❶

The University Club was built in 1899 as an elite club for gentlemen

American Craft Museum
This is a showcase for crafts – from ceramics to furniture ❻

St. Thomas' Church
Much of the interior carving was designed by sculptor Lee Lawrie ❹

★ Museum of Modern Art
One of the world's finest collections of modern art ❺

Museum of Television and Radio
Exhibitions, seasons of special screenings, live events and a vast library of historic broadcasts are offered at this media museum ❽

Fifth Avenue subway (lines E, V)

Saks Fifth Avenue has offered goods in impeccable taste to generations of New Yorkers. *(See p311.)*

★ St. Patrick's Cathedral
This, the largest Catholic cathedral in the United States, is a magnificent Gothic Revival building ❾

Olympic Tower
combines offices, apartments and a skylit atrium within its sleek walls.

Villard Houses
Five handsome brownstone houses now form part of the New York Palace Hotel ❿

STAR SIGHTS

★ **Museum of Modern Art**

★ **St. Patrick's Cathedral**

Paley Park is a tiny green oasis, known as a "vest-pocket" park.

Trump Tower
Donald Trump's tower houses many expensive shops **2**

IBM Building
A restful atrium is to be found at the base of this polished black granite building **3**

Sony Building has a very distinctive "chippendale" top.

Lever House
This building is one of the most prominent "glass-box" buildings in New York **14**

N

Park Avenue Plaza
is a bulky glass prism containing an airy atrium.

Racquet Club, a Renaissance palazzo–style building, provides squash and tennis courts for its members.

St. Bartholomew's Church
A Byzantine dome sets this place apart from other midtown churches **11**

M
51st Street subway (line 6)

LOCATOR MAP
See Manhattan Map pp12–13

KEY

– – – Suggested route

0 meters	100
0 yards	100

Tiffany & Company is renowned for its discreet luxury. The store contains many precious jewels. *(See p321.)*

General Electric Building
The spiky pinnacle of this building, built in 1931, is meant to symbolize electrical waves **12**

Waldorf-Astoria
Old-world elegance has attracted many famous guests to this hotel, including the late Duke and Duchess of Windsor **13**

Window display at Bergdorf Goodman *(see p311)*

Fifth Avenue ❶

Map 4 E1–16 F1. **M** *5th Ave-53rd St.*

IN 1883, WHEN William Henry Vanderbilt built his mansion at Fifth Avenue and 51st Street, he started a trend that resulted in palatial residences stretching as far as Central Park, built for top families such as the Astors, Belmonts and Goulds. Only a few remain to attest to the grandeur of the era.

One of these is the Cartier store at 651 Fifth Avenue, originally the home of Morton F. Plant, millionaire and commodore of the New York Yacht Club. As retailers swept north up the avenue – a trend that began in 1906 – society gradually moved to better locations uptown. In 1917, Plant moved to a new mansion at 86th Street, and legend has it that he traded his old home to Pierre Cartier for a perfectly matched string of pearls.

Fifth Avenue has been synonymous with luxury goods ever since. From Cartier at 52nd Street to Tiffany and Berg-dorf Goodman at 57th, you will find a range of famous brands symbolizing wealth and social standing today, just as Vanderbilt and Astor did more than a century ago.

Trump Tower ❷

725 5th Ave. **Map** 12 F3. **℃** *(212) 832-2000.* **M** *5th Ave-53rd St.* **Garden level, shops** ◯ *10am–6pm Mon–Sat, noon–5pm Sun.* **Building** ◯ *10am–7pm daily. See **History** p31.* ◙ ♿ **Concerts.** ▮▮ ▯ ▯ ▯
W www.trumponline.com

A GLITTERING, exorbitantly expensive apartment and office tower rises above a lavish six-story atrium with layers of exclusive shops and cafés. Designed in 1983 by Der Scutt of Swanke, Hayden, Connell & Partners, the public space has pink marble, a waterfall, mirrors and glitz. It is the most opulent example of the trend toward vertical shopping centers. The tower is a flamboyant monument to affluence by the developer Donald Trump, a symbol of the excesses of the 1980s. Next door, 727 Fifth Avenue is a complete contrast: the location of Tiffany & Co., the prestigious jewelers founded in 1837. Famed for exquisite window displays, the store uses understated but elegant blue packaging as a status symbol in itself. Tiffany's was immortalized by Truman Capote's 1958 novel *Breakfast at Tiffany's.*

Interior of the Trump Tower atrium

Entrance to Tiffany and Co., the exclusive jewelry emporium

IBM Building ❸

580 Madison Ave. **Map** 12 F3. **℃** *(212) 745-3500.* **M** *5th Ave.* **Garden Plaza** ◯ *8am–10pm daily.* ◙ ♿ **Newseum/NY** **℃** *317-7503.* ◯ *10am– 5:30pm Mon–Sat.* W www.newseum.org

THIS 43-STORY tower was designed by Edward Larrabee Barnes. Completed in 1983, it is a sleek, five-sided prism of gray-green polished granite, with a cantilevered corner at 57th Street. The Garden Plaza is open to the public. Near the atrium is a work by American sculptor Michael Heizer, entitled *Levitated Mass.* Inside a low, stain-less steel tank is a huge slab of granite which seems to float on air while beneath it, a sheet of water flows.

A new photo-journalism gallery, Newseum/NY, features exhibits, films, and lectures designed to further the public's under-standing of First Amendment issues and journalism.

St. Thomas' Church ❹

1 W 53rd St. **Map** 12 F4. ⚹ *(212) 757-7013.* Ⓜ *5th Ave–53rd St.* ⚬ *7am–6pm daily.* ✝ *frequent.* ⚹ ♿ ⚹ *after 11am service & concerts* Ⓦ *www.saintthomaschurch.org*

THIS IS THE FOURTH home for this parish and the second on this site. Today's church was built between 1909 and 1914 to replace an earlier structure destroyed in a fire in 1905. The previous building had provided the setting for most of the glittering high society weddings of the late 19th century. The most lavish of these was in 1895 when heiress Consuela Vanderbilt married the English duke of Marlborough.

The limestone building, in French–Gothic style, has a single asymmetrical tower and an off-center nave, novel solutions to the architectural problems posed by its corner position. The richly carved, shimmering white screens behind the altar were designed by architect Bertram Goodhue and sculptor Lee Lawrie. Carvings in the choir stalls, dating from the 1920s, include modern inventions such as the telephone, Presidents Roosevelt and Wilson, and Lee Lawrie himself.

Silver chalice at the Craft Museum

Museum of Modern Art ❺

See pp170–73.

American Craft Museum ❻

40 W 53rd St. **Map** 12 F4. ⚹ *(212) 956-3535.* Ⓜ *5th Ave–53rd St.* ⚬ *10am–6pm Fri–Wed, 10am–8pm Thu.* ⚹ ⚹ ♿ ⚹ *Lectures, films.* Ⓦ *www.americancraftmuseum.org*

THERE IS NO BETTER place to experience the vitality of contemporary American crafts than this, the showcase home of the American Crafts Council. On display are handmade quilts, ceramics, glass, textiles, wood, silver, furniture, paper and metalwork drawn from the museum's extensive crafts collection, which date from 1900. Founded in a brownstone on this site in 1956, the museum reopened in 1987 in the three-story atrium of an office tower. The reception desk was designed and carved in maple by James Schneider. The displays are not for sale but the store has excellent items by some wonderful American artists.

American Folk Art Museum ❼

45 W 53rd St. **Map** 12 F4. ⚹ *(212) 265-1040.* Ⓜ *5th Ave–53rd St.* ⚬ *10:30am–5:30pm Wed, Thu, Sat–Sun, 10:30am–7:30pm Fri.* ♿ ⚹ Ⓦ *www.folkartmuseum.org*

THE PERMANENT home for the appreciation and study of American folk art is here, in the first free-standing art museum built in New York since 1966. Designed by the innovative architectural firm of Tod Williams Billie Tsien & Associates and built in 2001, the structure is clad in panels of white tombasil, a white bronze alloy. The museum has 30,000 sq ft (2,787 sq m) of exhibition space on eight levels. The museum still retains the Eva and Morris Feld Gallery at the Lincoln Square location *(see p213).*

Museum of Television and Radio ❽

25 W 52nd St. **Map** 12 F4. ⚹ *(212) 621-6800.* Ⓜ *5th Ave–53rd St.* ⚬ *noon–6pm Tue–Sun (8pm Thu). Theaters and screening rooms close 9pm Fri.* ⚬ *public hols.* ⚹ ⚹ ♿ ⚹ ⚹ Ⓦ *www.mtr.org*

IN THIS one-of-a-kind repository museum, visitors can watch and listen to news and a collection of entertain-

Beatles Paul, Ringo and John on the "Ed Sullivan Show" in 1964

ment and sports documentaries from radio and television's earliest days to the present. Pop fans can see the early Beatles or a young Elvis Presley making his television debut. Sports enthusiasts can relive classic Olympic competitions. World War II footage might be chosen by students of history or by those who lived through the war. Six choices at any one time can be selected from a computer catalogue that covers a library of over 50,000 programs. The selections are then played on small private areas. There are larger screening areas and a theater for 200, where retrospectives of artists, directors and topics are shown. There are also photo exhibits, posters and memorabilia.

The museum was the brainchild of William S. Paley, a former head of the CBS TV network. It opened in 1975 as the Museum of Broadcasting on East 53rd Street. It proved so popular that in 1991 it moved into this hi-tech $50 million home in a building reminiscent of an antique radio set.

1960s television star Lucille Ball

The Museum of Modern Art 🄞

Museum facade on 54th Street

Moma contains one of the world's most comprehensive collections of modern art. Founded in 1929, it set the standard for museums of its kind. Following an expansion program, MoMA in Midtown reopened in 2004. The renovated building provides gallery space over six floors, almost twice that of the old museum. Expanses of glass create abundant natural light, and offer inviting views of the sculpture garden.

Sculpture Garden
The Abby Aldrich Rockefeller Sculpture Garden is a beautiful and restful space.

STAR PAINTINGS

★ **The Starry Night by Vincent Van Gogh**

★ **Les Demoiselles d'Avignon by Pablo Picasso**

Christina's World
(1948) Andrew Wyeth contrasts an overwhelming horizon with the minutely-studied surroundings of his handicapped neighbor.

Bird in Space *(c. 1928)*
Constantin Brancusi's elegant bronze sculpture captures the sheer essence of flight.

GALLERY GUIDE
The sculpture garden is on the first floor. The contemporary art, print, and media galleries are on the second floor. Painting and sculpture are exhibited on the second, fourth, and fifth floors. Architecture and design, photography, and drawings are all on the third floor. Changing exhibitions are displayed on the third and sixth floors. Films are shown on the lower level.

Sculpture garden

First floor

Main entran

Sixth floor

Fifth floor

Fourth floor

Third floor

Second floor

VISITORS' CHECKLIST

11 West 53rd St between Fifth Ave & Avenue of the Americas. **Map** 12 F4. ☎ *(212) 708-9400.* Ⓜ *5th Ave-53rd St.* 🚌 *M1, M2, M3, M4, M27, M50.* ◐ *10:30am–5:30pm, Wed–Mon, 10:30am–8pm Fri.* ● *Tue, Dec 25.* 🔓 Ⓦ www.moma.org

La Clownesse *(1896)*
This is typical of Henri de Toulouse-Lautrec's portraits of Parisian entertainers.

Water Lilies *(c. 1920)*
Claude Monet's late triptych is a vast artwork that creates a glowing, serene environment.

★ **Les Demoiselles d'Avignon**
Pablo Picasso's 1907 portrait of five prostitutes included two male clients in its early drafts. These were later left out to enhance his complex feelings about women.

KEY TO FLOOR PLAN

☐ Contemporary Art
☐ Media
☐ Prints and Illustrated books
☐ Architecture and Design
☐ Drawings
☐ Photography
☐ Paintings and Sculpture
☐ Special exhibitions
☐ Non-exhibition space
☐ Non-accessible space

★ **The Starry Night** *(1889)*
The small size of Vincent Van Gogh's work belies its passion. This turbulent night scene remains one of the most popular paintings in the collection.

Exploring the Collection

THE MUSEUM OF MODERN ART has approximately 100,000 works of art ranging from Post-Impressionist classics to an unrivaled collection of modern and contemporary art, from fine examples of design to early masterpieces of photography and film.

1880s To 1940s
PAINTING AND SCULPTURE

The Persistence of Memory by the Surrealist Salvador Dalí (1931)

PAUL CEZANNE'S monumental *The Bather* and Vincent van Gogh's passionate and transcendent *The Starry Night* are two of the seminal works in the museum's collection of late 19th-century painting. Both Fauvism and Expressionism are well represented with works by Matisse, Derain, Kirchner and others, while Pablo Picasso's *Les Demoiselles d'Avignon* marks a transition to a new style of painting.

The collection also has an unparalleled number of Cubist paintings, providing an overview of a movement that radically challenged our perception of the world. Among the vast range are Picasso's *Girl with a Mandolin*, Georges Braque's *Man with a Guitar* and *Soda*, and *Guitar and Flowers* by Juan Gris. Works by the Futurists, who brought color and movement to Cubism to depict the dynamic modern world, include Gino Severini's *Dynamic Hieroglyphic of the Bal Tabarin* and *Dynamism of a Soccer Player* by Umberto Boccioni, plus works by Balla, Carrà and Villon.

The geometric abstract art of the Constructivists is included in a strong representation of Lissitzky, Malevich and Rodchenko: De Stijl's influence is seen in paintings by Piet Mondrian, such as *Broadway Boogie Woogie*. There is a large body of work by Matisse, such as *Dance I* and *The Red Studio*. Dalí, Miró and Ernst feature among the bizarre, strangely beautiful Surrealist works.

POSTWAR PAINTING AND SCULPTURE

THE EXTENSIVE collection of postwar art includes works by Bacon and Dubuffet, and has a particularly strong representation of American artists. The collection of Abstract Expressionist art, for example, includes Jackson Pollock's *One [Number 31, 1950]*, Willem de Kooning's *Women, I*, Arshile Gorky's *Agony* and *Red, Brown, and*

The Bather, an oil painting by French Impressionist artist Paul Cézanne

Black by Mark Rothko. Other notable works include Jasper Johns' *Flag* and Robert Rauschenberg's *First Landing Jump*, composed of urban refuse, and *Bed*, made of bed linen. The Pop Art collection includes Roy Lichtenstein's *Girl with Ball* and *Drowning Girl*, Andy Warhol's famous *Gold Marilyn Monroe* and Claes Oldenburg's *Giant Soft Fan*.

Works after about 1965 include pieces by Judd, Flavin, Serra and Beuys among many others.

DRAWINGS AND OTHER WORKS ON PAPER

Man with a Hat by Pablo Picasso (1912), in collage and charcoal

MORE THAN 7,000 artworks ranging in size from tiny preparatory pieces to large mural-sized works are among MoMA's holdings. Many drawings use conventional materials, such as pencil, charcoal, pen and ink, pastel, and watercolor. However, there are also collages and mixed-media works composed of paper ephemera, natural products, and man-made goods.

The collection provides an overview of Modernism, from the late 19th century to the present day, including movements such as Cubism, Dadaism, and Surrealism. Drawings by famous and well-established artists, such as Picasso, Miró, and Johns, are exhibited alongside a growing number of works by talented emerging artists.

PRINTS AND ILLUSTRATED BOOKS

American Indian Theme II by Roy Lichtenstein (1980)

ALL SIGNIFICANT art movements from the 1880s onwards are represented in this extensive collection, which provides an overview of printed art. With more than 50,000 items in the department's holdings, there are wide-ranging examples of historical and contemporary printmaking. Works created using traditional techniques (such as lithographs, etchings, screenprints, and woodcuts), are displayed alongside pieces created using more experimental techniques.

There are some particularly fine examples of works by Pablo Picasso, who is widely considered to be the most important printmaker of the 20th century. There are also many illustrations and prints by other artists including Redon, Munch, Matisse, Dubuffet, Johns, Lichtenstein, and Warhol. The works are displayed in the galleries on a rotating basis.

PHOTOGRAPHY

THE PHOTOGRAPHY collection begins with the invention of the medium around 1840. It includes pictures by fine artists, journalists, scientists and entrepreneurs, as well as amateur photographers.

Among the highlights of the collection are some of the best known works by American and European photographers including Atget, Stieglitz, Lange, Arbus, Steichen, Cartier-Bresson and Kertesz. There is also a range of contemporary practitioners,

FILM DEPARTMENT

With a collection of some 10,000 films and four million stills, the collection can offer a wide range of programs, including retrospectives of individual directors and actors, films in specific genres and experimental work, as well as a broad range of other exhibitions. Film conservation is a key part of the department's work. Today's top directors are donating copies of their films to help fund this expensive but vital work.

Film still of Charlie Chaplin and Jackie Coogan in *The Kid* (1921)

most notably Friedlander, Sherman and Nixon.

The photographers have covered an extensive variety of subject matter in both colour and black and white–delicate landscapes, scenes of urban desolation, abstract imagery and stylish portraiture, including some

Sunday on the Banks of the Marne, photographed by Henri Cartier-Bresson in 1939

beautiful silver-gelatin print nudes by the French Surrealist Man Ray. Together, they form a complete history of photographic art and represent one of the finest collections in existence.

ARCHITECTURE AND DESIGN

THE MUSEUM of Modern Art was the first art museum to include utilitarian objects in its collection. These range from household appliances such as stereo equipment, furniture, lighting, textiles and glassware to industrial ball bearings and silicon chips. Architecture is represented in the collection of photographs, scale models, and drawings of buildings that have been or might have been built.

Graphic design is shown in typography and posters. Larger exhibits that look as if they belong in a museum of transportation include Pinin Farina's Cisitalia car and the Bell helicopter.

Reclining rocking chair of steam-bent beech and cane by Gebrüder Thonet (around 1900)

St. Patrick's Cathedral ⑨

See pp176–7.

Villard Houses ⑩

457 Madison Ave (New York Palace Hotel). **Map** 13 A4. **C** *(212) 935-3960.* **M** *51st St.* **Urban Center** ◯ *11am– 5pm Mon–Wed, Fri, Sat.* ◙ ♿ ▢ ⓦ *www.mas.org*

HENRY VILLARD WAS a Bavarian immigrant who became publisher of the *New York Evening Post* and founder of the Northern Pacific Railroad. In 1881, he bought the land opposite St. Patrick's Cathedral and hired McKim, Mead & White to design town houses, one for himself, the rest for sale. The inspired result has six four-story houses built around a central court opening to the street and the church. The south wing was Villard's, but financial difficulties forced him to sell before it was finished.

Ownership passed to the Roman Catholic Archdiocese, but the houses were threatened when the church outgrew its space in the 1970s. The problem was solved when the Helmsley chain purchased air rights for the 51-story Helmsley (now New York) Palace Hotel. The south wing became the formal entrance to the hotel and the grand public rooms of the Villard suite, now restored to their former glory, house French restaurant, Le Cirque 2000. The Urban Center occupies the north wing, and its bookshop is the best place in New York to find architectural books on the city.

Villard Houses, now the entrance to the New York Palace Hotel

St. Bartholomew's Church

St. Bartholomew's Church ⑪

109 E 50th St. **Map** 13 A4. **C** *(212) 378-0200.* **M** *51st St.* ◯ *8am–6pm daily (to 7:30pm Thu & 8:30pm Sun).* ◫ *frequent* ◙ ♿ **Lectures, concerts.** ▢ Ⓨ *after 9 & 11am Sunday services.* ⓦ *www.stbarts.org*

KNOWN FONDLY TO New Yorkers as "St. Bart's," this Byzantine structure with its ornate detail, pinkish brick, open terrace and a polychromed gold dome brought color and variety to Park Avenue in 1919.

Architect Bertram Goodhue incorporated into the design the Romanesque entrance portico created by Stanford White for the original 1903 St. Bartholomew's on Madison Avenue, and marble columns from the earlier church were used in the chapel.

St. Bartholomew's musical programs are well known, their Jazz Nativity being a favorite. They concentrate on classical, choral and organ music.

General Electric Building ⑫

570 Lexington Ave. **Map** 13 A4. **M** *Lexington Ave.* ● *to the public.*

IN 1931 ARCHITECTS Cross & Cross were commissioned to design a skyscraper that would be in keeping with its neighbor, St. Bartholomew's Church. Not an easy task, but the result won unanimous acclaim. The colors were chosen to blend and contrast, and the design of the tower complemented the church's polychrome dome.

The General Electric Building on Lexington Avenue

View the pair from the corner of Park and 50th to see how well it works. However, the General Electric is no mere backdrop but a work of art in its own right and a favorite part of the city skyline. It is an Art Deco gem from its chrome and marble lobby to its spiky "radio waves" crown.

Walk one block north on Lexington Avenue to find a place much cherished by movie fans. It is right at this spot that Marilyn Monroe, in a billowing white frock, stood so memorably in the breeze from the Lexington Avenue subway grating in the movie *The Seven-Year Itch*.

Waldorf–Astoria ⑬

301 Park Ave. **Map** 13 A5. 📞 (212) 355-3000. Ⓜ Lexington Ave, 53rd St. See **Where to Stay** p280
Ⓦ www.waldorf.com

THIS ART DECO classic, which covers an entire city block, was designed by Schultze & Weaver in 1931. The original Hotel at 34th Street was demolished to make way for the Empire State Building.

Winston Churchill and New York philanthropist Grover Whalen at the Waldorf–Astoria in 1946

Still deservedly one of New York's most prestigious hotels, the Waldorf–Astoria serves, too, as a reminder of a more glamorous era in the city's history. The 625-ft (190-m) twin towers, where the Duke and Duchess of Windsor lived, have hosted numerous celebrities, including every US president since 1931. The giant lobby clock, executed for the Chicago World's Fair of 1893, is from the original hotel, and the piano in the Peacock Alley cocktail lounge belonged to Cole Porter when he was a resident of the hotel's exclusive Towers.

Lever House ⑭

390 Park Ave. **Map** 13 A4. 📞 (212) 888-1260. Ⓜ 5th Ave-53rd St. **Lobby and building** ⬤ to the public. Call for additional information.
Ⓦ www.leverhouse.com

IMAGINE A PARK AVENUE lined with sturdy, residential buildings – and then imagine the sensation when they were suddenly reflected here in the first of the city's glass-walled skyscrapers, one of the most influential buildings of the modern era. The design, by

The pool at the Four Seasons in the Seagram Building

Skidmore, Owings & Merrill, is simply two rectangular slabs of stainless steel and glass, one laid horizontally, the other stacked to stand tall above it, to allow light in from every side. The crisp and bright design was intended to symbolize many of the Lever Brothers' products – they make soaps and other cleaning products. Revolutionary though it was in 1952, Lever House is now dwarfed by its many imitators, but its importance as an architectural pacesetter remains undiminished. The new Lever House restaurant is a VIP scene.

Lever House on Park Avenue

Seagram Building ⑮

375 Park Ave. **Map** 13 A4. 📞 (212) 572-7000. Ⓜ 5th Ave-53rd St. ⬤ 9am–5pm Mon–Fri. 🔲 3pm Tue. 🍽

SAMUEL BRONFMAN, the late head of Seagram distillers, was prepared to put up an ordinary commercial building until his architect daughter, Phyllis Lambert, intervened and persuaded him to go to the best – Mies van der Rohe.

The result, which is widely considered the best of the many Modernist buildings of the 1950s, consists of two rectangles of bronze and glass that let the light pour in.

Within is the exclusive Four Seasons Restaurant (see p292), a landmark in its own right. Designer Philip Johnson has created two linked rooms, with the centerpiece of one a pool, and the other a bar that is topped by a quivering Richard Lippold sculpture.

Office workers at lunch in the spacious Citigroup atrium

Citigroup Center ⑯

153 E 53rd St. **Map** 13 A4. Ⓜ 53rd St-Lexington Ave. **Open** 7am–11pm daily. 🍽 🕇 **St. Peter's Lutheran Church** 📞 (212) 935-2200. ⬤ 9am–9pm daily. 🕇 12:15pm Mon–Fri, 6pm Wed, 8:45am & 11am Sun. **Jazz vespers** 5pm Sun. **Concerts** daily except Mon. **Theater at St. Peter's Church** 📞 (212) 239-6200.
Ⓦ www.saintpeters.org

AN ALUMINUM-CLAD spire built on ten-story stilts with a sliced-off roof, Citigroup Center is unique; it caused a sensation when it was completed in 1978. The unusual base design had to incorporate St. Peter's Lutheran Church. The church is separate both in space and design, a granite sculpture below a corner of the tower. Step inside to see the striking interior and the Erol Beker Chapel by sculptor Louise Nevelson. The church is well known for its organ concerts, jazz vespers, and theater presentations. Citigroup's slanting top never functioned as a solar panel as intended, but it is an unmistakable landmark on the skyline.

Saint Patrick's Cathedral ❾

T HE ROMAN CATHOLIC Church originally intended this site for use as a cemetery, but in 1850 Archbishop John Hughes decided to build a cathedral instead. Many thought that it was foolish to build so far beyond the (then) city limits, but Hughes went ahead anyway. Architect James Renwick built New York's finest Gothic Revival building, the largest Catholic cathedral in the United States. The cathedral, which seats 2,500 people, was completed in 1878, though the spires were added from 1885 to 1888.

Fifth Avenue facade

Lady Chapel ★
This chapel honors the Blessed Virgin. The stained-glass windows portray the mysteries of the rosary.

Pièta
American sculptor William O. Partridge created this statue of the Pièta in 1906; it stands at the side of the Lady Chapel.

★ Baldachin
The great baldachin rising over the high altar is made entirely of bronze. Statues of the saints and prophets adorn the four piers supporting the canopy.

STAR FEATURES

★ Baldachin

★ Great Bronze Doors

★ Lady Chapel

★ Great Organ and Rose Window

Cathedral Facade
The exterior wall is built of white marble. The spires rise 330 ft (101 m) above the pavement.

Stations of the Cross
Carved of Caen stone in Holland, these reliefs won first prize in the field of religious art at the Chicago World's Fair in 1893.

VISITORS' CHECKLIST

5th Ave and 50th St.
Map 12 F4. (*(212) 753-2261.*
M *6 to 51st St.; E, F to Fifth Ave.* M1, M2, M3, M4.
○ *7:30am–8:30pm daily.*
✝ *frequent Mon–Sat; 7, 8, 9, 10:15am & 12 noon, 1, 4 & 5:30pm Sun.*
Concerts & lectures.

Shrine of St. Elizabeth Ann Seton
The bronze statue and screen depict the life of the first American to be canonized a saint. She founded the Sisters of Charity (see p76).

Great Organ ★ and Rose Window
Measuring 26 ft (8 m) in diameter, the rose window shines above the great organ, which has more than 7,000 pipes.

Main entrance

Great Bronze Doors ★
The massive doors weigh 20,000 lb (9,000 kg) and are adorned with important religious figures in New York.

Central Synagogue

652 Lexington Ave. **Map** 13 A4.
(212) 838–5122. **M** 51st St, Lexington
Ave. ◆ by appt. ☆ 6pm Fri Jan–Dec,
10.30am Sat (Sep–Jun), 10am Sat (Jul–
Aug). **W** www.centralsynagogue.org

THIS IS NEW YORK'S
oldest building in
continuous use as a
synagogue. It was
designed in 1870 by
Silesian-born Henry
Fernbach, America's
first prominent Jewish
architect. He also
designed some of
SoHo's finest cast-iron
buildings. Now com-
pletely restored after a
1999 fire, the Synagogue
considered the city's
best example of
Moorish-Islamic Revival
architecture. The con-
gregation was originally
founded in 1846 as
Ahawath Chesed (Love
of Mercy) by 18 newly
arrived immigrants,
most of them from
Bohemia, on Ludlow
Street on the Lower
East Side.

The stenciled interior is a
colorful mix of red, blue,
ocher and gilt and was
inspired by Victorian
prints of a Moorish
Palace in Spain
called the
Alhambra.

**Banded
"horseshoe"
arches** are an
Hispano-
Mooresque
design.

The ark holds the
sacred scrolls
of the Jewish Holy
Book, The Torah.

The facade
is an understated
Moorish design in
local brownstone.

The twin towers represent the
two columns that stood outside
Solomon's Temple. The domed
minarets, which rise
122 ft (37 m), are onion-shaped
and made of green copper.

Sutton Place and Beekman Place ⑱

Map 13 C3, 13 C5. **M** 59th St.

SUTTON PLACE IS A posh and
pleasant neighborhood,
delightfully devoid of busy
traffic, made up of elegant
low-rise apartment houses
and town houses designed by
noted architects. The arrival of
New York society in the 1920s
transformed an area that had
once been the province of
factories and tenements.
Three Sutton Square is the
residence of the secretary-
general of the United Nations.

Look beyond Sutton Square
and 59th Street for a glimpse
of Riverview Terrace, a
private street of five ivy-
covered brownstones fronting
on the river. The tiny parks at
the end of 55th Street and
jutting out at 57th Street offer
views of the river and the
Queensboro Bridge.

Smaller than Sutton Place,
and even more tranquil, is
Beekman Place, a virtually
private two-block enclave
of 1920s town houses and
some small-scale apartments.
Famous residents here have
included Gloria Vanderbilt,
Rex Harrison, Irving Berlin
and members of the large
Rockefeller family.

After much neighborhood
opposition, Bridgemarket
opened in 2000. Located
between the huge vaults
under the Queensboro
Bridge, there is an upscale
Terence Conran's for
housewares, two Guastavino's
restaurants, and a Food

**Park at Sutton Place, looking toward Queensboro Bridge and
Roosevelt Island**

Emporium. A fountain-blessed plaza is being considered.

At Turtle Bay Gardens, two rows of brownstone houses dating from the 1860s hide a charming Italianate garden. Among the residents enticed by this privacy have been the film stars Tyrone Power and Katharine Hepburn, composer Stephen Sondheim, and writer E.B. White.

Roosevelt Island ⑲

Map 14 D2. Ⓜ *59th St. Tram, Roosevelt Island station (F).* Ⓦ *www.rioc.com*

Since 1976 a Swiss cable car has offered a quick ride across the East River to Roosevelt Island, with eagle's-eye views of the city and the Queensboro Bridge.

Near the tram station are the remains of the Blackwell farmhouse, which stood from 1796 to 1804 and gave the island its name until the 1920s, when real estate development began. From the 1920s to the 1970s, the island housed a succession of hospitals, an almshouse, a jail, a workhouse and an insane asylum, and became known as Welfare Island.

In 1927, Mae West was held in the penitentiary here for eight days after a "lewd performance." She requested, and got, her silk lingerie to wear under her prison uniform. The ruins of 19th-century hospitals still remain, as does an 1872 lighthouse built by an asylum inmate.

The tram departs from 2nd Avenue at 60th Street and affords a thrilling ride and some fine city views.

Bloomingdale's store sign

Bloomingdale's ⑳

1000 3rd Ave. **Map** 13 A3. Ⓒ *(212) 705-2000.* Ⓜ *59th St.* Ⓞ *10am– 8:30pm Mon–Fri, 10am–7pm Sat, 11am–7pm Sun. See **Shopping** p311.* Ⓦ *www.bloomingdales.com*

For a while in the booming 1980s, "Bloomies" was synonymous with the good life. Founded by Joseph and Lyman Bloomingdale in 1872, this famous department store had a bargain-basement image until the 3rd Avenue El was taken down in the 1960s. Then came the store's transformation to the epitome of trendy, sophisticated shopping. But the late 1980s brought new ownership and eventual bankruptcy. While not as flashy as in the past, Bloomingdale's is open every day and remains one of the city's best-stocked stores. A second store has recently opened in Soho.

Fuller Building ㉑

41 E 57th St. **Map** 13 A3. *Peter Findlay Gallery.* Ⓒ *(212) 644-4433; James Goodman Gallery.* Ⓒ *(212) 583-3737.* Ⓞ *10am–6pm Tue–Sat.* Ⓜ *59th St.*

This slim-towered black, gray and white 1929 beauty by Walker & Gillette is a prime example of geometric Art Deco design. The striking statues on either side of the clock above the entry are by Elie Nadelman. Step inside to see the intricate mosaic tile floors; one panel shows the Fuller Company's

former home in the Flatiron Building. The Fuller Building is a hive of exclusive art galleries, most of which are open to the public daily.

French Renaissance–style facade of the Plaza Hotel

Plaza Hotel ㉒

5th Ave.& Central Park South **Map** 12 F3. Ⓒ *(212) 759-3000.* Ⓜ *59th St. See **Where to Stay** p281.*

The city's grande dame of hotels was designed by Henry J. Hardenbergh, known for the Dakota *(see p216)* and the original Waldorf–Astoria. Completed in 1907 at the exorbitant cost of $12.5 million, the Plaza was proclaimed "the best hotel in the world," with 800 rooms, 500 baths, a two-story ballroom, five marble staircases, and 14- to 17-room apartments for such families as the Vanderbilts and the Goulds *(see p49)*.

The 18-story cast-iron structure resembles a French Renaissance château on a larger scale. Much of the interior decoration came from Europe. The Palm Court still has mirrored walls and Italian carvings of the four seasons as supporting columns.

Former owner Donald Trump restored the hotel's original glitter (too much of it for some) with elaborate new Bavarian glass chandeliers, lush carpet and miles of gold leaf. Public areas have been refurbished without losing their original ambience.

The clock statues above the Fuller Building entrance

UPPER EAST SIDE

AT THE TURN of the century, New York society moved to the Upper East Side – and stayed. Many of the Beaux Arts mansions are now museums and embassies, but the well-to-do still occupy grand apartment buildings on Fifth and Park avenues. Chic shops and galleries line

African urn, Metropolitan Museum of Art

Madison Avenue. Farther east, the area includes what is left of German Yorkville in the East 80s, Hungarian Yorkville to the south and little Bohemia, with its Czech population, below 78th Street. Many of these ethnic groups have left the area, but their churches, restaurants, and shops still remain.

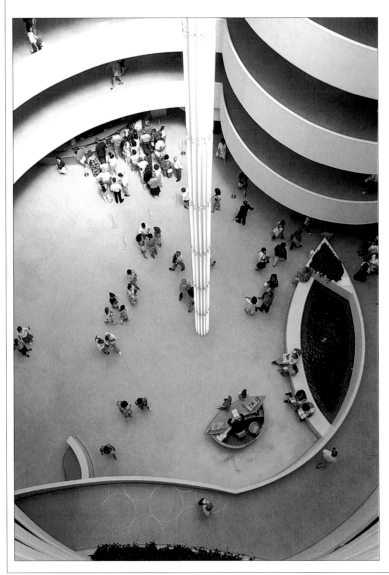

Looking down into the lobby of the Guggenheim Museum

SIGHTS AT A GLANCE

Historic Streets and Buildings

Seventh Regiment Armory ⑩
Henderson Place ⑭
Gracie Mansion ⑯

Museums and Galleries

Neue Galerie New York ①
Jewish Museum ②
Cooper-Hewitt National Design Museum ③
National Academy of Design ④
Solomon R. Guggenheim Museum pp186–87 ⑤
Metropolitan Museum of Art pp188–95 ⑥
Whitney Museum of American Art pp198–99 ⑦
Frick Collection pp200–1 ⑧
Asia Society ⑨
Society of Illustrators ⑫
Mount Vernon Hotel Museum and Garden ⑬
Museum of the City of New York ⑲

Churches and Synagogues

Temple Emanu-El ⑪
Church of the Holy Trinity ⑰
St. Nicholas Russian Orthodox Cathedral ⑱

Parks and Squares

Carl Schurz Park ⑮

GETTING THERE

The Lexington Ave 4 and 5 express trains stop at 59th and 86th streets. The local (No. 6) also stops at 68th, 77th and 96th streets. Buses include: M1, M2, M3 and M4 on Fifth/Madison Aves, M101/102 on Lexington/Third and M15 on First/Second. The crosstown buses are the M66, M72, M79, M86 and M96.

SEE ALSO

• **Street Finder**,
  maps 12–13, 16–17

• **East Side Walk** pp262–63

• **Where to Stay** pp281–82

• **Restaurants** p290

KEY

  Street-by-Street map

Ⓜ Subway station

⛴ Ferry terminal

🚁 Heliport

0 meters   500

0 yards   500

Statue of Diana, National Academy of Design

Street by Street: Museum Mile

Many of New York's museums are clustered on the Upper East Side, in homes ranging from the former Frick and Carnegie mansions to the modernistic Guggenheim, designed by Frank Lloyd Wright. The displays are as varied as the architecture, running the gamut from old masters to photographs to decorative arts. Presiding over the scene is the vast Metropolitan Museum of Art, America's answer to the Louvre. Many of the museums stay open late on Tuesday evenings, and some offer free admission.

Jewish Museum
The most extensive collection of Judaica in the world is housed here. It includes coins, archaeological objects and ceremonial and religious artifacts **2**

Cooper-Hewitt National ★ Design Museum
Ceramics, glass, furniture and textiles are well represented here **3**

The Church of the Heavenly Rest was built in 1929 in the Gothic style. The madonna in the pulpit is by sculptor Malvina Hoffman.

National Academy of Design
The Academy, founded in 1825, moved here in 1940. Its fine collection includes paintings and sculptures by its members **4**

Graham House is an apartment building with a splendid Beaux Arts entrance. It was built in 1892.

★ Solomon R. Guggenheim Museum
Floodlit at dusk, architect Frank Lloyd Wright's building looks purple. It is in the form of a spiral. Take the elevator to the top and walk down to see one of the world's best collections of modern art **5**

STAR SIGHTS

★ Solomon R. Guggenheim Museum

★ Cooper-Hewitt Museum

The facade of the Squadron A Armory is all that remains of the original building. It is now the west wall of the playground of Hunter High School. The school was built to complement the style of the armory.

Public basketball court

To 96th Street subway (2 blocks)

The William G. Loew Mansion (1931), now part of the Spence School, is in the "American Adams" style.

The Synod of Bishops of the Russian Orthodox Church Outside of Russia is housed in a lovely 1918 mansion.

Night Presence IV (1972), a modern work in rusting steel, was created by Louise Nevelson. Some New Yorkers feel it is out of place among its staid, old-fashioned neighbors on Park Avenue.

At **120 and 122 East 92nd Street** are two of the few wooden houses left in Manhattan. Built in 1859 and 1871, respectively, they have a charming Italianate air.

The Marx Brothers spent their boyhoods in a three-bedroom apartment in a modest row house at 179 East 93rd Street.

LOCATOR MAP
See Manhattan Map pp12–13

UPPER WEST SIDE
CENTRAL PARK
East Side
Hell Gate
UPPER EAST SIDE
Roosevelt I.
UPPER MIDTOWN
Queens

KEY

– – – Suggested route

0 meters 100
0 yards 100

Neue Galerie New York ❶

1048 5th Ave at E 86th St. **Map** 16 F3.
🅲 *(212) 628-6200.* Ⓜ *86th St.*
🚌 *M1–4.* ◯ *11am–9pm Fri, 11am–*
6pm Sat–Mon. 🚫 📷 🔓 *Café 9am–*
6pm Mon–Wed, 9am–9pm Thu–Sun.
🎫 ♿ Ⓦ *www.neuegalerie.org*

THIS MUSEUM was founded
by art dealer Serge
Sabarsky and philanthropist
Ronald Lauder. The objective
of this museum is to collect,
research and exhibit the fine
and decorative arts of
Germany and Austria from
the early 20th century.

The Louis XIII-style Beaux-
Arts structure was completed
in 1914 by Carrere & Hastings,
who also designed and built
the New York Public Library.
The building has been
designated a landmark
and is considered to
be one of the most
distinguished build-
ings ever erected on
Fifth Avenue. Once
occupied by Mrs. Cornelius
Vanderbilt III, the mansion
was purchased by Lauder and
Sabarsky in 1994. The ground
floor houses the entrance, a
bookshop, and the Café
Sabarsky, which draws its
inspiration from the Viennese
cafés of old. The second floor
is devoted to the works of
Klimt, Schiele, and Wiener
Werkstätte objects. The upper
floors feature works from Der
Blaue Reiter (artists such as
Klee, Kandinsky), the Bauhaus
(Feininger, Schlemmer) and
Die Brücke (Mies van der
Rohe, Breuer).

Jewish Museum ❷

1109 5th Ave. **Map** 16 F2.
🅲 *(212) 423-3200.* Ⓜ *86th St,*
96th St. ◯ *11am–5:45pm Sun–Wed,*
11am–8pm Thu, 11am–3pm Fri.
● *Sat, public & Jewish hols.*
🚫 📷 ♿ 🔓 ▭ 🎫
Ⓦ *www.jewishmuseum.org*

THE EXQUISITE château-like
residence of Felix M.
Warburg, financier and leader
of the Jewish community, was
designed by C.P.H. Gilbert in
1908. It now houses one of

the world's largest collections
of Jewish fine and ceremonial
art, and historical Judaica. The
stonework in a new extension
is by the stonemasons of St.
John the Divine *(see pp224–5)*.

Objects have been brought
here from all over the world,
some at great risk of persecution to the donors. Covering
4,000 years, artifacts include
Torah crowns, candelabras,
kiddush cups, plates, scrolls
and silver ceremonial objects.

There is a Torah ark from
the Benguiat Collection, the
exquisite faience entrance
wall of a 16th-century Persian
synagogue and the powerful
Holocaust by sculptor George
Segal. Changing exhibitions
reflect Jewish life and
experience around
the world.

19th-century
ewer and basin from Istanbul
at the Jewish Museum

Cooper-Hewitt National Design Museum ❸

2 E 91st St. **Map** 16 F2. 🅲 *(212) 849-*
8400. Ⓜ *86th St, 96th St.* ◯ *10am–*
5pm Tue–Thu (to 9pm Fri & 6pm Sat),
noon–6pm Sun. ● *public hols.* 📷
♿ 📷 🎫 Ⓦ *www.ndm.si.edu*

ONE OF THE largest design
collections in the world,
this museum occupies the
former home of industrialist
Andrew Carnegie. The
collection was amassed by the
Hewitt sisters, Amy, Eleanor
and Sarah. The museum
opened in 1897 at Cooper
Union *(see p118)*; the
Smithsonian Institution acquired the collections in 1967,
and the Carnegie Corporation
offered the mansion.

Carnegie asked for "the most
modest, plainest and most
roomy house in New York,"
but the house set new trends

Cooper-Hewitt Museum entrance

with central heating, private
elevator, and air-conditioning.
Note the wooden staircase,
rich paneling and carving,
and the sunny solarium.

National Academy of Design ❹

1083 5th Ave. **Map** 16 F3. 🅲 *(212)*
369-4880. Ⓜ *86th St.* ◯ *noon–5pm*
Wed–Thu, 11am–6pm Fri–Sun. ● *pub-*
lic hols. 📷 *except 5–6pm Fri.* 🚫 ♿
🎫 Ⓦ *www.nationalacademy.org*

MORE THAN 6,000 paintings,
drawings and sculptures,
including works by Thomas
Eakins, Winslow Homer,
Raphael Soyer and Frank
Lloyd Wright, comprise the
collection of the National
Academy of Design, founded
in 1825 by a group of artists.
The group's mission was
(and is) to train artists and
exhibit their work. In 1940,
Archer Huntington, an art
patron and philanthropist,
donated his house, an
attractive building with
patterned marble floors and
decorative plaster ceilings.
The grand entrance foyer has
a statue of Diana by sculptor
Anna Hyatt Huntington.

Statue of Diana in the National
Academy of Design entrance foyer

Solomon R. Guggenheim Museum **5**

See pp186–7.

Metropolitan Museum of Art **6**

See pp188–95.

Whitney Museum of American Art **7**

See pp198–9.

Frick Collection **8**

See pp200–1.

Asia Society **9**

725 Park Ave. **Map** 13 A1. *(212) 288-6400. Events: 517-NEWS.* **M** *68th St.* ◯ *11am–6pm Tue–Sun, Fri–9pm.* ● *public hols.* ◉ ● *12:30pm Tue–Sat, 6:30pm Fri, 2:30pm Sun.* Ø ● ▯ ▢ ▭ www.asiasociety.org

F̲OUNDED BY John D. Rockefeller III in 1956 to increase understanding of Asian culture, the society is a forum for 30 countries from Japan to Iran, Central Asia to Australia.

The 1981 eight-story building was designed by

South Asian sculpture at the Asia Society

Edward Larrabee Barnes and is made of red granite. After a complete renovation in 2001, the museum has greatly increased gallery space. One gallery is permanently devoted to Rockefeller's own collection of Asian sculptures, amassed by him and his wife on frequent trips to the East.

Changing exhibits show a wide variety of Asian arts, and the society has a full program of films, dance, concerts, and lectures and well-stocked bookshop.

Entrance Hall of the Seventh Regiment Armory

Seventh Regiment Armory **10**

643 Park Ave. **Map** 13 A2. *(212) 452-3067.* **M** *68th St.* ◯ *Mon–Fri by appt only.* ● *public hols.* Ø ● ☑ ▮ *(212) 744-4107.*

F̲ROM THE WAR of 1812 through two world wars, the Seventh Regiment has played a vital role. They were an elite corps of "gentlemen soldiers" from prominent families, and their armory is unlike any other in the US. Within the stern fortresslike exterior are extraordinary rooms filled with lavish furnishings of the Victorian era, objets d'art and regimental memorabilia.

The design by Charles W. Clinton, a veteran of the regiment, had offices facing Park Avenue, with a vast drill hall stretching behind to Lexington Avenue. The reception rooms include the Veterans' Room and the Library by Louis Comfort Tiffany. The drill hall is now the site of the Winter Antiques Show *(see p53)* and a favorite place to hold the city's many charity balls.

Temple Emanu-El **11**

1 E 65th St. **Map** 12 F2. *(212) 744-1400.* **M** *68th St, 60th St.* ◯ *10am–5pm Sun–Fri, 12:30pm–4:45pm Sat (last adm on Fri 3:30pm)* ● *Jewish hols.* ✦ *5:30pm Sun–Thu, 5:15pm Fri, 10:30am Sat.* ◉ ● ☑ ▯ ▭ www.emanuelnyc.org

T̲HIS IMPRESSIVE limestone edifice of 1929 is one of the largest synagogues in the world, seating 2,500 in the main sanctuary alone. It is home to the oldest Reform congregation in New York. Among the many fine details are the bronze grille doors of the Ark, and stained glass showing the Shield of David and the Lion of Judah. The dominant feature of the Fifth Avenue exterior is the great recessed arch enclosing a magnificent wheel window. The Beth-El Chapel is a twin-domed structure with a Byzantine influence.

The synagogue stands on the site of the palatial home of the legendary society hostess Mrs. William Astor. She left her midtown mansion when her nephew, who was feuding with her, built the Waldorf Hotel next door. The formidable Mrs. Astor moved to the Upper East Side, taking society with her, while her son built the Astoria Hotel on the site of her previous home.

The Ark at Temple Emanu-El

The Solomon R. Guggenheim Museum ❺

Home to one of the world's finest collections of modern and contemporary art, the building itself is perhaps the museum's greatest masterpiece. Designed by architect Frank Lloyd Wright, the shell-like façade is a New York landmark. The spiral ramp curves down and inward from the dome, passing works by major 19th-, 20th-, and 21st-century artists. The museum is due to undergo major works to restore the exterior which has been plagued by cracks. The two-year restoration programme will begin in March 2005 and continue over a two year period, during which the museum will remain open.

Fifth Avenue facade

Paris Through the Window
The vibrant colors of Marc Chagall's 1913 masterpiece illumine the canvas, conjuring up images of a magical and mysterious city where nothing is quite what it appears to be.

Small Rotunda

Sculpture terrace

Main entrance

Woman Ironing *(1904)*
A work from Pablo Picasso's Blue Period, this painting is his quintessential image of hard work and fatigue.

Yellow Cow *(1911)*
Franz Marc's work was influenced by a German back-to-nature movement.

Nude *(1917)*
This sleeping figure is typical of Amedeo Modigliani's stylized work.

MUSEUM GUIDE

The Great Rotunda features special exhibitions. The Small Rotunda shows some of the museum's celebrated Impressionist and Post-Impressionist holdings. The new Tower galleries feature exhibitions of work from the permanent collection as well as contemporary pieces. A fifth-floor sculpture terrace overlooks Central Park. Not all of the collection is on display at any one time.

Tower

Great
Rotunda

VISITORS' CHECKLIST

1071 5th Ave at 89th St.
Map 16 F3. 423-3500.
4, 5, 6 to 86th St. M1, M2,
M3, M4. 10am–5:45pm Sat–
Wed, 10am–8pm Fri. Dec 25,
Jan 1. **Concerts,
lectures, performing art series.**
W www.guggenheim.org

Before the Mirror *(1876)
In trying to capture the flavor of 19th-century society, Edouard Manet often used the image of the courtesan.*

Woman Holding a Vase
Fernand Léger incorporated elements of Cubism into this work from 1927.

Black Lines *(1913) This is one of Vasily Kandinsky's earliest examples of his work in "non-objective" art.*

Woman with Yellow Hair
(1931) The gentle, voluptuous figure of Picasso's mistress often appears in his work.

FRANK LLOYD WRIGHT

During his lifetime, Wright was considered the great innovator of American architecture. Characteristic of his work are Prairie-style homes and office buildings of concrete slabs, glass bricks and tubing. Wright received the Guggenheim commission in 1942 and it was completed after his death in 1959, his only New York building.

Interior of the Guggenheim's Great Rotunda

Metropolitan Museum of Art ❻

Founded in 1870 by a group of artists and philanthropists who dreamed of an American arts institution to rival those of Europe, this collection is thought to be the most comprehensive in the Western world. Works date from prehistoric times to the present. The museum opened here in 1880 and houses collections from all continents. Part of the first floor is under renovation, but will reopen in 2007 with a new Roman Court and Etruscan gallery.

The entrance of the Metropolitan Museum of Art

Robert Lehman Collection

★ **Gertrude Stein** (1905–6) *This portrait of the American writer Gertrude Stein is by Pablo Picasso. The masklike face is evidence of his debt to African and Roman art.*

Pendant Mask *The kingdom of Benin (now part of Nigeria) was renowned for its art. This mask was made in the 16th century.*

Seated Man with Harp *This statuette was made in the Cyclades c.3,000 BC.*

GALLERY GUIDE

Most of the collections are housed on the two main floors. Works from 19 curatorial areas are in the permanent galleries, with designated sections for temporary exhibitions. Central on the first and second floors are European painting, sculpture, and decorative art. The Costume Institute is situated on the ground level, directly below the Egyptian galleries on the first floor.

The Marriage Feast at C *This rare 16th-century pa painting by Juan de Flan(is part of the Linsky Colle(*

Bust of Diderot (1773)
Jean Antoine Houdon's bust was made for a Russian count.

★ **Portrait of the Princesse de Broglie**
This portrait, painted in 1853, was J.A.D. Ingres' last.

VISITORS' CHECKLIST

1000 Fifth Ave. **Map** 16 F4.
⌂ *(212) 535-7710.* **Ⓜ** *4, 5, 6 to 86th St.* **🚌** *M1, M2, M3, M4.*
○ *9:30am–5:30pm Sun & Tue–Thu, 9:30am–9pm Fri, Sat.*
● *Jan 1, Thanksgiving, Dec 25.*
Concerts, lectures, film & video presentations.
W www.metmuseum.org

First floor

Stairs to Costume Institute

Main entrance

Byzantine Galleries
This marble panel with a Griffin is from Greece or the Balkans (c.1250). It is just one of the pieces on display in the Byzantine Galleries.

STAR EXHIBITS

★ **Temple of Dendur**

★ **Portrait of the Princesse de Broglie by Ingres**

★ **Gertrude Stein by Pablo Picasso**

★ **Byzantine Galleries**

KEY TO FLOOR PLAN

	European painting, sculpture and decorative arts
	Art of Africa, Oceania, and the Americas
	Modern art
	American art
	Egyptian art
	Greek and Roman art
	Medieval and Byzantine art
	Arms and armor
	Non-exhibition space

English Armor
This was made for Sir George Clifford around 1580.

★ **Temple of Dendur** *(15 BC)*
The Roman emperor Augustus built this three-room temple. He is shown in its reliefs making offerings.

Metropolitan Museum of Art: Upper Levels

Marrakech
This 1964 work is one of Frank Stella's "Moroccan" paintings. Within a square format, fluorescent strips form the painting's main focus.

Sculpture Garden
These modern sculptures, on top of the Modern Art wing, are changed annually.

Card Players *(1890)*
Paul Cézanne departed here from his traditional landscapes, still lifes and portraits to paint this scene of peasants intently playing cards.

Under renovation

First floor

Second floor

★ Cypresses *(1889)*
Vincent Van Gogh painted this the year before he died. The heavy brushstrokes and the swirling style mark his later work.

Eagle-headed Winged Being Pollinating the Sacred Tree *(about 900 BC)*
This relief comes from an Assyrian palace.

STAR EXHIBITS

- ★ **Self-portrait of 1660 by Rembrandt**

- ★ **George Washington Crossing the Delaware by Leutze**

- ★ **Cypresses by Vincent Van Gogh**

- ★ **Diptych by Jan van Eyck**

★ Diptych
(1425–30)
*Flemish painter
Jan van Eyck was
one of the earliest
masters of oil
painting. These
scenes of the
Crucifixion and
Last Judgment
show him to be
a forerunner of
realism, too.*

★ Washington Crossing the Delaware
*In 1851 Emanuel Gottlieb Leutze painted
this romanticized – and inaccurate –
view of the famous crossing.*

KEY TO FLOOR PLAN

- ☐ European painting, sculpture and decorative arts
- ☐ Art of Africa, Oceania and the Americas
- ☐ Ancient Near Eastern and Islamic art
- ☐ Twentieth-century art
- ☐ American art
- ☐ Asian art
- ☐ Greek and Roman art
- ☐ Musical instruments
- ☐ Drawings, prints and photographs
- ☐ Non-exhibition space
- ☐ Special exhibitions

Astor Court

The Death of Socrates *(1787)
Jacques-Louis David shows
Socrates about to take poison
rather than renounce his beliefs.*

★ Self-portrait *(1660)
Rembrandt painted almost
100 self-portraits. This one
shows him at the age of 54.*

THE ASTOR COURT

In 1979, 27 crafts-people from China, responsible for the care of Souzhou's historic gardens, came to New York to repli-cate a Ming-style scholar's garden in the Metropolitan Museum. They used centuries-old techniques and hand-made tools that had been passed down for generations. It was the first cultural exchange between the United States and the People's Republic of China. The result is a quiet garden for meditation, a Western parallel to Souzhou's Garden of the Master of the Fishing Nets.

Exploring the Metropolitan

THE TREASURES OF "THE MET" include a vast collection of American art and more than 2,500 European paintings, including masterpieces by Rembrandt and Vermeer. There are also many Islamic exhibits, plus the greatest collection of Egyptian art outside Cairo.

AFRICA, OCEANIA AND THE AMERICAS

A painted gold funerary mask (10th–14th century) from the necropolis of Batán Grande, Peru

NELSON ROCKEFELLER built the Michael C. Rockefeller Wing in 1982 in memory of his son, who lost his life on an art-finding expedition in New Guinea. The wing showcases a superb collection of over 1,600 objects from Africa, the islands of the Pacific and the Americas.

Among the African works, the ivory and bronze sculptures from the royal kingdom of Benin (Nigeria) are outstanding, as is the wooden sculpture by the Dogon, Bamana and Senufo peoples of Mali. From the Pacific come carvings by the Asmat people of New Guinea and decorations and masks from the Melanesian and Polynesian islands. From Mexico and Central and South America come pre-Columbian gold, ceramics and stonework. The wing also contains fine Native American artifacts by the Inuit and other groups.

AMERICAN ART

GILBERT STUART's first portrait of George Washington, George Caleb Bingham's *Fur Traders Descending the Missouri*, John Singer Sargent's notorious portrait of *Madame X*, and the monumental *Washington Crossing the*

Delaware by Emanuel Leutze are among the icons of the American Wing. It holds one of the world's finest collections of American painting, including several works by Edward Hopper, and sculpture and decorative arts from colonial times to this century.

Period rooms, with original woodwork and furnishings, range from the saloon hall in which George Washington celebrated his last birthday to the elegant prairie-style living room from the Little house in Minnesota, designed by Frank Lloyd Wright in 1912.

Engelhard Court is an indoor sculpture garden with large-scale architectural elements, including the lovely stained-glass and mosaic loggia from Louis Comfort Tiffany's Long Island estate and the facade of an 1824 United States Branch Bank that stood on Wall Street.

The Lighthouse at Two Lights (1929) by Edward Hopper

ANCIENT NEAR EASTERN AND ISLAMIC ART

MASSIVE STONE SCULPTURES of human-headed winged lions, once guardians of the 9th-century BC Assyrian

Mysterious in identity and origin, a rare 5,000-year-old copper head from the Near East

palace of Assurnasirpal II, sit at the entrance to the Ancient Near Eastern galleries. Inside is a collection spanning 8,000 years, rich in Iranian bronzes, Anatolian ivories, Sumerian sculptures, and Achaemenian and Sassanian works in silver and gold. An adjacent gallery area displays the diversity of Islamic art from the 7th to the 19th century; glass and metalwork from Egypt, Syria and Mesopotamia; royal miniatures from the courts of Persia and Mughal India; rugs of the 16th and 17th centuries; and an 18th-century room from Syria.

ARMS AND ARMOR

MOUNTED KNIGHTS in full armor charge at each other across the equestrian court here. These galleries are a favorite with children and anyone moved by medieval romance or thrilled by power.

There are suits of armor, rapiers and sabers with hilts of precious stones and gold, firearms inlaid with ivory and mother-of-pearl, plus colorful heraldic banners and shields.

The pistol of Holy Roman Emperor Charles V (16th century)

Highlights include the armor of gentleman-pirate Sir George Clifford, a favorite of Queen Elizabeth I. The rainbow-colored armor of a 14th-century Japanese shogun and a collection of Wild West revolvers that once belonged to gunmaker Samuel Colt are also exhibited here.

ASIAN ART

The Old Plum, a Japanese paper screen from the early Edo period (about 1650)

MANY OUTSTANDING galleries contain masterpieces of Chinese, Japanese, Korean, Indian and Southeast Asian art, dating from the second millennium BC to the 20th century. A full-scale Ming-style Chinese scholar's garden was built by craftspeople from Souzhou as part of the first cultural exchange between the United States and the People's Republic of China. The museum also has one of the finest collections of Sung and Yuan paintings in the world, Chinese Buddhist monumental sculptures, fine Chinese ceramics and jade and an important display of the arts of ancient China.

The full range of Japanese arts is represented in a breathtaking suite of 11 galleries featuring chronological and thematic displays of Japanese lacquer, ceramics, painting, sculpture, textiles and screens. Indian, Southeast Asian and Korean galleries display superb sculptures and other arts from these regions.

COSTUME INSTITUTE

THERE IS ALWAYS a portion of the 75,000-piece collection of costumes, dating from the 17th century to the present, on display in these new state-of-the-art galleries. Here, the Institute maintains a definitive compendium of fashionable dress, from the elaborately embroidered dresses of the late 1600s to the shocking-pink evening dresses of Elsa Schiaparelli, complete with hats, scarves, gloves, handbags and other accessories. There are also the designs of Worth, Quant and Balenciaga, as well as gowns from the Napoleonic and Victorian eras, the costumes of the Ballets Russes and even David Bowie's sequined jockstrap.

The regional portion of the collection is rich with folk costumes from Europe, Asia, Africa and the Americas.

The Institute is so sophisticated in its understanding of conservation techniques that it has been called upon to advise NASA on the cleaning of astronauts' spacesuits.

A 17th-century European silk-and-satin doublet

DRAWINGS, PRINTS AND PHOTOGRAPHS

A NEW GALLERY regularly displays selections from the museum's incredible holdings of drawings, prints, etchings and photographs. The

Michelangelo's studies of a Libyan Sibyl for the ceiling of the Sistine Chapel (1508)

drawings collection is especially rich in Italian and French art from the 15th to the 19th century. Specific exhibits of the drawings in this collection are shown on a rotating basis because of the light-sensitive nature of works on paper.

Highlights among the 11,000 drawings include works by Michelangelo, Leonardo da Vinci, Raphael, Ingres, Goya, Rubens, Rembrandt, Tiepolo and Seurat.

The encyclopedic print collection of nearly 1.5 million images and the 14,000 illustrated books includes major works by virtually every master printmaker, from an early German woodcut called *Virgin and Child* to some of Dürer's most accomplished works and Goya's *The Giant*. Influential gallery-owner Alfred Stieglitz's donation of his own extensive collection of photographs brought here such gems as Edward Steichen's *The Flatiron*. It formed the core of a photography collection that is now also particularly strong in Modernist works dating from between the world wars.

Ephemera such as posters and advertisements form another part of this collection.

EGYPTIAN ART

O NE OF THE MUSEUM'S finest and best-loved areas is the ancient Egyptian wing, which displays every one of its thousands of holdings – from the prehistoric period to the 8th century AD. Objects range from the fragmented jasper lips of a 15th-century BC queen to the massive Temple of Dendur. Other amazing archaeological finds, most of them from museum-sponsored expeditions undertaken early in the 20th century, include sculptures of the notorious Queen Hatshepsut, who seized the Theban throne in the 16th century BC; 100 carved reliefs of Amenhotpe IV's reign; and tomb figures like the blue faïence hippo that has become the museum's mascot.

Queen Tiye, wife of Amenhotpe III (1417–1379 BC)

EUROPEAN PAINTING, SCULPTURE AND DECORATIVE ARTS

T HE HEART of the museum is its awe-inspiring collection of 3,000 European paintings. The Italian works include

Young Woman with a Water Jug (1660) by Jan Vermeer

Botticelli's *Last Communion of Saint Jerome* and Bronzino's *Portrait of a Young Man*. The Dutch and Flemish canvases are among the finest in the world, with Brueghel's *The Harvesters*, several works by Rubens and Van Dyck, over a dozen Rembrandts and more Vermeers than any other museum. The collection also has masterpieces by Spanish artists El Greco, Velázquez and Goya, and by French artists Poussin and Watteau. Some of the finest Impressionist and Post impressionist canvases reside here: 34 Monets, including *Terrace at Sainte-Adresse*; 18 Cézannes; and Van Gogh's *Cypresses*.
In the Kravis wing and adjacent galleries are works from the 60,000-object collection of European sculpture and decorative arts, such as Tullio Lombardo's marble statue of Adam; a bronze statuette of a rearing horse, after a model by Leonardo; and dozens of pieces by Degas and Rodin. Period settings include the patio from a 16th-century

Spanish castle and a series of ornate 18th-century French domestic interiors known as the Wrightsman Rooms. The Petrie European Sculpture Court features French and Italian sculpture in a beautiful garden setting reminiscent of Versailles in France.

GREEK AND ROMAN ART

A ROMAN SARCOPHAGUS from Tarsus, donated in 1870, was the first work of art in the Met's collections. It can still be seen in the museum's superbly restored Greek and Roman galleries, along with breathtaking wall panels from a villa that was buried under the lava of Vesuvius in AD 79, Etruscan mirrors, Roman portrait busts, exquisite objects in glass and silver and hundreds of Greek vases. A monumental 7th-century BC statue of a youth shows the movement toward naturalism in sculpture, and the Hellenistic *Old Market Woman* demonstrates how the Greeks had mastered realism by the 2nd century BC.

An amphora by Exekias, showing a wedding (6th century BC)

LEHMAN COLLECTION

W HAT HAD BEEN one of the the finest private art collections in the world, that of investment banker Robert Lehman, came to the museum in 1969. The Lehman Wing is a dramatic glass pyramid housing an extraordinarily varied collection rich in Old Masters and 19th-century French paintings, drawings,

EGYPTIAN TOMB MODELS

In 1920, a Met researcher's light illuminated a room, hitherto undiscovered for 2,000 years, in the tomb of the nobleman Mekutra. Within were 24 tiny, perfect replicas of his daily life, to ensure his comfort in the next world – his house and garden, fleet of ships and herd of cattle. Mekutra himself is there, too, on his boat, inhaling a lotus's scent and enjoying the music of his singer and harpist.

A panel from the stained-glass *Death of the Virgin* window, from the 12th-century cathedral of Saint Pierre in Troyes, France

bronzes, Renaissance majolica, Venetian glass, furniture and enamels. Among the canvases are works by north–European masters; Dutch and Spanish paintings, French masterworks, Post impressionists and Fauves.

MEDIEVAL ART

THE METROPOLITAN's medieval collection includes works dating from the 4th to the 16th century, roughly from the fall of Rome to the beginning of the Renaissance. It is split between the main museum and its uptown branch, the Cloisters *(see pp234 – 7)*. In the main building are a chalice once thought to be the Holy Grail, six silver Byzantine plates showing scenes from the life of David, a 1301 pulpit by Giovanni Pisano in the shape of an eagle, several monumental sculptures of the Virgin and Child, plus a huge choir screen from Spain. Other exhibits include Migration jewelry, liturgical vessels, stained glass, ivories and 14th- and 15-century tapestries.

MUSICAL INSTRUMENTS

THE WORLD'S OLDEST piano, Andrés Segovia's guitars and a sitar shaped like a peacock are some of the features of a broad and sometimes quirky collection of musical instruments that spans six continents and dates from prehistory to the present. The instruments illustrate the history of music and performance, and most of them are conserved to remain in playable condition.

Worth particular mention are instruments from the European courts of the Middle Ages and the Renaissance; rare violins; spinets and harpsichords; instruments inlaid with precious materials; a fully equipped traditional violin-maker's work-shop; there are also African drums, Asian *pi-pas*, or lutes; and Native American flutes. Visitors can use audio equipment to hear many of the instruments playing the music of their day.

Stradivari violin from Cremona, Italy (1691)

MODERN ART

SINCE ITS FOUNDATION in 1870, the museum has been acquiring contemporary art, but it was not until 1987 that a permanent home for 20th-century art was built – the Lila Acheson Wallace Wing. Other museums in New York have larger collections of modern art, but this display space is considered among the finest. European and American works from 1900 onward are featured on three levels, starting with Europeans such as Picasso, Kandinsky and Bonnard. The collection's greatest strength lies in its collection of modern American art, with works by New York school "The Eight," including John Sloan; such Modernists as Charles Demuth and Georgia O'Keeffe; American Regionalist Grant Wood; Abstract Expressionists Willem de Kooning; and such Color Field painters as Clyfford Still.

Grant Wood's view of *The Mid-night Ride of Paul Revere* (1931)

Special areas of the wing house Art Nouveau and Art Deco furniture and metalwork; a large collection of works on paper by Paul Klee; and the Sculpture Gallery, with its large-scale sculptures and canvases.

Gems of the collection include Picasso's portrait of Gertrude Stein, Matisse's *Nasturtiums* and *"Dance,1"* Demuth's *I Saw the Figure 5 in Gold*, Jackson Pollock's *Autumn Rhythm* and Andy Warhol's last self-portrait.

Each year the Cantor Roof Garden at the top of the wing features a new installation of contemporary sculpture, especially dramatic against the backdrop of the New York skyline and Central Park.

....

Book cover (1916) by illustrator N.C. Wyeth

Society of Illustrators ⓬

128 E 63rd St. **Map** 13 A2. ☎ *(212)
838-2560.* Ⓜ *Lexington Ave.* ◐
*10am–5pm Wed–Fri, 10am–8pm Tue,
noon–4pm Sat.* ⊙ ♿ *restricted.* ☑
🔲 Ⓦ *www.societyillustrators.org*

Established in 1901, this
society was formed to
promote the illustrator's art.
Its notable roster included
Charles Dana Gibson, N.C.
Wyeth and Howard Pyle. It
was at first concerned with
education and public service,
and held occasional exhibits.
In 1981, the Museum of
American Illustration opened
in two galleries. Changing
thematic exhibitions show the
history of book and magazine
illustration, with an annual
exhibition of the year's finest
American illustrations.

Mount Vernon Hotel Museum ⓭

421 E 61st St. **Map** 13 C3. ☎ *(212)
838-6878.* Ⓜ *Lexington Ave, 59th
St.* ◐ *11am–4pm Tue–Sun (Tues in
Jun & Jul: to 9pm).* ● *Aug, public hols.*
🔲 Ø ☑ 🔲 Ⓦ *www.mvhm.org*

Built in 1799, the Mount
Vernon Hotel Museum and
Garden was once a country
day hotel for New Yorkers
who needed a quite escape
from the crowded city, then

only at the south
end of the island.
The stone building
sits on land once
owned by Abigail
Adams Smith,
daughter of
President John
Adams.

It was acquired
by the Colonial
Dames of America
in 1924 and turned
into a charming re-
creation of a Federal
home. Costumed
guides show visitors
through the rooms,
pointing out the
treasures, including
Chinese porcelain,
Aubusson carpets,
Sheraton chests
and a Duncan
Phyfe sofa. In one
bedroom there is even a
baby's cradle and children's
toys. An 18th-century-style
garden has been planted
around the house.

Henderson Place ⓮

Map 18 D3. Ⓜ *86th St.*

**Queen Anne row houses
at Henderson Place**

Now surrounded by mod-
ern apartment blocks, this
enclave of 24 red-brick Queen
Anne row houses was built in
1882. The row houses were
commissioned by John C.
Henderson, a hat-maker, as a
self-contained community.
The elegant Lamb & Rich
design has gray slate roof
gables, pediments, parapets,
chimneys and dormer
windows forming patterns,
and a turret marking the
corner of each block.

Carl Schurz Park promenade

Carl Schurz Park ⓯

Map 18 D3. Ⓜ *86th St.*

Laid out in 1891, this park
along the East River has a
wide promenade over the
East River Drive. It offers fine
vistas of the river and the
turbulent waters of Hell Gate,
where the river meets Long
Island Sound. It is named
after Carl Schurz, a native
who became Secretary of the
Interior (1869–75). The first
part of the promenade is the
John Finlay Walk, named for
an editor of the *New York
Times* known for his hiking
prowess. One of the city's
most pleasant green escapes,
the park's grassy areas are
filled with basking New
Yorkers on sunny days.

Gracie Mansion ⓰

East End Ave at 88th St. **Map** 18 D3.
☎ *(212) 570-4751.* Ⓜ *86th St.*
🚌 *M86.* ◐ *Apr–mid Nov:10am,
11am, 1pm, 2pm Wed for prebooked
guided tours only.* 🔲 Ø ♿ 🔲

This gracious, balconied
wooden 1799 country
home is the official mayor's
residence. Built by wealthy
merchant Archibald Gracie, it
is one of the best Federal
houses left in New York.

Acquired by the city in
1887, it was the first home of
the Museum of the City of
New York. In 1942 it became
the official Mayoral Residence.
When Fiorello La Guardia
moved in after nine years in

Front view of Gracie Mansion

office, preferring it to a 75-room palace on Riverside Drive, he said that even the modest Gracie Mansion was too fancy for him. "The Little Flower" (from Fiorello) had fought corruption in the city.

Church of the Holy Trinity ⑰

316 E 88th St. **Map** 17 B3. ☎ (212) 289-4100. Ⓜ 86th St. ◷ 9am–5pm Mon–Fri, 7:30am–2pm Sun. ✝ 8:45am Mon–Fri, 8am, 9am, 11am, 6pm Sun. 📷 Ⓦ www.holytrinity-nyc.org

Arched doorway of the Church of the Holy Trinity

Delightfully placed in a serene garden setting, this church was constructed in 1889 of glowing golden brick and terra-cotta in French Renaissance style. It boasts one of New York's best bell towers, which holds a handsome wrought-iron clock with brass hands. The arched doorway is richly decorated with carved images of the saints and prophets.

The complex was donated by Serena Rhinelander in memory of her father and grandfather. The land was part of the Rhinelander farm, which the family had owned for 100 years.

Farther down at 350 E. 88th Street is the Rhinelander Children's Center, also a gift, and the headquarters of the Children's Aid Society.

St. Nicholas Russian Orthodox Cathedral ⑱

15 E 97th St. **Map** 16 F1. ☎ (212) 876-2190. Ⓜ 96 St. ◷ by appt. ✝ 10am, 6pm Sat, 10am, 5pm Sun (Russian). 📷 Ⓦ www.russianchurchusa.org

This really is "Moscow on the Hudson." Built in Muscovite Baroque style in 1902, it has five onion domes crowned with crosses, and blue and yellow tiles on a red brick and white stone facade. Among the early worshipers were White Russians who had fled the first uprisings at home, mostly intellectuals and aristocrats who soon became a part of New York society. Later, there were more waves of refugees, dissidents and defectors.

The cathedral now serves a scattered community, and the congregation is small. Mass is celebrated in Russian with great pomp and dignity.

The cathedral is filled with the scent of incense. The high central sanctuary has marble columns with blue and white trim above. Ornate wooden screens trimmed with gold enclose the altar. It is unique, an unexpected find on a side street in this staid part of Manhattan.

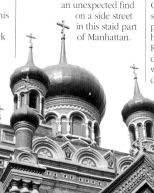

Facade and domes of St. Nicholas Russian Cathedral

Facade of the Museum of the City of New York

Museum of the City of New York ⑲

1220 5th Ave at 103rd St. **Map** 21 C5. ☎ (212) 534-1672. Ⓜ 103rd St. ◷ 10am–5pm Wed–Sat, 12–5pm Sun. ● public hols. **Donations welcome.** 📷 ♿ 🅿 ✝ Ⓦ www.mcny.org

Founded in 1923 and at first housed in Gracie Mansion, this museum is dedicated to New York's development from its earliest beginnings, shown in costumes, paintings, furnishings, toys and a range of fascinating memorabilia.

Housed in this handsome Georgian Colonial building since 1932, it is noted for its period rooms from actual homes, including John D. Rockefeller's bedroom and dressing room, and for its wonderful collection of toys, dolls and dollhouses dating from 1769. Start with *The Big Apple* video, then visit the exhibition, "Broadway! 125 Years of Musical Theater." The second floor has a magnificent collection of silver objects dating from 1678 to 1984. The Alexander Hamilton Gallery contains furniture and paintings that once belonged to the first Secretary of the Treasury.

The impressive collection housed in the basement includes antique fire equipment, paintings, maps and prints all relating to city history.

Whitney Museum of American Art ❼

T HE WHITNEY MUSEUM is the foremost showcase for American art from the 20th–21st centuries. It was founded in 1930 by sculptor Gertrude Vanderbilt Whitney after the Metropolitan Museum of Art turned down her collection of works by living artists such as Bellows and Hopper. In 1966 the museum moved to the present inverted pyramid building designed by Marcel Breuer. The Whitney Biennial show is the most significant survey of new trends in American art.

The cantilevered facade of the Whitney Museum

Green Coca-Cola Bottles
Andy Warhol's 1962 work is a commentary on mass production and monopoly.

The White Calico Flower
Georgia O'Keeffe's enlarged flower paintings have an abstract quality, as in this 1931 example.

Little Big Painting
The 1965 work by Roy Lichtenstein is a comic critique of Abstract Expressionist painting.

MUSEUM GUIDE
The Leonard and Evelyn Lauder galleries on the fifth floor have permanant collections, showing works by Calder, O'Keefe and Hopper. Changing exhibitions occupy the second, third and fourth floors.

Early Sunday Morning *(1930)*
Edward Hopper's paintings often convey the emptiness of American city life.

Dempsey and Firpo
In 1924, George Bellows depicted one of the most famous prizefights of the century.

VISITORS' CHECKLIST

945 Madison Ave. **Map** 17 A5.
570-3600. M 6 to 77th St.
M1, M2, M3, M4, 30, M72,
M79. ◯ 11am–6pm Tue–Thu,
Sat–Sun, 1–9pm Fri. ● public
hols. Lectures,
film/video presentations.
W www.whitney.org

Three Flags *(1958)*
Jasper Johns's use of familiar objects in an abstract form was influential in the development of Pop art.

Owh! In San Paõ *(1951)*
In this painting by Stuart Davis, abstract forms are combined with lettering to create a unique and distinctive American style.

Circus *(1926–31)*
Alexander Calder's fanciful creation is always on display.

Tango *(1919)*
This is considered Polish-born Elie Nadelman's greatest wood sculpture.

Hudson River Landscape *(1951)*
This steel sculpture is one of David Smith's most influential works.

Frick Collection ❾

THE PRICELESS ART collection of steel magnate Henry Clay Frick (1849–1919) is exhibited in a residential setting amid the furnishings of his opulent mansion, providing a rare glimpse of how the extremely wealthy lived in New York's gilded age. Frick intended the collection to be a memorial to himself and bequeathed the entire house to the nation on his death. The collection includes old master paintings, French furniture, Limoges enamels and Oriental rugs.

★ Lady Meux (1881)
Before marrying a brewery baron, the coquettish young Lady Meux was an actress. This was Whistler's second of three portraits of her.

The Harbor of Dieppe (1826)
J.M.W. Turner was criticized by some skeptical contemporaries for depicting this northern European port suffused with light.

**Colonnade
Garden
Court**

The White Horse (1819)
John Constable based this painting on a familiar scene from his Suffolk home.

Library

**West
Gallery**

**Limoges
Enamel**
The collection of enamels includes The Seven Sorrows of the Virgin *(1500–50).*

STAR PAINTINGS

- **★ Sir Thomas More by Hans Holbein**

- **★ Mall in St. James's Park by Thomas Gainsborough**

- **★ Officer and Laughing Girl by Johannes Vermeer**

- **★ Lady Meux by James McNeill Whistler**

★ Sir Thomas More (1527)
Holbein's portrait of Henry VIII's Lord Chancellor was painted eight years before More's execution for treason.

**Living
Hall**

GALLERY GUIDE
Of special interest are the skylit West Gallery, with oils by Vermeer, Hals and Rembrandt; the East Gallery, featuring Van Dyck; the Oval Room featuring Whistler; the Library and Dining Room, with English works; and the Living Hall with works by Titian, Bellini and Holbein.

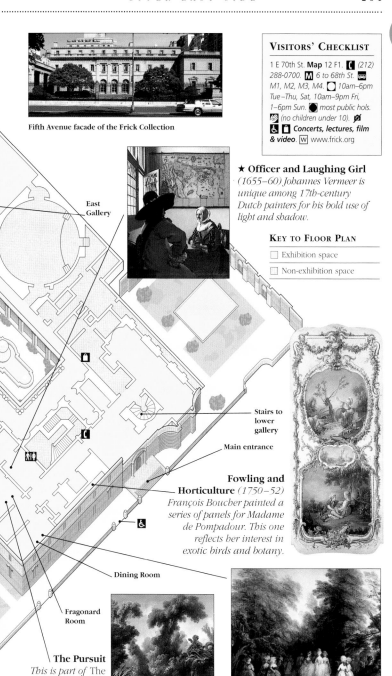

Fifth Avenue facade of the Frick Collection

VISITORS' CHECKLIST

1 E 70th St. **Map** 12 F1. ((212)
288-0700. **M** 6 to 68th St.
M1, M2, M3, M4. ○ 10am–6pm
Tue–Thu, Sat, 10am–9pm Fri,
1–6pm Sun. ● most public hols.
(no children under 10).
Concerts, lectures, film
& video. W www.frick.org

East
Gallery

★ **Officer and Laughing Girl**
(1655–60) Johannes Vermeer is
unique among 17th-century
Dutch painters for his bold use of
light and shadow.

KEY TO FLOOR PLAN

☐ Exhibition space

☐ Non-exhibition space

Stairs to
lower
gallery

Main entrance

**Fowling and
Horticulture** (1750–52)
François Boucher painted a
series of panels for Madame
de Pompadour. This one
reflects her interest in
exotic birds and botany.

Dining Room

Fragonard
Room

The Pursuit
This is part of The
Progress of Love
(1771–3 and 1790–
91), by Jean-Honoré
Fragonard. The series
of paintings depicts
the events of an
idealized courtship.

★ **Mall in St. James's Park** (1783)
The three central figures in Thomas
Gainsborough's London landscape
may be the daughters of George III.

CENTRAL PARK

THE CITY'S "BACKYARD" was created in 1858 by Frederick Law Olmsted and Calvert Vaux on an unpromising site of quarries, pig farms, swampland and shacks. Ten million cartloads of stone and earth turned it into the lush 843-acre (340-ha) park of today. There are scenic hills, lakes and lush meadows, dotted throughout with out-

Statues, Delacorte Theater *(see p206)*

crops of Manhattan bedrock and planted with more than 500,000 trees and shrubs. Over the years the park has blossomed, with playgrounds and skating rinks, plus ball fields and spaces for every activity from chess and croquet to concerts and events. Cars are banned on weekends, giving bicyclists, in-line skaters and joggers the right-of-way.

SIGHTS AT A GLANCE

Historic Buildings
The Dairy ❶
Belvedere Castle ❸

Monuments and Statues
Strawberry Fields ❷
Bethesda Fountain and Terrace ❺
Bow Bridge ❹

SEE ALSO
- **Street Finder**, maps 12, 16
- **Restaurants** p290

Ⓦ www.centralparknyc.org

GETTING THERE
Subway lines A, B, C and D run the length of the park on the Upper West Side, with stops at 59th, 72nd, 81st, 86th, 96th and 103rd Sts. The 59th St/Columbus Circle stop is served by the 1 and 9 Broadway/7th Ave lines, the 8th Ave lines; the W and R Broadway local trains stop at 57th St and 5th Ave at the southern end of the park. Bus routes M1, M2, M3 and M4 run along the eastern edge of the park.

Lakes and Gardens
Conservatory Water ❻
Central Park Wildlife Center ❼
Conservatory Garden ❽

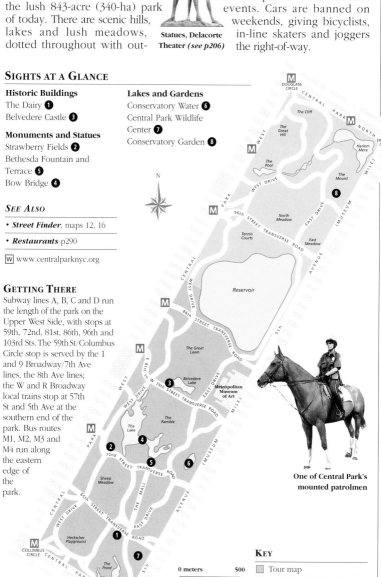

One of Central Park's mounted patrolmen

KEY
▢ Tour map
Ⓜ Subway station

0 meters 500
0 yards 500

◁ **Bird's-eye view of the park**

A Tour of Central Park

O N A SHORT VISIT, a walking tour
from 59th to 79th streets takes in
some of Central Park's loveliest
features, from the de nse wooded
Ramble to the open formal spaces
of Bethesda Terrace. Along the way,
you will see artificial lakes and some
of the 30 graceful bridges and arches, no
two alike, that link some 58 miles (93 km)
of footpaths, bridle paths and roads in the
park. In summer the park is often several
degrees cooler than the city streets around
it, and thus is a favorite retreat.

★ **Strawberry Fields**
*One of the park's most
visited spots, this
peaceful area was
created in memory
of John Lennon,
who lived nearby* ❷

★ **Bethesda Fountain and Terrace**
*The richly ornamented formal terrace
overlooks the Lake and the wooded shores
of the Ramble* ❺

Wollman Rink was restored
in the 1980s for future
generations of skaters by
tycoon Donald Trump.

**Central Park
Wildlife
Center**
*Three climate
zones are home
to over 100
species of
animals* ❼

**The
Pond**

Plaza Hotel
(see p179)

Frick Collection
(see pp200–1)

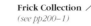

Hans Christian Andersen's
statue is a favorite Central
Park landmark for children.
It is on the west side of
Conservatory Water
and is a popular
site for
storytelling
in the
summer.

★ **The Dairy**
*This Victorian Gothic building
houses the Visitor Center. Make it
your first stop and pick up a
calendar of park events* ❶

Bow Bridge
This cast-iron bridge links the Ramble with Cherry Hill by a graceful arch, 60 ft (18 m) above the Lake **4**

LOCATOR MAP
See Manhattan Map pp12–13

Alice in Wonderland is immortalized in bronze at the northern end of Conservatory Water, along with her friends the Cheshire Cat, the Mad Hatter and the Dormouse. Children love to slide down her toadstool seat.

STAR SIGHTS
★ **The Dairy**
★ **Strawberry Fields**
★ **Belvedere Castle**
★ **Bethesda Fountain**
★ **Conservatory Water**

American Museum of Natural History *(see pp214–15)*

kota lding p216)

San Remo Apartments *(see p212)*

GREAT LAWN

Metropolitan Museum *(see pp188–95)*

Obelisk

The Ramble is a wooded area of 37 acres (15 ha), crisscrossed by paths and streams. It is a paradise for bird-watchers – over 250 species have been spotted in the park, which is on the Atlantic migration flyway.

Reservoir

Guggenheim Museum *(see pp186–87)*

★ Belvedere Castle
From the terraces there are unequaled views of the city and surrounding park. Within the stone walls is the Central Park Learning Center **3**

★ Conservatory Water
From March to November, this is the scene of model boat races each Saturday. Many of the tiny craft are stored in the boathouse that adjoins the Lake **6**

The Carousel, part of the park's Children's District

The Dairy ❶

Map 12 F2.
[(212) 794-6564.
Ⓜ Fifth Ave. ◯ 10am–5pm
Tue–Sun. **Slide show.** ⬛
Ⓦ www.centralparknyc.org

NOW USED AS the park information center, this charming building of natural stone was planned as part of the "Children's District" of the park, which included a playground, the Carousel, a Children's Cottage and stable. In 1873, there were cows grazing on the meadows in front of the Dairy, a ewe and her lambs feeding nearby, and chickens, guinea fowl and peacocks roaming the lawn. City children could get fresh milk and other refreshments here. Over the years, the Dairy deteriorated, being used as a shed until restoration in 1979, done according to original photographs and drawings. The Dairy is the place to begin exploring the lush and leafy park; maps and details of events can be obtained here. The less energetic can rent chess and checkers sets for use on the pretty inlaid boards of the *kinderberg*, the charming little "children's hill" nearby.

Strawberry Fields ❷

Map 12 E1. Ⓜ 72nd St.

THE RESTORATION of this teardrop-shaped section of the park was Yoko Ono's tribute in memory of her slain husband, John Lennon. They lived in the Dakota apartments overlooking this spot *(see p216)*. Gifts for the garden came from all over the world. A mosaic set in the pathway, inscribed with the word *Imagine* (named for Lennon's famous song), was a gift from the city of Naples in Italy.

This broad expanse of the park's landscape was designed by Vaux and Olmsted. Now it is an international peace garden, with 161 species of plants (one from every country of the world), including jetbead, roses, witch hazel, birches – and strawberries.

Belvedere Castle ❸

Map 16 E4. [(212) 772-0210.
Ⓜ 81st St. ◯ 10am–5pm Tue–Sun.
◉ ♿ to main floor only.

THIS STONE CASTLE atop Vista Rock, complete with tower and turrets, offers one of the best views of the park and the city from its lookout on the rooftop. Inside is the Henry Luce Nature Observatory, with a delightful exhibit telling inquisitive young visitors about the surprising variety of wildlife to be found in the park.

The view to the north from the castle allows you to look down into

Belvedere Castle with its lookout over the park

the Delacorte Theater, home to the free productions of Shakespeare in the Park every summer, featuring big-name stars *(see p335)*. The theater was the gift of George T. Delacorte. Publisher and founder of Dell paperbacks, Delacorte was a delightful philanthropist who was responsible for many of the park's pleasures.

Bow Bridge ❹

Map 16 E5. Ⓜ 72nd St.

THIS IS ONE of the park's seven original cast-iron bridges and is considered one of the finest. It was designed by Vaux as a bow tying together the two large sections of the lake. In the 19th century, when the Lake was used for ice skating, a red ball was hoisted from a bell tower on Vista Rock to signal that the ice was safe. The bridge offers expansive views of the park and the buildings bordering it on both the east and west sides.

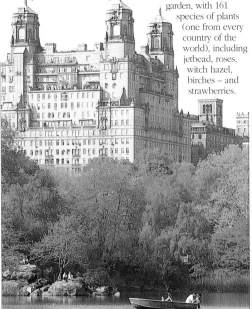

A tranquil scene in Central Park, overlooked by exclusive apartments

An 1864 print of Bethesda Fountain and Terrace

Bethesda Fountain and Terrace ❺

Map 12 E1. Ⓜ *72nd St.*

SITUATED BETWEEN the Lake and the Mall, this is the architectural heart of the park, a formal element in the naturalistic landscape. The fountain was dedicated in 1873. The statue, *Angel of the Waters*, marked the opening of the Croton Aqueduct system in 1842, bringing the city its first supply of pure water; its name refers to a biblical account of a healing angel at the pool of Bethesda in Jerusalem. The Spanish-style detailing, such as the sculptured double staircase, tiles and friezes, is by Jacob Wrey Mould.

The terrace is one of the best spots to relax and take in some people-watching.

Conservatory Water ❻

Map 16 F5. Ⓜ *77th St.*

BETTER KNOWN as the Model Boat Pond, this stretch of water is home to model yacht races every weekend.

At the north end of the lake, a sculpture of Alice in Wonderland is a delight for children. It was commissioned by George T. Delacorte in honor of his wife. He himself is immortalized in caricature as the Mad Hatter. On the west bank, free story hours are held at a statue of Hans Christian Andersen, portrayed reading from his own story, "The Ugly Duck-ling," while its hero waddles at his feet. Like that of Alice, this statue is climbed on by small children, who especially like to snuggle in the author's lap.

Conservatory Water's literary links continue into adolescence: it is here that J.D. Salinger's Holden Caulfield comes to tell the ducks his troubles in *The Catcher in the Rye*.

Central Park Wildlife Center ❼

Map 12 F2. 📞 *(212) 439-6500.* Ⓜ *Fifth Ave between 63rd and 66th sts.* ⏰ *10am–5pm Mon–Fri, 10am–5:30pm Sat, Sun; Nov–Mar: 10am–4:30 daily.* 🅦 *www.wcs.org/zoos; nyzoosandaquarium.com/142123*

REOPENED IN 1988 after four years of reconstruction, this imaginative zoo won plaudits for its creative and humane use of small space. More than 130 species of animals are represented in three climate zones, the Tropics, the Polar Circle and the California coast. An equatorial rain forest is home to monkeys and free-flying birds, while penguins and polar bears populate an Arctic landscape that allows views both above and under water. At the Tisch Children's Zoo children can get close to goats, sheep, cows and pot-bellied pigs. By its entrance is the much-loved Delacorte Clock, which plays nursery rhymes every half hour, as bronze musical animals (such as a goat playing pan pipes) circle around it. Toward Willowdell Arch is another favorite – the memorial to Balto, leader of a team of huskies that made a heroic journey across Alaska with serum for a diphtheria epidemic.

Statue of Balto, the heroic husky sled dog

Conservatory Garden ❽

Map 21 B5. Ⓜ *Central Pk N, 103rd St.* 📞 *(212) 860-1382.* ⏰ *8am–dusk.* ♿

THE VANDERBILT GATE on Fifth Avenue is the entry to a six-acre park containing three formal gardens. Each one represents a different national landscape style. The Central Garden, with a large lawn, yew hedges, crabapple trees, and a wisteria pergola recreates an Italian style. The South Garden, spilling over with perennials, represents an English style, with a bronze statue in the reflecting pool of Mary and Dickon, from Frances Hodgson Burnett's *The Secret Garden*. Beyond is a slope with thousands of native wildflowers, spreading into the park beyond. The North Garden, in the French style, centers around the bronze *Fountain of the Three Dancing Maidens*. It puts on a brief but brilliant display of annuals each summer.

Polar bear in the Wildlife Center

UPPER WEST SIDE

HIS AREA became residential in the 1870s, when the Ninth Avenue El *(see pp24-5)* made commuting to midtown possible. The Dakota, the city's first luxury apartment house, was built here in 1884, and the streets were graded and leveled. Buildings sprang up on Broadway and Central

Indian mask, Museum of Natural History

Park West, and cross streets, dating from the 1890s, still retain fine brownstone row houses. The area is bustling and diverse with many cultural institutions, including the American Museum of Natural History, Lincoln Center, and the new Columbus Square complex for Time Warner and CNN.

SIGHTS AT A GLANCE

Historic Streets and Buildings
Twin Towers of Central Park West ①
Columbus Circle ⑦
The Dakota ⑨
Pomander Walk ⑬
Riverside Drive and Park ⑭
The Dorilton ⑰

Museums and Galleries
New-York Historical Society ⑩
American Museum of Natural History pp214–15 ⑪
Hayden Planetarium ⑫
Children's Museum of Manhattan ⑮

Famous Theaters
Lincoln Center for the Performing Arts ②
New York State Theater ③
Metropolitan Opera House ④
Lincoln Center Theater ⑤
Avery Fisher Hall ⑥

Landmark Hotels and Restaurants
Hotel des Artistes ⑧
The Ansonia ⑯

GETTING THERE
By subway, take the 6th Ave B or D, the 7th Ave/Broadway 2 and 3, or the 8th Ave A and C trains. By bus, the M10 (Central Park West), M7, M11, M104 and M5 or the M66, M72, M79, M86 and M96 crosstown buses.

Stone figure on the facade of the Hotel des Artistes

KEY

▨	Street-by-Street map
Ⓜ	Subway station

SEE ALSO

• *Street Finder*, maps 11, 15

• *Where to Stay* pp282–3

• *Restaurants* p290

0 meters	500
0 yards	500

◁ **The facade of 14 Riverside Drive**

Street by Street: Lincoln Center

Lincoln Center was conceived when both the Metropolitan Opera House and the New York Philharmonic required homes, and a large tract on Manhattan's west side was in dire need of revitalization. The notion of a single complex where different performing arts could exist side by side seems natural today, but in the 1950s it was considered both daring and risky. Today Lincoln Center has proved itself by drawing audiences of five million each year. Proximity to its halls prompts both performers and arts lovers to live nearby.

★ **Lincoln Center for the Performing Arts**
Dance, music and theater come together in this fine contemporary complex. It is also a great place to sit around the reflecting fountain and people-watch ❷

Lincoln Center Theater
The Vivian Beaumont and the Mitzi E. Newhouse theaters are both housed in this building ❺

Composer Leonard Bernstein's
famous musical *West Side Story*, which was based on the Romeo and Juliet theme, was set in the impoverished streets around what is now Lincoln Center. Bernstein was later instrumental in setting up the large music complex.

The Guggenheim Bandshell
in Damrosch Park is the site of free concerts.

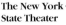

The New York State Theater
This is the home of the New York City Ballet, as well as an opera company. The theater seats 2,737 people ❸

The College Board Building is an Art Deco delight that now houses condominiums and the administrative offices of the College Board, developers of the college entrance exam.

Metropolitan Opera House
Lincoln Center's focus is the Opera House. The café at the top of the lobby offers wonderful plaza views ❹

American Folk Art Museum
Quilting and naïve painting are some of the arts displayed here ❼

Early American quilt

★ **Hotel des Artistes**
Artists Isadora Duncan, Noël Coward and Norman Rockwell once lived here. It also houses a much-praised restaurant (see p295) ❽

James Dean once lived in a one-room apartment on the top floor at 19 West 68th Street.

LOCATOR MAP
see Manhattan Map pp12–13

KEY

– – – Suggested route

| 0 meters | 100 |
| 0 yards | 100 |

To 72nd Street subway (4 blocks)

An **ABC-TV** sound stage for soap operas is housed in this castle-like building, formerly an armory.

55 Central Park West is the Art Deco apartment building that featured in the film *Ghostbusters*.

The Society for Ethical Culture was one of the city's first Art Nouveau buildings. It also houses a school.

To 59th Street subway (2 blocks)

Central Park West is home to many celebrities, who like the privacy of its exclusive apartments.

Century Apartments
The Century's twin towers are visible from the park, making it a New York landmark ❶

STAR SIGHTS

★ **Lincoln Center**

★ **Hotel des Artistes**

The San Remo, a twin-towered apartment house designed by Emery Roth

Twin Towers of Central Park West ❶

Map 12 D1, 12 D2, 16 D3, 16 D5.
Ⓜ *59th St-Columbus Circle, 72nd St.*
⬤ *to public.*

AMONG THE MOST familiar landmarks on the New York skyline are the five twin-towered apartment houses on Central Park West. Built between 1929 and 1931, before the Great Depression halted all luxury construction, they are among the most highly sought-after residences in New York.

Admired today for their grace and architectural detail, they were designed in response to a city planning law allowing taller apartments if set backs and towers were used.

Emery Roth designed the San Remo (145 CPW), whose tenants have included Dustin Hoffman, Paul Simon and Diane Keaton. Turned down by the residents' committee, Madonna went to live close by at 1 West 64th Street. The towers of the Eldorado (300 CPW), also designed by Roth, were home to

Groucho Marx, Marilyn Monroe, and Richard Dreyfuss. The Majestic (115 CPW) and the Century (25 CPW) are both sleek classics by Art Deco designer Irwin S. Chanin.

Lincoln Center for the Performing Arts ❷

Map 11 C2. 📞 *(212) 546-2656.* Ⓜ *65th St.* ♿ 🚻 *875-5350.* 🚻 📷
See Entertainment pp338–9.
🌐 *www.lincolncenter.org*

IN MAY 1959, President Eisenhower traveled to New York to turn a shovelful of earth, Leonard Bernstein lifted his baton, the New York Philharmonic and the Juilliard Choir broke into the Hallelujah Chorus – and the

city's most important cultural center was born. It soon covered 15 acres (6 ha) on the site of the slums that had been the setting for Bernstein's classic musical *West Side Story*. The plaza fountain is by Philip Johnson, and the sculpture, *Reclining Figure*, is by Henry Moore.

Jazz at the Lincoln Center has developed a state-of-the-art facility dedicated to jazz performances. It forms part of a major new complex at Columbus Circle *(see p213.)*

New York State Theater ❸

Lincoln Center. **Map** 11 D2. 📞 *(212) 870-5570.* Ⓜ *66th St.* ♿ 🚻 🚻
📷 *See Entertainment pp334–5.*
🌐 *www.nycballet.com*

THE HOME BASE for the highly acclaimed New York City Ballet and the New York City Opera, a troupe devoted to presenting opera at popular prices, is a Philip Johnson design. It was inaugurated in 1964.

Gargantuan white marble sculptures by Elie Nadelman dominate the vast four-story foyer. The theater seats 2,800 people. Because of its rhine-stone lights and chandeliers both inside and out, some have described the theater as "a little jewel box."

Metropolitan Opera House ❹

Lincoln Center. **Map** 11 D2. 📞 *(212) 362-6000.* Ⓜ *66th St.* ♿ 🚻 🚻
📷 *See Entertainment pp338–9.* 🌐
www.metopera.org; www.abt.org

HOME TO THE Metropolitan Opera Company and the American Ballet Theater, "the Met" is the most spectacular of Lincoln Center's buildings. Five great arched windows offer views of the opulent foyer and two radiant murals by Marc Chagall. (You can't see them in the mornings when they are pro-tected from the sun.)

Central plaza at Lincoln Center

Inside there are curved white marble stairs, miles of plush red carpeting and exquisite starburst crystal chandeliers

Free open-air concerts are held at the Guggenheim Bandshell

that are raised to the ceiling just before each performance. All the greats have sung here, including Maria Callas, Jessye Norman and Luciano Pavarotti. First nights are glittering, star-studded occasions.

The Guggenheim Bandshell, in Damrosch Park next to the Met, is a popular concert site with music from opera to jazz. The high point of the season is the Lincoln Center Out-of-Doors Festival that takes place in August.

Lincoln Center Theater ❺

Lincoln Center, 150 W 65th St. **Map** 11 C2. ☎ *(212) 362-7600 (Beaumont and Newhouse), (212) 870-1630 (Library).* 800-432 7250 (tickets) Ⓜ *66th St.* ♿ ✔ 🍽 🏪 See *Entertainment pp338–9.* Ⓦ *www.lct.org*

Tᴡᴏ ᴛʜᴇᴀᴛᴇʀꜱ ᴍᴀᴋᴇ up this innovative complex, presenting eclectic and often experimental drama.

The theaters are the 1000-seat Vivian Beaumont and the more intimate 280-seat Mitzi E. Newhouse.

Works by some of New York's best modern playwrights have been featured at the Beaumont. The theater's inaugural performance in 1962 was Arthur Miller's *After the Fall*.

The size of the Newhouse suits workshop-style plays, but it can still make the news with theatrical gems such as

Robin Williams and Steve Martin in a production of Samuel Beckett's *Waiting for Godot*. The New York Public Library for the Performing Arts houses exhibits including audio cylinders of early Met performances and original scores and playbills.

Avery Fisher Hall ❻

Lincoln Center. **Map** 11 C2. ☎ *(212) 875-5030.* Ⓜ *66th St.* ♿ ✔ 🍽 See *Entertainment p338–9.* Ⓦ *www.newyorkphilharmonic.org*

Lᴏᴄᴀᴛᴇᴅ ᴀᴛ ᴛʜᴇ northern end of the Lincoln Center Plaza, Avery Fisher Hall is home to America's oldest orchestra, the New York Philharmonic. It also provides a stage for some of the Lincoln Center's own performers, and the Mostly Mozart Festival. When the venue opened in 1962 as the Philharmonic Hall, critics initially complained about the acoustics. Several structural modifications, however, have rendered the hall an acoustic gem, comparing favorably with other great classical concert halls around the world. For a small fee, the public can attend rehearsals on Thursday mornings in the 2,738-seat auditorium.

Columbus Circle ❼

Columbus Circle, New York. **Map** 12 D3. Ⓜ *59th St.*

Pʀᴇꜱɪᴅɪɴɢ ᴏᴠᴇʀ this urban plaza at the corner of Central Park is a marble statue of explorer Christopher Columbus, perched on top of a tall granite column. The statue is one of the few remaining original features in this circle – which has become one of the largest building projects in New York's history.

New multi-use skyscrapers have been erected, attracting

national and international businesses. Global media company Time Warner has its headquarters in a new 80-storey skyscraper. The 2.8 million sq ft (260,000 sq m) building provides a retail, entertainment, and restaurant facility. Facilities include shops such as Hugo Boss, Williams-Sonoma, and Borders Books; dining at Per Se and Jean-George Vongerichten's Steakhouse; and the sixth hotel in the Mandarin Oriental chain.

The Time Warner Center is also home to Jazz at the Lincoln Center. The two venues here – The Frederic P. Rose Concert Hall and The Allen Room – together with a jazz club and education center, comprise the world's first performing arts facility dedicated to jazz.

Other notable buildings in Columbus Circle include Hearst House designed by British architect Norman Foster, Trump International Hotel, and the Maine Monument.

Hotel des Artistes ❽

1 W 67th St. **Map** 12 D2. ☎ *(212) 362- 6700.* Ⓜ *72nd St.*

Bᴜɪʟᴛ ɪɴ 1918 by George Mort Pollard, these two-story apartments were intended as working artists' studios but have attracted a variety of interesting tenants, including Alexander Woollcott, Norman Rockwell, Isadora Duncan, Rudolph Valentino and Noël Coward. The Café des Artistes is well known for its misty, romantic Howard Chandler Christy murals and its fine cuisine.

Decorative figure on the Hotel des Artistes

American Museum of Natural History ⓫

THIS IS ONE OF THE world's largest natural history museums. Since the original building opened in 1877, the complex has grown to cover four city blocks, and today holds more than 30 million specimens and artifacts. The most popular areas are the dinosaurs, and the newly-renovated Milstein Hall of Ocean Life. The new Rose Center for Earth and Space includes the Hayden Planetarium (see p216).

The facade on 77th Street

STAR EXHIBITS

★ Barosaurus

★ Blue Whale

★ Haida Canoe

★ Star of India

★ Star of India

This 563-carat gem is the world's largest blue star sapphire. Found in Sri Lanka, it was given to the museum by J.P. Morgan in 1900.

GALLERY GUIDE

Enter at Central Park West onto the second floor to view the Barosaurus exhibit, African, Asian, Central and South American peoples and animals. First floor exhibits include ocean life, meteors, minerals and gems, and the Hall of Biodiversity. North American Indians, birds and reptiles occupy the third floor. Dinosaurs, fossil fishes and early mammals are on the fourth floor.

★ Blue Whale

The blue whale is the largest animal, living or extinct. Its weight can exceed 100 tons. This replica is based on a female captured off South America in 1925.

★ Haida Canoe

This 63-ft (19.2-m) seafaring war canoe of the Haida Indians was carved from the trunk of a single cedar. It stands in the 77th Street foyer.

Entrance on W. 77th St

Dinosaurs

Fourth
floor

Third
floor

Second
floor

First floor

Rose Center
for Earth
and Space
(see p216)

Central
Park West
entrance

(see p216)

VISITORS' CHECKLIST

Central Park West at 79th St. **Map**
16 D5. [(212) 769-5100. M B,
C to 81st St. M7, M10, M11,
M79, M104. ◯ 10am–5:45pm
daily. (Rose Center open until
8:45pm Fri.) **Donation**. 📷 ♿
🎒 🚻 🖥 w www.amnh.org

Komodo Dragons
The largest living lizards, which can grow to 10 ft (3 m), live on Komodo and other Indonesian islands.

African Elephants
Four of the elephants in this group were collected and mounted in the 1920s by Carl Akeley, who created the museum's Hall of African Mammals.

★ Barosaurus
This exhibit, which shows the skeletons of a mother Barosaurus rearing up to protect her baby from an attacking predator, was cast from original fossils. The plant-eating dinosaur lived 140 million years ago.

Giant Sequoia
Sequoias are among the world's longest-lived plants. This section has 1,342 annual rings and measures more than 16 ft (4.8 m) across.

KEY TO FLOOR PLAN

- ☐ Dinosaurs and other fossil vertebrates
- ☐ Birds
- ☐ Fishes
- ☐ Mammals
- ☐ Meteorites, minerals and gems
- ☐ Human cultures
- ☐ Human biology and evolution
- ☐ Amphibians and reptiles
- ☐ Environment and ecology
- ☐ Rose Center for Earth and Space
- ☐ Special exhibitions
- ☐ Non-exhibition space

The Dakota **9**

1 W 72nd St. **Map** 12 D1. **M** *72nd St.* ● *to the public.*

THE NAME AND STYLE reflect the fact that this apartment building was truly "way out West" when Henry J. Hardenbergh, the architect responsible for the Plaza Hotel, designed it in 1880–84. It was New York's first luxury apartment house and was originally surrounded by squatters' shacks and wandering farm animals. Commissioned by Edward S. Clark, heir to the Singer sewing machine fortune, it is one of the city's most prestigious addresses.

The Dakota's 65 luxurious apartments have had many famous owners, including Judy Garland, Lauren Bacall, Leonard Bernstein and Boris Karloff, whose ghost is said to haunt the place. It was the setting for the film *Rosemary's Baby*, and the site of the tragic murder of former Beatle John Lennon. His widow, Yoko Ono, still lives here.

Carved Indian head over the entrance to the Dakota

New-York Historical Society **10**

170 Central Park West/77th St. **Map** 16 D5. **[** (212) 873-3400. **M** 81st St. **Galleries** ○ 10am–6pm Tue–Sun. **Library** ○ 10am–5pm Tue–Sun (Tue–Fri in summer). ● public hols. ⊘ & ⊘ ⊙ **W** www.nyhistory.org

AUDUBON'S ORIGINAL *Birds of America* prints and over 150 Tiffany lamps are among the treasures of New York's

The Rose Center for Earth and Space

oldest museum. Founded in 1804, the Society has a wide collection of paintings and decorative arts dating back to the 17th century. The portrait collection includes Gilbert Stuart's *George Washington*. There is fine furniture from the Federal period, plus an exceptional silver display.

American Museum of Natural History **11**

See pp214–15.

Hayden Planetarium **12**

Central Park West at 81st St. **Map** 16 D4. **[** (212) 769-5100, for Space Show tickets: (212) 769-5200. **M** 81st St. **W** www.amnh.org/rose

ON THE NORTHERN side of the American Museum of Natural History is the Hayden Planetarium, the centerpiece of the spectacular new Rose Center for Earth and Space, designed by Polshek and Partners. Housed within an 87-ft sphere, the Planetarium contains a technologically advanced Space Theater, the Cosmic Pathway, a 350-ft spiral ramp with a timeline chronicling 13 billion years of evolution, and a Big Bang Theater. The Hall of Planet Earth, centered around rock samples and using state-of-the-art computer and video displays explaining how the Earth works, explores our geologic history. Exhibits in the Hall of the Universe present the discoveries of modern

astrophysics. Four zones feature hands-on interactive exhibits. Seen from the street at night, the Rose Center is simply breathtaking; the exhibits inside prove that, as Carl Sagan said, "We are starstuff."

Pomander Walk **13**

261–7 W 94th St. **Map** 15 C2. **M** 72nd St.

LOOK THROUGH the gate for a delightful surprise – a double row of tiny town houses built in 1921 to look like the London mews setting of a popular play of the same name. It was much favored as a home by movie actors, including Rosalind Russell, Humphrey Bogart and the Gish sisters.

Facade of Pomander Walk town house

Riverside Drive and Park **14**

Map 15 B4. **M** 103rd St.

RIVERSIDE DRIVE is one of the city's most attractive streets – broad, with shaded, and lovely views of the Hudson River. It is lined with the opulent original town houses as well as newer apartment buildings. At 40–46, 74–77, 81–89 and 105–107 Riverside Drive are houses designed at the end of the 19th century by local architect Clarence F. True.

The curved gables, bays and arched windows seem to suit the curves of the road and the flow of the river.

The bizarrely named Cliff Dwellers' Apartments at 243 is a 1914 building with a frieze showing early Arizona cliff dwellers, complete with masks, buffalo skulls, mountain lions and rattlesnakes.

Riverside Park was designed by Frederick Law Olmsted in 1880. He also laid out Central Park *(see pp202–5).*

Soldiers' and Sailors' monument in Riverside Park

Children's Museum of Manhattan **⑮**

212 W 83rd St. **Map** 15 C4. **C** *(212) 721-1234.* **M** *86th St.* ◯ *10am–5pm Wed–Sun (Jul–Aug: Tue–Sun).* ● *Jan 1, Dec 25, Thanksgiving.* ▓ ◙ ☕ ▣ ⓦ *www.cmom.org*

THIS PARTICULARLY imaginative participatory museum was founded in 1973 on the premise that children learn best through play. The Body Odyssey shows kids what they're made of in a fun-filled scientific ride through the body. The HP Inventor Center transports kids to this digital domain where they can rethink, revise, and reshape design solutions. The Time Warner Center for Media transforms children into budding camera operators,

Children's Museum entrance

newscasters, animators, and technicians in a state-of-the-art TV studio. On weekends and holidays there are guest performers from puppeteers to storytellers in the 150-seat theater. On Saturdays children can make their own books. There is also a gallery for free play and a Word Play area for early language acquisition.

The Ansonia **⑯**

2109 Broadway. **Map** 11 C1. **M** *72nd St.* ● *to the public.*

THIS BEAUX ARTS gem was built in 1899 by William Earl Dodge Stokes, heir to the Phelps Dodge Company fortune, who brought French architect Paul E.M. Duboy to design a building to rival the Dakota. The hotel was converted to a condominium in 1992. The most prominent features are the round corner tower and the two-story mansard roof adorned with single and double dormers. The building had a roof garden (complete with Dodge's menagerie: ducks,

Distinctive rounded turret of the Ansonia Hotel

chickens and a tame bear) and two swimming pools.

The hotel's thick, sound-muffling walls soon made it a favorite with the musical stars of yesteryear. Florenz Ziegfeld, Arturo Toscanini, Enrico Caruso, Igor Stravinsky and Lily Pons were once regular guests there.

The Dorilton **⑰**

171 W 71st St. **Map** 15 C5. **M** *72nd St.* ● *to the public.*

OPULENT DETAIL and an impressive high mansard roof adorn this apartment house. On the West 71st Street side of the building is a nine-story-high gateway. To the modern eye, the Dorilton is gloriously elaborate, but when it was first built in 1902 it provoked this reaction, reported by the *Architectural Record*: "The sight of it makes

Balcony on the Dorilton, supported by groaning figures

strong men swear and weak women shrink affrighted."

What would the critics have made of the Alexandria Condominium, at 135 West 70th Street, just a block away? Built in 1927 as the Pythian Temple, its current name stems from the lavish Egyptian-style motifs that adorned this former Masonic lodge. Many were stripped away when the building was converted to a condominium, but you can still see what the polychrome designs were like. There are lotus leaves, hieroglyphics, ornately carved columns, mythical beasts, and, in majestic splendor on the roof, two seated pharaohs.

MORNINGSIDE HEIGHTS AND HARLEM

MORNINGSIDE HEIGHTS, near the Hudson River, is home to Columbia University and two of the city's finest churches. Farther east is Hamilton Heights, situated on the border of Harlem, America's most famous black community. One way to see its highlights, which are spread over a large area, is

St. Francis of Assisi, Museo del Barrio

with one of the various tours offered, including a Sunday morning tour *(see p353)*. Many tours start in Hamilton Heights, move east to the St. Nicholas Historic District, stop to enjoy the gospel choir at the Abyssinian Baptist Church, and end with a southern-style brunch at Sylvia's, Harlem's best-known restaurant.

Louis Armstrong in a stained-glass window at the new Cotton Club

SIGHTS AT A GLANCE

Historic Streets and Buildings

Columbia University **1**
St. Paul's Chapel **2**
Low Library **3**
Grant's Tomb **6**
City College of the City University of New York **7**
Hamilton Grange National Memorial **8**
Hamilton Heights Historic District **9**
St. Nicholas Historic District **10**
Mount Morris Historical District **17**

Museums and Galleries

Schomburg Center for Research into Black Culture **12**
Studio Museum in Harlem **16**
Museo del Barrio **19**

Famous Theaters

Harlem YMCA **13**
Apollo Theater **15**

Churches

Cathedral of St. John the Divine pp224–25 **4**
Riverside Church **5**
Abyssinian Baptist Church **11**

Parks and Squares

Marcus Garvey Park **18**

Landmark Restaurants

Sylvia's **14**

GETTING THERE

By subway, take the 7th Ave/ Broadway local 1 train to 116th St./Columbia University. The M4, M5, M11 and M104 buses serve the area. For Harlem, take the A, B, C or D lines to 125th St, or the M1, M2, M7 or M101/102 buses.

Carved stone column, Cathedral of St. John the Divine

SEE ALSO

0 meters   500

0 yards   500

KEY

Street-by-Street map

M Subway station

Street by Street: Columbia University

A GREAT UNIVERSITY is as much spirit as buildings. After admiring the architecture, linger awhile on Columbia's central quadrangle in front of the Low Library, where you will see the jeans-clad future leaders of America meeting and mingling between classes. Across from the campus on both Broadway and Amsterdam Avenue are the coffee-houses and cafés where students engage in lengthy philosophical arguments, debate the topics of the day or simply unwind.

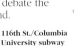

Alma Mater was sculpted by Daniel Chester French in 1903 and survived a bomb blast in the 1968 student demonstrations.

116th St./Columbia University subway (lines 1, 9)

The School of Journalism is one of Columbia's many McKim, Mead & White buildings. Founded in 1912 by publisher Joseph Pulitzer, it is the home of the Pulitzer Prize awarded for the best in letters and music.

Butler Library is Columbia's main library.

Low Library
With its imposing facade and high dome, the library dominates the main quadrangle. McKim, Mead & White designed it in 1895–97 ❸

★ **Central Quadrangle**
Columbia's first buildings were designed by McKim, Mead & White and built around a central quadrangle. This view looks across the quad toward Butler Library ❶

St. Paul's Chapel
esigned by the architects Howells &
kes in 1907, this church is known
for its fine woodwork and magnificent vaulted interior. It is full of
light and has fine acoustics **2**

LOCATOR MAP
See Manhattan Map pp12–13

KEY

– – – Suggested route

0 meters   100

0 yards   100

**The Sherman
Fairchild
Center** was
built in 1977
to house the
university's
life sciences
departments.

Student demonstrations put
Columbia University in the news in
1968. The demonstrations were
sparked by the university's plan to
build a gymnasium in nearby
Morningside Park. The protests forced
the university to build elsewhere.

The Eglise de Notre Dame was built for
a French-speaking congregation. Behind
the altar is a replica of the grotto at
Lourdes, France, the gift of a woman
who believed her son was healed there.

★ **Cathedral of St.
John the Divine**
*If this Neo-Gothic
cathedral is ever
finished, it will be
the largest in the
world. Although one third of the
structure has not yet been built, it
can hold 10,000 parishioners* **4**

**Carved
stonework**
decorates the
facade of the
Cathedral.

STAR SIGHTS

★ **Columbia
University**

★ **Cathedral of St.
John the Divine**

Alma Mater statue at Low Library, Columbia University

Columbia University ●

Main entrance at W 116th St. **Map** 20 E3. 🅲 *(212) 854-4900.* Ⓜ *116th St-Columbia Univ.* Ⓚ Ⓦ www.columbia.edu

THIS IS THE third location of one of America's oldest universities. Founded in 1754 as King's College, it was first situated close to where the World Trade Center stood.

In 1814, when a move uptown was proposed, the university approached the authorities for funding but was instead given a plot of land valued at $75,000, on which to build a new home. The university never built on the land itself, but leased it out and spent the years from 1857 to 1897 in buildings nearby. It finally sold the plot in 1985 to the leaseholders, Rockefeller Center Inc., for the sum of $400 million.

The present campus was begun in 1897 on the site of the Bloomingdale Insane Asylum. Architect Charles

McKim placed the university on a terrace, serenely above street level. Its spacious lawns and plazas still create a sense of contrast in the busy city.

Columbia, an Ivy League School, is noted for its law, medicine and journalism schools. Its distinguished faculty and alumni, past and present, include over 50 Nobel laureates. Famous alumni include Isaac Asimov, J.D. Salinger, James Cagney and Joan Rivers. Across the street is the affiliated Barnard College, a highly selective liberal arts college for women.

St. Paul's Chapel ●

Columbia University. **Map** 20 E3.
🅲 *(212) 854-1487 concert info.*
Ⓜ *116th St-Columbia Univ.*
🕙 *10am–11pm Mon–Sat (term time),*
10am–4pm (breaks). 🕔 *Sun.* 📷 Ⓚ

Interior brick vaulting of St. Paul's Chapel dome

COLUMBIA'S MOST outstanding building, built in 1904, is a mix of Italian Renaissance, Byzantine and Gothic. The interior Guastavino vaulting is of intricate patterns of aged red brick; the whole chapel is bathed in light from above.

The free organ concerts are an exceptionally fine way to appreciate the beauty and acoustics of this church. The Aeolian-Skinner pipe organ is renowned for its fine tone.

Facade of St. Paul's Chapel

Low Library ●

Columbia University. **Map** 20 E3.
Ⓜ *116th St-Columbia Univ.*

A CLASSICAL, columned building atop three flights of stone stairs, the library was donated by Seth Low, a former mayor and college president. The statue in front of it, *Alma Mater* by Daniel Chester French, became familiar as the backdrop to the many 1968 anti–Vietnam War student demonstrations. The building is now used as offices, and its rotunda for a variety of academic and ceremonial purposes. The books were moved in 1932 to Butler Library, across the quadrangle. The university's library collections total some six million volumes.

Cathedral of St. John the Divine ●

See p224–5.

Riverside Church ●

490 Riverside Dr at 122nd St. **Map** 20 D2. 🅲 *(212) 870-6700.* Ⓜ *116th St-Columbia Univ.* 🕙 *10:30am–5pm Tue–Sun.* 🕔 *10:45am Sun.* 📷 *with prior permission.* Ⓚ Ⓚ *Carillon bell concerts* 🅲 *(212) 870-6784. noon, 3pm Sun.* **Theater** 🅲 *(212) 864-2929.*
📧 Ⓦ www.theriversidechurchny.org

A 21-STORY STEEL frame with a Gothic exterior, the church design was inspired by the cathedral at Chartres. It was lavishly funded by John D. Rockefeller, Jr., in 1930. The Laura Spelman Rockefeller Memorial Carillon (in honor of Rockefeller's mother) is the largest in the world, with 74

Columbia University's main courtyard and the Low Library

bells. The 20-ton Bourdon, or hour bell, is the largest and heaviest tuned carillon bell ever cast. The organ, with its 22,000 pipes, is among the largest in the world.

At the rear of the second gallery is a figure by Jacob Epstein, *Christ in Majesty,* cast in plaster and covered in gold leaf. Another Epstein statue, *Madonna and Child,* stands in the court next to the cloister. The panels of the chancel screen honor eight men and women whose lives have exemplified the teachings of Christ. They range from Socrates and Michelangelo to Florence Nightingale and Booker T. Washington.

For quiet reflection, enter the small, secluded Christ Chapel, patterned after an 11th-century Romanesque church in France. For views, take the elevator to the 20th floor and then walk the 140 steps to the top of the 392-ft (120-m) bell tower for a fine panorama of Upper Manhattan from the windy observation deck. (This is definitely not recommended when the bells are tolling.)

Mosaic mural in Grant's Tomb showing Grant (right) and Robert E. Lee

Grant's Tomb ❻

W 122nd St and Riverside Dr.
Map 20 D2. ☎ *(212) 666-1640.*
Ⓜ *116th St-Columbia Univ.*
🕐 *9am–5pm daily.* ⬤ *Jan 1,
Thanksgiving, Dec 25.* 📷 ♿ 🚻
Ⓦ *www.nps.gov/gegr*

THIS GRANDIOSE monument honors America's 18th president, Ulysses S. Grant, the commanding general of the Union forces in the Civil War.

The mausoleum contains the coffins of General Grant and his wife, in accordance with the president's last wish that they be buried together. After Grant's death in 1885, more than 90,000 Americans contributed $600,000 to build the sepulcher, which was inspired by Mausoleus's tomb at Halicarnassus, one of the Seven Wonders of the Ancient World. The

General Grant on a Civil War campaign

tomb was dedicated on what would have been Grant's 75th birthday, April 27, 1897. The parade of 50,000 people, along with a flotilla of 10 American and 5 European warships, took more than seven hours to pass in review.

The interior was inspired by Napoleon's tomb at Les Invalides in Paris. Each sarcophagus weighs 8.5 tons. Two exhibit rooms feature displays on Grant's personal life and his presidential and military career.

Surrounding the north and east sides of the building are 17 sinuously curved mosaic benches that seem totally out of keeping with the formal architecture of the tomb. They were designed in the early 1970s by the Chilean-born Brooklyn artist Pedro Silva and built by 1,200 local volunteers under his supervision. The benches were inspired by the Spanish architect Antonio Gaudi's work in Barcelona. The mosaics depict subjects ranging from the Inuits to New York taxis to Donald Duck.

A short walk north of Grant's Tomb is another monument. An unadorned urn on a pedestal marks the resting place of a young child who fell from the riverbank and drowned. His grieving father placed a marker that reads simply "Erected to the memory of an amiable child, St. Clair Pollock, died 15 July 1797 in his fifth year of his age."

The 21-story Riverside Church, from the north

Cathedral of St. John the Divine ❹

Cram's Gothic West Front

Sᴛᴀʀᴛᴇᴅ ɪɴ 1892 and still only two-thirds finished, this will be the largest cathedral in the world. The interior is over 600 ft (180 m) long and 146 ft (45 m) wide. It was originally designed in Romanesque style by Heins and LaFarge; Ralph Adams Cram took over the project in 1911, devising a Gothic nave and west front. Medieval construction methods, such as stone supporting buttresses, continue to be used to complete the cathedral, which is also a venue for theater, music and avant-garde art.

Choir
Each of the choir's columns is 55 ft (17 m) tall and made of polished gray granite.

Nave
Rising to a height of over 100 ft (30 m), the piers of the nave are topped by graceful stone arches.

Rose Window ★
Completed in 1933, the stylized motif of the Great Rose is symbolic of the many facets of the Christian Church.

STAR FEATURES

★ **Rose Window**

★ **West Front Entrance**

★ **Bay Altars**

★ **Peace Fountain**

★ West Front Entrance
The portals of the cathedral's west front are adorned with many fine stone carvings. Some are recreations of medieval religious sculpture, but others have modern themes. This apocalyptic vision of New York's skyline, by local stonemason Joe Kinkannon, seems almost to predict the events of September 11, 2001 (see p54).

★ Peace Fountain
The sculpture is the creation of Greg Wyatt and represents nature in its many forms. It stands within a granite basin on the Great Lawn, south of the cathedral.

VISITORS' CHECKLIST

1047 Amsterdam Ave at W 112th St. **Map** 20 E4. *(212) 316-7540.* **M** *1, 9 to Cathedral Pkwy (110th St).* M4, M5, M7, M11, M104. *7am–6pm Mon–Sat, 1–7pm Sun.* *Vespers 6pm Sun.* **Donations.** *Concerts, plays, exhibitions, gardens.* **W** www.stjohndivine.org

Baptistry
The Gothic Baptistry has Italian, French and Spanish influences.

THE FINISHED DESIGN

Crossing tower

West towers

South transept

It will cost approximately $400 million to complete the cathedral. The south transept, crossing tower and west towers have yet to be finished. When the money is raised, the proposed design will take at least another 50 years to complete.

St. Ambrose Chapel
Named after a 4th-century Italian bishop, the chapel is decorated with Renaissance-style ironwork.

★ Bay Altars
The bay altar windows are devoted to human endeavor. The sports window shows feats of skill and strength.

Pulpit

Bishop's Chair
This is a copy from the Henry VII chapel in Westminster Abbey.

TIMELINE

1823 Cathedral planned for Washington Square	**1891** Site chosen and designated Cathedral Parkway	**1909** Pulpit designed by Henry Vaughan **1911** Cram design replaces earlier ones	**1967** Bronze lamps from former Penn Station installed on front steps
1800	1850	1900	1950
1873 Charter granted **1888** Competition to design cathedral won by Heins & LaFarge **1892** December 27 (St. John's Day), cornerstone laid		**1916** Ground broken for nave **1941** Work halted by World War II and does not resume until 1978	**1978** Third phase of building begins, and Stonemasons' Yard opened

City College of the City University of New York ❼

Main entrance at W. 138th St. and Convent Ave. **Map** 19 A2. **C** *(212) 650-7000*. **M** *137th St-City College.* **W** www.ccny.cuny.edu

Sᴇᴛ ʜɪɢʜ on a hill adjoining Hamilton Heights, the original Gothic quadrangle of this college, built between 1903 and 1907, is very impressive. The material used for the buildings is Manhattan schist, a stone that had been excavated in building the IRT subway. Later, contemporary buildings were added to the school, which enrolls nearly 15,000 students.

Once free to all residents of New York, City College still offers an education at low tuition rates. Three-quarters of the students are from minority groups, and a large number of them are the first in their families to attend college.

Shepard Archway at City College of the City University of New York

Hamilton Grange National Memorial ❽

287 Convent Ave. **Map** 19 A1. **C** *(212) 283-5154*. **M** *137th St-City College.* **○** *9am–5pm Fri–Sun.* **●** *public hols.* **📷 ▣** *hourly.* **W** www.nps.gov/hagr

Sǫᴜᴇᴇᴢᴇᴅ ʙᴇᴛᴡᴇᴇɴ a church and apartments is one of the city's most historic buildings, the 1802 columned wooden country home of Alexander Hamilton. He was one of the architects of the federal government system, first secretary of the treasury and founder of the National

Statue of Alexander Hamilton at Hamilton Grange

Bank. It is his face that appears on the $10 bill. Hamilton lived in The Grange for the last two years of his life. He was killed in a duel with political rival Aaron Burr in 1804.

The house was acquired by St. Luke's Episcopal Church in 1889 and moved two blocks to this "temporary" site, where it is open and always awaiting relocation and renovation.

Hamilton Heights Historic District ❾

W 141st–W 145th St. and Convent Ave. **Map** 19 A1. **M** *137th St-City College.*

Oʀɪɢɪɴᴀʟʟʏ ᴛʜɪꜱ was a setting for the impressive country estates of the wealthy. Also known as Harlem Heights, it was developed during the 1880s following the extension of the El line *(see p24)* into the neighborhood. The privacy of the enclave, on a high hill above Harlem, made it a very desirable location.

The section known as Sugar Hill was highly favored by Harlem's elite – US Supreme Court Justice Thurgood Marshall, notable jazz musicians Count Basie, Duke

Ellington and Cab Calloway, and world champion boxer Sugar Ray Robinson have all lived there.

The handsome three- and four-story stone row houses were built between 1886 and 1906 mixing Flemish, Romanesque and Tudor influences. In fine condition, many are used as residences by the faculty of City College.

Row houses in Hamilton Heights

St. Nicholas Historic District ❿

202–250 W 138th & W 139th St. **Map** 19 B2. **M** *135th St (B, C).*

A STARTLING CONTRAST to the rundown surroundings, the two blocks here, known as the King Model Houses, were built in 1891 when Harlem was considered a neighborhood for New York's gentry. They still comprise one of the city's most distinctive examples of row townhouses.

The developer, David King, chose three leading architects, who succeeded in blending their different styles to create a harmonious whole. The most famous of these was the firm of McKim, Mead & White,

Houses in St. Nicholas district

Adam Clayton Powell, Jr. (in dark suit) during a civil rights campaign

designers of the Pierpont Morgan Library *(see pp162-3)* and Villard Houses *(see p174)*, who were responsible for the northernmost row of solid brick Renaissance palaces. Their homes featured ground floor entrances rather than the typical New York brownstone stoops. Also, the elaborate parlor floors have ornate wrought-iron balconies below, as well as carved decorative medallions above their windows.

The Georgian buildings designed by Price and Luce are built of buff brick with white stone trim. James Brown Lord's designs of buildings, also Georgian in architectural style, feels much closer to Victorian, with outstanding red brick facades and bases constructed of brownstone.

Successful blacks were attracted here in the 1920s and 1930s, giving it the nickname Strivers' Row. Among them were celebrated musicians W. C. Handy and Eubie Blake.

Abyssinian Baptist Church **⓫**

132 W. 138th St. **Map** 19 C2.
[*(212) 862-7474.* **M** *135th St (B, C, 2, 3).* **⛪** *9am, 11am Sun. Groups of 10 or more need reservations.*

Nᴇᴡ ʏᴏʀᴋ's ᴏʟᴅᴇsᴛ black church, founded in 1808, became famous through its charismatic pastor Adam Clayton Powell, Jr. (1908–72), a congressman and civil rights

leader. Under his leadership it became the most powerful black church in America. A room in the church houses memorabilia from his life.

The church, a fine 1923 Gothic building, welcomes properly dressed visitors to Sunday services and to hear its superb gospel choir.

Schomburg Center for Research into Black Culture **⓬**

515 Malcolm X Blvd. **Map** 19 C2.
[*(212) 491-2200, (212) 491-2265 for tours.* **M** *135th St. (2, 3).* **◯** *hours vary – call to check.* **●** *Mon, Sun, public hols.* **♿ 🗖 🗖**
W *www.schomburgcenter.org*

Hᴏᴜsᴇᴅ ɪɴ a sleek contemporary complex opened in 1991, this is the largest research center of black and African culture in the United States. The immense collection was assembled by the late Arthur Schomburg, a black man of Puerto Rican descent, who was told by a teacher that there was no such thing as "black history." The Carnegie

Kurt Weill, Elmer Rice and Langston Hughes at the Schomburg Center

Corporation bought the collection in 1926 and gave it to the New York Public Library; Schomburg was made curator in 1932.

The library was the unofficial meeting place for writers involved in what later became known as the black literary renaissance of the 1920s, including Langston Hughes, W.E.B. Du Bois, Zora Neale Hurston and many other great writers of the day. It also hosted many literary gatherings and poetry readings.

The Schomburg Library has excellent facilities for conserving and making available the archive's treasures, which include rare books, photos, movies, art and recordings. The library was planned and designed to double as a cultural center and includes a theater and two art galleries, which feature changing shows of art and photography.

Harlem YMCA **⓭**

180 W 135th St. **Map** 19 C3.
[*281-4100.* **M** *135th St (2, 3).*

Sociologist W.E.B. Du Bois

Pᴀᴜʟ ʀᴏʙᴇsᴏɴ and many others made their first stage appearances here in the early 1920s. The Krigqa Players, organized by W.E.B. Du Bois in the basement in 1928, was founded to counter the derogatory images of blacks often presented in Broadway reviews of the time. The "Y" also provided temporary lodgings for some notable new arrivals in Harlem, including writer Ralph Ellison.

Gospel singers performing at Sylvia's during Sunday brunch

Sylvia's ⓮

328 Lenox Ave. **Map** 21 B1.
📞 *(212) 996-0660.* Ⓜ *125th St (2,3).*
🌐 *www.sylviassoulfood.com*

Harlem's best-known soul food restaurant serves up southern-fried or smothered chicken, spicy ribs, black-eyed peas, collard greens, candied yams, sweet potato pie and other Southern delicacies

Sylvia's

(see p287). Sunday brunch is served to the accompaniment of Gospel singers.

Take some time to explore the market at the corner of 125th Street and Lenox Avenue (opposite Sylvia's), extending for a block or more in either direction. This isn't a food market: it sells African clothing, jewelry and art of varying quality.

Apollo Theater ⓯

253 W 125th St. **Map** 21 A1.
📞 *(212) 531-5300, (212) 531-5301 (events).* Ⓜ *125th St (A, B, C, D).*
◯ *at showtimes. See Entertainment p341.* 🌐 *www.apollotheater.com*

The Apollo opened in 1913 as a whites-only opera house. Its great fame came when Frank Schiffman, a white entrepreneur, took over in 1934. He then opened the

theater to all races and turned it into Harlem's best-known showcase, with great artists such as Bessie Smith, Billie Holiday, Duke Ellington, and Dinah Washington.
Wednesday Amateur Nights, (begun in 1935) with winners

Apollo Theater

determined by audience applause, were famous, and there was a long waiting list for performers. These amateur nights launched the careers of Sarah Vaughan, Pearl Bailey, James Brown and Gladys Knight, among others, and they still attract hopefuls.

The Apollo was *the* place during the swing band era; following World War II, a new generation of musicians, such as Charlie "Bird" Parker, Dizzy Gillespie, Thelonius Monk and Aretha Franklin, continued the tradition.

Rescued from decline and refurbished in the 1980s, the Apollo once again features top black entertainers and hosts Amateur Nights.

Studio Museum in Harlem ⓰

144 W 125th St. **Map** 21 B2.
📞 *864-4500.* Ⓜ *125th St (2, 3).*
◯ *12–6pm Wed–Fri & Sun, 10am–6pm Sat.* ● *public hols.*
🚫 *except Sat.* 🅿 ♿ 🎞 **Lectures, children's programs, films.** 🏠
📷 🌐 *www.StudioMuseumin Harlem.org*

The museum was founded in 1967 in a loft on upper Fifth Avenue with the mission of becoming the premier center for the collection and exhibition of the art and artifacts of African-Americans.

The present premises, a five-story building on Harlem's main commercial street, was donated to the museum by the New York Bank for Savings in 1979. There are galleries on two levels for changing exhibitions featuring artists and cultural themes, and three galleries are devoted to the permanent collection of works by major black artists.

The photographic archives comprise one of the most

Exhibition space at the Studio Museum in Harlem

complete records in existence of Harlem in its heyday. A side door opens onto a small sculpture garden.

In addition to its excellent exhibitions, the Studio Museum also maintains a national artist-in-residence program, and offers regular lectures, seminars, children's programs and film festivals. An excellent small shop sells a range of books and African crafts.

Mount Morris Historical District ⑰

W 119th–W 124th Sts. **Map** 21 B2. Ⓜ *125th St (2, 3).*

Yᴏᴜ ᴄᴀɴ ᴘʟᴀɪɴʟʏ see that the late 19th-century Victorian-style town houses near Marcus Garvey Park were once grand. This was a favorite neighborhood of German Jews moving up in the world from the Lower East Side. Time has not been kind, and this district shows how the area has deteriorated.

A few impressive churches, such as St. Martin's Episcopal Church, remain. There are also some interesting juxta-positions of faiths to be seen: the columned Mount Olivet Baptist Church, at 201 Lenox Avenue, was once Temple Israel, one of the most imposing synagogues in the

St. Martin's Episcopal Church on Lenox Avenue

city; and at the Ethiopian Hebrew Congregation, 1 West 123rd Street, housed in a former mansion, the choir sings in Hebrew on Saturdays.

Marcus Garvey Park ⑱

120th–124th Sts. **Map** 21 B2. Ⓜ *125th St (2,3).*

The flamboyant black nationalist leader Marcus Garvey

Tʜɪs ʜɪʟʟʏ, ʀᴏᴄᴋʏ, two-block square of green is the site of New York's last fire watchtower, an open cast-iron structure built in 1856, with spiral stairs leading to the observation deck. The bell below the deck sounded the alarm. It may be best to view it from a distance, however, if you have any doubts about your safety. Previously known as Mount Morris Park, it was renamed in 1973 in honor of Marcus Garvey. He came to Harlem from Jamaica in 1916 and founded the Universal Negro Improvement Association, which promoted self-help, racial pride and a back-to-Africa movement.

Museo del Barrio ⑲

1230 5th Ave. **Map** 21 C5. ⎰ *(212) 831-7272.* Ⓜ *103rd St (6).* ◑ *11am–5pm Wed–Sun (to 8pm Thu).* ● *Jan 1, Thanksgiving, Dec 25.* **Donation expected.** ⍉ ⛨ ⌨ ⩘ *www.elmuseo.org*

Fᴏᴜɴᴅᴇᴅ ɪɴ 1969, this is North America's only museum devoted to Latin American art, specializing in the culture of Puerto Rico. Exhibitions feature contemporary painting and sculpture, folk art and historical artifacts. The stars of the perma-nent collection are about 240 wooden Santos, carvings of the saints by folk artisans and a reconstructed *bodega* or Latino corner grocery. Exhibits change often, but some of the Santos are always on display. The pre-Columbian collection contains rare artifacts from the Caribbean. Situated at the far end of Museum Mile, this unusual museum attempts to bridge the gap between the lofty Upper East Side and the cultural heritage of El Barrio (Spanish Harlem).

Folk art at the Museo del Barrio: one of the *Three Wise Men* (left) and the *Omnipotent Hand*

FARTHER AFIELD

THOUGH OFFICIALLY part of New York City, the boroughs outside Manhattan are quite different in feel and spirit. They are residential and don't have the famous skyscrapers that are associated with New York. The difference is evident even in the way residents describe a trip to Manhattan as "going into the city." Yet the outlying areas boast many attractions, including the city's biggest zoo, botanical gardens, museums, beaches and sports arenas. For a guided walk around Brooklyn see pages 264–65.

SIGHTS AT A GLANCE

Historic Streets and Buildings
Morris-Jumel Mansion ❷
George Washington Bridge ❸
Wave Hill ❺
Yankee Stadium ❿
Grand Army Plaza ⓲
Park Slope Historic District ⓳
Historic Richmond Town ㉔
Alice Austen House ㉗

Museums and Galleries
Audubon Terrace ❶
The Cloisters pp234–37 ❹
Van Cortlandt House Museum ❻
New York Hall of Science ⓭
American Museum of the Moving Image and Kaufman Astoria Studio ⓮
Brooklyn Children's Museum ⓰
Brooklyn Museum pp248–51 ㉑
Jacques Marchais Museum of Tibetan Art ㉕
PS1 Museum of Modern Art (MoMA), Queens ⓯
Snug Harbor Cultural Center ㉖

Parks and Gardens
New York Botanical Garden pp240–41 ❽
Bronx Zoo pp242–43 ❾
Flushing Meadow-Corona Park ⓬
Prospect Park ⓴
Brooklyn Botanic Garden ㉒

Famous Theaters
Brooklyn Academy of Music ⓱

Cemeteries
Woodlawn Cemetery ❼

Beaches
City Island ⓫
Coney Island ㉓
Jamaica Bay Wildlife Refuge Center ㉘
Jones Beach State Park ㉙

KEY

▨ Main sightseeing areas

0 kilometers   5
0 miles   3

N

SIGHTS OUTSIDE THE CENTER

The Bronx

Upper Manhattan

Queens

Brooklyn

Staten Island

◁ Jamaica Bay

Upper Manhattan

It was in upper Manhattan that the 18th-century Dutch settlers established their farms. Now a suburban area with little of the bustle of downtown Manhattan, it is a good place to escape the inner city for some relaxed museum and landmark sightseeing. The Cloisters (see pp234–37) displays a magnificent collection of medieval art, housed within original European buildings of the period. A piece of New York history is found at the Morris-Jumel Mansion in north Harlem. From his headquarters here, George Washington mounted the defense of Manhattan in 1776.

Audubon Terrace ❶

Broadway at 155th St. **M** *157th St.*
American Numismatic Society
((212) 234-3130. ** 9am–
4:30pm Tue–Fri. ** **
W www. amnumsoc.org
**American Academy of Arts and
Letters (** (212) 368-5900.
** 1–4pm Thu–Sun. ** **Hispanic
Society of America (** (212) 926-
2234. ** 10am–4:30pm Tue–Sat,
1–4pm Sun. ** public hols. **Donations**.
** ** **W** www.hispanicsociety.org

This 1908 complex of Classical Revival buildings by Charles Pratt Huntington is named after naturalist John James Audubon, whose estate once included this land. Audubon is buried in nearby Trinity Cemetery. His grave-

Facade of the American Academy of Arts and Letters

stone, a Celtic cross, bears the symbolic images of this adventurous artist's career: the birds he painted, his palette and brushes, and his rifles.

The complex was funded by the architect's cousin, civic benefactor Archer Milton Huntington. His dream was that it should be a center of culture and study. A central plaza contains statues by his wife, the sculptress Anna Hyatt Huntington.

Audubon Terrace contains several theme museums that are worth seeking out. The American Numismatic Society is the leading American museum devoted to coinage and medals, and has one of the world's best collections,

with half a million photos and illustrations of coins. A permanent exhibition called "The World of Coins" traces the historical and political role of money, and there is a vast library.

The American Academy of Arts and Letters was set up to honor American writers, artists, and composers, and 75 honorary members from overseas. On the roll are writers John Steinbeck and Mark Twain, painters Andrew Wyeth and Edward Hopper, and the composer Aaron Copland. Exhibitions feature members' work. The library (for scholars, by appointment) has old manuscripts and first editions.

Bronze door at the academy

The Hispanic Society of America is a public museum and library based upon the personal collection of Archer M. Huntington. The Spanish Renaissance-style main gallery holds works by Goya, El Greco and Velázquez. There are one-month exhibitions from March through May, and on one Sunday in late October the building is open to the public.

Statue of El Cid by Anna Hyatt Huntington at Audubon Terrace

Morris-Jumel Mansion ❷

Corner W 160th St and Edgecombe Ave. 【 *(212) 923-8008.* Ⓜ *163rd St.* 🕙 *10am–4pm Wed–Sun.* ⬤ *public hols.* 🈲 ◎ 🈲 *by appt.* 🈲 Ⓦ *www. morrisjumel.org*

Tʜɪꜱ ɪꜱ ᴏɴᴇ of New York's few pre-Revolutionary buildings. Now a museum with nine restored period rooms, it was built in 1765 for Roger Morris. His former military colleague George Washington used it as temp-orary headquarters while defending Manhattan in 1776. In 1810 it was bought and updated by Stephen Jumel, a merchant of French-Caribbean descent, and his wife Eliza. The pair furnished the house with souvenirs of many visits to France. Her boudoir has a "dolphin" chair, reputedly bought from Napoleon. Eliza's social climbing and love affairs scandalized New York society. It was rumored that she let her husband bleed to death in 1832 so she could inherit his fortune. She later married Aaron Burr, aged 77, and divorced him three years later on the day he died.

The exterior of the Palladian-style, wood-sided Georgian house with classical portico and octagonal wing has been restored. The museum exhibits include many original Jumel pieces.

The 3,500-ft (1,065-m) span of the George Washington Bridge

George Washington Bridge ❸

Ⓜ *175th St.* Ⓦ *www.panynj.gov*

Fʀᴇɴᴄʜ ᴀʀᴄʜɪᴛᴇᴄᴛ Le Corbusier called this "the only seat of grace in the disordered city." While not as famous a landmark as its Brooklyn equivalent, this bridge by engineer Othmar Ammann and his architect Cass Gilbert has its own character and history. Plans for a bridge linking Manhattan to New Jersey had been in the pipeline for more than 60 years before the Port of New York Authority raised the $59 million to fund the project. It was Ammann

The lighthouse under Washington Bridge

who suggested a road bridge rather than the more expensive rail link. Work began in 1927 and the bridge was opened in 1931: first across were two young roller skaters from the Bronx. Today it is a vital link for commuter traffic and is in constant use.

Cass Gilbert had plans to clad the two towers with masonry but funds did not permit it, leaving an elegant skeletal structure 600 ft (183 m) in height and 3,500 ft (1,065 m) long.

Ammann had also allowed for a second deck in his plan, and this lower deck was added in 1962, increasing the bridge's capacity enormously. Now the eastbound toll collection shows a traffic level of over 53 million cars per year.

Below the eastern tower is a lighthouse that was saved from possible demolition in 1951 by public pressure. Many thousands of young New Yorkers and children all around the world have loved the bedtime story *The Little Red Lighthouse and the Great Gray Bridge,* and wrote letters to save the lighthouse. Author Hildegarde Hoyt Swift wove the tale around her two favorite New York landmarks.

The bridge is also home to the world's largest free-flying American flag, which is hung out on major federal holidays.

The Cloisters ❹

See pp234–37.

Morris-Jumel Mansion, built in 1765, with its original colossal portico

The Cloisters ❹

The Cloisters seen from Fort Tryon Park

THIS WORLD-FAMOUS museum of medieval art resides in a building constructed from 1934 to 1938, incorporating medieval cloisters, chapels and halls. Sculptor George Grey Barnard founded the museum in 1914; John D. Rockefeller, Jr. funded the Metropolitan Museum of Art's 1925 purchase of the collection and donated the site at Fort Tryon Park and also the land on the New Jersey side of the Hudson, directly across from The Cloisters.

Tomb Effigy of Jean d'Alluye
This tomb immortalizes the 13th-century Crusader.

Langon Chapel

Pontaut Chapter House

Gothic Chapel

★ **Unicorn Tapestries**
The set of beautifully preserved tapestries, woven in Brussels around 1500, depicts the quest and capture of the mythical unicorn.

STAR EXHIBITS

★ Unicorn Tapestries

★ Belles Heures de Jean, Duc de Berry

★ Annunciation Triptych by Robert Campin

Boppard Stained-Glass Lancets *(1440–47)*
Below the lancet of Saint Catherine, angels display the arms of the coopers' guild, of which Catherine was patron.

Bonnefort Cloister

Glass Gallery

Trie Cloister

★ **Annunciation Triptych** *(about 1425)*
The Campin Room is the location of this Robert Campin of Tournai small triptych, a magnificent example of early Flemish painting.

Saint-Guilhem Cloister
Intricate floral ornamentation can be found on the capitals of this cloister.

Romanesque Hall

Upper floor

Lower floor

Main entrance

VISITORS' CHECKLIST

Fort Tryon Park. *(212) 923-3700.* M *A to 190th St (exit via elevator).* M4. *Mar–Oct: 9:30am–5:15pm Tue–Sun; Nov–Feb: 9:30am–4:45pm Tue–Sun.* *Jan 1, Thanksgiving, Dec 25.* **Donations.** *No videos.* *book in advance.* **Concerts.** W *www.metmuseum.org*

Virgin and Child Frescoes
This 12th-century fresco is from the Catalonian church of San Juan de Tredós.

KEY TO FLOOR PLAN

☐ Exhibition space

☐ Non-exhibition space

Cuxa Cloister
The reconstructed 12th-century cloister features Romanesque architectural detail and motifs.

Enthroned Virgin and Child
This elaborately carved ivory sculpture was made in England during the late 13th century.

GALLERY GUIDE
The museum is organized roughly in chronological order. It starts with the Romanesque period (1000 AD) and moves to the Gothic (1150 to 1520). Sculptures, stained glass, paintings and the gardens are on the lower floor. The Unicorn Tapestries are on the upper floor.

★ **Belles Heures**
This book of hours, commissioned by Jean, Duc de Berry, is among a rotating installation of exquisite illuminated books and folios.

Exploring The Cloisters

K NOWN PARTICULARLY for its Romanesque and
Gothic architectural sculpture, The Cloisters
collection also includes illuminated manuscripts,
stained glass, metalwork, enamels, ivories and
paintings. Among its tapestries is the renowned
Unicorn series. The Cloisters' splendid medieval
complex is unrivaled in North America.

ROMANESQUE ART

**A lifesized 12th-century Spanish
crucifix portraying Christ as the
King of Heaven**

F ANCIFUL BEASTS and people,
acanthus blossoms and
scrollwork top the columns
around The Cloisters. Many
are in the Romanesque style
that flourished in the 11th
and 12th centuries. The
museum has numerous
masterpieces of Romanesque
art and architecture, showing
the style's powerful rounded
arches and intricate details.
Highly embellished capitals
and warm, pink marble typify
the 12th-century Cuxa Cloister
from the Pyrenees in France.
A griffin, a dragon, a centaur
and a basilisk are among the
creatures parading over the
Narbonne Arch nearby.
    In a more solemn style, the
apse from the church of
Saint-Martín in Fuentidueña,
Spain, is a massive rounded
vault constructed from 3,300
blocks of limestone. It is
decorated with a 12th-century
fresco of the Virgin and Child
and has a golden-crowned
Christ depicted as triumphant
over death.
    More than 800 years ago,
Benedictine and Cistercian
monks sat on the cold stone
benches in the Pontaut Chapter
House. By the 19th century it
had become so neglected that
it was used as a stable. Its
ribbed vaulting is a foretaste of
the Gothic style to come.

**A 16th-century Flemish boxwood
rosary bead from the Treasury**

GOTHIC ART

W HERE ROMANESQUE art
was solid, the Gothic
style that followed (from 1150
to around 1520) was open,
with pointed arches, glowing
stained-glass windows and
three-dimensional sculpture.
Gothic depictions of the Virgin
and Child display exquisite
craftsmanship.
    The Gothic Chapel's
brilliantly colored windows
show scenes and figures from
biblical stories. Lifesized tomb
sculptures include the effigy
of the Crusader knight Jean
d'Alluye. During the 1790s,

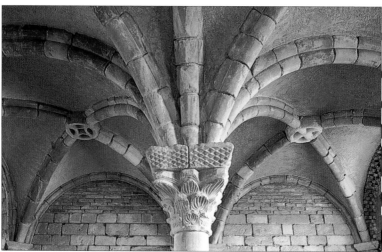

Vaulted ceiling of the Pontaut Chapter House

the statue's original home, La Clarté-Dieu Abbey in France, was vandalized, and the statue was used to bridge a stream.

In the Boppard Room, the lives of the saints are told in marvelous late Gothic stained glass from Germany.

Robert Campin's Flemish masterwork, the *Annunciation* altarpiece, is the focus of the Campin Room. It is an intimate room with furnishings that might have belonged to a wealthy 15th-century family.

MEDIEVAL GARDENS

More than 300 varieties of plants grown in the Middle Ages can be found in The Cloisters' gardens. The Bonnefont Cloister has herbal, medicinal and cooking plants. The Trie Cloister features plants shown in the *Unicorn Tapestries* and reveals the use of flowers in medieval symbolism: roses (for the Virgin Mary), pansies (the Holy Trinity) and daisies (the eye of Christ).

Bonnefont Cloister

THE TAPESTRIES

T HE CLOISTERS' tapestries are full of rich imagery and symbolism, and are among the museum's most highly prized treasures. The four *Nine Heroes Tapestries* bear the coat of arms of Jean, Duc de Berry, who was a brother of the King of France and one of the greatest art patrons of the Middle Ages. These tapestries are one of only two sets that survived from the late 14th century; the other set belonged to Jean's brother, Louis, Duc d'Anjou.

Nine great heroes of the past – three pagan, three Hebrew, three Christian – are shown with members of the medieval court, from cardinals, knights and damsels to musicians.

In an adjacent room is the magnificent *Hunt of the Unicorn*, a series of seven tapestries woven in Brussels around 1500. It depicts the symbolic hunt of the mythical unicorn and capture by a maiden.

Although they were misused in the 19th century to protect fruit trees from frost damage,

the tapestries are remarkably well preserved. They are also astonishing in detail, with

Julius Caesar, entertained by court musicians, in a *Nine Heroes* tapestry

literally hundreds of minutely observed plants and animals. Their story can be read as a tale of courtly love, but the series is also an allegory for the Crucifixion and the Resurrection of Christ.

THE TREASURY

I N MEDIEVAL TIMES, precious objects were stored in sanctuaries for safekeeping. At The Cloisters, they are found in the Treasury.

The collection includes several Gothic illuminated "books of hours." These were used for the private devotions of the nobility, such as the Limbourg brothers' *Belles Heures*, made for Jean, Duc de Berry, in 1410, and the tiny, palm-sized version by Gothic master Jean Pucelle for the Queen of France, around 1325.

Other religious artifacts range from a 13th-century English ivory Virgin to the 14th-century silver gilt and enamel reliquary shrine thought to have belonged to Queen Elizabeth of Hungary, along with censers, chalices, candlesticks and crucifixes.

Curiosities here include the "Monkey Cup," an enameled beaker probably made for the 15th-century Burgundian court, showing mischievous monkeys robbing a sleeping peddler; an intricately carved rosary bead the size of a walnut; a 13th-century boat-shaped, jeweled saltcellar; and a full set of playing cards dating to the 15th century.

Hunting images and symbols depicted on a 15th-century deck of playing cards

The west parlor of the Van Cortlandt House Museum

The Bronx

ONCE A prosperous suburb with a famous Grand Concourse lined with apartment buildings for the wealthy, the Bronx has now become an unfortunate symbol of urban decay. Still, diverse ethnic communities, unique resources and charming areas, such as Riverdale at the northern end, remain. Two major attractions are the Bronx Zoo and the New York Botanical Garden. There is also a new golf course at Ferry Point Park and Fulton Fish Market has relocated here. Yankee Stadium, now over 50 years old, is still a favorite for baseball fans.

Wave Hill ❺

W 249th St. and Independence Ave, Riverdale. ▐ (718) 549-3200. Ⓜ 231st St. then bus Bx7, 10, 24. ◯ 9am–5:30pm Tue–Sun (to 9pm Wed Jun–Jul, to 4:30pm mid-Oct to mid-Apr). ◙ free Tue, 9am–noon Sat, Dec–Feb. ⓦ www.wavehill.org

THIS 28-ACRE (11-ha) oasis of calm and beauty, boasts fine views over to the New Jersey Palisades across the Hudson River. The former estate of financier and conservationist George W. Perkins, Wave Hill has had a long series of distinguished tenants, including Theodore Roosevelt, Mark Twain and

Arturo Toscanini. Perkins also owned neighboring estates, underneath which he built a subterranean recreation center complete with bowling alley, and a tunnel leading into the main building.

The house and the grounds are open to the public. The house is frequently used for concerts. They often take place in the grand Armor Hall, designed in 1928 for Bashford Dean, who was then the curator of the collection of arms and armor at the Metropolitan Museum of Art.

The gardens were originally designed by Viennese landscape gardener, Albert Millard. There are also greenhouses, lawns, an herb garden and woodlands. Exhibitions range from sculpture to horticulture.

The adjoining Riverdale Park has attractive woodland and paths along the river.

The interior of the grand Armor Hall at Wave Hill

Van Cortlandt House Museum ❻

Van Cortlandt Park. ▐ (718) 543-3344. Ⓜ 242nd St, Van Cortlandt Park. ◯ 10am–3pm Tue–Fri, 11am–4pm Sat, Sun (last adm: 30 mins before closing). ◙ most public hols. ◙ ◙ ◙ ◙ See *The History of New York* pp18–19. ⓦ www.vancortlandthouse.org

The facade of Van Cortlandt House

A RESTORED 1748 Georgian Colonial country manor built of rough stone, the Bronx's oldest building was the family home of Frederick Van Cortlandt, a New Yorker who inherited great wealth and was related to many influential families of his day.

The dining room was used as one of General George Washington's headquarters; the ground behind the house was once the scene of skirmishing during the Revolutionary War.

The interior has American period furnishings as well as a superb collection of delftware and a complete 17th-century Dutch bedroom.

On the exterior, look for the carved faces in the keystones over the windows.

Woodlawn Cemetery ❼

Jerome and Bainbridge Aves.
📞 (718) 920-0500. Ⓜ Woodlawn.
🕐 9am–4:30pm daily. **Office** ◗
public hols. 🚫 ♿ 🎫

F OR A GLIMPSE into another kind of social history, visit Woodlawn Cemetery, the burial place of many a wealthy and distinguished New Yorker.

Memorials and tombstones are set in beautiful grounds. F.W. Woolworth and many members of his family are interred in a mausoleum

Entrance to the Woolworth mausoleum

only a little less ornate than the building that carries the family name. The pink marble vault of meat magnate Herman Armour is oddly reminiscent of a ham.

Other New York notables buried here include Mayor Fiorello La Guardia, Roland Macy, the founder of the great department store, author Herman Melville and jazz legend Duke Ellington.

New York Botanical Garden ❽

See pp240–41.

Bronx Zoo/ Wildlife Conservation Park ❾

See pp242–43.

Yankee Stadium ❿

E 161st St at River Ave, Highbridge.
📞 (718) 293-6000. Ⓜ 161st St.
Tours: daily at noon (except on game afternoons), no reservations required.
See **Entertainment** pp344–45.
🆆 www.yankees.com

T HIS IS THE HOME of the New York Yankees baseball team. Among Yankee heroes are two of the greatest players

of all time: Babe Ruth and Joe DiMaggio (who was also famous for marrying the actress Marilyn Monroe in 1954). In 1921 left-hander Babe Ruth, wearing the Yankees' distinctive pinstripes, hit the stadium's first home run – against the Boston Red Sox, his former team. The stadium was completed two years later by Jacob Ruppert, the owner of the Yankees, and became known as "the house that Ruth built".

The Stadium had a face-lift in the mid-1970s, and now seats up to 54,000 people who come for sports, concerts and other events. One of the largest annual gatherings has been that of the Jehovas Witnesses and in 1950, 123,707 people attended in a single day. In 1965 Pope Paul VI celebrated mass before a crowd of more than 80,000. It was the first visit to North America by a Pope – the second was made in 1979 when John Paul II also visited the Stadium.

The Yankees remain one of the top teams in the American League. Going to watch a game is a great New York experience. There are four Yankee Clubhouse stores in New York where tickets for tours and games can be purchased.

Joe DiMaggio in action at Yankee Stadium in 1941

City Island ⓫

Ⓜ 6 to Pelham Parkway, then Bx29 to City Island. **Museum** 190 Fordham St. 🕐 1pm–5pm Wed & Sun. 🆆 www.cityisland.com

S ITUATED off the northeast shore of the Bronx and surrounded by Long Island Sound, City Island is a small nautical outpost with a very New England feel and offers a refreshing change of pace. Its scenic marinas are filled with sailboats, and its seafood restaurants would satisfy any sailor's appetite. Several America's Cup winners have been built in its boatyards. The City Island Museum is in one of the island's most historic buildings, the old Public School 17, built on an Indian burial ground at a high point on the island.

City Island is linked to the Bronx by bridge. To the north on the mainland is Orchard Beach, a crescent of white sand edged with 1930s bathing huts. The beach is popular with area residents, and it can be uncomfortably crowded and dirty.

An old tugboat moored at one of City Island's piers

The New York Botanical Garden ●

Hibiscus

THE NEW YORK Botanical Garden is 250 acres of dazzling beauty and hands-on enjoyment. From the nation's most glorious Victorian glasshouse to the 12-acre Everett Children's Adventure Garden, it is alive with things to discover. One of the oldest and largest botanical gardens in the world, it has 48 gardens and plant collections, and 50 acres of uncut forest. The spectacular Enid A. Haupt Conservatory has been wonderfully restored as *A World of Plants*, with misty tropical rain forests and dramatic deserts.

Entrance to Enid A. Haupt Conservatory

Season.
Exhibitio
Galler

Deserts of Africa

Rock Garden
Rock outcroppings, streams, a waterfall, and a flower-rimmed pond create an alpine habitat for plants from around the world ④

Historic Forest
One of New York City's last surviving natural forest areas includes red oak, white ash, tulip trees, and birch ⑤

Deserts of the Americas

Everett Children's Adventure Garden *Kids can discover the wonders of ecology and plants* ⑧

LOCATOR MAP

Peggy Rockefeller Rose Garden
Over 2,700 rose bushes have been planted in the Rose Garden, laid out in 1988 according to the 1916 design ⑦

Palms of the Americas Gallery

100 majestic palms soar into a 90-ft glass dome. A tranquil reflecting pool is surrounded by tropical plants.

VISITORS' CHECKLIST

Kazimiroff Blvd, Bronx River Parkway (Exit 7W).
📞 (718) 817-8700.
Ⓜ 4, D to Bedford Park Blvd.
🚌 Bx26. ◯ Nov–Mar: 10am–5pm Tue–Sun; Apr–Oct: 10am–6pm Tue–Sun ⬤ Mon, public hols. 📷 🔌 ✉ 🖥
🎫 *Lectures*. Ⓦ www.nybg.org

The Enid A. Haupt Conservatory consists of 11 interconnecting glass galleries housing *A World of Plants*, including rain forests, deserts, aquatic plants, and seasonal exhibitions ①

Garden Cafe
This is a delightful spot to enjoy a meal. You can eat outside on terraces overlooking beautiful gardens ⑥

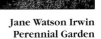

Conservatory

Jane Watson Irwin Perennial Garden
Flowering perennials are arranged in dramatic patterns according to height, shade, color and blooming time ②

Tropical Lowland Rain Forest Gallery

Courtyard Pool

Leon Levy Visitor Center
This modern pavilion, which opened in 2004, has a shop, a cafe, and a visitor orientation facility ⑨

Aquatic Plants and Vines Gallery

Tropical Upland Rainforest Gallery

Tram
The half-hour tour of the gardens provides information about horticultural, educational, and botanical research programs. Passengers can alight at a number of stops to explore the gardens before reboarding ③

Bronx Zoo ❾

OPENED IN 1899, the Bronx Zoo is the largest urban zoo in the US, home to more than 4,000 animals of 500 species, living in realistic representations of their natural habitats. The zoo is a leader in the perpetuation of endangered species, such as the Indian rhinoceros and the snow leopard. Its 265 acres of woods, streams and parklands include, in season, a children's zoo a butterfly zone, and a shuttle train that transports visitors around the sprawling park. Visitors are also free to walk around. For the best overview of the park areas take the Skyfari cable car (also open seasonally).

★ The Congo Gorilla Forest
This award winning replica of central African rain forest is home to gorillas, monkeys, and a host of other animals.

Skyfari cable car

Mouse-House

W
M

World of Darkness

Carter Giraffe Building

★ African Plains
Zebras, lions, cheetahs and gazelles roam the African Plains. Predators and prey are separated by a moat.

Africa
Oryxes find shelter under an African hut.

Asia entrance

Camel Rides
Children enjoy such seasonal experiences as camel rides and other attractions.

Bengali Express monorail

★ JungleWorld
A climate-controlled tropical rain forest harbors mammals, birds and reptiles from South Asia. The animals are kept apart from visitors by ravines, streams and cliffs.

Monkeys in JungleWorld

Baboon Reserve
Visitors walk along a dry riverbed to see wildlife in an Ethiopian mountain habitat.

Children's Zoo
Kids can crawl through a prairie dog tunnel, climb on a spiderweb, try on a turtle shell, and pet and feed the animals.

World of Reptiles

The Zoo Center
houses elephants, rhinos and tapirs.

Southern Boulevard entrance

Aquatic Bird House

Aitken Aviary

VISITORS' CHECKLIST

Fordham Rd /Bronx River Pkwy.
📞 *(718) 367-1010.* Ⓜ *2, 5 to Pelham Pkwy.* 🚄 *to Fordham Station.* 🚌 *Bx9, Bx12, Bx19, Bx22, Bx36, Bx39, Bx40, Bx42, BxM11 express bus, Q44.* ⏰ *Nov–Mar: 10am–4:30pm daily; Apr–Oct: 10am–5pm daily (5:30pm Sat & Sun).* 🎫 *free Wed.* ♿ ♿
✓ 🍴 ⭐ *Children's Zoo.*
🖥 *www.bronxzoo.com*

STAR FEATURES

★ **Wild Asia**

★ **African Plains**

★ **JungleWorld**

★ **World of Birds**

★ **Congo Gorilla Forest**

★ **Tiger Mountain**

Rainey Gate entrance

Monkey House

★ **World of Birds**
Exotic birds soar free in the lush surroundings of a rain forest. An artificial waterfall rushes down a 50-ft (15-m) fiberglass cliff in this walk-through habitat.

Greater hornbill

Bronxdale entrance

Himalayan Highlands
endangered species, such as snow leopards and red pandas, are kept here.

★ **Wild Asia**
The Bengali Express monorail journeys through forests and meadows of an Asian habitat, where elephants, rhinoceroses and Siberian tigers roam free.

★ **Tiger Mountain**
These magnificent animals are on view all year. Only one inch of glass separates visitors from the wild cats.

Queens

A BIG, SPRAWLING borough, Queens has a wide variety of attractions and residential and commercial areas, including Long Island City, where exciting new museums and restaurants are springing up all over. Development of the borough accelerated after 1909, when the construction of Queensboro Bridge made commuting easier. The city's main airports are here, and there are many different ethnic enclaves including the Greek neighborhood of Astoria and the various Asian communities in Flushing.

A 1900 Mutoscope at the Museum of the Moving Image

Flushing Meadow–Corona Park ⑫

Ⓜ *Willets Point-Shea Stadium. See* **Entertainment** *pp344–45.*

T HE SITE of New York's two World's Fairs now offers expansive waterside picnic grounds and a multitude of attractions. These include the 50,000-seat Shea Stadium, the home of the New York Mets baseball team and a popular site for rock concerts. Flushing Meadow is also home to the US Tennis Center, where the prestigious United States Open is played. The courts are open for would-be Agassis, Grafs and Everts for the remainder of the year. In the 1920s this area was known as the Corona Dump, a nightmarish place of salt marshes and great piles of smoldering trash. In *The Great Gatsby*, author F. Scott Fitzgerald dubbed it the "valley of ashes." It reeked of rotting garbage and glowed red at night. New York's Parks' Commissioner Robert Moses was the driving force behind its transformation. A whole mountain of rubbish was removed and the river was totally re-channeled. The marsh was drained and sewage works were built, helping to restore the area. This site was to serve as the site for the 1939 World's Fair, at which a world on the brink of war saluted the elusive notion of world peace.

The Unisphere, symbol of the 1964 fair, still dominates the remains of the fairground. This giant hollow ball of green steel, built by the US Steel Corporation, is 12 stories high and weighs a massive 350 tons.

The 1964 World's Fair Unisphere at Flushing Meadow-Corona Park

New York Hall of Science ⑬

46th Ave and 111th St Flushing Meadows, Corona Park. Ⓒ *(718) 699-0005.* Ⓜ *111th St.* ⊙ *Sep–Jun: 9:30am–2pm Tue–Thu, 9:30am–5pm Fri, noon–5pm Sat–Sun; Jul–Aug: 9:30am–2pm Mon, 9:30am–5pm Tue–Fri, 10:30am–6pm Sat–Sun.* ● *public hols.* 🎦 📷 ♿ 🅿 📡 Ⓦ *www.nyhallsci.org*

T HE SCIENCE PAVILION built for the 1964 World's Fair was designed with stained glass set in concrete panels. It is now a hands-on museum for science and technology, with exhibits on color, light and physics. Kids love the giant video screens, interactive video, and laser optical exhibits.

The concrete curtain wall of the New York Hall of Science

American Museum of the Moving Image and Kaufman Astoria Studio ⑭

35th Ave at 36th St, Astoria. **Museum** Ⓒ *(718) 784-4520.* **Studio** Ⓒ *(718) 784-0077.* Ⓜ *36th St.* **Museum** ☐ *noon–5pm Wed, Thu, noon–8pm Fri, 11am–6:30pm Sat, Sun. Screenings: 6:30pm Sat, Sun.* 🎦 **Studio** ● *to public.* 📷 ♿ 🅿 Ⓦ *www.ammi.org*

I N NEW YORK's filmmaking heyday, Rudolph Valentino, W.C. Fields, the Marx Brothers and Gloria Swanson all made films in the Astoria Studio, the largest studio in the city, opened in 1920 by Paramount Pictures. When the movies went west, the army took over, making training films from 1941 to 1971.

The complex stood empty until 1977 when Astoria Motion Picture and Television Foundation was founded to

Poster at the Museum of the Moving Image

largest moviemaking facilities on the East Coast. *The Cotton Club* and Woody Allen's *Radio Days* were filmed here.

In 1981 one of the studio buildings was transformed into the American Museum of the Moving Image, with interactive displays on production and theaters for the screening of movies and television.

There is a lot of memorabilia on display, from Ben Hur's chariot to Star Trek costumes. The main gallery draws from the permanent collection of over 85,000 movie artifacts. The Museum offers seminars, and a 200-seat theater has film and video programs, from early silent movies, with live music, to the avant-garde.

PS1 MoMA, Queens ⑮

22–25 Jackson Ave at 46th Ave, Long Island City. 🄲 *(718) 784-2084.* Ⓜ *E, V to 23rd St-Ely Ave; 7 to 45 Road-Courthouse Square; G to Court St or 21 St-Van Alst.* 🚌 *B61, Q67.* 🄾 *noon–6pm Thu–Mon.* ⬤ *Tue & Wed.* 🈲 🅰 📷 🆆 www.ps1.org

HOUSED IN an elementary school, PS1 was founded in 1971 under a scheme to transform abandoned New York City buildings into exhibition, performance and studio spaces for artists. The museum is affiliated to the Museum of Modern Art *(see pp170–73)* and is one of the oldest art organisations in the US devoted solely to modern art. Temporary exhibitions are hosted alongside permanent works and many pieces are interactive. In summer, music is performed in the courtyard.

preserve it. *The Wiz*, a musical starring Michael Jackson and Diana Ross, was made here, helping to pay for restoration. Today, the studios house the

Brooklyn

The bandstand at Prospect Park *(see p246)*

IF BROOKLYN were a separate city, it would be the country's fourth largest. It has a character all of its own. Many entertainment greats – Mel Brooks, Phil Silvers, Woody Allen and Neil Simon among them – celebrate their birthplace with great affection and humor. Brooklyn is the ultimate melting pot, with West Indians, Hasidic Jews, Russians, Italians and Arabs living side by side. Among the diverse neighborhoods are the historic residential districts of Park Slope and Brooklyn Heights.

Brooklyn Children's Museum ⑯

145 Brooklyn Ave. 🄲 *(718) 735-4400.* Ⓜ *Kingston.* 🄾 *1–6pm Tue–Fri, 11am–6pm Sat, Sun; Jul & Aug: 1–6pm Wed–Fri, 11am–6pm Sat, Sun.* **Rooftop Theater** 🄾 *6:30–8pm Fri, 10am–5pm Sat–Sun.* ⬤ *Jan 1, Jul 4, Labor Day, Thanksgiving, Dec 25.* **Donation.** 🅰 📷 🆆 www.bchildmus.org

THE BROOKLYN Children's Museum was the first to be designed especially for children and was founded in 1899. Since then, it has been a model, inspiration and consultant to the development of more than 250 museums for children across the country and all over the world. Housed in a high-tech, specially designed underground building dating from 1976, it is one of the most imaginative children's museums anywhere.

The layout of the building is a maze of complex interconnected

passageways running off the main "people tube" – a huge drainage pipe that connects the four levels. This is not a passive place where children are meant to stand around and stare – the emphasis is on involvement and hands-on exhibits. Everywhere you look there are curiosities to be discovered, experienced, made or played with. There is even a walk-on piano like the one in the film *Big* – children of every age find it quite irresistible.

Special exhibitions and events are designed to help children learn about the planet, resolve their fears or problems, understand other cultures and discover the past. The squeals of laughter and delight that are always heard are a sign of this well-designed and clever museum's success in teaching children and the young at heart.

A mask from the Children's Museum

The facade of the Brooklyn Academy of Music

Brooklyn Academy of Music ⓱

30 Lafayette Ave. **[** *(718) 636-4100.* **M** *Atlantic Ave.* 🅿 🦽 🚻 **W** www.bam.org See **Entertainment** *pp338–9.*

HOME TO THE Brooklyn Philharmonic, the Academy (known as BAM) is Brooklyn's leading cultural venue and the oldest, founded in 1858. It offers outstanding performances, often tending toward the innovative and avant-garde.

The classic 1908 building was designed by Herts & Tallant, and inaugurated with a production of Gounod's opera *Faust* featuring the Neapolitan tenor Enrico Caruso. The greats who have performed here includes actress Sarah Bernhardt, ballerina Anna Pavlova, musicians Pablo Casals and Sergei Rachmaninoff, poets Edna St. Vincent Millay and Carl Sandburg, and statesman Winston Churchill. Many international touring groups have made appearances here, including Britain's Royal Shakespeare Company.

The BAM Next Wave Festival has presented contemporary artists such as musicians David Byrne and Philip Glass and choreographers Pina Bausch and Mark Morris. The BAM also runs the Harvey Theater nearby, a movie theater now used for dance, drama and music events. BAM Rose Cinemas show first-run independent films and BAMcinématek has classics, retrospectives, festivals and sneak previews.

Grand Army Plaza ⓲

Plaza St at Flatbush Ave. **[** *(718) 965-8951.* **M** *Grand Army Plaza.* **Arch** ◯ *for occasional exhibitions.*

The Soldiers' and Sailors' Arch at Grand Army Plaza

FREDERICK LAW OLMSTED and Calvert Vaux laid out this grand oval in 1870 as a gateway to Prospect Park. The Soldiers' and Sailors' Arch and its sculptures were added in 1892 as a tribute to the Union Army. The bust of John F. Kennedy here is the only official New York monument to him.

In June, the plaza is the center of the Welcome Back to Brooklyn Festival for the famous – and not-so-famous – people born in Brooklyn.

Park Slope Historic District ⓳

Streets from Prospect Park W below Flatbush Ave, to 8th/7th/5th avenues. **M** *Grand Army Plaza.*

Relief work on the Montauk Club

THIS WONDERFUL enclave of beautiful Victorian town houses was developed on the edge of Prospect Park in the 1880s. It served the upper-middle-class professionals who were able to commute into Manhattan after the Brooklyn Bridge was opened in 1883. The shady streets are lined with two- to five-story houses in every architectural style popular in the late 19th century, some with the towers, turrets and curlicues so representative of the era. Particularly fine examples are in Romanesque Revival style, with rounded entry arches.

The Montauk Club at 25 Eighth Avenue combines the style of Venice's Ca' d'Oro palazzo with the friezes and gargoyles of the Montauk Indians, after whom this popular 19th-century gathering place was named.

Prospect Park ⓴

[*(718) 965-8969.* 🎭 *(718) 965-8999.* **M** *Grand Army Plaza.* 🎵 *(718) 788-8500.* **W** www.prospectpark.org

DESIGNERS OLMSTED and Vaux considered this park, opened in 1867, better than their earlier Central Park. The Long Meadow, a sweep of broad lawns and grand vistas, is the longest unbroken swath of green space in New York.

Olmsted's belief was that "a feeling of relief is experienced by entering them [the parks] on escaping from the cramped, confining and controlling circumstances of the streets of the town." That

The facade of the Brooklyn Public Library on Grand Army Plaza

vision is still as true today as it was a century ago.

Among the many notable features are Stanford White's colonnaded Croquet Shelter, and the pools and weeping willows of the Vale of Cashmere. The Music Grove bandstand shows Japanese influences and hosts both jazz and classical music concerts throughout the summer.

A favorite feature of the park is the Camperdown Elm, an ancient and twisted tree planted in 1872. The Friends of Prospect Park raise money to keep it and all the park trees healthy. This old elm has inspired many poems and paintings. Prospect Park has a wide variety of landscapes, from classical gardens dotted with statues to rocky glens with running brooks. A guided tour with a ranger is the best way to see the park.

Carousel horse in Prospect Park

Brooklyn Museum ㉑

See pp248–51.

Brooklyn Botanic Garden ㉒

900 Washington Ave. 📞 *(718) 623-7200.* Ⓜ *Prospect Pk, Eastern Pkwy.* **Grounds** ◯ *Apr–Sep: 8am–6pm Tue–Fri (10am Sat, Sun & hols); Oct–Mar: 8am–4:30pm (10am Sat & Sun).* ● *Jan 1, Thanksgiving, Dec 25.* 💳 *for Japanese Garden, free Tue & Sat (10am–noon).* 📷 ♿ 🎁 🍴 ◯ Ⓦ *www.bbg.org*

T HOUGH IT is not vast in size, you will find that this 50-acre (20-ha) garden holds many delights. The area was designed by the Olmsted Brothers in 1910 and features

A beluga whale at the New York Aquarium

a traditional Elizabethan-style "knot" herb garden and one of North America's largest collections of roses.

The central showpiece is a Japanese hill-and-pond garden, complete with a teahouse and Shinto shrine. In late April and early May the park promenade is aglow with delicate Japanese cherry blossoms, which have prompted an annual festival featuring typical Japanese culture, food and music.

April is also the time for tourists to appreciate Magnolia Plaza, where some 80 trees display their beautiful, creamy blossoms against a backdrop of daffodils on Boulder Hill.

The Fragrance Garden is planted in raised beds, where the heavily scented, textured and flavored plants are all labeled in Braille, giving blind visitors an opportunity to identify them as well.

The new conservatory now houses one of America's largest bonsai collections and some rare rain forest trees, which are providing scientists with medicinal extracts to produce life-saving drugs.

Brooklyn Botanic Garden lily pond

Coney Island ㉓

Ⓜ *Stillwell Ave, Coney Island.* 📞 *(718) 372 5159.* Ⓦ *www.coneyisland.com* **New York Aquarium** *Boardwalk and W 8th St, Coney Island.* 📞 *(718) 265-FISH.* ◯ *10am–5pm Mon–Fri, 10am–5:30pm Sat, Sun & hols (Jun–Aug: to 6pm Mon–Fri & 7pm Sat, Sun & hols; Nov–Mar: to 4:30pm daily).* 💳 Ⓦ *www.nyaquarium.com* **Coney Island Museum** *128 Surf Ave, nr W 12th St.* 📞 *(718) 372 5159.* ◯ *12–sundown Sat, Sun.* 💳 Ⓦ *www.coneyislandusa.com*

I N THE MID-19TH century, Brooklyn poet Walt Whitman composed many of his works on Coney Island, at that time untamed Atlantic coastline. By the 1920s, Coney Island was starting to bill itself as the "World's Largest Playground." Three huge fairgrounds built by 1904 (Luna Park, Dreamland and Steeplechase Park) provided a combination of hair-raising rides and nearby beaches. The subway arrived in 1920, and the 1921 boardwalk ensured Coney Island's popularity throughout the Depression.

A main attraction is the **New York Aquarium**, on 14 acres by the sea, with 350 species. The **Coney Island Museum** has memorabilia, relics of old rides, and souvenirs. Coney Island is still exciting: the boardwalk yields ocean views and the Cyclone roller coaster evokes screams. The Mermaid Parade in June is a major annual event.

Brooklyn Museum ㉑

W HEN IT OPENED in 1897, the Brooklyn Museum building, designed to be the largest cultural edifice in the world, was the greatest achievement of New York architects McKim, Mead & White. Though only one-sixth completed, the museum is today one of the most impressive cultural institutions in the United States, with a permanent encyclopedic collection of some 1.5 million objects, which are housed in a grand structure of 560,000 sq ft (41,805 sq m).

North facade, designed by McKim, Mead & Whi

KEY TO FLOOR PLAN

- [ ] Arts of Africa and the Americas
- [ ] Asian art
- [ ] Prints, drawings and photographs
- [ ] Williamsburg Murals
- [ ] Egyptian and Classical art
- [ ] Decorative arts
- [ ] Painting and sculpture
- [ ] Special exhibitions
- [ ] Non-exhibition space

★ **Female Figurine**
5000 years old, this rare statuette is a highlight of the museum's impressive Egyptian collection.

Iris and B. Cantor Auditorium

Chinese Jar
Cobalt blue fishes and water plants adorn this 14th-century Yuan dynasty blue-and-white ceramic jar.

★ **Beaded Crown**
This 19th century crown from Nigeria is the ultimate symbol of Yoruba kingship.

Third floor

Mezzanin Gallery

Second floor

South entrance

First fl

Morris A. and Meyer Schapiro W

Main entrance

★ **An Out of Doors Study** (1889)
Sargent's portrait of French artist Paul Helleu and his wife Alice was painted during the couple's visit to the Sargent family at Fladbury.

Fifth floor

VISITORS' CHECKLIST

200 Eastern Pkwy, Brooklyn. (718) 638-5000. M 2, 3 to Eastern Parkway/Brooklyn Museum. B41, B69, B67, B71. 10am–5pm Wed–Fri, 11am–6pm Sat, 11am–11pm first Sat in month, 11am–6pm Sun. Jan 1, Thanksgiving, Dec 25. **Donation expected.** Concerts, lectures. www.brooklynmuseum.org

ce visible orage

Theatre

Luce Center for American Art

★ **Winter Scene in Brooklyn** (1820)
Francis Guy's depiction of downtown Brooklyn is from the American Identities Collection.

Fourth floor

Alexander the Great
The military leader was portrayed in alabaster in the 1st century BC.

Ibis Coffin (332–330 BC)
The sacred bird of ancient Egypt merited a splendid coffin of gold leaf and silver.

Moorish Smoking Room (1865)
This room is from a house on West 54th Street, bought by J D Rockefeller in 1884.

GALLERY GUIDE
The collection is on five floors, with African and New World art on the first; prints, drawings and Asian art on the second; Egyptian, Classical, and European painting and sculpture on the third; decorative art on the fourth; and American art on the fifth. There is special exhibition space on the first and fourth floors.

STAR EXHIBITS

★ **Female Figurine**

★ **Beaded Crown**

★ **Winter Scene in Brooklyn by Francis Guy**

★ **An Out of Doors Study, by John Singer Sargent**

Exploring the Collection

THE BROOKLYN MUSEUM houses one of the finest art collections in the United States. Its strengths include an outstanding collection of Native American art from the Southwest; 28 American period rooms; exquisite pieces of ancient Egyptian and Islamic art; and important American and European paintings.

Seated Buddha torso in limestone, from India (late 3rd century AD)

ARTS OF AFRICA, THE PACIFIC, AND THE AMERICAS

THE BROOKLYN Museum set a precedent in the United States in 1923 by exhibiting African objects as works of art rather than artifacts. Since then, the African art collection has grown steadily in both importance and size.

Exhibits include a rare intricately carved ivory gong from the Benin kingdom of 16th-century Nigeria, one of only five in existence.

The museum also has a notable collection of Native American work, including totem poles, textiles and pottery. A 19th-century deerskin shirt, once worn by a chief of the Blackfoot tribe, depicts his brave and daring exploits in battle.

Ancient American artistic traditions are represented by Peruvian textiles, Central American gold and Mexican sculpture. A beautifully preserved tunic from Peru, dating from AD 600, is so tightly woven that its vibrant symbolic designs appear to have been painted onto the cloth rather than woven in the traditional way.

The Oceanic collection includes sculpture from the Solomon Islands, Papua New Guinea and New Zealand.

ASIAN ART

CHANGING EXHIBITIONS from the museum's permanent collection of Chinese, Japanese, Korean, Indian, Southeast Asian and Islamic art are always on display. Japanese and Chinese paintings, Indian miniatures and Islamic calligraphy complement the Asian sculpture, textiles and ceramics. The collections of Japanese folk art, Chinese cloisonné (enamel work) and Oriental carpets are of particular note. Good examples of Buddhist art range from a variety of Chinese, Indian and Southeast Asian Buddhas to a mandala-patterned temple banner from 14th-century Tibet, painted in rich, luminous watercolors.

DECORATIVE ARTS

THE FOCUS of the decorative arts department is a very stylish assembly of 28 superb American period rooms.

The earliest is from a 17th-century Brooklyn Dutch house. It served as a parlor, dining room and sleeping area, with the enclosed "bed boxes" built against the wall opposite the fireplace. The Moorish Smoking Room, from John D. Rockefeller's brownstone house, is an opulent example of elegant New York living during the 1880s. In complete contrast, the most recent room is a 1928–30 Art Deco study from a Park Avenue apartment, including a walk-in bar that was hidden behind paneling during the Prohibition era *(see pp28-29).*

Normandie **chrome pitcher, by Peter Müller-Munk (1935)**

Blackfoot tribe deerskin shirt, decorated with porcupine quills and glass beads (19th century)

Also on exhibit is a wide selection from the museum's vast collection of furniture, ceramics, glass, pewter, silver and metalware, including a 1930s pitcher whose shape was inspired by the stacks of the ocean liner *Normandie*.

EGYPTIAN, CLASSICAL AND ANCIENT MIDDLE EASTERN ART

RECOGNIZED AS among the world's finest, the Egyptian collection holds many masterpieces. It begins with an early female figure dating from 3500 BC, and encompasses sculptures, statues, tomb paintings and reliefs as well as funerary paraphernalia. Of the latter, the most unusual is the coffin of an ibis, probably recovered from the vast animal cemetery of Tuna el-Gebel in Middle Egypt. The ibis was a sacred bird representing the god Thoth, and this coffin is made of solid silver and wood overlaid with gold leaf, with rock crystal for the bird's eyes. These galleries have been renovated into a state-of-the-art, high-tech installation.

Among the artifacts from the Greek and Roman civilizations are statuary, pottery, bronzes, jewelry and mosaics.

Among the Ancient Near and Middle Eastern exhibits are an extensive collection of pottery and 12 alabaster reliefs from the Assyrian palace of King Ashur-nasir-pal II. These date from around 883-859 BC and depict the king fighting, overseeing his crops and purifying the "sacred tree," a major icon in Assyrian religion.

PAINTING AND SCULPTURE

THIS SECTION contains works from the 14th century to the present, including a well-known and outstanding 19th-century French art collection with works by Degas, Rodin, Monet, Cézanne, Matisse and Pissarro. It also boasts one of the largest holdings of Spanish

Pierre de Wiessant (about 1886) by Auguste Rodin, from his *Burghers of Calais* group

Colonial paintings and one of the best collections of North American paintings to be found in the United States.

The museum's 20th-century American collection includes, appropriately, *Brooklyn Bridge* by Georgia O'Keeffe.

The Sculpture Garden has a collection of architectural ornamentation taken from demolished New York buildings, including statues that were rescued from the original Penn Station.

PRINTS, DRAWINGS AND PHOTOGRAPHS

THE PRINTS section displays examples by many masters, ranging from a rare woodcut print by Dürer entitled *The Great Triumphal Chariot* and works by Piranesi to an excellent Impressionist and Post-Impressionist collection. This includes works by Toulouse-Lautrec and Mary Cassatt, the only American woman associated with the Impressionist movement. There are lithographs by James McNeill Whistler, Winslow Homer engravings, and a superb selection of

Rotherhide, an etching by James McNeill Whistler (1860)

drawings by Fragonard, Paul Klee, Van Gogh, Picasso and Gorky, among others, many of them in black and white.

The photography collection consists mainly of works by major 20th-century American photographers, including a 1924 portrait of Mary Pickford by Edward Steichen and work by Margaret Bourke-White, Berenice Abbott and Robert Mapplethorpe. All of these artworks are constantly rotated for conservation purposes.

Sandstone reliefs from Thebes in Egypt (around 760–656 BC), depicting the great god Amun-Re and his consort Mut

Staten Island

APART FROM the famous ferry ride, Staten Island and its attractions are not well known to New Yorkers in general. Residents feel so ignored, in fact, that they've talked about seceding from the city. Visitors who venture beyond the ferry terminal, however, will be pleasantly surprised to find hills, lakes and greenery, with expanses of open space, amazing harbor views and well-preserved early New York buildings. One of the biggest surprises here is a cache of Tibetan art that is hidden away in a replica of a Buddhist temple.

Historic Richmond Town ㉔

441 Clarke Ave. **C** *(718) 351-1611.* **S74** *S74 from ferry.* ○ *Sep–May: 1–5pm, Wed–Sun; Jun–Aug: 10am–5pm Wed–Sat, 1–5pm Sun.* ⬛ ⊙ ⬛ ⬛
Ⓦ *www.historicrichmondtown.org*

THERE ARE now 29 buildings, 14 of which are open to the public, in New York's only restored village and outdoor museum. The village was first named Coccles-town, after the local shellfish, but was soon corrupted to "Cuckoldstown," much to the annoyance of the

Cologne at the General Store

residents. By the end of the Revolutionary War the new name of Richmondtown had been adopted. It was the county seat until Staten Island was made part of the city in 1898, and has been preserved as an example of an early New York settlement.

The Voorlezer House, built in the Dutch era before 1696, is the oldest elementary

school to be found in the country. The Stephens General Store, which opened in 1837, doubled as the local post office. It has been well restored, right down to the contents of the shelves. The complex, set on 100 acres (40 ha), includes wagon sheds, a courthouse built in 1837, houses, several shops and a tavern. There are also several seasonal workshops where traditional rural crafts are demonstrated to visitors.

St. Andrew's Church, dating to 1708, and its old graveyard are just across the Mill Pond stream, and the Historical Society Museum is in the County Clerk's and Surrogate's Office. The toy room is a delight.

Jacques Marchais Museum of Tibetan Art ㉕

338 Lighthouse Ave. **C** *(718) 987-3500.* **S74** *S74 from ferry.* ○ *1–5pm Wed–Sun.* ● *public hols.* ⬛ ⊙ ⬛
⬛ Ⓦ *www.tibetanmuseum.com*

AHILLTOP provides a very tranquil setting for one of the largest collections of privately owned Tibetan art outside Tibet. The main building is a replica of a mountain temple with an authentic altar

The Voorlezer House at Richmond Town

in three tiers, crowded with gold, silver and bronze figures.

Another building is used as a library. The garden has some stone sculptures, including life-size Buddhas. The museum was built in 1947 by Mrs. Harry Klauber, a dealer in Asian art trading under the name of Jacques Marchais. The Dalai Lama ⚑ paid his first visit here in 1991.

A gazebo at the Snug Harbor Cultural Center

Snug Harbor Cultural Center ㉖

1000 Richmond Terrace. **C** *(718) 448-2500.* **S40** *S40 from ferry to Snug Harbor Gate.* **Grounds** ○ *dawn–dusk daily.* **Art Gallery** ○ *10am–5pm Tue–Sun.* ⬛ *donation.* **Children's Museum** ○ *noon–5pm (summer 11am–5pm) Tue–Sun.* ● *Jan 1, Thanksgiving, Dec 25.* ⬛ *limited.* ⬛ ⬛
Ⓦ *www.snug-harbor.org*

FOUNDED IN 1801 as a haven for aged sailors, Snug Harbor is now an arts center complex of 28 buildings in various stages of restoration. There are five stately Greek Revival gems, from 1831 to 1880. the oldest, the Main Hall, is the **Newhouse Center for Contemporary Art**, but the

Sacred sculpture at the Jacques Marchais Center of Tibetan Art

ships at sea in the stained-glass windows are a reminder of its origins. Other buildings house the award-winning **Staten Island Children's Museum** and the Veterans Memorial Hall, used for indoor performances. A sculpture festival and summer shows are held on the lawns. The Staten Island Botanical Garden has a noted orchid collection and a beautiful rose garden.

Snug Harbor is the legacy of a Scottish sailor, Robert Richard Randall, who became rich in the Revolutionary War, some say by piracy, and bequeathed his wealth to care for seamen. The property was bought so that the sailors could enjoy its harbor views.

Clear Comfort, Alice Austen's lifetime residence

Alice Austen House ㉗

2 Hylan Blvd. (718) 816-4506.
S 51 from ferry to Hylan Blvd.
noon–5pm Thu–Sun. Jan, Feb, public hols. **Donation**
limited.
www.aliceausten.org

THIS SMALL COTTAGE built around 1690 has the delightful name of Comfort Cottage. It was the home of the photographer Alice Austen, born in 1866, who lived in this house for most of her life. She documented life on the island, in Manhattan, and also on trips to other parts of the country and on her travels to Europe. She lost all her money in the stock market crash of 1929, and her poverty forced her into a public poorhouse at the age of 84. One year later, her photographic talent was finally recognized by *Life* magazine, which published an article about her, earning her enough money to enter a nursing home. She left 3,500 negatives dating from 1880 to 1930. Today, the Friends of Alice Austen House mounts exhibitions of her best work.

Even Farther Afield

The village of Broad Channel at Jamaica Bay

Jamaica Bay Wildlife Refuge Center ㉘

Cross Bay Blvd at Broad Channel.
(718) 318-4340. Broad Channel. Sunrise to sunset; visitor center: 8:30am–5pm daily.
www.nps.gov/gate

THE MARSHES and uplands of the Refuge cover an area almost the size of Manhattan. Over 300 species of birds live here either seasonally or all year round. On the main Atlantic migratory path, the Refuge is at its best in spring and autumn, when the skies are filled with skeins of geese and ducks. The park rangers lead hikes and nature walks for weekend visitors – be sure to wear suitable shoes and clothes, and take along a zoom-lens camera or binoculars to get the best from your visit. The only village is Broad Channel, a small collection of houses on pilings on the Cross Bay Boulevard. The Refuge and a 10-mile (16-km) stretch of beach and boardwalk at Rockaway, are accessible by subway straight from Manhattan.

Jones Beach State Park ㉙

(516) 785-1600. Long Island Railroad: Penn Station to Jones Beach (late May–Labor Day). (718) 217-5477. **Jones Beach Theater**. (516) 221-1000. **Beaches**.
all year late May –Labor Day.
www.nysparks.state.ny.us/parks

JONES BEACH was the creation of New York's Parks' Commissioner Robert Moses (*see p244*), who transformed this narrow spit of land into Long Island's most accessible and popular beach in 1929. There are sand dunes, surf on the Atlantic side and sheltered water in the bay. There is also miniature golf, swimming pools, restaurants and the Jones Beach Theater, which hosts a variety of open-air concerts in the summer.

Robert Moses State Park is on the next island to the east, Fire Island, which is over 30 miles (48 km) long, yet less than 900 yds (800 m) across. Areas of the island are totally unspoiled and unpopulated, with long stretches of white sands, making it a great place for walking and bicycling in peaceful surroundings.

Fire Island's communities are small and very varied – some are favored by singles looking for the company of the opposite sex, others are sedate and family-orientated, others are favorites with New York's large gay community.

Sunbathers basking at Jones Beach

FOUR GUIDED WALKS

WALKING IN NEW YORK is an excellent way to discover the human scale of the city. The following ten pages explore the unique character and charm of New York through four thematic walks. These range from an exploration of Greenwich Village and SoHo's literary and artistic connections *(see pp258–9)* to a trip across the Brooklyn Bridge for spectacular views and a glimpse of 19th-century New York *(see pp264–5)*.

In addition, each of the 15 areas of Manhattan described in the *Area by Area* section of this book has a short

Sculpture outside US Custom House, Lower Manhattan

walk on its *Street-by-Street* map, taking you past many of the interesting sights in that area. Various organizations and enthusiasts run walking tours of the city. These range from serious appraisals of architectural history to a guide to the ghosts of Broadway. Details of tour organizers are listed on page 353, or you can consult *Time Out New York* magazine. As in any major city, take extra care of your personal belongings while walking *(see p356–7)*. Plan your route ahead; walk only during daylight hours; and, whenever possible, go in a group.

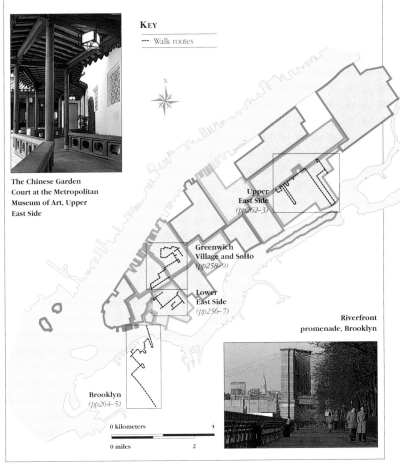

KEY

‑‑‑ Walk routes

N

The Chinese Garden Court at the Metropolitan Museum of Art, Upper East Side

Upper East Side *(pp262–3)*

Greenwich Village and SoHo *(pp258–9)*

Lower East Side *(pp256–7)*

Riverfront promenade, Brooklyn

Brooklyn *(pp264–5)*

0 kilometers   4

0 miles   2

◁ **Relaxing on Grove Street, Greenwich Village**

A 90-Minute Walk in the Lower East Side

This walk is through old immigrant neighborhoods that have given New York its unique flavor, and illustrates the ever-changing texture of the city as neighborhoods are rediscovered and one set of newcomers replaces another. Along the way you can experience a variety of cultures and cuisines. Sunday is the best day for local color. See more about Lower East Side on pages 92-99.

The Lower East Side

Begin on East Houston Street, the border between the Lower East Side and the East Village, where some of the best traditional Jewish cuisine can be found at Yonah Schimmel Knish Bakery ① (137) and Russ & Daughters ② (179), run by the grandson of the founder and famed for smoked fish and caviar. Katz's Delicatessen ③ (205) has been a fixture for over 100 years. Continue to Norfolk Street and turn right to see the Angel Orensanz Cultural Center ④, housed in New York's oldest synagogue building.

Turn right on Rivington for another synagogue survivor, the

An 1885 iron from the Lower East Side Tenement Museum ⑥

Congregation Shaarai Shomoyim First Romanian-American Congregation ⑤ in a handsome 1890 brick building. The interior, while shabby, is still impressive.

The Lower East Side has been discovered by hip young New Yorkers and is now home to cutting-edge boutiques, trendy clubs and restaurants. On Rivington cool young fashion shops share the blocks with the old.

Make a left onto Orchard Street, the traditional center of the Jewish Lower East Side. Pushcarts that lined the block are gone and the sidewalk stands sell mostly cheap merchandise, but many stores offer discount designer leather and fashion. All are closed on Saturday, so Sunday is the busiest day.

A must stop for historians is the Lower East Side Tenement Museum ⑥ (90 Orchard). An original tenement has been restored to show how three immigrant families lived from 1874 to the 1930s.

A detour across Broome Street on Orchard brings you to Guss Pickles ⑦ (85–7) a new location for an old-timer, the inspiration for the 1988 film *Crossing Delancey*. Customers still line up for the crunchy pickles sold from barrels.

Come back to Broome and turn left for another

unique survivor, the Kehila Kedosha Janina Synagogue and Museum ⑧ (280 Broome), a small but fascinating congregation with a little upstairs museum.

Another left along Eldridge will take you, beyond Canal Street, to the grand Eldridge Street Synagogue ⑨, the first Eastern European synagogue in New York, open again after extensive restoration.

KEY

— Walk route

- - Detour route

※ Good viewing point

Ⓜ Subway station

TIPS FOR WALKERS

Starting point: East Houston St.
Length: 2 miles (3.2 km).
Getting there: Take the subway F or V to Second Avenue; exit one East Houston at Eldridge. Other stops: F to Delancey, J, M, Z to Essex. The M15 bus stops on East Houston and on the corner of Delancey and Allen Streets, M14 and M9 run along Essex Street. Returning from Chinatown-Little Italy, Canal Street station is served by the J, M, N, Q, R, W and 6 trains.
Stopping-off points: Little Italy's cafes are perfect for coffee and luscious cakes. For more substantial fare, Sweet-n-Tart at 20 Mott Street is recommended for Chinese food, or for Italian on Mulberry Street, Il Cortile (125) or Il Palazzo (151). For Jewish dairy delicacies such as blintzes, try Ratner's Dairy Restaurant at 138 Delancey Street.

KENMARE S

CENTRE STREET

MOTT STREET

ELIZABETH STREET

ⓘⒸ GRA

Ⓜ Canal Street

BAYARD ST

MULBERRY ST

MOTT ST

⑫

⑪

⑬

⑩ ※ CANA

BOWERY

DIVISION

EAST BROADW

HESTER

0 meters

0 yards 500

Clothes vendors at Orchard Street market

Guss' Pickle Company ⑦

Chinatown

Turn around and return to Canal Street, pausing to admire the spire of the Chrysler Building and the city skyline in view in the distance from Eldridge. Turn left and cross the Bowery, where many jewelry shops remain, remnants of the city's original Diamond District ⑩ As you continue, the shops give way to stalls selling an exotic array of vegetables, and butcher shops with rows of roast ducks in

to taste unusual fare. For spiritual sustenance. visit the Eastern States Buddhist Temple ⑪ in Mott Street.

At Bayard Street, turn left to see all the Chinese political posters and messages on the Wall of Democracy, then turn back and walk to Mulberry Street. The curve next to Columbus Park was Mulberry Bend ⑫, once notorious for gang murders and mayhem.

An Italian deli in Little Italy ⑬

Pretzel seller on Orchard Street

the windows. At 200 Canal Street is Kam Man Food Products. One of the largest Chinese markets in the area, it is a fascinating place to explore. Turn left from Canal to Mott Street and you'll know you are right in the heart of Chinatown by all the Chinese neon signs. Even the banks and phone booths are shaped like pagodas. There are hundreds of restaurants here, from holes-in-the-wall to haute cuisine, all offering a chance

Little Italy

Walk up Mulberry Street toward Grand Street and you are suddenly in Little Italy ⑬. Small in area though it is, and encroached on by Chinatown, this is a colorful few blocks of old-world restaurants, coffee shops, and stores selling homemade pasta, sausages, breads and pastries. The Italian population has dwindled over the years, but a staunch group of merchants remain, determined to retain the area's Italian atmosphere. Their stronghold is Mulberry Street between Broome and Canal streets, with a few shops holding their own on Grand Street near Mulberry. If you continue to walk on Grand, however, you are quickly back into Chinatown.

The big event of the year is the Feast of San Gennaro, named for the patron saint of Naples. For 11 nights in September, Mulberry Street is jammed locals and visitors enjoying the parades and the Italian food, with rows of sizzling sausages stalls.

Kam Man Food Products at 200 Canal Street

A 90-Minute Walk in Greenwich Village and SoHo

A STROLL THROUGH the patchwork quilt of streets in Greenwich Village takes you to where New York's best-known writers and artists have lived, worked and played, and ends with a tour of SoHo's galleries and museums, where today's artists show their work. For more details on sights in Greenwich Village, see pages 106–13, and for SoHo sights, see pages 100–5.

Author Mark Twain, who lived on 10th Street

Facade in Washington Mews ⑬

West 10th Street
The junction of 8th Street and 6th Avenue ① has many book, music and clothing stores nearby. Walk up Sixth to West Ninth Street to see (on the left) Jefferson Market Courthouse ②.

Turn right at West 10th Street ③ to the Alexander Onassis Center for Hellenic Studies. A passageway at the front once led up to the Tile Club, a gathering place for the artists of the Tenth Street Studio, where Augustus Saint-Gaudens, John LaFarge and Winslow Homer lived. Mark Twain lived at 24 West 10th Street, and Edward Albee at 50 West 10th.

Back across Sixth Avenue is Milligan Place ④, a cluster of 19th-century houses, and Patchin Place ⑤, where the poets e e cummings and John Masefield both lived.

Farther on is the Ninth Circle bar ⑥ which, when it first opened in 1898, was known as "Regnaneschi's." It was the subject of John Sloan's painting *Regnaneschi's Saturday Night*. Playwright Edward Albee first saw the question "Who's afraid of Virginia Woolf?" scrawled on a mirror here.

The doorway of Chumley's ⑩

Greenwich Village
Turn left at Waverly Place past the Three Lives Bookstore, a typical Village literary gathering spot, to Christopher Street and to the triangular Northern Dispensary ⑦.

Follow Grove Street along Christopher Park to Sheridan Square, the busy hub of the Village. The Circle Repertory Theater ⑧, which premiered plays by Pulitzer Prizewinner Lanford Wilson, is now closed.

Cross Seventh Avenue and bear left on to Grove Street. At the corner of Bedford Street, you can't miss "Twin Peaks" ⑨, a home for artists in the 1920s. Turn right to see Bedford: the unmarked door is Chumley's ⑩, a saloon not much changed since 1928 when it was a speakeasy *(see p28)*. Writers Dylan Thomas, Simone de Beauvoir, Ernest Hemingway, William Faulkner, J.D. Salinger, Jack Kerouac and many others drank here. Covers of their books line the walls. 75 Bedford is the narrowest house in the Village, and was once the home of feminist poet Edna St. Vincent Millay.

Walk up Carmine to Sixth Avenue and turn right at Waverly Place. At 116 Waverly ⑪, Anne Charlotte Lynch, an English teacher, held weekly gatherings in her town house for such eminent friends as Herman Melville and Edgar Allan Poe, who gave his first reading of *The Raven* here.

A detour left of half a block will bring you to MacDougal Alley ⑫, a lane of carriage houses in which Gertrude Vanderbilt Whitney had her studio. She opened the first Whitney Museum here in 1932, just behind the studio.

TIPS FOR WALKERS

Starting point: 8th St/6th Ave.
Length: 2 miles (3.2 km).
Getting there: Take subway train A, B, C, D, E, F or V to West Fourth Street-Washington Square station (Eighth Street exit). Fifth Avenue buses M2 and M3 stop at Eighth Street. From here, walk one block west to Sixth. The M5 bus loops around Washington Square back to Sixth Avenue and Eighth Street.
Stopping-off points: The Pink Tea Cup, 42 Grove Street, is good for lunch. The SoHo Kitchen & Bar, 103 Greene Street, is a typical soaring SoHo space, also known for its superb selection of wines.

Washington Square

Back on MacDougal, turn left to Washington Square North, to see the finest Greek Revival houses in the United States. Built of red brick, they have marble balustrades and entrances flanked by columns. Writer Henry James set his *Washington Square* in No. 18, his grandmother's home.

Washington Square Park and Arch

Pause at Fifth Avenue to look back at Washington Square Park, with its famous Washington Square Arch. Go across to Two Fifth Avenue; opposite is Washington Mews ⑬, an elegant carriage house complex. John Dos Passos, Edward Hopper and Rockwell Kent lived in the studio at No. 14a at various times.

Go back up Washington Square North, past some elegant houses. Writer Edith Wharton lived at Seven Washington Square North. Walk beneath the arch and across Washington Square Park. On the left as you leave the park, is the fine Judson Memorial Church and Tower ⑭ by Stanford White and the NYU Loeb Student Center. The Center was once a boarding house, known as the "house of genius," and is where Theodore Dreiser wrote *An American Tragedy*.

SoHo

Walk south on Thompson, a typical Village street lined with clubs, cafés and shops. Turn left at Houston, SoHo's northern limit, and right on West Broadway, lined with some of the city's most famous galleries along with a large number of chic and arty boutiques.

Turn left at Spring Street for yet more tempting shops, then right at Greene Street ⑮, which is the heart of the Cast-Iron Historic District. Many of these fine buildings now house clusters of art galleries.

Turn left at the end of Greene Street to Canal Street, the end of SoHo, to see how quickly the atmosphere of New York can change. This noisy street is full of hawkers and discount electronics stores. You can explore bargains for the next two blocks and then turn left up Broadway, soon finding yourself on the cutting edge of art, at the New Museum of Contemporary Art at 583 Broadway *(see p105)*.

Cast-iron facade, Greene Street ⑮

KEY

— **Walk route**

☆ **Good viewing point**

Ⓜ **Subway station**

0 meters 500
0 yards 500

A Two-Hour Walk in the Upper East Side

A PROMENADE ALONG upper Fifth Avenue and its environs will take you past the best remaining examples of New York's turn-of-the-century gilded age. A detour through the old German district of Yorkville leads to a riverside stroll to Gracie Mansion, official residence of the city's mayor, dating from 1799. For details on Upper East Side sights, see pages 180–201.

| 0 meters | 500 |
| 0 yards | 500 |

From the Frick to the Met

Begin at the Frick mansion ①, built for coal magnate Henry Clay Frick in 1913–14. Allow some extra time to see Frick's art collection *(pp200–1)*. Many such mansions were built as New York's first families outdid each other with miniature Versailles, Loire-style châteaux and even Venetian palazzos. Most of the ones still standing have now become either institutions or museums. The apartment building opposite the Frick is typical of those where today's affluent New Yorkers live.

Church of the Holy Trinity ⑰

East on 70th are two of the city's top art galleries, the Knoedler Gallery and Hirschl & Adler ②. Walk up Madison to the corner of 72nd Street, to the big Polo-Ralph Lauren store ③, the 1898 French Renaissance home of Gertrude Rhinelander Waldo. Wander inside to see the elegant restored interior.

Walk back toward Fifth on the north side of 72nd, past two 1890s limestone beauties, now the Lycée Français de New York ④. Continue along Fifth Avenue to 73rd Street. Turn east to 11, Joseph Pulitzer's former home ⑤.

A few blocks on, between Lexington and Third, is a fine row of town houses ⑥. Back on Fifth, walk to 75th Street, to see No. 1,

KEY

— Walk route

※ Good viewing point

Ⓜ Subway station

Ukrainian Institute of America ⑩

the former residence of Edward S. Harkness, son of a founder of Standard Oil. It is now the Common-Fund ⑦. At 1 East 78th, the tobacco millionaire James B. Duke's 18th-century French-style château is now the New York University Institute of Fine Arts ⑧. At 79th Street and Fifth, the former home of financier Payne Whitney, is the French Embassy ⑨ and 2 East 79th is the Ukrainian Institute of America ⑩. On the southeast corner of 82nd is Duke-Semans House ⑪, one of the few grand Fifth Avenue residences still privately owned. Save another full day for The Metropolitan Museum of Art ⑫ at 82nd.

Carl Schurz Park Promenade

TIPS FOR WALKERS

Starting point: Frick Collection.
Length: 3 miles (4.8 km).
Getting there: Take subway train 6 to 68th Street and Lexington, then walk west (left) three blocks to Fifth Avenue. Or take the M1, M2, M3 or M4 bus up Madison Avenue to 70th Street and walk one block west.
Stopping-off points: The cafés at the Whitney and Guggenheim museums are pleasant. M.Rohr's Cafe is at 303 E85/2nd Ave and Mocca Hungarian is at 1588 2nd Ave/82nd, or try the Heidelberg Café on Second Avenue off 86th Street. Madison Avenue between 92nd and 93rd has many places to eat, including Sarabeth's Kitchen, with its excellent weekend brunch.

Yorkville

Turn east on 86th Street for the vestiges of German Yorkville – Bremen House ⑬, cross Second Avenue, then turn right to the Heidelberg Café and German deli, Schaller & Weber ⑭. For a restful stop, try Mocca Hungarian or M.Rohr's cafe on Second Avenue.

East River and Gracie Mansion

Henderson Place ⑮ at East End Avenue is a cluster of 24 red-brick Queen Anne town houses. Carl Schurz Park opposite was named after the city's most prominent German immigrant, editor of *Harper's Weekly* and the *New York Post*. The park promenade atop the east River Drive leads to a view of Hell Gate, where the Harlem River, Long Island Sound and New York harbor meet. From the walkway you can see the back of Gracie Mansion ⑯, the mayor's official residence. The path west along the fence leads to a better view. Walk west on 88th Street past the Church of the Holy Trinity ⑰ and at Lexington Avenue go to 92nd Street and west past two of the few wooden houses left in Manhattan ⑱.

The Cooper-Hewitt Museum ⑳

Carnegie Hill

Back on Fifth Avenue, turn downtown past the Felix Warburg Mansion of 1908, now the Jewish Museum ⑲, and continue to 91st Street and the huge Andrew Carnegie home, now the Cooper-Hewitt Museum ⑳. Built in 1902 in the style of an English country manor, it gave the area the unofficial name of Carnegie Hill. The James Burden House ㉑ at 7 East 91st Street, built for Vanderbilt heiress Adele Sloan in 1905, has a spiral staircase under a stained glass skylight that was known in society as "the stairway to heaven." At 1 East 91st, the financier Otto Kahn's Italian Renaissance-style residence was a show-place with a drive-through porch and interior courtyard. It is now the Convent of the Sacred Heart School.

Wooden houses on 92nd Street ⑱

A Three-Hour Walk in Brooklyn

A TRIP ACROSS New York's most famous crossing leads
to Brooklyn Heights, the city's first suburb. This
neighborhood has a 19th-century feel, mixed with a
hint of Middle Eastern cultures. The riverfront
promenade has unrivaled views of Manhattan. For more
details on sights in Brooklyn, see pages 245–51.

**Brooklyn Bridge-
Worth Street** M
550yards/500m

Fire Station on Old Fulton Street

Fulton Ferry Landing

About 3,580 ft (1 km) long, the
Brooklyn Bridge span yields
thrilling views of the lower
New York skyline and prize
photo opportunities. Take a
taxi, or, if feeling energetic,
walk across to Brooklyn.

On the far side, follow the
Tillary Street sign to the right,
turn right at the bottom of the
stairs, then take the first path
through the park and walk
down Cadman Plaza West ①
under the Brooklyn-Queens
Expressway; here Cadman
becomes Old Fulton Street.
You can see the bridge on the
right as you head to the river
at Water Street and the Fulton
Ferry landing ②. During the
Revolutionary War, George

Washington's
troops fled
to Manhattan
from here. In
1814, this was
the depot for the
ferry connecting
Brooklyn and
Manhattan Island.
This transformed
Brooklyn Heights
from a predomin-
antly farming area
to a residential
district. The area
is full of charac-
ter and is still a
very popular
place to live. To
the right is the
River Café ③.

Eagle Warehouse ④

This restaurant's fine cuisine
and spectacular views of the
Manhattan skyline make it
one of New York's most
exceptional dining spots.

Brooklyn Heights

From the landing, turn right
to steep Everitt Street up
Columbia Heights, past the
former Eagle Warehouse ④ of
1893 to Middagh Street and
along the streets of
Brooklyn Heights.
24 Middagh ⑤ is
one of the oldest,
built in 1824.

Next turn right on
Willow and left on
Cranberry; here the
town houses range
from wooden
clapboards to brick
Federal-style to
brownstones.
Except for cars and
a few modern
buildings, you could
be in the 19th
century.

Many famous peo-
ple have lived here.
Truman Capote
wrote *Breakfast at
Tiffany's* and *In
Cold Blood* in the
basement of 70

Willow,
and
Arthur
Miller
once
owned 155
Willow. Walt
Whitman lived
on Cranberry
Street when
he was
editor of the
Brooklyn Eagle.
He set the type
for his *Leaves of
Grass* at a print
shop near the
corner of Cranberry
and Fulton. The town
houses now on the site are
called Whitman Close.

Turn right along Hicks.
The Hicks family, local
farmers, inspired the name
"hick" for a
yokel. Turn
left on Orange
Street to the
Plymouth
Church ⑥,
home of
Henry Ward
Beecher, an
antislavery
preacher.
His sister,

Entrance to the River Café

**Truman Capote with
feathered friend**

Harriet Beecher Stowe, wrote *Uncle Tom's Cabin*. At Clark Street are marquees of once-luxurious hotels, such as the Towers. Follow Clark Street to 142 Columbia Heights, where Norman Mailer lives ⑦. Invalid Washington Roebling lived at 110 – using a telescope, he directed the construction of Brooklyn Bridge from his room.

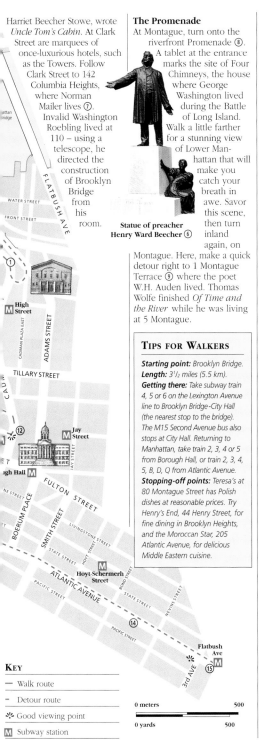

Statue of preacher
Henry Ward Beecher ⑥

The Promenade

At Montague, turn onto the riverfront Promenade ⑧. A tablet at the entrance marks the site of Four Chimneys, the house where George Washington lived during the Battle of Long Island. Walk a little farther for a stunning view of Lower Manhattan that will make you catch your breath in awe. Savor this scene, then turn inland again, on Montague. Here, make a quick detour right to 1 Montague Terrace ⑨ where the poet W.H. Auden lived. Thomas Wolfe finished *Of Time and the River* while he was living at 5 Montague.

The old Montague Street trolley,
which led to the river and the ferry

Montague and Clinton Streets

Once back on Montague Street, walk to the heart of Brooklyn Heights, with all its cafés and boutiques. The baseball team, the Brooklyn Dodgers, got their name from dodging the trolley cars that once ran down the street. Walk to the intersection of Montague and Clinton to see the stained glass of the 1834 Church of St. Ann and the Holy Trinity ⑩. Walk a block left on Clinton to Pierrepont Street for the Brooklyn Historical Society ⑪. A block farther, at Court Street, is the 1849 Borough Hall ⑫, and the subway taking you back to Manhattan.

Brooklyn's Dodgers, who got their
name from dodging trolley cars

Atlantic Avenue

Another option is to stay on Clinton and walk five short blocks to Atlantic Avenue. A left turn here leads to a whole string of Middle Eastern emporia ⑬, such as Sahadi Imports at 187 Atlantic Avenue, with a huge selection of foods. The Damascus Bakery at 195 makes the most delicious filo pastries. Various shops sell Arabic books, tapes, publications, and CDs. Two blocks on are numerous antique shops ⑭. At Flatbush Avenue, look left to the Brooklyn Academy of Music ⑮ and the grand front of the Williamsburg Savings Bank. Watch for signs to the subway back to Manhattan.

> ### TIPS FOR WALKERS
>
> **Starting point:** Brooklyn Bridge.
> **Length:** 3 1/2 miles (5.5 km).
> **Getting there:** Take subway train 4, 5 or 6 on the Lexington Avenue line to Brooklyn Bridge-City Hall (the nearest stop to the bridge). The M15 Second Avenue bus also stops at City Hall. Returning to Manhattan, take train 2, 3, 4 or 5 from Borough Hall, or train 2, 3, 4, 5, B, D, Q from Atlantic Avenue.
> **Stopping-off points:** Teresa's at 80 Montague Street has Polish dishes at reasonable prices. Try Henry's End, 44 Henry Street, for fine dining in Brooklyn Heights, and the Moroccan Star, 205 Atlantic Avenue, for delicious Middle Eastern cuisine.

KEY

— Walk route

- Detour route

☀ Good viewing point

Ⓜ Subway station

0 meters   500

0 yards   500

TRAVELERS' NEEDS

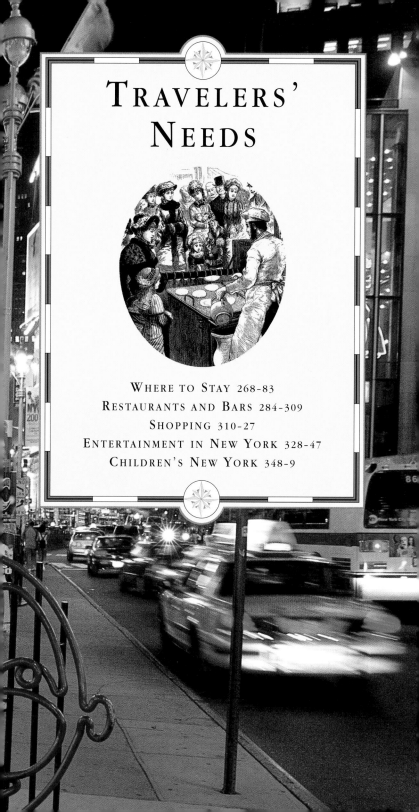

WHERE TO STAY

W ITH OVER 65,000 hotel rooms available, New York offers something for everyone. The top hotels are not quite as expensive as those in Paris or London, but the best news for visitors is the increase in budget hotels. While many of these are basic rather than charming, they offer good value. Other budget options are furnished apartments and studios and bed and breakfast in private homes, as well as youth hostels and YMCAs. From an inspection of over 200 hotels in New York, we have selected the best of their kind. *Choosing a Hotel (pp272–83)* contains detailed descriptions of the hotels, which will help you select the one best suited to your needs. Many of the hotels have a website address to enable you to book a room via the internet.

Cole Porter's piano, in the Waldorf–Astoria bar *(see p281)*

Bathroom at the Paramount Hotel *(see p277)*

WHERE TO LOOK

T HE EAST SIDE, roughly between 59th and 77th streets, is the traditional location for luxury hotels, but the renovation of certain landmark midtown properties, such as the St. Regis, and new hotels in famous chains from the Far East, such as the Peninsula Group, have increased competition in this price range.

Business travelers tend to favor midtown, especially the moderately priced hotels lining Lexington Avenue near Grand Central Terminal.

Those seeking relative quiet with access to midtown should look in the Murray Hill area, while theater lovers should note the revival of the Times Square area. Hotels within walking distance of theaters offer an advantage, since performances tend to end at the same time and cabs are hard to come by.

There are a number of good, inexpensive hotels around Herald Square, which is convenient for shopping. The Upper West Side hotels are also less expensive. This popular residential area is convenient for Lincoln Center and offers easy access to public transportation.

The **New York Convention and Visitors Bureau** publishes a free, annually updated leaflet called "The New York Hotel Guide," listing current rates, toll-free numbers and fax numbers. Staff will offer advice about hotels but do not make reservations.

HOTEL PRICES

S OME HOTELS offer seasonal promotional rates and other off-peak reductions. For example, business travelers vacate hotels at the end of the working week, and you can take advantage of bargain weekend deals, even in luxury hotels, as prices drop *(see Special Rates p270)*. There is a growing number of all-suite hotels available in every price category. Suites offer extra space plus cooking facilities and a refrigerator. Most suites can accommodate up to four people, which makes them popular with families.

Café Botanica at the Essex House Hotel *(see p278)*

HIDDEN EXTRAS

W HEN CALCULATING the cost of hotels in New York, it is not enough simply to take into consideration the quoted room price. Hotel rooms have long been subject to extra taxes, but the former sliding scale, which favored rates under $100, has now given way to a blanket 13.625% hotel tax, plus $2 per night per room fee.

Several hotels now include continental breakfast in the room price. This is a big

Lobby phones, to reach a guest staying in the hotel.

Suite at the Millennium *(see p278)*

saving, since standard hotel continental breakfast prices, before tax and tip, start at about $5 and soar to around $30 in some of the luxury hotels. To save money, head for the nearest deli or coffee shop and leave the hotel to business people having power breakfasts.

Hotel telephone charges are always high; it is much less expensive to use the pay phone in the lobby, particularly when you are calling overseas.

Tips are expected. Staff who take your luggage to the room are usually tipped a minimum of $1 per bag – more in a luxury hotel. The concierge need not be tipped for normal services such as arranging transportation or making dinner reservations, but should be rewarded for exceptional services.

When you order from room service, check the menu to see whether a service charge will also be included in the bill; if not, a 15–20% tip is customary. Solo travelers will find that single room rates are usually at least 80% of the double rate and are sometimes the same as for two people.

FACILITIES

ALTHOUGH you'd expect hotel rooms in New York City to be noisy, most windows are double- or even triple-glazed to keep out the noise. Air-conditioning is a standard feature, so there is no need to open the windows in hot weather. Even so, some rooms are obviously quieter than others, if they are at the back of the hotel or overlooking a courtyard – check when reserving.

Television, radio and at least one telephone are usually provided in every room, even in modest lodgings, and most hotel bedrooms have private bathrooms. In budget and mid-priced hotels a shower, rather than a tub is the norm. Many mid-range hotels now offer fax outlets and machines in each room, a health club or exercise room and a full concierge service. Luxury facilities include mini-bars in the room, dual phones, private phone message systems and electronic checkout.

The hotels listed here are all within a few minutes' walk of a large number of shops and restaurants. Very few hotels have their own parking, but valets may park your car in areas reserved for guests' use in nearby garages. A reduced (but still expensive) daily parking fee is normally offered. If there is no concierge at the hotel, front desk staff will be able to help with tourist information and to answer any queries.

The Art Deco lobby of the Edison Hotel *(see p276)*

DIRECTORY

TOURIST OFFICE

New York Convention and Visitors Bureau
810 7th Ave, NY, NY 10019. **Map** 12 E4.
[(212) 484-1222. Publications available at JFK Airport. W www.nycvisit.com

SUITE HOTELS

Manhattan East Suite Hotels
One reservation number serves all of the following suite hotels:

[(212) 465-3700. Toll Free 1-800-637-8483.
@ info@mesuite.com
W www.mesuite.com

Beekman Tower
3 Mitchell Pl. **Map** 13 C5.

The Benjamin
125 E 50th St. **Map** 13 B4.

Dumont Plaza
150 E 34th St. **Map** 9 A2.

Eastgate Tower
222 E 39th St. **Map** 9 B1.

Lyden Gardens
215 E 64th St. **Map** 13 B2.

Lyden House
320 E 53rd St. **Map** 13 B4.

Plaza Fifty
155 E 50th St. **Map** 13 B4.

Shelburne–Murray Hill
303 Lexington Ave. **Map** 9 A2.

Southgate Tower
371 7th Ave. **Map** 8 E3.

Surrey
20 E 76th St. **Map** 17 A5.

RESERVATION AGENCIES

Hotel Reservations A Meegan Services
JFK International Airport, Jamaica, NY 11430.
[(718) 995-9292.
FAX (718) 995-4439.

DISCOUNT RESERVATION SERVICE

Express
[(303) 440-8481.
FAX (303) 440-0166.
W www.express-res.com

Hotel con-x-ions
[(212) 840-8686.
FAX (212) 221-8686. W www.hotelconxions.com

Quikbook
[(212) 779 7666;
1-800-522-9991.
W www.quikbook.com

How to Reserve

It is advisable to make hotel reservations at least one month in advance. While it's unlikely that the hotel will be fully booked, you may well find that the best rooms and suites have been taken, especially if a major convention is taking place. The busiest periods are at Easter, the New York Marathon week in late October or early November, Thanksgiving and Christmas.

Reserve directly with the hotel by telephone, letter, fax or internet. Written confirmation of your telephone booking will be required, probably with a deposit as a guarantee of your arrival; any cancellation fees may be deducted from this. You can pay by credit card, international bank draft or money order, or US traveler's check. Advise the staff if you are going to arrive at the hotel after 6pm or you will lose your reservation, unless you have prepaid with a credit card.

You can also book a hotel through your travel agent or airline. Most hotels have a toll-free telephone number for use in the United States, but these numbers do not

work from Europe and the UK. If the hotel is part of an international chain, an affiliated hotel in your country should be able to reserve a room for you.

Special Rates

Hotels are busiest during the week, when business travelers are in the city, so most of them offer budget packages to encourage more weekend business. It's often possible to move from a standard to a luxury room for the weekend at the same rate.

A lower corporate rate is

Lobby of the St. Regis Hotel *(see p279)*

usually available to employees of large companies. Quite often, reservation clerks will grant corporate discounts on request without asking for a company affiliation.

Some reservation agencies offer discount rates. A good travel agent should be able to get the best current rates, but compare prices by contacting directly a discount reservation service such as Express or Quikbook*(see p269)*, which offers discounts between 20% and 50%, depending on the time of year. You reserve by credit card and receive a voucher, which you present to the hotel.

Package tours can also provide savings on the usual price. These rates may not oblige you to stay with a tour group, only to use their air and hotel arrangements. They may also include airport transfers, an additional saving. Airlines frequently have special deals, particularly during slow travel seasons. A knowledgeable travel agent should be able to tell you the current best deals, but newspapers often advertise special, limited offers that can be booked directly. At off-peak times you may net even bigger savings than with the package plans.

DIRECTORY

DISABLED TRAVELERS

Mayor's Office for People with Disabilities
52 Chambers St, Room 206, 10007.
📞 *(212) 788-2830.*
w www.nyc.gov

BED & BREAKFAST

Abode Bed and Breakfast Inc.
📞 *(212) 472-2000 or (800) 835-8880*
w www.abodenyc.com

At Home in NY
📞 *(212) 956-3125*
FAX *(212) 247-3294.*

Bed & Breakfast (& Books)
35 W 92nd St, Apt 2C, NY 10025
📞 *(212) 865-8740*

Country Inn The City
📞 *(212) 580-4183*
w www.countryinnthe city.com

B & B Network in New York
130 Barrow St, Suite 508, 10014. 📞 *(212) 645-8134 or (800) 900-8134.*

Jim's Deli!
w www.jimsdeli.com

Homestay New York
📞 *(718) 434-2071*
w www.homestayny.com

All Around the Town
📞 *(212) 675-5600 or (800) 443-3800.*

Urban Ventures, Inc.
📞 *(212) 594-5650.*
w www.nyurban ventures.com

YOUTH HOSTELS AND DORMITORIES

Hosteling International, NY
891 Amsterdam Ave at W 103rd St, NY, NY 10025. **Map** 20 E5.
📞 *(212) 932-2300.*

92nd St Y
1395 Lexington Ave, NY 10128. **Map** 17 A2.
📞 *(212) 415-5650.*

YMCA-Vanderbilt
224 E 47th St, 10017.
Map 13 A5.
📞 *(212) 756-9600.*

YMCA-West Side
5 W 63rd St, 10023.
Map 12 D2.
📞 *(212) 875-4273.*

STUDENT LODGINGS

NYU Summer Housing
8 Washington Place, NY, NY 10003. 📞 *(212) 998-4621.*

AIRPORT HOTELS

*See p364-5 for details of the hotels to be found at JFK and **Newark** airports.*

DISABLED TRAVELERS

BY LAW, NEW hotels must provide facilities for disabled visitors, and many older buildings have been renovated to comply, too. Guide dogs are allowed in most hotels, but it is advisable to check when reserving.

This guide's disabled access information is based upon each hotel's own assessment of its suitability. Let the hotel know of any specific needs when booking. The **Mayor's Office for People With Disabilities** also offers information about hotels.

TRAVELING WITH CHILDREN

AMERICAN HOTELS generally have a very welcoming attitude toward children. Cots or cribs and lists of baby-sitters are normally widely available, and most hotel restaurants are happy to cater to young guests.

Traveling with children can be cheaper than anticipated. Many hotels do not charge for children if they stay in their parents' room, or make only a small charge for an extra bed. There is usually a limit of one or two children per room in these cases, and most hotels stipulate that the children must be under a certain age, often 12. Parents of older children are expected to pay the full price, although the age limit is occasionally extended to 18. Ask about family rates when reserving.

BED-AND-BREAKFAST

THERE IS AN increasing number of bed-and-breakfast accommodations to be had in private apartments. This varies from a room in an apartment with an owner-host in residence to an entire apartment to yourself, with its own kitchen and bathroom, yours while the owner is away.

Staying in a private apartment enables you to feel at home in a New York neighborhood and to visit local restaurants, usually far more reasonably priced than

Entrance to the Peninsula Hotel *(see p281)*

those in tourist areas. Bed-and-breakfast lodgings can be found through many free booking services. Some booking agencies have a two-night minimum. Rates for unhosted apartments vary from about $70 to $200, and for a double room range from $60 to $90 a night, depending on whether you have a private bathroom. There is a wide range of apartments, from spacious and luxurious to cramped and dowdy. Your costs will rise if the address is remote, requiring frequent cabs. Ask about location and amenities when you reserve.

YOUTH AND BUDGET ACCOMMODATIONS

A YOUTH HOSTEL and many YMCA dormitories offer lodgings for those on a tight budget. For the longer-term visitor, the **92nd Street Y**, a nonsectarian hostel and lively cultural center situated in the Upper East Side, has good-value rooms from about $30 to $50 a night.

There are no campsites in Manhattan, and, sadly, youth hostels are not as prevalent in New York as they are in large European cities.

Sky-high swimming pool at a luxury hotel

USING THE LISTINGS

Hotel listings are on pages 272–83. Each hotel is listed according to its area and price category. The symbols after each hotel's address summarize the facilities it offers.

🛏 all rooms with bath and/or shower unless otherwise indicated
1 single-rate rooms available
🛏 rooms for more than 2 people available, or an extra bed can be put in a double room
24 24-hour room service
TV television in all rooms
Y minibar in all rooms
🚭 nonsmoking rooms available
🏞 rooms with good view available
▤ air-conditioning in all rooms
🏋 gym/fitness facilities available in hotel
🏊 swimming pool in hotel
📠 business facilities: message-taking service, fax machine for guests, desk and telephone in each room, and meeting room within hotel
🧒 children's facilities: cribs/cots, baby-sitting service
♿ wheelchair access
🛗 elevator
🐕 pets allowed in bedrooms (always check when reserving)
P valet parking available
🌳 garden/terrace open to guests
Y bar
🍴 restaurant
ℹ tourist information desk or personnel
💳 Credit cards accepted:
AE American Express
DC Diners Club
MC MasterCard/Access
V VISA
JCB Japanese Credit Bureau

Price categories for a double room with bath per night, including tax and service during tourist season:
⑤ under $150
⑤⑤ $150–$250
⑤⑤⑤ $250–$350
⑤⑤⑤⑤ $350–$450
⑤⑤⑤⑤⑤ over $450

Choosing a Hotel

THESE HOTELS have been selected across a wide price range for their good value, facilities, and location; they are listed area by area, starting with Lower Manhattan and moving on to hotels farther outside the city. Within each area, the hotels are listed by price category, from the least expensive to the most expensive. For map references, see pages 388–409.

	CREDIT CARDS	NUMBER OF ROOMS	RESTAURANT	AIR CONDITIONING	QUIET LOCATION

LOWER MANHATTAN

EMBASSY SUITES NEW YORK W www.embassysuites.com $ $ $
102 North End Ave., NY, NY 10281. **Map** 1 A2. ((212) 945-0100. FAX (212) 945-3012.
This all-suite hotel towers over Battery Park City. Large, comfortable accommodation with high-speed internet connection. Modern art dresses up the chain-standard design. Harbor views and discounted weekend rates.

| AE DC JCB MC V | 463 | ● | ▦ | ● |

HOLIDAY INN WALL STREET W www.holidayinnwsd.com $ $ $
15 Gold St., NY, NY 10038. **Map** 2 D2. ((212) 232-7800. FAX (212) 269-9569.
Wall Street's most technologically mature hotel was designed with business travelers in mind. Standard features include a desk and personal computer with CD/DVD drive, fax/copier/color printer, ergonomic chair, portable phones, even supplies like paper clips. SMART rooms feature laptops. Good buffet breakfast.

| AE DC JCB MC V | 138 | ● | ▦ | |

RITZ-CARLTON BATTERY PARK W www.ritzcarlton.com $ $ $ $
2 West St., NY, NY 10004. **Map** 1 B4. ((212) 344-0800. FAX (212) 344-3801.
This hotel features superlative amenities with fabulous views of New York harbor and the Statue of Liberty. Special attention is paid to children, who can also visit the Skyscraper Museum on site.

| AE DC JCB MC V | 298 | ● | ▦ | |

SOHO AND TRIBECA

COSMOPOLITAN HOTEL – TRIBECA W www.cosmohotel.com $
95 W. Broadway, NY, NY 10007. **Map** 1 B1. ((212) 566-1900. FAX (212) 566-6909.
In the heart of hip TriBeCa is one of Manhattan's best budget hotels. Rooms are petite but well maintained and pleasantly furnished; with tiny but pristine bathrooms. The location is super-convenient, and a wealth of first-rate restaurants are within walking distance. Highly recommended.

| AE DC JCB MC V | 105 | | ▦ | |

HOLIDAY INN DOWNTOWN/SOHO W www.holiday-inn.com $ $ $
138 Lafayette St., NY, NY 10013. **Map** 4 F5. ((212) 966-8898. FAX (212) 966-3933.
The hotel itself is nothing special, but travelers with an eye for trends will love the bustling edge-of-Chinatown location. Boutique-lined SoHo is just steps away, as is Nolita, downtown's hip neighborhood of the moment. Rooms are rather bland but comfortable enough. A well-regarded Cantonese restaurant is on site.

| AE DC JCB MC V | 227 | ● | ▦ | |

60 THOMPSON W www.60thompson.com $ $ $ $
60 Thompson St., NY, NY 10012. **Map** 4 D4. ((212) 431-0400. FAX (212) 431-0200.
Despite its chic modernist lines, this smallish newcomer boasts a warm, and surprisingly domestic, ambiance. Done in a soothing celadon-and-mahogany palette, rooms are plush and well equipped, with DVD and CD players, Internet access, and marble baths. Location is first rate.

| AE DC JCB MC V | 100 | ● | ▦ | |

TRIBECA GRAND HOTEL W www.tribecagrand.com $ $ $ $ $
2 Sixth Ave., NY, NY 10013. **Map** 3 E5. ((212) 519-6600. FAX (212) 519-6700.
Smart design is the key at this chic luxury hotel just south of SoHo. Sumptuous textiles, clean-lined custom furnishings, and cutting-edge technology, including a screening room, unite luxury and utility. A soaring atrium is home to a celebrity-studded lounge scene.

| AE DC JCB MC V | 203 | ● | ▦ | |

LOWER EAST SIDE

OFF SOHO SUITES HOTEL W www.offsoho.com $
11 Rivington St., NY, NY 10002. **Map** 5 A3. ((212) 979-9808. FAX (212) 979-9801.
It used to be that this budget hotel was in no-man's-land – but hip downtown has expanded so much as to practically embrace it. Decor is nonexistent and beds are a bit too firm, but rooms are well tended. Deluxe suites have a fully outfitted kitchen and bath, while economy suites share facilities.

| AE DC JCB MC V | 38 | ● | ▦ | |

Price categories for a standard double room per night, inclusive of breakfast, service charges and any additional taxes such as VAT: Ⓢ under $150 ⓈⓈ $150–$250 ⓈⓈⓈ $250–$350 ⓈⓈⓈⓈ $350–$450 ⓈⓈⓈⓈⓈ over $450	**RESTAURANT** Hotel restaurant or dining room usually open to non-residents unless otherwise stated. **AIR CONDITIONING** In-room units or central AC. **QUIET LOCATION** Quiet residential location or quiet street in a busy area. **CREDIT CARDS** Indicates which credit cards are accepted: *AE* American Express; *DC* Diners Club; *JCB*; *MC* MasterCard/Access; *V* VISA.	CREDIT CARDS	NUMBER OF ROOMS	RESTAURANT	AIR CONDITIONING	QUIET LOCATION

	CREDIT CARDS	NUMBER OF ROOMS	RESTAURANT	AIR CONDITIONING	QUIET LOCATION
HOWARD JOHNSON'S EXPRESS INN W www.hojo.com ⓈⓈ 135 E. Houston St., NY, NY 10002. **Map** 5 A3. 📞 *(212) 358-8844.* **FAX** *(212) 473-3500.* Located at the nexus of the Lower East Side and the East Village, this hotel is perfect for checking out the downtown scene. Rooms are well-equipped – some have microwaves and small fridges. Local calls are free and breakfast is included in the price. 🔳 1️⃣ ▦ TV 🔼 ⏚ ♿	AE DC MC V	46		▪	

EAST VILLAGE

	CREDIT CARDS	NUMBER OF ROOMS	RESTAURANT	AIR CONDITIONING	QUIET LOCATION
ST. MARK'S HOTEL W www.stmarkshotel.qpg.com Ⓢ 2 St. Mark's Place, NY, NY 10003. **Map** 4 F1. 📞 *(212) 674-0100.* **FAX** *(212) 420-0854.* In a city where ancient carpet and dingy walls are the norm in budget hotels, this bright and clean hotel offers welcome relief. Oak-and-marble hallways lead to sparse but neat rooms with small bathrooms. Shop-lined St. Mark's Place features a constant parade of tattooed youth, so don't expect quiet. 🔳 TV	AE DC JCB MC V	70		▪	
UNION SQUARE INN W www.unionsquareinn.com ⓈⓈ 209 E. 14th St., NY, NY 10003. **Map** 4 F1. 📞 *(212) 614-0500.* **FAX** *(212) 614-0512.* Here's a wonderful find for discerning travelers who want standard comforts at a reasonable price. Rooms are small but boast high-quality mattresses and brand-new bathrooms. There are no views and services are minimal, but the value is tops. A basic breakfast is included. 🔳 1️⃣ ▦ TV	AE DC JCB MC V	40		▪	

GREENWICH VILLAGE

	CREDIT CARDS	NUMBER OF ROOMS	RESTAURANT	AIR CONDITIONING	QUIET LOCATION
ABINGDON GUEST HOUSE W www.abingdonguesthouse.com/beta ⓈⓈ 13 Eighth Ave., NY, NY 10014. **Map** 3 C1. 📞 *(212) 243-5384.* **FAX** *(212) 807-7473.* This absolutely lovely guest house is located in the brownstone-lined, boutique-dotted West Village, one of the city's most charming neighborhoods. Each artfully decorated room is outfitted with first-rate comforts. Best for independent-minded travelers, since there is no resident innkeeper. No breakfast included, but a coffee bar is downstairs. 🔳 ▦ TV 🔼	AE DC JCB MC V	9		▪	
WASHINGTON SQUARE HOTEL W www.wshotel.com ⓈⓈ 103 Waverly Place, NY, NY 10011. **Map** 4 D2. 📞 *(212) 777-9515.* **FAX** *(212) 979-8373.* This hotel faces Washington Square Park in the heart of New York University territory. A surprisingly smart marble lobby leads to small but recently freshened rooms. Rates are a bit high, but the bustling location is great for bar-hoppers and live-music fans. The restaurant is very good. 🔳 1️⃣ TV 🔼 🔼 ♦ 🍽	AE DC JCB MC V	170	●	▪	
HOTEL GANSEVOORT W www.hotelgansevoort.com ⓈⓈⓈⓈ 18 Ninth Ave., NY, NY 10014. **Map** 3 B1. 📞 *(212) 206-6780.* **FAX** *(212) 255-5858.* The hottest new addition to New York's luxury hotel scene, and the first luxury hotel to open in the Meatpacking District. Special features include high ceilings, feather bedding and plasma screens. There is also a spa and amazing views from the rooftop garden. 🔳 ▦ 24 TV 🔼 🔼 ♦ 🍽 ≋ 🍽 🛁 🏋	AE DC JCB MC V	187	●	▪	●

GRAMERCY & THE FLATIRON DISTRICT

	CREDIT CARDS	NUMBER OF ROOMS	RESTAURANT	AIR CONDITIONING	QUIET LOCATION
HOTEL 17 W www.hotel17ny.com Ⓢ 225 E. 17th St., NY, NY 10003. **Map** 9 B5. 📞 *(212) 475-2845.* **FAX** *(212) 677-8178.* A hip reputation belies this budget hotel's essential austerity. Rooms are tiny, dark, and basic, with a TV, sink, and hairdryer rounding out the amenities. Still, the location and the price are right. Weekly rates are a bargain. Best for young travelers. 1️⃣ ▦ TV 🔼	JCB MC V	120		▪	
MURRAY HILL INN W www.murrayhillinn.com Ⓢ 143 E. 30th St., NY, NY 10016. **Map** 9 A3. 📞 *(212) 683-6900.* **FAX** *(212) 545-0103.* Rooms are small, simple, and utterly unstylish, but this well-managed walk-up hotel overflows with good value. Rooms with private bathrooms are nicest, but shared bathrooms (spotless) are fine for shoestring travelers. 1️⃣ ▦ TV	AE DC JCB MC V	50		▪	●

For key to symbols see back flap

Price categories for a standard double room per night, inclusive of breakfast, service charges and any additional taxes such as VAT:

⑤ under $150
⑤⑤ $150–$250
⑤⑤⑤ $250–$350
⑤⑤⑤⑤ $350–$450
⑤⑤⑤⑤⑤ over $450

RESTAURANT
Hotel restaurant or dining room usually open to non-residents unless otherwise stated.
AIR CONDITIONING
In-room units or central AC.
QUIET LOCATION
Quiet residential location or quiet street in a busy area.
CREDIT CARDS
Indicates which credit cards are accepted: *AE* American Express; *DC* Diners Club; *JCB*; *MC* MasterCard/Access; *V* Visa.

	CREDIT CARDS	NUMBER OF ROOMS	RESTAURANT	AIR CONDITIONING	QUIET LOCATION
GERSHWIN HOTEL w www.gershwinhotel.com ⑤⑤ 7 E. 27th St., NY, NY 10016. **Map** 8 F3. ☎ *(212) 545-8000.* **FAX** *(212) 684-5546.* This Andy Warhol-inspired hotel sets a postmodern tone with lipstick colors, cartoonish furniture, and remarkably high-quality pop art. Rooms are attractive, bright, and stylishly outfitted. 🔲 ① 🏨 TV ↻ ✦ 🍴 🐾 ⚹	AE DC JCB MC V	150	●	■	
GRAMERCY PARK HOTEL w www.gramercyparkhotel.com ⑤⑤ 2 Lexington Ave., NY, NY 10010. **Map** 9 A4. ☎ *(212) 475-4320.* **FAX** *(212) 505-0535.* Huge rooms and an appealing old-world ambiance are the keynotes here. Accommodation is stuck in the 1970s, but even standard rooms are large enough for families; suites and park-view rooms have small kitchenettes. An extra-special amenity: guests have access to Gramercy Park, off-limits to everyone else save a few area residents. 🔲 ① 🏨 TV ↻ ✦ 🍴 🐾 ⚹	AE DC JCB MC V	509	●	■	●
RAMADA INN EASTSIDE w www.applecorehotels.com ⑤⑤ 161 Lexington Ave., NY, NY 10016. **Map** 9 A3. ☎ *(212) 545-1800.* **FAX** *(212) 790-2760.* This unremarkable hotel is notable for its better-than-budget facilities and often heavily discounted rates. Rooms are small and spartan. Always ask for a better rate – if you're quoted more than $175, stay elsewhere. 🔲 ① TV ↻ ✦ 🍴 🐾 ⚹	AE DC JCB MC V	95		■	
THIRTY THIRTY w www.thirtythirty-nyc.com ⑤⑤ 30 E. 30th St., NY, NY 10016. **Map** 9 A3. ☎ *(212) 689-1900.* **FAX** *(212) 689-0023.* This stylish hotel is ideal for travelers who want a great value and a dash of panache. A sleek lobby leads to small but comfortable rooms that boast smart modern decor. A good number of twin-bedded rooms are available, and a few larger rooms have kitchenettes. 🔲 ① TV ↻ ✦ 🍴	AE DC JCB MC V	240		■	
ROGER WILLIAMS HOTEL w www.rogerwilliamshotel.com ⑤⑤⑤ 131 Madison Ave., NY, NY 10016. **Map** 9 A3. ☎ *(212) 448-7000.* **FAX** *(212) 448-7007.* This stylish hotel boasts attractive rooms with blond-wood, modern furnishings, VCRs, and CD players. A great staff and a wealth of free goodies – continental breakfast, all-day serve-yourself cappuccino and cookies, video and CD lending – makes it even more attractive. 🔲 🏨 TV ↻ ✦ 🍴 🐾 ⚹	AE DC JCB MC V	200		■	
HOTEL GIRAFFE w www.hotelgiraffe.com ⑤⑤⑤⑤ 365 Park Ave. South, NY, NY 10016. **Map** 9 A4. ☎ *(212) 685-7700.* **FAX** *(212) 685-7771.* The Flatiron District's finest hotel brims with inspired elegance – rich textiles and custom furnishings. Amenities include CD players and granite bathrooms; deluxe rooms have French doors onto a juliet balcony. Complimentary breakfast, plus a stylish Euro-Asian fusion restaurant. 🔲 🏨 TV ↻ ✦ 🍴 🐾 ⚹	AE DC JCB MC V	73	●	■	
INN AT IRVING PLACE w www.innatirving.com ⑤⑤⑤⑤ 56 Irving Place, NY, NY 10003. **Map** 9 A5. ☎ *(212) 533-4600.* **FAX** *(212) 533-4611.* This impeccably run ultra-Victorian inn, housed in adjoining brownstones, is outfitted in high period style. Each room boasts high-quality antiques and a beautiful bathroom, plus VCR and CD player. Complimentary breakfast is served in the salon, which also presents the city's best high tea. 🔲 🏨 TV ✦ 🍴	AE DC JCB MC V	12	●	■	●

CHELSEA & THE GARMENT DISTRICT

	CREDIT CARDS	NUMBER OF ROOMS	RESTAURANT	AIR CONDITIONING	QUIET LOCATION
AMERICANA INN w www.newyorkhotel.com ⑤ 69 W. 38th St., NY, NY 10018. **Map** 8 F1. ☎ *(212) 840-6700.* **FAX** *(212) 840-1830.* Linoleum floors lend an institutional feel, but otherwise this is a winner in the budget-basic price category. Rooms – which have private sinks – and baths are bright and spotless. The location is central, and the friendly, professional service is of a higher caliber than most in this price range. ① 🏨 TV ↻ ✦ ⚹	AE DC JCB MC V	50		■	
CHELSEA INTERNATIONAL HOSTEL w www.chelseahostel.com ⑤ 251 W. 20th St., NY, NY 10011. **Map** 8 D5. ☎ *(212) 647-0010.* **FAX** *(212) 727-7289.* A warren of low-rise buildings framing a central square comprise one of the city's best hostels. Private doubles and dorm beds are available. Facilities include two well-equipped kitchens, TV lounges, and laundry machines. ①	AE DC JCB MC V	57			

CHELSEA LODGE W www.chelsealodge.com $ | AE DC JCB MC V | 22
318 W. 20th St., NY, NY 10011. **Map** 8 D5. ((212) 243-4499. FAX (212) 243-7852.
A beautifully restored townhouse in the Chelsea Historic District hides this delightful budget hotel. A private sink and stall shower are in the room, so guests only have to share toilets. The impeccably maintained rooms are small but overflow with country charm. A real find!

COLONIAL HOUSE INN W www.colonialhouseinn.com $ | MC V | 20
318 W. 22nd St., NY, NY 10011. **Map** 8 D4. ((212) 243-9669. FAX (212) 633-1612.
This lovely brownstone caters to a gay crowd but welcomes everybody. Rooms are small and simple but nicely maintained; almost half have private baths, and a few have working fireplaces. Continental breakfast is included.

HOTEL WOLCOTT W www.wolcott.com $ | AE DC JCB MC V | 250
4 W. 31st St., NY, NY 10001. **Map** 8 F3. ((212) 268-2900. FAX (212) 563-0096.
Extensive facilities, large rooms, and low rates make this a good option for value-conscious travelers, especially families. Rooms are plain but fine; internet access on your TV is a bonus for those who use email. The staff is helpful, and there are coin-operated laundry machines.

CHELSEA INN W www.chelseainn.com $$ | AE DC JCB MC V | 26
46 W. 17th St., NY, NY 10011. **Map** 8 F5. ((212) 645-8989. FAX (212) 645-1903.
Two 19th-century brownstones house an eclectic mix of rooms and suites, about two-thirds of which have private bathrooms. Mix-and-match furnishings and well-worn textiles add a tenement feel, but everything is clean. Rooms with shared bath often price around $100.

CHELSEA SAVOY HOTEL W www.chelseasavoynyc.com $$ | AE JCB MC V | 90
204 W. 23rd St., NY, NY 10011. **Map** 8 E4. ((212) 929-9353. FAX (212) 741-6309.
This modern hotel has won a committed clientele with its generic but consistent comforts. Built from scratch a few years back, its hallways are wide, rooms pleasant. Rates include continental breakfast.

COMFORT INN MANHATTAN W www.comfortinnmanhattan.com $$ | AE DC JCB MC V | 131
42 W. 35th St., NY, NY 10001. **Map** 8 F2. ((212) 947-0200. FAX (212) 594-3047.
Recently bestowed with a hospitality award for outstanding service by its head office, this characterless but reliably comfortable chain hotel is just a few strides from the Empire State Building and other major midtown attractions. Rooms are well-kept, nicely appointed, and remarkably large by city standards. Rates include continental breakfast.

HOTEL CHELSEA W www.hotelchelsea.com $$ | AE JCB MC V | 400
222 W. 23rd St., NY, NY 10011. **Map** 8 E4. ((212) 243-3700. FAX (212) 675-5531.
This legendary artists' haven has housed famous names from Sandra Bernhardt to Sid Vicious, who killed girlfriend Nancy Spungen here in a seminal moment of punk history. About 100 rooms are available to short-term visitors with a bohemian spirit. Rooms are large and eccentrically outfitted with generally older furnishings.

HOTEL METRO W www.hotelmetronyc.com $$ | AE DC JCB MC V | 179
45 W. 35th St., NY, NY 10001. **Map** 8 F2. ((212) 947-2500. FAX (212) 279-1310.
This Art Deco delight is midtown's best mid-priced hotel. Rooms are larger and more attractive than most in this price range, and comforts are first-rate. The restaurant is very good, rates include breakfast, and the roof terrace boasts views of the Empire State Building. Excellent for families.

INN ON 23RD W www.innon23rd.com $$ | AE DC JCB MC V | 14
131 W. 23rd St., NY, NY 10011. **Map** 8 E4. ((212) 463-0330. FAX (212) 463-0302.
This wonderful inn offers a just-right blend of bed-and-breakfast charm and real-hotel amenities. Rooms and suites are impeccably outfitted, including pillowtop beds and plush Turkish terry towels in the bathrooms. The innkeepers serve a generous continental breakfast.

RED ROOF INN W www.redroof.com $$ | AE DC JCB MC V | 172
6 W. 32nd St., NY, NY 10001. **Map** 8 F3. ((212) 643-7100. FAX (212) 643-7101.
This premier urban outpost of the middle-America motel chain is a rousing success thanks to comfortable, freshly outfitted rooms and professional service. On-screen internet access is a bonus. It is located in a safe, bustling block, lined with affordable Korean restaurants and convenient to sightseeing and shopping. Rates include breakfast.

Price categories for a standard double room per night, inclusive of breakfast, service charges and any additional taxes such as VAT: $ under $150 $$ $150–$250 $$$ $250–$350 $$$$ $350–$450 $$$$$ over $450	**RESTAURANT** Hotel restaurant or dining room usually open to non-residents unless otherwise stated. **AIR CONDITIONING** In room units or central AC. **QUIET LOCATION** Quiet residential location or quiet street in a busy area. **CREDIT CARDS** Indicates which credit cards are accepted: *AE* American Express; *DC* Diners Club; JCB; *MC* MasterCard/Access; *V* Visa.	**CREDIT CARDS**	**NUMBER OF ROOMS**	**RESTAURANT**	**AIR CONDITIONING**	**QUIET LOCATION**

HOLIDAY INN/MARTINIQUE ON BROADWAY W www.holiday-inn.com $$$ 49 W. 32nd St., NY, NY 10001. **Map** 8 F3 **[** (212) 736-3800. **FAX** (212) 277-2702. This fine branch of the reliable Holiday Inn chain is housed in a landmark French-Renaissance building. Rooms are chain standard once you move past the marble lobby. The Little Korea location offers affordable Asian dining at all hours. Rates are high, so ask for discounts. ⬛⬛⬛⬛⬛⬛⬛⬛⬛⬛⬛	AE DC JCB MC V	532	●	▪	

THEATER DISTRICT

BIG APPLE HOSTEL W www.bigapplehostel.com $ 119 W. 45th St., New York, NY 10036. **Map** 12 E5. **[** (212) 302-2603. **FAX** (212) 302-2605. New York's best hostel caters to a world of young travelers with super-clean accommodation and a prime location. Most beds are in dormitories, but a few private doubles are available. Everything is newer and nicer than at most hostels. Book well in advance. ⬛⬛⬛	MC V	39			
PARK SAVOY HOTEL W www.parksavoy.com $ 158 W. 58th St., New York, NY 10019. **Map** 12 E3. **[** (212) 245-5755. **FAX** (212) 765-0668. This plain-Jane hotel offers basic accommodation in an excellent location: the best part of midtown, a block from Central Park. Rooms are spartan and not well maintained, but everything is clean. Some are big enough to accommodate four. The front desk is friendly but keeps service to a minimum. ⬛⬛⬛⬛⬛	AE MC V	70	●	▪	
BELVEDERE HOTEL W www.newyorkhotel.com $$ 319 W. 48th St., New York, NY 10036. **Map** 12 D5. **[** (212) 245-7000. **FAX** (212) 245-4455. This pleasing mid-range hotel is much smarter than most hotels in this price category and area. Rooms are good-sized, comfortable, and attractive. On site is a festive and hugely popular Brazilian steakhouse, but good restaurants abound in the area. A good choice for families. ⬛⬛⬛⬛⬛⬛⬛⬛	AE DC JCB MC V	400	●	▪	
BEST WESTERN PRESIDENT HOTEL W www.bestwestern.com $$ 234 W. 48th St., New York, NY 10036. **Map** 12 E5. **[** (212) 246-8800. **FAX** (212) 974-3922. This well-run chain hotel boasts small but just-fine rooms in a good location. Executive rooms feature a large desk and a new bathroom, but standard rooms do the job for most. Junior suites have a fold-out sofa for children. Two high-priced penthouse suites seem totally out of place. ⬛⬛⬛⬛⬛⬛⬛	AE DC JCB MC V	334	●	▪	
BROADWAY INN W www.broadwayinn.com $$ 264 W. 46th St., New York, NY 10036. **Map** 12 D5. **[** (212) 997-9200. **FAX** (212) 768-2807. Part B&B, part hotel, the Broadway Inn is a haven of tranquility and good taste in the heart of the Theater District. Rooms are simply but tastefully decorated with an Art-Deco flair. Breakfast is served in the charming library-style sitting room. Service is unparalleled in this price category. ⬛⬛⬛⬛⬛	AE DC JCB MC V	41		▪	
COMFORT INN MIDTOWN W www.comfortinn.com $$ 129 W. 46th St., New York, NY 10036. **Map** 12 E5. **[** (212) 221-2600. **FAX** (212) 764-7481. A recent renovation has transformed a formerly dour hotel into an attractive mid-priced option in a prime location. A marble-and-mahogany lobby leads to petite but pleasant guestrooms that have cheerful Americana-style decor; they are best suited to two travelers at most. ⬛⬛⬛⬛⬛⬛	AE DC JCB MC V	79		▪	
DAYS HOTEL MIDTOWN W www.daysinn.com $$ 790 Eighth Ave., New York, NY 10019. **Map** 12 D5. **[** (212) 581-7000. **FAX** (212) 974-0291. The tone is generic at this somewhat institutional hotel. The value is best when rates are $125 or lower. A decent New York-style coffee shop/deli is on site, plus a French bistro, Pigalle. ⬛⬛⬛⬛⬛⬛⬛⬛	AE DC JCB MC V	367	●	▪	
HOTEL EDISON W www.edisonhotelnyc.com $$ 228 W. 47th St., New York, NY 10036. **Map** 12 E5. **[** (212) 840-5000. **FAX** (212) 596-6850. This mammoth hotel is a good choice for travelers who want a comfortable room in a prime location. Quad rooms suit families well. Facilities include a cheap and perennially popular coffee shop/deli. ⬛⬛⬛⬛⬛⬛⬛⬛⬛⬛	AE DC JCB MC V	800	●	▪	

HUDSON �W www.hudsonhotel.com or www.ianschragerhotels.com $$ | AE DC JCB MC V | 1000
356 W. 58th St., New York, NY 10019. **Map** 12 D3. **(** (212) 554-6000. **FAX** (212) 554-6139.
This creation from the Ian Schrager/Philippe Starck team brims with riotous, eye-popping design. Rooms are beautiful but tiny – best for those who value style and scene over space. Public spaces often overflow with revelers. Expect more in the way of attitude than service. 🛏 24 TV 🔼 🏊 Ⓨ Ⓨ 🎏 🛗

MAYFAIR HOTEL �W www.mayfairnewyork.com $$ | AE DC MC V | 78
242 W. 49th St., New York, NY 10019. **Map** 12 D5. **(** (212) 586-0300. **FAX** (212) 307-5226.
Beware – rooms are miniscule at the Mayfair. But they're also comfortable and modern, service is extra-friendly, and the location is prime for theatergoing. Rates climb too high in the fall, but rooms are excellent value until then. The French bistro is worth enjoying even if you don't stay. 🛏 1 TV 🔼 🏊

WYNDHAM �W www.hotelwyndham.com $$ | AE DC MC V | 134
42 W. 58th St., New York, NY 10019. **Map** 12 F3. **(** (212) 753-3500. **FAX** (212) 754-5638.
Extra-large rooms at low, low prices. The individually decorated rooms and suites swing wildly between tacky and gorgeous, but they're all well maintained. The location (near Fifth Avenue and Central Park) is stellar. 🛏 🏋 TV 🔼 🏃

ALGONQUIN �W www.algonquinhotel.com $$$ | AE DC JCB MC V | 174
59 W. 44th St., NY, NY 10036. **Map** 12 F5. **(** (212) 840-6800. **FAX** (212) 944-1419.
This fully restored legend – home to Dorothy Parker's literary "Round Table" of the 1920s – is one of Midtown's most evocative hotels. Rooms are smallish but comfortable; the literary-themed suites make a worthy splurge. Off the glorious mahogany-paneled lobby – still ideal for socializing – is the Oak Room for star-quality cabaret. 🛏 24 TV 🔼 🏊 Ⓨ 🎏

BLAKELY HOTEL �W www.blakelynewyork.com $$$ | AE DC JCB MC V | 115
136 W. 55th St., New York, NY 10019. **Map** 12 E4. **(** (212) 245-1800. **FAX** (212) 582-8332.
Excellent package deals – often including Broadway show tickets – regularly make this good value even better. The spacious rooms are well appointed and have kitchenettes. Suites are well priced, but two queen beds make even standard rooms large enough for families. 🛏 1 🏋 TV 🔼 🏊 Ⓨ 🎏 🛗 🏃 ♿

CASABLANCA HOTEL �W www.casablancahotel.com $$$ | AE DC JCB MC V | 48
147 W. 43rd St., New York, NY 10036. **Map** 8 E1. **(** (212) 869-1212. **FAX** (212) 391-7585.
This stylish, Moroccan-themed hotel is enchanting – and the location is ideal for theatergoers. Rooms are not large, but are nicely outfitted in polished rattan and boast high-quality details. Breakfast and all-day cappucino are served in the fireplace lounge. 🛏 TV 🔼 Ⓨ 🛗

DOUBLETREE GUEST SUITES �W www.nyc.doubletreehotels.com $$$ | AE DC JCB MC V | 460
1568 Broadway, New York, NY 10036. **Map** 12 E5. **(** (212) 719-1600. **FAX** (212) 921-5212.
This all-suite hotel towing over Times Square more than compensates for its lack of personality with first-rate facilities and a central location. Some suites are designed for families, others are ideally suited to business travelers. A "Kids Club" playroom adds to the family appeal. 🛏 🏋 24 TV 🔼 🏊 Ⓨ Ⓨ 🎏 🛗 🏃 ♿

HILTON TIMES SQUARE �W www.timessquare.hilton.com $$$ | AE DC JCB MC V | 444
234 W. 42nd St., New York, NY 10036. **Map** 8 E1. **(** (212) 840-8222. **FAX** (212) 840-5516.
This Hilton surpasses its chain-hotel status with larger-than-standard rooms and a sophisticated air throughout. Rooms don't begin until the 23rd floor, so they're quiet despite the location. A pleasing restaurant from famous-name chef Larry Forgione adds to the appeal. 🛏 🏋 24 TV 🔼 🏊 Ⓨ Ⓨ 🎏 🛗 🏃 ♿

MANSFIELD �W www.mansfieldhotel.com $$$ | AE DC JCB MC V | 124
12 W. 44th St., New York, NY 10036. **Map** 12 E5. **(** (212) 944-6050. **FAX** (212) 764-4477.
This 1905 hotel fuses romance and modernism in rooms that are smallish but very inviting. Natural-fiber rugs cover ebony-stained floors and sleighbeds wear Belgian linens. All-day cappucinos included. 🛏 🏋 TV 🔼 🏊 Ⓨ

PARAMOUNT �W www.ianschragerhotels.com $$$ | AE DC JCB MC V | 610
235 W. 46th St., New York, NY 10036. **Map** 12 D5. **(** (212) 764-5500. **FAX** (212) 354-5237.
Hotelier Ian Schrager set the high design/low price standard for a decade ago, and it's still going strong. The miniscule rooms are all whites and grays, with compact stainless-steel bath and gilt-framed classic work doubling as art and headboard. Weekend rates often hover around $150. 🛏 24 🔼 Ⓨ Ⓨ 🎏 🛗 🏃

SOFITEL NEW YORK �W www.sofitel.com $$$ | AE DC JCB MC V | 398
45 W. 44th St., New York, NY. **Map** 12 F5. **(** (212) 354-8844. **FAX** (212) 354-2480.
This smart hotel is a welcome addition to the Theater District, with its dramatic blend of classic and modern. Rooms are spacious and beautifully designed. Some executive suites have terraces. 🛏 TV 🔼 🏊 Ⓨ Ⓨ 🎏 🛗 ♿

For key to symbols see back flap

Price categories for a standard double room per night, inclusive of breakfast, service charges and any additional taxes such as VAT: $ under $150 $$ $150–$250 $$$ $250–$350 $$$$ $350–$450 $$$$$ over $450	**RESTAURANT** Hotel restaurant or dining room usually open to non-residents unless otherwise stated. **AIR CONDITIONING** In-room units or central AC. **QUIET LOCATION** Quiet residential location or quiet street in a busy area. **CREDIT CARDS** Indicates which credit cards are accepted: *AE* American Express; *DC* Diners Club; *JCB*; *MC* MasterCard/Access; *V* VISA.	CREDIT CARDS	NUMBER OF ROOMS	RESTAURANT	AIR CONDITIONING	QUIET LOCATION

ESSEX HOUSE – A WESTIN HOTEL W www.westin.com $$$$$
160 Central Park South, New York, NY 10019. **Map** 12 E3. ((212) 247-0300.
FAX 212-315-1839. This ornate tower overlooking Central Park sparkles in full Art-Deco splendor. The reason to stay is the Westin Heavenly Bed, offering a genuinely celestial sleeping experience. Alain Ducasse *(see p295)* is one of New York's most coveted restaurant reservations.

| AE DC JCB MC V | 501 | ● | ■ | |

LE PARKER MERIDIEN W www.parkermeridien.com $$$$$
118 W. 57th St., New York, NY 10019. **Map** 12 E3. ((212) 245-5000. FAX (212) 708-7477.
The rooms here are modern, attractive, and functional, and facilities are excellent: two terrific restaurants, a creative cocktail bar, and one of the best hotel gyms in town (with spa services).

| AE DC JCB MC V | 730 | ● | ■ | |

MICHELANGELO W www.michaelangelohotel.com $$$$$
152 W. 51st St., New York, NY 10019. **Map** 12 F4. ((212) 765-0505. FAX (212) 581-7618.
This elegant hotel exudes Italian style, from the Vivaldi in the lobby to the Baci chocolates at bedtime. Each oversized room is warmly dressed in either Art Deco, Neoclassical, or country French style; bathrooms have Italian marble.

| AE DC JCB MC V | 178 | ● | ■ | |

MILLENNIUM BROADWAY W www.millennium-hotels.com $$$$
145 W. 44th St., New York, NY 10036. **Map** 12 E5. ((212) 768-4400. FAX (212) 768-0847.
Large rooms are outfitted in a smart deco style with comfy club chairs. The real perks come in the Premier tower, whose designer rooms manage to be both sleek and cozy. Club-level and Premier rooms include breakfast and cocktails served in a private lounge.

| AE DC JCB MC V | 752 | ● | ■ | |

MUSE W www.themusehotel.com $$$$
130 W. 46th St., New York, NY 10036. **Map** 12 E5. ((212) 485-2400. FAX (212) 485-2900.
If you want the intimate tone and personal service of a boutique hotel without the hard-edged modern design that often accompanies it, check into this classic-meets-contemporary newcomer, where the emphasis is on comfort, functionality, and service.

| AE DC JCB MC V | 200 | ● | ■ | |

ROYALTON W www.ianschragerhotels.com $$$$
44 W. 44th St., New York, NY 10036. **Map** 12 F5. ((212) 869-4400. FAX (212) 869-8965.
This super-stylish hotel may be the best effort from hotel pioneer Ian Schrager. An fashionable lounge scene occupies the lobby. Rooms are gorgeously designed on a loose cruise-ship theme (white cotton, mahogany, slate) complete with porthole windows.

| AE DC JCB MC V | 205 | ● | ■ | |

TIME W www.thetimeny.com $$$$
224 W. 49th St., New York, NY 10019. **Map** 12 D5. ((212) 320-2900. FAX (212) 320-2904.
Rooms are decorated in a black-and-cream Cubist scheme accented with one of three vivid colors: red, yellow, or blue. Rooms are efficient, but some are small. Rates are high, but specials are common.

| AE DC JCB MC V | 200 | ● | ■ | |

W TIMES SQUARE W www.whotels.com $$$$
1567 Broadway, New York, NY 10036. **Map** 12 E5. ((212) 930-7400. FAX (212) 930-7500.
Design-conscious travelers looking for a heart-of-Times Square location in addition to high style will enjoy this new addition to the fashionable "W" hotel chain with its trendy Blue Fin restaurant.

| AE DC JCB MC V | 509 | ● | ■ | |

CHAMBERS W www.chambers-ahotel.com $$$$$
15 W. 56th St., New York, NY 10019. **Map** 12 F3. ((212) 974-5656. FAX (212) 974-5657.
Situated in the heart of midtown, this place radiates downtown style from tip to toe with a sleek urban vibe. Expect Tibetan rugs, cashmere throws, and mood-setting candles as well as cutting-edge art. Town restaurant has received excellent notices.

| AE DC JCB MC V | 77 | ● | ■ | |

RITZ-CARLTON, NEW YORK W www.ritzcarlton.com $$$$$ AE DC JCB MC V **287**
50 Central Park South, New York, NY 10019. **Map** 12 F3. [212) 308-9100. FAX (212) 207 8831.
This reliable luxury chain's first midtown hotel debuted in 2002. Expect all of
the classic Ritz-Carlton hallmarks, which blend traditional stylings and premier
comforts: state-of-the-art technology, a full-service spa, and staff who never
say "no."

ST. REGIS NEW YORK W www.stregis.com $$$$$ AE DC JCB MC V **408**
2 E. 55th St., New York, NY 10022. **Map** 12 F4. [212) 753-4500. FAX (212) 787-3447.
This Beaux-Arts jewel is awash in luxury: crystal chandeliers, oriental carpets,
gilt-framed oils, Louis XIV antiques. Service is formal but impeccable. Lespinasse
(see p297) is one of only a fistful of *New York Times* four-star-winning
restaurants.

LOWER MIDTOWN

HOTEL GRAND UNION W www.hotelgrandunion.com $ AE DC JCB MC V **95**
34 E. 32nd St., New York, NY 10016. **Map** 9 A3. [212) 683-5890. FAX (212) 689-7397.
The Grand Union is justifiably popular with value-minded travelers. Rooms
verge on ugly, but they boast all the required comforts, and the maintenance
level is very high. Some are large enough for families. The staff is more
helpful than most in this price range.

CLARION HOTEL FIFTH AVENUE W www.hotelchoice.com $$ AE DC JCB MC V **189**
3 E. 40th St., New York, NY 10016. **Map** 8 F1. [212) 447-1500. FAX (212) 213-0972.
This freshly renovated chain hotel offers excellent value in a pricey neigh-
borhood. Rooms are outfitted in comfort with a hint of smart Art-Deco
style. The location – near New York Public Library and Grand Central
Terminal – is convenient for the Theater District but cleaner and quieter.

DUMONT AFFINIA W www.mesuite.com $$$ AE DC JCB MC V **248**
150 E. 34th St., New York, NY 10016. **Map** 9 A2. [212) 481-7600. FAX (212) 889-8856.
This all-suite hotel is great for those who value space and comfort over high
style. Trappings include fully appointed kitchens with microwave (the staff
will even do your shopping). There are executive workstations for work-
minded travelers and a spa for business men.

DYLAN W www.dylanhotel.com $$$ AE DC JCB MC V **197**
52 E. 41st St., New York, NY 10017. **Map** p 9 A1. [212) 338-0500. FAX (212) 338-0569.
This recently unveiled boutique hotel prizes form over function a bit too
much. Still, rooms are spacious by city standards. The excellently reviewed
French restaurant Virot is appeal enough.

LIBRARY HOTEL W www.libraryhotel.com $$$ AE DC JCB MC V **60**
299 Madison Ave., New York, NY 10017. **Map** 9 A1. [212) 983-4500. FAX (212) 499-9099.
The best among the bevy of new boutiques is this charmer, an understated
but beautiful haven. Each room boasts a unique theme, ranging from Fairy
Tales to Erotic Literature. Breakfast and all-day snacks are laid out in a cozy
lounge that doubles as – what else? – a well-stocked library.

FITZPATRICK GRAND CENTRAL HOTEL W www.fitzpatrickhotels.com $$$$ AE DC JCB MC V **155**
141 E. 44th St., New York, NY 10017. **Map** 13 A5. [212) 351-6800. FAX (212) 818-1747.
This lovely hotel is steps from Grand Central Terminal. Rooms surpass the
business-hotel standard with luxury fabrics and colors, and half-canopied
beds. The Liam Neeson penthouse offers marble-adorned luxury. A genuine
pub is on site.

MORGANS W www.ianschragerhotels.com $$$$ AE DC JCB MC V **154**
237 Madison Ave., New York, NY 10016. **Map** 9 A2. [212) 686-0300. FAX (212) 779-8352.
Opened in 1984, Ian Schrager's first boutique hotel is still going
strong, catering to a chic clientele that likes a low profile. Beware,
though – some rooms can be mighty small. Rates include breakfast.

W THE COURT/W THE TUSCANY $$$$ AE DC JCB MC V **320**
120-130 E. 39th St., New York, NY 10016. **Map** 9 A1. W www.whotels.com
Court: [212-685-1100. FAX 212-889-0287. Tuscany: [212) 685-1600. FAX (212) 779-8352.
This matched set of boutique-style hotels boasts beautifully designed
rooms that excel at both form and function. The Court is home to the super-
trendy bar-and-lounge scene, while the Tuscany features a more relaxed
ambiance and slightly larger rooms.

Price categories for a standard double room per night, inclusive of breakfast, service charges and any additional taxes such as VAT:

$(\$)$ under $150
$(\$)(\$)$ $150–$250
$(\$)(\$)(\$)$ $250–$350
$(\$)(\$)(\$)(\$)$ $350–$450
$(\$)(\$)(\$)(\$)(\$)$ over $450

RESTAURANT
Hotel restaurant or dining room usually open to non-residents unless otherwise stated.
AIR CONDITIONING
In-room units or central AC.
QUIET LOCATION
Quiet residential location or quiet street in a busy area.
CREDIT CARDS
Indicates which credit cards are accepted: *AE* American Express; *DC* Diners Club; *JCB*; *MC* MasterCard/Access; *V* Visa.

	CREDIT CARDS	NUMBER OF ROOMS	RESTAURANT	AIR CONDITIONING	QUIET LOCATION
BRYANT PARK w www.bryantparkhotel.com $(\$)(\$)(\$)(\$)(\$)$ 40 W. 40th St., New York, NY 10018. **Map** 8 F1. **(** (212) 869-0100. **FAX** (212) 869-4446. This hotel occupies the stunning American Radiator Building in an appealing midtown pocket: across from the charming Bryant Park, around the corner from the New York Public Library. Appointments bespeak cutting-edge luxury, and 24-hour butler service is among the perks. There is also a 70-person screening room.	AE DC JCB MC V	128	●	■	
KITANO w www.kitano.com or www.summithotels.com $(\$)(\$)(\$)(\$)(\$)$ 66 Park Ave., New York, NY 10016. **Map** 9 A2. **(** (212) 885-7000. **FAX** (212) 885-7100. This elegant Japanese-owned hotel is a sea of tranquility in the bustle, chaos, and excitement of the city. Hotel rooms are elegantly appointed havens of restful Japanese luxury. The Kaiseki cuisine in the restaurant is exceptional, and the service is flawless.	AE DC JCB MC V	149	●	■	●

UPPER MIDTOWN

	CREDIT CARDS	NUMBER OF ROOMS	RESTAURANT	AIR CONDITIONING	QUIET LOCATION
HABITAT HOTEL w www.habitatny.com $(\$)$ 130 E. 57th St., New York, NY 10022. **Map** 13 A3. **(** (212) 753-8841. **FAX** (212) 838-4767. The Habitat successfully fuses budget rates and designer comforts, but beware – most rooms are narrow, with a bed and pull-out trundle in lieu of a real double or twins. Most share hall baths but have in-room sinks. The location is great for shoppers. Ask about discounts for European travelers.	AE DC JCB MC V	300	●	■	
PICKWICK ARMS w www.pickwickarms.com $(\$)$ 230 E. 51st St., New York, NY 10022. **Map** 13 B4. **(** (212) 355-0300. **FAX** (212) 755-5029. Despite its location in a prestigious neighborhood, the Pickwick remains a beacon for budget travelers (although refurbishment is bringing in higher prices). Some rooms are tiny, but everything is clean and management is professional. About two-thirds of rooms have private baths.	AE DC JCB MC V	320	●	■	
KIMBERLY HOTEL w www.kimberlyhotel.com $(\$)(\$)(\$)$ 145 E. 50th St., New York, NY 10022. **Map** 13 A5. **(** (212) 755-0400. **FAX** (212) 486-6915. This low-profile hotel boasts mostly apartment-style one- and two-bedroom suites featuring home comforts, such as a full-size kitchen, dining area, and large, well-appointed rooms. Excellent for families and business travelers staying a while. Check for discounts and packages.	AE DC JCB MC V	185	●	■	●
METROPOLITAN HOTEL w www.metropolitanhotelnyc.com $(\$)(\$)(\$)$ 569 Lexington Ave., New York, NY 10022. **Map** 13 A4. **(** (212) 752-7000. **FAX** 212-758-6311. Previously Loews New York, the hotel continues to keep prices reasonable and caters to value-minded business travelers and child-toting families with equal aplomb.	AE DC JCB MC V	722	●	■	
ROGER SMITH w www.rogersmith.com $(\$)(\$)(\$)$ 501 Lexington Ave., New York, NY 10017. **Map** 13 A5. **(** (212) 755-1400. **FAX** (212) 758-4061. This pleasant hotel infuses creature comforts with a few artsy twists. Rooms are generous and individually decorated, mostly in a classic Americana style. Suites have microwaves and VCRs, and VIP rooms have whirlpool tubs. Rates include breakfast. Popular with up-and-coming rockers.	AE DC JCB MC V	130	●	■	
SWISSÔTEL NEW YORK – THE DRAKE w www.swissotel.com $(\$)(\$)(\$)$ 440 Park Ave., New York, NY 10022. **Map** 13 A3. **(** (212) 421-0900. **FAX** (212) 371-4190. Built in 1929, this Park Avenue dowager boasts a loyal following due to a great location, sophisticated European ambiance, and rooms that are excellent value. Some rooms have terraces.	AE DC JCB MC V	495	●	■	
BENJAMIN w www.thebenjamin.com $(\$)(\$)(\$)(\$)$ 125 E. 50th St., New York, NY 10022. **Map** 13 A4. **(** (212) 715-2500. **FAX** (212) 715-2525. This low-key hotel boasts well-outfitted rooms decorated in a Neoclassical-meets-modern style. Each has a gourmet kitchenette, and a work desk wired for high-tech travelers. The pillow menu will guarantee a good night's sleep. Facilities include a restaurant and a spa.	AE DC JCB MC V	209	●	■	

OMNI BERKSHIRE PLACE W www.omnihotels.com $$$$
21 E. 52nd St., New York, NY 10022. **Map** 12 F4. ((212) 753-7800. FAX (212) 754-5018.
This refined hotel is first-rate on all fronts, from the comfortable decor to the impeccable service. Extensive business facilities serve corporate travelers, the neighborhood is great for shoppers, and the hotel caters to families, too. Check for discounted weekend rates.

AE DC JCB MC V | 396

WALDORF-ASTORIA/WALDORF TOWERS W www.hilton.com $$$$
301 Park Ave., New York, NY 10022. **Map** 13 A5. ((212) 355-3000. FAX (212) 872-7272.
This New York legend is as great as ever. Rates are very reasonable in the main hotel, considering the glamorous air, extra-large rooms, and first-class dining and amenities. The exclusive Waldorf Towers has 24-hour butler service and a solid reputation for discretion.

AE DC JCB MC V | 1242

NEW YORK PALACE W www.newyorkpalace.com $$$$$
455 Madison Ave., New York, NY 10022. **Map** 13 A4. ((212) 888-7000. FAX (212) 303-6000.
This splendid hotel is housed in the landmark 1882 Villard Houses and a 55-story modern tower. The main hotel overflows with opulent old-world style, while the more exclusive tower boasts a refined contemporary-Deco style and around-the-clock butler service. Excellent on-site dining includes legendary Le Cirque 2000 *(see p296)*.

AE DC JCB MC V | 896

PENINSULA – NEW YORK W www.peninsula.com $$$$$
700 Fifth Ave., New York, NY 10019. **Map** 12 F4. ((212) 956-2888. FAX (212) 903-3949.
A stunning Beaux-Arts structure houses New York's best ultra-luxury hotel. Huge rooms are done in an Art Nouveau style, with big work desks and 21st-century technology. The rooftop spa offers pampering and relaxation.

AE DC JCB MC V | 239

PLAZA HOTEL W www.fairmont.com/the plaza/ $$$$$
768 Fifth Ave., New York, NY 10019. **Map** 12 F3. ((212) 759-3000. FAX (212) 759-3167.
The star of countless Hollywood films – and stage for even more high-society affairs – this 1907 French Renaissance palace continues to reign as New York's most glamorous address. The refined Fairmont hotels group has freshened the opulent period interiors and added a terrific new spa, but tourist crowds often undermine the elegance.

AE DC JCB MC V | 805

UPPER EAST SIDE

FRANKLIN W www.franklinhotel.com $$$
164 E. 87th St., New York, NY 10128. **Map** 17 A3. ((212) 369-1000. FAX (212) 369-8000.
The modern Franklin is more subway-convenient than sister hotel the Wales (below), but beware: rooms are miniscule. Sleekly designed and luxuriously equipped – with pillowtop beds wearing romantic sheer canopies, plus VCRs and CD players – they're nevertheless best for light packers and short-term stays. Continental breakfast and all-day cappuccino included.

AE DC JCB MC V | 48

HOTEL WALES W www.waleshotel.com $$$
1295 Madison Ave., New York, NY 10128. **Map** 17 A2. ((212) 876-6000. FAX (212) 860-7000. This quirky Victorian-style hotel offers pleasant relief in an expensive neighborhood. Comforts include beds dressed in Belgian linens, VCRs, and CD players. Rates include breakfast and self-serve cappuccino all day. Sarabeth's is a favorite for homestyle cooking and afternoon tea.

AE DC JCB MC V | 87

SURREY HOTEL W www.mesuite.com $$$
20 E. 76th St., New York, NY 10021. **Map** 17 A5. ((212) 288-3700. FAX (212) 628-1549.
Experience the high life for less at this lovely all-suite hotel. The Old World suites are spacious and pleasing from tip to toe; each one has a fully equipped kitchen. In-suite dining, from Cafe Boulud *(see p295)*, one of New York's finest restaurants, is reason enough to stay.

AE DC JCB MC V | 130

CARLYLE W www.thecarlyle.com $$$$$
35 E. 76th St., New York, NY 10021. **Map** 17 A5. ((212) 744-1600. FAX (212) 717-4682.
One of New York's most legendary and refined hotels, the Carlyle epitomizes Upper East Side elegance. Drawn in by the low-profile luxury and faultless service, generations of movie stars and world leaders have stayed in the beautifully appointed rooms and suites.

AE DC JCB MC V | 180

PIERRE W www.fourseasons.com/pierre/index.htm $$$$$
2 E. 61st St., New York, NY 10021. **Map** 12 F3. ((212) 838-8000. FAX (212) 940-8109.
Live like a royal at this elegantly residential, very European hotel, with opulent classical interiors. The old-world ambiance is extremely formal – with doormen and gloved elevator operators – but not uninvitingly so. Business travelers are better off elsewhere.

AE DC JCB MC V | 203

For key to symbols see back flap

| | | **Price categories** for a standard double room per night, inclusive of breakfast, service charges and any additional taxes such as VAT: $⑤ under \$150; ⑤⑤ \$150–\$250; ⑤⑤⑤ \$250–\$350; ⑤⑤⑤⑤ \$350–\$450; ⑤⑤⑤⑤⑤ over \$450$ | **RESTAURANT** Hotel restaurant or dining room usually open to non-residents unless otherwise stated. **AIR CONDITIONING** In-room units or central AC. **QUIET LOCATION** Quiet residential location or quiet street in a busy area. **CREDIT CARDS** Indicates which credit cards are accepted: *AE* American Express; *DC* Diners Club; *JCB*; *MC* MasterCard/Access; *V* VISA. |

	CREDIT CARDS	**NUMBER OF ROOMS**	**RESTAURANT**	**AIR CONDITIONING**	**QUIET LOCATION**
SHERRY-NETHERLAND w www.sherrynetherland.com ⑤⑤⑤⑤⑤ 781 Fifth Ave., New York, NY 10022. **Map** 12 F3. *(212) 355-2800.* **FAX** *(212) 319-4306.* No other hotel simulates genteel New York apartment living as well the Sherry. Mammoth rooms and suites are elegantly outfitted, and the service is impeccable. Rates include breakfast at exclusive Cipriani's, a favorite among power brokers.	AE DC JCB MC V	77	●	■	
STANHOPE w stanhopepark.hyatt.com ⑤⑤⑤⑤⑤ 995 Fifth Ave., New York, NY 10028. **Map** 16 F4. *(212) 774-1234.* **FAX** *(212) 517-0088.* This bright and elegant member of the Park Hyatt chain is ideal for museum lovers, since the Metropolitan Museum of Art is just across the street. The Versailles-inspired lobby displays Louis XIV antiques and museum-quality tapestries. Excellent through and through.	AE DC JCB MC V	185	●	■	●

UPPER WEST SIDE

	CREDIT CARDS	**NUMBER OF ROOMS**	**RESTAURANT**	**AIR CONDITIONING**	**QUIET LOCATION**
AMSTERDAM INN w www.amsterdaminn.com ⑤ 340 Amsterdam Ave., New York, NY 10023. **Map** 15 C5. *(212) 579-7500.* **FAX** 212-579-6127. Rooms are narrow and basic, but everything is fairly new and well maintained at this walk-up hotel. Bathrooms, both shared and private, are some of the nicest around for the money. Note that some "doubles" have single beds with a pull-out trundle rather than a real bed for two.	AE DC JCB MC V	25		■	
HOSTELLING INTERNATIONAL – NEW YORK w www.hinewyork.org ⑤ 891 Amsterdam Ave., New York, NY 10025. **Map** 20 E5. *(212) 932-2300.* **FAX** *(212) 932-2574.* This mammoth, square-block-sized hostel feels like an international college dormitory, complete with coffee bar and cafeteria, game room, a common kitchen, coin-operated laundry, a lounge with Internet-access machines, and a large yard with picnic tables. Travelers must be 18 years or older.	AE DC JCB MC V	628	●		
HOTEL NEWTON w www.newyorkhotel.com ⑤ 2528 Broadway, New York, NY 10025. **Map** 15 C2. *(212) 678-6500.* **FAX** *(212) 678-6758.* This clean, attractive, and professionally run hotel is a front-runner in the budget category. Rooms are large, with good, firm beds and nice bathrooms; some rooms are large enough for four.	AE DC JCB MC V	110	●	■	
JAZZ ON THE PARK w www.jazzhostel.com ⑤ 36 W. 106th St., New York, NY 10025. **Map** 21 A5. *(212) 932-1600.* **FAX** *(212) 932-1700.* This funky, artsy hostel brings a downtown vibe to the Upper West Side. A coffeehouse with live music most evenings lends a party atmosphere. Dorm rooms are basic, and bathrooms are decent. Expect a young, energetic, international crowd. A second location has opened at 57th Street and Lexington.	AE DC JCB MC V	220	●		
BELLECLAIRE HOTEL w www.hotelbelleclaire.com ⑤⑤ 250 W. 77th St., New York, NY 10024. **Map** 15 C5. *(212) 362-7700.* **FAX** *(212) 362-1004.* This recently renovated hotel has sparsely equipped but rather stylish rooms, with simple contemporary furnishings, cushioned headboards, and small bathrooms. A handful of rooms with shared baths go for as little as \$109. Two-bedroom/one-bath family suites are also available.	AE DC JCB MC V	180		■	
EXCELSIOR HOTEL w www.excelsiorhotelny.com ⑤⑤ 45 W. 81st St., New York, NY 10024. **Map** 16 D4. *(212) 362-9200.* **FAX** *(212) 580-3972.* This hotel offers high-quality comforts, directly across from the Museum of Natural History and steps from Central Park. Rooms are attractive and comfortable, with pretty bathrooms.	AE DC JCB MC V	196		■	
HOTEL BEACON w www.beaconhotel.com ⑤⑤ 2130 Broadway, New York, NY 10023. **Map** 15 C5. *(212) 787-1100.* **FAX** *(212) 724-0839.* The Beacon is one of the city's best-value hotels, especially for families. The rooms won't win style awards, but each has a modern kitchenette and most accommodate four. One-bedroom and two-bedroom/two-bath suites are good value. Washer/dryers are another family-friendly plus.	AE DC JCB MC V	236	●	■	

MILBURN w www.milburnhotel.com $$ | AE DC JCB MC V | 114
242 W. 76th St., New York, NY 10023. **Map** 15 C5. ((212) 362-1006. FAX (212) 721-5476.
This well-priced all-suite hotel is an excellent choice for families, or any
traveler who desires the comforts of home. Suites compensate for their lack of
style with a wealth of amenities, including modern bathrooms and well-
equipped kitchenettes. A helpful staff, laundry facilities, and a better-than-
average exercise room add to the value. 🛏 🎏 TV ↥ ⚡ 🍴 🔊 🕴 ⛐

ON THE AVE w www.ontheave-nyc.com $$ | AE DC JCB MC V | 251
2178 Broadway, New York, NY 10024. **Map** 15 C5. ((212) 362-1100. FAX (212) 787-9521.
Travelers with an eye for modern design and a mid-range budget will like this
stylish hotel. Rooms feature Scandinavian-style modular furniture, natural-
hued textiles, and attractive art. Beds should be a bit more plush, but
accommodation is comfortable overall. Cheaper rooms are smallish; the
deluxe category offers the best space-for-money ratio. 🛏 TV ↥ ⚡ ⛐ 🕴

QUALITY HOTEL ON BROADWAY $$ | AE DC JCB MC V | 350
w www.qualityhotelny.com
215 W. 94th St., New York, NY 10025. **Map** 15 C.2 ((212) 866-6400. FAX (212) 866-1357.
This nicely renovated chain hotel offers a subway-convenient location and good-
sized, if generic, guestrooms. Bathrooms are spacious by New York standards.
Some rooms have refrigerators and/or kitchenettes. The formerly sketchy neighborhood is now one of Uptown's most pleasant, and affordable dining options
abound. Rates sometimes plummet, so ask for discounts. 🛏 🎏 TV ↥ ⚡ 🕴

LUCERNE w www.newyorkhotel.com $$$ | AE DC JCB MC V | 250
201 W. 79th St., New York, NY 10024. **Map** 15 C4. ((212) 875-1000. FAX (212) 579-2408.
A distinctive 1903 building houses one of the city's best mid-priced hotels.
Service is the key note. The extremely well-kept rooms are outfitted in a
comfortable and attractive colonial Americana style; suites have kitchenettes
and minibars. A stylish grill hosts live jazz and blues. Rates, which include
continental breakfast, often drop well below $250. 🛏 🎏 TV ↥ ⚡ 🍸 🍴 🔊 🕴

MAYFLOWER HOTEL w www.mayflowerhotel.com $$$ | AE DC JCB MC V | 365
15 Central Park West, New York, NY 10023. ((212) 265-0060. FAX (212) 265-0227.
The prime location – in an upscale residential neighborhood at Central Park
West, just a shout from Lincoln Center and the Theater District – is the best
feature of this perfectly fine but otherwise undistinctive hotel. Rooms are
extra-large, traditionally styled, and comfortable. Extensive facilities include a
pleasant restaurant overlooking the park. 🛏 1 🎏 TV ↥ ⚡ 🍸 🍴 🕴

INN NEW YORK CITY w www.innnewyorkcity.com $$$$$ | AE DC JCB MC V | 4
266 W. 71st St., New York, NY 10023. **Map** 11 C1. ((212) 580-1900. FAX (212) 580-4437.
Expect ultra-luxury at this sparkling gem of a guesthouse, housed in a
gorgeous late 19th-century brownstone that has been restored to better-than-
new. Each spectacularly appointed suite has its own theme – Opera, Library,
Vermont, or Spa. Brilliant touches include bounteous in-suite breakfast
cupboards. Ridiculously expensive, but worth it. 🛏 🎏 TV ⚡ 🍸

MANDARIN ORIENTAL w www.mandarinoriental.com/hotelsite/ $$$$$ | AE DC MC V | 251
80 Columbus Circle, New York, NY 10019. **Map** 12 D3. ((212) 805-8800. FAX (212) 805-8888.
Opened in November 2003, this hotel offers sophisticated and luxuriously
appointed guestrooms including 48 suites with stunning views of Central
Park and the Manhattan skyline. There are excellent fitness facilities including
a lap pool and spa. The chic MObar on the 35th floor also boasts panoramic
views of the park. 🛏 1 🎏 24 TV ↥ ⚡ 🍸 🎵 🍴 ⛐

TRUMP INTERNATIONAL HOTEL & TOWER w www.trumpintl.com $$$$$ | AE DC JCB MC V | 167
1 Central Park West, New York, NY 10023. **Map** 12 D3. ((212) 299-1000. FAX (212) 299-1150.
Housed in a freestanding tower overlooking Central Park, this luxuriously
modern hotel is one of the city's finest. Smartly designed rooms are softened
with soothing Tuscan hues; floor-to-ceiling windows allow for unobstructed
city or park views. Each guest is assigned a personal concierge, making
service unparalleled. Jean Georges just may be New York's best restaurant.
🛏 🎏 24 TV ↥ ⚡ 🍸 🍴 🔊 🕴 ⛐

MORNINGSIDE HEIGHTS & HARLEM

SUGAR HILL INTERNATIONAL HOUSE w www.sugarhillhostel.com $ | AE MC V | 25
722 St. Nicholas Ave., New York, NY 10031. **Map** 19 A1. ((212) 926-7030.
This quiet, well-run, all-nonsmoking hostel offers two-dozen dorm beds
to shoestring travelers. Bunks fill spacious, high-ceilinged rooms; a few double
rooms are available to early arrivals. Security is good, there is a common kitchen,
and the kind owners are happy to offer advice. 1 🎏 ⚡

For key to symbols see back flap

RESTAURANTS AND BARS

NEW YORKERS love to eat well, and there are more than 25,000 restaurants in the five boroughs catering to their wishes. City dwellers avidly read restaurant reviews in magazines such as *New York* to ensure that they are seen in the latest fashionable eatery. "In" places and cuisine change with great regularity, while some favorite places simply remain

The classic Manhattan cocktail

popular. The restaurants in our listings have been selected as the best that New York can offer. *Choosing a Restaurant* on pages 288–90 will help narrow down your choice, and the information on pages 291–303 will fill out all the details. For lighter refreshment and casual meals, see *Light Meals and Snacks* on pages 304–305.

RESTAURANT MENUS

MEALS IN MOST of the better restaurants consist of three courses: the appetizer (or starter), an entrée (the main course) and a dessert. Virtually all New York restaurants, except fast-food places, serve you rolls or bread and butter just after you're seated, at no extra charge – it's all part of the expected service. In some fine restaurants you may be offered a complimentary appetizer, such as a small

Street-corner hot dog stand

dollop of mousse or a tiny triangle of quiche. Appetizers at the better restaurants are often the chef's most creative dishes – many diners request two appetizers and no entrée. Italian menus offer a pasta dish as a course before the main course, but in many places pasta is considered a main course. Coffee or tea and a dessert ordinarily conclude the meal in restaurants above the coffee-shop level. Your coffee cup may be refilled until you refuse any more. The cheeseboard used to be a rarity in New York restaurants, although some of the better establishments now feature one on the menu.

PRICES

YOU WILL ALWAYS find a restaurant in New York to suit your budget. At inexpensive coffee shops, diners and fast food chains, $10 will buy you a filling meal. There are also hundreds of acceptable, even first-rate, restaurants where you can eat well at a moderate cost – around $25 per person for a filling and decent meal, not including drinks – in attractive surroundings. For dinner at a trendy New American venue with a star chef, the bill could be upward of $70 to $100 per person, excluding drinks. Many top restaurants do, however, offer fixed-price (or, as they are known in New York, prix-fixe) meals. These are normally much cheaper than items on the à la carte menu. Lunch is also less expensive than dinner in such places, and because of the profusion of business diners, lunch is also the busiest period of the day.

TAXES AND TIPPING

NEW YORK CITY sales tax of 8.25% will be added to your bill. Service is not usually included. Tipping can run from 10% at a coffee shop to 20% at the fanciest places, with 15% an average fair tip. Many people just double the sales tax for a tip.

The bill is known as the "check" in the US. Commonly

A typical New York deli *(see p304)*

accepted credit cards are VISA, MasterCard and American Express. Traveler's checks are taken in many restaurants. Luncheonettes and coffee shops accept cash only. In fast-food chains, you order at the counter and pay cash in advance. Some other types of establishment take only cash.

DINING ON A BUDGET

DESPITE THE TALES of $200 business lunches, there are ways to stretch a meal budget in New York.

Order fewer courses than you would normally. American portions are huge, and an appetizer is often big enough for a light main course. You could share one with your companion or choose two appetizers and no entrée.

"Specials of the day" may be more expensive than items on the printed menu, so be sure to check prices.

Ask your waiter if there is a prix-fixe menu. Many expensive restaurants offer this at lunch and dinner – in the early evening it may often be called the pre-theater menu. Or try a prix-fixe lunch buffet. These are popular in

McSorley's Old Ale House

Indian restaurants and other places and are very reasonably priced meals.

Go to bars featuring "happy hours." They often offer a variety of hors d'oeuvres, like Spanish *tapas*, which can make a meal in themselves. If you want to simply see inside the restaurants every visitor has heard about, just go to have a drink and soak up the atmosphere. Avoid breakfast in your hotel. Even its coffee shop is likely to be more expensive than an outside coffee shop or deli. Many restaurants post their menus or will let you see them before you are seated, good for checking prices in advance.

HOURS

BREAKFAST HOURS are usually from 7 to 10:30 or 11am. Sunday brunch is a popular meal, served at most better restaurants between about 11am and 3pm. Lunch runs from 11:30am or noon to 2:30pm at most places, but the busiest time of the day

Poolside dining at the Four Seasons Hotel

is 1pm. Dinner is usually served from 5:30 to 6pm onward. The most popular time is around 7:30 to 8pm.

Some restaurants stop serving at 10pm during the week, or 11pm on Friday and Saturday. Certain informal restaurants, especially Chinese, are open from 11:30am to 10pm. Coffee shops are open long hours, from 7am to midnight or even 24 hours.

DRESS CODES

FEW RESTAURANTS demand that male diners dress formally, though a jacket is required at classy restaurants, and jacket and tie at the very best. At most places, for both men and women, "casual but

Dining in style at the Oyster Bar in Grand Central Terminal

chic" suffices. Women tend to dress up when dining at the expensive restaurants. If unsure, check the dress code when making a reservation.

RESERVATIONS

IT IS PRUDENT to make reservations at any restaurant above the luncheonette/fast food level, especially on weekends. A few of the trendiest restaurants won't even accept reservations except for groups of six or more. It is essential to make reservations for lunch at a midtown restaurant. But you may still have to wait at the bar, even if you have booked a table.

SMOKING

SMOKING IS now illegal in all bars and restaurants. The only exceptions are owner-operated bars that have special smoking rooms.

CHILDREN

WHEN EATING out with children, ask if there's a child's menu with half-portions. The prices are reduced, sometimes by half. Children are accepted in most New York restaurants, but if yours are unpredictable stick to casual spots, Chinatown Chinese or family-run Italian restaurants, burger bars, delis, cafés, fast food chains and luncheonettes. A few of the better restaurants have facilities for babies or toddlers; others may not be so well equipped. Dining out in the more formal New York restaurants is certainly not a family affair.

WHEELCHAIR ACCESS

WHILE MANY restaurants may be able to accommodate a wheelchair, it is always best to mention your requirements when making your reservation. Many smaller places cannot cater to disabled customers because of lack of space.

USING THE LISTINGS
Key to symbols in the listings on pp291–303.

🕿 telephone number
w website address
V vegetarian or vegetarian specialties
🍽 outdoor eating
🕭 wheelchair access to all or part of restaurant
T jacket and tie required
🎵 live music
🍷 excellent wine list
★ highly recommended
💳 credit cards accepted
AE American Express
DC Diners Club
MC MasterCard/Access
V VISA
JCB Japanese Credit Bureau

Price categories for a three-course meal for one, including a half-bottle of house wine and extra charges such as sales tax and a 15–20% tip:

$ Under $25
$$ $25–$35
$$$ $35–$50
$$$$ $50–$70
$$$$$ Over $70

What to Eat in New York

THE VARIETY OF FOOD found in New York is as varied as its cultural and ethnic makeup, and you can find virtually any food you want. For a hearty simple meal, such as marinated vegetables, pasta or salami and cheese, visit one of the Italian restaurants found in every neighborhood. For a more sophisticated meal try a Japanese restaurant for sushi and sashimi – as good in New York as anywhere in Japan. Or try such traditional Jewish foods as pastrami, blintzes and bagels, found in most delis and coffee shops. Spicy curries can be found in the many Indian restaurants around Manhattan. If you are really hungry, visit a steakhouse for juicy steaks, fresh seafood and some especially wicked desserts.

Bagel
This chewy Jewish bread roll is most popularly served with lox (smoked salmon) and cream cheese.

Pancakes
Thick, sweet pancakes are usually served with maple syrup as breakfast. Fresh or dried fruit may be mixed into the batter before cooking.

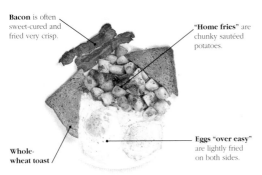

Bacon is often sweet-cured and fried very crisp.

"Home fries" are chunky sautéed potatoes.

Whole-wheat toast

Eggs "over easy" are lightly fried on both sides.

Breakfast or Brunch
Breakfast (or brunch if eaten midmorning) can consist of anything from home fries, eggs, bacon and toast to sweet pancakes or croissants, often with unlimited coffee.

French Toast
A breakfast dish of sliced bread dipped in egg then fried and often served with syrup.

Egg Cream
This drink is made with milk, chocolate syrup and carbonated soda water.

Corned Beef on Rye
Cured beef is served on rye bread with mild mustard and a pickle dill gherkin.

Burger and Fries "To Go"
A hamburger and french fries may come with salad and onion rings.

Giant Pretzel
This baked bread twist is sold on many street corners.

Clam Chowder
The Manhattan version of this shellfish soup is made with tomatoes and garnished with crackers.

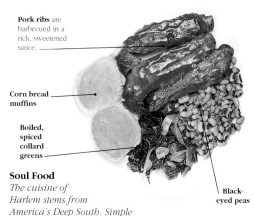

Pork ribs are barbecued in a rich, sweetened sauce.

Corn bread muffins

Boiled, spiced collard greens

Soul Food
The cuisine of Harlem stems from America's Deep South. Simple foods are cooked with spices for a unique flavor.

Black-eyed peas

Pizza
The street food of Italian festivals is available all over the city – this uptown version is topped with artichoke hearts.

Sushi
Japanese cuisine, like this ultrafresh raw fish and rice, is a New York favorite.

Dim Sum
Tiny steamed dumplings, stuffed with fish, meat or vegetables, are a specialty of Chinese cuisine.

Waldorf Salad
Created in the 1930s at the Waldorf Hotel, it's made out of apples, nuts and lettuce.

Cappuccino and Cookies
Frothy coffee sprinkled with chocolate is served with cookies in New York cafés.

Apple Pie à la Mode
This traditional American dessert is only "à la mode" when served with ice cream.

New York Cheesecake
This thick, baked Jewish dessert may be served plain or glazed with fruit.

Banana Split
Some New York ice cream concoctions will feed a family. No one will mind if you order extra spoons and share.

Choosing a Restaurant

THE RESTAURANTS in this section have been selected for their good value or exceptional food. The chart highlights some factors that may influence your choice. For details see pages 293–303. Details of *Light Meals and Snacks* are on pages 304–6 and for some of New York's best *Bars* see pages 307–9.

	Page Number	Fixed-Price Menu	Late Opening	Children's Facilities	Tables Outside	Sunday Night Opening	Vegetarian Dishes	Seafood Specialties
LOWER MANHATTAN								
14 Wall Street Restaurant *(French)* $$$$	295							
Bayard's *(French)* $$$$$	295							
SEAPORT AND THE CIVIC CENTER								
Cabana *(Latin American/Carribean)* $$	302		●	●		●		
Bridge Café *(American)* $$$	291		●	●		●	●	
LOWER EAST SIDE								
Golden Unicorn *(Chinese)* $	303			●		●		
Grand Sichuan *(Chinese)* ★ $	303					●		
Da Nico *(Italian)* $$	297	●	●	●	●	●	●	
Il Palazzo *(Italian)* $$	298			●	●	●		
Joe's Shanghai *(Chinese)* $$	303			●		●	●	
Canton *(Chinese)* ★ $$$	303					●		
Prune *(American)* $$$	293	●				●	●	
Sammy's Roumanian Steakhouse *(European)* $$$	300		●					
71 Clinton Fresh Food *(American)* $$$	293			●			●	
The Tasting Room *(American)* $$$	293	●				●		
SOHO AND TRIBECA								
Tennessee Mountain *(American Regional)* $	294	●	●	●		●		
Kin Khao *(Thai)* $$	303		●			●	●	
Le Pescadou *(French)* $$	296	●	●		●	●	●	●
Dos Caminos *(Latin American/Carribean)* $$$	302	●				●		
Le Jardin Bistro *(French)* $$$	296			●	●			
Le Zinc *(French)* $$$	296		●			●		
Lupa *(Italian)* ★ $$$	299			●		●		
Provence *(French)* $$$	297			●	●	●		
Aquagrill *(Seafood)* ★ $$$$	300					●	●	●
Montrachet *(French)* $$$$	297	●						
Bouley *(French)* $$$$$	295	●				●		
Chanterelle *(French)* $$$$$	295	●						
Danube *(European)* $$$$$	299	●					●	
GREENWICH VILLAGE								
Café de Bruxelles *(European)* $$	299			●		●		
Rio Mar *(European)* $$	299		●			●		
Home *(American)* $$	292	●		●	●	●	●	
Il Bagatto *(Italian)* $$	298			●		●	●	
Pearl Oyster Bar *(Seafood)* $$	301			●				●
Blue Hill *(American)* $$$	291			●		●		
Blue Ribbon Bakery *(American)* $$$	291		●			●		
Japonica *(Asian)* $$$	303						●	●
Da Silvano *(Italian)* $$$$	297				●	●	●	
Babbo *(Italian)* ★ $$$$	297					●		
Gotham Bar & Grill *(American)* $$$$	292			●			●	
Il Mulino *(Italian)* ★ $$$$	298						●	
One if by Land, Two if by Sea *(American)* $$$$	293	●				●	●	

Price categories include a three-course meal for one, half a bottle of house wine, tax, and a 15–20% tip.
$ under $25
$$ $25–$35
$$$ $35–$50
$$$$ $50–$70
$$$$$ over $70.

★ Means highly recommended.

FIXED-PRICE MENU
A fixed price for a set meal that is less expensive than normal menu prices.
LATE OPENING
Last orders at or after 11:30pm excluding Sunday.
CHILDREN'S FACILITIES
High chairs and/or child portions.
TABLES OUTSIDE
Garden or courtyard with outside tables.
VEGETARIAN DISHES
Vegetarian restaurant, or restaurant with good vegetarian selection.

	Page Number	Fixed-Price Menu	Late Opening	Children's Facilities	Tables Outside	Sunday Night Opening	Vegetarian Dishes	Seafood Specialties
EAST VILLAGE								
Great Jones Café (American Regional) $	294		■	●			■	●
First (American) $$$	292		■	●		●	■	●
GRAMERCY AND THE FLATIRON DISTRICT								
Craft (American) $$	291	●				●	■	
Blue Water Grill (Seafood) $$$	301	●	■		■	●		●
Bolo (European) $$$$	299	●				●		
Eleven Madison Park (American) $$$$	292	●				●	■	
I Trulli (Italian) ★ $$$$	298				■		■	
Mesa Grill (American Regional) ★ $$$$	294					●	■	
Patria (Latin American) ★ $$$$	302	●	■			●		
Periyali (Greek) $$$$	300							
Union Square Café (American) ★ $$$$	293			●		●	■	
Gramercy Tavern (American) ★ $$$$$	292	●				●	■	
Union Pacific (American) $$$$$	293	●					■	
Veritas (American) $$$$$	294	●				●	■	
CHELSEA AND THE GARMENT DISTRICT								
Rocking Horse Café (Latin American) $$	302		■				■	
Bottino (Italian) $$$	297			●	■	●	■	
The Red Cat (American) $$$	293					●	■	
AZ (American) ★ $$$$	291	●	■			●	■	
Da Umberto (Italian) $$$$	297						■	
Le Madri (Italian) $$$$	298					●	■	
THEATER DISTRICT								
Virgil's Real Barbecue (American Regional) $	294			●		●		
Becco (Italian) ★ $$	297	●	■	●		●	■	
Joe's Shanghai (Chinese) ★ $$	303			●		●	■	●
Turkish Cuisine (Turkish) $$	300	●	■		■		■	
Churrasccaria Plataforma (Latin American) ★ $$$	302	●	■			●		
Jezebel (American Regional) $$$	294						■	
Molyvos (Greek) ★ $$$	300		■					
Orso (Italian) ★ $$$	299					●		
Esca (Seafood) $$$	301				■			●
Beacon (American) $$$$	291					●	■	
Osteria del Circo (Italian) $$$$	299						■	
Le Bernardin (Seafood) ★ $$$$$	301							●
Alain Ducasse at the Essex House (French) $$$$$	295							
LOWER MIDTOWN								
The Oyster Bar and Restaurant (Seafood) ★ $$$	301			●				●
Asia de Cuba (Latin American/Caribbean) $$$$	301		■			●		
Michael Jordan's – The Steak House (American) $$$$	292			●		●		
UPPER MIDTOWN								
Dallas Bar-B-Cue (American) $	291	●	■			●		
La Bonne Soupe (French) $$	296		■	●	■	●		
Dawat (Indian) $$$	303			●		●	■	

For key to symbols see p285

Price categories include a three-course meal for one, half a bottle of house wine, tax, and a 15–20% tip.
$ under $25
$$ $25–$35
$$$ $35–$50
$$$$ $50–$70
$$$$$ over $70.

★ Means highly recommended.

FIXED-PRICE MENU A fixed price for a set meal that is less expensive than normal menu prices.
LATE OPENING Last orders at or after 11:30pm excluding Sunday.
CHILDREN'S FACILITIES High chairs and/or child portions.
TABLES OUTSIDE Garden or courtyard with outside tables.
VEGETARIAN DISHES Vegetarian restaurant, or restaurant with good vegetarian selection.

Restaurant	Price	Page Number	Fixed-Price Menu	Late Opening	Children's Facilities	Tables Outside	Sunday Opening	Vegetarian Dishes	Seafood Specialties
Rosa Mexicano (Latin American)	$$$	302					●	▪	
Shun Lee Palace (Chinese) ★	$$$	303	●		●		●		
Felidia (Italian)	$$$	298	●	●			●		
Guastavino's Restaurant and Club (French)	$$$$	296	●				●		
Inagiku (Japanese)	$$$	303			▪		●		
Aquavit (European) ★	$$$$$	299	●						●
Four Seasons (American)	$$$$$	292	●						
La Grenouille (French) ★	$$$$$	296							
Lespinasse (French) ★	$$$$$	297							
March (American)	$$$$$	292	●					●	
Oceana (Seafood)	$$$$$	301	●						●
UPPER EAST SIDE									
Mocca Hungarian Restaurant (European)	$	299	●		●		●		
Cabana (Latin American/Caribbean)	$$	302		▪	●		●	▪	
Pioneer Restaurant and Bar (Seafood)	$$	301	●	▪					●
Maya (Latin American)	$$$	302			●		●	▪	
Orsay (French)	$$$	297			●		●		
Erminia (Italian)	$$$$	298						▪	
Aureole (American)	$$$$$	291				▪		▪	
Café Boulud (French)	$$$$$	295					●	▪	
Le Cirque 2000 (French) ★	$$$$$	296					●		
Daniel (French) ★	$$$$$	295	●						
CENTRAL PARK									
Tavern on the Green (American)	$$$$	293	●		●	▪	●	▪	
UPPER WEST SIDE									
Gennaro (Italian)	$$	298			●			▪	
Santa Fe (American Regional)	$$	294					●		
Café Luxembourg (French)	$$$	295	●			▪	●		
Calle Ocho (Latin American/Caribbean)	$$$	302		▪			●		
Fiorello Café (Italian)	$$$	298		▪		▪	●		
Pasha (Turkish)	$$$	300			●		●	▪	
Rosa Mexicano (Latin American/Caribbean) ★	$$$	302			●		●	▪	
Café des Artistes (French)	$$$$	295			●		●		
Jean George (French)	$$$$$	296	●						
Picholine (European) ★	$$$$$	299	●				●		
MORNINGSIDE HEIGHTS AND HARLEM									
Copeland's (American Regional)	$	294		▪	●		●	▪	
Terrace in the Sky (European)	$$$$	300							
BROOKLYN									
Peter Luger (American)	$$$$	293			●		●		
River Café (American) ★	$$$$$	293	●			▪	●	▪	
QUEENS									
Elias Corner (Seafood)	$	301			●	▪	●		●
S'Agapo (Greek/Middle Eastern/Afghan)	$$$	300		▪		▪		▪	

Price categories include a three-course meal for one, half a bottle of house wine, tax, and a 15–20% tip.
$ under $25
$$ $25–$35
$$$ $35–$50
$$$$ $50–$70
$$$$$ over $70.

LATE OPENING
Last orders at or after 11:30pm excluding Sunday.
BAR DINING
Snacks, light meals or appetizers, served at the bar or at tables in the bar area.
FIXED-PRICE MENU
A fixed price for a set meal that is usually less expensive that normal menu prices.
SUNDAY OPENING
Brunch and/or dinner served on Sunday.
TABLES OUTSIDE
Garden or courtyard with outside tables.

			LATE OPENING	BAR DINING	FIXED-PRICE MENU	SUNDAY OPENING	TABLES OUTSIDE

AMERICAN

AUREOLE — $$$$$
34 East 61st St. **Map** 13 A3. ((212) 319-1660. W www.charliepalmer.com
Chef Charlie Palmer has won numerous awards for his progressive American fare, served in a flower-filled converted townhouse setting that does justice to the elegant cuisine. Aureole ranks among New York's top restaurants. ○ L Mon–Fri; D Mon–Sat. ▯ ▤ AE, MC, V.

LATE OPENING	BAR DINING	FIXED-PRICE MENU	SUNDAY OPENING	TABLES OUTSIDE
			●	

AZ — $$$$
21 West 17th St. **Map** 8 F5. ((212) 691-8888. W www.aznyc.com
The New American/Asian fusion creates magic at this innovative star, where every dish is delicious. The triplex building features a wall of water and a chic and charming rooftop space beneath a greenhouse. The prix-fixe lunch is an excellent buy. ○ D daily. �& ★ ▤ AE, MC, V.

| ● | | ● | ▦ | |

BEACON — $$$$
25 West 56th St. **Map** 11 C3. ((212) 332-0500. W www.beaconnyc.com
The spare, tri-level space is striking, the American menu highly praised, especially the rustic dishes from the wood-burning oven. Moods change with the levels, busy at the bar, intimate upstairs, and cozy near the open kitchen. ○ L Mon–Fri; D Mon–Sun. �& ▤ AE, MC, V.

| | ▦ | ● | ▦ | |

BLUE HILL — $$$
75 Washington Pl. **Map** 4 E2. ((212) 539-1776. W www.bluehillnyc.com
This intimate Greenwich Village restaurant is known for inventive New American fare that uses garden-fresh produce of the season, from two chefs who trained under David Bouley. Given the caliber of the food, the prices are reasonable. ○ D daily. ▤ AE MC, V.

| | | | ▦ | ● |

BLUE RIBBON BAKERY — $$$
33 Downing St. **Map** 4 D3. ((212) 337-0404. W www.blueribbonbakery.com
More than a bakery, this bi-level Village favorite has an enormous, eclectic menu that ranges from old-fashioned American comfort foods to sophisticated French-inspired fare, plus sandwiches on bread freshly baked in their brick oven, a notable cheese selection, and many "small plates" if you want to do some sampling. ○ L, D daily. �& ▤ AE, MC, V.

| ● | | | ▦ | |

BRIDGE CAFÉ — $$$
279 Water St. **Map** 2 D2. ((212) 227-3344. W www.bridgecafe.citysearch.com
Hidden in the shadows of the Brooklyn Bridge is city's oldest continuously operating tavern, a quaint wooden building circa 1794, with checked tablecloths, authentic old New York ambience, and a surprisingly sophisticated American menu. The Sunday brunch is also highly recommended. ○ L Mon–Fri, Sun; D daily. �& ▤ AE, MC, V.

| | | | ▦ | |

CRAFT — $$
43 East 19th St. **Map** 9 A5. ((212) 780-0880. W www.craftrestaurant.com
Talented Tom Colicchio of Gramercy Tavern has a new place around the corner where the emphasis is on simple preparation of highest quality, and absolutely fresh ingredients from small, specialized local farms and purveyors. The results have critics cheering. ○ L Mon–Fri; D Mon–Sun. �& ▤ AE, MC, V.

| | ▦ | ● | ▦ | |

DALLAS BAR-B-CUE — $
1265 Third Avenue. **Map** 13 B1. ((212) 772-9393.
The tacky neon and tile atmosphere is not particularly inspiring, but their enormous portions of barbequed ribs and chicken served with thick-sliced cornbread, low prices, and over-sized margaritas keep the restaurant constantly busy. ○ D, L Mon–Sat. �& ▤ AE, MC, V.

| ● | ▦ | ● | | ● |

Price categories include a
three-course meal for one,
half a bottle of house wine,
tax, and a 15–20% tip.
⑤ under $25
⑤⑤ $25–$35
⑤⑤⑤ $35–$50
⑤⑤⑤⑤ $50–$70
⑤⑤⑤⑤⑤ over $70

LATE OPENING
Last orders at or after 11:30pm excluding Sunday.
BAR DINING
Snacks, light meals or appetizers, served at the bar or at
tables in the bar area.
FIXED-PRICE MENU
A fixed price for a set meal that is usually less expensive
that normal menu prices.
SUNDAY OPENING
Brunch and/or dinner served on Sunday.
TABLES OUTSIDE
Garden or courtyard with outside tables.

	LATE OPENING	BAR DINING	FIXED-PRICE MENU	SUNDAY OPENING	TABLES OUTSIDE
ELEVEN MADISON PARK ⑤⑤⑤⑤ 11 Madison Ave. **Map** 9 A4. 【 *(212) 889-0905.* Restaurateur Danny Meyer has single-handedly made Madison Square Park chic with this soaring, three-story, Art Deco setting in the old Metropolitan Life Building. His typically imaginative New American cuisine is offered. The ambience is elegant but never stuffy. ◯ L, D daily. 🍴 🔊 📧 *AE, MC, V.*	■	●	■		
FIRST ⑤⑤⑤ 87 First Ave. **Map** 5 A2. 【 *(212) 674-3823.* ⓦ *www.first.citysearch.com* Where do chefs go when they get off work? For many the answer is this late-opening café, where the black-clad East Village crowd is not alone in discovering Sammy DeMarco's great New American fare. ◯ D daily; Brunch Sun. 🔊 📧 *AE, MC, V.*	●			■	
FOUR SEASONS ⑤⑤⑤⑤⑤ 99 East 52nd St. **Map** 13 A4. 【 *(212) 754-9494.* ⓦ *www.fourseasonsrestaurant.com* Restaurants come and go, but this gracious New York institution with landmark decor by Philip Johnson seems to go on forever, always among the top-rated for American/Continental food. The Grill Room is still the prime place for power lunches, and the Pool Room is a perfect setting for special-occasion dinners. ◯ L Mon–Fri; D Mon–Sat. 🍴 🔊 📧 *AE, MC, V.*	■	●			
GOTHAM BAR AND GRILL ⑤⑤⑤⑤⑤ 12 East 12th St. **Map** 4 E1. 【 *(212) 620-4020.* ⓦ *www.gothambarandgrill.com* Chef Alfred Portale has long been known for his "vertical food," artful layers of delicious and elegant New American fare. The lofty columned space manages to convey a mood that is both sophisticated and casual. The fixed-price three-course lunch is a great buy. ◯ L Mon–Fri; D daily. 🍴 📧 *AE, MC, V.*					
GRAMERCY TAVERN ⑤⑤⑤⑤⑤ 42 East 20th St. **Map** 9 A5. 【 *(212) 477-0777.* ⓦ *www.gramercytavern.com* Another Danny Meyer success, this is perhaps New York's most unpretentious fine dining, with the beams, antiques, and comfortable rustic ambience of a country inn, and a hospitable, knowledgeable staff. Tom Colicchio's inventive American cuisine is universally praised. No reservations needed for the less expensive Tavern Room. ◯ L Mon–Sat; Sun in Tavern; D daily. 🍴 🔊 ★ 📧 *AE, MC, V.*	■	●	■		
HOME ⑤⑤ 20 Cornelia St. **Map** 4 D2. 【 *(212) 243-9579.* Food like Mom used to make (provided she was a terrific cook) keeps this small, narrow café crowded. Entrees are lovingly prepared, many seasoned with the signature homemade catsup. The patio behind is a breath of fresh air in summer. ◯ L, D daily. 🔊 📧 *AE, MC, V.*				■	
MARCH ⑤⑤⑤⑤⑤ 405 East 58th St. **Map** 13 C3. 【 *(212) 754-6272.* ⓦ *www.marchrestaurant.com* Another elite dining spot, featuring a romantic setting in a gracious townhouse and a creative menu from star chef Wayne Nish. The recently expanded restaurant now has a skylit downstairs dining room. Menus make the most of the season's fresh produce, and the four-to-seven course prix-fixe dinners are memorable. ◯ D Mon–Sun. 🍴 🔊 📧 *AE, MC, V.*			●	■	
MICHAEL JORDAN'S – THE STEAK HOUSE ⓦ *www.theglaziergroup.com* ⑤⑤⑤⑤ Grand Central Terminal, West Balcony. **Map** 9 A1. 【 *(212) 655-2300.* The basketball great has scored again with this steak house and cigar bar overlooking the grand spaces of freshly renovated Grand Central Terminal. Order a steak with light-as-air french fries and creamed spinach, and revel in an All-American classic dinner. But don't come on a hot summer day; the terminal is not air-conditioned. ◯ L, D daily. 🍴 🔊 📧 *AE, MC, V.*				■	

ONE IF BY LAND, TWO IF BY SEA $$$$$
17 Barrow St. **Map** 3 C3. (212) 225-8649. w www.oneifbyland.com
Romance is in the air in this charming, landmark Greenwich Village
townhouse. Elegant New American/Continental fare comes with firelight,
flickering candles, flowers and a tinkling piano. If you want to propose or
celebrate a special anniversary, this is the place. D daily. AE, MC, V.

PETER LUGER   w www.peterluger.com $$$$
178 Broadway, Williamsburg, Brooklyn. (718) 387-7400.
There's nothing more all-American than a great steak, and nobody does it
better than Peter Luger. The gritty beer-hall ambience and remote location
don't discourage beef lovers. Don't even think about coming without a
reservation--and still expect a wait. L, D daily. AE, MC, V.

PRUNE $$$
54 East 1st St. **Map** 5 A3. (212) 677-6221.
Short on space but long on creativity, this unpretentious East Village café
serves original, reasonably priced American home cooking with multi-cultural,
sometimes quirky touches. Reservations are hard to come by, but it's worth
the effort. D daily; brunch Sat–Sun. AE, MC, V.

THE RED CAT $$$
227 Tenth Ave. **Map** 7 C4. (212) 242-1122. w www.theredcat.com
Red banquettes and red accent plates are just the start of the warmth at this
modern neighborhood place, stylish but still friendly and with first-rate
American fare with Mediterranean accents. Don't miss the parmesan frites with
mustard aioli. D daily. AE, MC, V.

RIVER CAFÉ $$$$$
One Water St, Brooklyn. **Map** 2 F2. (718) 522-5200 w www.rivercafe.com
New York's most spectacular view is from this Brooklyn standout, and the
New American fare is worthy of the romantic setting. The signature Chocolate
Duo dessert includes a chocolate marquise mini-Brooklyn Bridge. If you can't
afford the dinner tab, come for drinks and light fare on the terrace. (No jeans,
please.) L Mon–Sat; Brunch Sun; D Daily. ★ AE, MC, V

71 CLINTON FRESH FOOD $$$
71 Clinton St. **Map** 5 B3. (212) 614-6960.
A sure sign of the changes on the Lower East Side is this hot and hip (albeit
cramped) storefront café gaining fame for the exciting creations of chef Wylie
Dufresne, formerly of Jean George, and drawing food lovers from all over
town. D Mon–Sat. AE, MC, V.

THE TASTING ROOM $$$
72 East 1st St. **Map** 5 A3. (212) 358-7831.
The praise is universal for this small New American entry in the East Village,
where the friendly, unhurried ambience is set by hostess Renee Alevras, and
the seasonal dishes of her husband, chef Colin Alevras, can be accompanied
by a choice of 300 American wines. Tasting portions are available for each
main course. D Tue–Sat. MC, V.

TAVERN ON THE GREEN $$$$
Central Park at West 67th St. **Map** 12 D2. (212) 873-3200.
The lush garden, with illuminated trees and lanterns, make the Tavern on the
Green a romantic spot. The restaurant is a popular choice for weddings and
other events, so reservations are highly recommended. The restaurant's
signature cheesecake has been prepared by the same person for 25 years.
L, D daily. AE, DC, MC, V.

UNION PACIFIC $$$$$
111 East 22nd St. **Map** 9 A4. (212) 995-8500. w www.unionpacificrestaurant.com
A waterfall at the entrance and a lofty vaulted-ceiling dining room set the
stage for a dramatic evening: Rocco DiSpirito's bold New American menu with
Pacific Rim influences is a big reason why this neighborhood is becoming a
major food destination. L Mon–Fri; D Mon–Sat. AE, MC, V.

UNION SQUARE CAFÉ $$$$
21 East 16th St. **Map** 9 A5. (212) 243-4020.
Restaurant entrepreneur Danny Meyer's first venue has been one of New
York's most popular since 1985, loved for delicious fare served in comfortable,
casual surroundings by a friendly staff. Chef Michael Romano's new takes on
American standards include the freshest ingredients from the neighboring
Union Square Greenmarket. L Mon–Sat; D daily. ★ AE, MC, V.

For key to symbols see back flap

	LATE OPENING	BAR DINING	FIXED-PRICE MENU	SUNDAY OPENING	TABLES OUTSIDE

Price categories include a three-course meal for one, half a bottle of house wine, tax, and a 15–20% tip.
⑤ under $25
⑤⑤ $25–$35
⑤⑤⑤ $35–$50
⑤⑤⑤⑤ $50–$70
⑤⑤⑤⑤⑤ over $70.

LATE OPENING
Last orders at or after 11:30pm excluding Sunday.
BAR DINING
Snacks, light meals or appetizers, served at the bar or at tables in the bar area.
FIXED-PRICE MENU
A fixed price for a set meal that is usually less expensive than normal menu prices.
SUNDAY OPENING
Brunch and/or dinner served on Sunday.
TABLES OUTSIDE
Garden or courtyard with outside tables.

VERITAS ⑤⑤⑤⑤⑤
43 East 20th St. **Map** 9 A5. **(** (212) 353-3700. **w** www.veritas-nyc.com
A wine list offering 1,300 selections and helpful sommeliers are the biggest draws, but the New American cuisine is quite outstanding on its own at this chic and sleek restaurant. Just 55 seats, so be sure to reserve ahead.
○ D daily. ▮ & ⊘ AE, MC, V.

| | ■ | ● | ■ | | |

AMERICAN REGIONAL

COPELAND'S ⑤
549 West 145th St. **Map** 19 A1. **(** (212) 234-2357.
Take your pick of Southern fried chicken, Maryland crab cakes, or Louisiana gumbo. You can't go wrong at this popular Harlem spot where folks like Bill Cosby and Danny Glover have been spotted, and the Sunday gospel brunch is the best around. Jazz adds to the atmosphere. ○ D Tue–Sun; Brunch Sun. &
⊘ AE, MC, V.

| ● | | | ■ | |

GREAT JONES CAFÉ ⑤
54 Great Jones St. **Map** 4 F2. **(** (212) 674-9304. **w** www.greatjonescafe.com
Cajun food lovers hie to this hole-in-the-wall NoHo neighborhood café for spicy gumbo made with andouille sausage, jambalaya, corn-meal fried catfish, and other delicious New Orleans fare. Don't expect atmosphere, but do expect a young, hip, local crowd. ○ D daily.

| ● | | | | |

JEZEBEL ⑤⑤⑤
630 Ninth Ave. **Map** 12 D5. **(** (212) 582-1045. **w** www.jezebelny.com
A setting of porch swings, antiques, and palms add up to just the place to sample soul food favorites like fried chicken, catfish, grits, and okra – and be sure to save room for the scrumptious homemade pies. The location near the Theater District is another plus. ○ D Tue–Sat. & ⊘ AE, DC, MC, V.

MESA GRILL ⑤⑤⑤⑤
102 Fifth Ave. **Map** 8 F5. **(** (212) 807-7400. **w** www.mesagrill.com
Celebrity chef Bobby Flay is a master of Southwestern cookery, and his creative menus, from roasted pumpkin and smoked chile soup to cumin crusted chicken, have kept the customers coming in droves for a decade. Even the corn muffins are delicious. Sit upstairs for less of the perpetual din.
○ L Mon–Fri; D daily; brunch Sat-Sun. ▮ & ★ ⊘ AE, MC, V.

| | ■ | | ■ | |

SANTA FE ⑤⑤
72 West 69th St. **Map** 12 D1. **(** (212) 724-0822.
A relaxing setting amid peach-colored walls adorned with colorful rugs, and the location near Lincoln Center, are among the reasons this Southwestern standby has been a favorite for years. Some of the best dishes are the Masa shrimp appetizer and chipotle chicken with rice, steamed vegetables, and grated cheese over refried beans. ○ L, D daily. ⊘ AE, DC, MC, V.

| | | | ■ | |

TENNESSEE MOUNTAIN ⑤
143 Spring St. **Map** 4 E4. **(** (212) 431-3993. **w** www.tnmountain.com
Housed in a landmark farmhouse built in 1807, Tennessee Mountain is famous for its huge portions of barbecued and smoked chicken and ribs and its recently added steak menu. Southern-style pulled pork and Texas-style smoked brisket are also provided, plus a broad range of lighter snacks and appetizers. Monday and Tuesday nights have an excellent-value all-you-can-eat special. ○ L, D daily. ⊘ AE, MC, V.

| ● | | ● | ■ | ● |

VIRGIL'S REAL BBQ ⑤
152 West 44th St. **Map** 12 E5. **(** (212) 921-9494.
This big, boisterous Theater District restaurant offers a tour of barbecue styles throughout the South, Memphis to Carolina to Texas, 10 different platters of beef, pork, or chicken with a variety of sauces. On the side come flaky buttermilk biscuits with honey-butter, collard greens, and other delicious Southern standards. ○ L, D daily. & ⊘ AE, MC, V.

| | | | ■ | |

FRENCH

ALAIN DUCASSE AT THE ESSEX HOUSE $⑤⑤⑤⑤⑤
155 West 58th St. **Map** 12 F3. ☎ *(212) 265-7300.* W *www.alain-ducasse.com*
The celebrated French chef has come to New York in grand style, with a
limited schedule in a posh, intimate 65-seat home with just one seating at
each meal – and New York's most expensive menu. No one questions the
quality of the food, only whether it is worth the stratospheric prices.
◻ D Mon–Sat. 🍴 & 🍽 *AE, MC, V.*

BAYARD'S $⑤⑤⑤⑤⑤
1 Hanover Sq. **Map** 1 C3. ☎ *(212) 514-9454.* W *www.bayards.com*
Formerly the New York Cotton Exchange and private club for traders, this
mansion has been beautifully restored in Old-World style, furnished with
period antiques and nautical paintings. The highly regarded chef uses only the
freshest and finest ingredients, and the wine list is extensive. A special
experience. ◻ D Mon–Sat. 🍴 & 🍽 *AE, MC, V.*

BOULEY BAKERY $⑤⑤⑤⑤⑤
120 West Broadway. **Map** 1 B1. ☎ *(212) 964-2525.* W *www.bouley.net*
There is, indeed, a bakery, but there is also a rather simple dining room
overseen by master chef David Bouley, and his New French cuisine will make
you forget everything but your happy palate. The attached bakery café serves
breakfast, brunch, and lunch sandwiches on Bouley's heavenly breads.
◻ L, D daily. 🍴 & 🍽 *AE, MC, V.*

CAFÉ BOULUD $⑤⑤⑤⑤
20 East 76th St. **Map** 16 F5. ☎ *(212) 772-2600.* W *www.danielnyc.com*
Since Daniel Boulud opened his Midtown palace, his first restaurant has
become a bit more casual. The food is superbly prepared, serious French, and
the tab is also serious. Menus feature classic dishes, specialties of the season,
"Le Potager," a celebration of vegetables, and "Le Voyage," dishes with more
exotic flavors. ◻ L Tue–Sat; D daily. & 🍽 *AE, MC, V.*

CAFÉ DES ARTISTES $⑤⑤⑤
1 West 67th St. **Map** 12 D2. ☎ *(212) 877-3500.* W *www.cafedesartistesnyc.com*
Once a haunt of artists who lived in the building, the café has long been a
favorite for the romantic floor-to-ceiling murals of naked nymphs by Howard
Christy. Some say the food has slipped, but the regulars, everyone from Peter
Jennings to Itzhak Perlman, don't seem to mind. ◻ L Mon–Fri; D daily;
brunch Sat–Sun. 🍴 🍷 🍽 *AE, MC, V.*

CAFÉ LUXEMBOURG $⑤⑤
200 W. 70th St. **Map** 11 C1. ☎ *(212) 873-7411.*
A neighborhood favorite for nearly 20 years, this is a classic art deco Parisian
bistro with a zinc-topped bar, antique mirrors, and a loyal, hip clientele that
sometimes includes movie stars. The steak *frite* can't be beat. ◻ L Mon–Sat;
D daily; brunch Sat, Sun. 🍽 *AE, MC, V.*

CHANTERELLE $⑤⑤⑤⑤⑤
2 Harrison St. **Map** 4 D5. ☎ *(212) 966-6960.* W *www.chanterellenyc.com*
A classic for two decades, this understated Tribeca dining room still ranks high
for its flawless New French food and gracious service. Chanterelle is ideal for
special occasions or any time you want to linger over a memorable three-hour
dinner. ◻ L Tue–Sat; D Mon–Sat. 🍴 & 🍽 *AE, MC, V.*

DANIEL $⑤⑤⑤⑤⑤
60 East 65th St. **Map** 13 A2. ☎ *(212) 288-0033.* W *www.danielnyc.com*
A shining star of the New York food world, Daniel Boulud presides in a
flower-filled, Venetian Renaissance-inspired dining room worthy of his
extraordinary talents. Seasonal menus with choices such as roasted squab with
spiced pineapple or black truffle-crusted cod are divine. Lunch is a less
astronomical opportunity to sample the master. ◻ D Mon–Sat.
🍴 & ★ 🍽 *AE, MC, V.*

14 WALL STREET RESTAURANT $⑤⑤⑤
14 Wall St. **Map** 1 C3. ☎ *(212) 233-2780.* W *www.14wallstreetrestaurant.com*
Once J.P. Morgan's private dining room, this penthouse with wonderful views
is a Wall Street expense-account favorite. The room with high ceilings, dark
wood trim, and vintage French posters is a handsome setting for generally fine
French cuisine. The service is impeccable, and there's a convivial bar for after
dinner. ◻ L, D Mon–Fri. & 🍽 *AE, MC, V.*

For key to symbols see back flap

<table>
<tr><td rowspan="2">Price categories include a three-course meal for one, half a bottle of house wine, tax, and a 15–20% tip.
⑤ under $25
⑤⑤ $25–$35
⑤⑤⑤ $35–$50
⑤⑤⑤⑤ $50–$70
⑤⑤⑤⑤⑤ over $70.</td></tr>
</table>

LATE OPENING
Last orders at or after 11:30pm excluding Sunday.
BAR DINING
Snacks, light meals or appetizers, served at the bar or at tables in the bar area.
FIXED-PRICE MENU
A fixed price for a set meal that is usually less expensive that normal menu prices.
SUNDAY OPENING
Brunch and/or dinner served on Sunday.
TABLES OUTSIDE
Garden or courtyard with outside tables.

	LATE OPENING	BAR DINING	FIXED-PRICE MENU	SUNDAY OPENING	TABLES OUTSIDE
GUASTAVINO'S RESTAURANT AND CLUB ⑤⑤⑤ 409 East 59th St. **Map** 13 C3. (212) 980-2455, Club (212) 421-6644. www.guastavinos.com Under the savvy guidance of London's Terence Conran, this has emerged as one of the city's great settings, beneath the 59th Street Bridge, with formal French dining upstairs in the Club beneath the arched Guastavino tiles, and a huge, usually packed brasserie and bar in the lofty spaces downstairs. L Mon–Fri; D Mon–Sun; Brunch Sat–Sun. ★ AE, MC, V.		■	●	■	
JEAN GEORGES ⑤⑤⑤⑤⑤ Trump International Hotel, 1 Central Park West. **Map** 12 D3. (212) 299-3900. Jean-George Vongerichten in his namesake restaurant turns out food that is among the very best in New York, transformed by the French master's delicate sauces and creative combinations. Adam Tihany has designed a polished, almost austere setting that does not upstage the four-star chef. L Mon–Fri; D Mon–Sat. ★ AE, MC, V.			●		
LA BONNE SOUPE ⑤⑤ 48 West 55th St. **Map** 12 F4. (212) 586-7650. www.labonnesoupe.com This cozy midtown haven for the thrifty, nearing its 30th birthday, exudes comfortable, old-fashioned French charm. Besides filling soups, including a classic onion soup, specials include fondues, quiches, omelets, and reasonably priced "plats du jour," steak *pomme frites* to *poulet* to sweetbreads. L, D daily. AE, MC, V.	●			■	●
LA GRENOUILLE ⑤⑤⑤⑤⑤ 3 East 52nd St. **Map** 12 F4. (212) 752-1495. La Grenouille maintains the highest standards of elegant French dining in a beautiful dining room with silk on the walls, velvet banquette,s and glorious flower bouquets everywhere. A classic since 1962, it remains one of the city's best restaurants year after year. L, D Tue–Sat. ★ AE, MC, V.					
LE CIRQUE 2000 ⑤⑤⑤⑤⑤ 455 Madison Ave. **Map** 13 A4. (212) 303-7788. www.lecirque.com Some love the bright neon and the playful curving furniture by Adam Tihany, although some find it jarring amid the gilded old world splendor of the landmark Villard Houses. But no one doubts that Le Cirque is one of the city's better French restaurants and for many the place to see and be seen. L Mon–Sat; D Mon–Sun. ★ AE, MC, V.		■		■	
LE JARDIN BISTRO ⑤⑤⑤ 25 Cleveland Pl. **Map** 4 F4. (212) 343-9599. www.lejardinbistro.com When the weather is warm, dining beneath an umbrella in this leafy SoHo garden is delightful. The reasonably priced menu of simple French favorites such as bouillabaise, coq au vin, or mussels is never a disappointment, the staff is pleasant, and the ambience is delightful in the small indoor café as well as in the garden. L, D daily. AE, MC, V.				■	●
LE PESCADOU ⑤⑤ 18 King Street. **Map** 4 D3. (212) 924-3434. Monet-style murals and a chandelier with shimmering baubles adorn this delightful French fishhouse. Their seasonally changing menu includes specialties such as traditional fish soup and fillet of salmon with a horseradish crust. In the winter months lamb and veal dishes are also served. L, D daily. AE, MC.	●	■	●	■	●
LE ZINC ⑤⑤⑤ 139 Duane St. **Map** 1 C1. (212) 513-0001. www.lezincnyc.com The proprietors of the very haute Chanterelle have opened a welcome informal bistro, open to 4am. The spare decor features creamy walls, bare tables, and wine bottles adorning the walls. Onion fritters and skate are recommended. L, D daily; brunch Sun. AE, MC, V.	●			■	

LESPINASSE $$$$$
2 East 55th St, St. Regis Hotel. **Map** 12 F3. ((212) 339-6719. W www.stregis.com
Opulent Louis XV surroundings, Waterford crystal, Limoges china, and
sumptuous formal French fare put this firmly in the top ranks of New York
restaurants, but be forewarned that the tab can be a painful ending to a
wonderful meal. ◯ L, D Tue–Sat. ▮ & ▮ ★ ✉ AE, MC, V.

MONTRACHET $$$$
239 West Broadway. **Map** 4 E5. ((212) 219-2777. W www.montrachet.net
This first of Drew Nieporent's restaurant empire, nearly two decades old,
continues to rank among the city's best, known for its comfortable, casual
decor, modern French cuisine, and exceptional wine list. The prix-fixe or tasting
menus are worth planning for. ◯ L Fri; D Mon–Sat. ▮ ★ ✉ AE, MC, V.

ORSAY $$$
1057-59 Lexington Ave. **Map** 17 A5. ((212) 517-6400. W www.orsayrestaurant.com
Replacing the late Mortimer's, society's favorite hangout, isn't easy, but this
chic French café has succeeded, drawing back the upscale clientele and many
others with authentic bistro fare served with flair by very French waiters.
◯ L, D daily. & ✉ AE, MC, V.

PROVENCE $$$
38 MacDougal St. **Map** 4 D3. ((212) 475-7500. W www.provence.citysearch.com
Popular for its Provençal atmosphere, outdoor garden, and reasonable prices,
this pictureque French café in SoHo is a romantic find. The menu features
traditional dishes such as bouillabaisse and roasted duck as well as more
"nouveau" additions. ◯ L, D daily. ✉ AE.

ITALIAN

BABBO $$$$$
110 Waverly Pl. **Map** 4 D2. ((212) 777-0303.
The setting in a century-old duplex Greenwich Village townhouse, with grand
stairway and skylight, and the inventive, rustic Italian country fare of notable
chef Mario Batali, make this one of the most popular of the many Italian
restaurants in the city; reserve well in advance. Sit upstairs for less crowded
surroundings. ◯ D daily. ▮ & ★ ✉ AE, MC, V.

BOTTINO $$$
246 10th Ave. **Map** 7 C4. ((212) 206-6766. W www.bottinonyc.com
A 100-year-old hardware store amid the booming Chelsea gallery scene has
been transformed into sleek minimalist modern space with Eames, Knoll, and
Bertoia furnishings. Bottino attracts a stylish crowd both day and night for
good Northern Italian fare and a lovely garden that is tented in winter.
◯ L Tue–Sat; D daily. ▮ ✉ AE, MC, V.

BECCO $$
355 West 46th St. **Map** 11 D5. ((212) 397-7597. W www.becconyc.com
A best-bet in the Theater District, popular Becco has bargain prix-fixe menus,
your choice of a generous antipasto with unlimited portions of three pastas of
the day, or Caesar salad with a main course, all well prepared under the
watchful eyes of the Bastianiches, who also own the upscale Felidia.
◯ L Mon–Sat; D daily. ▮ ★ ✉ AE, MC, V.

DA NICO $$
164 Mulberry St. **Map** 4 F3. ((212) 343-1212. W www.littleitalynyc.com/danico
A rustic setting and a wonderful courtyard garden make this family-run
restaurant one of the favorites in Little Italy. Take your pick of southern or
northern Italian standards, an antipasto bar, and 16 kinds of pizza, and don't
miss the tiramisu for dessert. ◯ L, D daily. & ✉ AE, MC, V.

DA SILVANO $$$
260 Sixth Ave. **Map** 4 D3. ((212) 982-2343.
Try for a table outside where you can watch for the celebrities, who are often
regulars at this neighborhood trattoria where chef/owner Silvano Marcetta has
presided for 25 years. The northern Italian fare is consistent, and the buzz is
even better. ◯ L, D daily. ▮ & ✉ AE, MC, V.

DA UMBERTO $$$
107 West 17th St. **Map** 8 E5. ((212) 989-0303.
Sophisticated Tuscan fare has kept them coming for years to this
unpretentious restaurant where a long list of daily specials uses the freshest
ingredients of the season. A regional wine list complements the food, and the
tiramisu is worth the calories. ◯ L Mon–Fri; D Mon–Sat. ▮ ✉ AE.

For key to symbols see back flap

Price categories include a three-course meal for one, half a bottle of house wine, tax, and a 15–20% tip.
$ under $25
$$ $25–$35
$$$ $35–$50
$$$$ $50–$70
$$$$$ over $70.

LATE OPENING
Last orders at or after 11:30pm excluding Sunday.
BAR DINING
Snacks, light meals or appetizers, served at the bar or at tables in the bar area.
FIXED-PRICE MENU
A fixed price for a set meal that is usually less expensive that normal menu prices.
SUNDAY OPENING
Brunch and/or dinner served on Sunday.
TABLES OUTSIDE
Garden or courtyard with outside tables.

	LATE OPENING	BAR DINING	FIXED-PRICE MENU	SUNDAY OPENING	TABLES OUTSIDE
ERMINIA $$$$ 250 East 83rd St. **Map** 17 B4. (212) 879-4284. Romance is in the air in this tiny, candlelit Italian with brick walls, beamed ceilings, and a fireplace. The well-prepared, authentic Italian classics and caring service add to the special feeling, and the homemade napoleon dessert is a great way to end the meal. ◯ D Mon–Sat. *AE*.					
FELIDIA $$$$ 243 East 58th St. **Map** 13 B3. (212) 758-1479. W www.lidiasitaly.com Exposed brick, wood paneling, and extravagant flowers in an East Side townhouse make a cozy setting for fine Northern Italian fare overseen by a popular TV chef, Lidia Bastianich. The wide-ranging seasonal menu includes creative pastas and risottos, along with seafood and meat dishes. The wine list offers more than 1,000 labels. ◯ L Mon–Fri; D Mon–Sat. *AE, MC, V.*			●		
FIORELLO'S CAFÉ $$$ 1900 Broadway. **Map** 12 D2. (212) 595-5330. The bountiful antipasto bar alone is enough reason to visit: you can have a seat on a stool and sample enough for a whole meal before heading for Lincoln Center, just across the street. But the thin crust pizzas are equally tempting, and there is a full Italian menu as well. ◯ L, D daily. *AE, MC, V.*	●	■		■	●
GENNARO $$ 665 Amsterdam Ave. **Map** 15 C2. (212) 665-5348. This tiny café serves the best Italian food on the Upper West Side, prepared to order by the owner/chef and at fair prices, which explains the constant lines (no reservations, but a current expansion should help). The antipasto is a meal in itself. ◯ D daily. ♿					
IL BAGATTO $$ 192 East 2nd St. **Map** 5 B2. (212) 228-0977. Even uptowners head for this East Village hangout between Avenues A & B, where the Italian food is good and the price is right. Expect a wait to get in and rushed service, but fans say it's worth it, and you can meet some neighborhood types while you wait. ◯ D Tue–Sun. *AE*.				■	
IL MULINO $$$$$ 86 West 3rd St. **Map** 4 D2. (212) 673-3783. Call weeks ahead if you hope for a reservation at the Greenwich Village restaurant many call Manhattan's best Italian. The Tuscan menu is not innovative, but the high quality is consistent, the portions large, the brick-walled, lamp-lit room is inviting, and the service warm and caring. The odds of a table are much better for lunch. ◯ L Mon–Fri; D Mon–Sat. ♿ ★ *AE, MC, V.*					
IL PALAZZO $$ 151 Mulberry St. **Map** 4 F4. (212) 343-7000. W www.littleitalynyc.com/ilpalazzo One of the better choices on Mulberry Street: cozy, candlelit, and non-touristy. The menu includes all the Italian favorites, including tempting pastries. The serene garden with a fountain out back is a summer delight. ◯ L, D daily. *AE, MC, V.*				■	●
I TRULLI $$$$ 122 East 27th St. **Map** 9 A3. (212) 481-7372. W www.itrulli.com Reviewers rave about this Gramercy favorite specializing in the Southern food of Puglia, accompanied by a notable wine list. (There's even more wine at the Enoteca I Trulli next door). With a cozy fireplace in winter and a summer garden, this is a winner for all seasons. ◯ L Mon–Fri; D Mon–Sat. ★ *AE, MC, V.*					●
LE MADRI $$$$ 168 West 18th St. **Map** 8 E5. (212) 727-8022. W www.lemadri.citysearch.com Casually elegant and known for flavorful Northern Italian cooking, this Chelsea old-timer attracts a well-heeled crowd who enjoy lusty dishes such as osso buco, and an Italian wine list with more than 200 choices. ◯ L Mon–Fri; D daily; Brunch Sun. Closed for lunch weekends July, Aug. *AE, MC, V.*				■	

LUPA ⑤⑤⑤
170 Thompson St. **Map** 4 F3. 🄲 *(212) 982-5089.* W *www.luparestaurant.com*
Informal and much less expensive than his Babbo, Mario Batali's rustic,
candle-lit Roman trattoria serves elegant fare at affordable prices: appetizers
like heavenly prosciutto with figs, and pastas such as squid ink tagliarini with
spicy calamari. You may have to wait for a seat, but you won't be sorry you
came. 🄻 L, D daily. 🄳 ★ 🄴 *AE, MC, V.*

ORSO ⑤⑤⑤
322 West 46th St. **Map** 12 D5. 🄲 *(212) 489-7212.* W *www.orsorestaurant.com*
If you are lucky enough to snag a reservation, you'll enjoy some of the Theater
District's best dining, with a splendid Italian menu that ranges from thin-crusted
pizzas to formal entrees, served in a sophisticated contemporary setting. Save
room for dessert; it's too good to miss. 🄻 L, D daily. 🄳 ★ 🄴 *AE, MC, V.*

OSTERIA DEL CIRCO ⑤⑤⑤⑤
120 West 55th St. **Map** 12 E4. 🄲 *(212) 265-3636.* W *www.osteriadelcirco.com*
The sons of Le Cirque 2000 owner Sirio Maccioni have created their own
whimsical circus motif with banners, jugglers, and saucy monkeys. They serve
tasty Tuscan fare from mother Egidiana's recipes, adding up to a lively (albeit
noisy) Theater District favorite. 🄻 L, Mon–Fri; D daily. 🄳 🄴 *AE, MC, V.*

EUROPEAN

AQUAVIT ⑤⑤⑤⑤⑤
13 West 54th St. **Map** 12 F4. 🄲 *(212) 307-7311.* W *www.savvydiner.com/newyork/aquavit*
A midtown townhouse decorated with contemporary Swedish art is the setting
for New York's top Scandinavian restaurant, serving Swedish-inspired cuisine
as interpreted an inventive chef, Marcus Samuelsson, whose presentation is as
exciting as his menus. The herring plate and the arctic char are highly
recommended. 🄻 L Mon–Fri; D daily; brunch Sun. 🄿 ★ 🄴 *AE, MC, V.*

BOLO ⑤⑤⑤⑤
23 East 22nd St. **Map** 9 A4. 🄲 *(212) 228-2200.* W *www.bolorestaurant.com*
A vibrant room filled with paintings is the venue for the Mesa Grill's creative
chef Bobby Flay, whose contemporary take on Spanish cuisine draws a
packed house. Grilled meats and rice dishes such as black squid ink risotto
and a tasty paella are specialties, and roast suckling pig is the feature every
Wednesday night. 🄻 L Mon–Fri; D Mon–Sun. 🄳 🄴 *AE, MC, V.*

CAFÉ DE BRUXELLES ⑤⑤
118 Greenwich Ave. **Map** 3 B1. 🄲 *(212) 206-1830.*
Ten kinds of mussels, crispy frites, and fabulous Belgian beer can't be beat
at this comfortable Greenwich Village restaurant, established long before
the current Belgian fad began in New York. Stews and seafood are also
excellent, and the Belgian chocolate desserts make all others seem
inadequate. 🄻 L, D daily. 🄴 *AE, MC, V.*

DANUBE ⑤⑤⑤⑤⑤
30 Hudson St. **Map** 1 B1. 🄲 *(212) 791-3771.*
The chemistry is just right at David Bouley's unusual Tribeca restaurant, offering light-as-air, "nouveau Austrian" food in an intimate new spin on an old-
world setting. It's all so warm and wonderful, nobody wants to leave. Wiener
schnitzel and spaetzle never had it so good. 🄻 D Mon–Sat. 🄳 ★ 🄴 *AE, MC, V.*

MOCCA HUNGARIAN RESTAURANT ⑤
1588 Second Ave. **Map** 17 B4. 🄲 *(212) 734-6470.*
Mocca brings to mind a simple European café with flowery china on the wall,
lace curtains, and old-fashioned lighting. Chicken paprikash, beef goulash,
stuffed cabbage, dumplings, and schnitzels are among the traditional choices.
All are reasonable, and the prix-fixe dinners are a real bargain. 🄻 L, D daily.

PICHOLINE ⑤⑤⑤⑤
35 West 64th St. **Map** 12 D2. 🄲 *(212) 724-8585.*
For fine dining in the Lincoln Center area, the top choice is Terrance
Brennan's elegant Mediterranean restaurant, where the chef's blending of
subtle flavors transforms every dish. The cheese course is famous – be sure to
save room. 🄻 L Sat; D Mon–Sun. 🄿 ★ 🄴 *AE, MC, V.*

RIO MAR ⑤⑤
245 West 16th St. **Map** 8 E5. 🄲 *(212) 727-2132.*
The generous free tapas at the bar of this hip Spanish taverna in the trendy
Meatpacking District just might fill you up, but upstairs you can enjoy big
helpings of classics like paella or arroz con pollo and sangria in a shabby-chic
dining room. 🄻 L, D daily. 🄴 *AE.*

LATE OPENING	BAR DINING	FIXED-PRICE MENU	SUNDAY OPENING	TABLES OUTSIDE

Price categories include a three-course meal for one, half a bottle of house wine, tax, and a 15–20% tip.
$ under $25
$$ $25–$35
$$$ $35–$50
$$$$ $50–$70
$$$$$ over $70.

LATE OPENING
Last orders at or after 11:30pm excluding Sunday.
BAR DINING
Snacks, light meals or appetizers, served at the bar or at tables in the bar area.
FIXED-PRICE MENU
A fixed price for a set meal that is usually less expensive that normal menu prices.
SUNDAY OPENING
Brunch and/or dinner served on Sunday.
TABLES OUTSIDE
Garden or courtyard with outside tables.

SAMMY'S ROUMANIAN STEAKHOUSE $$$
157 Chrystie St. **Map** 5 A4. ((212) 673-0330.
It looks like a Jewish wedding every night, with balloons everywhere and diners dancing the *hora* in the aisles. The skirt steaks, chopped liver, and *shmaltz* (chicken fat) on the table will freak your cholesterol level, and you'll enjoy every minute. ☐ D daily. & ⊠ AE, MC, V.

(Late Opening ●)

TERRACE IN THE SKY $$$$
400 West 119th St. **Map** 20 F3. ((212) 666-9490. w www.terraceinthesky.com
Way off the beaten path, this dimly lit, elegant rooftop restaurant near Columbia University is so romantic that many weddings are held here. The view from the dining room is fine, from the terrace divine, the harpist adds to the ambience, and the Continental fare lives up to the setting. ☐ L Tue–Fri; D Tue–Sat. & ⊠ AE, MC, V.

GREEK/MIDDLE EASTERN/AFGHAN

MOLYVOS $$$
871 Seventh Ave. **Map** 12 E4. ((212) 582-7500. w www.molyvos.com
Owner John Livanos (also of the upscale Oceana) comes from the fishing village of Molyvos, and he has done his hometown proud with this handsome Theater District restaurant in warm Mediterranean hues, where traditional Greek cooking is elevated to haute cuisine. ☐ L, D daily. & ★ ⊠ AE, MC, V.

(Late Opening ●)

PASHA $$$
70 West 71st St. **Map** 12 D1. ((212) 579-8751.
All is serene in this spacious, skylit, Turkish restaurant a few blocks from Lincoln Center. Tiny appetizer lamb dumplings with mint are delicious, as is the chicken stuffed with rice, pistachios, and currants, served on spinach, and many eggplant dishes, including the lamb with eggplant and tomatoes. ☐ D daily. ⊠ AE, MC, V.

(Sunday Opening ■)

PERIYALI $$$$
35 West 20th St. **Map** 8 F5. ((212) 463-7890. w www.periyali.com
A billowing, canopied ceiling and white stucco walls set the scene for ultra-sophisticated Greek dining. The double grilled lamb chop and creative fish dishes put Greek food into gourmet territory, and the list of Greek wines is incomparable. Periyali was the first to elevate Greek cuisine to fine dining and continues to set the standard. ☐ L Mon–Fri; D Mon–Sat. ❚ ⊠ AE, MC, V.

(Bar Dining ■)

S'AGAPO $$
34-21 34th Ave near 35th St, Astoria, Queens. ((718) 626-0303.
The name means "I love you" in Greek, and it's apt for this cheerful spot with wonderful Greek food, especially grilled fish. There is music on weekends and a terrace for summer evenings. ☐ L, D daily. ⊠ MC, V.

(Late Opening ● Tables Outside ●)

TURKISH CUISINE $$
631 Ninth Avenue. **Map** 12 D5. ((212) 397-9650.
This restaurant serves amazing food at a reasonable price, but the interior is low-key. Shish kebabs and a large colorful platter of appetizers, including hummus, tabbouleh, baba ganouj, and stuffed grape leaves, are just some of the highlights on the menu. ☐ L, D daily. & ⊠ AE, MC, V.

(Late Opening ● Sunday Opening ● Tables Outside ■ ●)

SEAFOOD

AQUAGRILL $$$$
210 Spring St. **Map** 4 D4. ((212) 274-0505.
Yellow walls, seashell lighting fixtures, and cushy banquettes are the setting for a trendy SoHo seafood haven with a spacious raw bar featuring oysters flown in daily. The fish is always the freshest, warm octopus salad is a classic, and anything on the menu can be ordered grilled, poached, or roasted. ☐ L Tue–Fri; D Tue–Sun; brunch Sat–Sun. ❚ ★ ⊠ AE, MC, V.

(Bar Dining ■ Sunday Opening ■)

BLUE WATER GRILL
31 Union Square West. **Map** 9 5A. **(** *(212) 675-9500.*
This perennially popular restaurant attracts a beautiful crowd to its
converted bank setting. Chef Steve Hanson serves up excellent
seafood and a great raw bar. L, D daily. *AE, MC, V.*

ELIAS CORNER
24-02 31st St at 24th Ave, Astoria, Queens. **(** *(718) 932-1510.*
The largest Greek community outside the motherland is a 15-minute subway
ride from Manhattan in Astoria, where Elias Corner serves wonderful fish
simply grilled with oil and oregano seasoning. On a summer evening in the
garden, with the hum of Greek conversation all around you, it might as well
be Athens. D daily.

ESCA
402 West 43rd St. **Map** 7 C1. **(** *(212) 564-7272.*
Chef Mario Batali, best known for Italian restaurants such as Babbo and
Lupa in the Village, has staged a Theater District smash hit by serving the
freshest of seafood, deliciously prepared with a Southern Italian accent. The
patio dining is a plus in warm weather. The only problem is getting a
reservation. L, D Mon–Sat. *AE, MC, V.*

LE BERNARDIN
155 West 51st St. **Map** 12 E4. **(** *(212) 489-1515.*
W *www.le-bernardin.com*
Seafood doesn't come any better than at this quietly luxurious French
restaurant lauded for revolutionizing the way fish is served in New York and
considered one of America's best restaurants. Chef Eric Lipert seems to have
no critics. Perfection has its price, but the meal will be memorable.
L Mon–Fri; D Mon–Sun. ★ *AE, MC, V.*

OCEANA
55 East 54th St. **Map** 13 A4. **(** *(212) 759-5941.*
W *www.oceanarestaurant.com*
Fitted with the look and intimacy of a posh private yacht, Oceana is a first-
class passage all the way, food to decor, reflected in a high tab, even for the
prix-fixe lunch. Upstairs is more masculine, with paneling, posters, and a
seafood bar serving raw oysters as well as main courses. L Mon–Fri;
D Mon–Sat. *AE, MC, V.*

THE OYSTER BAR AND RESTAURANT
Grand Central Station, lower level, 42nd St and Lexington Ave. **Map** 9 A1.
(*(212) 490-6650.* W *www.oysterbarny.com*
A New York classic beneath a vaulted ceiling of Guastavino tiles, this big,
bustling, 90-year-old restaurant serves only the finest seafood, from the formal
menu with as many as 30 choices, to the long raw bar with two dozen kinds
of oysters. L Mon–Fri; D Mon–Sat. ★ *AE, MC, V.*

PEARL OYSTER BAR
18 Cornelia St. **Map** 4 D2. **(** *(212) 691-8211.*
New England-style informality is the mood, and Maine lobster rolls rival
oysters as the favorite dish at this Greenwich Village seafood haven whose
only fault may be that it is too popular. If you don't want to stand in line,
come for lunch. *MC, V.*

PIONEER RESTAURANT AND BAR
1303 Third Avenue. **Map** 17 B5. **(** *(212) 717-6600.*
Large portions of seafood such as warm lobster salad, crab cakes,
and clam chowder are the main draw at this popular restaurant. The
best seats are at the back where you get a view of their pretty garden,
which almost makes you forget that you are eating in the city.
Daily, L, D. *AE, MC, V.*

LATIN AMERICAN / CARIBBEAN

ASIA DE CUBA
Morgans Hotel, 237 Madison Ave. **Map** 9 A2. **(** *(212) 726-7755.*
Sit on the balcony to enjoy people-watching, or join the downstairs
communal table for 36. Either way, you'll enjoy Philippe Starck's
ultra-hip interior, and the buzz that hasn't let up since the restaurant
opened. As the name suggests, the unusual menu is a blend of Asian
and Caribbean flavors. L Mon–Fri; D daily. *AE, MC, V.*

<table>
<tr><td colspan="2">

Price categories include a three-course meal for one, half a bottle of house wine, tax, and a 15–20% tip.
$ under $25
$$ $25–$35
$$$ $35–$50
$$$$ $50–$70
$$$$$ over $70.

</td><td>

LATE OPENING
Last orders at or after 11:30pm excluding Sunday.
BAR DINING
Snacks, light meals or appetizers, served at the bar or at tables in the bar area.
FIXED-PRICE MENU
A fixed price for a set meal that is usually less expensive that normal menu prices.
SUNDAY OPENING
Brunch and/or dinner served on Sunday.
TABLES OUTSIDE
Garden or courtyard with outside tables.

</td></tr>
</table>

	LATE OPENING	BAR DINING	FIXED-PRICE MENU	SUNDAY OPENING	TABLES OUTSIDE

CABANA W www.cabana.citysearch.com. $$
1022 Third Ave. **Map** 13 B2. ☎ (212) 980-5678. **Also at**
Pier 17, South Street Seaport. **Map** 2 E2. ☎ (212) 406-1155.
Latin flavor and background music enliven this favorite with two locations, serving a Cuban/Caribbean menu that features sizzling platters and dishes such as coconut shrimp, empanadas, arroz con pollo, and Jamaican jerk chicken. Order a pina colada or margarita and pretend you're in the islands.
◻ L, D daily. ♿ 🍽 *AE, MC, V.*

(Row values: LATE OPENING ●, SUNDAY OPENING ▪)

CALLE OCHO $$$
446 Columbus Ave. **Map** 16 D4. ☎ (212) 873-5025
Every night feels like a party at this loud and lively spot named for the Cuban area of Miami, always filled with beautiful people and pulsing with Latin rhythm. The chef is Cuban, but his sophisticated modern dishes are inspired by Latin cuisine from Peru to Puerto Rico.
◻ D daily; brunch Sun. ♿ 🍽 *AE, DC, MC, V.*

(Row values: LATE OPENING ●, SUNDAY OPENING ▪)

CHURRASCCARIA PLATAFORMA W www.churrasccariaplataforma.com $$$
318 West 49th St, Belvedere Hotel. **Map** 12 D5. ☎ (212) 245-0505.
A Brazilian carnival for carnivores, with carvers offering all-you-can-eat servings of prime rib, suckling pig, lamb, chicken – 20 choices in all – plus a 40-foot salad bar with anything from carpaccio to sushi, along with exotic greens, all for a reasonable prix-fixe tab. ◻ L, D daily. ♿ ★ 🍽 *AE, MC, V.*

(Row values: LATE OPENING ●, FIXED-PRICE MENU ●, SUNDAY OPENING ▪)

DOS CAMINOS SOHO $$$
475 West Broadway. **Map** 4 E3. ☎ (212) 277-4300.
The Mexican menu may be upscale, but the prices are reasonable. Be sure to try the guacamole mashed-to-order. There are 150 tequilas to choose from, but the signature cocktail is a prickly pear margarita.
◻ L, D daily. ♿ 🍽 *AE, MC, V.*

(Row values: FIXED-PRICE MENU ●, SUNDAY OPENING ▪)

MAYA $$$
1191 First Ave. ☎ (212) 585-1818. **Map** 13 C2. W www.maya.citysearch.com
A major reason that Mexican cuisine is being treated with new respect, Maya chef Richard Sandoval serves up sophisticated and delicate main courses and wonderful side dishes in a lovely peach-hued setting. The only drawback is the sound level; dine early to avoid the din. ◻ D daily. ♿ 🍽 *AE, MC, V.*

(Row values: SUNDAY OPENING ▪)

PATRIA $$$$$
250 Park Ave South. **Map** 9 A5. ☎ (212) 777-6211. W www.patrianyc.com
Latin American gone gourmet, creative dishes beautifully presented in a festive setting of mosaic murals and terrazzo floors, draws crowds despite the steep prix-fixe tab. Come for the $20 lunch to sample the excellent fare at an affordable price. ◻ L Mon–Fri; D Mon–Sun. 🍴 ★ 🍽 *AE, MC, V.*

(Row values: LATE OPENING ●, BAR DINING ▪, FIXED-PRICE MENU ●, SUNDAY OPENING ▪)

ROCKING HORSE CAFÉ $$
182 Eighth Ave. **Map** 8 D5. ☎ (212) 463-9511. W www.rockinghorse.citysearch.com
The place rocks all right, always packed with diners even after a recent expansion. They come for the great margaritas and excellent Mexican food, with new takes on the traditional, all at reasonable prices.
◻ L, D daily. 🍽 *AE, MC, V.*

(Row values: LATE OPENING ●)

ROSA MEXICANO $$$
1063 First Ave. **Map** 13 C4. ☎ (212) 753-7407. **Also at**
61 Columbus Ave. **Map** 12 D2. ☎ (212) 977-7700. W www.rosamexicano.com
New York's first gourmet Mexican restaurant, now with a festive West Side sibling, has colorful decor and food that would do credit to a French chef. But while the food is wonderful, what many people remember most here are the guacamole made at the table and the power-packed margaritas.
◻ D daily. ♿ ★ 🍽 *AE, DC, V*

(Row values: SUNDAY OPENING ▪)

ASIAN

CANTON $$$
45 Division St. **Map** 5 A5. ⓒ (212) 226-4441.
Those who prefer the milder tastes of Cantonese food will find it at its best here. Refined atmosphere and service lure many local diners as well as visitors, even though the prices are a bit high for Chinatown. Let the waiter guide your choices and you'll have an excellent meal. ◐ L, D Wed–Sun. ★

GOLDEN UNICORN $
18 East Broadway. **Map** 4 E5. ⓒ (212) 941-0911.
Dim sum is the star here, but all the dishes are well prepared in this third-floor restaurant in typical Hong Kong style, which means big, flashy, crowded, and noisy. The larger the group the better, so you can taste more of the specialties. ◐ L, D daily. ♿ ✔ AE, MC, V.

GRAND SICHUAN $
125 Canal St. **Map** 4 E5. ⓒ (212) 625-9212.
For those who favor the spicy seasonings of China's Szechwan province, this is a Chinatown find, a no-frills storefront with little ambience but authentic specialties of the region at reasonable prices. The good reputation has spawned two uptown siblings at 229 Ninth Avenue and 745 Ninth Avenue. ◐ L, D daily. ★ ✔ AE, MC, V.

INAGIKU $$$$
Waldorf-Astoria Hotel, 111 East 49th St. **Map** 13 A5. ⓒ (212) 355-0440.
Ⓦ www.inagiku.com
Specialties at this beautifully formal Japanese restaurant are the tempura and the traditional Kaiseki, a full-course dinner with dozen or so dishes served in a designated order. ◐ L Mon–Fri; D daily. ♿ ✔ AE, MC, V.

JAPONICA $$$
100 University Place. **Map** 4 E1. ⓒ (212) 243-7752.
The excellent sushi makes this a draw for professionals and sushi lovers – but NYU students are also regulars. The menu features many types of tuna. The service is friendly. ♿ ◐ L, D daily. ✔ AE.

JOE'S SHANGHAI $$
9 Pell St. **Map** 4 F5. ⓒ (212) 233-8888;
24 West 56th St. **Map** 11 C3. ⓒ (212) 333-3868.
Both the Chinatown and Midtown locations are branches of a Flushing restaurant famous for its soup dumplings (look for "steamed buns" on the menu) with delicious broth that spurts out when you take a bite. The rest of the moderately priced Shanghai menu is admirable as well. ◐ L, D daily. ★

KIN KHAO $$
171 Spring St. **Map** 4 E4. ⓒ (212) 966-3939.
The name means "eat rice" in Thai but that's only the beginning of a vast menu offering regional Thai and Bangkok cuisine. Be sure to make reservations; the Soho location is very popular especially on weekends. Save room for the sticky-rice and papaya dessert. ◐ D daily. ✔ AE, MC, V.

SHUN LEE PALACE $$$
155 East 55th St. **Map** 13 A4. ⓒ (212) 371-8844. Ⓦ www.shunleepalace.com
For decades this handsome dining room has been considered New York's premiere Chinese restaurant. Owner Michael Tong sets the elegant mood, and the Cantonese/Szechuan blend menu never disappoints. Casseroles are among the specialties, along with Beijing duck and dishes such as crispy prawn with passion fruit. Choices include a spa menu. ◐ L, D daily. ♿ ★ ✔ AE, MC, V.

INDIAN

DAWAT $$$
210 East 58th St. **Map** 13 B3. ⓒ (212) 355-7555. Ⓦ www.restaurant.com/dawat
One of the more attractive and upscale Indian dining places in the city, Dawat features recipes inspired by Madhur Jaffrey, a noted Indian cookbook author. It is known for generous portions and signature dishes such as salmon rubbed in coriander chutney and steamed in a banana leaf. ◐ L Mon–Sat; D Mon–Sun. ♿ ✔ AE, MC, V.

For key to symbols see back flap

Light Meals and Snacks

YOU CAN GET A SNACK almost anywhere and anytime in Manhattan. New Yorkers seem to eat endlessly – on street corners, in bars, luncheonettes, delis, before and after work, and long into the night. Casual eating in New York might include soft pretzels or char-roasted chestnuts from a corner stand; a huge sandwich from a deli; a Greek *gyro* sandwich (roasted lamb in pita bread) from street vendors; a pretheater snack at a café or coffee bar; or a post-party binge at an all-night diner or bistro. While street fare is generally cheap, the quality and culinary skills vary greatly.

DELIS

DELICATESSENS are a New York institution, a great source for a hefty lunchtime sandwich. Try the wonderful corned beef and pastrami sandwiches at the famous **Carnegie Delicatessen**, considered by many to be New York's best deli.

Some delis, such as **Katz's Deli**, cater to those who enjoy traditional kosher food. Most deli business is, however, takeout and as such delis are bustling places serving huge sandwiches at relatively cheap prices. Counter staff are typically surly and impatient, and rudeness has almost become a trademark of the **Stage Deli**, which is now more of a tourist stop than the showbiz favorite it used to be.

For New York ethnic Jewish flavor, try the **Second Avenue Delicatessen**, well-known for its homemade soups, pickles, corned beef sandwiches, chopped liver, and other kosher goodies. **Zabar's** is a takeout heaven for yuppies who put up with the crowds for superb smoked fish, pickles, and salads. Aficionados say the best pastrami sandwiches and other favorites are to be found at **Pastrami King** in Queens.

CAFÉS, BISTROS AND BRASSERIES

CAFÉS, BISTROS, and the larger brasseries have become "in" places in New York in recent years. Try **Balthazar** on Spring St. for "brilliantly faux" everything except the menu, which is stellar. The **Café Centro**, above Grand Central, is particularly busy and noisy during lunchtime, and is a favorite with business types. The Provençal/Mediterranean fare includes fish soups and some succulent desserts. **The Brasserie** on W 33rd, a longtime landmark, has had an elegant remodeling. **Bistro du Nord** on Madison Avenue has a variety of good French/American fare with an inventive flair. Downtown, **The Odeon** is a TriBeCa favorite for its brasserie menu and late hours. **Raoul's** in SoHo is a French bistro with a relaxed ambience that keeps artists and other habitués coming back for reliable, informal food. **Elephant and Castle**, a minimally decorated café, is a Greenwich Village standby for soup-salad-omelette lunches and other light snacks. Its real forte is breakfast and brunch, served in ample portions at modest prices. The bar scene is lively too. Tiny **Chez Jacqueline** is also a favored Village spot. Its French bistro fare and proximity to several off-Broadway theaters make it popular with the young, hip, and international crowd for a moderately priced dinner or late supper.

In the Theater District, try the Cuban **Victor's Café 52**. Large, lively, and Latin, it is known for authentic Cuban food served in giant portions at medium prices. **Chez Josephine** is an exuberant bistro-cabaret with live jazz piano playing. The scene is the main attraction here, and the French food is excellent. **La Boite en Bois**, small but delightfully French, serves delicious French bistro food and is conveniently close to Lincoln Center. In the same vicinity is **Vince and Eddie's**, a tiny gem known for reliable, often superb American food.

Sarabeth's, on the Upper West Side, defies categorizing, but might best be dubbed a café. The best time to visit is for breakfast or weekend brunch, when families wolf down waffles, French toast, pancakes, and omelettes. There are two other branches, one of which is located in the Whitney Museum of Art.

The Gramercy Park area's **Les Halles** is about as all-out French bistro as New York gets. At its late-night peak, the decibel level is high, but regulars think the *frites* and beef dishes are worth the noise and crowds.

PIZZERIAS

PIZZA IS AVAILABLE all over New York, from street stands and fast-food places that sell it by the slice for a few dollars, to a traditional Neapolitan pizzeria.

Some pizzerias offer something more. **Arturo's Pizzeria** uses a coal oven for crisp, thin-crusted bases with the added incongruence of live jazz. **Mezzogiorno** has a Tuscan menu and wonderful pizzas with unusual toppings. The crowded **Mezzaluna** also specializes in brick-oven, thin-crusted pizza, as does **John's Pizzeria**, whose many fans (including Woody Allen) consider it to be Manhattan's best.

Brooklyn boasts a top pizzeria in Coney Island's **Totonno Pizzeria**, which is well worth the trip for real pizza aficionados, though it also has a Manhattan branch. Generally, pizza parlors are good places to go for a cheap, simple meal, especially with children. Most places won't take reservations, so popular ones may have long lines.

HAMBURGER PLACES

YOUR NOSE may lead you to some of the cheaper burger and hot dog stands on the street. However, there are many places in New York where you can buy a better quality burger, even though prices for a top grade all-beef burger can go up to $10.

Hamburger Harry's offers reasonably priced, large, juicy, and mesquite-grilled burgers, with a choice of over a dozen toppings and a huge fresh salad. **Hard Rock Café** is a well-known chain which serves hearty portions in a lively atmosphere.

Bright and basic, the five outlets of **Jackson Hole** offer fat, juicy, meaty burgers in 28 varieties popular with kids. Adults might prefer less glare and smarter décor, but they will like the low prices. It's also a good place to try the quintessential New York drink, the egg cream (see p286).

The **Beer Bar** at Café Centro is where professional types like to hang out. Besides an unusual beer menu, the burgers are delicious.

New York's best burgers may well be found at the **Corner Bistro** in Greenwich Village. Not only are the burgers tasty and reasonably priced, but the beer selection is good, too, and the 4am closing makes this a great late-night stop.

DINERS AND LUNCHEONETTES

DINERS and luncheonettes, also called sandwich or coffee shops, can be found all over town. Food is usually indifferent but served in huge, cheap platefuls. Despite the name luncheonette, such places are usually open from breakfast until late evening, and you can stop in at almost any hour for coffee and something basic and filling to eat.

A recent trend with diners has seen 1990s replicas of the old 1930s cheap-eats places. One such retro-diner is the chic Empire Diner (see p136). The **Broadway Diner** in Midtown is a faithful re-creation of a 1940s diner. It offers a good American breakfast, including thick-cut fries and homemade corned beef hash with poached eggs.

Jerry's attracts a SoHo art and celebrity crowd who love the inventive sandwiches, salads, desserts and huge breakfasts. Also attracting a hip art crowd is **Florent**, a West Village diner with reliable French food served around the clock. **Big Nick's** is the best place for a pizza, hamburger, or breakfast on the Upper West Side. **The Coffee Shop** in Union Square serves Brazilian-American fare and is open all night.

On the Upper East Side, Eli Zabar's **E.A.T.** sells top quality, but pricey Jewish favorites – like mushroom-barley soup and challah bread, as well as some sinful desserts. Devotees swear by **Viand**, a spic-and-span East Side luncheonette, with cheap, ample American breakfasts, good burgers, egg creams, and the best turkey sandwiches in town. **Veselka** is not the usual New York sandwich shop – what makes it special is the Polish/Ukrainian food, all at rock-bottom prices.

TEAROOMS

ABOUT THE ONLY PLACE you can be absolutely sure of getting a cup of real, brewed tea is at a formal, prix fixe afternoon tea in a lounge at one of New York's pricier hotels, from 3pm to 5pm.

Afternoon tea in the **Plaza Hotel**'s Palm Court has cream cakes and hot buttered scones galore. For an extra stylish tea, on Chippendale furniture, visit the **Carlyle** hotel. The **Hotel Pierre** offers one of the better buys in hotel prix fixe teas. Tea at the **Waldorf–Astoria** comes with Devonshire cream, while the elegant tea at the **Stanhope** hotel is abundant enough to carry you through to a late dinner.

A variation on tea themes can be found in a new chain of teahouses called **Saint's Alp**. These delightful spots serving frothy, flavored, colorful tea drinks poured over crushed ice can be found at 51 Mott Street near Chinatown and in the new Times Square area. Teatime, Japanese style, can be enjoyed at **The Tea Box** located in the Takashimaya department store.

COFFEE AND CAKES

YOU CAN GET a decent cup of coffee for as little as 75 cents, with endless free refills, at most diners, luncheonettes, and coffee shops. There is a new trend for coffee bars that serve a variety of gourmet and specialty coffees, such as cappuccino, espresso and caffè latte. Some ice cream parlors and patisseries also serve good coffee, along with decadently luscious pastries.

Coffee houses such as **Caffè Vivaldi** offer relatively cheap coffees, teas, and desserts served on marble tables while **Joe** boasts the world's best espresso machine. **Caffè Ferrara**, going strong since 1892, has moderately priced Italian pastries, good coffee, and outdoor seating. **Caffè Dante** is a favorite with students who like to sit outside in warm weather. **DT·UT** has places downtown and uptown and is kid-friendly and comfortable.

The European-style outdoor **Fledermaus Café**, in the South Street Seaport, serves fine coffee and is a good place to watch the passing scene.

The **Hungarian Pastry Shop** has a range of Austro-Hungarian delights and views of St John the Divine. Located in the Hotel Edison, **Café Edison** offers good-priced food in an Art Nouveau setting. **Sant' Ambroeus** is a luxurious outpost of the Milanese pasticceria, with decadent desserts and espresso bar. In addition to home delivery of pies or cakes, **Dessert Delivery** have a nifty cafe for tasting the pastries and coffee. Try **Serendipity 3**, famous for its Victoriana, ice cream creations, coffee, and mid-afternoon snacks. **Barnes & Noble Café** is a happy refuge for coffee and a pastry while browsing the bookstore. **Mudspot** is the new permanent digs for a couple who used to sell potent coffee from a bright orange van. And, like them or not, you can't ignore **Starbucks**, which has dozens of locations around town.

DIRECTORY

LOWER EAST SIDE

Caffè Ferrara
195 Grand St.
Map 4 F4.

Fledermaus Café
199 Water St. **Map** 2 E2.

Katz's Deli
205 E Houston St.
Map 5 A3.

Saint's Alp
51 Mott St
Map 4 F 4.

SoHo AND TRiBeCa

Jerry's
101 Prince St. **Map** 4 D3.

Mezzogiorno
195 Spring St.
Map 4 D4.

Odeon
145 W Broadway.
Map 1 B1.

Raoul's
180 Prince St. **Map** 4 D3.

GREENWICH VILLAGE

Arturo's Pizzeria
106 W Houston St.
Map 4 E3.

Balthazar
80 Spring St. **Map** 4 E4.

Caffè Dante
79 MacDougal St.
Map 4 D3.

Caffè Vivaldi
32 Jones St. **Map** 3 C2.

Chez Jacqueline
73 MacDougal St.
Map 4 D2.

Corner Bistro
331 W 4th St.
Map 3 C1.

Elephant and Castle
68 Greenwich Ave.
Map 3 C1.

Florent
69 Gansevoort St
Map 3 B1.

Joe
141 Waverly Place.
Map 3 C1.

EAST VILLAGE

DT-UT
41 Avenue B.
Map 5 B2.

Mudspot
307 E 9th St.
Map 4 F1.

Second Avenue Delicatessen
156 2nd Ave.
Map 4 F1.

Veselka
144 2nd Ave.
Map 4 F1.

GRAMERCY AND THE FLATIRON

The Coffee Shop
29 Union Sq.
Map 9 A5.

Les Halles
411 Park Ave.
Map 9 A3.

THEATER DISTRICT

Broadway Diner
1726 Broadway.
Map 12 E4.

Café Edison
Edison Hotel, 228 W 47th
St. **Map** 12 D5.

Carnegie Delicatessen
854 7th Ave.
Map 12 E4.

Chez Josephine
414 W 42nd St.
Map 7 B1.

Hamburger Harry's
145 W 45th St.
Map 12 E4.

Hard Rock Café
221 W 57th St.
Map 12 E3.

Stage Deli
834 7th Ave.
Map 12 E4.

Victor's Café 52
236 W 52nd St.
Map 11 B4.

EAST SIDE MIDTOWN

Beer Bar at Café Centro
MetLife Building,
200 Park Ave. **Map** 9 A2.

UPPER MIDTOWN

Barnes & Noble Café
Citicorp Building,
160 E. 54th St. **Map** 13 A4.

Brasserie
100 E 53rd St. **Map** 13 A4.

Plaza Hotel
Palm Court, 768 5th Ave.
Map 12 F3.

The Tea Box
Takashimaya, 693 5th Ave.
Map 12 F2.

Waldorf–Astoria
301 Park Ave.
Map 13 A5.

UPPER EAST SIDE

Bistro du Nord
1312 Madison Ave.
Map 17 A2.

Carlyle
35 E 76th St.
Map 17 A5.

Dessert Delivery
350 E. 55th St.
C *(212) 838-5411*
Map 13 B4.

DT-UT
1626 2nd Ave.
Map 17 B4.

E.A.T.
1064 Madison Ave.
Map 17 A4.

Hotel Pierre
2 E 61st St.
Map 12 F3.

Jackson Hole
232 E 64th St.
Map 13 B2.

John's Pizzeria
408 E 64th St.
Map 13 C2.
One of several branches.

Mezzaluna
1295 3rd Ave.
Map 17 B5.

Payard Patisserie
1032 Lexington Ave.
Map 13 A1.

Sant' Ambroeus
1000 Madison Ave.
Map 17 A5.

Serendipity 3
225 E 60th St.
Map 13 B3.

Stanhope
995 5th Ave.
Map 17 A4.

Viand
1011 Madison Ave.
Map 17 A5.

UPPER WEST SIDE

Big Nick's
2175 Broadway at 77th.
Map 15 C5.

La Boite en Bois
75 W 68th St.
Map 11 C1.

Sarabeth's
423 Amsterdam Ave.
Map 15 C4.

Whitney Museum
945 Madison Ave.
Map 17 A5.

Vince and Eddie's
70 W 68th St.
Map 11 C1.

Zabar's
2245 Broadway.
Map 15 C2.

MORNINGSIDE HEIGHTS AND HARLEM

The Hungarian Pastry Shop
Amsterdam & 109th St.
Map 20 E4.

BROOKLYN

Totonno Pizzeria
1524 Neptune Ave.
Map 7 C5.

QUEENS

Pastrami King
124 Queens Blvd,
Kew Gardens.

New York Bars

NEW YORK BARS play a huge role in the life and culture of the city. Many New Yorkers spend the evening in a succession of bars, because each usually offers something more than just alcohol. There may be additional inducements, like excellent food, live music, dancing, or a particularly large selection of beers. Brew pubs, which serve meals and brew beer on the premises, are a recent phenomenon. Bars suiting every taste and budget are to be found all over the city.

RULES AND CONVENTIONS

BARS GENERALLY stay open from around 11am to midnight. Some stay open to 2 or 4am, when they must close by law. Many bars have a "happy hour" between 5pm and 7pm, when they offer twofers (two drinks for the price of one) and a variety of free snacks. Bartenders also have the right to refuse to serve anyone they consider having had too much to drink. Smoking is banned from New York bars and is only allowed outside or in specially ventilated rooms.

The legal minimum drinking age is 21; if the bartender suspects you are younger, you'll be "carded," or asked to show some identification to prove your age. Children are not usually taken into bars.

It is common to "run a tab" and pay your bill just before you leave. Tipping the bartender is expected – 10% of the bill or about 50 cents for a single drink. Shots are not premeasured, so if you want a bigger drink, it can help to "belly up" to the bar and tip the bartender accordingly for his or her generosity. If you sit at a table, you'll be served there and be charged more.

A round of drinks can be expensive. A good way to save money is by buying a quart (95 cl) or a half gallon (190 cl) pitcher of beer.

Avoid the "free drinks for ladies" bars, which are often just pick-up joints. Some of New York's pubs did not admit women until forced by law to do so, a few years ago. Even today, many women feel uncomfortable drinking alone in certain places.

WHAT TO DRINK

YOU CAN GET almost any alcoholic drink you want in New York bars; the most popular drink is ice-cold beer. Mainstream bars serve standard beers from big producers like Budweiser, Coors, and Miller, and high-profile imports such as Bass ale, Becks and Heineken, and even draft Guinness. Old pubs and certain chic new bars, have a much wider variety of beers, imported and small domestics. These include locally made products by some of New York's microbreweries, and the popular Brooklyn Lager. Microbrewery products are flavorful beers often based on traditional European styles.

Other popular drinks include cocktails; rum and coke; dry martinis; Scotch or bourbon, either "straight up" (without ice) or on the rocks (with ice); vodka-and-tonic and gin-and-tonic. The "Cosmopolitan" is very New York – vodka and grapefruit in a Martini. A range of Martinis made with vodka are also popular.

Wine is widely available at bars, although the "wine bar" concept has been replaced by the "olive bar" and champagne bars, such as **Flute**.

FOOD

ALL BARS SERVE some sort of food throughout the day. It is usually convenience food like burgers, fries, salads, sandwiches and small snacks like delicious spicy chicken wings. Happy hour is an excellent time to fill up on free snacks and hot hors d'oeuvres in New York bars. Most bar kitchens stop serving food just before midnight.

FASHIONABLE BARS

YOU MAY have to line up to watch the bored and beautiful at **BB's**, formerly the Bowery Bar and once a gas station. Though it's for members only, you should know about **Bungalow 8**. Also hot are **Lot 61** and **Suite 16**. Much more fun is the funky late night scene at **Bar Six**, a West Village hangout for the cool and quirky, with microbrewery beers and food that has a Moroccan accent. Also downtown is **SoHo Kitchen and Bar**, a handsome loftlike space with tiered dining areas, a long brick bar, good pizzas, a lengthy wine list containing some 400 wines, and a good range of beers. The **Odeon** on Broadway is another good place to catch the lively SoHo–TriBeCa scene.

On the Upper East Side, the bar at **Swifty's** is a place to observe what passes these days for high society without paying steep prices for the restaurant's ordinary food.

There is a new vogue for cigar bars that encourage smokers. **The Cigar Room at Trumpets** has a 36 premium cigar menu and a large single malt Scotch list. Its attached *intime* dining room is also cigar-friendly. At **Bar and Books** you can inhale, sip, and nibble snacks before a fireplace in a club-like library setting, with live jazz on weekends. In the same venue is the Beekman Bar and Book.

BARS WITH VIEWS

TAKE THE ELEVATOR to the 26th floor of the Art Deco **Beekman Tower** for unsurpassed views of the city plus piano music to set the mood. Also spectacular is the **Pentop Bar and Terrace** at the Peninsula Hotel, the **Stone Rose Lounge** and **Rise** at the Ritz-Carlton in Battery Park. In warm weather **BP Café** is the latest Midtown scene. The **Tavern on the Green** has magical views of Central Park. Inside, the glitz may overwhelm you, but the garden is a delight.

HISTORIC AND LITERARY BARS

IF YOU SAMPLE only one New York bar, it should probably be **McSorley's Old Ale House**, an Irish saloon, often dubbed "McSurly's" because of the staff. It's been on the same site since 1854, making it one of New York's oldest bars. It offers a good choice of beers and a tasty lunch. Try the chili.

The Ear Inn dates from 1812 when the first tavern opened on this SoHo site. Now the haunt of poets and writers, its dark, cramped interior and long wooden bar ooze authenticity.

Greenwich Village has some of the city's oldest bars, such as **Chumley's**, which retains its character as a Prohibition-era speakeasy. It's particularly snug in winter, when an open fire burns in the hearth.

Dylan Thomas's old favorite, the **White Horse Tavern**, is an unpretentious 1880s landmark still going strong and crowded with literary and collegiate types. There's an outdoor café used in warm weather.

Peculier Pub is a beer-lover's paradise, with over 360 varieties of beer from all over the world. You must, however, be willing to tolerate the sometimes snappish and uninformed staff.

A good, though rather touristy, place for a drink in the financial district is the atmospheric **Fraunces Tavern**, first built in 1719 (see p76). Another oldie, dating to 1864, is **Pete's Tavern**, a prime hangout in the Gramercy Park area that is busy until 2am. It is known for its Victoriana, its house brew called Pete's Ale, and the many beers on tap. In the same area, the **Old Town Bar** has been a typically Irish pub since 1892 and is now favored largely by advertising types.

No longer the celebrity scene it once was, **Sardi's** is still a hangout for *New York Times* reporters and is worth a stop to inspect the "who's who" celebrity caricatures lining the walls and for the generous drinks served in the second floor bar.

After work, crowds head to **P. J. Clarke's**, a long time favorite New York saloon dating back to the 1890s, with Irish bartenders and an incredibly bustling *après*-office scene. **Elaine's**, also on the East Side, remains a haunt of New York and visiting literary types. Sit close to Elaine's table where the meeting-and-greeting action takes place. The food is nothing much.

Near Carnegie Hall is the unobtrusive **P. J. Carney's**, which has been a watering hole for musicians and artists since 1927. It serves Irish ales and a good shepherd's pie.

YOUNG HANGOUTS

BREW PUBS, where the house beer is brewed on the premises, are currently the rage with the 20s-to-30s crowd, as are bars with sizable beer lists that feature a variety of microbrewery and imported beers. **The Chelsea Brewing Company** is a large, fun-filled brewpub situated in the Chelsea Piers sports complex, overlooking the Hudson River. In the nearby Gramercy neighborhood you will find the **Heartland Brewery**, which is the busiest, and, some think, best of the new brew pubs, with five beers, including the outstanding India Pale Ale, and many seasonals, such as cranberry and pumpkin ales.

The **Westside Brewing Company** uptown is a favorite youth and neighborhood hangout, popular for its house ales and fruit beers. Although a little pricy, serious beer drinkers will enjoy the 170 draft and bottled Belgian beers on offer at **Burp Castle**. For homesick Brits, the **Manchester** is a name to reckon with. In a cozy publike setting, you'll find Watneys or Newcastle Brown Ale on tap, just two of 18 draft beers and 40 bottled ones not widely available in New York.

In the East Village is bustling **d.b.a.**. Depending on whom you ask, the initials might stand for "don't bother to ask" or "draft beer available". There are 14 draft beers on tap, along with scores of microbrews and 50 single malt whiskeys to choose from.

A popular beer stop uptown for the college-age crowd is the loud and noisy **Brother Jimmy's BBQ**, where you can snack on old-fashioned southern barbequed ribs.

Park Slope Brewery Company, in two Brooklyn locations, is another brew pub favored by the young for its 12 home brews and seasonal beers, as well as its decent pub grub and lively ambience.

SINGLES BARS

THE CHANCE TO MEET new people is offered in singles bars, which are still extremely popular. These are located all over the city, with a large concentration in midtown on the East Side. Prices in such places can be inflated, with beer costing $3 and up.

The Art Deco styled **Beer Bar**, with its interesting beer list and beer-tasting menus, is currently new and "with it." There is a frenetic singles scene at **Live Bait**, which is good for model-gazing and for its passable southern food.

GAY AND LESBIAN BARS

GAY BARS CAN be be found in Greenwich Village, with many also in SoHo, the East Village, Chelsea, and Murray Hill. Lesbian bars are mostly in Greenwich Village and the East Village. For current listings, check the *Native* newspaper and the *Village Voice* or call the Gay and Lesbian Switchboard (see p343).

HOTEL BARS

CENTRALLY LOCATED in midtown, the Algonquin Hotel (see p143) was a famous literary haunt in the 1920s and early 1930s. Its Lobby Bar and Blue Bar are both good places for a quiet pre-dinner or pretheater drink.

The round bar in the handsome lobby lounge of the trendy **Royalton Hotel** is a perfect spot for a drink while watching the theatrical crowds drifting in and out. This is a favorite meeting place for Conde-Nast staffers. Also in the Theater District, the **Whiskey Bar** in the Paramount Hotel has floor-to-ceiling windows and is usually frequented by fashion and theater types. In Lower Midtown is the **Sun Garden**, a glassed-in, tiered space, particularly pleasant on bright afternoons when the sun streams through the glass.

The **Bull and Bear** in the Waldorf–Astoria, dating back to the Prohibition era, exudes comfort and a sense of history. There are many exotic drinks and Bull and Bear ale on tap.

Uptown, the **Oak Room** at the Plaza Hotel is a posh place to impress people, drink, and converse in earnest tones –

but at a high price. The **King Cole Room** at the St. Regis Hotel is named after the mural behind the bar, by Maxfield Parrish, which adds color to a stylish room.

For nostalgic British visitors and anglophile New Yorkers, **Journeys** in the Essex House Hotel has an English club ambience, with hunting prints and mahogany paneling.

Drinks are a bargain at **Randolfs** in the Warwick Hotel where free snacks are served during happy hour.

The **Maritime Lobby Bar** in the Maritime Hotel features a kitschy seafaring theme and draws a young and trendy crowd thanks to a roaring fire in winter and a large outdoor terrace in summer. The glass-floored **Lobby Bar** at Ian Shrager's trendy Hudson Hotel is a regular hotspot, or join the *Sex in the City* crowd in Rande Gerber's Whiskey Blue bar in one of the boutique W Hotels.

DIRECTORY

LOWER MANHATTAN

BB's
40 E 4th St. **Map** 4 F2.

Fraunces Tavern
54 Pearl St. **Map** 1 C4.

Rise
2 West St. **Map** 1 B4.

Stone Rose Lounge
10 Columbus Circle, 45th Floor. **Map** 12 D3.

SOHO AND TRIBECA

The Ear Inn
326 Spring St. **Map** 3 C4.

The Odeon
145 W Broadway.
Map 4 E4.

SoHo Kitchen and Bar
103 Greene St. **Map** 4 E3.

GREENWICH VILLAGE

Bar Six
502 6th Ave. **Map** 4 D1.

Chumley's
86 Bedford St. **Map** 3 C2.

Peculier Pub
145 Bleecker St. **Map** 4 D3.

White Horse Tavern
567 Hudson St. **Map** 3 C1.

EAST VILLAGE

Burp Castle
41 E 7th St. **Map** 4 F2.

d.b.a.
41 1st Ave. **Map** 5 A1.

McSorley's Old Ale House
15 E 7th St. **Map** 4 F2.

GRAMERCY

Flute
40 E 20th St. **Map** 9 A5.

Heartland Brewery
35 Union Square W.
Map 9 A5.

Live Bait
14 E 23rd St. **Map** 8 F4.

Old Town Bar
45 E 18th St. **Map** 8 F5.

Pete's Tavern
129 E 18th St. **Map** 9 A5.

CHELSEA AND THE GARMENT DISTRICT

Bungalow 8
515 W 27th St. **Map** 7 C3.

Chelsea Brewing Company
Pier 59 11th Ave.
Map 7 B5.

Lot 61
550 W 21st St. **Map** 7 C4.

Maritime Lobby Bar
363 W 16th St. **Map** 8 D5.

Suite 16
127 8th Ave. **Map** 8 D5.

THEATER DISTRICT

BP Café
476 5th Ave. **Map** 8 F1.

P. J. Carney's
906 7th Ave.
Map 12 E3.

Lobby Bar
Hudson Hotel, 356 W 58th St. **Map** 12 D3.

Randolfs
Warwick Hotel, 65 W 54th St. **Map** 12 F4.

Royalton Hotel
44 W 44th St. Fifth Ave.
Map 12 F5

Sardi's
234 W 44th St. **Map** 12 F5.

Whiskey Bar
Paramount Hotel, 235 W 46th St. **Map** 12 E5.

LOWER MIDTOWN

Beer Bar
Metlife Bldg, 200 Park Ave. **Map** 9 A2.

BP Café
Bryant Park, 25 W 40th St.
Map 7 B1.

The Cigar Room at Trumpets
Grand Hyatt Hotel, Grand Central Station, E 42nd St. **Map** 13 A5.

Sun Garden
Grand Hyatt Hotel, Grand Central, 42nd St.
Map 9 A1.

UPPER MIDTOWN

Bar and Books
889 1st Ave. **Map** 13 C2.

Beekman Tower
3 Mitchell Place.
Map 13 C5.

Bull and Bear
Ground fl, Waldorf–Astoria Hotel, Lexington Ave at E 49th St. **Map** 13 A5.

King Cole Room
St Regis Hotel, 2 E 55th St.
Map 12 F5.

Manchester
920 2nd Ave. **Map** 13 B5.

Oak Room
Plaza Hotel, 768 5th Ave.
Map 12 F3.

Pentop Bar and Terrace
700 5th Avenue.
Map 12 F5.

P. J. Clarke's
915 3rd Ave. **Map** 13 B4.

UPPER EAST SIDE

Brother Jimmy's BBQ
1485 1st Ave. **Map** 17 C3.

Elaine's
1703 2nd Ave. **Map** 17 B4.

Swifty's
1007 Lexington Ave.
Map 17 A5.

UPPER WEST SIDE

Journeys
Essex House Hotel, 160 Central Park S.
Map 12 E3.

Tavern on the Green
Central Park, W 67th St.
Map 12 D2.

Westside Brewing Company
340 Amsterdam Ave.
Map 15 C2.

BROOKLYN

Park Slope Brewing Company
40 Van Dyke St.

SHOPPING

A VISITOR to New York will inevitably include shopping in his or her action plan. The city is the consumer capital of the world: a shopper's paradise that is a constant source of entertainment, with dazzling window displays and a staggering variety of goods for sale. Everything is available here, from high fashion to rare children's

Tiffany's clock

books, state-of-the-art electronics and a mouthwatering array of exotic food. Whether you are looking for a personal Hovercraft, read-in-the-dark eyeglass attachments, a designer bed for your pet gerbil or a Wurlitzer jukebox, this is the city of your dreams. Whether you have $50,000 or $5, New York is the place to spend it.

BEST BUYS

NEW YORK is a bargain hunter's dream, with huge discounts on anything from household goods to designer clothes. Some of the best shops are on Orchard Street and Grand Street on the Lower East Side, where designer goods are sold at

The 1920s-style Henri Bendel store (see p311)

20–50% below the retail price. You can find just about every imaginable item of clothing here, in addition to tableware, shoes, home furnishings and electronics. Shops in this area are closed on Saturday – the Jewish Sabbath – but are usually open all day Sunday.

Another great area for fashion bargain hunters is the trendy Garment District, roughly between Sixth and Eighth avenues from 30th to 40th Street. The hub of it – Seventh Avenue – was renamed as Fashion Avenue in the early 1970s. Here, many different designers and manufacturers have showrooms, some of which are open to the public. They also have sales of many of their samples, announced on notices posted around the

area. Often the best time to go and visit these stores is just before one of the major gift-giving holidays.

SALES

ONE WORD you are likely to see all over the city, no matter what time of year you visit, is "Sale." So before you pay full price for anything, check the sale goods first. The best sales are during New York's sale seasons, which run from mid-June until the end of July and from December 26 until February. For information, look for ads in the local papers. A word of warning: along midtown Fifth Avenue there are signs announcing "Lost Our Lease" sales. But many of the shops have had these signs up for years and are best avoided.

HOW TO PAY

MOST SHOPS accept major credit cards, although there will often be a minimum purchase price. If you want to use your traveler's checks, identification is needed. Personal checks drawn in another currency will be refused. Some stores only take cash, especially during sales.

Designer dress at a New York sale

The Bulgari entrance at Hotel Pierre (see p281)

OPENING HOURS

MOST SHOPS in New York are normally open from 10am to 6pm, Monday to Saturday. Many department stores, though, are open all day Sunday and until 9pm at least two nights a week. The best time to avoid crowds is weekday mornings. The most crowded times are lunch hours (noon to 2:30pm), Saturday mornings, sales and holidays.

TAXES

THERE IS NO city 8.25% sales tax on clothing and shoes under $110, but you may still be asked to pay duty on goods at customs if you exceed the allowance. However, if the goods are sent direct, you won't have to pay sales tax.

SHOPPING TOURS

IF YOU CAN'T FACE the thought of braving the stores by yourself, why not go on one of the many shopping tours available in New York? Apart from visiting the main department stores, options include a visit to private designer showrooms, auction houses and fashion shows. Some operators will customize tours to suit your requirements.

Convention Tours Unlimited
📞 *(212) 545-1160.*

Doorway to Design
📞 *(212) 221-1111.*

Guide Service of New York
📞 *(212) 408-3332.*

The Intrepid New Yorker
📞 *(212) 750-0400.*

Window displays at Bloomingdale's *(see p179)*

DEPARTMENT STORES

MOST OF NEW YORK'S large department stores are in midtown Manhattan. Be sure to allow plenty of time to explore the ones you are interested in, because all these stores tend to be enormous, with an amazing range of goods. If at all possible, avoid going at weekends and around vacation times – the crowds can be overwhelming. Prices are often high, but you can still find some bargains during the sales.

Stores such as Saks Fifth Avenue, Bloomingdale's and Macy's provide a diverse and extraordinary range of shopping services, including actually doing the shopping for you. But then you would

miss out on what may be the shopping experience of a lifetime.

Barney's New York is a favorite among young professional New Yorkers. It specializes in excellent, but reassuringly expensive, designer clothes.

Bergdorf Goodman is luxurious, very elegant and understated. It carries high-quality contemporary fashions at high prices, specializing in European designers. The men's store is right across the street.

Almost every visitor to New York includes **Bloomingdale's** (see p179) on their sightseeing list. Bloomingdale's is the Hollywood film star of the department stores, with many eye-catching displays and seductive goods. Its ambience is that of a luxurious wonderland, filled with young and old New Yorkers seeking out the newest in fashion. The linen and the fine china departments have an undisputed reputation for quality. Check out the gourmet food section– it has a shop devoted entirely to caviar. Extensive shopping services and amenities include a noted restaurant, Le Train Bleu, with its view of the Queensboro Bridge.

Everything found in **Henri Bendel's**, from the Art Deco jewels to beautiful handmade shoes, is displayed as though each were a priceless work of art. The store, which is laid out in a series of 1920s-style boutiques, is exclusive and sophisticated, and it has an excellent selection of creative and innovative women's fashions.

Lord & Taylor is renowned for its classic and much more conservative fashions for men

A magnificent display offering household goods

and women. The store places an emphasis on US designers. You need comfortable shoes and lots of spare time to wander around.

Macy's, the self-proclaimed largest store in the world (see p132–3), sprawls over an entire city block. It has ten floors and sells everything imaginable from can openers to massive antiques.

Saks Fifth Avenue is synonymous with style and elegance. It has long been considered one of the city's high-quality department stores, with service to match. It sells stunning designer clothes for men, women and children.

ADDRESSES

Barney's New York
660 Madison Ave.
Map 13 A3.
📞 *(212) 826-8900.*

Bergdorf Goodman
754 5th Ave. **Map** 12 F3.
📞 *(212) 753-7300.*

Bloomingdale's
1000 3rd Ave. **Map** 13 B3.
📞 *(212) 705-2000.*

Henri Bendel
712 5th Ave. **Map** 12 F4.
📞 *(212) 247-1100.*

Lord & Taylor
424 5th Ave. **Map** 8 F1.
📞 *(212) 391-3344.*

Macy's
151 W 34th St. **Map** 8 E2.
📞 *(212) 695-4400.*

Saks Fifth Avenue
611 5th Ave. **Map** 12 F4.
📞 *(212) 753-4000.*

New York's Best: Shopping

Designer shoes from Madison Avenue

IN A CITY where you can literally shop 24 hours a day, the best plan is to shop the way New Yorkers do, by neighborhood. Each has its own character and specialties. Here are highlights of the best shopping districts – where they are and what you will find in each. If time is very tight, head for one of the huge department stores *(see p311),* or if window shopping is your preference, stroll along Fifth Avenue, home to Manhattan's most glittering stores *(see opposite).* For great bargains in a truly ethnic area, try the Lower East Side.

Greenwich and East Villages
Explore around Eighth Street and St. Mark's Place for shoes and avant-garde fashions, books, ethnic goods and flea markets. Move to lower Broadway for antiques (often "retro" 20th century). (See pp108–9 and pp116–17.)

SoHo
The area bordered by Sixth Avenue, Lafayette, Houston and Canal streets is bustling with contemporary art galleries, antiques, crafts, exclusive gifts, and clothes from designer flagships. Weekend brunchtime gallery-hopping is very popular. (See pp102–3.)

Lower East Side
On Sundays New Yorkers flock to Canal, Delancey, Orchard and Essex streets for great bargains in fashions, shoes, jewelry, electronic and household goods, heading up to NoLita for trendy fashions. (See pp94–95.)

Greenwich Village

SoHo and TriBeCa

Seaport and the Civic Center

Lower East

Lower Manhattan

South Street Seaport
This is a browser's paradise of crafts, gifts, toys, souvenirs, antiquarian and new books, and antiques with a seafaring connection. (See pp82–83.)

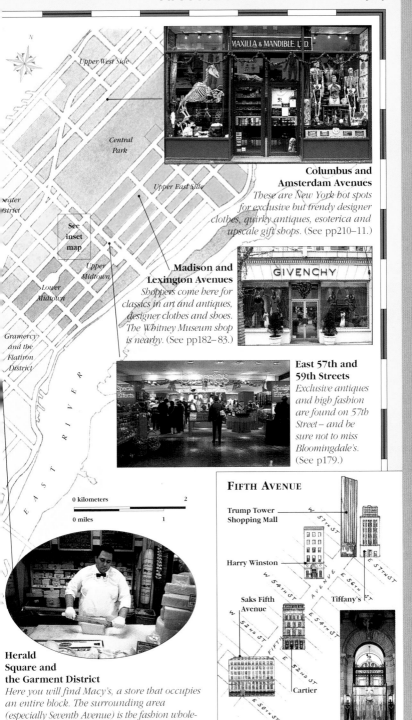

Columbus and Amsterdam Avenues
These are New York hot spots for exclusive but trendy designer clothes, quirky antiques, esoterica and upscale gift shops. (See pp210–11.)

Madison and Lexington Avenues
Shoppers come here for classics in art and antiques, designer clothes and shoes. The Whitney Museum shop is nearby. (See pp182–83.)

East 57th and 59th Streets
Exclusive antiques and high fashion are found on 57th Street – and be sure not to miss Bloomingdale's. (See p179.)

Herald Square and the Garment District
Here you will find Macy's, a store that occupies an entire block. The surrounding area (especially Seventh Avenue) is the fashion wholesale center with major discounts during sales – but some stores accept only cash. (See pp130–31.)

FIFTH AVENUE

Trump Tower Shopping Mall

Harry Winston

Saks Fifth Avenue

Tiffany's

Cartier

From Saks to Tiffany's
Leading retailers have their flagship store on world-famous Fifth Avenue.

Harry Winston
(see p320)

New York Originals

N EW YORK IS A CITY where just about any kind of
shop, no matter how esoteric, will always attract
customers. Dozens of tiny shops scattered around the
city specialize in unusual merchandise, from butterflies
and bones to traditional Tibetan treasures and
Shamrock sprigs from Ireland. Coming across these in
some tucked-away corner is what makes shopping in
New York such an entertaining experience.

SPECIALTY SHOPS

F OR BEAUTIFUL BRASS, onyx
and pewter chess sets, and
the opportunity to play a
decent game, make a move to
the **Chess Shop**. For every
type of pen **Arthur Brown &
Bros.** stocks an enormous
range, including such names
as Mont Blanc and Schaeffer.
Big City Kites and Darts has
kites in different kinds of
weird and wonderful shapes
from fiery dragons to cuddly
teddy bears, plus enough
accessories to satisfy even the
most dedicated kite flyer. For
those with a bit more energy,
Blades sells and rents out
skates and also the trendiest
skateboards plus all the safety
equipment to go with them.

If you're looking for
different or unusual buttons,
a visit to **Tender Buttons**,
which stocks millions, is a
must. Whether you want
enamel, wood or Navajo
silver buttons – or perhaps
want your own buttons made
into cuff links or earrings –
here you'll find just what you
want – and more.

Leo Kaplan Ltd. is the
place to go if you are a keen
collector of paperweights and
Rita Ford's Music Boxes, a
19th-century style shop,
stocks a tuneful and extensive
range of music boxes.

The **New York Firefighter's
Friend** sells an intriguing range
of items related to fire-fighting,
including toy fire engines, fire-
men's jackets, badges, scaled-
down uniforms for children,
stuffed toy dalmatians and a
wide selection of T-shirts
including a popular one with
NYFD (New York Fire Department) on one side and "Keep
back 200 feet" on the other.

For the true romantic who
wants to impress, everything
sold by **Only Hearts** is
heart-shaped, including pillows,
soap and jewelry. If you are
artistic, or if you wish to buy
a present for someone who
is, visit the **Pearl Paint Co.**,
which stocks everything you
could need. The **Magickal
Childe** is an occult emporium
full of potions, tarot cards and
fragrant incense (note: there's
no phone here and hours are
erratic). Step straight into the
space age at **Star Magic** to
buy celestial maps, holograms,
prisms and scientific toys.
Forbidden Planet is a
science fiction megastore
with everything from comics
to models for the true fan.

Cologne made especially for
George Washington and the
official soap of the White
House during the Eisenhower
era are just some of the many
fascinating items for sale at
Caswell-Massey Ltd., the
oldest pharmacy in the city.

Guitar gurus will want to
visit **Rudy's**, Manny's or Sam
Ash's guitar shop. Not only is
there a chance you'll bump
into Eric Clapton or Lou Reed –
both have their guitars made in
this area – but you'll find the
widest and best choice of
instruments in the city.

Bibliophiles will find a range
of gifts in both the **New York
Public Library Shop** *(see
p144)* (such as bookends of
the lions guarding the main
entrance) and the **Morgan
Library shop** *(see pp162–3)*,
including bookmarks and
writing paper.

University logos and college
colors dominate the many
knickknacks and accessories
are at **The Yale Club** gift shop
and **The Princeton Club**.

Hebrew Religious Articles
carries one of the largest
selections of Jewish religious
items in the city.

The Cathedral Shop at the
Cathedral of St. John the Divine
is a large store selling books,
artworks, herbs, jewelry and
religious items made locally.

MEMORABILIA

A T LINCOLN CENTER, the
**Metropolitan Opera
Shop** has records, cards,
librettos, small binoculars and
many other opera-related
items. The **Performing Arts
Shop** downstairs is a real
treasure trove of theater,
opera, ballet and music
memorabilia. For theater fans,
everything from scripts and
vocal scores to CDs can be
found at **Broadway New
York**. For thousands of rare
and classic film stills and
posters visit **Jerry Ohlinger's
Movie Material Store**.

The **Carnegie Hall Shop**
carries musically themed
cards, T-shirts, games,
posters, tote bags and much
more. For something truly
original and very American,
be sure to visit **Lost City Arts**
and **Urban Archaeology** in
SoHo. Between these two
shops, you'll unearth all sorts
of relics from America's past,
from Barbie Doll lunch boxes
to furniture from traditional
ice-cream parlors.

TOYS, GAMES AND GADGETS

F OR CHILDREN'S GIFTS, don't
miss the legendary **F.A.O.
Schwarz**. This is a massive
store crammed from floor to
ceiling with luxury toy cars,
enormous stuffed animals and
every kind of electronic toy
imaginable. There are
shoulder-to-shoulder crowds
at Christmas, when you might
have to line up to get in.

The **Children's General
Store** is one of the city's
newest – and cleverest –
children's toy stores.

The Enchanted Forest
(see p102) is a magical
experience for children. Its
handmade toys are artfully
displayed among the trees of
the delightful interior, built by
a theatrical set designer.

Penny Whistle Toys sells a
huge selection of quality toys,
games and all kinds of dolls.

For games for both children and adults, the **Game Show** has puzzles and games galore, from real classics like Monopoly to the latest yuppie favorite. **Red Caboose** is for fans of model railways. On three floors, the **Toys 'R' Us** flagship glass building on Broadway is the largest toy store in the world, with a 60 ft (20 m) ferris wheel.

Dinosaur Hill on Second Avenue offers handmade puppets and toys, mobiles, and beautifully made children's clothes. It's expensive but worth it.

MUSEUM SHOPS

SOME OF NEW YORK's best souvenirs can be found in the city's many museum shops. In addition to the usual range of books, posters and cards, there are reproductions of the exhibits on display, including jewelry and sculpture. The **American Craft Museum** (see p169) has an excellent selection of American crafts as well as original works for sale. In addition to realistic model dinosaurs, rubber animals, minerals, and rocks, the **American Museum of Natural History** (see

pp214–15) has a variety of recycled products and earth-awareness gifts, which include posters, bags and T-shirts with environmental messages, and a large selection Native American handicrafts. There is also a kids' shop with reasonably priced items such as shell sets, magnets and toys.

The **Asia Society Bookstore and Gift Shop** (see p185) has a striking selection of Oriental prints, posters, art books, toys and jewelry. Items related to interior design are offered at the **Cooper-Hewitt** (see p184). One of New York's largest collections of Jewish ceremonial objects, including menorahs and Kiddush cups, books and jewelry, is found in the small shop at the **Jewish Museum** (see p184).

For reproduction prints of famous paintings and other exquisite gifts a visit to the **Metropolitan Museum of Art** (see pp188–95) gift shop is a must. There is also an enormous book department and a children's gift shop. The traditional **American Folk Art Museum** (see p213) prides itself on its American country crafts, including

wooden toys, quilts and weathervanes, which are mostly original. Works by craftspeople who currently have pieces on display in the museum are also sold.

The **Museum of the City of New York** (see p197), specializes in pictures of old New York. The **Museum of Modern Art/MOMA Design Store** (see pp170–73) has a highly praised selection of innovative home furnishings, toys and kitchenware inspired by international designers such as Frank Lloyd Wright and Le Corbusier. The store will remain open during the reconstruction.

For a selection of nautical items, including charts, maps, model ships and scrimshaw, go to the **South Street Seaport Museum Shops** (see pp82–85). The **Whitney Museum's Shop** (see pp198–9) stocks American-made items, including jewelry, wooden toys, books and posters complementing current exhibitions. The **Museum of Jewish Heritage** (see p77) has a gift shop with an unusual array of gifts, souvenirs and educational material about Jewish life. Open to ticketed visitors only.

THE BEST OF THE IMPORTS

NEW YORK is a massive melting pot of different nationalities, cultures and ethnic groups, all of which have made their mark on New York's diverse culture in one way or another. Many ethnic shops specialize in food or goods of a particular group. Some of the most interesting and unusual shops include **Alaska on Madison**, which has a huge collection of Eskimo art, and the **Chinese Porcelain Company,** for exquisite Chinese decorative arts and furniture. **Pearl River Mart** has been a staple for Asian goods for thirty years, and **Himalayan Crafts and Tours** stocks every-thing from paintings to

Tibetan rugs. **Sweet Life**, on the Lower East Side, is a tiny but charming old-fashioned candy shop with delicacies from around the world. **Things Japanese** has beautifully made crafts and unusual books. **Surma** is a Ukrainian general store that sells hand painted eggs and linens. **Common Ground** sells Native American arts, and **Astro Gems** has a large collection of jewelry and mineral specimens from Africa and Asia.

ADDRESSES

Alaska on Madison
937 Madison Ave. **Map** 17 A1.
((212) 879-1782.

Astro Gems
185 Madison Ave. **Map** 9 A2.
((212) 889-9000.

Chinese Porcelain Company
475 Park Ave. **Map** 13 A3.
((212) 838-7744.

Common Ground
19 Greenwich Ave. **Map** 1 B1.
((212) 989-4178.

Himalayan Crafts and Tours
2007 Broadway. **Map** 11 C1.
((212) 787-8500.

Pearl River Mart
477 Broadway. **Map** 4 E4.
((212) 431-4770.

Sweet Life
63 Hester St.
Map 5 B4.
((212) 598-0092.

Surma
11 E 7th St. **Map** 4 F2.
((212) 477-0729.

Things Japanese
127 E 60th St.
Map 13 A3.
((212) 371-4661.

DIRECTORY

SPECIALTY SHOPS

Arthur Brown & Bros.
2 W 46th St.
Map 12 F5.
☎ (212) 575-5555.

Big City Kites and Darts
1210 Lexington Ave.
Map 17 A4.
☎ (212) 472-2623.

Blades
120 W 72nd St.
Map 11 C1.
☎ (212) 787-3911.
One of several branches.

Caswell-Massey Ltd.
518 Lexington Ave.
Map 13 A5.
☎ (212) 755-2254.

The Cathedral Shop
Cathedral of St. John the Divine, 1047 Amsterdam Ave. **Map** 20 E4.
☎ (212) 222-7200.

Hebrew Religious Articles
45 Essex St. **Map** 5 B4.
☎ (212) 674-1770.

Leo Kaplan Ltd.
967 Madison Ave.
Map 17 A5.
☎ (212) 249-6766.

Magickal Childe
35 W 19th St.
Map 8 F5.

Morgan Library Shop
Madison Ave at 36th St.
Map 9 A2.
☎ (212) 685-0610.

New York Firefighter's Friend
263 Lafayette St.
Map 4 F3.
☎ (212) 226-3142.

New York Public Library Shop
5th Ave at 42nd St.
Map 8 F1.
☎ (212) 930-0678.

Only Hearts
386 Columbus Ave.
Map 15 D5.
☎ (212) 724-5608.

Pearl Paint Co
308 Canal St.
Map 4 E5.
☎ (212) 431-7932.

The Princeton Club
15 W 43rd St. **Map** 8 F1.
☎ (212) 596-1200.

Rita Ford's Music Boxes
19 E 65th St. **Map** 12 F2.
☎ (212) 535-6717.

Rudy's
169 W 48th St. **Map** 12 E5.
☎ (212) 391-1699.

Star Magic
745 Broadway. **Map** 4 E2.
☎ (212) 228-7770.

Tender Buttons
143 E 62nd St.
Map 13 A2.
☎ (212) 758-7004.

The Chess Shop
230 Thompson St.
Map 4 D3.
☎ (212) 475-9580.

The Yale Club
50 Vanderbilt Ave.
Map 13 A5.
☎ (212) 661-2070.

MEMORABILIA

Broadway New York
1 Shubert Alley.
Map 12 E5.
☎ (212) 944-4133.

The Carnegie Hall Shop
881 7th Ave.
Map 12 E3.
☎ (212) 903-9610.

Forbidden Planet
840 Broadway.
Map 4 E1.
☎ (212) 473-1576.

Jerry Ohlinger's Movie Material Store
242 W 14th St.
Map 3 C1.
☎ (212) 989-0869.

Lost City Arts
18 Cooper Sq.
Map 4 F2.
☎ (212) 375-0500.

Metropolitan Opera Shop
Metropolitan Opera House, Lincoln Center, 136 W 65th St.
Map 11 C2.
☎ (212) 580-4090.

Performing Arts Shop
Metropolitan Opera House, Lincoln Center, 136 W 65th St.
Map 11 C2.
☎ (917) 441-1195.

Urban Archaeology
143 Franklin St.
Map 4 D5.
☎ (212) 431-6969.

TOYS, GAMES AND GADGETS

The Children's General Store
Grand Central Station.
Map 9 A1.
☎ (212) 682-0004.

The Enchanted Forest
85 Mercer St.
Map 4 E4.
☎ (212) 925-6677.

Dinosaur Hill
306 E 9th/2nd Ave.
Map 4 F1.
☎ (212) 473-5850.

F.A.O. Schwarz
767 5th Ave.
Map 12 F3.
☎ (212) 644-9400.

Game Show
1240 Lexington Ave.
Map 17 A4.
☎ (212) 472-8011.
One of several branches.

Penny Whistle Toys
448 Columbus Ave.
Map 16 D4.
☎ (212) 873-9090.
One of several branches.

Red Caboose
23 W 45th St.
Map 12 F5.
☎ (212) 575-0155.

Toys 'R' Us
1530 Broadway, Times Square.
Map 8 E2.
☎ 594-8697.

MUSEUM SHOPS

American Craft Museum
40 W 53rd St. **Map** 12 F4.
☎ (212) 956-3535.

American Folk Art Museum
45 W 53rd St. **Map** 12 F4.
☎ (212) 265-1040.

American Museum of Natural History
W 79th St at Central Park West. **Map** 16 D5.
☎ (212) 769-5100.

Asia Society Bookstore and Gift Shop
725 Park Ave. **Map** 13 A1.
☎ (212) 288-6400.

Cooper-Hewitt
2 E 91st St. **Map** 16 F2.
☎ (212) 860-6878.

Jewish Museum
1109 5th Ave. **Map** 16 F2.
☎ (212) 423-3200.

Metropolitan Museum of Art
5th Ave at 82nd St.
Map 16 F4.
☎ (212) 535-7710.

Museum of the City of New York
5th Ave at 103rd St.
Map 21 C5.
☎ (212) 534-1672.

Museum of Jewish Heritage
18 First Place,
Battery Park City.
Map 1 B4.
☎ (646) 437-4200.

Museum of Modern Art/MOMA Design Store
44 W 53rd St.
Map 12 F4.
☎ (212) 767-1050.

South St. Seaport Museum Shops
207 Front St. **Map** 2 D2.
☎ (212) 748-8600.

The Whitney Museum's Store Next Door
943 Madison Ave.
Map 13 A1.
☎ (212) 570-3676.

Fashion

Whether you're looking for a secondhand pair of 501s or the kind of ballgown Ivana Trump would be proud to wear, you're sure to find it in New York. The city is the fashion capital of America and an important center of clothing manufacture and design. New York's clothing stores, like its restaurants, reflect the city's dramatically different styles and cultures. To save time it's probably best to visit one area at a time and wander from store to store. Alternatively, visit one of the major department stores for an excellent selection of fashion for everyone.

AMERICAN DESIGNERS

Many American designers sell their creations in boutiques within the large department stores, or have exclusive shops of their own. One of the most famous is Geoffrey Beene, known for sophisticated looks that are casual and comfortable.

Bill Blass is the king of American fashion whose clothes feature loads of different colors, wild patterns, innovative shapes and a lot of wit. Liz Claiborne's designs are always elegantly simple, casual and reasonably priced, including everything you could possibly need from tennis whites to casual professional wear for women.

Marc Jacobs, known for his sportswear, has his own label and store in Greenwich Village. James Galanos is an exclusive designer for the rich and famous, making one-of-a-kind *couture* clothes, and Betsey Johnson is popular with women able to wear figure-hugging fashions in fabulous fabrics.

In the last decade, Donna Karan has become a name that appears everywhere. Her simple, stylish and great-looking designs work for everything from work-out clothes to black tie wear. Calvin Klein now has his name on place settings and sunglasses in addition to underwear, jeans and a whole range of clothes. He is renowned for comfortable, sensuous and well-fitting – as well as very hip – looks. Ralph Lauren is well known for his aristocratic and expensive clothes, a "look"

favored by the exclusive and posh Ivy League, horsey set. For those with a taste for more experimental designs, Joan Vass specializes in moderately priced but exciting, colorful and innovative knitwear.

DISCOUNT DESIGNER CLOTHES

If you're on the lookout for discount designer clothes, **Designer Resale**, **Encore** and **Michael's** sell a wide range. Oscar de la Renta, Ungaro and Armani are just some of the leading labels available. Clothes are either new or worn but near-perfect.

One of New York City's best kept secrets is the **Century 21 Department Store** in lower Manhattan. The designer discount emporium has reopened in its original location and sells European and American designer fashions discounted up to an amazing 75 per cent off regular retail prices.

MEN'S CLOTHES

In the center of midtown, you'll find two of the city's most highly regarded mens-wear stores: **Brooks Brothers** and **Paul Stuart**. Brooks Brothers is something of a New York institution, famous for its traditional, conservative clothing such as smart button-down shirts and Chinos. There's an ultra-conservative woman's line too. Paul Stuart prides itself on its very British look and offers a stylish array of superbly tailored fashions.

Go to the high-quality department store **Bergdorf Goodman Men** to find beautifully made Turnbull & Asser shirts and marvelous suits by Gianfranco Ferré or Hugo Boss.

Barney's New York has one of the most comprehensive men's departments in America, with a truly massive range of clothes and accessories. **Rothman's** offers international styles at great bargain prices.

The Custom Shop Shirtmakers specializes in custom-made suits and shirts in beautiful materials. Go to **Burberry Limited** if you are looking for classic British trenchcoats and traditional outdoor wear.

J. Press sells classic, conservative yet elegant clothes while **John Varvatos** is famous for luxurious, sporty designs with superb detail. Uptown designer menswear boutiques include the renowned **Beau Brummel** with a selection of very stylish European clothes and **Thomas Pink** whose bright colors and fine fabrics make this store a celebrity favorite. Many of these men's stores also carry striking women's fashions. Watch for the new Hickey-Freeman store on 5th Avenue for a wide range of men's traditional clothing.

CHILDREN'S CLOTHES

In addition to an excellent selection within the large department stores, there are several shops around the city that sell children's clothing exclusively. A good example is **Bonpoint**, which has a world of French-style charm. **GapKids** and **BabyGap** shops, often in the **Gap** shops, have comfortable, long-lasting cotton overalls, sweat pants, denim jackets, sweatshirts and leggings. The wonderfully named **Peanut Butter & Jane** sells trendy but particularly comfortable togs. **Space Kiddets** has everything from booties to Western wear.

Women's Clothes

WOMEN'S FASHION is subject to design trends, and New York stores keep pace with them all. Most of the city's most fashionable shops are found in the midtown area around Madison and Fifth avenues. These include some of the major department stores (see p311), which stock a range of American designers, including Donna Karan, Ralph Lauren and Bill Blass.

Leading international names such as **Chanel**, **Fendi**, and **Valentino** also have shops here, as does one of the outstanding American designers, **Geoffrey Beene**. There is also a handful of popular ready-to-wear stores, including **Ann Taylor**, which is much favored by young, busy professionals looking for stylish, comfortable clothing.

Right at the heart of this area stands the pink-marbled Trump Tower, which houses a selection of exclusive shops. Madison Avenue is packed with designers for the smart set, who have everything you could ever need, including **Givenchy** who sells show-stopping formal gowns at phenomenal prices, Valentino who has classic Italian clothes and **Emanuel Ungaro** who is relatively unintimidating and has something to suit most tastes and physiques from beautifully tailored jackets to more matronly full-figured and boldly patterned print dresses. **Missoni** is famous for richly textured sweaters in sumptuous wools and colorful patterns. **Yves St Laurent Rive Gauche** has evening gowns, one-of-a-kind jackets, silks and extravagant blouses and beautifully cut pants suits.

Sophisticated Italian looks are also available from Italian style kings **Giorgio Armani** and **Gianni Versace**. **Dolce & Gabbana** sells only unique, one-of-a-kind Italian clothing. **Gucci**, one of the oldest Italian shops in America, is only for the wealthy and status-conscious.

The Upper West Side has many shops competing for attention with contemporary fashions, including **Betsey Johnson's** shop, with her whimsical, relatively inexpensive designs. **Calvin Klein** now has a store on the East Side, specializing in ultra-hip, casual fashions. **French Connection** is known for its affordable separates, both casual and for the office. **Scoop** is *the* place to get a little black dress.

The villages – the East Village in particular – are the best places to go for second-hand clothing and 1950s rock 'n' roll gear, with ever-changing interesting shops run by new and young designers and art school graduates. For a range of affordable, well-cut clothes from classic to casual, try **APC**.

Cheap Jack's carries a huge selection of second-hand Levi's as well as hundreds of denim and leather jackets. **Loehmann's** offers discounted fashion clothes, and it's the place to shop if you want top-of-the-line fashions at unbelievable discounts. **Big Drop** has a great selection of perfectly fitting little black dresses. **Screaming Mimi's** is where you could unearth that pair of velvet bell-bottoms or go-go boots you've always dreamed of having. A more mainstream shop is **The Gap**, a chain store selling lots of moderately-priced, casual and comfortable clothes for men, women and children.

Recently SoHo has come to rival Madison Avenue for designer boutiques specializing in expensive but interesting clothes – the fashions here are far more avant-garde. You'll find **Yohji Yamamoto**, among other exclusive stores. **Comme des Garçons** sells minimalist Japanese chic.

Cynthia Rowley is a prominent New York designer who sells flirty fashions for women and **What Comes Around Goes Around** is the place to go for vintage jeans.

Size Chart

For Australian sizes follow the British and American conversions.

Children's clothing

American	2-3	4-5	6-6x	7-8	10	12	14	16 (size)
British	2-3	4-5	6-7	8-9	10-11	12	14	14+ (years)
Continental	2-3	4-5	6-7	8-9	10-11	12	14	14+ (years)

Children's shoes

American	7½	8½	9½	10½	11½	12½	13½	1½	2½	
British	7	8	9	10	11	12	13	1	2	
Continental	24	25½	27	28	29	30	32	33	34	

Women's dresses, coats and skirts

American	4	6	8	10	12	14	16	18
British	6	8	10	12	14	16	18	20
Continental	38	40	42	44	46	48	50	52

Women's blouses and sweaters

American	6	8	10	12	14	16	18
British	30	32	34	36	38	40	42
Continental	40	42	44	46	48	50	52

Women's shoes

American	5	6	7	8	9	10	11
British	3	4	5	6	7	8	9
Continental	36	37	38	39	40	41	44

Men's suits

American	34	36	38	40	42	44	46	48
British	34	36	38	40	42	44	46	48
Continental	44	46	48	50	52	54	56	58

Men's shirts

American	14	15	15½	16	16½	17	17½	18
British	14	15	15½	16	16½	17	17½	18
Continental	36	38	39	41	42	43	44	45

Men's shoes

American	7	7½	8	8½	9½	10½	11	11½
British	6	7	7½	8	9	10	11	12
Continental	39	40	41	42	43	44	45	46

DIRECTORY

DISCOUNT DESIGNER CLOTHES

Designer Resale
324 E 81st St. **Map** 17 B4.
(212) 734-3639.

Encore
1132 Madison Ave.
Map 17 A4.
(212) 879-2850.

Michael's
1041 Madison Ave.
Map 17 A5.
(212) 737-7273.

Century 21 Department Store
22 Cortland St. **Map** 1 C2.
(212) 227-9092.

MEN'S CLOTHES

Barney's New York
660 Madison Ave.
Map 13 A3.
(212) 593-7800.

Beau Brummel
347 West Broadway.
Map 4 E3.
(212) 219-2666.
One of several branches.

Bergdorf Goodman Men
754 5th Ave. **Map** 12 F3.
(212) 753-7300.

Brooks Brothers
346 Madison Ave.
Map 9 A1.
(212) 682-8800.

Burberry Limited
9 E 57th St. **Map** 12 F3.
(212) 371-5010.

The Custom Shop Shirtmakers
618 5th Ave. **Map** 12 F4.
(212) 245-2499.
One of several branches.

J. Press
7 E 44th St. **Map** 12 F5.
(212) 687-7642.

John Varvatos
149 Mercer St.
Map 4 E3.
(212) 965-0700.

Paul Stuart
350 Madison Ave.
Map 13 A5.
(212) 682-0320.

Polo/Ralph Lauren
Madison Ave at 72nd St.
Map 13 A1.
(212) 606-2100.

Rothman's
200 Park Ave South.
Map 9 A5.
(212) 777-7400.

Thomas Pink
520 Madison Ave.
Map 13 A4.
(212) 838-1928.

CHILDREN'S CLOTHES

Bonpoint
1269 Madison Ave.
Map 17 A3.
(212) 722-7720.

GapKids
60 W 34th St. **Map** 8 F2.
(212) 760-1268.
One of several branches.

Peanut Butter & Jane
617 Hudson St.
Map 3 B1.
(212) 620-7952.

Space Kiddets
46 E 21st St. **Map** 8 F4.
(212) 420-9878.

WOMEN'S CLOTHES

Ann Taylor
645 Madison Ave.
Map 13 A3.
(212) 832-2010.
One of several branches.

APC
131 Mercer St.
Map 4 E3.
(212) 966-9685.

Betsey Johnson
248 Columbus Ave.
Map 16 D4.
(212) 362-3364.
One of several branches.

Big Drop
174 Spring St.
Map 3 C4.
(212) 966-4299.

Calvin Klein
654 Madison Ave.
Map 13 A3.
(212) 292-9000.

Chanel
15 E 57th St.
Map 12 F3.
(212) 355-5050.

Cheap Jack's
841 Broadway.
Map 4 E1.
(212) 777-9564.

Comme des Garçons
520 W 22nd St.
Map 8 F3.
(212) 604-9200.

Cynthia Rowley
112 Wooster St.
Map 4 E4.
(212) 334-1144.

Emanuel Ungaro
792 Madison Ave.
Map 13 A2.
(212) 249-4090.

Fendi
720 5th Ave.
Map 12 F3.
(212) 767-0100.

French Connection
304 Columbus Ave.
Map 12 D1.
(212) 473-4486.
One of several branches.

The Gap
250 W 57th St.
Map 12 D3.
(212) 315-2250.
One of many branches.

Geoffrey Beene
309 5th Ave.
Map 8 F3.
(212) 725-9647.

Gianni Versace
815 Madison Ave.
Map 13 A2.
(212) 744-6868.

Giorgio Armani
760 Madison Ave.
Map 13 A2.
(212) 988-9191.

Givenchy
710 Madison Ave.
Map 13 A1.
(212) 688-4338.

Gucci
685 5th Ave.
Map 12 F4.
(212) 826-2600.

Loehmann's
101 Seventh Ave.
Map 8 E1.
(212) 352-0856.

Missoni
1009 Madison Ave.
Map 13 A1.
(212) 517-9339.

Dolce & Gabbana
434 W Broadway.
Map 4 E3.
(212) 965-8000.

Saks Fifth Avenue
611 Fifth Ave. **Map** 12 F4.
(212) 753-4000.

Scoop
532 Broadway (near Spring St).
Map 4 E4.
(212) 925-2886.
One of two branches.

Screaming Mimi's
382 Lafayette St.
Map 4 F2.
(212) 677-6464.

Valentino
747 Madison Ave.
Map 13 A2.
(212) 772-6969.

What Comes Around Goes Around
351 West Broadway.
Map 4 E4.
(212) 343-9303.

Yohji Yamamoto
103 Grand St.
Map 4 E4.
(212) 966-9066.

Yves St Laurent Rive Gauche
859 Madison Ave.
Map 13 A1.
(212) 517-7400.

Accessories

IN ADDITION TO the following shops, all of the major Manhattan department stores have extensive accessory departments stocking a range of hats, gloves, bags, jewelry, watches, scarves, shoes and umbrellas.

JEWELRY

MIDTOWN FIFTH AVENUE is where to find the most dazzling jewelers. By day, windows glisten with gems from around the world; by night they are empty – the jewels safely locked away. The most sensational shops are all within a couple of blocks of one another and include the museum-like **Harry Winston**, which show-cases its coveted jewels from around the world. **Buccellati** is well respected for its innovative Italian creations and excellent workmanship. **Bulgari** has an impressive collection that ranges in price from a mere couple of hundred to over a million dollars.

Housed in a Renaissance-style palazzo, **Cartier** is a jewel in itself and sells its beautiful baubles at unthinkable prices. **Tiffany & Co.** has ten floors of glittering crystal, diamonds and other jewels just waiting to be packed up for you and taken away in the store's signature sky blue boxes.

Diamond Row, a one-block area on 47th Street (between Fifth and Sixth avenues), is lined with shops displaying hundreds of thousands of dollars worth of diamonds, gold, pearls and other exotic jewels from around the world. Try not to miss the **Jewelry Exchange**, a complex where 60 different crafts-people sell their ware direct to the public. Boisterous bargaining is very much alive here, so be prepared to play the game.

HATS

NEW YORK'S OLDEST hat shop is **Worth & Worth**, which also has the largest collection of hats in the city. You can get everything you could possibly want here, ranging from original Australian bush hats to silk toppers, to slouch hats and boaters. Check out **Larisa/L&R Design Studios** for custom-designed hats for women and strange cold-weather hats for men. **Suzanne Millinery** is the hat-maker to the stars, as she has proved very popular with celebrities such as Whoopi Goldberg and Ivana Trump.

UMBRELLAS

THE MINUTE IT STARTS to rain in New York, hundreds of street vendors selling umbrellas seem to sprout like mush-rooms. Their umbrellas, which sell at just a few dollars, are without doubt the cheapest in the city, but unlikely to last much longer than the downpour itself. For good-quality umbrellas, you'll find a fine selection of Briggs of London at **Worth & Worth**. There is a wide range of different sizes, trendy patterns and traditional tartans and stripes at **Barney's New York**, and there's always Macy's for the usual sizes and styles. World-famous **Gucci** has umbrellas to match its ties. There are expensive and telescopic ones found at **Hanae Mori**, and doorman-sized ones in solid black or in the university's traditional colors of black and orange at **The Princeton Club. The Yale Club** has blue ones emblazoned with a white "Y".

HANDBAGS AND BRIEFCASES

TWICE A YEAR, during the January and August sales, a serpentine line of buyers wraps around the corner of 48th Street and Madison Avenue waiting to get into **Crouch & Fitzgerald.** An old New York institution, selling handbags, briefcases and luggage. All the well-known brands are sold here, including Judith Leiber, Ghurka, Dooney & Bourke and Louis Vuitton, as well as the firm's own line. Elsewhere in the city are such exclusive shops as **Bottega Veneta** and **Prada**, where handbags are displayed like precious art, with prices to match. Younger and trendier places include **Furla**, well-respected for its Italian designs, and the stylish **Il Bisonte**. Current must-have designer Rafé Totengco's soft suede pastel pouches are found at **TG-170** and **Big Drop. The Coach Store** is known for its simple, classic leather handbags.

For discount designer handbags go to the legendary **Fine & Klein,** and for bargain briefcases from slim envelopes to thick lawyer's bags, a visit to the **Altman Luggage Company** is a must.

SHOES AND BOOTS

MANHATTAN shoe stores are famous for their exten-sive selections of shoes and boots, and if you shop around you are sure to find what you want at a reasonable price.

Most of the large depart-ment stores in New York also have shoe departments where you can find designer-label shoes in addition to other brands. **Bloomingdale's** *(see p179)* has a huge women's footwear department, and **Brooks Brothers** has one of the best selections of tradi-tional men's shoes in the city.

For both men's and women's shoes, the most exclusive shops are around the midtown area. **Martinez Valero** has beautiful shoes made from suede and leather, in various elegant styles. **Ferragamo** sells classic styles crafted in Florence. Go to **Botticelli** for whimsical shoe fashions. The best new place is **Jeffrey's** for excellent selection. For stylish shoes at decent prices, head for **Sigerson Morrison** in Little Italy.

For cowboy boots, head for **Billy Martin's**. There's an enormous selection of handmade boots, from basic, no-frills "ropers," which real American cowboys wear, to crocodile leather boots that sell for thousands of dollars. Billy Martin's stocks western garb and accessories, so you dress in western gear from head to toe. For beautiful custom-made boots, try **Buffalo Chips Bootery**.

For the latest and best in children's shoes, **East Side Kids** stocks the trendiest fashions for kids. **Little Eric** has unusual, eye-catching footwear and **Shoofly** has imported shoes in all styles. **Harry's** carries a wonderful selection of sensible shoes.

For discounted shoes, the greatest concentration of shops is around West 34th Street and West 8th Street between Fifth and Sixth Avenues, and Orchard Street on the Lower East Side.

LINGERIE

EXPENSIVE imports from Europe, which are sexy yet elegant, can be found at **La Petite Coquette**.

More affordable is **Victoria's Secret**, which offers two floors of beautifully made lingerie in satin, silk and many other fine fabrics.

DIRECTORY

JEWELRY

Buccellati
46 E 57th Ave.
Map 12 F3.
((212) 308-2900.

Bulgari
730 5th Ave.
Map 12 F3.
((212) 315-9000.

Cartier
653 5th Ave.
Map 12 F4.
((212) 753-0111.

Harry Winston
718 5th Ave.
Map 12 F3.
((212) 245-2000.

Jewelry Exchange
15 W 47th St.
Map 12 F5.

Tiffany & Co
5th Ave at 57th St.
Map 12 F3.
((212) 755-8000.

HATS

Larisa Hats
342 7th Ave/29th St.
Map 8 E3.
((212) 695-8989.

Suzanne Millinery
27 East 61 St.
Map 13 A3.
((212) 593-3232.

Worth & Worth
101 W 55th St, Suite 3N
Map 12 E4.
((212) 265-2887.

UMBRELLAS

Barney's New York
See p311.

Gucci
685 5th Ave.
Map 12 F4.
((212) 826-2600.

Hanae Mori
27 E 79th St.
Map 16 F5.
((212) 472-2352.

The Princeton Club
15 W 43rd St.
Map 8 F1.
((212) 596-1200.

Worth & Worth
See Hats.

The Yale Club
50 Vanderbilt Ave.
Map 13 A5.
((212) 661-2070.

HANDBAGS AND BRIEFCASES

Altman Luggage Company
135 Orchard St.
Map 5 A3.
((212) 254-7275.

Big Drop
174 Spring St.
Map 4 F4.
((212) 966-4299.

Il Bisonte
120 Sullivan St.
Map 4 D4.
((212) 966-8773.

Bottega Veneta
635 Madison Ave.
Map 13 A3.
((212) 371-5511.

The Coach Store
595 Madison Ave.
Map 13 A3.
((212) 754-0041.

Crouch & Fitzgerald
400 Madison Ave.
Map 13 A5.
((212) 755-5888.

Fine & Klein
119 Orchard St.
Map 5 A3.
((212) 674-6720.

Furla
727 Madison Ave.
Map 13 A3.
((212) 755-8986.
One of two branches.

Prada
45 E 57th St. **Map** 12 F3.
((212) 308-2332.

TG-170
170 Ludlow St.
Map 5 A3.
((212) 995-8660.

SHOES AND BOOTS

Billy Martin's
220 E 60th St.
Map 13 B3.
((212) 861-3100.

Botticelli
620 5th Ave. **Map** 12 F4.
((212) 582-6313.

Bloomingdale's
See p311.

Brooks Brothers
See p319.

Buffalo Chips Bootery
355 W Broadway. **Map** 4 E4. ((212) 625-8400.

East Side Kids
1298 Madison Ave.
Map 17 A2.
((212) 360-5000.

Ferragamo
661 5th Ave.
Map 12 F3.
((212) 759-3822.

Harry's
2299 Broadway.
Map 15 C2.
((212) 874-2035.

Jeffrey's
449 W 14th St.
Map 3 B1.
((212) 206-1272.

Little Eric
1331 3rd Ave.
Map 17 B5.
((212) 288-8987.

Shoofly
465 Amsterdam Ave.
Map 15 C4.
((212) 580-4390.

Martinez Valero
1029 Third Ave.
Map 13 B3.
((212) 753-1822.

Sigerson Morrison
28 Prince St.
Map 4 F3.
((212) 219-3893.

LINGERIE

La Petite Coquette
51 University Place.
Map 4 E1.
((212) 473-2478.

Victoria's Secret
34 E 57th St.
Map 12 F3.
((212) 758-5592.
One of several branches.

Books and Music

As the publishing capital of America, it's not surprising that New York has the country's best selection of bookstores. These range from vast general interest stores to hundreds of esoteric bookstores specializing in everything from sci-fi to suspense, selling new books and old. Music lovers will also find sounds for all tastes at reasonable prices, plus thousands of rare recordings.

GENERAL INTEREST BOOKSTORES

One of the most well-known of New York's bookstores – for best prices as well as selection of titles – is **Barnes & Noble** on Fifth Avenue, reputedly the world's largest bookstore and packed high with over three million books on every imaginable subject. There are branches all over the City, plus the sales annex across the street, with amazing bargains.

Several blocks away is the main branch of New York's famous **Strand Book Store**. The Strand, as those in the know refer to it, has an astonishing two million copies of new and secondhand books. There is also a large rare book room for first editions.

Gryphon Bookshop is as comprehensive as its music counterpart, as it stocks an enormous collection of used books and country/bluegrass LPs. **12th Street Books** has a good selection of new and used books, and art books. Both branches of **Borders Books & Music** offer a choice of CDs and books of all genres.

In midtown, **Rizzoli** has an enormous selection of photography, foreign language, music and art books plus children's books and videos. **Gotham Book Mart**, a New York institution, is a tiny shop with hundreds of out-of-print books and limited editions.

Shakespeare & Co. offers a sensational selection of titles and is open late every night.

SPECIALTY BOOKSTORES

For the best selection of art books in the city, visit **Hacker Art Books**. **Urban Center Books** has titles on urban planning and other conservation issues. The city's largest selection of theatrical books and publications is found at **Drama Book Shop**. Jewish books and music abound at **J. Levine Judaica**. Rare books, books out-of-print and old books about New York are the *raison d'être* of **JN Bartfield Books**. The **Biography Bookshop** is the only midtown store specializing in diaries, letters, biographies and auto-biographies. Theater buffs should try **Applause Theater & Cinema Books**.

For hundreds of titles on science, business, technology and computers visit **McGraw-Hill Bookstore**.

Books on murder and suspense are the focus of two shops: **Murder Ink** and **Mysterious Bookshop**.

Try **Forbidden Planet** for old and new science fiction books and comics. The **Village Comics** has thousands of old and new comics to suit all tastes.

Bank Street Book Store has one of the best selections of current children's books. Visit **Books of Wonder** for a variety of hardcover and rare children's books.

Travelers' Choice specializes in travel guides, maps, videos and travel accessories. **The Complete Traveler** also stocks a wide selection of brand-new and antique travel books and guides for your trip, on everywhere from Alabama to Zimbabwe. The staff is very knowledgeable and more than helpful.

For an excellent range of maps visit the large **Rand McNally Map & Travel Store** and the **Hagstrom Map & Travel Store**. Cookbooks are on the menu at **Kitchen Arts & Letters**, with many out-of-print books and first editions. Radicals should head for **Revolution Books** or **St. Mark's Bookstore,** which also has an excellent selection of literary and art titles.

The **Oscar Wilde Memorial Bookshop** has a wide selection of gay and lesbian texts.

RECORDS, TAPES AND COMPACT DISCS

The best Manhattan record-store chain is **Tower Records**, whose three stores have everything from bebop to rap. **HMV** and **Virgin** follow a close second. **J&R Music World** is a complete home entertainment store with one of the best CD selections in the city.

For out-of-print records, go to **Gryphon Records**, a treasure trove for collectors with an excellent choice of classical, jazz and opera recordings. **Footlight Records** is for lovers of Broadway musicals and film soundtracks, and **House of Oldies** has a massive stock of deleted and rare records to suit all tastes. **Bleecker Bob's Golden Oldies** Record Shop has everything from imports, rock and punk to rare jazz. Try **Midnight Records** for imports, reissues, American garage rock and psychedelia.

One of the oldest record stores in New York is **Vinylmania**. This is a must-stop for anyone looking for deep-house vinyl, or house music on CD. True music enthusiasts should head to **Other Music**, which stocks obscure gems, from hot electronica to 70's free jazz.

SHEET MUSIC

Just behind Carnegie Hall is one of the best stores for classical sheet music, **Joseph Patelson Music House Ltd**. The **Frank Music Company** has a huge collection of classical music scores. **Charles Colin Publications** specializes in jazz. For chart music and pop tunes try **Colony Record and Music Center** in the Brill Building.

DIRECTORY

GENERAL INTEREST BOOKSTORES

Barnes & Noble
105 5th Ave. **Map** 8 F5.
((212) 807-0099.
One of many branches.

Borders Books & Music
461 Park Avenue.
Map 17 A3.
((212) 980-6785.
One of two branches.

Gotham Book Mart
41 W 47th St. **Map** 12 F5.
((212) 719-4448.

Gryphon Bookshop
2246 Broadway.
Map 15 C4.
((212) 362-0706.

Rizzoli
31 W 57th St.
Map 12 F3.
((212) 759-2424.
One of several branches.

Shakespeare & Co
716 Broadway.
Map 4 E2.
((212) 529-1330.

939 Lexington Ave.
Map 13 A1.
((212) 570-0201.

Strand Book Store
828 Broadway.
Map 4 E1.
((212) 473-1452.

12th Street Books
11 East 12th St.
Map 4 F1.
((212) 645-4340.

SPECIALTY BOOKSTORES

Applause Theater & Cinema Books
211 W 71st St.
Map 11 C1.
((212) 496-7511.

Drama Book Store
723 7th Ave.
Map 12 E5.
((212) 944-0595.

Bank Street Book Store
610 W 112th St.
Map 21 A4.
((212) 678-1654.

Biography Bookshop
400 Bleecker St.
Map 3 C2.
((212) 807-8655.

Books of Wonder
16 W 18th St.
Map 8 E5.
((212) 989-3270.

The Complete Traveler
199 Madison Ave.
Map 9 A2.
((212) 685-9007

Forbidden Planet
840 Broadway.
Map 4 E1.
((212) 473-1576.

Hacker Art Books
45 W 57th St.
Map 12 F3.
((212) 688-7600.

Hagstrom Map & Travel Store
57 W 43rd St.
Map 8 F1.
((212) 398-1222.

J. Levine Judaica
5 W 30th St.
Map 8 F3.
((212) 695-6888.

JN Bartfield Books
30 W 57th St.
Map 12 F3.
((212) 245-8890.

Kitchen Arts & Letters
1435 Lexington Ave.
Map 17 A2.
((212) 876-5550.

McGraw-Hill Bookstore
1221 6th Ave.
Map 12 E4.
((212) 512-4100.

Murder Ink
2486 Broadway.
Map 15 C2.
((212) 362-8905.

Mysterious Bookshop
129 W 56th St.
Map 12 E3.
((212) 765-0900.

Oscar Wilde Memorial Bookshop
15 Christopher St.
Map 3 C2.
((212) 255-8097.

Rand McNally Map & Travel Store
150 E 52nd St.
Map 13 A4.
((212) 758-7488.

Revolution Books
9 W 19th St.
Map 7 C5.
((212) 691-3345.

St. Mark's Bookshop
31 3rd Ave.
Map 5 A2.
((212) 260-7853.

Travelers' Choice
2 Wooster St.
Map 4 E4.
((212) 941-1535.

Urban Center Books
457 Madison Ave.
Map 13 A4.
((212) 935-3592.

Village Comics
214 Sullivan St.
Map 4 D2.
((212) 777-2770.

RECORDS, TAPES, COMPACT DISCS

Bleecker Bob's Golden Oldies
118 W 3rd St.
Map 4 D2.
((212) 475-9677.

Footlight Records
113 E 12th St.
Map 4 F1.
((212) 533-1572.

Gryphon Records
233 W 72nd St.
Map 11 D1.
((212) 874-1588.

HMV
57 W 34 St.
Map 8 E2.
((212) 681-6700.
One of several branches.

House of Oldies
35 Carmine St.
Map 4 D3.
((212) 243-0500.

J&R Music World
31 Park Row.
Map 1 C2.
((212) 238-9100.

Midnight Records
263 W 23rd St.
Map 8 D4.
((212) 675-2768.

Other Music
15 E 4th St. **Map** 4 F2.
((212) 477-8150.

Tower Records
1961 Broadway.
Map 11 C1.
((212) 799-2500.
One of three branches.

Vinylmania
60 Carmine St.
Map 4 D3.
((212) 924-7223.

Virgin Megastore
45th & Broadway.
Map 12 E5.
((212) 921-1020.
One of several branches.

SHEET MUSIC

Charles Colin Publications
315 W 53rd St.
Map 12 D4.
((212) 581-1480.

Colony Record and Music Center
1619 Broadway.
Map 12 E4.
((212) 265-2050.

Frank Music Company
244 W 54th St.
Map 12 D4.
((212) 582-1999.

Joseph Patelson Music House Ltd
160 W 56th St.
Map 12 E4.
((212) 757-5587.

Art and Antiques

ANY ART-LOVING VISITOR to New York could easily spend several days gallery-hopping around the several hundred galleries found throughout New York. Antique lovers can find an exciting variety of goods, including Americana and many bargains, at the many flea markets; or they can browse through European and American fine antiques in one of the more exclusive antiques centers. To find out what's happening, pick up the free monthly *Art Now Gallery Guide,* available at most galleries, or check the local papers.

ART GALLERIES

ONE OF THE MOST well known galleries in New York is **Leo Castelli**, an important showcase for Pop Art during the early 1960s and now spotlighting new artists. **Mary Boone Gallery** features Neo-Expressionist artists such as Julian Schnabel. **Pace Wildenstein Gallery** exhibits current stars, especially well-known painter-photographers, and the trendy gallery **Gorney, Bravin & Lee** deals in contemporary art and sculpture. The **John Weber Gallery** features new talent but is famous for its many Minimalists and Conceptualists. **Postmasters** is a treasure trove of conceptual pieces.

The venerable **Swann Galleries** has prints, books, maps, posters, autographs and photographs; **Marian Goodman Gallery** features the European avant-garde.

Chelsea is a good center for galleries and the **Mathew Marks Gallery** and **Marienne Boesky Gallery** are usually worth a visit. The **Gagosian Gallery** exhibits paintings by modern masters, with great works by Lichtenstein and Johns. It also has an outlet in the Upper East Side where you can find **Knoedler & Company**, and the **Hirschl & Adler Galleries** with a good selection of European and American fine art.

AMERICAN FOLK ART

IF YOU'RE in the market for American folk art, go to **Susan Parrish Antiques** for a selection of hooked rugs and other Americana. Similar goods are at **Laura Fisher**, who sells everything from decoys to hooked rugs.

ANTIQUES CENTERS AND SECONDHAND ANTIQUES

IN ADDITION TO hundreds of small shops selling everything from tiger teeth to multimillion-dollar paintings, Manhattan is home to **The Manhattan Art & Antiques Center**, which has dozens of dealers under one roof. The **Chelsea Antiques Building** is home to more than 100 galleries of antiques over twelve floors. Collectibles include Hollywood memorabilia and rare personal items of stars like Garbo and Bogart. **Irving Barber Shop Antiques** is filled with fabulous secondhand finds at astoundingly good prices.

AMERICAN FURNITURE

FOR FURNITURE from the 17th- 18th- and 19th-centuries, try **Bernard & S. Dean Levy**, **Eagles Antiques**, or **Leigh Keno American Furniture**. **Judith & James Milne** sell early American country furniture and a splendid collection of quilts. Go to **Woodard & Greenstein American Antiques & Quilts** for a truly wonderful selection of Shaker pieces.

Collectors of Art Deco or Art Nouveau furniture should pay a visit to **Alan Moss**, which is full of furniture and decorative items. **Macklowe Gallery & Modernism** has a massive collection of fine Art Nouveau furniture. **Lillian Nassau** has Tiffany lamps and many Art Nouveau and Art Deco pieces.

New York has a handful of retro shops, though numbers are growing all the time. Two of the best are **Depression Modern** and **Mood Indigo**, which have treasures from the 1930s and 1940s.

INTERNATIONAL ANTIQUES

IF YOU'RE LOOKING for English antiques, try **Florian Papp** and **Kentshire Galleries**. For European pieces, you'll have plenty of choices; try **Betty Jane Bart Antiques**, **Kurt Gluckselig Antiques**, **The Little Antique Shop**, **Linda Horn Antiques**, **La Belle Epoque**, and **Les Pierres**. Oriental dealers include **Doris Leslie Blau**, **E. & J. Frankel** and **Flying Cranes Antiques**.

FLEA MARKETS

NEW YORK HAS a number of year-round weekend markets. Most flea markets officially open at 9 or 10am, but the haggling starts as early as 6am. If you arrive early, you could unearth some valuable piece of cultural Americana like a Barbie lunch box or a Soupy Sales record.

Visit the **Annex Antiques Fair and Flea Market** for everything from secondhand clothing to antique furniture. The weekend **Canal Street Flea Market** has bric-a-brac; the **Columbus Avenue Flea Market** has new and secondhand clothing and furniture. For information on all street fairs and flea markets, check Friday's *The New York Times.*

AUCTION HOUSES

MANHATTAN'S TWO most celebrated auction houses are **Christie's** and **Sotheby's**, selling collectibles ranging from coins, jewels, and vintage wines to fine and decorative arts. **William Doyle Galleries** and **Phillips Fine Art Auctioneers** are both well-respected names for fine art, jewelry, and antiques. Items for sale are previewed several days before the auctions, so check the Friday and Sunday *Times.*

DIRECTORY

ART GALLERIES

Gagosian Gallery
555 W 24th St.
Map 7 C4.
📞 *(212) 741-1111.*

Gorney, Bravin & Lee
534 W 26 St.
Map 7 C4.
📞 *(212) 352-8372.*

Hirschl & Adler Galleries
21 E 70th St.
Map 12 F1.
📞 *(212) 535-8810.*
One of several branches.

John Weber Gallery
530 W 25th St, Suite 19.
Map 7 C4.
📞 *(212) 691-5711.*

Knoedler & Company
19 E 70th St.
Map 13 A1.
📞 *(212) 794-0550.*

Leo Castelli
18 E 77th St.
Map 17 A5.
📞 *(212) 249-4470.*

Marian Goodman Gallery
24 W 57th St.
Map 12 F3.
📞 *(212) 977-7160.*

Marienne Boesky Gallery
535 W 22nd St.
Map 7 C4.
📞 *(212) 680-9889.*

Mary Boone Gallery
745 5th Ave.
Map 12 F3.
📞 *(212) 752-2929.*

Mathew Marks Gallery
523 W 24th St.
Map 7 C4.
📞 *(212) 243-0200.*

Pace Wildenstein Gallery
534 W 25th St.
Map 7 C4.
📞 *(212) 929-7000.*

Postmasters
459 W 19th St. **Map** 7 C5
📞 *(212) 727-3323.*

Swann Galleries
104 E 25th St.
Map 9 A4.
📞 *(212) 254-4710.*

AMERICAN FOLK ART

Laura Fisher
Manhattan Art & Antiques Center, 1050 2nd Ave.
Map 13 B4.
📞 *(212) 838-2596.*

Susan Parrish Antiques
390 Bleecker St.
Map 3 C2.
📞 *(212) 645-5020.*

ANTIQUE CENTERS AND SECOND-HAND ANTIQUES

Chelsea Antiques Building
110 W 25th St. **Map** 8 F4.
📞 *(212) 929-0909.*

Irving Barber Shop Antiques
210 E 21st St.
Map 9 A4.
no phone.

The Manhattan Arts & Antiques Center
1050 2nd Ave.
Map 13 A3.
📞 *(212) 355-4400.*

AMERICAN FURNITURE

Alan Moss
436 Lafayette St.
Map 4 F2.
📞 *(212) 473-1310.*

Bernard & S. Dean Levy
24 E 84th St.
Map 16 F4.
📞 *(212) 628-7088.*

Depression Modern
150 Sullivan St.
Map 4 D3.
📞 *(212) 982-5699.*

Eagles Antiques
1097 Madison Ave.
Map 17 A5.
📞 *(212) 861-8797.*

Judith & James Milne
506 E 74th St. **Map** 17 C5.
📞 *(212) 472-0107.*

Leigh Keno American Furniture
127 E 69th St. **Map** 17 A5.
📞 *(212) 734-2381.*

Lillian Nassau
220 E 57th St. **Map** 13 B3.
📞 *(212) 759-6062.*

Macklowe Gallery & Modernism
667 Madison Ave.
Map 13 A3.
📞 *(212) 644-6400.*

Mood Indigo
181 Prince St. **Map** 4 E3.
📞 *(212) 254-1176.*

Woodard & Greenstein American Antiques
506 E 74th St. **Map** 17 A5.
📞 *(212) 988-2906.*

INTERNATIONAL ANTIQUES

La Belle Epoque
280 Columbus Ave.
Map 12 D1.
📞 *(212) 362-1770.*

Betty Jane Bart Antiques
1225 Madison Ave.
Map 17 A3.
📞 *(212) 410-2702.*

Doris Leslie Blau
724 5th Ave. **Map** 12 F3.
📞 *(212) 586-5511.*
By appointment only.

E & J Frankel
1040 Madison Ave.
Map 17 A5.
📞 *(212) 879-5733.*

Florian Papp
962 Madison Ave. **Map** 17 A5. 📞 *(212) 288-6770.*

Flying Cranes Antiques
1050 2nd Ave. **Map** 13 B4.
📞 *(212) 223-4600.*

Kentshire Galleries
37 E 12th St. **Map** 4 E1.
📞 *(212) 673-6644.*

Kurt Gluckselig Antiques
200 E 58th St.
Map 13 B3.
📞 *(212) 758-1805.*

Linda Horn Antiques
1015 Madison Ave.
Map 17 A5.
📞 *(212) 772-1122.*

The Little Antique Shop
44 E 11th St.
Map 4 E1.
📞 *(212) 673-5173.*

Les Pierres
367 Bleecker St. **Map** 3 C2.
📞 *(212) 243-7740.*

FLEA MARKETS

Annex Antiques Fair and Flea Market
24th to 27th Sts at 6th Ave.
Map 8 E4.
📞 *(212) 243-5343.*
Open Sat and Sun.

Canal Street Flea Market
335 Canal St. **Map** 4 E5.
Open every weekend Mar–Dec.

Columbus Avenue Flea Market
Columbus Ave, between 76th and 77th St.
Map 16 D5.
📞 *(212) 877-7371.*
Open Sun.

AUCTION HOUSES

Christie's
20 Rockefeller Plaza.
Map 12 F5.
📞 *(212) 636-2000.*

Sotheby's
1334 York Ave.
Map 13 C1.
📞 *(212) 606-7000.*

William Doyle
175 E 87th St. **Map** 17 A3. 📞 *(212) 427-2730.*

Phillips Fine Art
450 W 15th St. **Map** 7 C5.
📞 *(212) 940-1200.*

Food and Household Goods

NEW YORK'S STRIKING cultural and ethnic diversity is celebrated in its food – the city's food shops provide a truly international feast. There is also a dazzling array of household goods, electronics and photographic equipment available almost everywhere you turn.

GOURMET GROCERIES

SCATTERED AROUND town are several famous food emporiums that are tourist attractions in themselves. Remember, too, to visit the department stores, which often rival the specialty food stores.

At **Dean & DeLuca**, a chic delicatessen, food has been elevated to an art form – don't miss the huge selection of take-out food. **Russ & Daughters**, one of the oldest gourmet shops, is known as an "appetizing" store, full of ethnic food and famous for smoked fish, cream cheese, chocolates and bagels. **The Gourmet Garage** sells all kinds of delicious fresh food, in particular organic produce. **Zabar's** is perhaps the finest food store in the world, with huge crowds jostling for the excellent smoked salmon, bagels, caviar, cheese and coffee.

William Poll offers picnic hampers as well as a great variety of prepared dishes. For pâté de foie gras, Scottish smoked salmon, and caviar, go to **Caviarteria**.

SPECIALTY FOOD AND WINE SHOPS

FABULOUS BREAD and cake shops abound but one of the best is **Poseidon Greek Bakery**, renowned for its filo pastry. **H & H Bagels** bakes 60,000 of the best bagels every day. **Vesuvio** has Italian bread and some unusual pepper biscuits. Try **Fung Wong** for delicious Chinese pastries or purchase a traditional Sicilian loaf from **A. Zito & Sons Bakery**.

For a choice of over 250 kinds of cheese, as well as olives and charcuterie, visit **Murray's Cheese Shop**. Great confectionery shops include **Li-Lac** for handmade chocolates and **Mondel**

Chocolates for chocolate animals. **Economy Candy** has a huge selection of dried fruit but for a real treat go to **Teuscher**, which has fresh champagne truffles flown in direct from Switzerland.

Myers of Keswick imports English food. For something more exotic, **Kam Man Food Products** is an Oriental grocery selling Chinese, Thai, and other oriental products. The **Italian Food Center** has great olive oils, dried pastas and sausages, and try **Raffeto's Corporation** for every kind of pasta. Go to **Jefferson Market** for meat and fish, and **Citarella** for its fine seafood. **Angelica's Herbs and Spices** has a selection of 2,000 varieties of herbs and spices.

For fine burgundies, **Acker, Merrall & Condit** is a good choice. Go to **Garnet Liquors** for fine wines and champagnes at bargain prices. **SoHo Wines and Spirits** has an extensive selection of single-malt Scotch whisky. **Sherry-Lehmann** is New York's leading wine merchant.

New York also has many fine coffee stores. Among the best are **Oren's**, **The Sensuous Bean** and **Porto Rico Importing Company**, each with a mouth-watering selection. For fruit and vegetables at reasonable prices, visit a farmers' market, but get there early. Among the most popular are **City Hall**, **Upper West Side**, **St. Mark's in-the-Bowery**, and **Union Square**. For information about the city's markets, phone: 788-7900.

HOUSEHOLD GOODS

MOST OF THE department stores offer a wide range of household goods. For a specialized shop, try **Broadway Panhandler**, a cook's heaven with outstanding baking and pastry-making

equipment. **Bridge Kitchenware** is a household name among most restaurateurs. **Williams-Sonoma** has many cooking utensils and cookbooks. **Zabar's** has a great selection of cooking utensils.

Baccarat, **Daum**, **Lalique** and **Villeroy & Boch** are where you'll find the finest crystal, china and silverware. Other fashionable shops include **Orrefors Kosta Boda** and **Tiffany & Co**. Go to **Avventura** for crystal and china and, for the best of inexpensive, utilitarian American china, visit **Fishs Eddy**. Also visit **Ceramica**, which stocks lovely handmade Italian pottery, and **La Terrine** and **Steuben Glass** for hand-painted ceramics.

Inexpensive linens can be found in most department stores, but for silk sheets and luxurious linens, visit **Porthault** and **Pratesi**. **ABC Carpet & Home** has an enviable reputation for home furnishings as does **Bed, Bath & Beyond** for its bed linens, kitchen and bath accessories. For the lowest prices, shop-hop on Grand Street on the Lower East Side.

ELECTRONICS AND PHOTOGRAPHIC EQUIPMENT

PERHAPS THE MOST competitive retailers in New York are the ones that sell electronics, and it pays to shop around. If you're buying electrical goods to take to Europe, make sure they have compatible voltages and formats (many in the US are made to different standards).

B & H Photo is where amateur and professional photographers can find everything they need. Another place for computer equipment is **CompUSA**. **J&R Music World** sells competitively priced equipment and has the best jazz CD selection in the city. **The Wiz** offers a wide range of equipment and games. Check the newspapers for **Willoughby's**; they have good sales on photographic equipment and supplies.

DIRECTORY

GOURMET GROCERIES

Caviarteria
502 Park Ave. **Map** 13 A3.
[(212) 759-7410.

Dean & DeLuca
560 Broadway. **Map** 4 E3.
[(212) 226-6800.

Gourmet Garage
435 Broome St. **Map** 4 E4.
[(212) 941-5850.
One of several branches.

Russ & Daughters
179 E Houston St.
Map 5 A3.
[(212) 475-4880.

William Poll
1051 Lexington Ave.
Map 17 A5.
[(212) 288-0501.

Zabar's
2245 Broadway.
Map 15 C4.
[(212) 787-2000.

SPECIALTY FOOD AND WINE SHOPS

A Zito & Sons Bakery
259 Bleecker St. **Map** 3 C2.
[(212) 929-6139.

Acker, Merrall & Condit
160 W 72nd St. **Map** 11 C1.
[(212) 787-1700.

Angelica's Herbs and Spices
147 1st Ave. **Map** 5 A1.
[(212) 677-1549.

Citarella
2135 Broadway.
Map 15 C5.
[(212) 874-0383.

City Hall Green Market
Centre St and Chambers St.
Map 1 C1.

Economy Candy
108 Rivington St. **Map** 5 A3.
[(212) 254-1531.

Fung Wong
41 Mott St. **Map** 4 F3.
[(212) 267-4037.

Garnet Liquors
929 Lexington Ave. **Map** 13
A1. [(212) 772-3211.

H & H Bagels
2239 Broadway. **Map** 15
C4. [(212) 595-8003.
One of two branches.

Italian Food Center
186 Grand St. **Map** 15 C4.
[(212) 925-2954.

Jefferson Market
450 Ave of the Americas.
Map 12 E5.
[(212) 533-3377.

Kam Man Market
200 Canal St. **Map** 4 F5.
[(212) 571-0330.

Li-Lac
120 Christopher St. **Map** 3
C2. [(212) 242-7374.

Mondel Chocolates
2913 Broadway.
Map 20 E3.
[(212) 864-2111.

Murray's Cheese Shop
257 Bleecker St. **Map** 3 C2.
[(888) 692-4339.

Myers of Keswick
634 Hudson St. **Map** 3 C2.
[(212) 691-4194.

Oren's
1144 Lexington Ave.
Map 17 A4.
[(212) 472-6830.

Porto Rico Importing Company
201 Bleecker St. **Map** 3 C2.
[(212) 477-5421.
One of several branches.

Poseidon Greek Bakery
629 9th Ave. **Map** 12 D5.
[(212) 757-6173.

Raffeto's Corporation
144 West Houston St.
Map 4 D3.
[(212) 777-1261.

St. Mark's in-the-Bowery Greenmarket
E 10th St at 2nd Ave.
Map 4 F1.

The Sensuous Bean
66 W 70th St. **Map** 12 D1.
[(212) 724-7725.

Sherry-Lehmann
679 Madison Ave.
Map 13 A3.
[(212) 838-7500.

SoHo Wines and Spirits
461 W Broadway.
Map 4 E4.
[(212) 777-4332.

Teuscher Chocolates
25 E 61st St. **Map** 12 F3.
[(212) 751-8482.
620 5th Ave. **Map** 12 F4.
[(212) 246-4416.

Union Square Greenmarket
E 17th St and Broadway.
Map 8 F5.

Upper West Side Greenmarket
Columbus Ave at 77th St.
Map 16 D5.

Vesuvio Bakery
160 Prince St. **Map** 4 E3.
[(212) 925-8248.

HOUSEHOLD GOODS

ABC Carpet & Home
888 Broadway.
Map 8 F5.
[(212) 473-3000.

Bed, Bath & Beyond
620 Ave of the Americas
Map 8 F5.
[(212) 255-3550.

Avventura
463 Amsterdam Ave.
Map 15 C4.
[(212) 769-2510.

Baccarat
625 Madison Ave.
Map 13 A3.
[(212) 826-4100.

Bridge Kitchenware
214 E 52nd St.
Map 13 B4.
[(212) 688-4220.

Broadway Panhandler
477 Broome St.
Map 4 E4.
[(212) 966-3434.

Ceramica
59 Thompson St.
Map 4 D4.
[(212) 941-1307.

Daum Boutique
694 Madison Ave.
Map 13 A3.
[(212) 355-2060.

Fishs Eddy
2176 Broadway.
Map 15 C5.
[(212) 873-8819.

Lalique
712 Madison Ave.
Map 13 A3.
[(212) 355-6550.

Orrefors Kosta Boda Crystal
685 Madison Ave.
Map 13 A3.
[(212) 752-1095.

Porthault
18 E 69th St. **Map** 12 F1.
[(212) 688-1660.

Pratesi
829 Madison Ave.
Map 13 A2.
[(212) 288-2315.

Steuben Glass
667 Madison Ave. **Map** 13
A3. [(212) 752-1441.

La Terrine
1024 Lexington Ave.
Map 13 A1.
[(212) 988-3366.

Tiffany & Co
See p321.

Villeroy & Boch
901 Broadway.
Map 8 F5.
[(212) 535-2500.

Williams-Sonoma
20 E 60th St. **Map** 13 A3.
[(212) 980-5155.
One of three branches.

Zabar's
See Gourmet Groceries.

ELECTRONICS AND PHOTOGRAPHIC EQUIPMENT

B & H Photo
420 9th Ave. **Map** 8 D2.
[(212) 444-6615.

J&R Music World
See p322.

The Wiz
555 5th Ave. **Map** 12 F5.
[(212) 557-7770.
One of several branches.

CompUSA
420 5th Ave. **Map** 8 F1.
[(212) 627-0222.

Willoughby's
138 W 32nd St. **Map** 8 E3.
[(212) 564-1600.

ENTERTAINMENT IN NEW YORK

NEW YORK CITY IS a non-stop entertainment extravaganza, every day, all year round. Whatever your taste, you can be sure the city will satisfy it on both a grand and an intimate scale. The challenge is to take advantage of as many of the entertainments as possible. If it's theater, you can enjoy a main-stream success on Broadway or take a chance on an experimental production in a loft. If it's music, there's the magnificence of opera at the Met or a jazz group blowing in a club in the Village. You can catch a spectacle of avant-garde dance in a café or try your own avant-garde dancing in one of the city's warehouse-sized clubs. Movie theaters abound. But perhaps best of all is wandering and watching the vast show that is New York.

Performance by the New York City Ballet

PRACTICAL INFORMATION

FIND OUT what events there are to choose from in the arts and leisure listings of the *New York Times* and the *Village Voice* newspapers and in *Time Out New York* and

TKTS discount ticket booth - great for last minute theater offers

The New Yorker magazines. These briefly describe the current entertainment and tell you which credit cards are accepted at the venue. At your hotel ask for *Where*, a free weekly magazine containing maps and information on the many attractions.

Hotel staff may be able to answer some of your questions and should also carry a wide selection of brochures and leaflets. In addition, they may be willing to reserve tickets for you. Some hotel TVs have a New York visitor information channel.

The New York Convention and Visitors Bureau, which is known as **NYC & Company** is the city's official source for everything to do and see in the city. Touch-screen kiosks provide information and sell general admission tickets to the city's top attractions.

Multilingual counselors, discount coupons, free maps, brochures, tour information and ATMs are available.

NYC On Stage is a telephone hotline for theater, dance and music events; **Broadway Line** gives brief descriptions of current shows, schedules and the different prices; **Moviefone** gives recorded information on all the films; and **ClubFone** has up-to-date information on nightlife.

BOOKING TICKETS

POPULAR SHOWS may be sold out for weeks ahead, so book early. Box offices are open daily, except Sundays, from 10am until one hour after the performance begins. Call in person, or phone the box office or a ticket agency and order your seats by credit card. The biggest agencies are

Bobby Short singing at the Café Carlyle (p343)

Telecharge, **Ticketmaster** and **Ticket Central**; they will charge a small fee of a few dollars. An independent ticket agent may also be able to find seats for you – try **Prestige Entertainment**; others are listed in the Yellow Pages. Fees vary according to demand. **Broadway Ticket Center** in the Times Square Visitors Center sells full-price tickets.

DISCOUNT TICKETS

ESTABLISHED in 1973 to the advantage of theaters and theater-goers alike, the non-profit TKTS company sells un-sold tickets on the day of the performance for all Broadway shows. Discounts range from 25% to 50%, but the price will include a small handling fee and must be paid for in cash or by traveler's check.

The **TKTS** booth at Duffy Square sells matinée tickets from 10am to 2pm every Wednesday and Saturday; evening tickets are sold from 3pm to 8pm, and Sunday tickets from 11am until 7:30pm. The booth at South Street Seaport sells evening tickets from 10am to 6pm from Monday through Thursday. All matinée tickets are sold the day before. Queues at these booths get long particularly during the vacation season.

You can purchase day-of-performance tickets from **Ticketmaster** at discounts of 10% to 25% (with a small commission

The Booth Theater on Broadway *(see p333)*

charge) by telephone. The **Hit Show Club** sells vouchers that can be exchanged at box offices for discounted tickets.

Some shows offer standing-room tickets on the day at a bargain price. It's often the only way to catch a sold-out show on short notice, but you might not get the best view.

"SCALPERS" AND TOUTS

IF YOU BUY from a "scalper" (a ticket tout), you risk getting tickets for the wrong day, counterfeit tickets, and paying outrageous prices. The police often monitor sports and theater venues for scalpers and their customers.

FREE TICKETS

FREE TICKETS to TV shows, concerts, and special events are sometimes offered at the **NYC & Company Visitor Information Center**, which is open from 8:30am to 6pm Monday to Friday and 9am to 5pm on weekends. Free or deeply discounted tickets to film or theater premieres are often advertised in the *New York Times, Daily News* or *Time Out New York*. The "Cheap Thrills" section in the *Village Voice* lists poetry readings, recitals, and experimental films. The New York Shakespeare Festival at the **Delacorte Theater** in Central Park offers free tickets – one ticket per person – on a

first-come, first-served basis. The line forms at noon on the day of the performance. Take a picnic basket and blankets for a very enjoyable day out.

Free tickets for TV video-taping sessions are available by writing to the networks or from their on-street agents at the **Rockefeller Center**.

Royale Theater in the heart of Broadway *(see p333)*

DISABLED ACCESS

BROADWAY THEATERS reserve a few spaces and cut-price tickets for the disabled. Call **Ticketmaster** or **Tele-charge** well in advance for informa-tion and to reserve tickets. For Off-Broadway theaters, call their box offices. Some theaters offer equipment for the hearing-impaired. **Tap** can arrange sign language for Broadway theaters.

USEFUL CONTACTS

Broadway Line
📞 *(212) 563-2929.*

ClubFone
📞 *(212) 777-2582.*

Delacorte Theater
Entrance via 81st St at Central Park W. **Map** 16 E4.
📞 *(212) 861-7277.*
🔳 www.publictheater.org
Summer time only.

Hit Show Club
8th floor, 630 9th Ave. **Map** 12 D5. 📞 *(212) 581-4211.*

Moviefone (see p337)

Movie Tickets Online
🔳 www.movietickets.com
🔳 www.fandango.com

Prestige Entertainment
📞 *(212) 697-7788.*

Network Tickets
ABC.
67th St and Columbus Ave.
📞 *(212) 456-3537.*
CBS.
524 W 57th St.
📞 *(212) 975-2476.*

New York Convention Center & Visitors Bureau (NYC & Co.)
810 7th Ave **Map** 12 E4.
📞 *(212) 484-1222.*
🔳 www.newyork.citysearch.com
🔳 www.nycvisit.com

NYC On Stage
1501 Broadway. **Map** 12 D2.
📞 *(212) 768-1818.*

Tap (Theatre Access Project)
📞 *(212) 221-1103 (Voice).*

Telecharge
📞 *(212) 239-6200, (800) 545-2559.* 🔳 www.telecharge.com

Ticket Central
📞 *(212) 279-4200.*
🔳 www.ticketcentral.org

Ticketmaster
📞 *(212) 307-4100.*
🔳 www.ticketmaster.com

TKTS
📞 *(212) 221-0013.*
Duffy Square. **Map** 12 E5.
South Street Seaport. **Map** 2 D2.

New York's Best: Entertainment

Greenwich Village jazz club

Nᴇᴡ ʏᴏʀᴋ is one of the great entertainment capitals of the world. Top names in every branch of the arts are drawn here to perform and often to live and work. Major sports events are also constant, and as for nightlife, New York lives up to its reputation as "the city that never sleeps." From the huge choice offered, there are some venues and events that stand out as classics of their kind; this selection has been chosen from the listings on pages 332 to 347 as among those not to be missed. Even if you experience only one of them, you will have been part of something as essentially New York as the Empire State Building.

Avalon
Nightclubs come and go, but this converted church has become a firm favorite with New York's night owls. (See p342.)

Madison Square Garden
Top sporting action is found at "the Garden," including home games for basketball's New York Knicks and ice hockey's Rangers, plus the Golden Gloves boxing tournament. (See p344.)

Film Forum
At New York's most stylish arts movie theater you can see the latest foreign and American independent releases or catch up with a classic in a wide range of retrospectives. (See p336.)

Village Vanguard
The jazz clubs of Greenwich Village have played host to all the great names in jazz. Fans can catch the stars of today and tomorrow at the world-famous Village Vanguard and the Blue Note. (See p340.)

Philharmonic Rehearsals
*The Thursday-morning
rehearsals at Avery Fisher
Hall are often open to
the public at a fraction of
the normal ticket price.*
(See p338.)

Metropolitan Opera House
*Reserve well ahead and prepare
to pay high prices to see the giants
of the opera world.* (See p338.)

**Shakespeare in
Central Park**
*If you are a
summer visitor,
set aside a time
to get one of
the rare free
tickets for the
Delacorte
Theater's open-air Shakespeare
featuring top Hollywood and
Broadway names.* (See p332.)

The Nutcracker
*The Christmas event for children of
every age is performed each year at
Lincoln Center by the New York City
Ballet.* (See p334.)

0 kilometers   2

0 miles   1

Public Theater
*Founded in 1954,
the Public has a
mandate to create
theater for all New
Yorkers. Its year-
round Shakespeare
Festival is part of
a commitment to
classical works,
but new plays are
also developed here.*
(See p118).

Carnegie Hall
*Conveniently situated in the
Theater District, Carnegie Hall is
famous the world over as a showcase for the best in the musical arts.
A backstage tour gives a fascinating insight into "the house that
music built."* (See p338.)

Theater and Dance

NEW YORK IS FAMOUS for its extravagant musicals and its ferocious critics. It is one of the world's greatest theater and dance centers, featuring every kind of production imaginable. Whether your preference is for the glitz and glamour of a Broadway blockbuster or something truly experimental, you'll find it here.

BROADWAY

BROADWAY HAS long been synonymous with New York's Theater District, but the majority of Broadway theaters are actually scattered between 41st and 53rd streets and from Sixth to Ninth Avenues, with a few around the much-improved Times Square. Most were built between 1910 and 1930, during the heyday of vaudeville and the famous Ziegfeld Follies. The **Lyceum** *(see p142)* is the oldest theater still in operation (1903), the **American Airlines Theater**, permanent home of the Roundabout Theater Co., is the newest, and the historic **Biltmore Theater** opened in 2003 after a 14-year closure.

Many Broadway theaters went through a slump in the 1980s but are now enjoying a revival, using big names to draw in the crowds and benefiting from the Times Square renewal. This is where you will find the "power productions" – the big, highly publicized dramas, musicals and revivals starring Hollywood luminaries in (it is hoped) sure-fire earners. Hits have included imports such as *Les Misérables;* New York originals like *Cats* and *The Producers;* the popular children's favorite *The Lion King;* and great revivals like *42nd Street.*

OFF-BROADWAY AND OFF-OFF-BROADWAY

THERE ARE about 20 Off-Broadway stages and 300 Off-Off-Broadway stages whose works will sometimes transfer to Broadway. Off-Broadway theaters have from 100 to 499 seats, and Off-Off-Broadway showplaces have fewer than 100. Both range from the well-appointed to the improvised, sited in lofts,

churches and even garages. Off-Broadway became very popular during the 1950s as a reaction to the commercialism of Broadway. It was also an ideal place for more cautious producers to try out works considered too avant-garde or unsuitable for Broadway at much lower operating costs. During the last two decades, Off-Off-Broadway theaters have become the venue for the more experimental pieces by these same producers.

Off-Broadway theaters are found all over Manhattan – from the **Douglas Fairbanks Theater**, where the irreverent *Forbidden Broadway* plays, to Central Park's open-air **Delacorte Theater**. Some are even in the traditional Broadway district, such as the **Manhattan Theater Club**. Farther afield are the **Brooklyn Academy of Music (BAM)** *(see p246),* and the **92nd Street Y**. In these venues you will always find lively, unusual and experimental showcases for new talent as well as lots of uninhibited productions.

The Off-Broadway theaters mounted the first productions in New York of the works of playwrights Sean O'Casey, Tennessee Williams, Eugene O'Neill, Samuel Beckett, Jean Genet, Eugene Ionesco and David Mamet. They host new and very often irreverent treatments of the classics, and every imaginable theatrical presentation is floated.

Sometimes a more intimate, smaller Off-Broadway stage suits a production better than a larger more established theater would, as proved by such long-running successes as *The Fantasticks* and the *Threepenny Opera*. Of course, there are flops occasionally – but that's show business.

PERFORMANCE THEATER

THIS EXTREMELY avant-garde art form can be found in several Off- and Off-Off-Broadway locations. Accurate descriptions and categorizations are almost impossible, but expect the bizarre and outlandish. The most likely venues to find this are **La MaMa**, **P.S. 122**, **HERE**, **92nd Street Y**, **Symphony Space** and the Joseph Papp **Public Theater** *(see p118).* The latter is perhaps the most influential theater in New York. It was founded in the 1950s by the late director Joseph Papp, who introduced neighborhood tours to bring theater to people who had never seen it before.

The Public Theater created hits like *Hair* and *A Chorus Line;* it is most famous for its free summer performances of Shakespeare at the Delacorte Theater in Central Park *(see p206).* It usually has several productions running, and at 6pm on the day of performance, "Quiktix" tickets (limited to two per person) are sold in the Public Theater lobby.

THEATER SCHOOLS

NEW YORK is the best place in the country to see actors learning their trade. Foremost among the acting schools is **The Actors' Studio**. The late Lee Strasberg, the advocate of method acting – in which the actor aims for complete identification with the character being played – was its guru. His students included Dustin Hoffman, Al Pacino and Marilyn Monroe. "In progress" productions feature trainees and are usually open to the public. Sandy Meisner trained many actors, including the late Lee Remick, at the **Neighborhood Playhouse School of the Theater**. Its plays are not open to the public. The **New Dramatists** began in 1949 to develop new playwrights, helping the careers of the likes of William Inge. Play readings are open to the public and free.

BROADWAY THEATERS

① Ambassador
219 W 49th St.
(212) 239-6200.

② Barrymore
243 W 47th St.
(212) 239-6200.

③ Belasco
111 W 44th St.
(212) 239-6200.

④ Booth
222 W 45th St.
(212) 239-6200.

⑤ Broadhurst
235 W 44th St.
(212) 239-6200.

⑥ Broadway
1681 Broadway.
(212) 239-6200.

⑦ Brooks Atkinson
256 W 47th St.
(212) 307-4100.

⑧ CORT
138 W 48th St.
(212) 239-6200.

⑨ Eugene O'Neill
230 W 49th St.
(212) 239-6200.

⑩ Gershwin
222 W 51st St.
(212) 307-4100.

⑪ John Golden
252 W 45th St.
(212) 239-6200.

⑫ Helen Hayes
240 W 44th St.
(212) 307-4100.

⑬ Imperial
249 W 45th St.
(212) 239-6200.

⑭ Longacre
220 W 48th St.
(212) 239-6200.

⑮ Lunt–Fontanne
205 W 46th St.
(212) 307-4747.

⑯ Lyceum
149 W 45th St.
(212) 239-6200.

⑰ Majestic
247 W 44th St.
(212) 239-6200.

⑱ Marquis
1535 Broadway.
(212) 307-4100.

⑲ Martin Beck
302 W 45th St.
(212) 239-6200.

⑳ Minskoff
200 W 45th St.
(212) 307-4100.

㉑ Music Box
239 W 45th St.
(212) 239-6200.

㉒ Nederlander
208 W 41st St.
(212) 307-4100.

㉓ Neil Simon
250 W 52nd St.
(212) 307-4100.

㉔ Palace
1564 Broadway.
(212) 307-4747.

㉕ Plymouth
236 W 45th St.
(212) 239-6200.

㉖ Richard Rodgers
226 W 46th St.
(212) 307-4100.

㉗ American Airlines Theater
227 W 42nd St.
(212) 719-1300.

㉘ Royale
242 W 45th St.
(212) 239-6200.

㉙ St. James
246 W 44th St.
(212) 239-6200.

㉚ Shubert
225 W 44th St.
(212) 239-6200.

㉛ Virginia
245 W 52nd St.
(212) 239-6200.

㉜ Walter Kerr
219 W 48th St.
(212) 239-6200.

㉝ Winter Garden
1634 Broadway.
(212) 239-6200.

For other theaters *see p335.*

BALLET

AT THE HEART of the dance world is Lincoln Center (see p212), where the New York City Ballet performs pieces in the **New York State Theater**. This company was created by the legendary brilliant choreographer George Balanchine (see p46) and is probably still the best in the world. The current director, Peter Martins, was one of Balanchine's best dancers and continues the strict policy of ensemble dancing rather than "star turns." The season runs from November to February and late April to early June. The ballet school at the **Juilliard Dance Theater** also presents a spring workshop every year, and this is a good chance to see budding stars.

The American Ballet Theater appears at the **Metropolitan Opera House**, which also hosts many visiting foreign companies, such as the Kirov, Bolshoi and Royal ballets. Its repertoire includes 19th-century classics, such as *Swan Lake*, and works by modern choreographers like Twyla Tharp and Paul Taylor.

CONTEMPORARY DANCE

NEW YORK is the center of many of the most important movements in modern dance. The **Dance Theater of Harlem** is world famous for its modern, traditional and ethnic productions. Other havens of experimental dance include the **92nd Street Y** and the **Merce Cunningham Studio** in Greenwich Village. The unusual **Dance Theater Workshop** has a packed program as well as an art gallery. **The Kitchen**, **La MaMa**, **Symphony Space** and **P.S. 122** are all multimedia venues with the latest in contemporary dance, performance art and avant-garde music. Choreographer Mark Morris's company performs at the brand new **Mark Morris Dance Center** in Brooklyn; **City Center** (see p146) is a favorite spot for dance fans. It used to house the New York City Ballet and the American Ballet Theater

before Lincoln Center was built. As well as featuring the Joffrey Ballet, City Center has held performances by all the great contemporary artists, including Alvin Ailey's blend of modern, jazz and blues and the companies of modern dance masters Merce Cunningham and Paul Taylor. Avoid the mezzanine as the view is restricted.

The city's single most active venue for dance is probably the **Joyce Theater,** where such well-established companies as the Feld Ballet, along with bold newcomers and visiting troupes, perform.

Each spring the Festival of Black Dance at the **Brooklyn Academy of Music (BAM)** (see p246) features everything from ethnic dance to hip-hop. During autumn the "Next Wave" festival of music and dance is held, celebrating international and American avant-garde dance and music. During winter the American Ballet Festival is held here.

During June, **New York University** (see p113) holds a Summer Residency Festival with lecture-demonstrations, rehearsals and performances, and **Dancing in the Streets** organizes summertime dance performances all over the city.

Throughout the month of August, **Lincoln Center Out of Doors** has a program of free dance events on the plaza, with such experimental groups as the American Tap Dance Orchestra.

The new **Duke Theater** presents many contemporary dance companies and participates in events such as the New York Tap Festival.

At different times of the year, **Radio City Music Hall** holds several spectacular shows, with different companies from all over the world. At Christmas and Easter, it features the famously precise Rockettes dance troupe.

Choreographers and dance companies frequently present works-in-progress and recitals to the public. Among the most interesting venues for these is **Alvin Ailey's Repertory Ensemble**, famous for promoting black cultural expression, which is opening

the country's largest dance facility in 2004. The **Hunter College Dance Company** performs new works by its student choreographers, and the **Isadora Duncan Dance Foundation** re-creates Duncan's original dances. To see contemporary choreographers the best place to go is **Juilliard Dance Theater**.

PRICES

THEATER is extremely expensive to produce, and ticket prices tend to reflect this. Even Off- and Off-Off-Broadway tickets are not cheap anymore. At one time, all tickets to previews of new plays sold at a much-reduced price, but not so today. Preview tickets are easier to get hold of, though, and it's fun to see a show before the reviews are in so you're able to make up your own mind.

For a Broadway theater ticket you can expect to pay $80 or more; for musicals, up to $100; Off-Broadway, $25 to $40. For dance, $20 to $50 is the usual range, with up to $115 for the American Ballet Theater.

TIMES OF PERFORMANCE

THE GENERAL RULES for theater hours are: closed on Mondays (except for most musicals), with matinees on Wednesdays, Saturdays and sometimes Sundays. Matinees usually begin at 2pm, with evening performances at 8pm. Be sure to check the correct dates and times of the performance beforehand.

BACKSTAGE TOURS AND LECTURES

FOR THOSE INTERESTED in the mechanics and anecdotes of the theater, your best bet is to go on one of the theater tours. The **92nd Street Y** organizes insider's views of the theater, with famous directors, actors and choreographers taking part. Writers are invited along to read or discuss their current works. **Radio City Music Hall** also holds tours.

DIRECTORY

OFF-BROADWAY

92nd Street Y
Lexington Ave.
Map 17 A2.
 (212) 415-5420.

Actors' Playhouse
100 Seventh Ave S.
Map 3 C1.
 (212) 463-0060.

American Place
111 W 46th St.
Map 12 E5.
 (212) 840-3074.

**Brooklyn
Academy of Music**
30 Lafayette St., Brooklyn.
 (718) 636-4100.

HERE Art Center
145 6th Ave.
Map 4 D4.
 (212) 647-0202.

**Circle in the
Square**
1633 Broadway.
Map 12 E4.
 (212) 239-6200.

Delacorte Theater
Central Park. (81st St.)
Map 16 E4.
 (212) 861-7277.
Summer time only.

**Douglas
Fairbanks Theater**
432 W 42nd St.
Map 7 C1.
 (212) 239-6200.

John Houseman
450 W 42nd St.
Map 7 C1.
 (212) 967-9077.

Lambs Theater
130 W 44th St.
Map 12 E5.
 (212) 997-1780.

**Manhattan
Theater Club**
311 W 43rd St.
Map 8 D1.
 (212) 399-3030.

**New York Theater
Workshop**
79 E 4th St. **Map** 4 F2.
 (212) 460-5475.

Public Theater
425 Lafayette St.
Map 4 F2.
 (212) 539-8500.

Symphony Space
2537 Broadway.
Map 15 C2.
 (212) 864-5400.

Vivian Beaumont
Lincoln Center.
Map 11 C2.
 (212) 362-7600.

OFF-OFF-BROADWAY

**Bouwerie Lane
Theater**
330 Bowery.
Map 4 F2.
 (212) 677-0060.

The Kitchen
512 W 19th St.
Map 7 C5.
 (212) 255-5793.

**Performing
Garage**
33 Wooster St.
Map 4 E4.
 (212) 966-3651.

**Theater at St.
Peter's Church**
Citigroup Center, 619
Lexington Ave.
Map 13 A4.
 (212) 935-5824.

PERFORMANCE
THEATER

La MaMa
74a E 4th St.
Map 4 F2.
 (212) 475-7710.

P.S. 122
150 First Ave.
Map 5 A1.
 (212) 477-5288.

Public Theater
See Off-Broadway.

THEATER SCHOOLS

**The Actors'
Studio**
432 W 44th St.
Map 11 C5.
 (212) 757-0870.

New Dramatists
424 W 44th.
Map 11 C5.
 (212) 757-6960.

DANCE

92nd Street Y
See Off-Broadway.

**Alvin Ailey American
Dance Center**
211 W 61st St.
Map 11 C3.
 (212) 767-0590.

**Brooklyn
Academy
of Music**
See Off-Broadway.

City Center
131 W 55th St.
Map 12 E4.
 (212) 581-7907.

**Dance Theater of
Harlem**
466 W 152nd St.
 (212) 690-2800.

**Dance Theater
Workshop**
219 W 19th St. **Map** 8 E5.
 (212) 924-0077.

**Dancing in the
Streets**
55 6th Ave. *(offices)*
 (212) 625-3505.

**Hunter College
Dance Company**
695 Park Ave.
Map 13 A1.
 (212) 772-4490.

**Isadora Duncan
Dance Foundation**
141 W 26th St.
Map 20 D2.
 (212) 691-5040.

Joyce Theater
175 Eighth Ave at 19th St.
Map 8 D5.
 (212) 242-0800.

**Juilliard Dance
Theater**
60 Lincoln Center Plaza,
W 65th St.
Map 11 C2.
 (212) 769-7406.

PERFORMANCE
VENUES

Duke Theater
229 W 42nd St.
Map 8 E1.
 (646) 223-3000.

The Kitchen
See Off-Off Broadway.

La MaMa
See Performance Theater.

**Lincoln Center
Out of Doors**
Lincoln Center, Broadway
at 64th St. **Map** 11 C2.
 (212) 362-6000.

Manhattan Center
311 W 34th St. **Map** 8
D2. (212) 279-7740.

Mark Morris
3 Lafayette St. (Brooklyn)
 (718) 624-8400.

**Merce Cunning-
ham Studio**
55 Bethune St. **Map** 3 B2.
 (212) 691-9751.

**Metropolitan
Opera House**
Lincoln Center,
Broadway at 65th St.
Map 11 C2.
 (212) 362-6000.

**New York State
Theater**
Lincoln Center, Broadway
at 65th St. **Map** 11 C2.
 (212) 870-5570.

**New York
University**
Tisch School of the Arts
(TSOA), 111 2nd Ave.
Map 4 F1. (212) 998-
1920.

P.S. 122
See Performance Theater.

**Radio City Music
Hall**
50th St at Ave of the
Americas. **Map** 12 F4.
 (212) 307-7171.

Symphony Space
See Off-Broadway.

BACKSTAGE TOURS

92nd Street Y
See Off-Broadway.

**Radio City Music
Hall**
 (212) 307-7171.

W **EVENTS GUIDE**
www.broadway.org
www.playbill.com
www.newyork.citysearch.
com

Movies

NEW YORK is a film buff's paradise. Apart from new US releases, which show months in advance of other countries, many classic and foreign films are screened here.

The city has always been the testing ground for new developments in films, and it continues to be a hotbed of new and innovative talent. Many of the movies' most famous directors – Spike Lee, Martin Scorsese and Woody Allen – were born and raised in New York, and the city's influence can be seen in many of their films. They, and others, can often be seen filming on the streets of the city; many of New York's landmarks have become famous after appearing in films. Most of the TV networks based in New York offer free tickets to the taping of their shows. Watching a show, such as *The David Letterman Show,* is popular with visitors.

FIRST-RUN MOVIES

NEW YORK REVIEWS and box office returns are so vital to a film's success that most major American films have their premieres in Manhattan's theaters. First-run films are shown mainly at the City Cinema chains, Loews, United Artists and Cineplex Odeon, which are scattered around the city. Some theaters have recorded information giving the names and duration of the different films showing, with starting times and ticket prices.

Programs start at 10am or 11am and are repeated every two to three hours until midnight. You should expect to line up for most evening and weekend performances of the more popular films. Making reservations using a credit card is possible at some

theaters for an additional charge of about $1 per ticket. Matinées (usually before 4pm) are easier to get into. Senior citizens pay a reduced price for tickets: the required age may be over 60, 62 or 65 depending on the policy of the theater.

NEW YORK FILM FESTIVAL

A HIGH POINT of the year for film buffs is the New York Film Festival, now in its third decade. Organized by the **Film Society of Lincoln Center**, the festival starts in late September and continues for two weeks at the many Lincoln Center theaters. Outstanding new films from the United States and abroad are entered in a competition that has no prizes except for the huge prestige of winning an award. Many of the films shown during the festival are later released and can usually be seen only in art houses.

FOREIGN FILMS AND ART HOUSES

FOR THE LATEST foreign and independent films, go to the **Angelika Film Center**, which has six screens and an upscale coffee bar. Other good places are the 4-screen **Rose Cinemas** at the Brooklyn Academy of Music, the stylish **Film Forum**, and **Lincoln Plaza Cinema**. The Plaza has a busy program of art and art foreign films. For Asian,

FILM RATINGS

Films in the United States are graded as follows:
G General audiences; all ages admitted.
PG Parental guidance suggested; some material unsuitable for children.
PG-13 Parents strongly cautioned; some material inappropriate for children under age 13.
R Restricted. Children under 17 need to be accompanied by a parent or an adult guardian.
NC-17 No children under 17 admitted.

ON LOCATION

Many New York locations have played starring roles in films. Here are a few:

The Brill Building (1141 Broadway) contained Burt Lancaster's penthouse in *Sweet Smell of Success.*
The Brooklyn Bridge was a great backdrop in Spike Lee's *Mo' Better Blues.*
Brooklyn Heights and the **Metropolitan Opera** appeared in *Moonstruck.*
Central Park has shown up in countless films, including *Love Story* and *Marathon Man.*
55 Central Park West will be remembered as Sigourney Weaver's home in *Ghostbusters.*
Chinatown played a major role in *Year of the Dragon.*
The Dakota was where Mia Farrow lived in the classic *Rosemary's Baby.*
The Empire State Building is still standing after *King Kong*'s last battle. The observation deck is where Cary Grant waited in vain in *Affair to Remember;* here Meg Ryan finally met Tom Hanks in *Sleepless in Seattle.*
Grand Central Station is famous for Robert Walker's meeting with Judy Garland in *Under the Clock* and the magical ballroom sequence in *The Fisher King.*
Harlem hosted the jazz musicians and dancers in *The Cotton Club.*
Katz's Deli was the setting for the café scene between Billy Crystal and Meg Ryan in *When Harry Met Sally...*
Little Italy appeared in *The Godfather I* and *II.*
Madison Square Garden was the setting for the dramatic climax of *The Manchurian Candidate.*
Tiffany & Co. was Audrey Hepburn's favorite shop in *Breakfast at Tiffany's.*
The United Nations Building featured in *North by Northwest.*
Washington Square Park was where Robert Redford and Jane Fonda walked *Barefoot in the Park.*

Asian, Indian and Chinese films, you should visit the **Asia Society**. The **French Institute** screens many French films with English subtitles and plays host to the Asian American International Film Festival. The **Quad Cinema** shows a wide selection of foreign films, often quite rare. **Cinema Village** runs special film events, such as the Festival of Animation.

The **Walter Reade Theater** houses the Film Society of the Lincoln Center, offering retrospectives of international movies as well as celebrations of contemporary works, such as the popular annual Spanish Cinema Now festival.

On weekends order tickets ahead of time and arrive 30 minutes in advance, especially for new releases.

CLASSIC FILMS AND MUSEUMS

RETROSPECTIVES OF films by particular directors or featuring specific actors are shown at the **Public Theater** and the **Whitney Museum of American Art** (see pp198–9), The **American Museum of the Moving Image** (see p244) screens old films and also has many exhibits of memorabilia from the film industry. The **Museum of Television & Radio** (see p169) has regular screenings of classic films; you can also see or hear specific television or radio programs. Students interested in classic, new and experimental movies will appreciate the huge wealth of material at the **Anthology Film Archives.**

The sky shows at the **Rose Center for Earth and Space** at the **American Museum of Natural History** are well worth a whole day's visit.

On summer evenings in Bryant Park, you can watch free classic movies, and on Saturday mornings, the **Film Society of Lincoln Center,** where special children's shows are held.

TELEVISION SHOWS

A NUMBER of TV programs originate in New York. By writing several months in advance, you may be able to see one being taped for broadcast. The popular David Letterman show is almost impossible to get tickets for, but tickets are available for *Saturday Night Live* at **NBC**; tickets may be found at NBC's desk in the Rockefeller Center (212 664-3700 for information). To request free tickets from **ABC** and **CBS**, write to each company individually.

Another good source of free tickets is the Times Square Visitors Information Bureau (see p352). On weekday mornings on Fifth Avenue around **Rockefeller Plaza**, free tickets for a number of TV programs are sometimes distributed by the program's production staff. There's absolutely no way that you can plan for this. It's simply a matter of good luck and being in the right place at the right time.

For those who want to get a glimpse behind the scenes of TV, NBC organizes tours around the studios, usually from 9am to 4pm Monday to Saturday.

CHOOSING WHAT TO SEE

I F YOU FEEL bewildered by the huge range of films offered in New York, check the listings in *New York* magazine, the *New York Times*, the *Village Voice* and *The New Yorker*. The following Internet guides give show times and locations:
w www.moviefone.com
w www.movietickets.com.

FILM HOUSES

ABC
See p329.

American Museum of the Moving Image
35th Ave and 36th St
Astoria, Queens.
((718) 784-0077.

American Museum of Natural History
Central Park W at 79th St.
Map 16 D5.
((212) 769-5650.

Angelika Film Center
18 W Houston St. **Map** 4
E3. ((212) 995-2000.

Anthology Film Archives
32 2nd Ave at 2nd St.
Map 5 C2.
((212) 505-5181.

Asia Society
725 Park Ave.
Map 13 A1.
((212) 517-2742.

Rose Cinemas
Brooklyn Academy of
Music.
((718) 623-2770.

CBS
See p329.

Cinema Village
22 E 12th St.
Map 4 F1.
((212) 924-3363.

Film Forum
209 W Houston St.
Map 3 C3.
((212) 727-8110.

French Institute
55 E 59th St.
Map 12 F3.
((212) 355-6160.

Lincoln Plaza Cinema
1886 Broadway.
Map 12 D2.
((212) 757-2280.

Moviefone
((212) 777-FILM.

Museum of Modern Art
11 W 53rd St.
Map 12 F4.
((212) 708-9480.

Museum of Television & Radio
25 W 52nd St.
Map 12 F4.
((212) 621-6600.

New York Film Festival
((212) 875-5600.

Public Theater
425 Lafayette St.
Map 4 F4.
((212) 539-8500.

Quad Cinema
34 W 13th St.
Map 4 D1.
((212) 255-8800.

Rockefeller Plaza
47th–50th St, 5th Ave.
Map 12 F5.

Walter Reade Theater/Film Society of the Lincoln Center
70 Lincoln Center Plaza.
Map 12 D2.
((212) 875-5600.

Whitney Museum of American Art
945 Madison Ave.
Map 13 A1.
((212) 570-3600.

Classical and Contemporary Music

N EW YORKERS HAVE A voracious appetite for music. Live concerts by the world's most celebrated musical performers may be enjoyed at famous halls throughout the year, and younger, newer artists and exotic imports always find receptive audiences.

TICKETS

F IND OUT WHAT you can choose from in New York by checking out the listings in the *New York Times* and the *Village Voice* and in *Time Out New York* and *The New Yorker* magazines.

CLASSICAL MUSIC

T HE ORCHESTRA in residence at **Avery Fisher Hall** in Lincoln Center (*see p213*) is the New York Philharmonic. It is also the annual site for the popular "Mostly Mozart" series and Young People's Concerts. **Alice Tully Hall**, in Lincoln Center, is an acoustic gem and home to the Chamber Music Society.

One of the world's premier concert halls is the revamped **Carnegie Hall** (*see p146*). Upstairs in the Weill Recital Hall there are quality performances for reasonable prices.

The **Brooklyn Academy of Music (BAM)** (*see p246*) is the home of the Brooklyn Philharmonic. The **New Jersey Performance Arts Center** in Newark is the newest star in the music venue crown. Classical music, dance, opera, jazz and world music all find an audience here.

The **Merkin Concert Hall** is host to some top chamber ensembles and soloists. For really excellent acoustics, go to the **Town Hall**. The **92nd Street Y's** Kaufmann Concert Hall also offers a lively menu of music and dance. There's also the **Frick Collection**

CLASSICAL RADIO
New York has three FM radio stations that broadcast classical music: WQXR at 96.3, the National Public Radio station WNYC at 93.9 and WKCR 89.9.

and **Symphony Space**, both of which offer a varied program ranging from gospel to Gershwin, classical to ethnic. The beautiful Grace Rainey Rogers Auditorium in the **Metropolitan Museum of Art** is for chamber music and soloists, while the **Florence Gould Hall**, at the Alliance Française, presents a varied program of chamber music and orchestral pieces.

The **Juilliard School of Music** and the **Mannes College of Music** are both considered excellent. Their students and faculties give free recitals, and there are shows by leading orchestras, chamber music groups and opera companies. The **Manhattan School of Music** offers an excellent program of over 400 events per year, from classical to jazz.

At 9:45am on the Thursdays of the New York Philharmonic concerts, the evening show is rehearsed at **Avery Fisher Hall** in Lincoln Center. Audiences are often admitted to listen, and rehearsal tickets are available at low prices. The **Kosciuszko Foundation** hosts the annual Chopin Competition. **Corpus Christi Church** has an active concert schedule, presenting such groups as the Tallis Scholars.

OPERA

D OMINATING the city's operatic scene is **Lincoln Center** (*see p212*), home to the New York City Opera, and the **Metropolitan Opera House**, which has its own opera company. The Met is the jewel in the crown, offering top international performers. More accessible and dynamic is the New York City Opera. Its performances range from *Madame Butterfly* to *South Pacific*, with subtitles above the stage to help the audience understand the plot.

Lower-priced quality performances are staged by the up-and-coming singers at the **Village Light Opera Group**, the **Amato Opera Theater**, the **Kaye Playhouse** at Hunter College, and the students at the **Juilliard Opera Center** in Lincoln Center.

CONTEMPORARY MUSIC

N EW YORK is one of the most important places in the world for contemporary music. Exotic, ethnic and experimental music is played in many first-rate venues. The **Brooklyn Academy of Music (BAM)** is the standard-bearer of the avant-garde. Each autumn the Academy holds a festival of music and dance called "Next Wave," which has helped launch many musical careers.

An annual festival of serious modern music called "Bang on a Can" is performed at the **Ethical Culture Society Hall** and features works by Steve Reich, Pierre Boulez and John Cage. Experimentalists, such as Davie Weinstein with his "audio-visual acid test" music – a mix of CD players, amplified instruments, keyboards and sound effects – perform at the **Dance Theater Workshop**.

Other venues include the **Asia Society** (*see p185*), with its jewel of a theater for many visiting Asian performers, and **St. Peter's Church**.

BACKSTAGE TOURS

B EHIND-THE-SCENES tours are offered by **Lincoln Center** and **Carnegie Hall**.

RELIGIOUS MUSIC

F EW EXPERIENCES are more moving than an Easter concert in the vast **Cathedral of St. John the Divine** (*see pp224–5*). Seasonal music is also offered at many of the city's museums and in almost every other available space – from Grand Central Terminal's main concourse (*see pp154–5*) to bank and hotel lobbies. For jazz vespers in a stunning modern building, visit **St.**

Peter's Church *(see p175)*. Most of these concerts are free, but you are encouraged to contribute.

ALFRESCO

FREE OUTDOOR summer concerts occur in **Bryant Park, Washington Square** and **Lincoln Center's Damrosch Park**. The annual concerts on Central Park's Great Lawn and in Brooklyn's Prospect Park are performed by the New York Philharmonic and the Metropolitan Opera. In good weather, strolling musicians perform at South Street Seaport, on the steps

of the **Metropolitan Museum of Art** *(see pp188–95)*, and in the area around Washington Square.

MUSIC FOR FREE

THROUGHOUT the year free musical performances are given at the **Citigroup Atrium** *(see p175)*, **The Cloisters** *(see pp234–7)* and the **Whitney Museum's** Philip Morris Building *(see p150)*. Sunday-afternoon recitals are held at **The Dairy** in Central Park *(see p206)*. You will also find music in the **Federal Hall** *(see p68)*, while at **Lincoln Center,**

don't miss the exciting free performances held in the **Juilliard School of Music**. Other very popular venues include the **Greenwich House Music School** (free student recitals) and the **Theodore Roosevelt Birthplace** *(see p125)*. Numerous free concerts and talks take place in the city's churches, including **St. Paul's Chapel** and **Trinity Church Wall Street.** *(see p68)*.

W INTERNET EVENTS GUIDE

www.culturefinder.com
www.nytoday.com
www.newyork.citysearch.com

MUSIC VENUES

92nd Street Y
1395 Lexington Ave.
Map 17 A2.
(*(212) 996-1100.*

Amato Opera Theater
319 Bowery at 2nd St.
Map 4 F2. (*(212) 228-8200.*

Asia Society
725 Park Ave. **Map** 13 A1.
(*(212) 288-6400.*

Brooklyn Academy of Music
30 Lafayette Ave, Brooklyn.
(*(718) 636-4100.*

Bryant Park
Map 8 F1.
(*(212) 768-4242.*

Carnegie Hall
881 7th Ave. **Map** 12 E3.
(*(212) 247-7800.*

Cathedral of St. John the Divine
1047 Amsterdam Ave and 112th St. **Map** 20 E4.
(*(212) 316-7540.*

Citigroup Atrium
Lexington Ave at 53rd St.
Map 13 A4.
(*(212) 559-6892.*

The Cloisters
Fort Tryon Park.
(*(212) 923-3700.*

Corpus Christi Church
529 W 121st St. **Map** 20 E2.
(*(212) 666-9350.*

The Dairy
Central Park at 65th St.
Map 12 F2.
(*(212) 794-6564.*

Dance Theater Workshop
See Dance p335.

Ethical Culture Society Hall
2 W 64th St.
Map 12 D2.
(*(212) 874-5210.*

Federal Hall
26 Wall St.
Map 1 C3.
(*(212) 825-6888.*

Florence Gould Hall (at the Alliance Française)
55 E 59th St.
Map 13 A3.
(*(212) 355-6160.*

Frick Collection
1 E 70th St.
Map 12 F1.
(*(212) 288-0700.*

Greenwich House Music School
46 Barrow St.
Map 3 C2.
(*(212) 242-4770.*

Kaye Playhouse (Hunter College)
695 Park Ave.
Map 13 A1.
(*(212) 772-4448.*

Kosciuszko Foundation
15 E 65th St. **Map** 12 F2
(*(212) 734-2130.*

Lincoln Center
155 W 65th St.
Map 11 C2.
(*(212) 546-2656.*

Tours for all venues at Lincoln Center can be arranged by calling:
(*(212) 875-5350.*

Alice Tully Hall
(*(212) 875-5050.*

Avery Fisher Hall
(*(212) 875-5030.*

Damrosch Park
(*(212) 875-5596.*

Juilliard Opera Center
(*(212) 769-7406.*

Juilliard School of Music
(*(212) 799-5000.*

Metropolitan Opera House
(*(212) 362-6000.*

Manhattan School of Music
120 Claremont Ave.
Map 20 E2.
(*(212) 749-2802.*

Mannes College of Music
150 W 85th St.
Map 15 D3.
(*(212) 580-0210.*

Merkin Hall
129 W 67th St.
Map 11 D2.
(*(212) 501-3330.*

Metropolitan Museum of Art
1000 5th Ave at 82nd St.
Map 16 F4.
(*(212) 535-7710.*

New Jersey Performance Arts Center
1 Center St, Newark, NJ.
(*(888) 466-5722.*

NYC On Stage
1501 Broadway.
Map 12 D2.
(*(212) 768-1818.*

St. Paul's Chapel
Broadway at Fulton St.
Map 1 C2.
(*(212) 602-0874.*

St. Peter's Church
54th St at Lexington Ave.
Map 13 A4.
(*(212) 935-2200.*

Symphony Space
2537 Broadway. **Map** 15 C2.
(*(212) 864-5400.*

Theodore Roosevelt Birthplace
28 E 20th St. **Map** 8 F5.
(*(212) 260-1616.*

Town Hall
123 W 43rd St. **Map** 8 E1.
(*(212) 997-1003.*

Trinity Church
Broadway at Wall St.
Map 1 C3.
(*(212) 602-0800.*

Village Light Opera Group
12 W 12th St. **Map** 4 D1.
(*(212) 243-6281.*

Washington Square
Map 4 D2.

Whitney Museum
120 Park Ave at 42nd St.
Map 9 A1.
(*(212) 663-2453.*

Rock, Jazz and World Music

THERE'S EVERY IMAGINABLE form of music in New York, from international stadium rock to the sounds of the 1960s, from Dixieland jazz or country blues, soul and world music to talented street musicians. The city's music scene changes at a dizzying pace, with many new arrivals (and departures) almost daily, so there's no way to predict what you may find when you arrive. Musical standards also vary.

PRICES AND PLACES

AT CLUBS, EXPECT to pay a cover charge and possibly a one- or two-drink minimum (at $5 or more) requirement. The prices for concerts range from $8 to $75 for the major venues, with about $12 to $25 the norm. Many of the smaller concert venues are arranged for seating in certain areas and dancing in others – often with different prices for each.

The top international bands are usually to be found in the huge arenas at **Shea Stadium** in Flushing Meadows or at the **Meadowlands** and **Madison Square Garden** (*see p133*). Here the likes of Elton John, Bruce Springsteen and the Stones perform. Tickets for these events sell out very fast, so buy as many as you need as soon as you hear of a concert, unless you don't mind paying a lot for them through an agent or a scalper. During the summer, big outdoor concerts are held at Jones Beach (*see p253*) and **Central Park SummerStage**.

Medium-sized venues for mainstream bands include the Art Deco palace of **Radio City Music Hall** and the **Beacon Theater**, by far the most popular live-music venues are in the Upper West Side area.

Many leading rock venues are basically bars with music. They will often book different bands every night, so check the listings in the *New York Times*, *Village Voice* or *Time Out New York* or phone the place to find out what's happening and at what time during that particular week.

ROCK MUSIC

ROCK COMES IN many forms: gothic, industrial, techno, psychedelic, post-punk funk, indie and alternative music are among the latest crazes. If you prefer to see more of a band than a giant video screen, the following venues have a much more intimate, friendly atmosphere. **CBGB**, New York's sleazy, dungeon-like cradle of new wave, launched such bands as Talking Heads and Blondie in the 1970s and is still a show-case for new indie bands.

The **Knitting Factory** has live jazz and new music while **The Mercury Lounge** is one of the most happening music spots, featuring hot new bands being groomed for MTV. **Irving Plaza** is where relatively unknown and sometimes known rock groups play, as do the occasional famous country and blues musicians.

Mega-star Bruce Springsteen played his first recorded concert in the 1970s at the **Bottom Line**, and it still remains a record industry showcase for new bands.

Bands appearing at the **Acme Underground** are mostly up-and-coming acts, given a chance to find fame in the rock music world.

The **Hammerstein Ballroom** at the Manhattan Center in midtown hosts techno, progressive and alternative bands. **Roulette** has avant-garde sounds performed by such appropriately named groups such as Woof, Quack and Miaow.

JAZZ

THE ORIGINAL Cotton Club and Connie's Inn, which were once crucibles of jazz, are long gone, as are the former speakeasies of West 52nd Street. But living legends such as Maynard Ferguson still play, while others carry on the old traditions of Dave Brubeck, Les Paul, Duke Ellington, Count Basie and other big bands.

In Greenwich Village, jazz temples from the 1930s survive and continue to foster great music. Foremost among them is the **Village Vanguard**, where some of the most highly revered jazz memories linger and newer ones are being fashioned by such groups as the McCoy Tyner and Branford Marsalis trios. **Blue Note** hosts big bands at high prices but has an excellent atmosphere.

The **Knitting Factory** and the well-known **Bottom Line** feature contemporary and avant-garde jazz; **Smoke** is an intimate nightspot offering a divergent roster of musicians.

Birdland features ex-Mingus alumni and musicians such as Bud Shank. Expect the great sounds of Dixieland jazz or small unknown groups in **Cajun**, a friendly New Orleans–style restaurant.

Café Carlyle, an East Side spot famed for mellow jazz pianist and singer Bobby Short, now also features clarinetist-filmmaker Woody Allen playing with Eddy Davis and his New Orleans Jazz Band.

A sophisticated club and restaurant, **Iridium** features progressive jazz. **Fez under Time Café** presents the Mingus Big Band workshop every Thursday. If you're in New York in June, don't miss the annual **JVC Jazz Festival**, where such famous jazz and blues icons as Oscar Peterson, Nina Simone and B.B. King play at various clubs all around Manhattan.

Jazz at Lincoln Center events are scheduled through-out the year, including concerts by the renowned Lincoln Center Jazz Orchestra under the direction of Wynton Marsalis. The music ranges from Duke Ellington's New York sounds to Johnny Dodds' traditional New Orleans-style jazz. Jazz at Lincoln Center now has its own home since it moved into the world's first performing arts center specifically for jazz. It is housed in the new Time Warner Center on Columbus Circle. A multi-room facility perched above Central Park, with bandstands posed against sparing walls of glass and a dance floor beneath the moon and stars.

Finally, Friday night at the **Rose Center** (at **AMNH**) offers live jazz concerts.

FOLK AND COUNTRY MUSIC

FOLK, ROCK MUSIC and R&B (rhythm and blues) can be found at the famed but much-faded **Bitter End**, which once showcased James Taylor and Joni

Mitchell but now specializes in promising new talent as does **Kenny's Castaways**. Also worth checking out is the **Sidewalk Café**.

BLUES, SOUL AND WORLD MUSIC

FOR BLUES, soul and world music, options include the **Apollo Theater** in Harlem (see p228). For nearly 60 years the near-legendary Wednesday Amateur Nights have been responsible for discovering and launching stars, including James Brown and Dionne Warwick.

The **Cotton Club** is no longer located in its original spot, but the modern venue offers good blues, jazz and a Sunday real Gospel brunch

on Harlem's main street. **Go** is a trendy club, decorated all in white. Don't miss "Mambo Mondays" with Nestor Torres at **SOB's** (Sounds of Brazil), a world music club specializing in Afro-Latin rhythms.

Terra Blues's bar doubles as an interesting music venue. The blues artists that appear here can range from authentic Chicago acoustic players to more modern blues acts.

A recent addition on the music scene is **C–Note**, a venue that has steadily gained in popularity, and finally, **Tonic** offers a mix of improv, jazz, and blues from a rotating cast of artists.

DIRECTORY

MUSIC VENUES

Beacon Theater
2124 Broadway.
Map 15 C5.
📞 (212) 496-7070.

Central Park SummerStage
Rumsey Playfield.
Map 12 F1.
📞 (212) 360-2777.

Madison Square Garden
7th Ave 33rd St.
Map 8 E2.
📞 (212) 465-6741.

Meadowlands
50 Route 120
East Rutherford, N J.
📞 (201) 935-3900.

Radio City Music Hall
See Dance p335.

Shea Stadium
126th St at Roosevelt Ave.
Flushing, Queens.
📞 (718) 507-8499.

ROCK MUSIC

Acme Underground
9 Great Jones St.
Map 4 F2.
📞 (212) 677-6963.

Bottom Line
15 W 4th St. **Map** 4 D2.
📞 (212) 228-6300.

CBGB
315 Bowery. **Map** 4 F2.
📞 (212) 982-4052.

Knitting Factory
74 Leonard St. **Map** 4 E5.
📞 (212) 219-3006.

Mercury Lounge
217 E Houston St.
Map 5 A3.
📞 (212) 260-4700.

Hammerstein Ballroom
311 W 34th St. **Map** 8 D2.
📞 (212) 279-7740.

Roulette
228 W Broadway. **Map** 4 E5.
📞 (212) 219-8242.

Irving Plaza
17 Irving Pl. **Map** 9 A5.
📞 (212) 777-6800.

JAZZ

Birdland
315 W 44th St. **Map** 12 D5.
📞 (212) 581-3080.

Blue Note
131 W 3rd St.
Map 4 D2.
📞 (212) 475-8592.

Café Carlyle
95 E 76th St.
Map 17 A5.
📞 (212) 744-1600.

Cajun
129 8th Ave. **Map** 8 D5.
📞 (212) 691-6174.

Fez under Time Café
380 Lafayette St.
Map 4 F2.
📞 (212) 533-2680.

Iridium
1650 Broadway.
Map 12 D2.
📞 (212) 582-2121.

Jazz at Lincoln Center
📞 (212) 258-9800.

JVC Jazz Festival
📞 (212) 501-1390.

Knitting Factory
See Rock Music.

Rose Center Jazz
79th St at CPW. **Map** 16 D5.
📞 (212) 769-5100.

Smoke
2751 Broadway. **Map** 20 E5.
📞 (212) 864-6662.

Village Vanguard
178 7th Ave South.
Map 3 C1.
📞 (212) 255-4037.

FOLK AND COUNTRY

Bitter End
147 Bleecker St. **Map** 4 E3.
📞 (212) 673-7030.

Kenny's Castaways
157 Bleecker St. **Map** 4 E3.
📞 (212) 473-9870.

Sidewalk Café
94 Ave A. **Map** 5 B2.
📞 (212) 473-7373.

BLUES, SOUL AND WORLD MUSIC

Apollo Theater
253 W 125 St. **Map** 19 A1.
📞 (212) 531-5300.

C–Note
157 Avenue C. **Map** 5 C2.
📞 (212) 677-8142.

Cotton Club
656 W 125th St.
Map 22 F2.
📞 (212) 663-7980.

Go
73 8th Ave.
Map 3 C1.
📞 (212) 463-0000.

SOB's
204 Varick St. **Map** 4 D3.
📞 (212) 243-4940.

Terra Blues
149 Bleecker St.
Map 4 E3.
📞 (212) 777-7776.

Tonic
107 Norfolk St.
Map 5 B4.
📞 (212) 358-7501.

Clubs, Dance Halls and Piano Bars

NEW YORK'S NIGHTLIFE and club scene is legendary, and deservedly so. Whatever your preference – be it for a noisy disco, stand-up comedy or the soothing melodies of a Harry Connick, Jr., sound-alike in a piano bar – you'll be really amazed at the choice. There was a rash of big discos in the 1980s, but relatively few of these have survived the recent trend toward the comfort and style of supper clubs.

WHEN AND WHERE

THE BEST and hippest time for clubbing is during the week – it's also a lot cheaper. Take a fair amount of money and some ID to prove that you're old enough to drink (which is over 21) – but beware, all the drinks are very expensive.

The trendiest clubs roll on until 4am or later. Fashions and club nights change all the time, so go to Tower Records on Broadway for all the latest leaflets, check club details in the listings magazines *(see p328)* and read the *Village Voice*. The most interesting places nowadays are often popularized by word of mouth. Your best bet is to go somewhere like the **Avalon** and hope someone will tell you where to go on to – often invitations to other clubs are given out there as well.

DANCING

NEW YORKERS thrive on music and dancing. The dance floors available all around the city range from the ever-popular **SOB's** – for jungle, reggae, soul, jazz, and salsa – to a few huge basketball-court-sized places, such as **Roseland**. This has ballroom dancing every Thursday and Sunday and is New York's classic Broadway ballroom, revealing a tantalizing glimpse of older Broadway culture. It also has a good megasize, 700-seater, restaurant with a fully stocked bar.

If you want to sample something really different, try **Barbetta**, where Boris and Yvgeny play a combination of gypsy music and Viennese waltzes. The **Copacabana**, which when it originally

opened starred the likes of Dean Martin and Frank Sinatra, is now a disco alternating with live bands. It also stages wild parties on the last Thursday of every month, with go-go boys, drag queens and disco divas.

The **Avalon**, which is a mixed venue with ground-floor dancing and spectator seats up in the balconies, was renovated in 1998, and the new, improved club is well worth a visit. It always advertises upcoming events. To reserve tickets ahead, call Ticketmaster *(see p329)*.

Some of the most popular clubs for dancing, which also feature the latest music groups, are Ritz, Acme Underground, Marquee, CBGB, Tramps, and the Knitting Factory *(see p341)*. Few of these have strict membership policies. Be sure to get there early and be prepared to line up for entry.

NIGHTCLUBS

NIGHTCLUBS are the places to see a show. New York shows are less flashy than in the 1940s and 1950s but they still boast a wide variety of acts. Expect to pay a cover charge; many of the clubs also require that you have at least two drinks.

The **Rainbow Grill** on the 65th floor of the RCA Building has a fine piano bar. The chic **Supper Club** surrounds you with gold lamé draperies and features big band music downstairs. Cabaret singers perform upstairs in their intimate Blue Room. **Joe's Pub** at the Public Theater has very decent food and offers the likes of John Hammond and Mo Tucker. Central Park has an indoors/outdoors club,

Tavern on the Green, which offers jazz in its Chestnut Room, and **Feinstein's at the Regency** is the epitome of classic cabaret.

GAY AND LESBIAN VENUES

THE PAST TWO decades have seen the arrival of clubs and restaurants specifically geared to gay and lesbian clientele. Although the entertainment is varied, transvestite revues predominate. Though all the clubs are open to heterosexuals and often to the opposite sex, too, some can make "interlopers" feel extremely uncomfortable. The current popular gay cabarets include the **Duplex**, which has a mix of stand-up comics, comedy sketches and singers. The very fashionable nightclubs and bars for men include the trendy uptown **Town House**, a piano bar with restaurant, and **Julius**, known as Greenwich Village's top neighborhood bar. **Don't Tell Mama** is a long-established gay bar that presents good musical revues and spoofs.

Henrietta Hudson and **Crazy Nanny's** cater solely to women, as does **Grolier**. **Marie's Crisis** piano bar is a mixed venue, and **Splash** is open daily with a happy hour between 5pm and 9pm.

The *Village Voice*, *HQ*, and *Next* have good listings of what's happening in the gay communities, and the *Gay Yellow Pages* covers the gay scene. If you need more information, phone the **Gay and Lesbian Switchboard**.

COMEDY SHOWCASES

MANY OF New York's best current comedy clubs or showcases have evolved from earlier "improvisational" comedy. Leading the pack are the **Boston Comedy Club**, the **Original Improv** and **Caroline's**. Also good for a visit are the **Comic Strip Live**, **Stand-Up New York**, **NY Comedy Club**, **55 Grove**

St., **Dangerfield's**, and **Comedy Cellar**. Each club presents a nightly batch of stand-up comics.

PIANO BARS AND HOTEL "ROOMS"

CABARETS HAVE become a New York institution. Such cozy, just-for-listening places are often called "rooms" and are located in hotels. Most operate from Tuesday to Saturday (usually with a cover charge or drink minimum), and most take credit cards.

The **Algonquin's** Oak Room has song stylists. For a classic piano lounge with a panoramic Manhattan view, visit the **Beekman Tower**. The "long-distance hummer" award goes to Bobby Short, who has played his piano for over 25 years at the Café Carlyle in the **Carlyle Hotel**. Woody Allen plays there on Mondays with Eddy Davis's New Orleans Jazz Band. Also in the Carlyle is Bemelman's Bar, with its whimsical murals; it attracts a relaxed crowd who enjoy first-class crooners.

For mainstream danceable music, the venerable **Rainbow Room** is still *the* place to dine and dance, just like in the old days.

Hear tinkling keys and fine songs in the lounge of the **Drake Swissôtel**. There's a piano player at the **Hilton Hotel's** Lobby Lounge, and Café Pierre's singer-pianist Kathleen Landis holds court at the **Pierre Hotel**. There's also piano music at the Ambassador Lounge in the **Millennium UN Plaza Hotel.**

Sports and Fitness

NEW YORKERS ARE SPORTS CRAZY, and there are activities to suit every taste. If you're a doer not a viewer, you can choose from health clubs and horseback riding to pumping iron and swimming, playing tennis or jogging. Spectator sports are provided by two professional baseball teams, two hockey teams, a basketball team and two football teams, while for tennis fans there are the US Open and Virginia Slims tournaments.

TICKETS

THE EASIEST WAY to get hold of your tickets is through Ticketron or Ticketmaster *(see p329)*. For the big games, you may need a ticket agent.

FOOTBALL

THE CITY'S two professional football teams are the New York Giants and the New York Jets. They both play their home games across the river at **Giants Stadium** in New Jersey. Tickets for the Giants are almost impossible to obtain, but they may be available for the Jets.

BASEBALL

TO CAPTURE the essence of this American institution, first time spectators should go to **Yankee Stadium**, home of the New York Yankees. **Shea Stadium**, the Mets' base, is also convenient. The season runs from April to September.

BASKETBALL

THE NEW YORK KNICKS play their home games from October to April at **Madison Square Garden**; you may also catch the ever-popular Harlem Globetrotters there.

BICYCLING

THE BEST PLACE to cycle is in Central Park during the weekend, when it is closed to cars. Bikes may be rented from **Central Park Bike Rentals**.

BOXING

PROFESSIONAL boxing matches are more often seen on Paramount's wide TV screen than in the flesh at **Madison Square Garden**.

FITNESS CENTERS, GYMS AND HEALTH CLUBS

MOST MAJOR HOTELS have fitness centers. Check out the **Chelsea Piers Sports & Entertainment Complex;** there's something for everyone at this enormous facility. Many commercial gyms and health clubs are open only to members. Members can use the facilities at a **Y**.

GOLF

PRACTICE YOUR swing at the **Randalls Island Golf Center, Chelsea Golf Club** or play mini-golf at the **Wollman Memorial Rink**. The city owns several courses in the boroughs, such as **Pelham Bay Park** in the Bronx and **Silver Lake** on Staten Island. For reservations, phone (212) 225-GOLF. **Ferry Point Golf Course** opens in the Bronx in 2004, with driving range and daily fees.

HORSEBACK RIDING AND RACING

THE ONLY riding stable in Manhattan is **Claremont Riding Academy**. You can ride in its indoor arena or go trotting in Central Park.
   Harness racing, in which horses pull sulkies (small carts), takes place year-round at **Yonkers Raceway**. Flat races are held daily, except Tuesday, October to May at the **Aqueduct Race Track**, and May to October at the **Belmont Park Race Track**.

ICE HOCKEY

FISTS AND ICE FLY when the New York Rangers meet their competition at **Madison Square Garden.** The season runs from October to April.

ICE-SKATING

THERE ARE THREE good places to go ice skating out of doors. One is the **Rockefeller Plaza Rink**, which looks beautiful at Christmas. The others are in Central Park: **Wollman Rink** and **Lasker Rink**. For indoor sites, try the **Sky Rink** at Chelsea Piers.

INDOOR SPORTS

CHELSEA PIERS has it all: roller rinks, bowling, indoor soccer, basketball, rock-climbing walls, fitness centers, golf, a field house for gymnastics, sports medicine and spa centers, and of course, swimming pools. This huge complex, spread over four old West Side piers, is open to all. As the ads say, "You gotta see this place!"

JOGGING

SOME PARKS are safe for joggers, others are not, so be guided by your concierge. None is safe after dark, at dusk or before dawn. The most popular route is around the reservoir in Central Park. The **International Running Center** has weekly running clinics and races, as does **Chelsea Piers**.

MARATHON

TO BE ONE of the 25,000 who enter the New York Marathon, you have to sign up six months in advance. The race is held on the first Sunday in November. Phone (212) 860-4455 for information.

SPORTS BARS

TOP BARS include **Time Out** or **Mickey Mantle's**, both of which have giant scoreboards and multiple video screens.

SWIMMING

MANY MANHATTAN hotels have pools with free access during your stay. You can also swim and surf at the

Surfside 3 Maritime Center at Chelsea Piers. For a day trip, go to Jones Beach State Park (see p253) along Long Island's shoreline.

TENNIS

THE TOP TENNIS tournament in New York is the US Open, played each August at the **National Tennis Center**. Also good is the women's Virginia Slims Championships in November at **Madison Square Garden** (see p133).

If you want to play tennis rather than watch it, look in the telephone directory under "Tennis Courts: Public and Private." For private courts,

you can expect to pay about $50–70 an hour. The **Manhattan Plaza Racquet Club** offers both courts and lessons by the hour. For public courts, you will need a $50 permit, available from the **NY City Parks & Recreation Department**. You will also need an identity card and a reservation.

TRACK AND FIELD

THE MILLROSE GAMES are normally held in early February, and the Amateur Athletic Union (AAU) championships, where most of the top athletes usually appear, are held in late

February at **Madison Square Garden**. Chelsea Piers also has a complete track and field complex.

OTHER ACTIVITIES

IN CENTRAL PARK, options include renting rowboats from **Loeb Boathouse** or playing chess – pick up the pieces from The Dairy (see p206). Bowling is available at **Chelsea Piers** and a few other lanes throughout the city. **Slate Billiards** and many bars offer pool and darts.

If you want something completely different, go to **Sheepshead Bay**,Brooklyn, and try deep-sea fishing.

SPORTS ADDRESSES

Aqueduct Race Track
Ozone Park, Queens.
(718) 641-4700.

Belmont Park Race Track
Hempstead Turnpike, Long Island.
(718) 641-4700.

Central Park Bike Rental
2 Columbus Circle.
Map 12 D3.
(212) 541-8759.

Chelsea Piers Sports & Entertainment Complex:
Piers 59–62 at 23rd St and 11th Ave (Hudson River). Map 7 B4-5.
(212) 336-6444. W
www.chelseapiers.com

Claremont Riding Academy
175 W 89th St.
Map 15 C3.
(212) 724-5100.

Giants Stadium
Meadowlands
East Rutherford, N J.
(201) 935-8111. W
www.giants.com

(516) 560-8200. W
www.newyorkjets.com

International Running Center
9 E 89th St.
Map 17 A3.
(212) 860-4455.

Lasker Ice Rink
Central Park Drive East at 108th St.
Map 21 B4.
(212) 534-7639.

Loeb Boathouse
Central Park.
Map 16 F5.
(212) 517-2233.

Madison Square Garden
7th Ave at 33rd St.
Map 8 E2.
(212) 465-6741.
W www.thegarden.com

Manhattan Plaza Racquet Club
450 W 43rd St.
Map 7 C1.
(212) 594-0554.

Mickey Mantle's
42 Central Park South.
Map 12 E3.
(212) 688-7777.

National Tennis Center
Flushing Meadow Park, Queens.
(718) 595-2420.
W www.usta.com

NY City Parks & Recreation Department
Arsenal Building
64th St and 5th Ave.
Map 12 F2.
(212) 408-0100.

Pelham Bay Park
The Bronx.
(718) 885-1461.

Plaza Rink
1 Rockefeller Plaza, 5th Ave.
Map 12 F5.
(212) 332-7654.

Printing House Fitness & Racquet Center
421 Hudson St. Map 3 C3.
(212) 243-7600.

Randalls Island Golf Center
Randalls Island.
Map 22 F2.
(212) 427-5689.

Shea Stadium
126th St at Roosevelt Ave, Flushing, Queens.
(718) 507-TIXX or (718) 507-8499.

Sheepshead Bay
(For information on fishing trips call Mike's Tackle.
(718) 646-9261.

Silver Lake
915 Victory Blvd
Staten Island.
(718) 447-5686 or (718) 225-4653.

Slate Billiards
54 W 21st St.
Map 8 E4.
(212) 989-0096.

Time Out
349 Amsterdam Ave.
Map 15 C5.
(212) 362-5400.

Wollman Rink
Central Park,
5th Ave at 59th St.
Map 12 F2.
(212) 439-6900.

Yankee Stadium
River Ave at 161st St,
The Bronx.
(718) 293-4300.

YMCA 47th St
224 E 47th St.
Map 13 B5.
(212) 756-9600.

Y at 92nd St
1395 Lexington Ave.
Map 17 A2.
(212) 415-5500.

YMCA West Side
5 W 63rd St.
Map 12 D2.
(212) 875-4100.

Yonkers Raceway
Yonkers,
Westchester County.
(914) 968-4200.

Late-Night New York

NEW YORK IS INDEED a city that never sleeps. If you wake up in the middle of the night – with a craving for fresh bread, a need to be entertained or an urge to watch the sun rise over the Manhattan skyline – there are always plenty of options to choose from.

BARS AND CLUBS

THE BEST and friendliest bars are often the Irish ones. **O'Flanagan's** or **Scruffy Duffy's** are both loud, have late-night dancing, and cater to regulars. Go for a late-night dry martini at the **Temple Bar**. The best piano bars are in the hotels: try the Café Carlyle in the **Carlyle Hotel**, Feinstein's at the **Regency**, or the Oak Room in the **Algonquin Hotel**.

For hot American jazz until 4am, go to **Joe's Pub** or the **Blue Note**. Traditional jazz and swing entertain the diners and dancers at the **Rainbow Room. Cornelia Street Café** is a snug and lively nook for prose, poetry and theater readings. Poetry, theater and Latin music can be found at the **Nuyorican Poets Café**. If you're in the Village, stop in at **Rose's Turn** for open mike, piano bar, and late-night ambience.

MIDNIGHT MOVIES

SPECIAL MIDNIGHT showings and a youthful crowd can be found at the Angelika Film Center and the Film Forum (see pp336–7). New multiplexes often show movies at midnight on weekends.

SHOPS

SHAKESPEARE & Company Booksellers on Broadway and the St. Mark's Bookshop are open until late. The Upper West Side branch of HMV is open until midnight, the East Side branch until 10pm. Both Tower Records branches shut at midnight, as does Gryphon Records. Bleecker Bob's Golden Oldies Record Shop stays open until 3am on weekends (see Shopping pp322-3). Check out **TLA Video** on 8th Street if you've forgotten to rent a movie tape – it's open

every day until midnight. Among the many Village clothing stores that stay open late on weekends is **Trash and Vaudeville** (open till 8pm on Fridays and Saturdays). For aspirin and other health essentials, two **Duane Reade** drugstores and **Rite Aid Pharmacy** are open 24 hours. **Love Drugstores** are usually open until midnight.

TAKE-OUT FOOD AND GROCERIES

A FEW TAKE-OUT food stores are open 24 hours a day, including the **Delmonico Gourmet Food Market** and the **West Side Supermarket**. Many Korean greengrocers also stay open all night. The **Food Emporium** is a supermarket chain usually open until midnight. On Saturdays, **Zabar's** stays open until midnight. Liquor stores are usually open until 10pm and many deliver.

For the best in bagels, go to **H & H Bagels**, **Bagels On The Square** and **Jumbo Bagels and Bialys**. There are many pizzerias and Chinese restaurants that stay open late, and most deliver.

DINING

CLUBBERS AND the trendy set often frequent **La Jumelle**, **Florent** and **Les Halles** for good French dishes. Twentysomethings will seek out the **Coffee Shop** for late-night beer and Brazilian food. You'll find delicious and legendary sandwiches at the **Carnegie Deli**. **Caffè Reggio** in Greenwich Village has been a favorite for late-night coffee and desserts since 1927. It is also possible to find good food in dinner clubs. **Le Bar Bat** is popular for its bat cave décor and Vietnamese

cuisine. **The Dead Poet** is a real Upper West Side neighborhood hangout, with live music, a lively bar: bring your own food. The other end of the scale is the glitzy **Rainbow Room** or **Rainbow Grill**. Cipriani's magic touch, good music, and the New York ambience make these two spots extra-special.

SPORTS

THERE IS round-the-clock play at **Slate Billiards** or until 5am at the **Billiard Club** on weekends. Have late-night beers and burgers with the New York University crowd at **Bowlmore Lanes** bowling alley.

SERVICES

MIDNIGHT EXPRESS CLEANERS picks up garments in Manhattan until midnight and has them ready the next day. Note that this service does not pick up or deliver to major hotels. On Thursdays hairdresser **George Michael of Madison Avenue/Madora Inc** is open until 10pm and will also make house calls.

TOURS AND VIEWS

ONE OF NEW YORK'S most enjoyable walks is along the Hudson River at the World Financial Center's **Battery Park City**, open (and safe) at all hours. Piers 16 and 17 at South Street Seaport attract strollers and revelers all night long and the **Harbour Lights** restaurant on Pier 17 is open until 4am for a middle of the night pick-me-up. Enjoy the city lights by taking a **Circle Line** two-hour tour of the nighttime harbor.

Try the Riverview Terrace at Sutton Place: the benches offer a peaceful and quiet place to watch the sun rise over the East River, Roosevelt Island and Queens. Two of the most sensational views with the Manhattan backdrop are (looking west) from the **River Café** and (looking east) from **Arthur's Landing** restaurant. Take a trip on the **Staten**

Island Ferry (see p76) to see the Statue of Liberty and the Manhattan skyline in the dawn light, or a take a taxi across Brooklyn Bridge (see pp86–9) to watch the sun rise over New York harbor. Go to the **Beekman Tower Hotel's** Top of the Tower for some panoramas of the city's East Side up to 1am. The ultimate view is from the **Empire State Building**: its Observation Deck (see pp134–5) stays open until midnight. **Rise**, the 14th-floor bar of the Ritz-Carlton Hotel in Battery park has great views of the harbor and Statue of Liberty.

Château Stables has rides in horse-drawn carriages and **Liberty Helicopters** run flights over the city at sunset. If you want something a little bit different, try **Marvelous Manhattan Tours'** escorted evening barhopping walks. And if you still can't sleep, visit the bustling **Fulton Fish Market** at 6am or stroll the Upper West Side and eat two hot dogs at the famous **Gray's Papaya**.

CHILDREN'S NEW YORK

YOUNG VISITORS soon catch the contagious excitement in the air in New York. Attractions for all ages abound, and plenty are designed especially for children. More than a dozen theater companies, two zoos and three imaginative museums are for just the young, backed up with special events at many museums and parks. The chance to visit a TV studio is a treat, and New York's own Big Apple Circus is a perennial delight. With more to do than can ever be squeezed into a single visit, you'll never hear the cry "I'm bored!" Best of all, there's no need to spend a fortune to have fun.

A young visitor making New York his very own playground

PRACTICAL ADVICE

NEW YORK is family-friendly. Many of its hotels allow children in parents' rooms free, and will supply cots or cribs if needed. Most museums charge half price or less for children, while others are free. Children under 44 in (112 cm) also ride free on subways and buses when accompanied by an adult. Travel between 9am and 4pm to avoid rush hours.

Supplies such as diapers and medicines are readily available, and the Rite Aid Pharmacy (see p357) is open 24 hours a day. Finding changing tables in public toilets is less easy, but no one objects if a counter is used. Best bets are the facilities in libraries, hotels and department stores. Most hotels will arrange babysitters; another reliable source is the **Baby Sitters' Guild**.

To find out more about the range of current activities for children, get a copy of the free quarterly calendar of events, available from the New York Convention and Visitors Bureau (see p352). Weekly listings can be found in *New York* magazine or *Time Out New York*.

NEW YORK ADVENTURES

THE CITY can seem like a giant amusement park for youngsters. Elevators whisk you sky-high for bird's-eye views from atop the world's highest buildings. You can set sail on the classic **Circle Line** tour around Manhattan; the sailboat **Pioneer** (see p84), or charter your own paddle-wheeler from the marina at E. 23rd St; or the free round-trip on the Staten Island Ferry (see p76). The Roosevelt Island Tram (see p179) is a Swiss cable car offering an airborne ride over the East River. Central Park (see pp202–7) is a source of rides of every kind – from the old-fashioned charm of the carousel to real horseback and ponycart rides. Children who prefer a faster pace can join the skate-boarders and in-line skaters who cruise around the traffic-free park every weekend.

Cooling off in a playground in Central Park

MUSEUMS

WHILE MANY of New York's museums appeal to all ages, some are designed just for the young. High on the list is the imaginative Children's Museum of Manhattan (see p217), a multimedia world in which children can produce their own videos and newscasts. Farther afield are the **Staten Island Children's Museum**, where a huge climb-through anthill is one of the favorite items, and the Brooklyn Children's Museum (see p245). The *Intrepid* Sea-Air-Space Museum (see p147) is a real air-craft carrier. Finally, no one should miss the spectacular new Hayden Planetarium and the dinosaur display at the American Museum of Natural History (see pp214–15).

OUTDOOR FUN

IN SUMMER, all of New York comes out to play. Central Park is a child's wonderland, from skating rinks to

Skating with Santa at Rockefeller Center

boating lakes, bicycle paths to miniature golf. The park has free entertainment galore – such as guided walks by park rangers on Saturdays, toy sailboat races and summer storytelling. The Central Park Wildlife Center and the smaller Tisch Children's Zoo are all-time favorites.

Children of all ages will be fascinated by the Bronx Zoo/Wildlife Conservation Park which is home to over 700 species *(see pp242–3)*.

Rockaway Beach and Coney Island *(see p247)* are just a subway ride away. Winter brings the chance to skate at Rockefeller Center *(see p142)* or in Central Park on a rink fringed with views of skyscrapers.

INDOOR FUN

NEW YORK children's theater is of a quality and variety matching that for adults. Some favorite companies are the **Paper Bag Players** and **Theaterworks USA**, whose shows sell out fast; get schedules and reserve seats early.

The **Swedish Marionette Theater** in Central Park has morning shows Tuesdays through Fridays, and Saturdays until 1pm.

The New York City Ballet's annual Christmas production of *The Nutcracker* at Lincoln Center *(see p212)* opens at about the same time that the **Big Apple Circus** sets up its tent nearby. Ringling Brothers and Barnum & Bailey Circus is in action at Madison Square Garden *(see p133)* for several weeks each spring.

Opportunities for youngsters to work off energy in winter are many, from indoor skating rinks to mini-golf and bowling alleys at **Chelsea Piers**.

Centerpiece clock at toy store F.A.O. Schwarz

SHOPPING

THERE WILL be no complaints about shopping trips if they include **F.A.O. Schwarz**, one of the world's biggest and best toy stores with a vast range of wonderful items. Another favorite among children is **Enchanted Forest**, and youngsters are welcomed for storytelling sessions at **Books of Wonder**.

EATING OUT

HAMBURGER-and-pasta joint Ottomanelli's Café is very popular with children, and even adults find it hard to finish their huge burgers. The lively **Hard Rock Café** is another hit, and most children enjoy the foods sold around Chinatown and Little Italy. Drop into the **China-. town Ice Cream Factory** for some strange and wonderful flavors. For a quick hot snack, try pizza-by-the-slice or pretzels and hot dogs from street vendors. There are also scores of fast food places, including White Castle, Burger King or McDonalds.

Storytelling session at South Street Seaport

DIRECTORY

PRACTICAL ADVICE

Baby Sitters' Guild
(212) 682-0227.

ADVENTURES

Circle Line
Pier 83, W 42nd St. **Map** 7 A1.
(212) 563-3200.

MUSEUMS

Staten Island Children's Museum
1000 Richmond Terr, Staten Is.
(718) 273-2060.

OUTDOOR FUN

Chelsea Piers
(212) 366-6800.
www.chelseapiers.com

Rockaway Beach
(718) 474-6400.

Swedish Cottage Marionette Theater
(212) 988-9093.

INDOOR FUN

Big Apple Circus
(212) 268-2500.

Paper Bag Players
(212) 663-0390.

Theaterworks USA
787 7th Ave. **Map** 12 E4.
(212) 627-7373.

SHOPPING

Books of Wonder
16 W 18th St. **Map** 8 C5.
(212) 989-3270.

Enchanted Forest
85 Mercer St. **Map** 4 E4.
(212) 925-6677.

F.A.O. Schwarz
767 Fifth Ave. **Map** 12 F3.
(212) 644-9400.

EATING OUT

Chinatown Ice Cream Factory
65 Bayard St. **Map** 4 F5.
(212) 608-4170.

Hard Rock Café
221 W 57th St. **Map** 12 E3.
(212) 459-9320.

Ottomanelli's Café
1626 York Ave. **Map** 17 C3.
(212) 772-7722.

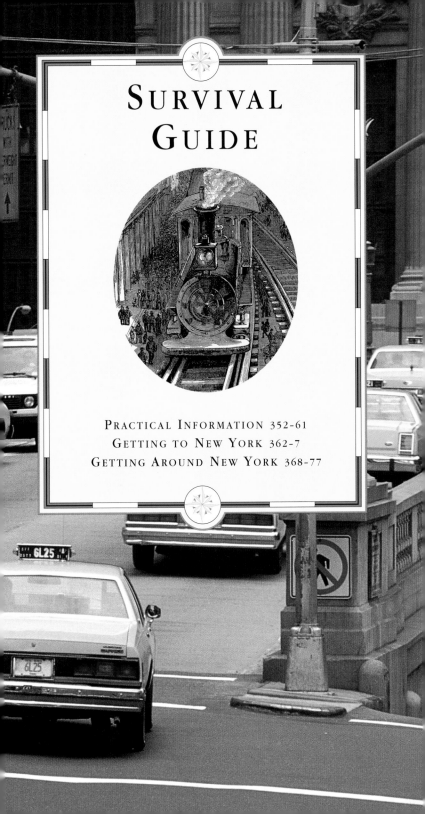

SURVIVAL
GUIDE

PRACTICAL INFORMATION

VISITORS TO New York are treated very much the same as anyone else. While you may not be given special treatment, as long as you follow a few guidelines on personal security *(see pp356–7)* you'll be able to explore the city as freely as any native New Yorker. Buses and subway trains *(pp372–5)* are reliable and

Visitors resting on the steps of the Metropolitan Museum of Art

cheap; there are lots of cash machines *(pp358–9)*, and money can be easily exchanged at banks, hotels and foreign money brokers. The wide range of prices offered by all the many hotels *(pp272–83)*, restaurants *(pp288–304)* and entertainment venues *(pp328–47)* means your New York trip can be both fun and affordable.

SIGHTSEEING TIPS

NEW YORK'S rush hours extend from 8 to 10am, 11:30am to 1:30pm and 4:30 to 6:30pm, Monday to Friday. During these times, every form of public transportation will be crowded, and the streets will be much harder to navigate on foot.

It's worth trying to visit a cluster of sights in the same area – see the *Street-by-Street* plans of each area – instead of exhausting yourself rushing from one distant attraction to another. Buses are a comfortable and reliable way to get around, and you'll see the city as you travel.

It's best to avoid passing through certain areas of the city, especially at particular times *(pp356–7)*. Public toilets in bus stations should be avoided. They attract drug users and the homeless. It is best to find a large hotel, department store, coffee shop or book-store if you need a restroom.

If you need help with street directions or feel a need to get off the street, ask a policeman or find a hotel doorman. There is one on duty at the entrance to most hotels 24 hours a day.

OPENING HOURS

BUSINESS HOURS are generally from 9am to 5pm with no lunchtime closing. Only banks close earlier, at 3pm, although some do have longer hours

(8am–6pm) and are open on Saturday mornings. Many museums close on Mondays and major holidays. Some open on Tuesday or Thursday evenings during certain seasons (phone for details).

MUSEUMS

IN NEW YORK, *museum* is used as a blanket term to include institutions that offer diverse holdings. The city's museums are described on pages 34 to 37. Museums either charge admission, starting at around $2, or ask for a "donation," which can be $6 to $9. There are discounts for senior citizens, students and children. The leading museums schedule free guided tours and lectures.

Museum Mile *(see pp182–3)*, on and near Fifth Avenue, groups a number of major museums close together. Of these, the Frick Collection and the Cooper-Hewitt are small enough to see in one or two hours, but the larger museums, the Guggenheim, Whitney, and Metropolitan, may take far longer than this.

Hotel doorman

ETIQUETTE

IT IS ILLEGAL to smoke in any public place or building in New York. Some restaurants now provide separate rooms for smokers, but it is best to phone ahead for details.

Business travelers need not bring a gift for their hosts. Such tokens are not expected

and may even be considered improper. If you do bring something, it should be something inexpensive and preferably representative of where you live.

Tipping is an integral part of New York life: for taxi drivers leave 10 to 15%; waiters 15 to 20%, cocktail waiters 15%, hotel room service 10% (when not added to the bill); coat check $1; hotel maids $1 or $2 per day after the first day; hotel bellhops about $1 per bag; hair stylists 15 to 20% and barbers 10 to 20%.

TOURIST INFORMATION

ADVICE ON ANY aspect of life in New York City is available from the **New York Convention and Visitors Bureau**, known as **NYC & Co.***(see pp328–9)*. Their 24-hour touch-tone phone service offers help outside office hours. Brochures and information kiosks can also be found at the walk-in office of the **Times Square Visitors Information Bureau**.

Hotel lobbies and museums have free literature racks, and all of the daily newspapers hold a wealth of information about what's going on where.

Useful information
NYC & Co, 810 7th Ave. **Map** 12 E4.
[C] *(212) 484-1222.* [W] www.nycvisit.
com [W] www.ci.nyc.ny.us [O] 8:30am–
6pm Mon–Fri; 9am–5pm Sat, Sun.
Times Square Visitors Center
1560 Broadway. **Map** 12 E5.
[W] www.timessquarebid.org
New York State information
[W] www.state.ny.us
On-line guide to everything in NYC:
[W] www.jimsdeli.com

ENTERTAINMENT LISTINGS

A NUMBER of inexpensive or even free publications listing current exhibitions and leisure activities are available at newsstands, hotels and galleries throughout New York.

Among the more popular ones are *New York* magazine, *The New Yorker's* "Goings On About Town" roster and *Time Out New York,* which list offerings at the city's many museums, clubs, theaters, galleries, restaurants, cinemas, colleges and libraries, plus impending auctions. The *Village Voice* focuses on events in SoHo, TriBeCa and Greenwich Village, plus other major cultural activity in the city. *The New York Times* Friday and Sunday editions list current visual and performing arts events in their respective "Weekend" and "Arts and Leisure" sections. *Art News* is a monthly magazine that lists major art events and auctions and reviews exhibits.

There are also various free magazines. The weekly *Where* is distributed through hotel concierges and lists major museums, their opening hours, locations and any exhibitions. *Art Now/New York Gallery Guide* is released in art galleries each month. It lists current exhibitions and has useful maps showing where they are located.

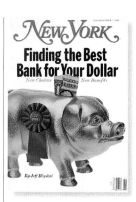

New York magazine has weekly comprehensive entertainment listings for all of New York

GUIDED TOURS

Whichever way you want to see New York – with the help of a pre-recorded walk or by an exciting trip in a helicopter, boat or horse-drawn carriage – organized sightseeing trips, planned by someone else, can save a lot of time, effort and often money. There are numerous companies to choose from, each providing plenty of local information.

Boat Tours
Circle Line
Sightseeing Yachts
Pier 83, W 42nd St.
Map 7 A1.
(*(212) 563-3200.*
A three-hour trip circum-navigating Manhattan.

Circle Line Statue of
Liberty Ferry
South Ferry, Battery Park.
Map 1 C4.
(*(212) 269-5755.*

Spirit of New York
W 23rd and 8th Ave.
Map 8 D4.
(*(866) 211-3805. Cruises
include lunch or dinner.*

Dept. of Transportation
Staten Island Ferry
South Ferry. **Map** 2 D4.
(*(212) 487-5761
or 5766.
Manhattan–Staten Island.*

World Yacht, Inc
Pier 81 W 41st St.

Map 7 A1.
(*(212) 630-8100.
Cruises include lunch,
dinner and onboard
entertainment.*

Carriage Tours
59th St at Fifth Ave and
along Central Park S.
*Horse-drawn carriages
gather outside the Plaza
Hotel (***Map** 12 F3),
*days and evenings. The
usual itinerary takes in
Central Park.*

Bus Tours
Allied Tours
165 W 46th St.
Map 12 E5.
(*(212) 869-5112.*

Gray Line of New York
42nd St and 8th Ave.
Map 8 D1.
(*(212) 397-2620.*

Short Line Tours/American
Sightseeing NY
166 W 46th St.
Map 12 F5.
(*(800) 631-8405.*

Bicycle Tours
Bite of the Apple Tours,
2 Columbus Circle, 59th St
& Broadway. **Map** 12 D3.
(*(212) 541-8759.
A two-hour spin around
Central Park. $20, or $30
with bike rental. 10am,
1pm, and 4pm.*

Walking Tours
Big Apple Greeters
1 Centre St, Suite 2035.
Map 4 F4.
(*(212) 669-8159.
Free tours by New York
natives.*

Big Onion Walking Tours
PO Box 250201, Columbia
University. **Map** 20 E3.
(*(212) 439-1090.
Historical and ethnic.*

Harlem Spirituals, Inc.
690 8th Ave. **Map** 8 D1.
(*(212) 757-0425.
Harlem's history and
culture. Apr–Oct only.*

Heritage Trails
*Four free do-it-yourself
historical trails begin at
Federal Hall; brochures at
Federal Hall.* **Map** 1 C3.

Museum of the City of
New York
103rd St and Fifth Ave.
Map 21 C5.
(*(212) 534-1672.
Architecture and history.*

NBC Studio Tour
30 Rockefeller Plaza.
Map 12 F5.
(*(212) 664-7174.*

92nd Street Y
1395 Lexington Ave.
Map 17 B5.
(*(212) 427-6000.
Culture and history.*

Talk-a-Walk
30 Waterside Plaza.
Map 9 C4.
(*(212) 686-0356.
Recorded itineraries.*

Carriage ride in Central Park

DISABLED TRAVELERS

DISABLED PEOPLE will find New York more accessible than most cities. All of the city's buses have ramps that can be lowered to help people in wheelchairs board. The buses also "kneel" to help those with restricted mobility.

Hotels, large stores and office buildings are also often well equipped for wheelchair access, and some museums offer tours for the deaf, blind and disabled. Several city theaters have systems to aid hearing-impaired patrons as do a growing number of telephones. *Access Guide to New York City*, free from the **Junior League of the City of New York**, lists buildings accessible to the disabled.

Useful information Junior League of the City of New York, 130 E 80th St. **Map** 17 A4. ☎ *(212) 288-6220*. The Mayor's Office for People with Disabilities. ☎ *(212) 788-2830*.

A New York city bus "kneeling" to help the elderly board

CUSTOMS AND IMMIGRATION

CITIZENS OF Britain, New Zealand, Australia, and 26 other countries do not need visas if they are staying in the US for 90 days or less. Canadians need only proof of citizenship and a photo ID. Students do need proper visas. All travelers need round-trip or onward passage tickets and must show proof they have $500 or more. Check with a US embassy or travel agent if in doubt.

Customs allowances per person when you enter the US

are 200 cigarettes, 50 cigars or 4.4 pounds (2 kilograms) of tobacco; no more than 2 pints (1 liter) of alcohol; gifts worth no more than $100; no meat or meat products (even in cans), seeds, growing plants or fresh fruit.

Upon arrival at one of New York's airports, follow signs stating "other than American passports" to immigration counters where your passport will then be inspected and stamped. Once you have reclaimed your baggage from the appropriate area (again, follow the signs), you will be approached by a Customs officer. He or she will examine the Customs declaration you should have received and filled in on your flight and direct you either toward the exit or to a Customs inspector who will then search your luggage. According to US Customs officials, only 5% of all travelers will have to have their luggage searched. There are no red or green Customs channels – you're cleared and free to go once the Customs officer has seen your fully completed declaration.

STUDENT TRAVELERS

MANY MUSEUMS and theaters allow students a discount on admission. To receive this, however, you will need to carry proof of your student status at all times.

An International Student ID Card can be purchased quite cheaply, provided you have the right credentials, from the **Council Travel**, which has two branches in New York. At the same time, ask for a copy of the *ISIC Student Handbook*. This invaluable booklet identifies places and services throughout the US that offer a range of discounts to card holders. Included are selected accommodations, various museums, theaters, tours, attractions, nightclubs and restaurants.

Although it is normally extremely difficult to obtain permission to work in the US, students are an exception to this rule, being eligible to work as part of exchange programs, or as interns. Any branch of the Student Travel Association in the UK, Australia or New Zealand will be able to help you with details of working holidays in New York. In London, contact the **Council on International Educational Exchange**.

STUDENT INFORMATION

Bunac
P.O. Box 430.
☎ *(203) 264-0901*.
Summertime only.

Council on International Educational Exchange
633 3rd Ave. **Map** 9 B1.
☎ *(212) 822-2600*.
52 Poland St, London W1V 4JQ
☎ *(207) 478-2000*.

Council Travel
254 Greene St. **Map** 4 E2. Also at 205 E 42nd St. **Map** 9 B1
☎ *(212) 254-2525, (800) 226-8624*.

CONVERSION CHART

Bear in mind that 1 US pint (0.5 liter) is a smaller measure than 1 UK pint (0.6 liter).

Imperial system:
1 inch = 2.5 centimeters
1 foot = 30 centimeters
1 mile = 1.6 kilometers
1 ounce = 28 grams
1 pound = 454 grams
1 US pint = 0.47 liter
1 US gallon = 3.8 liters

Metric system:
1 millimeter = 0.04 inch
1 centimeter = 0.4 inch
1 meter = 3 feet 3 inches
1 kilometer = 0.6 mile
1 gram = 0.04 ounce

International Student ID Card

New York
daily newspapers

A newspaper
vending machine

NEWSPAPERS, TELEVISION AND RADIO

YOU CAN BUY foreign newspapers, usually the previous day's issue, at **Universal News**, airports, hotels and newsstands near international business areas like the World Financial Center or Wall Street.

TV program schedules can be found in the weekly *TV Guide* magazine and the television section of the Sunday edition of *The New York Times*.

The choice of TV stations available in New York is vast. CBS operates on channel 2, NBC on channel 4, ABC on channel 7 and WNYW (Fox) on channel 5. PBS offers cultural and educational fare, including some vintage BBC programs, on channel 13. Cable TV offers everything from the Arts and Entertainment Network (channel 16) to public access programs.

AM radio stations include WCBS News (880AM) and WFAN Sports (660AM). Some FM stations are WNEW rock (102.7FM), WBGO jazz (88.3FM) and WQXR classical (96.3FM).

Information Universal News, 234 W 42 **Map** 8 D1. ((212) 221-1809.

ELECTRICAL APPLIANCES

ALL AMERICAN electric current flows at a standardized 110 to 120 volts AC (alternating current). You will need to bring an adapter plug and a voltage convertor that fits standard US electrical outlets. US plugs have two flat prongs.

Most modern New York hotels provide wall-mounted electric hair dryers in bathrooms. In addition, some hotels have wall plugs capable of powering both 110- and 220-volt electric shavers, but little else – not even radios. It can, in fact, be dangerous to connect anything more powerful. If you bring along sophisticated electrical appliances with you, be certain to take a battery pack as well. You will also need an adapter to recharge your spare batteries.

Few New York hotel rooms provide irons or coffee-makers. However, room service should be able to provide you with an iron upon request.

Standard plug

EMBASSIES AND CONSULATES

Australia
150 E 42nd St. **Map** 9 A1.
((212) 351-6500.
w www.australianyc.org

Britain
845 Third Ave. **Map** 13 B4.
((212) 745-0200.
w www.britainusa.com/ny

Canada
1251 Sixth Ave at 50th St. **Map** 12 E4. ((212) 596-1628.
w www.canada-ny.org

Ireland
345 Park Ave. **Map** 13 A4.
((212) 319-2555.
w www.irelandemb.org

New Zealand
37 Observatory Circle, NW, Washington, DC 20008.
((202) 328-4800. w www.nzemb.org

RELIGIOUS SERVICES

THERE ARE SOME 4,000 places of worship in New York, catering to almost any faith. Most hotels have lists of local organizations and service times. Among the leading churches and temples are:

Baptist
Riverside Church
122nd St at Riverside Dr.
Map 20 D2.
((212) 870-6700.

Catholic
St. Patrick's Cathedral
Fifth Ave at 50th St.
Map 12 F4.
((212) 753-2261.

Episcopal
St. Bartholomew's
109 E 50th St. **Map** 13 A4.
((212) 378-0200.

Jewish
Reform
Temple Emanu-El
Fifth Ave at 65th St.
Map 12 F2.
((212) 744-1400.

Orthodox
Fifth Avenue Synagogue
5 E 62nd St. **Map** 12 F2.
((212) 838-2122.

Lutheran
St. Peter's
619 Lexington Ave. **Map** 17 A4.
((212) 935-2200.

Methodist
Christ Church United Methodist
520 Park Ave. **Map** 13 A3.
((212) 838-3036.

Riverside Church

Personal Security and Health

Police badge

IN 1998, NEW YORK was rated the safest among large US cities with a population of more than one million. This ranks New York 166th among cities with population of over one hundred thousand. The city's police force concentrates on foot and bicycle patrols in tourist areas, and security has been beefed up in midtown, in the transportation system and at airports. While there are places where any traveler would be foolish to tread after dark – and sometimes in daylight – if you keep your wits about you and stick to the following guidelines, you should enjoy a trouble-free visit.

New York City police patrol using a range of transportation

LAW ENFORCEMENT

THE NEW YORK police department has around-the-clock foot, horse, bike and car patrols. These are concentrated in specific areas at critical times – for instance, the theater district during show times. There are police who ride the subways and buses, and the recent dramatic drop in crime statistics reflects this.

You may also see youths wearing red berets. As their T-shirts proclaim, they are Guardian Angels. Always unarmed, these safety patrols "police" the subways and midtown streets. Although tolerated by the police and often a welcome sight, they have no official powers.

GUIDELINES ON SAFETY

UNDER THE LEADERSHIP of former mayor Rudolph Giuliani, New York became a relatively safe place to roam. Common sense still rules, however, so be alert and walk as if you know where you're going. Avoid eye

contact and confrontations with down-and-outs. If someone asks you for money, be careful and do not be drawn into conversation.

Avoid deserted streets. At night, if you can't afford a taxi, try to travel with a group and keep away from the Lower East Side, Chinatown, midtown west of Broadway (except Lincoln Center and Times Square) and any place off the beaten path. The Financial District (except for the World Financial Center) is deserted after business hours, and some TriBeCa and SoHo streets can be risky after dark.

Parks are often used for drug dealing. They are safest when there is a crowd for a rally, concert or other event, although you should still take precautions to avoid being pick-pocketed. If you want to go for a jog, ask your hotel concierge for a map of safe routes and follow his or her advice. When walking in the park or street, keep your wallet in an inconspicuous

place and have enough change handy for phone calls and bus fares. It's best not to have to dig into your purse or wallet while standing in line. Never stop to count your money on the street, and be aware of strangers watching at bank machines. Defeat purse snatchers by carrying your bag with the clasp facing toward you and the shoulder strap across your body.

Leave valuable jewelry at home or stored at your hotel; do not allow anyone except hotel and airport personnel to carry your luggage or parcels; and stow your valuables and camera in a locked suitcase or closet safe when you leave your hotel room.

Mounted police officers patrolling the streets to keep the city safe

LOST AND FOUND

THE CHANCES are poor of recovering anything lost in New York City. There is no city-wide lost and found. The lost-and-found rooms at Grand Central and Penn Station, however, are well-run with helpful staff. Most taxi and transport firms also have lost and found departments.

In the event of loss or theft, report all missing items to the police and make sure you get a copy of the police report for

As a general rule, be alert when you walk down the street

Cap and badge worn by city police

your insurance claim. Keep a record of your valuables' serial numbers and receipts as proof of possession.

USEFUL INFORMATION

Lost and Found Offices
Bus and subway services
((212) 712-4500.

Taxis
((212) 692-8294.

Stolen or Lost Credit Cards
American Express
((800) 528-4800 (free).

Diners Club
((800) 234-6377 (free).

JCB
((800) 366-4522 (free).

MasterCard
((800) 627-8372 (free).

VISA
((800) 336-8472 (free).

TRAVEL INSURANCE

TRAVEL INSURANCE is highly recommended, mainly because of the high cost of medical care. There are many types of coverage, with prices dependent on the length of your trip and the number of people covered on the policy.
Among the most important features are: accidental death, dismemberment, emergency medical and dental care, trip cancellation, and baggage and travel document loss. There are many policies that include all these items. Your travel agent or insurance company should recommend a suitable policy.

MEDICAL TREATMENT

BE PREPARED to undergo an expensive experience: some of the city's practitioners and facilities are among the

best around, and medical fees in the US are unregulated. Be sure to protect yourself well with insurance. A few physicians and dentists may accept credit cards, but they are much more likely to want payment in cash or traveler's checks. Hospitals accept most credit cards *(see p358)*.

A 24-hour pharmacy, one of several in the city

EMERGENCIES

IN THE EVENT of your being involved in a medical emergency, proceed at once to a **Hospital Emergency Room**. Should you need an ambulance, telephone 911 and one will be sent. If your medical insurance is properly in order, you won't have to worry about costs.
Unless you are impoverished, it is better to avoid the city-owned hospitals listed in the telephone book Blue Pages. Instead, choose one of the many private hospitals listed in the Yellow Pages. Dial 411 and ask the operator to give you the number of the nearest public or private hospital. Other options include asking your hotel to call a doctor or dentist to visit you in your room, or finding one yourself through the **NY Hotel Urgent Medical Services**, **Dial-A-Doctor** or **NYU Dental Care**. For more general advice and information call **Travelers' Aid**, a national organization geared to helping travelers.

CRISIS INFORMATION

All Emergencies
(*911 (or 0). This alerts police, fire and medical services.*

Crime Victims Hot Line
(*(212) 577-7777.*

Dial-A-Doctor
(*(212) 971-9692.*

Hospital Emergency Rooms
St. Vincent's, 11th St and Seventh Ave. **Map** 3 C1.
(*(212) 604-7998.*

St. Luke's Roosevelt.
58th St and Ninth Ave. **Map** 12 D3. (*(212) 523-6800.*

National Organization for Women (NOW)
(*(212) 627-9895.*

NY Hotel Urgent Medical Services
(*(212) 737-1212.*

NYU Dental Care
345 E 24th St/1st Ave.
Map 9 B4.
(*(212) 998-9800 (9am–6:30pm Mon–Thu, 9am–4pm Fri), (212) 998-9828 (weekends and after 9pm).*

Pharmacy (24-hour)
Rite Aid, 50th St./8th Ave.
Map 12 D4. (*(212) 247-8384.*

Poison Control Center
(*(212) 764-7667.*

Sex Crimes Report Line
(*(212) 267-7273.*

Travelers' Aid
JFK Airport, Terminal 410.
(*(718) 656-4870.*

New York ambulance

Banking and Currency

NEW YORK IS THE NATION's banking center. It has a wealth of local, regional and major national banks, plus some retail branches of the leading foreign banks. Fleet Bank and Barclays are well represented in New York; the banks of Australia, Canada, Ireland, Scotland, Tokyo, and Turkey all have offices or branches.

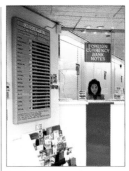

Foreign currency exchange counter at Chequepoint USA

BANKING

NEW YORK banks are generally open weekdays from 9am to 3pm. There are, however, a number of banks that open earlier or close late evening to suit commuters' needs. Tellers are behind a counter. At most banks, all the tellers will cash traveler's checks and exchange your foreign currency.

Automated teller machine (ATM)

AUTOMATED TELLER MACHINES

A CONVENIENT development in banking has been the introduction of the automated teller machine (ATM). These are found in nearly all bank lobbies and enable you to obtain American currency 24 hours a day by electronically tapping into your own bank account. ATMs usually issue American banknotes in $20 denominations.

Before you leave for New York, check with your bank about which New York City banks and ATM systems will accept your bank card and what fees and commissions will be charged on each transaction. Most ATM machines are in either the

Cirrus or Plus network. They accept various US bank cards, MasterCard and VISA cards and certain others. Among the many advantages of ATMs is the swift, secure exchange of your money at the wholesale rate used between the banks when they make their million-dollar deals.

On a more cautionary note, be aware of your surroundings when using an unlocked ATM. It is best to use them only in daylight hours or when the streets are crowded.

CREDIT CARDS

MASTERCARD, American Express, VISA, JCB and Diners Card are widely accepted throughout the United States, regardless of which company or bank issues them. These cards can also be used to obtain cash advances from various ATM machines. They may also be upgraded to confer higher spending limits. In the US you can use a credit card to pay for nearly everything imaginable, from groceries to restaurant and hotel bills, and telephone orders for movie and theater tickets. Major expenses such as tours, travel packages and expensive rentals are all best paid for by credit card. Try to avoid carrying huge sums of money around with you.

CASHING CHECKS

DOLLAR TRAVELER's checks issued by American Express and Thomas Cook are widely accepted without a fee by most of New York's department stores, shops, hotels and restaurants. Traveler's checks in other currencies, including sterling, are not universally accepted. They can usually be

exchanged by your hotel cashier, but may require a visit to a bank. Exchange rates are printed daily in the *New York Times* and *Wall Street Journal*, and may be posted in bank windows. American Express checks are exchanged without a fee at American Express offices. Major hotels have cashiers to exchange traveler's checks.

Foreign exchange brokers are few. Among the most solidly established are **Travelex Currency Services Inc.** and **American Express**. The ones listed on the opposite page have late hours. Others are listed in the city's telephone Yellow Pages under *Foreign Money Brokers*. Expect to pay a fee, which will vary widely from one place to the next, plus a commission.

Chase Manhattan Bank offers exchange in more than 400 locations and there are scores of hole-in-the-wall check-cashing shops in Manhattan. They are listed in the Yellow Pages classified section. They may not be willing to cash your traveler's checks though, and they are very unlikely to accept or cash foreign checks.

EXCHANGE ADDRESSES

Travelex Currency Services Inc.
1590 Broadway
Map 12 E5.
C *(212) 265-6063.*
One of several branches.

American Express
See p359.

Coins

American coins come in 50-, 25-, 10-, 5- and 1-cent pieces. The new gold-tone $1 coins are now in circulation as are the State quarters, which feature an historical scene on one side. Each value of coin has a popular name: 25-cent pieces are called quarters, 10-cent pieces are called dimes, 5-cent pieces called nickels and 1-cent pieces called pennies.

**25- cent coin
(a quarter)**

**10- cent coin
(a dime)**

**5- cent coin
(a nickel)**

**1- cent coin
(a penny)**

**A one-dollar coin
or 'buck'**

Bank Notes (Bills)

Units of currency in the United States are dollars and cents. There are 100 cents to a dollar. Notes come in $1, $5, $10, $20, $50 and $100s. All bills are green, so check the amount carefully. The new $20 and $50 bills with new security features are now in circulation; they have larger numbers when compared to the old notes.

1- dollar bill ($1)

5- dollar bill ($5)

10- dollar bill ($50)

20- dollar bill ($20)

50- dollar bill ($50)

100- dollar bill ($100)

FINANCIAL SERVICES

American Express
822 Lexington Ave. **Map** 13 A2.
(212) 758-6510. 9am–6pm
Mon–Fri, 10am–4pm Sat.
Helpline (800) 221-7282

**Avis Currency
Exchange**
Grand Central Terminal.
Map 9 A1. (212) 661-7600.
10am–8pm Mon–Fri,
noon–8pm Sat & Sun.

Cirrus/MasterCard
(800) 424-7787

Chequepoint USA
22 Central Park South.
Map 12 F3. (212) 750-2400.
8am–8pm daily.

VISA Plus
(800) 843-7587

Travelex
1590 Broadway. **Map** 12 E5.
(212) 265-6063. 9am–
7pm Mon–Sat, 9am–5pm Sun.
Also at: 317 Madison Ave
(212) 883-0400.
(800) CURRENCY.
9am–5pm Mon–Sun.
www.us.thomascook.com

Using New York's Phones

Sign for public payphones

Pᴜʙʟɪᴄ ᴘᴀʏ ᴘʜᴏɴᴇꜱ can be found at many street corners, in hotel and office lobbies, restaurants, bars, theaters, and department stores. Few use credit cards, but you can now buy prepaid phone cards. Most phones are coin-operated and take 5-, 10- and 25-cent coins. In 2003 Neptune 800 internet payphones were introduced to the streets of New York. These have a color monitor, keyboard, and webcam, and offer customers internet access at 25 cents per minute.

NEW YORK TIME

New York is on Eastern Standard Time. When making international calls, calculate the time in the country you are calling. For the UK add 5 hours; for Australia add 15 hours; and for New Zealand add 17 hours.

PUBLIC TELEPHONES

Tʜᴇ ꜱᴛᴀɴᴅᴀʀᴅ pay phone has a hand receiver and 12-button key pad and is pillar- or wall-mounted. In some locations the pay phone may belong to an independent company. The independents are often more expensive and less reliable. Regulations require each public pay phone to post information about charges, toll-free numbers and how to make calls using other carriers. Look

for the Verizon logo on the box to be sure the phone will reach all numbers at standard rates. To complain about service, call the **Public Service Commission**.

Useful information
Public Service Commission [C] (800) 342-3355 (tollfree number).
To check e-mail
Times Square Visitors Center,1560 Broadway, **Map** 12 E5; NY Computer Cafe, 247 E 57th St. [C] (212) 872-1704 **Map** 13 B3; many New York Public Libraries have Internet desks, but there is usually a time limit for use.

Independently operated pay phone

PAY PHONE CHARGES

Wɪᴛʜɪɴ the New York boroughs, the standard charge, around 25 cents, buys three minutes' talking time. If your call lasts longer, the operator will request additional payment.

Many newsstands now sell prepaid phone cards for long-distance calls; they can be bought in $5, $10, and $25 amounts. The cards offer substantial savings compared to standard rates. However, the calls are connected over the Internet and so the sound quality may not be as good as calls using a standard carrier.

USING A COIN-OPERATED PHONE

1 Lift the receiver.

3 Dial or press the number.

Coins
Make sure you have the correct coins available before you dial.

5 cents

10 cents

25 cents

2 Insert the necessary coin or coins. The coin drops as soon as you insert it.

4 If you do not want to complete your call or it does not get through, retrieve the coin(s) by pressing the coin return.

5 If the call is answered and you talk longer than the allotted three minutes, the operator will interrupt and ask you to deposit more coins. Pay phones do not give change.

A typical public pay phone stand

International long-distance rates for calls dialed direct vary from country to country. For calls to the UK, the discount rate starts at 1pm, then drops to an economy rate from 6pm until 7am the next day.

USEFUL NUMBERS

Directory Inquiries
☏ *411; 10-10-9000.*

Main Post Office
☏ *(212) 967-8585.*

Operator Assistance
☏ *0.*

Speaking Clock
☏ *(212) 976-1616.*

International Directory Inquiries
☏ *00.*

REACHING THE RIGHT NUMBER

• Five area codes are used in New York: 212 , 917, 646 for Manhattan; the other boroughs use 718 and 347. Calls to 800, 888, and 877 numbers are free.
• To call a number outside your own area, first dial 1. For example, to dial Queens from Manhattan dial 1 (718) (number). To call inside your area, dial the area code first.
• To call long distance from a pay phone: dial 0 followed by the area code and then the number. The operator will answer and tell you how much money you need to deposit.
• To make an international direct call: dial 011 followed by the country code (New Zealand: 64; Australia: 61; UK: 44), then the city or area code (minus the first 0) and the local number.
• To make an international call via the operator: dial 01 followed by the country code, the city code (minus the first 0) and then the local number.
• International Directory Inquiries are on 00. International operator assistance is on 01.
• **In an emergency, phone 911.**

Sending A Letter

US postal service logo

APART FROM post offices, letters can be mailed at your hotel concierge desk (which usually also sells stamps); in letter slots in office building lobbies; in air, rail and bus terminals; and in the occasional street mailbox. These are always painted blue, or red, white and blue. Mail in most mailboxes is not picked up on weekends. Post offices are shown on the *Street Finder* maps (*see pp378–9*).

POSTAL SERVICES

THE CITY's main **General Post Office** is open 24 hours a day. Stamps can be bought here or from branch offices (a handy one is in the Empire State Building) or from coin-operated machines in pharmacies, department stores and bus and train stations. All letters go first class.

The post office offers three special delivery services: **Express Mail** service for next-day delivery, **Priority Mail** service for two-day delivery, and **International Express Mail** for overseas. Priority Mail will also pick up letters on weekdays for an extra charge. Private express mail can be arranged through hotel

Colorful US stamps

concierges or with one of the delivery services listed in the telephone book.

Useful information
General Post Office, 421 8th Ave.
Map 8 D2. ☏ *(212) 967-8585.*
☏ *(800) 222-1811* Priority and Express Mail.
☏ *(800) 463-3339* FedEx.
☏ *(800) 225-5345* DHL.
☏ *(800) 742-5877* UPS.
Internet guides
ⓦ www.bigyellow.com
ⓦ www.usps.com

HELD MAIL

MAIL will be held for you for 30 days at the General Post Office's General Delivery window. Mail can be sent to any local post office by giving the zip code or name. Address mail with: Name, General Delivery, US Post Office, New York, NY 10001.

Express Mail **Priority Mail**

Standard mailbox

Mailboxes
Mailboxes can be few and far between on New York streets, and it may be easier to find a post office (see Street Finder pp378–9). Instructions on how to use each mailbox are written on the box. If you use Express or Priority services, weigh your letters at a post office to figure out the postage needed.

GETTING TO NEW YORK

MANY INTERNATIONAL airlines have direct flights to New York. It is also very well served by charter and domestic services. Price wars between airlines have reduced fares, and domestic flights now prove a viable alternative to bus and train tickets; group tour package prices are often

Grand Central Terminal

unbeatable. The *QE2* is one of several cruise ships that dock in the city. Long-distance trains serving New York are clean and comfortable. Interstate and long distance buses have air-conditioning, video screens and on-board toilets. For information on arriving in New York see the map on pages 366–7.

AIR TRAVEL

NEW YORK CAN be reached by air direct from most major cities. The flight from London takes about eight hours. However, there are no direct flights from Australia or New Zealand. Instead, the airlines fly to the West coast, which takes around 14 hours, land, refuel and then continue on to New York.

Among the main carriers to New York are **Air Canada**, **Delta**, **Continental**, **British Airways**, **American Airlines**, **Virgin Atlantic** and **United Airlines**. All international flights arrive at Newark or JFK airports *(see pp364–5)*.

APEX (Advance Purchase Excursion) tickets for the scheduled airlines are usually the cheapest return fares apart from package tours. But they must be bought in advance and are valid for a stay of 7 to 30 days. Some airlines offer cheaper fares if you limit your stay to specified periods. Senior citizens may also receive discounts on some flights.

AIRLINE NUMBERS

Air Canada **(** *(888) 247-2262.*
w www.aircanada.ca

American Airlines **(** *(800) 433-7300.*
w www.aa.com

British Airways **(** *(800) 247-9297.*
w www.british-airways.com

Continental **(** *(800) 231-0856.*
w www.flycontinental.com

Delta **(** *(800) 241-4141.*
w www. delta.com

United Airlines **(** *(800) 241-6522*
w www.ual.com

Virgin Atlantic **(** *(800) 862-8621*
w www.fly.virgin.com

OCEAN TRAVEL

NEW YORK IS a regular port of call for many cruise liners, in addition to the *QE2*, which docks there, via Southampton, 25 times a year. You can also take the *QE2* from New York to Australia and New Zealand. Ocean travel offers an expensive but

Long-distance Greyhound bus

relaxing way of traveling to New York. Ships dock at the Hudson River piers in midtown Manhattan.

LONG-DISTANCE BUSES

ALL LONG-DISTANCE buses such as **Greyhound Lines** arrive in the city at the **Port Authority Bus Terminal**. Buses from here also connect with the three airports. With over 6,000 buses arriving and leaving daily and carrying some 172,000 passengers, the atmosphere is chaotic. Many hotels are also accessible directly from the terminal.
Useful information Greyhound Bus Lines **(** *(800) 231-2222. (24 hrs).*
w www.greyhound.com Port Authority Bus Terminal. W 40th St and Eighth Ave. **Map** 8 D1. **(** *(212) 564-8484 (24 hrs).* **w** www.panynj.gov

TRAIN TRAVEL

AMTRAK TRAINS from Canada, upstate New York, southern, northeastern and western states all stop at Penn Station *(see p376)*. Metro-North lines from upstate New York and Connecticut arrive at Grand Central Terminal *(see p376)*.

Ocean liner anchored in Manhattan

New York Airports

THE THREE MAIN airports (Newark, JFK and La Guardia) are all well connected to central Manhattan. Look for uniformed "skycaps" – scarlet-capped porters wearing distinctive badges, who will help you with your luggage. Never trust anyone else to help carry your bags – you may never see them again. Taxi dispatchers will help you into a licensed taxi at the taxi area.

GETTING INTO MANHATTAN

THE GROUND Transportation center at each airport will give you information on the ways you can continue your trip. The most useful services, operating from LaGuardia and JFK, are the **New York Airport Service** and **Super Shuttle**. The former stops at Grand Central; the latter will drop you anywhere in Manhattan. New Jersey Transit buses and **Olympia Airport Express** also go to and from each airport into the city. The fare on the Olympia vans is one of the best bargains.

Shared vehicle rides are offered at JFK and LaGuardia by **Classic Airport Share Ride** and **Connecticut Limo**. You can sometimes share a taxi or one of the independent (gypsy) cabs into Manhattan. For the price of a subway ride, the "A" line connects with a shuttle bus and takes passengers to and from JFK. The M60 city bus also goes to and from LaGuardia. Most of the car rental firms have courtesy telephones at the baggage-claim areas. Telephone numbers and web addresses for your advance reservations are listed on page 370.

Taxi dispatcher

BUS COMPANIES

New York Airport Service
☎ (718) 875-8200.

Classic Airport Share Ride
☎ (631) 567-5100. 🖥 www.classictrans.com

Super Shuttle
☎ 212-BLUE VAN. 🖥 www.supershuttle.com

Olympia Airport Express
☎ (212) 964-6233. 🖥 www.olympiabus.com

Connecticut Limo
☎ (800) 472-5466. 🖥 www.ctlimo.com

LA GUARDIA (LGA)

PRINCIPALLY SERVING business travelers, La Guardia lies 8 miles (13 km) east of Manhattan on the north side of Long Island in Queens.

Upon arrival, you can rent luggage trolleys from the baggage-claim area next to the luggage carousels. Skycaps are on hand to assist you. Baggage can also be left in the Tele-Trip business center on the departure level. Foreign exchange desks are located around the Central Terminal.

Uniformed taxi dispatchers at the airport are on duty at peak hours. Only use yellow taxis licensed by the city. The cost of tolls, plus a small surcharge after 8pm and all day Sunday, will be added to the fare shown on the meter (about $25–$40 to midtown).

Useful information Airport Information Service ☎ (718) 533-3400. 🖥 www.laguardiaairport.com 🖥 www.panynj.gov

Transatlantic jet

PLAN OF LA GUARDIA AIRPORT

A frequent free bus service runs between each of the terminals and parking areas. Buses and taxis into the city and its suburbs depart from the first floor of the Central Terminal building.

Central Terminal building

Marine Air Terminal

Delta Shuttle Terminal

USAirways Terminal

USAirways Shuttle

Delta Terminal

Grand Central Parkway to New York

KEY

🅿 Parking

🚌 Bus service between terminals

JFK Airport

NEW YORK'S main airport, JFK, is 15 miles (24 km) southeast of Manhattan, in the borough of Queens. American Airlines, British Airways, Delta, TWA, and United have their own arrivals buildings, with customs and immigration facilities. Other international airlines use Terminals 1, 2 or 4. Note that the terminals have been recently renumbered. A $10 billion airport expansion includes a new terminal for American Airlines.

Main Hall at the International Arrivals Building, JFK

Airport information signs at JFK

Luggage trolleys are free on arrival in the meeting area. Foreign exchange offices are located in all terminals.

Transportation to Manhattan can be arranged 24 hours a day at the Ground Transportation desk on the ground level near the baggage-claim. Courtesy phones are provided by car rental companies. Most have shuttle service to their rental offices. Taxis wait outside terminals. A trip to Manhattan takes up to an hour; there is a flat fee of $45 plus tolls. The

New York Airport Service bus is reliable, safe, and operates 24 hours. For early morning flights there are hotels near the airport. Hotels can be booked at the Meegan Services desk.

A light-rail system, AirTrain JFK, began service to the Howard Beach terminal at the end of 2002, and started service to Jamaica Airtrain terminal in 2003, providing direct onward connections to the city subway.

Useful Addresses

Airport Information Service
(718) 244-4444.

Best Western JFK Airport
138–10 135th Ave, Queens.
(718) 322-8700.

Holiday Inn JFK
144–02 135th Ave, Queens.
(718) 659-0200.

Helicopter Flight Services (212) 355-0801. W www.heliny.com; Liberty Helicopters (888) 692-4354.

American Airlines (8)
British Airways United Airlines (7)
Terminal 9
TWA (6) (Domestic flights)
Van Wyck Expressway to New York
Terminal 1
TWA (5) (International flights)
Garage
Terminal 2
Terminal (4)

Key

🚌 Parking
Ⓟ Bus stops for all buses

Delta Airlines (3)

Plan of JFK Airport

Free Airline Connection buses operate between terminals – allow half an hour for distant connections. They usually leave every 5–15 minutes, 24 hours a day. For a faster, but more expensive, transfer, take a taxi. All buses and cabs leave from clearly marked stands just outside the air terminal arrival areas.

NEWARK AIRPORT

Bus terminal at Newark Airport

KEY

🅿 Parking

🚌 Bus stop

— Inter-terminal monorail

Terminal B
(International Arrivals)

Terminal C

Terminal C-3

Marriott Hotel

Terminal A

Roads to Manhattan

PLAN OF NEWARK AIRPORT

A monorail links all three terminals with the parking lots. Free Airline Connection buses offer a 24-hour service between terminals every 5–15 minutes. Allow about 30 minutes for the farthest terminals. Taxis are also available. All buses and taxis leave from outside the air terminal arrival areas.

NEWARK, NEW YORK'S second largest international airport, is about 16 miles (26 km) southwest of Manhattan, in New Jersey.

All international flights arrive at Terminal "B." Baggage trolleys are free for arriving international passengers. There is no baggage room. Foreign exchange desks are available in each terminal.

The Ground Transportation services desk, open 24 hours a day, is next to the baggage-claim area. Courtesy phones are provided by limousine and car rental firms. Many of these have a free shuttle service to their rental offices.

There are taxi stands located outside most arrival areas. Uniformed taxi dispatchers will also help you hail a cab. Never accept a ride into town from anyone who approaches you in the terminal: they may not have insurance and could charge an outrageous fare.

The trip into Manhattan takes about 40–60 minutes and will cost you up to $50.

Buses to Manhattan can take 40 minutes to over an hour, but cost about $12. Electronic boards around the terminal list departure times. A direct train service, AirTrain Newark (www.airtrain newark.com), takes 20 minutes to New York Penn Station and costs $11.55.

For early morning flights, there are hotels located in and around the airport grounds. City hotels can be booked on arrival through the courtesy phones that are linked

directly to various Manhattan hotels. At Newark, these are located in all the terminals.

USEFUL ADDRESSES

Port Authority at Newark Airport
📞 *(888) 397-4636.*
🅆 www.newarkairport.com

Holiday Inn International
1000 Spring St, Elizabeth, N J.
📞 *(800) 465-4329.*

Marriott Hotel
Newark Airport grounds.
📞 *(800) 228-9290.*

Arrival and departure monitors at Newark Airport

Arriving in New York

THIS MAP SHOWS the links between New York's three airports and the center of Manhattan. It also illustrates rail connections linking New York to the rest of the United States and Canada. Travel information, including travel times for subway, bus, rail and helicopter services, is listed in each information box. The passenger ship terminal, New York's key point of arrival for the flood of post-war immigrants, is located a short distance from the center of Manhattan. Port Authority Bus Terminal, on the West Side, provides services across the city.

Ships at the passenger terminal

KEY

✈	Airport *see pp363–5*
⚓	Seaport *see p362*
🚆	Rail link *see p362*
🚌	Bus station/link *see p362*
🚁	Helicopter links *see p364*
—	New York Airport Service and Super Shuttle *see p363*
—	Helicopters *see p364*
—	Long Island Rail Road *see pp376–7*
—	New Jersey Transit buses *see p363*
—	Olympia Airport Express *see p363*
—	Shuttle bus *see p364*
—	Subway A *see p374*

⚓ **PASSENGER SHIP TERMINAL**
Piers 88–92 for QE2 and other cruise ship arrivals and departures.

Passenger Ship Terminal

🚌 **PORT AUTHORITY BUS TERMINAL**
All long-distance buses arrive and depart here; links to all city airports.

Port Authority Bus Terminal

🚆 **PENN STATION**
Long-distance trains serve the US and **Canada**; *commuter trains to* **Long Island** *and* **New Jersey**; *AirTrain Newark to* **Newark Airport**.
🚆 *Amtrak, Long Island Rail Road and New Jersey Transit services.*
Ⓜ *A, C, E, 1, 2, 3, 9.*

Penn Station

Chelsea and the Garment District

Greenwich Village

Super Shuttle buses take passengers to any point between 23rd and 63rd streets

SoHo and TriBeCa

East Village

Seaport and the Civic Center

Lower East Side

✈ **NEWARK**
Bus to Manhattan every 20–30 mins.
🚌 **Olympia Airport Express** *every 20–30 mins to* **Penn Station** *and* **Grand Central Terminal**.
🚌 **New Jersey Transit** *buses every 15–20 mins to the* **Port Authority Bus Terminal**.
🚆 *AirTrain to* **Penn Station**.
🚁 *Chartered helicopters to 34th St. heliport.*

Lower Manhattan

Pier 11

Amtrak railroad train

Grand Central Terminal

Morningside Heights and Harlem

Upper West Side

Central Park

Upper East Side

✈ **LA GUARDIA**

Buses to Grand Central Terminal every 20 mins. Train services every 5–10 mins. Water shuttle to city center.

🚌 **New York Airport Service** *every 20–30 mins to* **Grand Central**, **Port Authority** *and hotels.*

🚌 **Super Shuttle** *service to your choice of destination.*

🚆 *Shuttle bus to* **Jamaica, Queens**, *station of the* **Long Island Rail Road** *every half hour; then trains every 5–10 mins to* **Penn Station** *(25 mins).*

🚁 **Chartered helicopter** *to midtown.*

🚆 **GRAND CENTRAL**

Daily commuter train service to upstate **New York** *and* **Connecticut**.

🚆 *Metro-North.*

Ⓜ *4, 5, 6, 7, S.*

Grand Central Terminal

Upper Midtown

Lower Midtown

East 34th St. Pier

NYC Heliport

Jamaica
🚆 *Long Island Rail Road.*
Airtrain JFK.

Chartered helicopter service to and from all three airports

✈ **JFK**

Bus service to Grand Central and Port Authority every 20 mins. Trains every 5–10 mins to Penn Station. Subway to city center.

🚌 **New York Airport Service** *every 20 mins to* **Grand Central, Port Authority Bus Terminal** *and midtown hotels (45 mins–1 hr).*

🚌 **Super Shuttle** *service to your choice of destination (see box at center of map).*

🚆 **AirTrain JFK** *to* **Howard Beach terminal** *with connections on to the city subway system.*

🚁 **Chartered helicopters** *make frequent departures from all airports to* **34th Street Heliport**.

The Port Authority of New York and New Jersey, operator of JFK, Newark and La Guardia airports, is investing $2.7 billion in AirTrain, a new rail link that will connect the airports to the city subway system.

Howard Beach
🚆 *AirTrain JFK.*

| 0 kilometers | | 2 |
| 0 miles | 1 | |

GETTING AROUND NEW YORK

WITH OVER SIX thousand miles of streets, walking around New York could prove difficult. But the city is a network of districts and many of the major sites can be visited area by area. Taxis are best for door-to-door transit but can be held up in traffic jams, especially during rush hours. The city's bus service is reliable and cheap but often slow. Subways are quick, reliable and cheap, and make stops throughout central Manhattan. There are weekly and day passes that are valid for all public transportation. These are the best value when visiting the sights of the city.

Stretch limousine, the preferred
vehicle for New York's glitterati

NEGOTIATING THE AVENUES AND STREETS

MANHATTAN'S avenues run approximately north to south; its streets (except in the older areas) run east to west. Fifth Avenue is used to divide East and West Street addresses; Five West 40th Street is, for example, a few doors west of Fifth Avenue on 40th Street, and Five East 40th is a few doors to the east.

Most streets in midtown are one-way. In general, traffic is eastbound on even-numbered streets and westbound on odd-numbered streets. Avenues also tend to be one-way, alternating northbound or southbound. First, Third (above 23rd Street), Madison, Eighth, Avenue of the Americas (6th Ave) and Tenth avenues, are all northbound, while Second, Lexington, Fifth, Seventh, and Ninth avenues and Broadway below 59th Street are southbound. There is two-way traffic on York, Park, Eleventh and Twelfth avenues and Broadway above 60th Street.

Although most city blocks north of Houston Street are rectangular, they are not very uniform: east–west blocks are three or even four times longer than north–south blocks.

Certain streets have more than one name, for instance, Avenue of the Americas is also Sixth Avenue. Note too that Park Avenue South is not the same as Park Avenue. Many intersections and plazas have titles commemorating people or events. The maps in this guide use the names most often used by New Yorkers.

Rush-hour gridlock in Manhattan

FINDING AN ADDRESS

A useful formula has been devised to help pinpoint any **Avenue Address**. By dropping the last digit of the address, dividing the remainder by 2, then adding or subtracting the **Key Number** given here, you will discover the nearest cross street. For example: To find No. 826 Lexington Avenue, first you have to drop the 6; divide 82 by 2, which is 41; then add **22** (the key number). Therefore, the nearest cross street is 63rd Street.

A road sign for Madison Avenue positioned at an
intersection with a street

Avenue Address	Key Number	Avenue Address	Key Number
1st Ave	+3	9th Ave	+13
2nd Ave	+3	10th Ave	+14
3rd Ave	+10	Amsterdam Ave	+60
4th Ave	+8	Audubon Ave	+165
5th Ave, up to 200	+13	Broadway above	
5th Ave, up to 400	+16	23rd St	-30
5th Ave, up to 600	+18	Central Park W, divide	
5th Ave, up to 775	+20	full number by 10	+60
5th Ave 775–1286,		Columbus Ave	+60
do not divide by 2	-18	Convent Ave	+127
5th Ave, up to 1500	+45	Lenox Ave	+110
5th Ave, up to 2000	+24	Lexington Ave	+22
(6th) Ave of the		Madison Ave	+26
Americas	-12	Park Ave	+35
7th Ave below		Park Ave South	+08
110th St	+12	Riverside Drive, divide	
7th Ave above		full number by 10	+72
110th St	+20	St Nicholas Ave	+110
8th Ave	+10	West End Ave	+60

PLANNING YOUR JOURNEY

THE STREETS and sidewalks are busiest during the rush hours – 8 to 10am, 11:30am to 1:30pm and 4:30 to 6:30pm, Monday to Friday. Throughout these periods it is better to face the crowds on foot than attempt any journey by bus, taxi or subway. At other times of day and during certain holiday periods *(see p53)*, the traffic is often much lighter and you should reach your destination quickly.

There are, of course, a few exceptions. Fifth Avenue should always be avoided on parade days (St. Patrick's Day and Thanksgiving Day are the worst). Celebrity visits or one of the regular demonstrations at City Hall *(see p90)* can cause major disruption to the traffic. The area around Seventh Avenue, south of 42nd Street, is likely to be busy during the day with the truck and handcart traffic of New York's garment industry.

WALKING

MOST INTERSECTIONS between avenues and streets have lampposts with name-markers and electric traffic signals. The traffic lights show red (stop) and green (go) for vehicles and "Walk–Don't Walk" for pedestrians. Most New Yorkers, however, rely on their own judgment rather than on the numerous "Walk" signs.

Remember that vehicles keep to the right. There are no

Pedestrian crossing

Do not cross the street

You may cross the street

Staten Island Ferry leaving Battery Park

Circle Line tour boat

FERRIES

There are two ferries of interest to visitors *(see also p353)*: the Circle Line runs a ferry to the Statue of Liberty and Ellis Island several times each day from Battery Park at the southern tip of Manhattan – W www.circleline.com. The 24-hour Staten Island ferry from Battery Park travels the channel and offers splendid views of lower Manhattan, the Statue of Liberty, Ellis Island, the bridges and Governors Island. The round trip is the best bargain in New York; it's free.

cautionary "Look Left" signs to alert you to the direction of oncoming traffic. There are, however, numerous one-way streets, so it's best to look both ways before you cross. Beware, too, of cars, trucks and taxis turning the corner behind you as you start to cross the street.

There are pedestrian crossings at some intersections. These are officially designated pedestrian crossing points (at Rockefeller Center for instance) and are closely monitored by the police. The city has a few underground walkways for pedestrians in Central Park.

WATER TAXI

THE NEW YORK water taxi arrived in 2002 and runs from East 90th Street Pier to Pier 84. Visit www.nywatertaxi. com for more information.

CYCLING

CYCLING IN THE city is safest on the park pathways (Central Park and along the East and Hudson rivers) in daylight hours. You can rent bikes at Columbus Circle or the Loeb Boathouse in Central Park.
Useful information
Central Park Bike Rental, 2 Columbus Circle. **Map** 12 D3. (*(212) 541-8759.*
W *www.centralparkbiketour.com*

Cyclist in Central Park

Driving in New York

H EAVY TRAFFIC AND EXPENSIVE rental cars make driving in New York a frustrating experience. You must wear a seat belt. The speed limit is 30 mph (48 km/h) – which is difficult to exceed because of Manhattan's pot-holes and traffic. Most streets are one-way, and there are traffic lights at every corner. Driving is on the right.

Busy traffic heading down Sixth Avenue

RENTING A CAR

T O RENT A CAR you must be at least 25 years old, or pay a surcharge. You will need a valid driver's license (for for-eign visitors an International Driver's License is useful), a passport, and a credit card or you will have to pay a deposit.

Unless you are adequately covered by your own insu-rance policy, you should also take out damage and liability protection, as vandalism and theft are common. Refill with gas before you return the car or you'll pay double the normal price for fuel. It is cheaper to rent a car in the city than at the airports.

TRAFFIC SIGNS

Black-and-white markings on many street crossings mean that pedestrians have right of way. At intersections, they indicate that traffic should keep out when the light is red. Unlike the rest of New York State, you can never turn right on a red light unless there is a sign indicating otherwise.

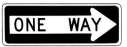

Traffic flows in a single direction

PARKING

P ARKING IN Manhattan is difficult and costly. Parking areas and parking garages post their rates at the entrance. Some hotels include parking charges in their room rates.

In some areas there are meters at the curb for short-term (20–60 minutes) parking. Don't be tempted to park at out-of-order meters – you may receive a parking ticket. Yellow street and curb markings mean no parking.

"Alternate-side" parking applies on most of the city's side streets. Cars may usually be left all day and night but must be moved to the other side of the street before 8am the next day. For specific information call the **Trans-portation Department**.

PENALTIES

I F YOU RECEIVE a parking ticket, you have seven days to pay the required fine or to appeal against it. If you have any queries about your ticket call the **Parking Violations Bureau** between 8:30am and 7pm on any weekday.

New York's tow-away crews are extremely active, and one-third of cars towed suffer damage. If you cannot find your car at its parking place, first of all call the traffic department's tow-away office. The pound is open 24 hours a day, Monday to Saturday. You can redeem your car for a hefty fine of $150, plus $10 per day storage fee. Traveler's checks, certified checks, money orders and cash are all accepted. There is an ATM machine *(see p358)* on the premises. If you have rented the car, the contract must be produced, and only the authorized driver may redeem the car. If the car is not at the pound, report it to the police.

Useful information

Police emergen-cies only **C** *911*; Parking Violations Bureau **C** *(718) 802-3636*; Traffic Dept, Tow Pound, Pier 76, W 38th St and 12th Ave. **Map** 7 1B; uptown at the 207th St. Pound **C** *(212) 788-7800*; Transportation Dept **C** *311*.

BRIDGE TOLLS

M OST MAJOR access routes in and out of New York City levy tolls. These vary in price from $1.50 for some of the smaller bridges, to $6.00 for the George Washington Bridge between New York and New Jersey. The bridges of the Triborough Bridge Authority charge $3.50 each way. All tolls must be paid in cash. Avoid E-Z Pass lanes, marked with purple signs, which are only for holders of pre-paid passes.

CAR RENTAL AGENCIES

I F YOU NEED TO rent a car while in New York, agencies are listed in the telephone directory under *Automobile Renting*. The major rental companies include:

Avis **C** *(800) 331-1212.*
w www.avis.com

Budget **C** *(800) 527-0700.*
w www.drivebudget.com

Dollar **C** *(800) 800-4000.*
w www.dollar.com

Hertz **C** *(800) 654-3131.*
w www.hertz.com

National **C** *(800) 227-7368.*
w www.nationalcar.com

Entry prohibited

50 mph (80 km/h) speed limit

Give way to all vehicles

Stop at intersection

New York's Taxis

New York taxi cab

ALL LICENSED TAXI cabs are yellow. If their roof numbers are lit up, they are available and can be flagged down. Occupied cabs have their top lights switched off. Taxis that are not on duty have their "Off-Duty" sign lit. Only licensed cabs are authorized to pick up people who hail them from the street; accepting a ride from anyone else can be dangerous and expensive.

TAKING A CAB

THERE ARE more than 12,000 Yellow Cabs in New York. Each one has a meter, and many can issue printed receipts. A taxi can carry up to four passengers with a single fare covering everyone on board.

Taxi stands are scarce; hotels, Penn Station and Grand Central Terminal are by far the best places to seek cabs.

Licensed taxis undergo periodic inspections and are insured against accidents and losses. Non-licensed or "gypsy" cabs are unlikely to have these safeguards, and are not recommended.

Once the cab driver accepts a passenger the meter starts ticking at $2.50. The fare increases 40 cents after each additional 292 yards (267 meters) or every 120 seconds of waiting time. There is an additional 50-cent charge between 8pm and 6am, and a $1 charge between 4pm and 8pm on weekdays.

A few drivers now accept credit cards but most will want to be paid in cash. Tip the driver about 15%.

Cab driving is a traditional occupation of newly arrived immigrants and, as such, communication can be a problem. Although owners of licensed cabs

```
I ♡ NEW YORK
TRIP#  004653
09:11AM 11-15-92
MEDALLION# 6N64
DIST       2.30
FARE $     6.00
TLC:212-221-TAXI
```

A printed receipt available from most taxi cabs

must pass exams in English comprehension and the layout of the city, they will not necessarily understand either. Make sure your driver understands exactly where you want to go before you start your ride.

By law, a driver must take you anywhere in the city unless the off-duty sign is lit and the roof light is off. The driver should not ask you your destination until after you've sat down, and must follow your requests not to smoke, to open or close a window, and to pick up or drop off passengers as you direct. If he or she doesn't comply you can report them to the **Taxi & Limousine Commission**.

Each yellow cab displays the driver's photograph and registered number next to the meter. Drivers can be sullen, or try to overcharge or not cooperate with some of your requests. Make a note of the driver's number or the license or receipt number (if you have requested one), and report it to the Commission.

Yellow taxi cabs dominating one of the city's avenues

TAXI NUMBERS

Taxi & Limousine Commission
《 (212) 692-8294 or (212) 676-1000 for general information.

Lost and Found
《 212-MK-TAXI

If you would prefer to use a taxi that has been radio-dispatched, rather than hailing one on the street, call:

Allstate Car & Limousine
《 (800) 453-4099 (toll free).

Chris Limousines
《 (718) 356-3232.

Tri-State and Limo Service
《 (212) 777-7171.

A meter will display your fare as it mounts up. Additional costs are then shown separately.

The roof-light illuminates the cab's number as well as the driver's "Off-Duty" sign.

Traveling by Bus

T HE CITY'S MORE THAN 4,000 blue-and-white buses
cover more than 200 routes in the five boroughs.
Many run 24 hours a day, every day. The buses are
modern, clean and air-conditioned. Traveling by bus is
a good way to take in many of New York's sights. Buses
are also considered safe and tend not to get crowded.
Smoking is forbidden on all public buses, and animals
except service animals (guide dogs) are not allowed.

The fare box is just inside the
entrance doors, next to the driver.

FARE

Y OU CAN PAY THE FARE on a
bus using a MetroCard
(see p374) or exact change
(these must be in coins
only). Bus drivers cannot
make change, and fare
boxes do not accept dollar
bills, half dollars or pennies.
You can buy the MetroCard
at any subway station booth.
   If you are need to take more
than one bus to reach your
destination, you are eligible
for a free transfer. If you pay
your bus fare with a Metro-
Card, a free bus-to-subway,
subway-to-local bus, or
local bus-to-bus transfer is
electronically placed on the
card. If you pay with exact
change, be sure to ask the
driver for a transfer ticket
when you pay.
   There are discount fares
for senior citizens and
the disabled. All buses can
"kneel," which helps elderly
people to board (see p354),
and they are also accessible
to wheelchairs via a lift
at the rear.

RECOGNIZING YOUR BUS
*Each bus stop serves more
than one route, so look for
the route number posted on
the lighted strip above the
windshield on the front of
the bus. Ask the driver if he
or she will be stopping at your
destination or close to it.*

Exit the bus through the
double doors toward the rear.

RIDING THE BUS

B USES WILL STOP only at the
designated bus stops.
They follow north–south
routes on the major avenues,
stopping every two or three
blocks. Crosstown buses,
running east–west, stop at
every block (see p368). Many
routes run a 24-hour daily
service, which becomes a lot
less frequent during the
evening and at night; other
bus services operate only
during the peak hours of 7am
to 10pm.
   Bus stops are marked by
red, white and blue signs and
yellow paint along the curb.
Most also have bus shelters.
A route map and schedule
is posted at each stop. When
you have identified your bus,
enter at the front door and
put your MetroCard in the
fare box. Request a transfer
if you will be changing to
another bus. The majority
of New York's bus drivers
are very friendly and will
call out your stop if you
ask them to.

Bus stops often have
three-sided, glass-
walled shelters.

This bus map shows the
route and main stopping-off
points for route M15.

To request a stop when
traveling on the bus, press
the yellow or black vertical
call strip between the
windows. A "Stop Requested"
sign near the driver will then
light up. If the bus is crowded,
it is worth starting to move
toward the exit door when
you are a few blocks from
your stop.
   Leave through the double
door located toward the rear
of the bus. The driver will
activate the door release as
soon as the bus has stopped,
but you then have to push
the yellow stripe on the door,
not the door itself. This
automatically opens the door
and keeps it open.

Route numbers appear on the
front and side of the bus.

Enter the bus through the
doors at the front.

LONG-DISTANCE & COMMUTER BUSES

Buses to the rest of the US and Canada leave from the **Port Authority Bus Terminal**. Another terminal, at the Manhattan end of the George Washington Bridge, is for local buses to northern New Jersey and New York's Rockland County.

Bus tickets at Port Authority are on sale in the main concourse. The long-distance bus companies, Greyhound, Peter Pan, and Adirondack and the commuter Short Line and NJ Transit have their own ticket counters. There are no reservations taken on any of these bus lines.

There are bathrooms open from 6am to 10pm, but caution is advised. The homeless congregate in Port Authority.

A Greyhound bus arriving in New York en route to Port Authority

BUS INFORMATION

Route Maps
Available from MTA, 370 Jay St, Brooklyn, NY 11201 or NYC Visitors Center, 810 7th Ave (212-484-1222).
MTA Travel Information
C (718) 330-1234 (24 hrs).
W www.mta.info

Port Authority Bus Terminal
West 40th St and Eighth Ave.
Map 8 D1. C (212) 564-8484.
W www.panynj.gov

George Washington Bridge Terminal
178th St. and Broadway. C (212) 564-1114. W www.panynj.gov

Lost Property
C (212) 712-4500.

SIGHTSEEING BY BUS

For a pleasant and cheap alternative to a tour bus, hop on a city bus and see New York with the New Yorkers. Bus routes M1 and M6 down Fifth and Seventh Avenues to the Battery, returning north via the Wall Street area, Madison Avenue, and Sixth Avenue. Route M5 gives fine views of the Hudson River as buses travel north on Riverside Drive to the George Washington Bridge at 178th Street. Route M104 travels from the United Nations at First Avenue across 42nd Street, through Times Square, then follows Broadway north by Lincoln Center to Columbia University at 125th Street.

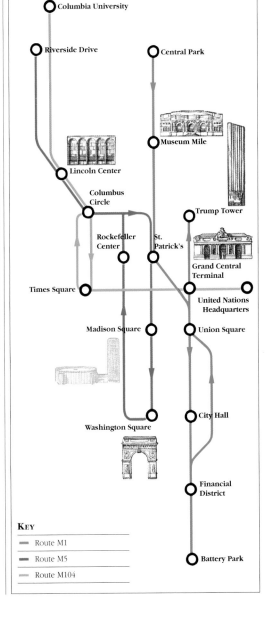

KEY

— Route M1
— Route M5
— Route M104

Using the Subway

New York subway logo

THE SUBWAY is the quickest and most reliable way to travel in the city. The vast system extends over 233 route miles (375 km) and has 468 stations. Most routes operate 24 hours a day throughout the year. Night services are less frequent, and fewer trains run on weekends. In the past few years the subway system has been completely upgraded, and the trains are now air-conditioned, well lit, safer and more comfortable.

NEW YORK SUBWAY

MANY SUBWAY entrances are marked by illuminated spheres: green where the station booth is manned around the clock, red means that there is restricted entry. Others are marked by a sign bearing the name of the station and the numbers or letters of the routes passing through it.

The subway system runs 24 hours a day, but not all routes operate at all times. The basic service is between 6am and midnight.

Bear in mind that there are two types of trains. Local trains stop at all stations, and express trains are faster and stop at fewer stations. Both types of stops are distinguished on every subway map.

In general, the safest, but most crowded, times to travel are between the rush hours of 9am to 4:30pm. Use common sense, stand in the "Off-Hour Waiting Area" on the platforms, and always be sure of where you are going when you use the subway. It is safe to travel to outer boroughs, although it is not a good idea for anyone to travel alone after 10pm. Use the central cars and avoid all eye contact with any unsavory characters.

In an emergency, contact either the station agent in the station booth or a member of the train crew in either the first car or in the middle of the train.

SUBWAY FARE

THE FARE is $2 no matter how far you travel. The MetroCard has replaced tokens as means of fare. A one-day FunPass for $7 for unlimited travel all day is one option for visitors. Other options are a $10 pass (good for 5 rides and one free ride), a $20 pass (good for 10 rides and two free rides), or a $21 pass for unlimited travel all week. MetroCard, which can also be used on buses *(see p372),* is sold at 3,500 locations around the city as well as at subway stations where you can pay with cash or credit card.

Subway information New York City Transit Authority [C] *(718) 330-1234.* Metrocard Customer Service [C] *(212) 638-7622.* [W] www.mta.info

READING THE SUBWAY MAP

Each route is identified on the subway map *(see inside back cover)* by color, by the names of the stations at each end of the line, and by a letter or number. For instance, the green (6) route links Woodlawn and Utica Avenues, and is served by number 4 trains. Local and express stops and interchange points are identified. The letters and numbers below the station names indicate which routes serve that particular station. A letter or number in heavy type indicates that trains on that route stop there between 6am and midnight; letters in lighter type mean that the route is served by a part-time service only; a boxed letter or number shows the last stop on the line. The maps posted in all the subway stations have a comprehensive guide that explains the trains and timetable of each route.

- **(A)** Line letter
- Local stop
- Express stop
- Express and local stop
- Free local transfers
- Free express transfers

42 Street– Times Square
N·R [S]
1·2·3 [7] 9

Express and local stops

Light type Part-time service

Boxed type Last stop on this line (full or part-time)

Free transfers from line to line

Bold type Full-time service

This station's green sphere shows that it is staffed continuously

MAKING A TRIP BY SUBWAY

Subways run north–south up and down the city on Lexington Avenue, 6th Avenue, 7th Avenue/ Broadway and 8th Avenue. The N, R, E, F and W trains to Queens run east to west.

Subway map

1 There is a map of the subway system on the back inside cover of this book. Large-scale maps are also positioned in prominent areas in every station. Maps are also available at www.mta.info

Booth with agent

2 Buy a MetroCard or token from a station subway booth or vending machine. The machines accept most credit cards and bills up to $50 but not pennies. You can also refill your MetroCard.

3 Use the card or token to pass through the turn-stile onto the platform.

Entry turnstile

4 Follow the directions for the train you want. For safety, stay in sight of the booth as you wait for your train; at night, stay in one of the yellow off-hours waiting areas.

Off-hours waiting area

5 Each train displays its route number or letter in the appropriate color and the names of the terminal stations.

Route indicator

6 Once aboard, you will find a system map next to the door on each side of the car. Newer trains have electronic ones that light up overhead. Stops are announced on the public address system, and you will see station names at each platform. The doors are operated by the conductor. For safety, be sure to enter a well-populated car.

7 After leaving the train, look for signs giving directions to the exit. If you need to change trains, just follow the signs to the connecting platforms.

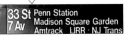

Traveling by Train

New York has two main train stations. Grand Central Terminal is served by commuter trains from New York's suburbs and Connecticut, while Pennsylvania (Penn) Station is the terminal for long-distance services from the rest of the US and also Canada. Most commuter trains have no buffet cars on board, so it's best to buy any food and drink you want before boarding the train. Seat reservations are available only on the long-distance intercity services.

An Amtrak train

GRAND CENTRAL TERMINAL

Grand Central Terminal *(see pp154–5)* on Park Avenue between 41st and 42nd streets is the main terminal for **Metro-North Railroad** trains (Hudson, New Haven and Harlem lines), which run north and east of New York and serve southwest Connecticut and Westchester, Dutchess, and Putnam counties. From Grand Central you might travel by train to such destinations as the Bronx Zoo *(see pp242–3)*, the New York

Botanical Garden and President Franklin D. Roosevelt's Hyde Park estate.

The 4, 5 and 6 trains on the green (Lexington) line and number 7 on the purple (Flushing) line serve Grand Central subway station, below the main terminal. A shuttle service links Grand Central to Times Square. Many bus lines stop at Grand Central.

PENN STATION

Penn station, between Seventh and Eighth avenues and from 31st to 33rd streets, is a modern terminal that was rebuilt in 1963 underneath the Madison Square Garden complex *(see p133)*. Commuter trains, New Jersey Transit trains and **Amtrak** trains from Canada and other parts of the US terminate at this station. There are no luggage trolleys, but redcap porters will help.

You will find taxis at street level. Buses run downtown on Seventh Avenue and uptown on Eighth Avenue. The blue (8th Avenue) subway lines, A, C, and E run on the Eighth Avenue side of the station; the red (Broadway) lines, 1, 2, 3 and 9 run on the Seventh Avenue side of the station. The ticket counters and waiting rooms are one level below; the trains leave from an even lower level.

From Penn Station, you could head out to New Jersey and Long Island or venture farther on Amtrak trains to

Canada, Philadelphia or Washington. Also in Penn Station are ticket offices and departure points of the **Long Island Rail Road (LIRR)**, mainly a commuter line, but with trains to such Long Island resorts, as the Hamptons, Montauk Point, and Fire Island.

PATH TRAINS

Path trains operate round the clock between New Jersey stations (Harrison, Hoboken, Jersey City and Newark) and Penn Station in Manhattan. They also stop at Christopher Street, the World Trade Center, 9th, 14th, 23rd and 33rd Streets and Avenue of the Americas (6th Avenue).

LIRR train at Penn Station

AMTRAK

Amtrak is the US national railroad passenger service linking New York with other US cities and Canada. Some Amtrak trains have cars with reclining seats; others have dining facilities and lounge cars. Sleeper cars are available on all long-distance routes. The new express trains operate on certain Amtrak routes, such as the **Acela** between Boston and Washington via New York.

Tickets can be bought at Penn Station, as well as from Amtrak Travel Centers. Buy your ticket before getting on the train as there is a penalty for buying tickets on board. Senior citizens receive a 15% discount; the conductor will ask for proof of age. There are no student discounts. Seat reservations made by phone with a credit card need to be made at least 10 days in advance of travel if you want the tickets mailed to you.

Amtrak also offers a Great American Vacations package and various promotional fares during the year. Ask for information when you book.

Long Island Rail Road logo

Grand Central Terminal

Information board at Penn Station

TICKETS AND TRAVEL

TICKETING AREAS at all train stations are well lit and generally crowded at all times of the day. Ticket offices will accept most credit cards, as well as cash. There are a variety of ticket types, most based on a one-way fare; a return fare is twice the single fare. If you are planning a number of trips, Metro-North and LIRR offer weekly and off-peak passes that will save you money.

Train times, destination and gate numbers are continually updated on numerous large information boards. Watch for signs indicating the major interim stops and transfer points, listed next to the gate for departing trains. Wait for the opening of the gate posted for your train. Metro-North and LIRR cars are all one class, and have no reserved seating. Amtrak trains offer both services. The conductor will ask to see your ticket after the train has left the station.

Penn Station and Grand Central Terminal have good facilities, including bathrooms, banks, shops, bars and restaurants.

TRAIN INFORMATION

Amtrak Travel Centers
☎ (800) USA-RAIL or (800) 872-7245. ⓦ www.amtrak.com

Acela
☎ (800) 523-8720.
ⓦ www.amtrak.com

Long Island Rail Road (LIRR)
☎ (718) 217-LIRR (Information).
☎ (212) 643 5228 (Lost property).
ⓦ www.mta.info

Metro-North
☎ (212) 532-4900 (Information).
☎ (212) 340-2555 (Lost property).
ⓦ www.mta.nyc.ny.us

PATH Trains
☎ (800) 234-7284.
ⓦ www.panynj.com

DAY TRIPS BY TRAIN

There are some beautiful places outside New York city, which, if your time allows, are well worth a visit. Below is a list of some recommended sights within 125 miles (200 km) of New York city center. For further details, call the New York Convention and Visitors Bureau (see p352).

Phillipsburg Manor, Tarrytown

Stony Brook
Peaceful north shore village. Entrance to the Three Villages historic district.
🚇 58 miles (93 km) east. Long Island Rail Road from Penn Station. 2 hrs.

The Hamptons
Chic bars and boutiques in a weathered, historic setting. The Beverly Hills of Long Island.
🚇 100 miles (161 km) east. Long Island Rail Road from Penn Station. 2 hrs, 50 min.

Montauk Point
State park on the easternmost tip of Long Island; windswept ocean views.
🚇 120 miles (193 km). LIRR from Penn Station. 3 hrs.

Westbury House, Old Westbury
John Phipps's 1906 re-creation of a Charles II mansion with exquisite English formal gardens.
🚇 24 miles (39 km) east. Long Island Rail Road from Penn Station. 40 min.

Tarrytown
Washington Irving's home "Sunnyside" and Jay Gould's mansion.
🚇 25 miles (40 km) north. Metro-North from Grand Central, then taxi. 40–50 min.

Hyde Park
Springwood estate of Franklin D. Roosevelt and the Vanderbilt mansion.
🚇 74 miles (119 km) north. Metro-North from Grand Central to Poughkeepsie, then bus. 2 hrs.

New Haven, Connecticut
Home of Yale University.
🚇 74 miles (119 km). Metro-North from Grand Central Terminal. 1 hr, 46 min.

Hartford, Connecticut
Mark Twain's riverboat-style house, Atheneum Museum and Old State House.
🚇 112 miles (180 km) north. Amtrak from Penn Station. 2 hrs, 45 min.

Winterthur, Delaware
Henry du Pont's collection of Early American art, museum and gardens.
🚇 116 miles (187 km) south. Amtrak from Penn Station to Wilmington, then bus to Winterthur. 2 hrs.

Yale University in New Haven, Connecticut

STREET FINDER

THE MAP REFERENCES given with all sights, hotels, restaurants, bars, shops and entertainment venues described in this book refer to the maps in this section (*see* How Map References Work *opposite*). These maps cover the whole of Manhattan. A complete index of street names and all the places of interest marked on the maps can be found on the following pages.

The key map *(below)* shows the areas covered by the *Street Finder*, within the various districts. The maps include all of Manhattan's sight-seeing areas (which are color-coded), with all the districts important for hotels, restaurants, bars, shops, theaters and entertainment.

Browsing at South Street Seaport

0 kilometers   2

0 miles   1

Inset on Map 1

KEY TO STREET FINDER

- ▢ Major sight
- ▢ Other sight
- ▢ Station building
- **M** Subway station
- 🚁 Heliport
- ⛴ Ferry terminal
- 🚌 Bus terminal
- 🚋 Tram terminal
- **P** Parking
- ℹ Tourist information office
- ✚ Hospital with emergency room
- 🚓 Police station
- ✝ Church
- ✡ Synagogue
- ⊠ Post office
- ═ Railroad line
- → One way street
- ━ Pedestrian street

SCALE OF MAP PAGES

0 meters	200
	1:12,500
0 yards	200

Inset on Map 19

HOW THE MAP REFERENCES WORK

The first figure tells you which Street Finder map to turn to.

Theodore Roosevelt Birthplace ❼

28 E 20th St. **Map 9 A5.** ☎ 260-
1616. **M** 14th St-Union Sq. ◯
9am–5pm Wed–Sun (last adm:
4:30pm). ● public hols. 🈂 ◎ ☑
Lectures, concerts, films & video.
🈂 **W** www.nps.gov/thrb

A letter and number give the grid reference. Letters go across the map's top and bottom, numbers on its sides.

The map continues on map 5 of the *Street Finder.*

Street Finder Index

Each place name is followed by its borough (unless in Manhattan) and then by its Street Finder reference

Each place name is followed by its borough (unless in Manhattan) and then by its Street Finder reference

Each place name is followed by its borough (unless in Manhattan) and then by its Street Finder reference

Each place name is followed by its borough (unless in Manhattan) and then by its Street Finder reference

A

▲
4

B

C

1

Manhattan
Community
College

HARRISON ST
INDEPENDENCE
PLAZA

JAY STREET

STAPLE STREET

HUDSON STREET

WASHINGTON
MARKET PARK

DUANE PARK

WEST BROADWAY

THOMAS

STREET

DUANE

STREET

Western Union
Building

TRIMBLE
PLACE

STREET

320TH

WORTH STREET

LAFAYETTE STREET

CENTRAL

PACE PLAZA

ANDRE
PLAZ

PIER 25

WEST

DUANE STREET

READE

STREET

READE

STREET

PACE

STREET

PIER 21

RIVER TERRACE

STREET

CHAMBERS

STREET

GREENWICH STREET

STREET

CHAMBERS

READE

STREET

Chambers St-
Church St

Surrogate's
Court/Hall of
Records

Chambers
Centre

M

STREET

WARREN

STREET

STREET

Chambers Street-
West Broadway M

STREET

CHAMBERS

Municipal
Building

PARK PLACE

STREET

MURRAY

STREET

WEST

WARREN

STREET

LOWER

Old NY County
Courthouse

Brooklyn
Bridge-
City Hall

PARK END AVENUE

STREET MURRAY

STREET

PARK
PLACE

MURRAY

CHURCH STREET

STREET

CITY

PARK
PLACE

City Hall

Park Place

M

PARK ROW

FRANCIS

BROADWAY

Pace
University

SPRU

BEEKMAN STREET

P

Irving Trust
Operation Center

Woolworth
Building

ST PETER'S STREET

Beekm
Downtow
Hospit

2

New York
Telephone
Company

BARCLAY

STREET

US Post Office

Federal
Office

World Trade
Center
Church Street

St Paul's Chapel

M
ANN

M

STREET

THEATRE ALLEY

BEEKMAN

VESEY

STREET

VESEY

STREET

M

FULTON

AT&T Building

FULTON

STREET

Fulton
Street

M

North Cove Yacht Harbor

World Financial
Center

NORTH END AVENUE

World Trade

Center Site

CHURCH STREET

DEY STREET

ST

NASSAU

JOHN

MAIDEN

DUTCH ST

STREE

Fulton
Street

M

NORTH COVE
YACHT HARBOR

CORTLANDT STREET

Merrill Lynch
Liberty Plaza

Federal
Reserve
Bank

PLA

LIBERTY

STREET

3

Battery
Park
City

American
Stock
Exchange

WESTSIDE HIGHWAY 9A (WEST ST)

WASHINGTON ST

ALBANY STREET

GREENWICH STREET

CEDAR

Cortland
Street

Chamber of
Commerce

THAMES ST

CEDAR

LIBERTY STREET SQUARE

Chase
Manhattan
Bank

LEGIC

STREE

HUDSON

PINE

CARLISLE ST

TRINITY

PLACE

PINE

STREET

Wall St

Federal

WALL STREET

RECTOR

PLACE

RECTOR

Rector Street-
Greenwich Street

M

Rector Street-
Trinity Place

M

Trinity
Church

WALL

STREET

Hall

Wall Street

M

New York
Stock Exchange

Broad St

M

WILLIAM STREET

PIN

STREE

LIBERTY PLAZA

WEST THAMES Street

EDGAR
STREET

JP WARD
STREET

EXCHANGE
ALLEY

NEW STREET

BROAD STREET

Bank of New
York

MANCE

HANOVER
SQUARE

COUNT

MILL
ALLEY

THIRD PLACE

River

SOUTH END AVENUE

SECOND PLACE

MORRIS
STREET

Cunard
Building

P

4

Hudson

SOUTH GARDENS

FIRST PLACE

Downtown
Athletic
Club

INTERNATIONAL

WESTSIDE
PLAZA

BATTERY PLACE

Bowling
Green

Bowling Green

M

US
Custom
House

WHITEHALL STREET

STONE

BEAVER

MARKETFIELD
STREET

SOUTH WILLIAM LANE

BRIDGE

STATE STREET

PEARL STREET

WATER STREET

Frauno
Tavern

BROAD STREET

STREET

Battery
Plaza

Battery Park
City Heliport

PIER A

Castle Clinton
National

BATTERY

Whitehall
Street

M

Shrine of Elizabeth
Ann Seton

PETER MINUIT
PLAZA

MOORE ST

BROAD STREET

Ellis
Island

PARK

The East Coast
War Memorial

FERRIES TO LIBERTY
AND ELLIS ISLANDS

SOUTH FERRY
PLAZA

SOUTH FERRY

BROOKLYN-
BATTERY TUNNEL

South Ferry

M

US Coast
Guard

Brooklyn Battery Tunnel

5

Liberty
Island

Statue of
Liberty

A

B

C

NORTH 9TH STREET
NORTH 8TH STREET
NORTH 7TH STREET
NORTH 6TH AVENUE STREET
NORTH 5TH STREET
NORTH AVENUE

KENT AVENUE
NORTH 4TH STREET
NORTH 3RD STREET

WYTHE STREET

BERRY STREET

RIVER STREET

METROPOLITAN AVENUE
#215
NORTH 1ST STREET

GRAND STREET

SOUTH 1ST STREET

SOUTH 2ND STREET

SOUTH 3RD STREET

SOUTH 4TH STREET

SOUTH 5TH STREET

EAST

Athletic
Field

RIVER

PARK

MANGIN STREET
BARUCH PLACE

Williamsburg Bridge

STREET
SOUTH

LEWIS STREET

STREET

EAST

RIVER

□ *Fireboat Station*

PARK

SAMUEL A
SPIEGEL SQUARE

STREET CHERRY STREET

*CORLEARS
HOOK PARK*

SOUTH 6TH STREET
DUNHAM PLACE
BERRY STREET
#399
BROADWAY
SOUTH 8TH STREET
WYTHE STREET

AVENUE

SOUTH 9TH ST

SOUTH 11TH ST

Wallabout
Channel

DIVISION AVENUE

*Corlears
Hook*

PIER 44

*US Naval Reserve
Center*

W a l l a b o u t   B a y

East

River

Belmont
Island

Queens - Midtown Tunnel 495

49TH STREET

50TH AVENUE

51ST AVENUE

2ND (KENT) AVENUE

VERNON BLVD

JACKSON AVENUE

BORDEN AVENUE

Vernon Jackson
Boulevard

M

**Long Island City
Station**

PULASKI Bridge

54TH (FLUSHING) AVENUE

55TH AVENUE

55TH STREET

56TH AVENUE

Newton Creek

MANHATTAN AVENUE #9315

BOX STREET

COMMERCIAL STREET

CLAY STREET

DUPONT STREET

FRANKLIN STREET

EAGLE STREET

WEST STREET

FREEMAN STREET

GREEN STREET

MANHATTAN STREET

HURON STREET

INDIA STREET

JAVA STREET

KENT STREET

GREENPOINT AVENUE

Manhattan
Marina

East

River

PIER 70

PIER 69

PIER 68

PIER 67

FRANKLIN DELANO ROOSEVELT DRIVE (EAST RIVER DRIVE)

AVENUE D

AVENUE C

EAST 16TH STREET

EAST 15TH STREET

A   17   B   C

MADISON   AVENUE

PARK   AVENUE

1

E A S T   S I D E

#760

#1250   #1364   #353

EAST   73RD   STREET
EAST   72ND   STREET   100»   200»   300»   72ND   STREET   400»   YORK
E A S T   71ST   STREET   71ST   STREET

Asia
Society

EAST   70TH   STREET   70TH   STREET   New York
Hospital

Hunter College   EAST   69TH   STREET   69TH   STREET

M   68th Street Hunter College-
Lexington Avenue
12   68TH   STREET   68TH   STREET   Memorial
Hospital

LEXINGTON   AVENUE

Seventh
Regiment
Armory

EAST   67TH   STREET   67TH   STREET
EAST   66TH   STREET   66TH   STREET

2

EAST   65TH   STREET   65TH   STREET
EAST   64TH   STREET   64TH   STREET
EAST   63RD   STREET   63RD   STREET

Museum of
American
Illustration

Society of
Illustrators

Lexington
Avenue
M   62ND   STREET   Abigail Adams
Smith Museum

EAST   62ND   STREET

THIRD   AVENUE   SECOND   AVENUE   FIRST   AVENUE

#1031   #951

#1066

#425   #695

East 60th
Street Heliport

EAST   61ST   STREET   61ST
M   59th Street
Lexington Avenue   EAST   60TH   STREET   EAST   60TH   STREET
Bloomingdale's
M   59TH   STREET   59TH   STREET

3

Fuller
Building   EAST   58TH   STREET   58TH   STREET   SUTTON   PLACE
E A S T   57TH   STREET   57TH   STREET
100»   200»   300»   400»
EAST   56TH   STREET   56TH   STREET

Central
Synagogue   EAST   55TH   STREET   55TH   STREET

Lever
House   Citicorp
Center   EAST   54TH   STREET   54TH
M   Lexington Avenue-
Third Avenue   53RD   STREET

4

PARK   AVENUE   Seagram
Building   EAST   53RD   STREET

Villard
Houses   General Electric
Building   EAST   52ND   STREET   52ND   STREET   FIRST   AVENUE

St Bartholomew's
Church   M   51st Street-
Lexington Avenue   EAST   51ST   STREET   51ST   STREET

12   Waldorf-
Astoria   EAST   50TH   STREET   50TH   STREET   BEEKMAN   PLACE

EAST   49TH   STREET   Japan Society   49TH   STREET

EAST   48TH   STREET   48TH   STREET

EAST   47TH   STREET   HAMMARSKJOLD PLAZA   UNITED NATIONS PLAZA

5

VANDERBILT   AVENUE

#260

EAST   46TH   STREET   46TH   STREET   United Nations
Headquarters

Helmsley
Building   EAST   45TH   STREET   45TH   STREET

MetLife
Building   Grand Central
Terminal   EAST   44TH   STREET   #702   #824   1&2 United
Nations Plaza

FRANKLIN D. ROOSEVELT DRIVE (EAST RIVER DRIVE)

A   9   B   C

1

BLACKWELL
PARK

Roosevelt   Island   Bridge

VERNON   BOULEVARD

36TH   AVENUE

9TH STREET

10TH STREET

11TH STREET

12TH STREET

13TH STREET

37TH   AVENUE

West Channel

FRANKLIN D ROOSEVELT DRIVE (EAST RIVER DRIVE)

East Channel

MAIN   STREET

38TH   AVENUE

L O N G

I S L A N D   C I T Y

2

40TH   AVENUE

13TH STREET

10TH STREET

12TH STREET

VERNON BOULEVARD

#4002

41ST   AVENUE

QUEENSBRIDGE
PARK

Q U E E N S

C O U N T Y

41ST ROAD

ROOSEVELT
ISLAND

AERIAL TRAMWAY
Queensboro Bridge

Queensboro   Bridge

QUEENS   PLAZA   NORTH

3

VERNON BOULEVARD

QUEENS   PLAZA   SOUTH

9TH STREET

10TH STREET

11TH STREET

12TH STREET

21ST STREET

WEST   ROAD

EAST   ROAD

43RD

43RD   ROAD

AVENUE

13TH STREET

#4302

#4802

9TH STREET

10TH STREET

West Channel

East Channel

44TH   AVENUE

44TH   ROAD

4

WEST   ROAD

EAST   ROAD

M 44th Drive

44TH   DRIVE

45TH   AVENUE

45TH   STREET

11TH   STREET

ROAD

45TH   AVENUE

VERNON

46TH   AVENUE

46TH   ROAD

5TH STREET

47TH   AVENUE

5

47TH   ROAD

STREET

JACKSON AVENUE

STREET

48TH   AVENUE

1

WEST 102ND STREET

WEST 101ST STREET

WEST 100TH STREET

WEST 99TH STREET

WEST 98TH STREET

WEST 97TH STREET

RIVERSIDE DRIVE EAST

RIVERSIDE DRIVE WEST

RIVERSIDE PARK

WEST END AVENUE

BROADWAY

AMSTERDAM AVENUE

2

WEST 96TH STREET

96th Street

WEST 95TH STREET

POMANDER WALK

WEST 94TH STREET

WEST 93RD STREET

WEST 92ND STREET

WEST 91ST STREET

JOAN OF ARC PARK

HENRY HUDSON PARKWAY

9 A

Hudson River

3

WEST 90TH STREET

WEST 89TH STREET

WEST 88TH STREET

WEST 87TH STREET

WEST 86TH STREET

WEST 85TH STREET

86th Street

Jewish Center

WEST END AVENUE

BROADWAY

AMSTERDAM AVENUE

4

RIVERSIDE PARK

RIVERSIDE DRIVE

EDGAR ALLAN POE STREET

WEST 83RD STREET

WEST 82ND STREET

WEST 81ST STREET

WEST 80TH STREET

WEST 79TH STREET

79th Street

Children's Museum of Manhattan

HENRY HUDSON PARKWAY

5

WEST 78TH STREET

WEST 77TH STREET

WEST 76TH STREET

WEST 75TH STREET

WEST 74TH STREET

Boat Basin

WEST END AVENUE

BROADWAY

AMSTERDAM AVENUE

Ansonia Hotel

A

B

C

MADISON AVENUE

EAST 101ST STREET

LEXINGTON

EAST 101ST STREET

FIRST

#1934

THIRD

#1800

EAST 100TH STREET

EAST 100TH STREET

PARK

EAST 99TH STREET

EAST 99TH STREET

AVENUE

EAST 98TH STREET

AVENUE

SECOND

EAST 97TH STREET

#1708

AVENUE

EAST 97TH STREET

#1855

#1236

EAST 96TH M STREET

EAST 96TH STREET

100» 96th Street

200»

300»

#1841

AVENUE

EAST 95TH STREET

#1695

EAST 95TH STREET

EAST 94TH STREET

EAST 94TH STREET

EAST 93RD STREET

EAST 93RD STREET

FRANKLIN D ROOSEVELT DRIVE (EAST RIVER DRIVE)

EAST 92ND STREET

EAST 92ND STREET

EAST 91ST STREET

EAST 91ST STREET

EAST 90TH STREET

LEXINGTON

THIRD

EAST 90TH STREET

SECOND

FIRST

YORK

EAST 89TH STREET

EAST 89TH STREET

EAST 88TH STREET

EAST 88TH STREET
Church of the Holy Trinity

#1602

PARK

EAST 87TH STREET

AVENUE

EAST 87TH STREET

AVENUE

AVENUE

#1833

#1044

AVENUE

EAST 86TH M STREET

EAST 86TH STREET

#1021

100» 86th Street

#1530

200»

#1511

300»

#1637

400»

#1610

500»

EAST 85TH STREET

EAST 85TH STREET

EAST 84TH STREET

EAST 84TH STREET

EAST 83RD STREET

EAST 83RD STREET

YORK

EAST 82ND STREET

EAST 82ND STREET

AVENUE

EAST 81ST STREET

EAST 81ST STREET

#903

EAST 80TH STREET

#1491

EAST 80TH STREET

#1513

#1498

EAST 79TH STREET

EAST 79TH STREET

MADISON AVENUE

100»

LEXINGTON

#1374

200»

300»

400»

#1496

500»

#1477

PARK

#878

EAST 78TH STREET

EAST 78TH STREET

SECOND

FIRST

YORK

CHEROKEE PL.

EAST 77TH M STREET

THIRD

77th Street

EAST 77TH STREET

Lenox Hill Hospital

AVENUE

AVENUE

AVENUE

EAST 76TH STREET

AVENUE

EAST 76TH STREET

Whitney Museum of American Art

EAST 75TH STREET

EAST 75TH STREET

AVENUE

EAST 74TH STREET

STREET

EAST 74TH STREET

#785

#1271

#1861

#1370

A

B

C

D E F

Triborough Bridge

East River

Hell Gate

1

SHORE BOULEVARD

ASTORIA PK SOUTH

Pot Cove

Harlem River

MILL
ROCK
PARK

26TH   AVENUE   4TH

12TH   STREET

14TH   STREET

9TH   STREET

2ND   STREET

3RD   STREET

1ST   STREET

27TH   STREET

8TH   STREET

AVENUE

28TH AVENUE

2

ASTORIA BOULEVARD

MAIN AVENUE

30TH   AVENUE

WELLING STREET

EAST END AVENUE

HENDERSON PL

Gracie
Mansion

CARL

SCHURZ

PARK

VERNON

30TH   STREET   ROAD

30TH   DRIVE

3

LIGHTHOUSE
PARK

Hallets
Cove

31ST   AVENUE

12TH   STREET

BOULEVARD

GRACIE SQ

GRACIE
TERRACE

ROOSEVELT
ISLAND

31ST   DRIVE

BROADWAY

33RD   AVENUE

33RD   ROAD

13TH   STREET

4

FRANKLIN D ROOSEVELT DRIVE (EAST RIVER DRIVE)

West Channel

MAIN   STREET

East Channel

RAINEY
PARK

34TH   STREET

9TH   STREET

10TH   STREET

11TH   STREET

12TH   STREET

VERNON

AVENUE

JOHN
JAY
PARK

BLACKWELL
PARK

35TH   AVENUE

BOULEVARD

5

D E F

H a r l e m   R i v e r

Willis Avenue Bridge

Triborough   Bridge

RANDALL'S

ISLAND

PARK

EAST 127TH STREET

EAST 126TH STREET

125th Street
M (MARTIN LUTHER KING, JR BOULEVARD)
100»   200»

LOUIS
GUVILLIER
PARK

FRANKLIN D ROOSEVELT DRIVE (EAST RIVER DRIVE)

PALADINO

RONALD E MCNAIR PLACE

SYLVAN PL

THIRD   AVENUE

SECOND   AVENUE

FIRST   AVENUE

PLEASANT   AVENUE

AVENUE

EAST 120TH STREET

EAST 119TH STREET

EAST 118TH STREET

EAST 117TH STREET

116th Street
M (LUIS   MUÑOZ   MARIN   BOULEVARD)
100»   200»   300»   400»

EAST 115TH STREET

EAST 114TH STREET

JEFFERSON

PARK

EAST 113TH STREET

EAST 112TH STREET

EAST 111TH STREET

M 110th Street
EAST 110TH STREET

EAST 109TH STREET

EAST 108TH STREET

Benjamin

Franklin

Plaza

EAST 107TH STREET

RECREATION

PIER

H a r l e m

R i v e r

SECOND   AVENUE

FIRST   AVENUE

THIRD   AVENUE

EAST 106TH STREET

EAST 105TH STREET

EAST 104TH STREET

M 103rd Street
EAST 103RD STREET

Foot Bridge

LEXINGTON   AVENUE

General Index

Acknowledgments

DORLING KINDERSLEY would like to thank the many people whose help and assistance contributed to the preparation of this book.

MAIN CONTRIBUTOR
Eleanor Berman has lived in New York for almost 40 years. Her travel articles are widely published and she is the author of *Away for the Weekend: New York*, a favorite since 1982. Her other books include *Away for the Weekend* guides for the Mid-Atlantic, New England and Northern California, *Travelling on Your Own* and *Reflections of Washington, DC*.

MUSEUM CONTRIBUTORS
Michelle Menendez, Lucy O'Brien, Heidi Rosenau, Elyse Topalian, Sally Williams.

DORLING KINDERSLEY wishes to thank the following editors and researchers at Websters International Publishers: Sandy Carr, Matthew Barrell, Sara Harper, Miriam Lloyd, Ava-Lee Tanner, Celia Woolfrey.

ADDITIONAL PHOTOGRAPHY
Edward Hueber, Eliot Kaufman, Karen Kent, Dave King, Norman McGrath, Howard Millard, Paul Solomon, Chuck Spang, Chris Stevens.

ADDITIONAL ILLUSTRATIONS
Steve Gyapay, Kevin Jones, Dinwiddie MacLaren, Janos Marffy, Chris D. Orr, Nick Shewring, John Woodcock.

CARTOGRAPHY
MAPS Andrew Heritage, James Mills-Hicks, Chez Picthall, John Plumer (Dorling Kindersley Cartography)
Advanced Illustration (Cheshire), Contour Publishing (Derby), Europmap Ltd (Berkshire). Street Finder maps: ERA-Maptec Ltd (Dublin) adapted with permission from original survey and mapping by Shobunsha (Japan).

CARTOGRAPHIC RESEARCH
Roger Bullen, Tony Chambers, Ruth Duxbury, Ailsa Heritage, Jayne Parsons, Laura Porter, Donna Rispoli, Joan Russell, Jill Tinsley, Andrew Thompson.

DESIGN AND EDITORIAL
MANAGING EDITOR Douglas Amrine
MANAGING ART EDITORS Stephen Knowlden, Geoff Manders
SENIOR EDITOR Georgina Matthews
SERIES DESIGN CONSULTANT Peter Luff
EDITORIAL DIRECTOR David Lamb
ART DIRECTOR Anne-Marie Bulat
PRODUCTION CONTROLLER Hilary Stephens
PICTURE RESEARCH Susan Mennell, Sarah Moule
DTP DESIGNER Andy Wilkinson
Keith Addison, Ron Boudreau, Linda Cabasin, Rebecca Carman, Michelle Clark, Sherry Collins, Carey Combe, Diana Craig, Maggie Crowley, Guy Dimond, Tom Fraser, Jo Gardner, Alex Gray, Marcus Hardy, Sasha Heseltine, Pippa Hurst, Kim Inglis, Jane Middleton, Helen Partington, Leigh Priest, Nicki Rawson, Marisa Renzullo, Ellen Root, Liz Rowe, Anaïs Scott, Anna Streiffert, Clare Sullivan, Andrew Szudek, Ros Walford.

SPECIAL ASSISTANCE
Beyer Blinder Belle, John Beatty at the Cotton Club, Peter Casey at the New York Public Library, Nicky Clifford, Linda Corcoran at the Bronx Zoo, Audrey Manley at the Morgan Library, Jane Fischer, Deborah Gaines at the New York Convention and Visitors Bureau, Dawn Geigerich at the Queens Museum of Art, Peggy Harrington at St. John the Divine, Pamela Herrick at the Van Cortlandt House, Marguerite Lavin at the Museum of the City of New York, Robert Makla at the Friends of Central Park, Gary Miller at the New York Stock Exchange, Laura Mogil at the American Museum of Natural History, Fred Olsson at the Shubert Organization, Dominique Palermo at the Police Academy Museum, Royal Canadian Pancake House, Lydia Ruth and Laura I. Fries at the Empire State Building, David Schwartz at the American Museum of the Moving Image, Joy Sienkiewicz at the South Street Seaport Museum, Barbara Orlando at the Metropolitan Transit Authority, the staff at the Lower East Side Tenement Museum, Msgr. Anthony Dalla Valla at St. Patrick's Cathedral.

RESEARCH ASSISTANCE
Christa Griffin, Bogdan Kaczorowski, Steve McClure, Sabra Moore, Jeff Mulligan, Marc Svensson, Vicky Weiner, Steven Weinstein.

PHOTOGRAPHIC REFERENCE
Duncan Petersen Publishers Ltd.

PHOTOGRAPHY PERMISSIONS
DORLING KINDERSLEY would like to thank the following for their kind permission to photograph at their establishments:
American Craft Museum, American Museum of Natural History, Aunt Len's Doll and Toy Museum, Balducci's, Home Savings of America, Brooklyn Children's Museum, The Cloisters, Columbia University, Eldridge Street Project, Federal Hall, Rockefeller Group, Trump Tower.

PICTURE CREDITS
t = top; tc = top center; tr = top right; cla = center left above; ca = center above; cra = center right above; cl = center left; c = center; cr = center right; clb = center left below; cb = center below; crb = center right below; bl = bottom left; bc = bottom center; br = bottom right.

Works of art have been reproduced with the permission of the following copyright holders:
© ADAGP, Paris and DACS, London 1993: 67cl (*Four Trees*, April 1971–July 1972, by Jean Dubuffet), 105cl, 170bl, 186tl, 187crb, 199crb; *Alice In Wonderland*, 1959 © Jose de Creeft/DACS, London/VAGA, New York 1993: 53cl, 205cl; © DACS 1993: 34tr, 113tc, 160tr (donated by the Norwegian Government, 1952), 171cb, 172cr, 186bl, 187cra, 187bl, 188cla; © Estate of STUART DAVIS/DACS, London/VAGA, New York 1993: 199cr; DK IMAGES: Judith Miller/Wallis & Wallis, Sussex 58br; © DEMART PRO ARTE BV/DACS 1993: 172cl; *The American Merchant Mariners Memorial*, 1991, © MARISOL ESCOBAR/DACS, London/VAGA, New York 1993: 55bc; © JASPER JOHNS/DACS, London/VAGA, New

York 1993: 199ca; © ROY LICHTENSTEIN/DACS 1993: 173tl, 198clb; © Estate of DAVID SMITH/DACS, London/VAGA, New York 1993: 199bl. © 1993 THE GEORGIA O'KEEFFE FOUNDATION/ARS, New York: 198c; © 1993 FRANK STELLA/ARS, New York: 190tr. By permission of ELLSWORTH KELLY: 35cr. By permission of E JAN NADELMAN: 199br. Printed by permission of the NORMAN ROCKWELL FAMILY TRUST © 1961 the Norman Rockwell Family Trust: 161br. © 1993 THE ANDY WARHOL FOUNDATION FOR THE VISUAL ARTS, INC: 198cla. © THE WHITNEY MUSEUM OF AMERICAN ART, NY: 35br (*The Brooklyn Bridge: Variation On An Old Theme*, 1939, by Joseph Stella), 198bl.

The Publishers are grateful to the following museums, companies and picture libraries for permission to reproduce their photographs:

AGENCE FRANCE PRESSE: Doug Kanter 31tr; ALAMY.COM: Bob Jones 109b; ALGONQUIN HOTEL, N.Y: 272bl; AMERICAN AIRLINES: 363tl; AMERICAN MUSEUM-HAYDEN PLANETARIUM, NY: D. Finnin 216t; AMERICAN MUSEUM OF THE MOVING IMAGE: Carson Collection © Bruce Polin 245t; AMERICAN MUSEUM OF NATURAL HISTORY, NY: 37bl, 214ca; AQUARIUS, UK: 169tr; ASHMOLEAN MUSEUM, Oxford: 15c; THE ASIA SOCIETY, NY: 185cl; AVERY ARCHITECTURAL AND FINE ART LIBRARY, Columbia University in the City of New York: 135cl; AVERY FISHER HALL: © N McGrath 1976 331tr.

© THE GEORGE BALANCHINE TRUST: *Apollo*, choreography by George Balanchine, photo by P Kolnik 5tc; *Stravinsky Violin Concerto*, choreography by George Balanchine, photo by P Kolnik 328tc; George Balanchine's *The Nutcracker*, SM, photo by P Kolnik 331cb; THE BETTMANN ARCHIVE, NY: 16bcl, 17cra, 17cr, 17bl, 18cl, 20cbr, 20bl, 20–21, 23br, 25cra, 26cla, 26cra, 26crb, 30cla, 31tl, 41tl, 43cbl, 47cr, 47bc, 49c, 54-55b, 71tl, 74cla, 79crb, 79br, 109bl, 175cla, 183br, 207t, 210cl, 223cr, 229t, 239tr, 265tr; BETTMANN NEWSPHOTOS/REUTERS: 31tr; BETTMANN/ UPI: 27cra, 27bc, 28bcr, 29br, 30cra, 30bl, 30br, 44cl, 47cra, 48cl, 49bl, 72c, 72ca, 78cl, 151c, 161c, 264br, 265cr; BLOOMINGDALE'S: 27cbr; BFI: courtesy of Paramount Pictures 46b; © Roy Export Company Establishment 173tr; THE BRITISH LIBRARY, London: 14; BROOKLYN HISTORICAL SOCIETY: (detail) 89tl; THE BROOKLYN MUSEUM: 36bl, 37c, 248c, 248cra, 248bl, 249t, 249cra, 249c, 249bl, 249b, 250t, 250br, 251ct, 251bl; Lewis Wick Hine, *Climbing Into The Promised Land*, 1908 – 34clb; J Kerr 248c, 250bl; P Warchol: 249cr; The Cantor Collection 251cl; Adam Husted 248t; BROWN BROTHERS: 67br, 71bl, 82cra, 90t, 104br.

CAMERA PRESS: 28cbr, 28bl, 31cb, 125cr; R Open 48tr; T Spencer 30cb; THE CARLYLE HOTEL, NY: 273tr, 328bc; CARNEGIE HALL: © H. Grossman 331br; J ALLAN CASH: 31bl, 362cr; CATHEDRAL OF ST. JOHN THE DIVINE: Greg Wyatt 1985, 225tl; CBS ENTERTAINMENT/DESILU TOO: "Vacation from Marriage" 169br; CHELSEA PIERS: Fred George 31bl; COLORIFIC!: A Clifton 373cl; Colorific/ Black Star: 79cra; T Cowell 221cr; R Fraser 74t; H Matsumoto 368cr, 371tr; D Moore 29bl; T Spiegel 13cr, 348tr; CORBIS: Bettmann 367c; Randy Duchaine 98br; Todd Gipstein 75t; Gail Mooney

205b; Bill Ross 10t; Steven E. Sutton 51b; Mike Zens 260–61. CULVER PICTURES, INC: (inset) 9, 17crb, 18cbl, 19bl, 21tl, 21br, 24tl, 24cl, 27cb, 27bl, 46tr, 47cb, 48br, 49tr, 74bl, 75cra, 75cb, 76tl, 78crb, 83c, 119bl, 122tc, 125bl, 135cr, 145c, 147cl, 227t, 227bc, 227cr, 259crb. DAILY EAGLE: (detail) 89cl; DAILY NEWS: 354tl, 354tr. ESSEX HOUSE, NY: 268cr; ESTO: P Aaron 330bl; MARY EVANS PICTURE LIBRARY: 22br, 46clb, 47br, 87br, 104bl.

CHRIS FAIRCLOUGH COLOUR LIBRARY: 369bcl; THE FORBES MAGAZINE COLLECTION, NY: 112tl; FOUR SEASONS HOTEL: Peter Vitale 273cr; FRAUNCES TAVERN MUSEUM, NY: From the exhibit "Come All You Gallant Heroes" The World of the Revolutionary Soldier December 4, 1991 to August 14, 1992: 20cla; Copyright THE FRICK COLLECTION, NY: 35bl (*St Francis In The Desert* by Giovanni Bellini), 200ca, 200cl, 200clb, 200b, 200tr, 201ca, 201cr, 201bc, 201br.

GARRARD THE CROWN JEWELLERS: 143c; THE SOLOMON R GUGGENHEIM MUSEUM, NY: *Blue, Green, Yellow, Orange, Red*, 1966, by Ellsworth Kelly, photo by D Aronowitz 35cr; photo by D Heald 186tl, 186bl, 186bc, 186br, 187t, 187cra, 187crb, 187bl.

ROBERT HARDING PICTURE LIBRARY: 362tc; HARPERS NEW MONTHLY MAGAZINE: 87tl; HARPERS WEEKLY: 351c; MILTON HEBALD: *Prospero and Miranda* 203t, *Romeo and Juliet* 331cr; THE HOTEL MILLENIUM, NY: 269tl. THE IMAGE BANK: front endpaper bl, 89br; P McConville 377c; M Melford 377br; P Miller 367tr; A Satterwhite 75br. THE JEWISH MUSEUM, NY: 182tr, 184c. Copyright © 1993 K-III MAGAZINE CORPORATION: All rights reserved. Reprinted with the permission of *New York* Magazine 352tr; THE KOBAL COLLECTION: 211tc; LEBRECHT MUSIC: Toby Wales 147t; FRANK LESLIE'S ILLUSTRATED NEWSPAPER: 86br, 87tr, 267c; LIBRARY OF CONGRESS: 18bc, 21cla, 25bl, 25br; LIFE MAGAZINE © Time Warner Inc/Katz/A Feininger: 8–9; GEORG JOHN LOBER: *Hans Christian Anderson*, 1956, 204br; THE LOWELL HOTEL, NY: 273cl; MARY ANN LYNCH: 310bc, 356cl.

MADISON SQUARE GARDEN: 132r, 330cr; MAGNUM PHOTOS: © H Cartier-Bresson 173c; Erwitt 33cr; G Peres 12br, 92; JACQUES MARCHAIS CENTER OF TIBETAN ART: 252bc; MASTERFILE UK: Gail Mooney 31br; METRO-NORTH COMMUTER RAILROAD: F English 154tr, 154cla; THE METROPOLITAN MUSEUM OF ART, NY: 33bl (*Young Woman With A Waterjug* by Johannes Vermeer), 35crb (*Figure of a Hippopotamus*, faience, Egypt, 12th Dynasty), 180tc, 188cla, 188clb, 188bc, 188br, 189tl, 189tr, 189cr, 189bl, (photo Al Mozell) 189br, 190tr, 190c, 190bl, 190br, 191tl, 191tr, 191c, 191bl, 192tl, 192tr, 192c, 192b, (detail) 193tl, 193tr, 193b, 194t, 194cl, 194cr, 194b, 195tl, 195cr, 195bl, 234tr, 234cl, 234cr, 234b, 235ca, 235cr, 235bl, 235br, 236tl, 236tr, 237tr, 237c, 237b; METROPOLITAN TRANSIT AUTHORITY: 372bca, 374t, 375cla/ca; Collection of THE MORGAN LIBRARY, NY: 34cr (*Blanche of Castille and King Louis IX of France, author dictating to a scribe*, moralized Bible, c1230), 162br, *Song of Los* David A. Loggie (gift of Mrs Landon K Thorne) 162la, *Biblia Latina* David

A. Loggie 162lb, 163tl, 163c, 163bl, 163br; MORRIS-JUMEL MANSION, INC NY: 17tl; A Rosario 21crb; THE MUSEUM OF THE CITY OF NEW YORK: 15b, 16cra, 16–17, 17tr, 18ca, 19crb (photo J Parnell), 20tl, 20cbl, 22tl (attributed to Samuel Lovett Waldo), 22cla, 22clb, 23cr, 23crb, 23bc, 24cb, 25tl, 25crb, 25cb, 26bl, 27tr, 28tl, 28cr, 29tc, 29c, 30tr, 35tr (silver porringer), 87cr (Talfour); THE MUSEUM OF MODERN ART, NY: 33ca (*The Starry Night* by Vincent Van Gogh, 1889), 34t (*The Goat* by Pablo Picasso, 1950), 6bl (Cisitalia "202" GT car), 165tc, 170c, 170bl, 171tc, © 2004 Photo Elizabeth Felicella, architectural rendering Kohn Pedersen Fox Associates, digital composite Robert Bowen 170tl, 171cra, 171crb, 171cb, 171bl, The Bather, c. 1885, Paul Cezanne 172bc, 172cl, 172cr, 173tl, 173b.

NATIONAL BASEBALL LIBRARY, Cooperstown, NY: 4tr, 23bl, 28cl; NATIONAL MUSEUM OF THE AMERICAN INDIAN/SMITHSONIAN INSTITUTION: 16c; NATIONAL PARK SERVICE: Ellis Island Immigration Museum 78ca, 78br; Statue of Liberty National Monument 75bl; THE NEW MUSEUM OF CONTEMPORARY ART, NY: 105cl; NEW YORK BOTANIC GARDEN: Tori Butt 240b, 241t/cl/b; Jason Green 240cr; Muriel Weinerman 241b; NEW YORK CITY FIRE DEPARTMENT: 357br; NEW YORK CITY TRANSIT AUTHORITY: 374bc; Phil Bartley 375tc, 375ca, 375cl; NEW YORK POLICE DEPARTMENT: Photo Dept 356cl; Collection of THE NEW YORK HISTORICAL SOCIETY: 47tr; THE NEW YORKER MAGAZINE INC: Cover drawing by Rea Irvin, © 1925, 1953, All rights reserved, 28bcl; THE NEW YORK PALACE, NY: 25tr; NEW YORK POST: 354tl; NEW YORK PUBLIC LIBRARY: Special Collection Office, Schomburg Center for Research in Black Culture 28ca, 29cla; Stokes Collection 21tr; NEW YORK STATE DEPARTMENT OF MOTOR VEHICLES: 370b; NEW YORK STOCK EXCHANGE: 71ra; THE NEW YORK TIMES: 354tl; NPA: © CNES 1993 10b; THE PENINSULA, NY: 271bc; PERFORMING ARTS LIBRARY: Clive Barda: 210bl; POPPERFOTO: 29cra, 29cr, 260cla; PLAZA HOTEL, NY: 272tr.

COLLECTION OF THE QUEENS MUSEUM OF ART: purchased with funds from the George and Mollie Wolfe World's Fair Fund 29cbr; Official souvenir, purchase 30cbr; RENSSELAER POLYTECHNIC INSTITUTE: 86–87, 87bl; REX FEATURES LTD: 376tl; Sipa-Press 52tr, 52br; Courtesy of the ROCKEFELLER CENTER © The Rockefeller Group, Inc: 29cbl. LUIS SANGUINO: *The Immigrants*, 1973, 256b; THE ST. REGIS, NY: 270c; SCIENTIFIC AMERICAN: 18 May 1878 edition 86tr; 9 November 1878 edition 88bl; THE SOCIETY OF ILLUSTRATORS: 196tl; SOUTH STREET SEAPORT MUSEUM: R.B. Merkel 83bl, 84bl; SPECTRUM COLOUR LIBRARY: 376bl; FRANK SPOONER

PICTURES: Gamma 158cl; Gamma/B Gysenbergh 367tl; Liaison/Gamma/ Anderson front endpaper clb, 158tl, 159cla; Liaison/Levy/Halebian: 42tr, 45c; Sygma/ A Tannenbaum 47ca; THEATER DEVELOPMENT FUND: David LeShay 328cl; TURNER ENTERTAINMENT COMPANY: 135br, 183br. UNITED NATIONS, NY: 159cra, 160tr, 160bc, 161tc, 161cla, 161br; UNITED NATIONS PHOTO: 158tr; © US POSTAL SERVICE: 361t, © THE US POSTAL SERVICE 1981: 361ca, © US POSTAL SERVICE 1991: 361c. Used with permission; UN PLAZA HYATT HOTEL, NY: 273bl.

© JACK VARTOOGIAN, NY: 61bc, 156t. JUDITH WELLER: *The Garment Worker* 128t; LUCIA WILSON CONSULTANCY: Ivar Mjell 2–3, 13br, 164; Collection of THE WHITNEY MUSEUM OF AMERICAN ART, NY: 198cla, 198c, 198clb, 199t, 199ca, 199cr, 199crb (purchase with funds from a public fundraising campaign in May 1982. One half of the funds were contributed by the Robert Wood Johnson Jr. Charitable Trust. Additional major donations were given by The Lauder Foundation; the Robert Lehman Foundation, Inc.; the Howard and Jean Lipman Foundation, Inc; an anonymous donor; The TM Evans Foundation, Inc.; MacAndrews & Forbes Group Incorporated; the DeWitt Wallace Fund, Inc; Martin & Agnes Gruss; Anne Phillips; Mr and Mrs Laurance S. Rockefeller; the Simon Foundation, Inc.; Marylou Whitney; Bankers Trust Company; Mr and Mrs Kenneth N Dayton; Joel and Anne Ehrenkranz; Irvin and Kenneth Feld; Flora Whitney Miller. More than 500 individuals from 26 states and abroad also contributed to the campaign), 199bl, 199br (purchased with funds from the Mr and Mrs Arthur G Altschul Purchase Fund, the Joan and Lester Avnet Purchase Fund, the Edgar William and Bernice Chrysler Garbisch Purchase Fund, the Mrs Robert C Graham Purchase Fund in honour of John I H Baur, the Mrs Percy Uris Purchase Fund and the Henry Schnakenberg Purchase Fund in honor of Juliana Force); WHEELER PICTURES: 78t; WILDLIFE CONSERVATION SOCIETY, BRONX ZOO: Dennis DeMello 242tr, 242bl; ROBERT WRIGHT: 41t, 138b, 140 (all four), 141tl/br, 154br, 155tl/r, 285tr, 356cl, 357c. YU YU YANG: *Untitled*, 1973, 57br.
All other images © Dorling Kindersley. See www.dkimages.com for further information.

JACKET
Front - DK PICTURE LIBRARY: Dave King b, cl; GETTY IMAGES: Joseph Pobereskin main image. Back - IMAGESTATE: Mark Segal t; The Solomon R. Guggenheim Foundation, New York: b. Spine - GETTY IMAGES: Joseph Pobereskin.

DORLING KINDERSLEY SPECIAL EDITIONS

DORLING KINDERSLEY books can be purchased in bulk quantities at discounted prices for use in promotions or as premiums.
We are also able to offer special editions and personalized jackets, corporate imprints, and excerpts from all of our books, tailored specifically to meet your own needs.

To find out more, please contact: (in the United Kingdom) – Sarah.Burgess@dk.com or SPECIAL SALES, DORLING KINDERSLEY LIMITED, 80 STRAND, LONDON WC2R 0RL; (in the United States) – SPECIAL MARKETS DEPARTMENT, DORLING KINDERSLEY, PUBLISHING INC., 375 HUDSON STREET, NEW YORK, NY 10014.

FOR PEACE OF MIND ABROAD,
WE'VE GOT IT COVERED

 DK INSURANCE PROVIDES YOU
WITH QUALITY WORLDWIDE
INSURANCE COVER

For an instant quote
go to **www.dk.com/travel-insurance**

Organised by Columbus Travel Insurance Services Ltd, 17 Devonshire Square, London EC2M 4SQ, UK
Underwritten by certain underwriters at Lloyd's and Professional Travel Insurance Company Ltd.

The Manhattan Subway

HOW TO USE THIS MAP

Transit Authority subway service operates 24 hours a day. On this map, **bold** identification letters or numbers below station names indicate that trains always operate between 6am and midnight. A light letter or number shows that the train does not run at all times or skips a station. Following the destruction of the World Trade Center (*see p54*) Cortlandt Street Station is temporarily closed. For more information call (718) 330-1234 or visit www.mta.nyc.ny.us/nyct/subway/index.

Throughout this guide, the subway station closest to each sight is listed. For more details on traveling on the New York subway, see pages 374–5.

- Local service only
- All trains stop (local and express service)
- Station served by one of two lines
- Free subway transfer
- Free out-of-system subway transfer (MetroCard only)
- Ⓜ Normal service
- ◆ Special rush hour or express service
- ---- Commuter rail service

Nights and weekends only

Part time service

Full time service

Station Name

Terminal

Wheelchair Accessible Stations

The following subway stations are accessible to wheelchair passengers. For further information, call (718) 568-585 (6am–9am daily), or 1(800) 734-6772 (24-hour).

Routes	Station
MANHATTAN	**Ⓐ** Inwood-207 Street
	Ⓐ 175 Street
	Ⓒ Ⓔ 50 Street/8 Avenue *southbound only*